Trade and Investment Prospects in Health Services

The high growth in India's healthcare sector and the emergence of reputed private players of international standard have created opportunities in trade, investment and collaboration. India is engaged in health services trade across all four modes. India's health services exports span segments as diverse as tele-medicine, medical value travel, clinical trials and the deployment of medical professionals to other countries. Foreign exchange earnings, as indicated by firm-level data, stood at ₹1.4 billion, with much of this accruing to smaller establishments engaged in wellness tourism and diagnostics exports. There is also growing interest among foreign players in entering India's medical devices, clinical research and trials, and pharmaceutical segments. Several are entering through joint ventures and through tie-ups in technology, training and research. The following section highlights India's export prospects in health services across the various modes of services trade.

1. *Prospects in Mode 1*

    According to health industry experts, India has considerable opportunities in several aspects of e-health, including tele-radiology, tele-diagnostics, tele-pathology, intensive care, ophthalmology, dermatology, psychiatry and, to some extent, in continuous online remote monitoring. Tele-medicine is provided to other countries by independent tele-medicine providers as well as reputed IT companies such as Wipro Limited, which is partnering with Manipal Hospitals to combine their IT and network security and protocols capabilities with the core medical competence of reputed hospitals. The Apollo Group in India exports e-health services; it provides tele-medicine services (consultation, diagnostic, tele-pathology, tele-radiology and so on) from its Apollo Gleneagles Hospital in Kolkata to patients in Bangladesh, Nepal, Bhutan and Myanmar; it also provides tele-diagnostic and tele-consultation services from its centre in Karaganda Oblastu in Kazakhstan to the Central Asian region.[18] The US and Singapore are important markets. The client base in the US for leading Indian tele-medicine providers has expanded from merely one hospital

---

[18] See http://www.apollohospdelhi.com/news/html (accessed November 2008).

to 60 hospitals in a few years.[19] The National Healthcare Group of Singapore has tied up with tele-medicine institutions in India to provide tele-radiology services to designated hospitals in Singapore. Contracts have been signed with Malaysia and Dubai. India's potential in cross-border e-health provision is driven by its cost advantages and the fact that specialised medical staff and doctors are involved in reporting and interpretation work. Indian radiologists report salaries that are 70 to 80 per cent lower than those in the US (Chanda, 2008). The recently proposed initiatives to provide medical advice through telemedicine and to create a network of hospitals for medical education and treatment under the 'Digital India' campaign is likely to further strengthen India's Mode 1 prospects and could potentially also open up opportunities for collaboration with foreign providers.

In addition to tele-medicine, India exports health services in other forms through Mode 1. It is an attractive market for healthcare business process outsourcing, such as medical transcriptions, billing, coding and data conversion, with potential cost savings of 20–30 per cent for client companies. For instance, Apollo Hospitals has partnered with Health Services America and Medstaff International in the US for billing, documenting clinical and administrative records, coding medical processes, and processing insurance claims for Medi-claim policyholders and third-party administrators. Outsourcing of pathology services is also emerging as a huge opportunity due to the high cost differential in India. Some Indian research laboratories and contract research organisations provide sophisticated tests, such as molecular diagnostics for autoimmune disorders, cytogenetics and diseases related to abnormalities in chromosomes and hormones. Some laboratories are able to offer a wide menu of more than 1,500 tests under one roof.

The clinical research and trials segment has grown significantly since the introduction of Trade Related Aspects of Intellectual Property Rights (TRIPs) and is estimated at around US$500 million in India today. India's clinical research market is projected to more than double and to cross US$1 billion by

---

[19] Based on discussions with a leading telemedicine exporter in India. The period referred to is 2005–2008.

2016, driven by its large population and low costs.[20] Clinical trials and research are mainly conducted by Contract Research Organisations (CROs) and some of the major Indian pharmaceutical companies. Several foreign companies do bioequivalence studies in India. At present, the business is mainly with the US. Healthcare providers such as Manipal Hospitals have set up centres in specific areas like stem cell research and clinical applications and also set up CROs (such as Acunova) to conduct clinical trials. These companies have received approval from the authorities of foreign governments (e.g. Malaysia) to conduct clinical trials, including fast-track clinical trials.

2. *Prospects in Mode 2*

One segment where India shows promising prospects is medical value travel. The medical tourism market in India was estimated at US$1.9 billion in 2011.[21] India's share in the global medical tourism industry was 3 per cent in 2013. According to government sources, in 2009 more than 110,000 foreign tourists from 65 countries visited India for medical treatment. However, more than 90 per cent of these inflows are from a few countries—the SAARC region (Maldives, Bangladesh and Afghanistan), the Middle East (Oman and the UAE) and Africa. Common treatments include cardiac surgery, knee replacement, eye surgery and organ transplants. Wellness tourism is another segment that is seen as holding much promise.

Several factors are contributing to the growth in medical tourism exports. Private sector initiatives to obtain international accreditation from the Joint Commission International (JCI), investments in healthcare infrastructure to attract medical tourists, the establishment of world-class hospitals and partnerships with international insurance and tourism companies and with hospitals and practitioners have contributed to India's medical tourism exports. India has a huge cost advantage, with one-eighth to one-fifth of costs for comparable treatments in the western countries. Table 8.4 compares the costs in India and several competing and source

[20] See http://www.thehindu.com/sci-tech/health/policy-and-issues/post-stringent-norms-clinical-trials-in-india-plummet/article4639976.ece (accessed 20 June 2013).

[21] http://www.oifc.in/Sectors/Healthcare/Healthcare-in-India (accessed 3 July 2013).

Table 8.4
Prices for Medical Tourism in Select Countries, 2010 (in US$)

Procedure	US	India	Thailand	Singapore	Malaysia	Mexico	UK
Heart bypass (CABG)	113,000	10,000	13,000	20,000	9,000	3,250	13,921
Heart valve replacement	150,000	9,500	11,000	13,000	9,000	18,000	
Angioplasty	47,000	11,000	10,000	13,000	11,000	15,000	8,000
Hip replacement	47,000	9,000	12,000	11,000	10,000	17,300	12,000
Knee replacement	48,000	8,500	10,000	13,000	8,000	14,650	10,162
Rhinoplasty	4,500	2,000	2,500	4,375	2,083	3,200	3,500
Tummy Tuck	6,400	2,900	3,500	6,250	3,903	3,000	4,810
Breast reduction	5,200	2,500	3,750	8,000	3,343	3,000	5,075
Breast implants	6,000	2,200	2,600	8,000	3,308	2,500	4,350
Crown	385	180	243	400	250	300	330
Dental implants	1,188	1,100	1,429	1,500	2,636	950	1,600

Source: Lunt et al. (2011), Table 1, p. 12.

countries in medical tourism while Box 8.1 highlights the nature of the engagement by various corporate hospitals in medical tourism exports.

India's medical tourism exports, however, remain constrained by the lack of insurance portability and lack of accreditation of healthcare providers by overseas health insurance trusts or private insurance companies.

Box 8.1: Corporate Hospitals Engaged in Medical Tourism

Apollo Hospital Enterprises

It has conducted 94,000 heart surgeries with a success rate of 99 per cent since its establishment.[22] It has a dedicated team for medical tourism that treated an estimated 60,000 overseas patients in 2009–2011, with patients coming mainly from East Africa, the Gulf (Oman and Yemen) and South Asia (Bangladesh and Nepal).

Escorts Heart and Research Institute

The hospital performs around 15,000 heart operations every year with a mortality rate of 0.8 per cent, which is lower than most hospitals in the US. The number of overseas patients doubled from 675 in the year 2000 to 1,200 in 2008.[23]

B. M. Birla Heart Research Centre

This super-specialty hospital for diagnosis, treatment and research related to cardiovascular diseases provides advanced heart care to patients from Bangladesh, Bhutan, Nepal, Mauritius, Hong Kong, Kenya and neighbouring countries.

Source: SACEPS (2011).

---

[22] http://ehealth.eletsonline.com/2011/01/the-indian-doctor-today-stands-tall-dr-prathap-c-reddy-apollo-hospitals-india/ (accessed 29 November 2013).

[23] http://dspace.iimk.ac.in/bitstream/2259/590/1/475-484.pdf (accessed 29 November 2013).

3. *Prospects in Mode 3*

There has been growing interest in recent years among foreign players and non-resident Indians in entering the Indian healthcare market. In addition, domestic and international financial institutions, private equity funds, venture capitalists and banks have begun to explore investment opportunities across a wide range of segments (drugs and pharmaceuticals, medical devices, hospitals, and others). In the hospitals and medical devices segment alone, there are reportedly at least 20 international players competing in the Indian healthcare market. These players enter mainly through joint ventures with Indian companies or through technology and training collaborations. Examples include Singapore's Pacific Healthcare, which has opened an international medical centre in Hyderabad in a joint venture with India's Vitae Healthcare; Singapore-based Parkway Group Healthcare PTE Ltd., which has entered through a joint venture with the Apollo Group to set up the Apollo Gleneagles hospital in Kolkata; the Columbia Asia Group, which has started its first US-style medical centre in Bangalore; and research, training and other forms of collaboration between hospitals in India and abroad. Such inflows have been facilitated by the liberal foreign investment regime in the health sector (Chanda, 2007; SACEPS, 2011).

There is a high degree of involvement by foreign players in the hi-tech medical devices segment, accounting for US$770 million; 90 per cent of the demand in this segment is met by imports from the US, Japan and Germany. Some foreign companies conduct the first 550 surgeries in India after the US Food and Drug Administration (FDA) approves a medical device or surgical treatment (Chanda, 2008). In the health insurance segment, the FDI limit has been relaxed, resulting in growing health insurance premiums and joint ventures by leading global health insurance players. The recently proposed increase in the FDI cap in insurance from 26 to 49 per cent and the focus of the Modi government on boosting Indian manufacturing across sectors, including through FDI in the health sector, can be expected to open up further opportunities for foreign companies in the health insurance and medical technologies segments.

There is also outward FDI by Indian hospitals, with a focus on the South Asia region. Major hospital groups like Apollo Hospitals and B.M. Birla Hospitals have established super-specialty or tertiary care outlets in other South Asian countries. Fortis Healthcare has recently established a joint venture in Sri Lanka for a super-specialty cardiac hospital (Asian Tribune, 2011). Several Indian hospitals have established their branches in Nepal, Sri Lanka and Bangladesh. Some, such as Manipal Hospitals, have also set up medical colleges in other South Asian countries.

4. *Prospects in Mode 4*

There is also scope for India to export healthcare workers, such as nurses and technicians, on a temporary basis and through institutional tie-ups with overseas establishments given its cost advantage and availability of manpower.[24] Table 8.5 highlights India's significance as a source of medical professionals for other countries.

Table 8.5

Top 20 Countries for Education of International Medical Graduate Physicians

Country	Number	Share (%)
India	51,330	20.4
Philippines	20,476	8 1
Pakistan	15,104	6 0
Mexico	13,817	5 4
Dominican Republic	8,082	3 2
Grenada	7,599	3 0
Dominica	6,793	2 7
Union of Soviet Socialist Republics (USSR)	6,450	2 6
China	5,912	2 3
Egypt	5,447	2 2
Iran	5,088	2 0
South Korea	4,815	1 9

(Table 8.5 Continued)

[24] However, once again, there are barriers in the form of licensing and certification requirements, immigration restrictions and cultural and social sensitivities.

(Table 8.5 Continued)

Country	Number	Share (%)
Italy	4,626	1 8
Germany	4,183	1 6
Spain	4,031	1 6
Syria	4,012	1 6
United Kingdom	3,696	1 5
Colombia	3,650	1 4
Montserrat	3,569	1 4
Nigeria	3,489	1 4

Source: AMA-IMG Section Governing Council (2013).

Available data on physician emigration, on medical education for international medical graduates in the US and on source country for J-1 visa physicians[25] reveal India's importance in the global market as a supplier of medical professionals. However, regulations concerning licensing and accreditation remain a barrier to the cross-border mobility of Indian healthcare professionals (Consumer Unity Trust Society, 2007).

Key Regulations

The healthcare sector is both over-and under-regulated in India. Areas of regulation which are pertinent to trade concern standards for medical establishments, accreditation of medical professionals and foreign direct investment. Regulations in some of these areas are still evolving, but there has been considerable streamlining in recent years to establish and improve standards and to improve governance.

1. *Standards and accreditation (Government of India, 2011)*
    The Ministry of Health & Family Welfare has developed Indian Public Health Standards (IPHS) for certain government clinical

---

[25] The J-1 visa is a scholar visa for those who wish to teach, lecture, study, research or get graduate medical education/training. See USCIS for data on different types of visas and the significance of India as a source country. Available at http://www.uscis.gov/ (accessed on 20 June 2013).

establishments, viz. Community Health Centres (CHC), Primary Health Centres (PHC) and Sub-Centres, that are implemented through administrative means. A few states and Union Territories have enacted laws for the registration and regulation of nursing and clinical establishments, but so far these do not cover laboratories and diagnostic centres. Standards have been established in recent years for medical establishments. The Clinical Establishments (Registration and Regulation) Act was passed in 2010 to address the need for regulating standards across a wide range of medical establishments (e.g. hospital, maternity homes, nursing homes, dispensaries, clinics and sanatoriums) and places offering pathological, chemical, diagnostic and laboratory services, whether incorporated or not. The Act aims at the compulsory registration of all clinical establishments in two stages, provisional at first and permanent thereafter. Clinical establishments are required to comply with the prescribed minimum standards at the time of permanent registration. Although there is no provision for periodic inspection, the registering authority has been given the power to conduct an inquiry or inspection of the clinical establishment at any time and to issue directions; it is also empowered to cancel the registration if it is satisfied that the conditions of registration are not being fulfilled. Further, it can restrain the clinical establishment from operating if there is imminent danger to the health and safety of patients. Penalties of up to ₹500,000 are imposed in case of contravention of the provisions of the Act. There is provision for appeal to the state government from orders rejecting or cancelling registration. The Act also envisages the establishment of a national council that has the responsibility for setting the minimum mandatory standards for all clinical establishments.

In 2006, the National Accreditation Board for Hospitals and Healthcare Providers (NABH) initiated an accreditation programme for secondary and tertiary hospitals. The latter is a constituent board of the Quality Council of India. The objective was to improve the quality of healthcare establishments in the country. As of now, accreditation of hospitals is a voluntary process that involves the evaluation of an organisation's compliance with pre-established performance standards. The organisation is granted accreditation if it is assessed as meeting an acceptable level of compliance, or it may be given conditional accreditation. NABH accreditation has been gradually taking off over the years. At present, there are over 180 NABH-accredited hospitals, mostly in the private sector. The NABH has also received international certification. There is also the National Accreditation Board for Laboratories (NABL) for accrediting diagnostic laboratories and facilities.

Medical professionals are regulated through central legislation, viz. the Indian Medical Councils Act (1956), the Indian Dental Council Act (1948) and the Indian Nursing Council Act (1947). These laws provide for setting up regulatory councils at the national and state levels. The national councils prescribe norms and standards of education, while the state councils deal primarily with registration and enforcement of these standards. There are rules for the registration of medical practitioners and separate regulations for professional conduct, etiquette and ethics. These Acts contain recommendatory guidelines such as on the use of drugs as well as mandatory rules, such as for the maintenance of medical records of indoor patients for a minimum period of three years and the maintenance of a register of certificates issued.

2. *Foreign investment regulations*

FDI inflows in hospitals and diagnostic centres amounted to US$1,597.3 million during the April 2000 to March 2013 period. FDI inflows in medical and surgical appliances stood at US$604.5 million and the drugs and pharmaceuticals sector attracted FDI worth US$10,318.7 million over the same period. From January 2000, up to 100 per cent FDI is permitted under the automatic route in hospitals in India. Thus, no government approval is required as long as the Indian company files with the regional office of the RBI within 30 days of receipt of inward remittances and files the required documents along with Form FC-GPR with that office within 30 days of issue of shares to non-resident investors.[26] Foreign investors are also permitted to hold a controlling stake in hospitals. Currently, approval from the FIPB

---

[26] Overseas Indian Facilitation Centre, Healthcare, December 2013, available at http://www.oifc.in/healthcare (accessed on 4 January 2013).

is only required for foreign investors with prior technical collaboration, but is allowed up to 100 per cent. Prior to January 2000, FDI in hospitals was permitted under the FIPB route; this meant that the FIPB would consider the investment proposals, take a decision and then the Indian company would file the papers with the RBI. Current regulations also permit other forms of capital mobilisation to be treated as FDI. For instance, Indian companies can raise foreign currency resources abroad up to 49 per cent through ADRs and GDRs under the automatic route, subject to specified conditions. Although the FDI regime is liberal in this sector, studies indicate that the extent of FDI in the main segment, i.e. the hospital industry, remains limited due to the high costs of real estate infrastructure, medical equipment and supplies, and various structural and resource constraints.

Challenges Facing India's Healthcare Sector

Despite the sector's rapid growth and potential, India's healthcare sector falls well below international benchmarks for physical infrastructure and manpower, and even falls below the standards in comparable developing countries. There is also a severe deficit of health infrastructure. The number of hospital beds per 1,000 persons stands at 0.9, which is less than half that of Brazil and China. The projected cumulative deficit for hospital beds in 2014 is around 2.8 million. If India is to meet the global average of 3 beds per 1,000 population, it will require 1.75 million additional hospital beds.[27]

There is also a shortage of human resources. An additional 310,000 doctors are required by 2022 to attain a ratio of one medical doctor per 1,000 persons (Government of India, 2011). As per the most recent World Health Organization Statistics,[28] there are 1.9 health workers per 1,000 persons, with 0.6 physicians per 1,000 persons compared to a world average of 1.5 and 1.3 nurses and midwives per 1,000 persons.

[27] http://www.oifc.in/Sectors/Healthcare/Healthcare-in-India (accessed on 3 July 2013).

[28] www.who.org (accessed on July 2013).

India ranked 53 among the 57 countries facing a human resource crisis in the health sector. These ratios are projected to remain below the existing world averages in the near future. To bridge the deficit in physical and human resource infrastructure in healthcare, India will require significant investment of around US$86 billion (FICCI, 2008).

These deficiencies are aggravated by the inequitable distribution of healthcare infrastructure within the country and the chronic and acute shortage of specialised and even basic facilities in rural and semi-urban areas. There is also the problem of a fragmented market structure and lack of economies of scale and standardisation, as the sector remains dominated by unorganised investors. Another challenge is the low level of insurance penetration, which remains below 10 per cent. Thus, India's healthcare sector needs to scale up considerably in terms of the availability and quality of its physical infrastructure as well as human resources so as to meet the growing demand and to benchmark itself against international standards. Although innovative business models and new forms of delivery such as tele-medicine are being used to address such gaps, large upfront investments are needed in the sector and the equity and accessibility challenges in this sector are considerable.

India–EU Relations in Health Services: Status, Opportunities, Challenges

The preceding discussion indicates that there are opportunities for Indian healthcare providers (professionals and establishments) to service the EU market. Some of these driving forces include advances in information and communication technology that make possible the electronic delivery of healthcare and ageing populations, personnel shortages, rising demand, escalating costs, financing constraints and long waiting lists for treatment in the EU. The initiation of healthcare reforms by several EU countries in order to contain operational costs, improve efficiency and redesign their health and technological infrastructure in order to give their populations greater choice and improved access to healthcare has created export opportunities for third countries like India whose private healthcare providers are increasingly aligning themselves with international standards and guidelines.

Primary Survey Findings on Status and Potential

To understand the status and prospects for expanding India–EU relations in health services, discussions were held with a wide range of practitioners in the healthcare sector (including doctors, researchers, radiologists and biotechnologists), senior management at leading Indian hospitals and industry experts based in Bangalore, Delhi, Kolkata, Mumbai and the UK. This was corroborated by information from secondary sources. The interviews were conducted in person and over the phone. The discussions aimed to understand the work being done by Indian healthcare providers for EU-based clients, the opportunities realised or perceived in the EU region and the main barriers to doing business with the EU in the healthcare sector. To validate these views and to get alternate perspectives, views were also solicited from industry association representatives, economic counsellors of select EU countries in New Delhi and the EC.

Discussions with stakeholders in government and industry on both sides suggest several segments for expanding bilateral relations and cooperation in the health sector. The six main opportunity segments highlighted were:

1. Tele-medicine with a particular stress on tele-radiology and more generally the integration of IT with healthcare delivery (bioinformatics, continuous monitoring and tele-diagnostics).
2. Conducting clinical trials and clinical research in India for EU-based pharmaceutical companies and Contract Research Organisations (CROs).
3. Back-office support functions in health services, such as medical transcription and revenue cycle management.
4. Medical tourism, especially for elected and out-of-pocket expenditure cases and for alternative therapies and treatments.
5. Temporary staffing by Indian health personnel, especially nurses, under establishment–establishment arrangements and through government-level agreements.
6. Collaborative ventures between universities, hospitals and research centres in medical education, research, training and product development.

Among the identified opportunity segments, stakeholders indicated greater optimism about export prospects in areas that are non-intrusive and those with minimal patient contact and interface, i.e. the tele-medicine, clinical trials and research, and back-office segments. There were mixed views about exploiting the medical value travel market in the EU given perception and regulatory issues and the predominance of the public sector in EU's healthcare delivery. Potential was also seen in the area of medical staffing and cross-border mobility of Indian health personnel, especially in the UK, although EU-wide prospects were perceived to be limited due to social, political and regulatory challenges.

The discussions indicated that the markets of interest in the EU depend on the segment. Segments of healthcare that require cultural and linguistic affinity are largely confined to the UK. The UK was perceived as the main market of interest across all the opportunity areas. In tele-medicine, the UK and the National Health Service (NHS) in particular was identified as the main client market for tele-medicine exports from India. Clinical trials and clinical research were perceived to be among the most promising areas for commercial and collaborative work with the EU; Germany and the Scandinavian countries are seen as prospective markets, either due to their pharmaceutical base or their inclination towards R&D and their acknowledgment of Indian expertise. In the area of personnel staffing and exchange, the UK (particularly the NHS) was identified as the main market, although some potential was also perceived in the more English-inclined countries of Scandinavia, Germany and the Netherlands. In medical tourism, apart from the UK, countries like Germany, France and the Scandinavian countries were perceived to be potential client markets given their inclination towards rehabilitative and alternative treatments and tourist interest in India.

1. *Tele-medicine*

Some Indian companies are setting up a commercial presence and partnerships to enter the EU market for tele-medicine since direct outsourcing of such work outside EU membership is not allowed at present. For example, Teleradiology Solutions, an Indian company engaged in tele-medicine exports, has incorporated a subsidiary in the EU called Teleradiology Europe. The subsidiary has a US-trained Dutch radiologist based in the Netherlands who interprets radiology reports for hospitals in the US. The subsidiary could undertake work within the EU since it is not subject to the outsourcing restrictions on patient data as long as the work is delivered from its local company in the EU. Thus, commercial presence in the EU is one way for tele-medicine providers to access the EU market. In anticipation of changes in data protection legislation that would enable outsourcing of such work to India, Teleradiology Solutions has already set up the aforementioned EU-based subsidiary. Meanwhile, it is also investing in a separate segment at its Bangalore office to cater to business in the EU. Manipal Hospitals is similarly using its overseas presence in the UK to tap the emerging business in tele-medicine; it has got a sub-contract from a private consortium that has an NHS contract for radiology reporting within the UK. This work is being done in collaboration with a UK-based company called 4 Ways Healthcare. The consortium handles the physical aspects of the delivery, while Manipal Hospitals, through a local delivery centre that it has set up in the UK, does the reporting work by sending its radiologists on rotation to the UK.

Several trade commissions from EU Member Countries, such as the Netherlands and Denmark, have shown an interest in expanding tele-medicine from India to their countries and could provide a platform for pushing these opportunities with their respective governments. Given the shortage of qualified persons in the EU and the e-health initiatives under consideration in the EU, there are opportunities in tele-medicine services for India.

2. *Clinical trials and research*

In the developed world, drug development is expensive because the patient pool is limited and the recruitment rate is slow. Several factors make India an ideal market for conducting clinical trials and research, and explain the enormous potential for doing such work for the EU. India is cost-effective for clinical trials given its huge population, diverse genetic pool, wide range of diseases, drug-naïve population, trained medical and technical manpower and good hospitals where such trials can be undertaken. Since drug development is highly capital-intensive and the R&D costs of MNCs for developing drugs and bringing them to the market have increased significantly, delays in clinical trials can be very expensive for a pharmaceutical company. Indian CROs can help pharmaceutical companies lower their costs and reduce the time to market drugs. It was noted that while the US is mainly outsourcing clinical trials to India because of its large market, the main motivation for European companies is to reduce their costs.

Companies in India, such as Biocon Limited and Clinigene International Limited, are conducting clinical trials for European pharmaceutical companies. Some Indian CROs have set up marketing offices in other countries, including in the EU, while others are acquiring companies in the EU and elsewhere to build their image and credibility. Business with Europe is, however, very small; whereas Eastern European countries are doing US$3 billion in clinical trials for Europe, India is doing only US$100 million worth of business.[29] Some Indian CROs are, however, holding discussions with companies in Europe, mainly from the UK, Germany and Italy. Sweden, Denmark, Germany and Finland have enquired about conducting clinical research and trials in India for a faster turnaround. Some areas of interest are Phase I and II studies on diabetes, oncology, neuropsychiatry, gastroenterology and stem cell research. There are also ongoing discussions with European bio-pharma companies for proof of concept for new drugs. The break-up of India's engagement with the EU in this area is not available, but the countries with the strongest pharmaceutical sectors, namely the UK and Germany, are seen to be the most important markets for India within the EU; the UK constitutes half the clinical trials market in Europe, followed by Germany. There is scope for research in experimental therapies for clinical trials that could be conducted by Indian companies or research centres in collaboration with European institutions and universities. There is also potential for partnerships between Indian and EU laboratories to get international certification for evaluation and testing.

3. *Medical tourism*

There are potential markets in the EU from which India could attract medical tourists. These include the UK, given the colonial, linguistic and social ties, and some countries in Eastern Europe, such as Poland, that are facing challenges in their healthcare system

---

[29] These numbers were provided by respondents.

following their transition from socialism. According to a survey conducted by the Treatment Abroad website, in 2007 over 70,000 British citizens travelled abroad for medical treatment, with India being the destination of choice.[30]

Indian providers perceive Eastern Europe as a good market for establishing tie-ups with institutions given the region's need for affordable healthcare, its shortage of quality medical infrastructure, the exodus of medical personnel from Eastern Europe to Western Europe following accession, and their possible affinity to India (due to good political relations in the past).

There is also some potential in the alternative medicine area, given the growing interest in the western countries for treatment of chronic disorders where allopathy fails to deliver. India has the potential to provide various streams of alternative medicine, including *panchkarma*, *ayurveda*, *unani*, *siddha* and homeopathy.

4. *Back-office processing*

Another segment where India could export health services to the EU is in back-office business process and support services. Although such work is at present being done for the US market, Indian health industry experts see scope for doing high-end back-office work in healthcare for the EU market. Specific activities include revenue cycle management, which involves handling patient bills and records to process reimbursements from insurance companies; such work involves specialised expertise and can be done for hospitals and physicians. Germany has recently expressed an interest in outsourcing medical transcription as well as other IT-enabled services to India to overcome its high costs and labour shortages in healthcare.

Another segment is medical coding and analysis of patient charts. For example, companies are examining procedures and assigning codes to these procedures for later analysis to ease reimbursement by insurance companies. Such coding work can be offered to the EU for data analysis and diagnostic purposes.

---

[30] Times of India, 3 March 2008. For details see 'Britons Oppose Sending NHS Patients to India', Times of India. 3 March 2008. Available at http://articles.timesofindia.indiatimes. com/2008-03-03/uk/27743553_1_three-hours-and-seven-and-a-half-nhs-britons (accessed on 5 July 2013).

There is a European Procedural Terminology that Indian companies can use for such coding work. This work could also be done using the data from clinical trials.

5. *Staffing*

Given the shortage of personnel in most EU countries, particularly in areas like nursing, there is scope for India to export medical personnel on a temporary basis to staff the national health systems of these countries. The main potential is in the UK and the key areas of staffing are nursing and paramedics. Medical management is another area where India is seen as having the technical capabilities to serve the EU market.

6. *Collaboration*

There is a lot of scope for collaboration on various fronts between India and the EU in the healthcare sector (services and products). Potential areas include medical education and training, staffing and exchange of personnel and research and product development. While the EU has shown little interest in setting up medical education campuses in India, there are possibilities for collaboration through technical tie-ups, dual degrees and twinning programmes that could be combined with a period of deployment and practical training in the EU following coursework. Since the EU has excellent hospitals with trained personnel and established processes in sub-specialty care, collaboration in postgraduate training would help raise Indian standards while also addressing labour shortages in those countries. The Danish authorities have expressed some interest in such collaboration. In addition, EU companies that are engaged in healthcare delivery, for example, the delivery of medical equipment and devices, could be part of this academic-cum-commercial relationship to impart training. However, language and lack of mutual recognition of standards and qualifications remain critical barriers to expanding such collaborative efforts.

The discussions also suggested scope to collaborate in knowledge process outsourcing of specialised and technical services for the healthcare industry, such as the design and production of medical devices and the testing of medical equipment; this would be facilitated by the emergence of corporate hospitals in India and the entry of foreign players in these segments.[31] Companies like Siemens and Philips that are engaged in the development and production of medical equipment are looking at India for research, design and prototype testing and as a market for such products. There are, however, constraints in the form of ethical regulations, liability and compensation concerns and the lack of international standards for registration of medical devices and technologies in India.

Survey Findings on Barriers

Discussions with a wide range of stakeholders concerned with India–EU relations in health services indicated several barriers faced by Indian healthcare providers, both establishments and personnel, in doing business with the EU. These barriers pertain to constraints at the EU-wide level and at the country level due to regulations in EU Member States. Most respondents emphasised three points that constrain bilateral relations in health services between India and the EU.

First, European markets are not well understood and Indian providers only have an understanding of the UK's NHS. There is only generic knowledge about the healthcare sector in other EU countries, and that too only in terms of awareness about the existing shortages of personnel and waiting times. Since each EU country has its own complex and evolved healthcare system, this lack of awareness automatically constrains the scope for providing healthcare services to the EU market.

Second, linguistic, social and cultural barriers constrain India's potential for delivering healthcare services to the EU. Healthcare is a highly personalised service where perceptions, attitudes and social and linguistic affinity play an important role. Thus, India's prospects are mainly limited to the UK market and a few EU countries that have English-speaking capabilities.

Third, the existing barriers to India's exports of health services to the EU are not really barriers but regulations that would be justified in any country to ensure safety, quality and consumer protection. Thus, the onus is on India to adopt a variety of regulatory measures, introduce

---

[31] Overseas companies are looking at corporate hospitals such as Escorts and Fortis to provide such tests.

reforms and align its own standards and regulations with international ones so as to leverage its capabilities in the health sector in the EU or for that matter in any other developed region. Thus, often the constraints are not due to external regulations but the lack of domestic regulatory frameworks or lack of enforcement of necessary regulations in this sector and, at times, with the operational and administrative aspects of the regulations in EU countries than with the regulations per se.

Discussions indicated regulatory and other barriers associated with each of the opportunity segments highlighted earlier. There are: (a) restrictions on outsourcing certain kinds of health services to providers outside the EU territory; (b) regulations related to data protection and data exclusivity; (c) accreditation and certification requirements for healthcare establishments and compliance with international or EU standards and guidelines; (d) restrictions on insurance portability restrictions and coverage; (e) recognition of professional qualifications and registration requirements; and (f) immigration and visa regulations that affect the mobility of providers. Respondents, however, noted that many of these regulations are warranted on the grounds of consumer protection, safety and national interest. Hence, whether or not these act as market access barriers has more to do with the way in which some of these are implemented administratively, as in the case of recognition issues, or with the underlying justification for certain regulations not being in line with ground realities. There are also national treatment barriers that place Indian health providers at a disadvantage vis-à-vis EU-based providers, thus undermining their market access in relation to competitor countries within the EU.

1. *Tele-medicine*
   Discussions highlighted constraints in the form of data protection regulations, lack of recognition of provider qualifications, contract issues and perception issues that adversely affect India's exports of tele-medicine services to the EU. The key aspects of these barriers and their effects on India's tele-medicine exports to the EU are highlighted in Table 8.6.
2. *Clinical trials and research*
   The constraints on outsourcing clinical trials and research work from the EU to India pertain to the rigour and standards of trials and analyses, data protection, accreditation and certification of

Table 8.6
Barriers to Tele-medicine between India and the EU

Problem	Features and Implications
Data protection, privacy, and information security issues[32]	• Bureaucratic EU data protection laws
	• Cumbersome database registration requirement with data protection authorities
	• Lack of harmonisation in data protection legislation among Member States
	• Data on EU patients cannot be sent outside the EU unless there is a legal basis for transfer, i.e. official adequacy finding to determine country has national laws to provide adequate level of data protection
	• India has not received adequacy determination from EU authorities, so it needs to legalise data transfer
	• Imposes additional compliance costs of security audits, fines, registration, contracts with client companies
	• Overcoming the constraints by setting up commercial presence in the EU and doing tele-medicine from within the EU
Recognition and accreditation requirements	• Expensive and time-consuming certification process
	• Multiple levels of verification
	• Stringent certification requirements for tele-radiology companies and providers
	• Registration required with each country's healthcare commission and concerned authorities
	• Compliance with EU Directives on data protection, consumer safety, etc.
	• Indemnity/insurance requirement
	• Cumbersome evaluation and documentation requirements
	• Competence determination tests
	• Language requirements
	• Residency requirements
	• Requirement to appear in person for registration
	• Re-certification, re-validation, re-licensure, regular appraisal requirements

(Table 8.6 Continued)

[32] Much of the discussion in this part is based on Johnson (2007), pp. 44–48.

(Table 8.6 Continued)

Problem	Features and Implications
	• Lack of harmonisation within EU
	• Implicit discrimination against non-EU providers
Contract issues	• Practical problems with malpractice insurance and liability policies in EU countries
	• Handling of breach of contract and jurisdictional issues in enforcing compliance
	• Costs imposed due to service line agreement clauses on prior consent, indemnity, non-disclosure, liability
	• Delays in executing contracts
Perception, attitudes, and stakeholder resistance	• Resistance to electronic delivery of healthcare in the EU
	• Cultural and social barriers
	• Language barriers, translation requirement for reports
	• Resistance from professional associations in EU due to concerns over employment losses

Source: Based on interviews conducted by the author.

laboratories and organisations conducting the trials and contract obligations. There are also issues of perception regarding India as a destination for clinical trials and research. As in the case of tele-medicine, there is a lack of awareness in Europe about India's capability as a destination for clinical trials and research; India has not been marketed sufficiently in Europe in this segment, since its focus has been on the US. Many of these regulations are perceived as necessary and not as barriers per se. In fact, the onus lies on India to address some of these concerns. Table 8.7 summarises the main constraints affecting clinical trials and research by India for EU countries.

3. *Medical Value Travel and Alternative Therapies/Treatments*
   Although there is scope for medical tourism by India, several factors limit the potential for medical value travel from the EU to India. These mainly pertain to the lack of insurance portability from the EU to India for reasons such as:

   (i) Restrictions on reimbursement of patients from the EU if travel to the exporting country exceeds a certain duration,

Table 8.7

Constraints on Clinical Trials and Research

Problem	Features and Implications
Standards and Accreditation	• Requirement to conform with client country guidelines often cumbersome
	• Accreditation of Indian laboratories required even if they conform to accepted global standards
	• Compliance costs of meeting documentation, audit, infra-structure, qualifications, training requirements
Norms for clinical trials	• Stringent requirements for informed consent, transparency, adherence to prescribed norms
Data protection	• India not perceived as data-secure
	• Data exclusivity contracts have to be signed
	• Detailed audits required
	• Costs of litigation
Personnel mobility	• Problems in getting visas for technical persons sent by Indian CROs to clients in EU—short duration, single entry

Source: Based on interviews conducted by the author.

effectively negating the possibility of India as a medical destination;

(ii) The relatively low share of non-insured and out-of-pocket paying patients in the EU that automatically limits the pool of patients who would opt for treatment in India;

(iii) The dominance of the public sector as a provider of insurance, which creates problems of political acceptability in allowing medical value travel to India and getting reimbursed by the national health insurance trusts in EU countries;

(iv) The lack of accreditation of Indian hospitals and the lack of recognition of Indian medical qualifications, which affect the scope for reimbursement for treatment in India.

In addition, perceptions regarding India as a healthcare provider also pose a challenge. Given that health is a perception-based sector and medical value travel involves a close interface between the doctor and the patient, attitudinal factors and India's lack of credibility as a medical tourist destination will constrain the

Table 8.8

Constraints to India's Medical Value Travel Exports to the EU

Problem	Features and Implications
Insurance portability regulations	• State insurance trusts and private insurance companies do not accept treatment in India for reimbursement
	• Flight time restrictions for UK patients (limited to 3 hours) for reimbursement from the NHS
	• Restrictions on reimbursement of alternative medicines and therapies for lack of scientific evidence and registration
Growing competition	• India at disadvantage relative to Eastern European countries on qualifications, e-health delivery, movement of persons, insurance portability
Perceptions	• Nationally sensitive issue, resistance to medical value travel by national health providers
	• Cultural, social, linguistic perceptions about India
	• Perceptions about India as a suitable destination for medical value travel

Source: Based on interviews conducted by the author.

extent of trade under this Mode between India and the EU. These issues fall under three categories, namely insurance portability, competition from within the EU and perceptions of the standards and quality of healthcare in India. These issues are summarised in Table 8.8.

4. *Back-office Support Functions*

While India can provide the EU with various support services in the healthcare sector, including revenue cycle management, medical coding, and analysis, there are three main constraints to tapping the EU market: accreditation and certification, the limited scope of the market in the EU, and data privacy and restrictions on international data transfer. These constraints are summarised in Table 8.9.

5. *Collaboration in education, training, research, and staffing*

While there is scope for collaboration with the EU on various fronts within the health services sector, discussions indicated that this potential remains unexploited for various reasons. Table 8.10 highlights constraints affecting specific areas for collaboration, such as in staffing, research and medical device testing.

Table 8.9

Constraints to India's Provision of Support Services in Healthcare to the EU

Problem	Features and Implications
Accreditation	• Certification required by concerned regulatory bodies in various segments (medical coding, analysis)
	• Additional requirements of continuing certification and evaluation
Limited scope in the EU	• Resistance to outsourcing back-office functions
Data privacy and restrictions on international data transfer	• India is not empanelled as data-secure by EU authorities
	• Restricts scope for data transfer and related outsourcing
	• Compliance costs of meeting EU and individual countries' data protection legislation

Source: Based on interviews conducted by the author.

Table 8.10

Constraints to Collaboration in Healthcare between India and the EU

Problem	Features and Implications
Political and social sensitivities	• Affect staffing and temporary movement of health personnel from India to EU countries
Recognition of qualifications	• Qualifications and experience of Indian health personnel not recognised in EU Member Countries
	• Re-certification and registration requirements impose additional costs on Indian doctors
Other regulatory issues	• Regulatory differences between India and the EU on ethics, liability and production and testing

Source: Based on interviews conducted by the author.

6. *Summing up the constraints*

As the segment-wise constraints above indicate, the most common barriers affecting India–EU relations in health services relate to accreditation and standards, data protection regulations, consumer protection and safety norms and detailed specifications for compliance with international or EU Member Country norms. It is also evident that Indian healthcare providers need to be compliant not only with the EU-level Directives but also with country-specific regulations, which complicates the provision of healthcare to the EU. Further, it is not clear to what extent acceptance in one EU Member Country translates into acceptance in other member countries. There are eligibility issues at the establishment level and at the individual provider level that can complicate the certification and registration process with EU authorities. It is also worth noting that there are requirements for registration and certification with multiple institutions and regulatory authorities, including healthcare commissions, local agencies and specialist registers. Adding to these constraints are perceptions related to social, linguistic and cultural factors that are very important in health services, which is human resource-intensive and involves close customer-service provider relations, trust and quality assurance.

Constraints in the Indian Market

Several domestic constraints also affect India's trade in health services with the EU. These constraints mainly relate to standards and accreditation, and to adequacies in India's legal and regulatory framework for health services. Table 8.11 summarises the main constraints within India that affect its ability to export health services to the EU.

As the summary of domestic constraints to realising the potential for expanding India–EU relations in health services indicates, the main constraints are institutional. Hence, a variety of domestic reforms and supporting policies are needed to promote bilateral health services trade.

Negotiating Approach in Health Services

As the preceding section highlights, numerous regulatory and other constraints impede the realisation of the potential for expanding India–EU relations in health services. These are indicative of the issues that need to be addressed in the India–EU BTIA and beyond. An examination of the multilateral and bilateral commitments made by India and the EU in health services indicates the stance taken by both sides in this sector, to what extent the identified constraints can be addressed through

Table 8.11
Domestic Constraints Affecting India's Health Services Exports to the EU

Constraint	Features and Implications
Accreditation and standards	• Absence of mutual recognition agreements with key markets, requiring Indian providers to undergo cumbersome certification and registration processes
	• Lack of recognition prevents Indian companies from drawing on overseas pool of medical manpower
	• Lack of standardisation in medical and nursing training in India
	• No regulatory body in some areas (paramedics)
	• Authentication systems not perceived to be credible
	• Lack of international accreditation by most Indian healthcare establishments, preventing medical value travel, insurance portability, clinical trials outsourcing
	• Lack of registration, standardisation and overseas recognition of alternative medicines and therapies
	• Lack of central laboratory accreditation that is recognised internationally (CAP)
Legal and regulatory framework	• Bureaucracy and delays in approval process for clinical trials
	• Delays in clearance for drug and sample shipments for testing
	• CROs require multiple clearances (from multiple ministries) to undertake clinical trials
	• Ethics approval process cumbersome, as multiple committees are involved
	• Absence of legislation in certain areas (movement of drugs within India, lack of procedural controls on use of medical devices)
	• Poor enforcement of registration for clinical trials
	• Slow regulatory clearances for bio-equivalence studies
	• Lack of clarity in guidelines for bio-technology products
	• Jurisdiction issues about dispute resolution, as India lacks a credible and efficient legal system
	• Gaps between India's clinical trials legislation and that of EU countries (e.g., requirement for pharmaceutical person for issuing drugs in the EU, not in India)

(Table 8.11 Continued)

(Table 8.11 Continued)

Constraint	Features and Implications
	• Concerns over violation of ethics by Indian CROs
Data protection	• Concerns over possible breach of data confidentiality after data submission to Indian regulatory body
	• Lack of strict firewalls for data leakage, guidelines on data exclusivity lacking, not strictly enforced
Insurance and Litigation	• Lack of insurance portability, public or private from EU (related to lack of recognition of Indian qualifications and establishments)
	• Malpractice liability issues: concerns over dispute resolution, jurisdiction, appropriate compensation
	• Absence of insurance in India in emerging areas of medicine: clinical trials require insurance abroad at a high cost
Other	• VAT and service tax charged on services of consultants monitoring clinical trials and reporting to client (export-oriented services usually exempt from service tax)
	• Delays in getting multiple entry visas for consultants monitoring clinical trials, short duration visas are typical
	• Delays in bringing certain medical devices into India affect medical device testing, research-related outsourcing

Source: Based on interviews conducted by the author.

negotiations and what India could expect in this sector under the BTIA. There are two important points in this regard. First, one must recognise that the EU is unlikely to offer India anything substantially more than what it has already committed to other countries or in the WTO. Second, given the special status of health services in the EU, which is excluded from the scope of the EU Services Directive (although there are initiatives to promote cooperation in cross-border healthcare on issues such as patient mobility, e-health and recognition of qualifications), this is likely to be a difficult sector to negotiate with the EU as a whole and bilateral country-specific arrangements hold more promise.

Multilateral Commitments and Offers by the EU

The health services sector is captured in two parts of the GATS schedules, i.e. in the health and social services sectoral schedules and in a subsector called medical, dental and midwives services under the business services sectoral schedule. The EC's commitments and offers show that the EC has made a very restrictive offer in health services and in the subsector of health professionals under business services (WTO, 1994a, 2003, 2005b). Most of the offers are unbound in Mode 1. This effectively means that outsourcing of health services, such as tele-medicine work, clinical trials, back-office support (medical coding and imaging) and tele-pathology, are not permitted cross-border by the EU, either by institutions like hospitals and laboratories, or by individual providers like doctors and radiologists. The only EU country that has unrestricted access under Mode 1 for hospital and other human health services is Hungary and the two countries that have made unrestricted offers in the social services subsector are Latvia and Lithuania. None of the major countries in the EU has provided market access for cross-border delivery of health and social services. The only two countries to have given unrestricted access for medical, dental and midwives services in the case of Mode 1 are Poland and Sweden, while the main markets of interest in the EU have not made commitments.

In Mode 2, market access is unrestricted in most countries under hospital services, which is the most pertinent for medical value travel. The potential of this market depends on the extent of insurance portability by public or private insurance providers and the out-of-pocket paying population. Likewise, while Mode 2 is relatively unrestricted for the professional services subsector in healthcare, issues of recognition and portability of insurance remain. Thus, the liberal market access in Mode 2 under both schedules may not translate into real market access for Indian providers, unless insurance and perception issues are addressed. In Mode 3, the offers are for the most part unrestricted in the main segment of concern, namely hospitals, but are restrictive and subject to limitations in the case of medical professionals under business services. These limitations take the form of economic needs tests, authorisation requirements and quantitative restrictions based on local needs assessment. There are implicit restrictions relating to standards, qualifications and certification. Across Modes 1 to 3, there are also no discernible improvements in the EC's initial and Revised Offer in health services relative to its GATS commitment. The lack of progressive liberalisation in this sector confirms the sensitive nature of this sector given issues of standards, qualifications and consumer protection.

As concerns the EC's Mode 4 commitments and offers, these are highly restrictive. For the two categories of service providers that are pertinent to India, namely contractual service suppliers and independent professionals, the EC's offers are unbound. The same is true for national treatment, which implies that the scope for differential and more restrictive treatment of foreign medical professionals in the EU remains. To the extent that Indian companies may be interested in setting up establishments in the EU and the associated mobility of professionals, the EU's unbound entries for intra-corporate transferees and business visitors for medical professionals under hospital and other health services and its many limitations on Mode 3, no market access has been granted under GATS. There is again no progressive improvement in the EC's Mode 4 offers relative to GATS in the categories of interest under health services.

India's commitments in health services are very liberal, with entries of *none* for Modes 1, 2, and 3 in both professional services subsectors pertinent to healthcare and under the health and social services sector (WTO, 1994b, 2004, 2005c). There are, however, some exceptions on the grounds of relevant technology and for publicly subsidised healthcare being limited to Indian nationals.

Bilateral Negotiations in Health Services: EC

In various EC agreements, there are provisions specific to the health services sector, while in others cross-cutting issues are addressed that are pertinent to trade in health services. The provisions on health mainly pertain to increasing collaboration between the two sides through exchange of information rather than commerce per se. For example, the EU–South Africa Trade, Development and Cooperation Agreement calls for cooperation through knowledge and experience sharing on programmes and improving the education and training of public health professionals. In the EU–Mexico Economic Partnership, Political Coordination and Cooperation Agreement, there is a similar thrust on collaboration in research, preventive medicine and other public health-related areas, and bilateral engagement in projects to improve public health and develop vocational training programmes.

There are also provisions on cross-cutting issues. For instance, the EU–Chile Comprehensive Free Trade Agreement specifically mentions the need to cooperate on standards, technical regulations and conformity assessment to avoid and reduce technical barriers to trade. There are provisions for regulatory cooperation, compatibility of technical regulations based on international and European standards and technical assistance to create a network of conformity assessment bodies on a non-discriminatory basis. Cooperation is envisaged to reduce gaps in standards, regulatory practices and business practices and the operation of systems on both sides. Likewise, in the EU–South Africa Trade, Development and Cooperation Agreement, there are provisions to promote greater use of international technical regulations, standards and conformity assessment procedures including sector-specific measures. There are also provisions calling for cooperation in quality management and assurance in select sectors of importance to South Africa, facilitation of technical assistance and capacity-building initiatives in accreditation and developing practical links between South African and European standardisation, accreditation and certification organisations. Such provisions are very relevant in the area of health services, as some of the main barriers pertain to differences in standards and regulations. As these agreements call for harmonisation of standards and the establishment of regulatory and other mechanisms to enable such harmonisation, they provide important cues for the BTIA.

With regard to the movement of persons, there are several provisions on mutual recognition and domestic regulations regarding qualifications and licensing. One relevant provision concerns the transitivity of recognition accorded by the Member States, which is relevant to health services. The provisions on mutual recognition of qualifications in the EU's bilateral agreements, though general in nature, provide grounds for institutional regulatory mechanisms that accord recognition to partner countries' service providers with greater transparency and speed and, if required, for temporary licensing provisions. Some bilateral agreements also call for cooperation between institutions of higher learning and in education and vocational training as well as links between specialised bodies in the EU and the partner country to facilitate the recognition of degrees and diplomas and the pooling and exchange of experience and technical resources. Such provisions create room for negotiating collaboration in research and training and the movement of personnel, which are relevant for India in the health services sector.

The EC's bilateral agreements also contain a separate article on data protection that includes provisions for cooperation to improve the level of protection accorded to the processing and transfer of personal data, taking into account international standards (which are provided in the Annex to the agreements). The provisions also call for technical assistance, exchange of information and joint initiatives in this area. Hence, personal data and issues of choice, notice, transfer and processing of sensitive personal data are a matter of concern for the EU in all its agreements and will also be important in the negotiations with India.

Overall, the specific and general provisions for the health sector contained in the EU's bilateral agreements with countries such as Chile, Mexico and South Africa are pertinent to the various constraints on India–EU relations in health services. They provide a basis for India–EU negotiations in this sector and provisions that could be adapted to suit India's interests in health services.

Bilateral Negotiations in Health Services: India

India, too, has addressed health services in its bilateral partnership and cooperation agreements through sector-specific and cross-cutting provisions. For instance, under the India–Singapore Comprehensive Economic Cooperation Agreement (CECA), several provisions are relevant to health services.[33] Apart from guaranteeing market access and national treatment in each other's market, the agreement also contains a provision for MRAs to facilitate the free movement of people across five professions, including the medical, dental and nursing professions in both countries. Professionals employed in 127 specific occupations, including the healthcare profession, are to be allowed entry and stay for up to a year or the duration of the contract, whichever is less. This list contains 35 occupations that fall under the health services sector. An important recent development in this regard is the agreement between India and Singapore to sign an MRA for nurses under the CECA, wherein Singapore has agreed to recognise degrees from four nursing institutions in India, after nearly a decade of intense negotiations between the two countries. This agreement will open up overseas employment opportunities for Indian nurses in the Singaporean market and could provide a basis for

[33] http://www.commerce.nic.in/ceca/toc.htm (accessed on November 2008).

similar MRAs with other partner countries such as Japan and Republic of Korea.[34]

The CECA also contains an education cooperation chapter to facilitate joint postgraduate programmes between reputed institutions in the two countries. Although medical training institutions are not explicitly covered under this education cooperation chapter, these provisions provide scope for facilitating linkages between reputed medical colleges in India and Singapore. However, in securing India's market access interests in Singapore, apart from medical value travel, Singapore has not committed in other segments such as tele-medicine, health services outsourcing and foreign direct investment in hospitals.

It is worth noting that India's commitments in health services under the CECA are more liberal than under GATS, although India has progressively liberalised even under GATS in its initial and Revised Offer, with full commitments in Modes 1 and 2 and raising its FDI ceiling in Mode 3. India's willingness to make liberal commitments under the CECA or GATS reflects its autonomous liberalisation in this sector since 2000.

Overall, the CECA provisions and commitments provide for increased cooperation and exchange between India and Singapore in the health services sector in both the professional and establishment segments. The commitments also indicate that both countries have been more willing to provide market access on a bilateral basis than under GATS. The provisions regarding MRAs and cooperation among training institutions are elements that India would seek to incorporate in its other bilateral agreements to address its interests in the health services sector.

The Way Forward

Going ahead, specific issues could be addressed under the ongoing India–EU BTIA negotiations and also bilaterally between India and select EU Member Countries. The negotiating agenda should consist of a cross-cutting approach to the health sector through a focus on cooperation and joint initiatives as well as efforts to remove sector-specific restrictions.

---

[34] The Modi government is pushing for a pact on the mutual recognition of qualifications with the ASEAN as part of the recently signed services and investment agreement signed with that bloc.

In addition, any negotiating strategy must be supplemented by domestic reforms and the introduction of regulatory frameworks and measures in India to address the identified domestic constraints.

A Cooperation Chapter

Collaboration opportunities need to be pursued in the context of the BTIA and beyond. This would have positive implications across all the identified opportunity segments in the EU. A cooperation chapter, either of a general cross-cutting nature or a chapter on cooperation specific to health services along the lines of the India–Singapore CECA chapter on cooperation under education services, could be negotiated. This chapter would need to include elements such as institutional tie-ups, exchange of faculty, students and trainees, research collaboration, cooperation on standards and recognition issues and the launching of joint programmes and pilot projects between India and EU countries. The text of the cooperation chapter should cover all broad aspects of collaboration in the healthcare sector, including:

1. Institutional tie-ups to help in the areas of tele-medicine and medical value travel.
2. Partnerships and affiliations among laboratories and research centres to facilitate work in the area of clinical trials, and global recognition and certification of Indian laboratories.
3. Tie-ups between laboratories in India and the EU, or Indian laboratories and EU universities to conduct clinical trials.
4. A possible reciprocal health agreement with select markets in the EU, along the lines of the agreements some of these countries have with non-member nations for treatments required during visits on emergency grounds.
5. Provisions to facilitate partnerships and collaboration among medical education and research institutions in India and the EU.
6. Institutional linkages in training between select institutions in the EU and India, pilot programmes on research and training on a joint basis to facilitate the certification of Indian medical professionals and postgraduate training possibilities.
7. Pilot programmes for staff deployment and exchange or medical value travel between select institutions on both sides.

8. Pilot programmes with the NHS to provide Indian doctors with additional training and certification from the UK Medical Board and for deployment in the UK on a three- or six-month rotation basis, for radiology reporting or to undertake clinical duties and return to their parent institution in India.

9. Temporary exchange of personnel in terms of sending surgical teams or nurses to the EU for limited periods.

10. Twinning programmes with coursework being done in India and the research and clinical work being done in the EU institution.

11. Visiting faculty and scholarly exchange in the medical profession.

12. Tie-ups between Indian hospitals/research centres and EU companies such as Siemens and Philips that develop medical devices and equipment for commercial and academic reasons.

The win–win outcome of such arrangements needs to be highlighted to the EU authorities. Not only will this enable Indian practitioners to get relevant skills and further the EU's aim of improving the healthcare system of its partner country (as stated in several of its other bilateral agreements), but it would also address the EU's manpower shortages and supplement its skill sets. Equivalence of qualifications could be ensured through twinning programmes, partnerships in education and affiliation between institutions on both sides in continuing education and research. This requires tiering Indian institutions and negotiations with the EU on the criteria for selecting the institutions that should be partnered with. This personnel exchange could also be done for laboratories, pharmacists, radiologists, paramedics and any health professionals where there are huge shortages in the EU countries. Private providers will also need to proactively push for such partnerships with EU institutions. A case in point is the tie-up between Max Healthcare and clusters of hospitals in the US to send nurses to those hospitals for work on a temporary basis. Contractual arrangements through temporary visas and strict return conditions could ensure that the personnel return on completion of their contracts.

Removing Restrictions on Cross-border Delivery

The negotiations on health could also focus on removing existing restrictions on the outsourcing of clinical data and patient information to India for services such as tele-radiology, tele-consulting, tele-imaging and medical coding. The Indian government must lobby with the concerned EU governments to enable such outsourcing outside the EU region. As Indian companies engaged in e-health have adopted international IT security standards, restrictions on the grounds of data privacy and IT security may not be warranted. This will require making the EU governments aware of the IT security systems in place in Indian companies and their compliance with internationally accepted protocols. The benefits from such outsourcing in terms of cost reduction and reduced wait time for EU public health systems need to be stressed. The model adopted by the Singapore National Health Care Group in outsourcing tele-radiology work to India could be suggested to the EU authorities. Singapore, which also has stringent quality assurance standards, has outsourced work from its national healthcare system to India by following a rigorous accreditation and auditing of Indian telemedicine providers by Singapore's National Healthcare Group.[35] Interested EU companies could use this model with select Indian companies. Efforts could be made to affiliate hospitals in the national health systems of selected EU countries with tele-medicine companies that meet all quality standards and data security norms, as in the Singapore model. There is also scope to include provisions regarding cooperation in healthcare to improve the public health systems of both countries through tele-medicine. This could include the negotiation of institutional affiliations between Indian and EU institutions for cross-border delivery. In this context, Prime Minister Modi's 'Digital India' initiative and the proposal to enable healthcare delivery to the poorest of the poor through telemedicine can create new collaborative opportunities with EU companies and public health agencies.

Facilitating Cross-border Patient Mobility and Insurance Portability

As was pointed out by most respondents, it will be important to highlight to the EU authorities through these negotiations and through trade and industry delegations the gains the EU could realise in terms of lower

---

[35] The Singapore Ministry of Health gave the Indian company interpretation tests, checked to ensure that the processes were robust and checked the credentials of the physicians at the Indian establishment. The success with the Singapore model, with turnarounds being reduced from 3 days to a few hours for X-ray reports, reduced costs and increased referrals, has proven to be a win-win for both sides.

costs and reduced waiting lists by allowing their patients to get treated in India. It is important to negotiate and remove the three-hour limit on flying time that is imposed by the NHS for reimbursement. In addition, the Indian government would need to get the public health systems of the EU countries, in particular the UK and perhaps others such as the Netherlands, Denmark and Germany, to accept treatment in India for reimbursement by the international health insurance trusts.

One way to address this issue is to get the NHS and other public health systems to select certain Indian healthcare establishments for reimbursement for select procedures such as cardiac surgeries, joint replacements and cosmetic surgeries where such a third country can be easily justified given the long waiting lists and shortage of personnel. Information needs to be disseminated about the Indian medical system, its reputed institutions and the procedures being done in India. The selection of institutions could include those that have received accreditation from internationally recognised sources, such as the JCI, coupled with additional audits by the authorities of the concerned government.

Another way to address the publicly insured pool of persons in the EU for medical tourism is to launch pilot projects on an institutional tie-up basis on a very limited scale. This tie-up can be made part of a larger institutional link, such as staff exchange, research and development, training and tele-medicine, to give more credibility and accountability to the Indian healthcare provider. Over time, the scale of such initiatives could be expanded to cover more institutions and procedures. The understanding with the public health authorities could also involve insurance providers like Bupa Global that could act as third-party administrators in such government–government schemes.

In addition to publicly insured patients and getting some understanding on reimbursement from national health systems, it is also important to arrive at an understanding with private health insurance companies. Although the share of privately insured patients is relatively small in EU countries, this segment can be tapped by making private health insurance companies like Bupa Global aware of the benefits that would accrue to them by covering treatments in India. Private health insurance companies have to be given an incentive to pay for patients to be treated in cheaper places like India and for this the government, along with private healthcare providers, needs to do some promotional work. Again, through trade and industry delegations, the insurance companies can be incentivised to accept establishments that have international accreditation and do an additional audit of the providers' clinical and privacy policies to decide whom to certify and for what kind of coverage. Thus, sensitisation and promotion of India's potential as a medical tourism destination for EU patients to the EU authorities and private insurance providers will be required.

Addressing Professional Mobility: Recognition and Visa Issues

Issues related to accreditation and standards are among the most important barriers to India–EU relations in health services. Whether it is medical tourism, tele-medicine, movement of personnel or clinical trials, the central issue is recognition of standards and qualifications. On issues of establishment (hospitals, laboratories and tele-medicine companies) standards that concern adherence to various protocols, one needs to create awareness among EU authorities about those that have international accreditation or affiliations through a tiering approach to healthcare establishments while also raising and harmonising internal standards within India. There should also be negotiations to facilitate the extension of such accreditation once accorded by one EU Member Country to other EU countries, with minimal additional requirements for bridging and registration.

In the area of recognition of professional qualifications, negotiations on mutual recognition are required for doctors, nurses, radiologists and medical coders. This will again require tiering the medical training institutions in India and providing the EU authorities with a list of high-quality institutions and a select list of occupations that can be supplemented with additional requirements to bridge any gaps in training. It will also be important to negotiate for streamlining registration and certification processes in the EU that are currently very cumbersome and time-consuming. As highlighted earlier, the recently negotiated MRA in nursing with Singapore provides a basis for similar limited agreements on mutual recognition with selected EU countries in specific segments of the health sector.

In the context of visas, the scope for granting specially classified visas in areas where EU countries have a shortage, such as for nurses, needs to be explored (as the US has done). The issue of an uneven playing field for Indian medical personnel due to the preference given to EU nationals by potential export markets like the UK also needs to be addressed. Industry associations in India need to lobby EU governments to remove the first preference in recruitment to EU nationals. The possibility of granting longer duration multiple-entry visas for select categories of technical and senior personnel in the health sector, such as in CROs, also needs to be explored.

Domestic Reforms and Policy Measures in India

Much of what has been outlined above for the negotiations needs to be supplemented and at times preceded by domestic reforms and the introduction of regulatory frameworks and measures in India. Some of the issues that need to be addressed internally are highlighted here.

1. *Standards and recognition*
   The main regulatory bottleneck is standards and recognition. The regulatory bodies in India's health sector must consider cross-certification of degrees with other countries. Mutual recognition would also need to be supported by a credential or ranking system of different medical institutions and colleges. This would not only facilitate outsourcing of work to India, medical value travel and other partnerships, but would also enable India to draw on Indian medical personnel who are trained in the EU, particularly the UK, and to get them to work in India, serving both the Indian and the EU markets. Recognition of Indian medical degrees on a mutual basis would enable the exchange of consumers and cooperation among institutions in India and the EU.

   Attempts at mutual recognition on a wider basis will need to be preceded by internal measures to raise standards in our own medical colleges and institutions. There is considerable divergence at present in our standards of training, qualifying exams and extent of clinical practice and exposure across different Indian medical training institutions and nursing and paramedic schools and colleges, unlike the US or the UK where there is a set standard and common qualifying exam. Thus, quality has to be standardised internally.

In other areas, too, there needs to be an alignment of India's norms and practices with the International Conference on Harmonisation (ICH) guidelines. International accreditation from the concerned authorities is required in various segments of clinical trials (such as cellular therapy and stem cell research). The Indian laboratory accreditation system has to be aligned with the globally recognised Certified Authorization Professional (CAP) certification in the US, which is also recognised in Europe. Conformity is also required in the area of medical devices with the introduction of more effective procedural controls and their enforcement. More Indian laboratories and CROs need to be accredited internationally by getting CAP certification; meanwhile, efforts need to be made to get our standards recognised by international standard-setting bodies.

2. *Insurance sector*

   Further opening up of the Indian insurance sector would enable more joint ventures between Indian and overseas insurance companies and would also make possible the provision of insurance by Indian companies to foreigners to cover treatment in India. Recent developments to raise the FDI cap in insurance are a welcome step in this direction. In addition, several transparency issues have to be sorted out in India. One of the main problems affecting the take-off and penetration of health insurance in India is the lack of standardisation and proper classification of services for pay-outs. Health insurance companies and providers need to arrive at a common nomenclature and classification of diseases and procedures, and agree on a tiering of institutions and products to arrive at a differential pricing model based on facilities, standards, personnel and treatments. Quality benchmarking and its enforcement through the accreditation process of hospitals will need to take off and foreign insurance companies must accept the accreditation process of Indian hospitals.

   To tap the out-of-pocket market for patients, there is also a need to develop attractive packages, such as in the area of alternative treatments and medicines. This will, however, require getting certain procedures and drugs registered with the Drug Controller General of India (DCGI). State governments will need to take these initiatives jointly with private providers and promotional campaigns will also be required.

Malpractice insurance is also important. At present, this has to be bought in the client country. Opening up the insurance sector could create possibilities for purchasing the policy in India and reduce this cost. Clinical trials insurance is another area that needs to emerge in India to cover CROs engaged in clinical trial work. Such policies are very expensive at present. More joint ventures and liberalisation of the insurance sector could see the emergence of Indian companies entering this segment of insurance.

Concluding Thoughts

As the preceding analysis has highlighted, there are several opportunity segments for enhancing bilateral relations between India and the EU in health services. However, there are also numerous constraints to realising this potential. First, as healthcare is dominated by the public sector in the EU, developing commercial relations with another country is likely to face resistance from internal stakeholders in the EU and any discussions with the EU have to involve the concerned public health authorities and institutions. Public versus private issues, equity implications, fiscal conditions, costs, consumer protection and standards are likely to be very important in shaping the prospects for bilateral relations in this sector. Second, the prospects are likely to be the greatest in those EU countries where there is a gradual shift towards private provision, as these markets are likely to be compelled to open up their healthcare systems externally in the near future. Third, given the scope for intra-regional trade in health services in terms of patient mobility or tele-medicine within the EU, India faces competitive challenges from member countries within the EU. For instance, in 2010 European countries imported €3 billion ($3.98 billion)[36] worth of health products and services. However, most of this trade was among European countries (OECD, 2012b). The sector is also currently in a state of flux within the EU, with member countries experimenting with cross-border cooperation among themselves and

[36] Converted using www.oanda.com using the average exchange rate for the year 2010 of 1 Euro = 1.3267 dollars.

debating a wide range of issues concerning regulatory coordination, harmonisation, consumer choice, safety and national interest. Finally, as the health services sector falls outside the scope of the EU Services Directive, the EU cannot be treated as a single regional market for health services exports. Thus, the health services sector poses special challenges due to its public good nature and its special status within the EU.

The priority should be to negotiate a chapter on cooperation that covers various regulations that have a bearing on the health services sector. In addition, three specific issues need to be focused on, both in the context of the chapter on cooperation and otherwise. The first pertains to specific restrictions maintained by the EU and using the negotiations to remove them. The second pertains to larger issues such as equivalence, recognition, standards and establishing mechanisms to either harmonise or agree on a selective basis for greater linkages between EU and Indian establishments and providers. The third pertains to administrative and operational issues in the way regulations are implemented and administered in the EU, which, if streamlined, could smooth existing relations in these areas.

One must, however, be pragmatic about what can be achieved through discussions in this sector under a BTIA. It would be unrealistic to expect any major progress in this sector under the BTIA. Therefore, the way forward would be to look beyond the BTIA and to launch joint programmes with select countries in the EU, on a pilot basis, in all possible segments of opportunity and to scale these initiatives depending on the outcome. A cooperation-based approach with demonstrable outcomes would probably yield more in this sector. Also, as stakeholder buy-in will be essential, including from politically sensitive constituents such as public health authorities and national insurance trusts in the EU, a limited and gradual approach is likely to be more appropriate.

These negotiating efforts have to be supported by active lobbying and promotional work by Indian industry associations and trade delegations to market India as a healthcare provider as well as consumer. India should highlight its importance as a healthcare market given its large population and its share in the global disease burden and, thus, its potential as a consumer of healthcare to show why it is in the EU's interests to expand its relationship with India in this sector. Meanwhile, a variety of internal measures and regulatory reforms need to be adopted in India if these bilateral initiatives are to be scalable and sustainable in the long run.

9

Environmental Services in the EU–India BTIA and Beyond

Aparna Sawhney

Introduction

Bilateral preferential and free trade agreements have become a strategic route for opening target country markets, particularly since multilateral negotiations have increasingly begun to falter and delay further liberalisation. The EU has pursued the path of bilateralism and regionalism with enthusiasm and has to its account the largest number of preferential trade agreements in the world.[1] The EU has increasingly pursued free trade agreements with developing countries as a means of

---

[1] The European Commission notifies different types of agreements in the WTO: intra-EU Custom Union accessions as well as bilateral Free Trade Agreements with countries in Europe, the Mediterranean, Latin America, the Middle East and South Africa. Typically, EC free trade agreements are accompanied by association agreements (EIAs). Besides the EC trade agreements, individual EU Members have bilateral FTAs with the EFTA (now consisting of the 4 non-EU countries of Iceland, Liechtenstein, Norway and Switzerland). The EFTA has separate bilateral FTAs with European, Middle Eastern, and Asian countries. See WTO website for details:

http://www.wto.org/english/tratop_e/region_e/summary_e.xls (accessed on 1 June 2015).

accessing new markets for its products and investment (Francois et al., 2005), as well as a means of exporting its regulations and non-trade objectives (Sally, 2007). Indeed, the European Council's strategy[2] seeks to integrate environmental issues in the external relations of the EU and its Member States.

Among the Asian developing countries, the EU is interested in establishing deeper commercial ties with the Indian economy through a bilateral trade and investment agreement (BTIA) to further liberalise trade in goods and services. Services and investment are priority areas in the agreement, and within the services negotiations the environmental service sector is a key sector where the EU has been seeking a more liberal commitment from India. More importantly, environmental aspects form an integral part of the entire BTIA since sustainable development remains an overarching goal in the EU's recent commercial deals. Indeed, the new national program of *Swachh Bharat Abhiyan* ('Clean India' Campaign), launched in October 2014, and aimed at creating a clean green India by 2019, has enhanced business opportunities in the environmental services.

According to Eurostat, the environmental goods and services sector, also called the environment industry/eco-industries, consists of a heterogeneous set of producers of goods and services aiming at the protection of the environment and the sustainable management of natural resources.[3] The sector is considered to be important and promising since its development can reduce pressure on the environment, create new jobs and be economically advantageous for business.[4] Indeed, the European eco-industry is considered to have great potential in contributing towards the Lisbon Agenda goals for growth and jobs with further improvement in its competitiveness (ECORYS, 2009). The EU has significant interest in exploring market opportunities beyond its borders, especially in developing countries (like India) where the eco-industry has not matured but where there is increasing demand for environmental services.

[2] Adopted in Barcelona on 11 March 2002.

[3] http://epp.eurostat.ec.europa.eu/statistics_explained/index.php/Environmental_goods_ and_services_sector (accessed on 26 March 2013).

[4] http://epp.eurostat.ec.europa.eu/statistics_explained/index.php/Environmental_goods_ and_services_sector (accessed on 26 March 2013).

In this chapter, we examine the bilateral trade and investment flows between India and the EU in the environmental services sector, and critical climate change issues that are of interest in the EU–India collaborative efforts in the field. It is essential to note at the outset that the environmental services sector is rather broad and overlaps with several other services including energy, engineering, architecture and design, and consulting. Thus, commitments in other proposed chapters of the BTIA impinge on the environmental services sector; however, in the analysis here, the focus remains on the environmental services sector as encapsulated within the services negotiations and the significance of climate change mitigation in light of the post-Kyoto goals. The rest of the chapter is organised as follows: The second section highlights the EU's environmental sustainability goal that forms an integral part of the BTIA and the significance of climate change mitigation. The third section outlines the coverage and classification of the environmental services sector, and briefly discusses the position of the EU and India in the global environmental services market and the clean energy sector. The fourth section reviews the extent to which the EU and India have liberalised this sector, in terms of commitments made multilaterally and in other preferential trade agreements. The fifth section analyses the environmental segments of trade interest to the EU and India, as well as actual trade in this sector. The sixth section examines the barriers faced by the environmental service providers. The seventh section provides a summary of the analysis and opportunities for India–EU collaboration in the environmental services sector, and the eighth section ends with suggestions for domestic reforms in India.

The Sustainable Development Chapter in EU BTIAs and Climate Change

While environmental services is included as one of the sectors within services liberalisation, the EU has also begun to incorporate a chapter on sustainable development within its new BTIAs, which allows the integration of the EU's non-trade goals in its commercial deals. For example, Chapter 13 of the EU–Korea FTA 2010 on *Trade and Sustainable Development* reaffirms the commitment of the partners to promote sustainable development at every level of their trade relationship while also committing to cooperate 'on the development of the *future* international climate change framework in accordance with the Bali Action Plan' (Article 13.5, paragraph 3, emphasis added). Moreover, the chapter encompasses a wider liberalisation goal for the environmental sector, stating that the:

> Parties shall strive to facilitate and promote trade and foreign direct investment in environmental goods and services, including environmental technologies, sustainable renewable energy, energy efficient products and services and eco-labelled goods, including through addressing related non-tariff barriers. (Article 13.6, para 2, EU–Korea FTA)

Sustainable development is a desirable goal for all nations, and particularly for an emerging economy like India, it is important to integrate environmental aspects in the economic growth process to ensure that the nation can sustain the growth rate for generations to come. The broad goal of sustainable development can be achieved through targeted environmental programmes and policies, and in this context, the activities in the environmental services sector fall within the realm of sustainable development. In particular, the proposed chapter on sustainable development within the EU–India BTIA stated that the agreement's 'Market Access chapters could provide commitments to *fast-track liberalisation of environmental goods and services*'.[5]

While the proposed sustainable development chapter observed that the agreement does not *seek to harmonise levels of environmental, labour and social protection*, yet it did indicate that the '*FTA could reflect commitments in... a set of core Multilateral Environmental Agreements* (MEAs)...the starting point could be recognition of the importance of adherence to and the effective implementation of the specific trade obligations set out in the fourteen core MEAs that have taken part in information exchange sessions under the auspices of the WTO Committee on Trade and Environment.'[6] The chapter also sought commitment on potential future environmental negotiations by indicating that the EU–India BTIA could include 'trade-related regulatory co-operation to achieving climate-change objectives and more generally

---

[5] 'Discussion Paper on Sustainable Development for EU-India FTA', EU text dated 17 September 2007. Emphasis added.

[6] 'Discussion Paper on Sustainable Development for EU-India FTA', EU text dated 17 September 2007. Emphasis added.

to ensure protection of sustainable energy and increased energy efficiency *for the post-2012 climate change strategy*' (emphasis added). This suggests that the agreement could infringe on regulatory aspects of environmental protection and future climate negotiations. The environmental regulatory framework is indeed key to the development of environmental goods and services, as the growth of this sector is driven by the needs created by these regulations, such as compliance with the environmental legislation and production target for energy from renewable sources (Eurostat–EC, 2009).

While the environmental services negotiations are conducted separately in the context of sectoral negotiations, the sustainable development chapter envisions wider environmental aspects in the EU–India BTIA (as in the EU–Korea FTA noted above). On the economic front, since one of the critical sectors in the climate change strategy is the renewable energy sector, trade in clean energy technology and equipment is likely to gain significance in pursuance of climate change mitigation.

Classification of the Environmental Services Sector

According to the OECD–Eurostat definition, the environmental industry or eco-industry includes activities that produce goods and services to measure, prevent, limit, minimise or correct environmental damage to water, air and soil, as well as problems related to waste, noise and eco-systems. This includes technologies, products and services that reduce environmental risk and minimise pollution and resources. Thus, the environment industry constitutes a heterogeneous set of economic activities to protect environmental damage to air, water, soil and problems relating to ecosystems and management of natural resources. Given the nature of the industry, it is important to note some of the key characteristics of the environmental services sector.

First, environmental services do not fall in the category of a coherent economic sector, unlike financial or IT services. Rather, the sector is dispersed across other traditional sectors of the economy including engineering and design, chemicals, construction and R&D. In other words, this services sector overlaps with other services sectors that are negotiated separately. It is, thus, possible that while the environmental sector is otherwise not open, liberalisation in other sectors could form a channel of trade for certain environmental services.

Second, environmental equipment and services are often provided in an integrated manner, especially in segments of water treatment and waste management. For example, technology, design and engineering of waste treatment systems fall under environmental services, but the provision of these environmental services are typically integrated with the provision of the associated equipment. This makes it difficult to track trade in environmental goods and services separately.

Third, given the above two characteristics of the sector, several environmental firms specialise in multiple segments of the environmental services sector along with the provision of equipment. Often a firm that is otherwise categorised as an infrastructure construction company may well be providing environmental services in turnkey projects, such as building water treatment plants or solid waste incinerators. Thus, while a separate environmental sector may not be identified in a country, it could well have environmental service providers that are operating under a different industry heading. Indeed, a recent US International Trade Commission (USITC) report noted that the analysis of the environmental services sector is 'complicated by the fact that several environmental services are provided by firms that primarily identify themselves as members of other industry sectors' (USITC, 2013:1–4).

The classification of environmental services for negotiating purposes in the multilateral forum of the WTO was made largely on the basis of the associated environmental media. In 1994, environmental services were classified into four distinct segments under the General Agreement on Trade in Services (GATS) as follows: (a) Sewage disposal services (CPC 9401); (b) Refuse disposal services (CPC 9402); (c) Sanitation and similar services (CPC 9403); and (d) Other services. The EU, however, has followed a more disaggregated seven-segment classification under Eurostat that distinguishes the *other services* into specific components. The seven segments are: (a) Water and wastewater management, CPC 9401; (b) Solid/hazardous waste management, CPC 9402 and CPC 9403; (c) Protection of ambient air and climate, CPC 9404; (d) Remediation and clean up of soil and waters, part of CPC 9406; (e) Noise and vibration abatement, CPC 9405; (f) Protection of biodiversity and landscape, parts of CPC 9406 not covered under D; (g) Other Environmental and ancillary Services, CPC 9409.

While the Eurostat/OECD classification seems broader than the GATS categorisation, the latter can be easily written in a more expanded form. Indeed, the WTO Secretariat reconciled the differences between the GATS' four-segment classification and the EU's seven-segment classification in 1998, with some reservations for sensitive segments such as water for human use, wholesale in scrap and services incidental to agriculture/foresting. Table 9.1 provides the correspondence between the different EU and the GATS environmental segments.

Table 9.1
EU Classification of Environmental Services and Corresponding GATS Segments

EU Classification	Corresponding GATS Classification
A. Water for human use and wastewater management Waste Water services (CPC 9401)	I. Sewage disposal services (CPC 9401) Excludes collection, purification and distribution services of water (in CPC 18000) Excludes construction, repair and alteration of sewers (in CPC 51330) (GATS 3B civil engineering construction services)
B. Solid and hazardous waste management (a) Refuse Disposal (CPC 9402) (b) Sanitation and similar (CPC 9403)	II. Refuse Disposal Services (CPC 9402) Excludes dealing and wholesale in waste and scrap (in CPC 62118 and 62278; GATS 4 distribution services) Excludes R&D services on environment issues (CPC 85; GATS 1C Business services (R&D) III. Sanitation and Similar Services (CPC 9403) Excludes disinfecting/exterminating services for buildings (in CPC 87401; GATS (1F)(o) – Other Business Building Cleaning Services.) Excludes pest control for agriculture (CPC 88110; GATS 1F(f) services incidental to agriculture, hunting and forestry.
C. Protection of ambient air and climate (CPC 9404)	IV. Other Cleaning Services of Exhaust Gases (CPC 9404)

(Table 9.1 Continued)

(Table 9.1 Continued)

EU Classification	Corresponding GATS Classification
D. Remediation and clean up of soil and waters (part of CPC 9406) Treatment, remediation of contaminated/polluted soil and water	D. Other Nature and Landscape Protection Services (CPC 9406)
E. Noise and vibration abatement (CPC 9405)	D. Other Noise and vibration abatement (CPC 9405)
F. Protection of biodiversity and landscape (parts of CPC 9406 not covered under D)	D. Other Nature and landscape protection services CPC 9406 Excludes forest and damage assessment and abatement services (in CPC 881, GATS 1F(f). Services incidental to agriculture, hunting and foresting)
G. Other Environmental and ancillary Services (CPC 9409)	D. Other Other environmental services nec, (CPC 9409)

Source: WTO (1998b) document S/C/W/46.

In this chapter, while analysing the EU and Indian environmental sectors, we follow the extended seven-segment classification of environmental services, since the EU has used its seven-segment classification in making offers under the Doha Round of negotiations and making its commitments in bilateral FTAs. India on the other hand, made its multilateral offers under GATS with the four-segment classification, and the EU too followed this classification for its GATS commitments. Thus, when discussing the WTO commitments and offers in the fourth section of this chapter, we retain the GATS' four-segment classification.

The EU and India in the Global Environmental Services Market

The global environmental services (ES) sector grew rapidly during the last decade (by 41 per cent during 2000–2009) to reach US$506 billion by market value in 2010.[7] The water utilities and water treatment services have constituted by far the largest share by revenue value (49 per cent), followed by solid and hazardous waste services (32 per cent) (USITC, 2013). However, the fastest growing ES segment has been the environmental consulting and engineering services segment, which grew by 73 per cent during the decade to reach US$52.2 billion in 2010.

The developed countries have continued to account for the largest environmental services markets, and in 2010, the US remained the largest with a share of 38 per cent of global environmental services revenue, followed by Western Europe with a share of 28 per cent. While Japan accounted for 11 per cent of the global environmental services market, the rest of Asia (including China and India) accounted for 8 per cent in 2010. While the market size of Latin America and the Asia-Pacific region (especially China and India) are small, these regions have experienced vibrant growth in their environmental markets. Table 9.2 depicts the relative sizes of the different environmental services segments and the largest country markets. The figures are based on the Environmental Business International (EBI) environmental services sector estimates, which do not cover the ambient air/climate change mitigation services.

Thus, while the EU is enthusiastic about liberalising the environmental sector worldwide, there is marked disparity in the market sizes and maturity levels in a developing country like India when compared to the EU. When we consider the water services market, which is by far the largest segment of the total ES market, we find that the dominant water services firms are from the EU, with a strong global presence through subsidiaries in both developed and developing countries. Table 9.3 gives a snapshot of the water services market in 2011. As evident from the table, the Indian water services market is less than one-tenth the size of the EU market, with the latter being home to the most mature water management firms in the world.

---

[7] Based on market revenue estimates from the Environmental Business International Inc., US. The EBI dollar value estimates, however, do not match with those from Market-Line since underlying coverage and value estimations are different. But the more important qualitative indications of relative market sizes of the specific segments and country market sizes are similar in both data sources. We quote from both the EBI as well as MarketLine estimates in this chapter for the years 2010 and 2011, respectively, highlighting the key players in the world market.

Table 9.2

Environmental Services Market 2010: Distribution across Segments and Regions

Segment	Share in Global ES Market	Key Regional/ Country Markets[a]
Water utilities and waste water management services	49%	US (36%), W. Europe (29%), Japan (8%)
Solid and hazardous waste management services	32%	US (38%), W. Europe (26%)
Remediation and industrial services	8%	US (33%), W. Europe (24%), Japan (13%)
Consulting & engineering	10%	
Analytical services	1%	
Total world market	*100%*	*US (38%), W. Europe (28%), Japan (11%)*

Source: USITC (2013) based on estimates from EBI.

Note: [a]Figures in parentheses give the relative size of the regional market in the global ES market for the corresponding segment.

Table 9.3

Water Services Market, 2011

Region	Value (billion US$)[a]	CAGR[b]	Leading Companies
EU-27	260.1	4%	Veolia Environnement (France), Suez Environnement (France), Hera S.p.A (Italy)
India	21.1	7%	Hyderabad Metropolitan Water Supply and Sewage Board, Ion Exchange, VA Tech Wabag
US	163.4	5%	American Water Works Co., Aqua America, California Water Services Group
China	54.0	3%	Beijing Capital Co, Beijing Enterprises Water Group, Nanhai Development Co
World	*725.2*		*Veolia Environnement, Veolia Water North America*

Source: USITC (2013) based on estimates from MarketLine.

Notes: [a]Absolute market sizes are based on MarketLine estimates and are not comparable to the estimates from EBI Inc.

[b]Compound annual growth rate over five years leading up to 2011 of the regional/country market.

The EU is enthusiastic about growth prospects in developing country environmental markets since Europe already has the first-mover advantage in several environmental technologies and services. The EU environmental companies have a competitive edge in several environmental segments, including water and wastewater management services (e.g. Vivendi Environnement S.A. and Suez S.A. from France), and solid and hazardous waste management services (e.g. RWE AG from Germany).

The environmental market in the EU, however, is quite heterogeneous since all members are not equally developed nor do they have identical regulations; it is also fragmented by size and language. Germany, the UK, France and Italy have the four largest national environmental markets in Europe (EBI, 2006). Spain has a comparatively smaller market but is expected to have good growth prospects. Among the newer Eastern European EU Members, Poland and the Czech Republic (members since 2004) have rather small markets that are more in the league of the Indian environmental sector.

The maturity and size of the national environmental sectors across EU Member States are clearly divided along the Western versus Central and Eastern European nations (newer EU Members). While the environmental sectors of West European countries are well-developed and have cutting-edge technology in the world market, the environmental sectors of Central and East European countries are small and just beginning to evolve; their environmental regulations are being upgraded and enforcement remains poor. Their accession to the EU was conditioned on the upgrading of national environmental regulations to stringent EU standards (*Acquis Communautaire*), as well as compliance based on a definite timetable (EBI, 2006:8–152). The new EU Members have been on the fast track for implementing EC environmental Directives, as part of their accession condition to the Union. The EU funding for environmental projects is several times the size of the entire Indian environmental sector. The projects are usually co-financed by national authorities, the European Investment Bank and the private sector. Sector-specific EU grants also offer assistance for environmental protection to EU Member States. However, it is important to note that tenders related to these grants (posted on the website of the European Commission) typically restrict participation to EU firms or are tied to EU content (USCS, 2007).

The implementation of new EU environmental Directives is also driving environmental market growth in the older EU Member States. While West European environmental sectors have low market growth in pollution abatement/environmental protection services, robust growth is expected in clean technology and resource efficiency. These business opportunities are again a reflection of the level of maturity of the environmental sector in the Western EU Members versus the newer Members (and India).

Compared to the EU environmental industry, the Indian domestic environmental industry is not an organised sector and has relatively small environmental service providers and less-diversified firms. On the whole, in India, two types of environmental firms are observed: large engineering firms offering environmental services as part of their equipment or technology package for pollution treatment and small (even micro) firms specialising in analytical environmental services, including environmental management systems facilitation, environmental audits, environmental impact assessment and development of environmental standards. The larger firms offer environmental services as an integrated package through large turnkey consulting projects. Such comprehensive project design and management includes the provision of engineering, construction, equipment and operation and maintenance of general utility facilities, such as water, pollution and waste management systems for industrial clients. These Indian firms are typically well-developed and large in terms of staff and scale of operations. However, large Indian firms remain small when compared to the European environmental multinationals.

Moreover, the Indian environmental industry has made little investment in R&D over the past decades, with the majority of the processes or technologies employed in the industry being generic with a few modifications. There are hardly any worthwhile patents taken up by the Indian industry on new processes or technologies except in ion-exchange resins and some membranes. However, some companies have made rapid strides in advancing technological capabilities in conventional environmental management. For instance, in renewable energy (pertinent for climate change mitigation efforts) and wastewater treatment, local firms have strengthened their ability to supply technologically superior products. Table 9.4 highlights the renewable energy-based power capacity installed (by technology) in

Table 9.4
Global Renewable Power Capacity (in GW) by Technology and Region, 2011

Region	Biomass	Geothermal	Tidal	Solar PV	CSP	Wind	Total Capacity
EU-27	26	0.9	0.2	51	1.1	94	174
Of which							
– Germany	7.2	~0	0	25	0	29	61
– Italy	2.1	0.8	0	13	~0	6.7	22
– Spain	0.8	0	~0	4.5	1.1	22	28
India	3.8	0	0	0.5	~0	16	20
Japan	3.3	0.5	0	4.9	0	2.5	11
US	13.7	3.1	~0	4	0.5	47	68
World	*72*	*11.2*	*0.5*	*70*	*1.8*	*238*	*390*

Source: Extracted from REN21 (2012) Table R2, p. 98.

India. Much of this has happened through indigenous efforts and through strategic partnerships with foreign companies.

It is important to note that as several of the Indian environmental firms are relatively new, they do not qualify for the large projects funded by multilateral organisations in the country, due to strict eligibility criteria that include past record, experience, turnover, product specifications and third-party guarantees.

Extent of Liberalisation in Environmental Sector of the EU and India

The EU has been particularly keen on India's commitments in environmental services for market access through Mode 3 (commercial presence), while Indian interest lies in the further liberalisation of the professional services through Mode 4 (movement of natural persons) in the EU given their respective factor abundance. This section examines the extent of liberalisation, particularly in terms of the FDI regime in India and foreign professional/labour entry (independent of commercial presence) in the EU.

Unilateral Liberalisation

In India, the existing regime allows foreign direct investment in environmental equipment and services under the automatic route with up to 100 per cent foreign equity holding. Environmental management and consulting is completely open with 100 per cent foreign equity, although foreign investment in infrastructure services has often been routed through the government's Foreign Investment Promotion Board—but even in the latter case automatic FDI approvals are increasingly allowed.[8] Construction development of townships and housing built-up infrastructure as well as those for industrial parks is open under the automatic route with 100 per cent equity. Infrastructure and common facilities include water supply, sewerage and common effluent treatment plants. In environmental equipment (typically offered with services) too, India allows FDI up to 100 per cent foreign equity under the automatic route. Investment under the automatic route in India signifies that central government approval is not required, and reflects the underlying decentralisation and promotion of private participation in infrastructure services at the state and municipal levels. This is also reflected in India's Revised Offer to the WTO in 2005 in which it scheduled commitments in sub-sectors such as refuse disposal services and sanitation services.

In July 2005, the Indian government further opened up environmental infrastructure services in new township construction with 100 per cent equity in 'built-up infrastructure and construction development projects ... including city and regional level infrastructure' under the automatic route.[9] As central government approvals are not required now for foreign investment in certain township construction, it has reduced bureaucratic barriers.

The EU has a liberal regime for foreign investment (Mode 3) in environmental services. However, reservations for public works and government-approved monopoly in certain infrastructure environmental services constitute the main market restrictions. Moreover, while capital movement is open, movement of foreign professionals face restrictions.

[8] FDI in infrastructure including roads, highways, tunnels, bridges, ports and harbours, generation and distribution of power is permitted and comes under automatic approval with 100 per cent foreign equity.

[9] The investment is conditional on a minimum size of US$10 million for wholly-owned subsidiaries and US$5 million for joint ventures with Indian partners. Foreign Exchange Management Regulations 2005: Notification No. FEMA 136/2005-RB dated 19 July 2005.

Multilateral Commitments and Offers in the WTO

The WTO environmental negotiations have been led by the EC since the Uruguay Round, and the EC made commitments in environmental services in 1994 under GATS. At that time, India, like most developing countries, refrained from making any commitments in the sector. This section discusses the multilateral commitments and offers in environmental services of India and the EU. It is noteworthy that while the actual trade regime in India is quite liberal (as indicated above), the WTO commitments and offers are more restrained. On the other hand, the EC's commitments and offers in the GATS mirror its actual trade regime.

Under the Doha Round of negotiations, India had not offered to open the environmental services sector initially (in 2003). In the Revised Offer in 2005, however, India offered to open the two environmental segments of refuse disposal services and sanitation services. On the other hand, the EC's offer in the environmental services sector remained virtually the same as its commitments. Much to the discontent of the developing countries, the EC continues to keep the movement of natural persons unbound (not offered to make any commitment), while foreign investment is completely open. Even in the EC's latest offer (October 2007) Mode 1 and Mode 4 are unbound for most states.[10] While Modes 2 and 3 are open for most states, these are unbound for the emerging East European Members. Comparing India's Revised Offer of 2005 with the EC's conditional Revised Offer of 2005 in environmental services, it is clear that, unlike the EC, India has no horizontal reservation for public utilities (national or local) for exclusive rights given to private operators. The EC has, however, maintained such reservations all through, and this directly impacts market access in environmental services such as sewage services, refuse disposal services and sanitation services, where local authorities hold a monopoly in providing services to the communities. Table 9.5 provides a comparative summary of the offers made by India and the EU in the environmental services sector under the Doha Round.

Within the two subsectors, namely *refuse disposal services* (CPC 9402) and *sanitation services* (CPC 9403), that India tabled in the Revised Offer of 2005, the offers are more liberal than those made by the

---

[10] WTO (2007) Council for Trade in Services, 'Notification from The European Communities and its Member States Pursuant to Article of the GATS', S/SECRET/11.

Table 9.5
Comparison of GATS Offers in Environmental Services, India vs. EC
(2005)

India	EC
No such horizontal reservation for public utilities at national or local level	*Horizontal restriction*: 'Public utilities may be subject to public monopolies or exclusive rights granted to private operators, under the horizontal commitments regulatory'. Effectively restricts market access in CPC 9401, 9402 and 9403, even when 'None' is reported.
I. Sewage Services (CPC 9401) Not offered	Mode 1 unbound (open in Estonia, Latvia and Lithuania). Modes 2 and 3 open in most (unbound in Cyprus, Finland, Hungary, Malta, Poland and Romania). Mode 4 is unbound in all states.
II. Refuse Disposal Services (CPC 9402) Modes 1 and 2 open. Mode 3 open subject to incorporation (FIPB approval in prior collaboration) Mode 4 is unbound.	Mode 1 unbound (open in Estonia and Hungary). Modes 2 and 3 are open for most (unbound in Cyprus, Malta, Poland and Romania). Mode 4 is unbound in all states.
III. Sanitation and Similar Services (CPC 9403) Mode 1 and 2 open. Mode 3 open subject to incorporation (FIPB approval in prior collaboration). Mode 4 is unbound.	Mode 1 unbound (open for Estonia, Hungary and Latvia). Modes 2 and 3 open for most (unbound in Cyprus, Finland, Malta, Poland and Romania). Mode 4 is unbound.
IV. Other environmental services: - *Protection of ambient air and climate (CPC 9404)* Not offered.	Mode 1 unbound (open for Estonia, Finland, Latvia, Poland and Romania). Modes 2 and 3 open for most (unbound in Cyprus, the Czech Republic, Hungary, Malta, the Slovak Republic and Slovenia). Mode 4 is unbound.

(Table 9.5 Continued)

(Table 9.5 Continued)

India	EC
- Noise and Vibration abatement (CPC 9405) Not offered	Mode 1 unbound (open for Estonia, Finland, Latvia, Poland, and Romania). Modes 2 & 3 unbound (open for Austria, Bulgaria, Estonia, Finland, Latvia, Lithuania, Poland, Romania and Sweden) Mode 4 unbound.
- Nature & landscape protection services (CPC 9406) Not offered	Mode 1 unbound (open for Estonia, Finland and Romania) Mode 2 and 3 open (unbound for Cyprus, the Czech Republic, Hungary, Malta, Poland and the Slovak Republic) Mode 4 unbound.
- Other ancillary services (CPC 9409) Not offered	Mode 1 unbound (open for Estonia, Finland, Poland and Romania). Modes 2 and 3 open (unbound for Bulgaria, Cyprus, the Czech Republic, Hungary, Malta, the Slovak Republic and Slovenia) Mode 4 unbound.

Source: Compiled by author from the WTO Revised Offer of India and the EU.

EC when compared Mode by Mode India put no restrictions in Modes 1 and 2 (unlike the EC which has Mode 1 as unbound), and Mode 3 is open, subject to incorporation (but unbound for EC members Cyprus, Malta, Poland and Romania—markets where new environmental projects have been financed). Mode 4, of course, is unbound for both partners.

The EC offer contained restrictions in other related services like *integrated engineering services* (CPC 8673), with application in environmental services like sanitation works (turnkey projects), Modes 1, 2 and 3 are not open for all states. Mode 1 is unbound for Cyprus, Greece, Italy, Malta, Portugal, Poland and Romania; Mode 2 is unbound for Bulgaria, Cyprus, Malta, Poland and Romania; Mode 3 is unbound for Bulgaria, Cyprus, the Czech Republic, Spain, Italy, Malta, Portugal, Poland and Romania. Mode 4 remains unbound for all.

Similarly, in engineering services (CPC 8672), engineering design, advisory and consulting, Mode 4 is unbound, with Bulgaria, Greece and Hungary requiring nationality/permanent residency conditions.

To the extent that larger Indian environmental service firms have engineering services as their key specialisation, market access in the emerging economies of EC is restricted. Since the environmental services sector also overlaps with a wide range of other professional services, any restrictions in those sectors immediately impinge on the openness of the environmental sector.

In concluding this section, we observe that while the capital- and technology-rich EC has kept Mode 3 completely open in the environmental services sector, and requests the developing countries to match that offer, it continues to restrain Mode 4 and Mode 1 that labour-abundant countries like India have been requesting. With unemployment continuing to haunt some of the European nations, it seems unlikely that the EC would like to open the gates for foreign nationals for short- or medium-term projects. While EU Members (such as Germany) had to allow the entry of foreign IT-professionals given the need for skilled computer personnel, it has given rise to domestic resistance against such a policy.

Liberalisation in Other Bilateral and Preferential Agreements

The EU's bilateral FTAs with emerging economies have included services liberalisation, including those with Chile, Mexico and Republic of Korea. The EC's offer in the environmental services sector in the WTO, under the current Doha Round, is representative of its commitment in the bilateral agreements with developing countries, as evident in the EU–Chile Association Agreement of 2002 (enforced in 2003). In particular, the EU has explicitly included water for human use (as in its Revised Offer of 2005) with Modes 2 and 3 open, but with Mode 1 and 4 unbound. The developing country partner, Chile, has left Modes 1 and 3 unbound, Mode 2 open and Mode 4 unbound in environmental services in its bilateral FTA with the EU.

In the more recent EU–South Korea FTA 2009 (enforced 2011), the EU did not explicitly table *water for human use,* but tabled wastewater services while retaining the horizontal reservations on public utilities (as in its WTO Revised Offer). Moreover, Mode 1 has continued to be unbound for all environmental services except consulting services.

Republic of Korea on the other hand, clearly distinguished between industrial and non-industrial waste management services (the latter includes public environmental services for households). Industrial wastewater services and refuse disposal services sectors have Mode 1 and Mode 4 unbound. Non-industrial wastewater services is even more restricted, with Modes 1, 3 and 4 unbound, while non-industrial refuse disposal has not even been tabled by Republic of Korea.

On the other hand, India's environmental services sector commitments in its bilateral free trade agreements mirror its WTO Revised Offer. This is evident in the more recent bilateral agreements, including the India–Korea Comprehensive Economic Partnership Agreement, 2009 (effective 2010), the India–Japan Economic Partnership Agreement 2010 (effective 2011), and the India–Malaysia Comprehensive Economic Cooperation Agreement (effective 2011). In each of these three bilateral agreements, India commitments in the environmental services sector are in refuse disposal services and in sanitation and similar services, leaving the industrial and non-industrial services in these subsectors equally open. In India, market access is restricted only under Mode 4 (unbound), while Modes 1, 2 and 3 are completely open for both Japan and Republic of Korea. For Malaysia, the Indian market has an additional restriction under Mode 3, subject to incorporation and a cap on foreign equity of 49 per cent (Malaysia has similar equity restrictions.).

Republic of Korea's commitment in the environmental services sector in its bilateral agreement with India is similar to the one with the EU. Republic of Korea has continued to distinguish between industrial and non-industrial core environmental services, opening only the industrial segment of sewage services and refuse disposal services. The distinction between industrial and non-industrial core environmental services is also found in Malaysia's market access commitments to India. Malaysia has tabled wastewater management of only industrial effluents and covers only those services contracted by the private sector, keeping all public works out of its purview.

Thus, comparing the depth of commitments made in the environmental services sector by the EU and India in their respective existing bilateral preferential agreements, their commitments are as deep as their offers under the GATS, WTO.

Trade Interests of India and the EU in Environmental Services and Clean Energy

Trade interests are driven by the competitive advantages of the environmental firms in the EU and India. The EU is home to the largest and most well-developed multinational environmental corporations that have a comparative advantage in the export of resource-saving and clean technologies and in technical expertise in the design and engineering of treatment and purification facilities.

Moreover, given the cross-cutting nature of the environmental sector, it promises to be one of the fastest-growing sectors of the future. Not surprisingly, the EU in its 2005 service liberalisation requests to 103 WTO Members noted that the environmental services sector is a key sector for the EC especially since European companies are world leaders in this sector. In 2006, plurilateral requests from the developed countries (including Australia, Canada, the EC, Japan, Republic of Korea, Norway, Switzerland, Chinese Taipei or Taiwan and the US) to developing countries specifically asked for the opening up of sewage, refuse disposal, sanitation, cleaning of exhaust gases, noise abatement, nature and landscape protection, and other environmental protection services.

In its bilateral negotiations, the EC requested that India provide greater market access in infrastructure environmental services including water, wastewater/sewage services and refuse disposal/sanitation services, which are the most significant segments in terms of market value. These services also fall in the realm of public procurement, and although foreign environmental firms have been granted projects by various municipalities across India, it has taken place out of choice rather than any multilateral commitment to open public procurement for transparent bids. Indeed, the EC considers government procurement (defined as purchasing activities of government entities, from purchase of paper clips to computer systems, wastewater plants, consulting services, etc.) to be arguably the largest trade sector sheltered from multilateral disciplines. Thus, the EC's demand for market access to Indian infrastructure environmental services would be a demand for (environmental) public procurement in India.

On the other hand, the Indian environmental sector is dependent on the import of technology, mostly from the US and the EU. Moreover, with environmental R&D being low in India, there is little scope for Indian service providers to find an export market for clean technology-based services in the EU.[11] However, the Indian environmental service providers are seen to be specialising and exporting (largely to other developing countries) engineering, consulting and analytical services.

The renewable energy sector in India has been growing rapidly, and the growth prospects continue to be strong since the 12th Five-Year Plan (2012–2017) envisions the share of renewable in total commercial energy use to be 15 per cent by 2020. The government has continued to offer a range of financial incentives to promote private investment in renewable energy through the last two decades, including tax holidays, 100 per cent accelerated depreciation and concessional import and customs duties on high-technology equipment and components for wind and solar energy.[12]

Although India has experienced robust growth in wind energy and created a niche in this energy form, it continues to be critically dependent on key technology component imports in the renewable sector. Since several EU Members, including Germany and Denmark, have established technological prowess in renewable energy (e.g. solar and wind), the growth of the Indian market offers new business opportunities.

In particular, under the renewable energy programme of India's National Action Plan on Climate Change 2008—a comprehensive policy to mitigate climate change and move the economy towards a low-carbon sustainable growth path—the share of solar[13] energy in the total energy mix will be increased significantly, while continuing to expand the scope of other renewable forms such as wind and biomass. According to a recent investment report, in 2011, India achieved its highest recorded annual investment growth in renewable energy (62 per cent), achieving a total investment of US$12 billion, of which US$4.7 billion was for solar, US$5.9 billion was for wind, US$0.9 billion was for solar biomass and waste-to-energy, and US$0.5 billion was for small hydro (UNEP, 2012:24). While the size of this investment is still small

[11] Although some Indian firms are now focusing on developing indigenous technology for bio-sanitisers for water and bio-soil remediation, establishing these in the international market will take a while.

[12] For example, given India's dependence on imported solar technology, the import tariff rates on solar PV cells and modules have been reduced substantially over the years, with a basic customs duty of zero and an applied tariff rate of 10 per cent in 2004.

[13] Under the National Solar Mission, launched in 2010.

compared to China (US$52 billion) and the US (US$51 billion), the sharp increase reflects India's recent policy focus on renewables. Thus, India seems to have entered a high growth phase of renewable-based energy under its new vision to pursue a low-carbon energy path.

For Indian environmental service providers gaining market access in EU countries, independent commercial presence would be more attractive. To this end, India, along with several developing countries, made a Mode 4-specific plurilateral request to developed countries, including the EU,[14] for three environmental service segments of sewage, refuse disposal and sanitation services among other indicative service sectors. The collective request sought new and improved market access for the categories of contractual service suppliers and independent professionals delinked from commercial presence.

The competitiveness global rankings of environmental firms reflect that Indian environmental service providers are mediocre by EU standards. Some Indian firms have succeeded in establishing a foot-hold in the South Asian, Middle Eastern and African markets since they are price competitive (vis-à-vis European/US/Japanese firms). But, the EU market remains out of bounds, as cutting-edge technology in clean production and resource efficiency are not in the realm of most Indian firms.

New business opportunities abound in Central and Eastern Europe nations (in new EU Member States of the Czech Republic, Poland and Hungary). However, these markets are dominated by mature firms from Western Europe and the US in addition to their native firms, the latter being comparable to Indian environmental firms (say, in Poland or the Czech Republic).

Trade between India and the EU in Environmental Services

Several European environmental corporations, including Vivendi Environnement S.A., Suez S.A. and Ondeo Industrial Solutions, have had operations in India for the past 10 years, but the market data does not capture these operations since they largely include government projects under public–private partnership and contractual engagements.

---

[14] The target group of countries included the US, the EU, Australia, Canada, Japan, New Zealand, Switzerland, Norway and Iceland.

In India, infrastructure environmental services (under government procurement) are as large as the size of the value of market transactions recorded by EBI Inc. in its estimate of the Indian ES market. For example, in one programme called the Jawaharlal Nehru National Urban Renewal Mission (JNNURM) launched in December 2005 (where the government investment is based on the needs of 63 Indian cities), ₹10,047 crore or US$2.2 billion was sanctioned for water supply, sewerage and solid waste management projects in 2006–2007. During the 11th Five-Year Plan (2007–2012), the Indian government invested €36.22 billion ($50.39 billion)[15] on urban water supply and sanitation, urban drainage and solid waste management.

Multinational environmental corporations, including EU firms such as Degremont (Suez S.A.) and Veolia (Veolia Environnement S.A.), have been invited to execute most of these projects in India—with no financial risk and assured return in these government procurement projects. In January 2008, Degremont (Suez S.A.) was awarded two government projects worth US$127 million to build a drinking water plant in Mumbai and a wastewater treatment and reuse facility in Delhi. Being world leaders in environmental services of water utilities, wastewater treatment and refuse disposal services, EU firms have a ready clientele in India (in both the government and private sectors) among those who can afford their services. This is especially evident in the government procurement sector in India, where EU firms have been granted several large infrastructure projects, given their expertise.

On the other hand, there is little trade potential for Indian environmental firms in the EU (even in the less mature markets of Eastern Europe). In the EU environmental market, Indian environmental firms find that they lack cutting-edge technology as well as the corporate reputation and project history required to successfully bid for projects. Besides the domination of European environmental corporations, there is also competition from US environmental firms that are world leaders in environmental consulting, engineering and analytical services. Moreover, given the regulatory barriers in the EU, the export of labour-intensive environmental services is also restricted. A few Indian firms,

---

[15] Converted using the average exchange rate for the period 1st April 2007–31st March 2012 using www.oanda.com as per the rate, 1Euro=1.3913 Dollars.

however, have begun to work for EU environmental firms in other Asian and African countries (responses from the firm survey are reported in the next section), where relatively cheaper Indian skills are employed by the large multinationals—but not for projects in the EU.

FDI Inflow in Non-conventional Energy in India

India has maintained a relatively open FDI regime in the Indian environmental infrastructure services—including sewage, refuse disposal and sanitation—that are also the target segments that the EC has been formally requesting for liberalisation. The actual FDI inflow in these areas, however, fails to reflect the extent of foreign participation in the Indian environmental infrastructure sector, which falls within the realm of government contractual services.

A summary of the FDI inflow in non-conventional energy in India during the past 10 years (January 2000 to December 2010) is reported in Table 9.6. As evident from the table, the major source of environmental FDI during the period 2000–2010 has been the US in the water and wastewater management segment. Among EU Members, Germany and France have been the source of FDI in non-conventional energy, followed by the Netherlands and the UK.

Table 9.6
FDI Inflow in Non-conventional Energy[16] in India, Select Countries 2000–2010

Country	FDI (₹ crore)	FDI (US$ million)
Mauritius	980.61	218.06
Singapore	518.36	107.02
Germany	61.38	15.04
France	55.48	12.15
Netherlands	32.18	7.15
US	32.47	7.23
UK	8.76	1.94

Source: Based on data from DIPP, January 2013.

[16] Non-conventional energy includes renewable energy.

Market Access Barriers in the Environmental Services Sector

Although the EU market for environmental services is largely open under Mode 3 as shown in Table 9.5, other regulations make market access difficult for service providers from India. This section also highlights the apprehensions of Indian environmental firms in entering the EU market, as well as the perceptions of established EU environmental firms operating in the Indian market.

Regulatory Barriers in the EU

As noted earlier, the EC has maintained a horizontal reservation for public utilities (national or local) and for exclusive rights given to private operators in the GATS offers (including the Revised Offer[17]; India does not have an equivalent horizontal condition in its GATS offers). This horizontal restriction also reflects the underlying public procurement policies in vogue in the EU, and impacts market access in environmental services such as sewage services, refuse disposal services and sanitation services, where local authorities hold a monopoly in providing services to the community.

The EU treaties also impose several restrictions. For example, the Protocol on Services of General Interest, Treaty of Lisbon (signed by 27 Members on 13 December 2007), in force since December 2009, covers services of general interest including services subject to specific public service obligation (e.g. waste management, water supply and wastewater treatment, among others). These services are not subject to a *'self-standing regulatory regime at the EU level'*, but specific Community rules such as public procurement and environmental and consumer protection legislation apply to certain aspects of this service (European Commission, 2007b:4). The EU allows wide discretion to national, regional and local authorities in providing, commissioning and organising services of general economic interest as close as possible to the needs of users (Article 1 of the Protocol). Thus, a country-by-country market entry approach would be required by Indian environmental firms in order to enter the EU. Moreover, in the European Commission internal market, several professions are regulated under the General System

[17] See WTO (2005b, 2005c and 2007).

Directive (Directive 1999/42/CE), where access is subject to legal, regulatory or administrative provisions on the possession of a specific qualification (regulated at the EC level as well as individual country level).

As noted earlier, restrictions by the EU Member States in related sectors such as engineering and integrated engineering services (CPC 8673) that have application in environmental services like sanitation works (turnkey projects) translate into barriers for the environmental services sector. To the extent that larger Indian environmental service firms have engineering services as their key specialisation, market access in the emerging economies of the EU is restricted. Since the environmental services sector overlaps with a wide range of other professional services, any restrictions in those sectors immediately impinge on the openness of the environmental services sector.

Thus, the prospects of Indian environmental firms finding a foothold in the EU market are rather small due to the dominance of large, mature and diversified corporations. Moreover, given that the environmental services market in the EU is driven by new technology, most Indian firms find it unfeasible even to enter this market (since they are dependent on older technology imported from the EU/US).

Market Access Barriers Perceived by Indian Environmental Firms

As indicated earlier, Indian environmental service firms consist mainly of small firms that provide ancillary environmental services (including environmental consulting, analytical services, auditing and certification) and larger engineering firms that offer turnkey project services. A survey of 20 Indian environmental firms in 2007–2008 covered both engineering firms offering environmental turnkey projects sometimes along with analytical services, as well as firms offering only analytical services. Among the 20 firms covered in the survey, most were found to be operating exclusively in India, while those with operations abroad had never entered the EU market. Indeed, most did not even consider the EC as a viable market for them to enter because the West European environmental markets are too mature, while in the less mature East European economies, West European and US corporations have a strong foothold. Moreover, corporate networking, firm reputation and project history make it virtually impossible for Indian businesses to venture into the EU environmental market.[18] Interestingly, some of the surveyed Indian environmental firms do projects for EU companies abroad, but do not want to set up operations in the EU since market opportunities there are limited. They, however, would like to continue to do more projects both in Europe as well as in East Asia, Africa and the Middle East for these EU firms.

Indian firms indicated that they perceived restrictions on labour mobility as the most significant barrier in the EU country markets. The Indian environmental firms also indicated that it is India's labour cost advantage that makes them competitive in developing countries, since they lag behind the technology used by the European firms.

Technological collaboration with European corporations is common among larger Indian environmental firms, but the latter sees such technical upgrading only as a means of improving their market image in Indian and other developing country markets and not as a tool to enter the EU markets.

The conjunction of regulatory barriers, nature of environmental service demand (high technology-based) in the EU and dominance of the northern firms inhibit the entry of Indian firms in the EU environmental sector.

Barriers in India Identified by EU Environmental Firms

Some of the leading environmental services' multinational firms have Indian operations since the environmental sector has good growth prospects. A survey of four European environmental MNCs in India during 2007–2008 provided their detailed perspectives on the Indian environmental sector. The respondents included Degremont (parent company SUEZ, France), Veolia Water (parent company Veolia Environment, France), ERM (parent company ERM, UK) and Agrinergy Consultancy (parent company Agrinergy, UK). Table 9.7 summarises the responses of the European firms on their expectations of the Indian environmental sector, as well as the barriers and problems faced in India.

Some of the European firms have been active in India for several decades, while others have entered the market more recently. It is

---

[18] Personal communication with Seema Arora, Head, CII-ITC Centre of Excellence for Sustainable Development, 13 November 2007.

Table 9.7
Market Perception of EU Environmental Firms in India

ES Subsector	Reason for Entry	Licensing, Approval & Project Bidding Problems	Other Problems
Water and wastewater services	• Market size, better growth prospects, and skilled Indian workforce. • Operations in India also help their exports abroad. • Huge market in India with no foreign competition.	• No problem in obtaining visas. • Bidding is transparent. • No problem in repatriation of profits. • Bureaucratic procedures long • No problem in licensing or approval, although norms in 27 state governments are different. • Bidding not transparent.	• Bribery is a problem, and have sometimes given bribes to obtain contracts. • Delays in project commencement result in financial problems for the firm. • Lack of clarity in tax structure. • Bureaucrats corrupt and most of the sanctioned project funds are pilfered.
Natural resource, health and safety management	• Good growth prospects.	• No licensing problem • Obtains Indian projects through international competitive bids. • Indian consultancy firms are not in the same league (small, lack international exposure and certification), so no competitive threat	• Local labour laws not conducive to expanding business in India. • Multiplicity and/or complexity of taxation (e.g., interstate VAT) and legal enforcement norms.
Climate change services.	• Good opportunity in Indian market. • Carbon services market competitive in India, with several firms offering services.	• No problem in licensing as client takes care of everything. UN approval required for carbon credit projects. • No visa problems.	• Cultural and linguistic problems.

Source: Compiled by the author.

noteworthy that all the firms found that entry into India is easy with no problems in obtaining visas, licences or approvals. The common complaint was regarding bureaucratic delays and bureaucratic corruption (with bribery being used to obtain contracts).

The European environmental firms also indicated that there is no clarity in taxation and enforcement of norms is poor. Interestingly, all in all, the problems highlighted are not particular to foreign operators, but apply to domestic operators too. In general, the major market challenges faced by foreign investors in India include infrastructure constraints imposed by poor road, railroad, port and airport facilities, disrupted power supply, limited telecommunications, etc.

Summing up

The new business opportunities in the EU environmental market are of two types: first, the demand for new resource-saving technology as well as engineering and design in the more mature West European markets; and second, the demand for more basic environmental services in the new EU Member Countries in Central and Eastern Europe. In both sets of markets, the scope for Indian environmental firms is limited. The analysis in this chapter highlighted the presence of several challenges for emerging Indian environmental service provided in the EU including: highly fragmented markets by size, language and local regulations across Member States; government restrictions in terms of carve-outs for environmental services in the realm of public monopolies (or private operators with government-granted exclusive rights); regulations for several environmental professionals; intense competition from native companies (especially mature corporations from France, Germany and the UK that command 60 per cent of the total EU environmental market); and, of course, intense competition from US firms besides the emerging firms from Poland, the Czech Republic, etc.

On the whole, the opportunities for Indian environmental firms are rather limited in the EU, since they continue to depend on technological imports from European firms. While Indian firms have labour cost advantages, restrictions in Mode 4 make it difficult for business visitors and contractual service suppliers to break into these diverse markets due to challenges in networking and establishing work history/reputation, besides, of course, the language problems. The 2007–2008 survey indicated that most Indian firms do not even consider ever venturing into the European market. They have instead focused on establishing a foothold in other developing countries in South Asia, Southeast Asia, Africa and the Middle East.

The EC has long requested India to make commitments in Mode 3 for infrastructure environmental services. Yet, the EC in its bilateral free trade agreements has not made commitments any deeper than those offered in the WTO (as noted in the case of the EC–Chile bilateral agreement). The commitments under Mode 4 and Mode 1 continue to be unbound, and environmental services in the purview of the national or local government bodies have been carved out of the commitments. Exclusive rights given to private players by government bodies are also carved out. Thus, the completely liberal commitments in Modes 2 and 3 in the EC do have conditional exceptions.

It is unlikely that the EC will offer anything deeper than what it has committed to in its other bilateral preferential treaties or committed/offered in the WTO. Repeated requests for a more open Mode 4 in GATS have not yielded any positive results from the EC. Moreover, in the face of dismal labour market performance within the EC, a liberal Mode 4 can hardly be expected at this time.

On the other hand, a liberal Indian Mode 3 in infrastructure environmental services (i.e. water, wastewater and solid waste management), which is of primary interest to the EU, has been the ground reality. The actual market access regime in India is even more open, allowing 100 per cent equity through the automatic route even in infrastructure ES which is otherwise under the purview of the government. Some infrastructure environmental services, in particular refuse disposal services and sanitation and similar services, have also featured in India's recent preferential bilateral agreements with Republic of Korea, Japan and Malaysia. Moreover, European environmental firms have been granted major infrastructure environmental contracts by various municipalities and government entities across India that do not get reflected in the market data. Multinational environmental firms have been executing large integrated infrastructure environmental projects awarded by local authorities, which indicates that environmental service imports have been under Modes 3 and 4.

It is important to note that despite the open regime for environmental investment, in practice actual environmental FDI has been negligible in India. Low FDI inflows reflect a poor market rate of return in the environmental segments, thus much of the foreign participation is still through the award of government contracts (i.e. infrastructure services under the purview of local governments). Indeed, the late 1990s witnessed the cancellation of several infrastructure environmental contracts in water and waste management services in developing countries across the world (especially in Southeast Asia and Latin America) by major environmental multinationals given the poor returns or public backlash in these countries.[19]

Collaborative Opportunities in the Environmental Services Sector

The Indian environmental goods and services sector is dependent on the import of environmental equipment and technology from the mature firms of the EU, Japan and the US. Among the different environmental segments, the EU has emerged as the most competitive in waste management and recycling[20] with proven strong specialisation in its external trade (ECORYS, 2009:97). India, thus, stands to gain from the EU in this sector through greater access to efficient waste management technology and services.

The EU–India collaborative efforts could be devoted to further the technological capacity of Indian environmental firms, by encouraging joint ventures in segments driven by rapid technological innovation, including clean energy. The EU is the leading region in the world for clean energy technology, including wind, solar and biomass. While China has emerged with a competitive advantage in clean energy equipment such as solar cells and panels, Germany continues to be one of the leading innovators in eco-technology (ECORYS, 2009:93).

---

[19] See Sawhney (2007) for a summary.
[20] The EU accounts for 50 per cent the global market by revenue (ECORYS, 2009:93).

While the scope for Indian environmental firms in the EU market may be limited, a few firms have successfully developed specialisation within niche environmental segments in the world market by building on licensed technology/high-tech component imports (e.g. Suzlon Energy Limited in wind energy). Indian environmental firms are also interested in market access (in Mode 4) for labour-intensive segments of environmental consulting, management and so on. However, given the discretion practiced (and allowed legally) by EC states and local authorities in government procurement, a country-by-country market entry approach is required by Indian environmental firms in order to enter the EU to exploit such niche opportunities. Thus, going forward, to encourage collaborative efforts in increasing market access for Indian environmental firms in the EU, country-specificity of barriers needs to be addressed.

Concluding Thoughts and Domestic Reforms

A large part of the environmental services continues to be implemented at the state and local levels (infrastructure environmental services), and any decision taken at the centre with regard to this sector impacts the state and local governments. Indeed, the operations of European multinational environmental corporations in India are to be found most notably in government procurement projects for water and waste disposal services. This has two important implications. First, the demand in the Indian environmental services market is relatively lower than expected and has not matured to the next level, i.e. beyond pollution abatement to pollution prevention. This also reflects, in turn, the poor enforcement of environmental regulations on the ground. Second, foreign environmental firms have focused on the minimal-commercial risk business model of taking on public assignments of building municipal water treatment facilities or waste disposal contracts (often through build-operate-transfer contracts).

The Indian environmental firm survey unanimously suggests that local players recognise that EC firms have a technological edge in this field but their service costs are higher; hence, the Indian players indicate that they are not threatened by the entry of multinationals in this field. It is important to add, however, that the survey covered a rather small group of environmental service providers in India, and the premise underlying their perception is that there will be no uncompetitive market practices (such as predatory price-cutting) on the part of large European firms with deep pockets.

Several environmental services segments—including that of water, wastewater and refusal services—require a strong regulatory institutional framework to curb monopolistic/anti-competitive practices and encourage competitive growth of the sector. Thus, in negotiating this sector, India needs to pay as much attention to strengthening the domestic regulatory and institutional framework.

- *Enhance demand for environmental services through effective enforcement of environmental regulations, including Renewable Portfolio Obligation for clean energy at the state level.* In order to enhance the growth of the environmental and clean energy sector, it is important to make demand grow in the domestic market. Increasing environmental awareness and enforcing the existing regulations would certainly help enhance the demand for environmental services in India.
- *Expand the supply capacity of environmental services.* Given the low provision of essential (infrastructure) environmental services such as clean water and sanitation facilities to the population, India has an urgent need to expand the supply capacity of this sector. However, the experience of several Asian developing countries through the 1990s (encouraging PPP in water and waste services) suggests that the policies of privatisation and liberalisation in environmental services by themselves will not be successful in the ultimate goal of building capacity in essential environmental infrastructure (Sawhney, 2007). Indeed, the nature of private contract is critical in determining whether and what kinds of actual technology transfer take place in developing countries; the mere presence of leading global environmental service providers in developing countries will not result in the much touted *win–win* situation (Sawhney, 2007).
- *Build in preferences for domestic environmental firms to ensure growth of the environmental sector.* The growth of environmental

service providers and renewable energy industry in countries such as China, Republic of Korea and Chinese Taipei, took place along with strategic government policies and increased environmental expenditure. All three countries followed import-substitution policies along with liberalisation to nurture the growth of their domestic environmental service providers. Indeed, through the 1990s, Republic of Korea encouraged privatisation and liberalisation in environmental services with preferences built in for domestic engineering firms. Domestic operators then subcontracted specialised services to foreign companies for, say, advanced technology. This strategy served the twin purpose of boosting the growth of the indigenous environmental firms while upgrading the environmental technology used to build environmental infrastructure in the country at the same time.

Domestic reforms, thus, need to be geared towards enhancing the demand for environmental services and also building domestic supply capacity. Thus, going forward, in maximising the returns in a collaborative relationship with the EU, we need to be cognisant of the long-term goal of sustainable development through a strong domestic environmental sector in India.

10

Here is the Market, Where is FDI? The Retail Sector in India and Opportunities for the EU

Tanu M. Goyal

Introduction

Retail is defined as all activities involved in the selling of goods or services directly to final consumers for their personal, non-business use via shops, markets, door-to-door selling, mail order or over the Internet where the buyer intends to consume the product through personal, family or household dues (Mukherjee and Patel, 2005). This sector is labour-intensive and it offers huge employment possibilities at low skill levels. In 2012, the global retail market was valued at US$15 trillion[1] and is forecast to reach an estimated US$20 trillion in 2017 with a compound annual growth rate (CAGR) of 3.9 per cent over the next six years (2012–2017).[2]

---

[1] http://www.marketresearch.com/First-Research-Inc-v3470/Retail-Sector-7509924/ (accessed on 12 June 2013).

[2] http://www.lucintel.com/reports/consumer_goods/global_retail_industry_2012_2017_trends_foreacast._january_2012.aspx (accessed on 12 June 2013).

Since the global slowdown in 2008, emerging markets, particularly in Asia and Latin America, are considered high-growth, high-potential markets by investors in the retail sector. In most emerging markets including India, the retail sector is largely unsaturated and there is immense scope for private investment. In India, the retail sector is the largest private sector and the second-largest employer after agriculture. In the past two decades, the sector has grown at a double-digit rate. One of the factors for this growth is the rise in income in India. India's real per capita income almost doubled between 2001–2002 and 2011–2012, while real private consumption expenditure increased at an average of 7.7 per cent between 2005–2006 and 2011–2012 (Images Multimedia Private Limited 2013). According to Images Multimedia Private Limited (2013), the Indian retail market is expected to grow at 15 per cent CAGR between 2012 and 2017. Modern/corporate retail growth is likely to surpass the growth of the overall retail market. According to Images Multimedia Private Limited (2014), modern retail grew by 30 per cent at an average during the last five years (since 2010) and is expected to gather pace over the next 2–3 years. As the growth of the modern/corporate sector in retail is faster than in the traditional/non-corporate sector, the sector is likely to lead to better quality jobs and secure employment.

The EU is the largest retail market in the world. The retail sector contributes around 4.2 per cent to the total value added in the EU and employs around 17.4 million people.[3] The EU has one of the largest numbers of foreign retailers. Among EU Members, in 2012 the UK had the largest number of foreign retailers followed by Spain (4th), France (6th), Germany (6th) and Italy (9th). In comparison, India was ranked 35th and China was ranked fifth in terms of the number of foreign retailers.[4] The EU also has the largest number of global retailers. According to Deloitte (2013), among the top 250 retailers in 2011, around 80 retailers were from the EU, within which Germany had the maximum number of global retailers. European retailers are also expanding their presence to other markets, particularly in developing countries in Asia, the Middle East and Latin America. There is a lot of interest among EU retailers in the Indian retail market.

---

[3] For details, see http://ec.europa.eu/internal_market/retail/index_en.htm (accessed on 27 August 2012).

[4] http://www.cbre.eu/emea_en/services/retail_leisure/how_global_is_the_business_of_retail (accessed on 15 November 2012).

India and the EU have complementarities in the retail sector. While the Indian retail market is growing and has enormous investment potential, the EU retail market is saturated. Moreover, since the EU market is facing a slowdown, EU retailers are diversifying their investments and targeting new markets. A number of EU retailers are investing in the Indian retail sector, due to the large consumer base and emergent demand in the country. Around 50 per cent of foreign investment in the Indian retail sector is from the EU. The economic reforms of the nineties propelled the entry of large corporates in the Indian retail sector and this led to the growth of modern/corporate retail. A number of Indian corporates have invested in this sector, and after the liberalisation of single-brand retail in 2006 they are keen to collaborate with EU retailers. Lately, a few Indian companies have also made investments in the EU market and others are exploring the possibilities of investment. EU retailers have technical knowledge, efficient supply-chain networks and a skilled workforce and, therefore, collaboration can facilitate the operations of Indian retailers in the EU market.

Despite the trade and investment potential, both India and the EU have restrictive foreign direct investment policies in the retail sector. While India largely has market access restrictions in the form of FDI limitations and associated conditions imposed on foreign retailers, the EU imposes regulatory barriers that can be difficult for foreign investors to meet. The two sides are already negotiating the sector under the WTO and the on-going India–EU BTIA. In the plurilateral negotiations of the WTO that began after the Hong Kong Ministerial Conference (December 2005), India is a recipient of requests in distribution services that include retail and the EU is a demandeur.[5] The EU has particularly requested for Mode 3 liberalisation. In the India–EU BTIA too, the EU is a demandeur. In September 2012, India liberalised the retail policy, however, unlike other sectors, there are no further reforms likely to take place in the store-based retail sector. The government has initiated discussions to undertake reforms in non-store retail format, which are likely to open opportunities for foreign retailers.

Given this background, this chapter provides an overview of the retail sector in India and in the EU and discusses how the two countries can

---

[5] For details, see http://commerce.nic.in/trade/Plurilateral%20Requests%20in%20 Distribution%20services.pdf (accessed on 27 August 2012).

enhance bilateral trade and investment in the retail sector through the India–EU BTIA.

Classification of the Retail Sector

India and the EU follow the GATS (MTN.GNS/W/120) classification in international negotiations for classifying retail trade. The retail sector falls under distributive trade services (Section 6, Division 62). With technology development and globalisation, new formats of retailing have emerged including both store and non-store retail formats. The international definition provides comprehensive coverage of both store and non-store formats, which was not present in the earlier definition. The GATS definition also takes into account evolving formats of store-based retail such as hypermarkets, supermarkets and specialised stores.

Retail trade is defined in the same way in India's National Industrial Classification (NIC) and the EU's statistical classification of economic activities in the European Community (NACE). In NIC 2008 and NACE Revision 2, wholesale and retail trade and repair of motor vehicles and motorcycles sector, referred to as distributive trades (Section G), which includes both store and non-store retail formats and within store-based retail both specialised and non-specialised retail formats are included.

Trends and Developments in the Retail Sector

Before the global slowdown, retail was regarded as a sunrise industry. However, the growth of the retail market has slowed in the past few years, due to the global economic crisis and slowing consumer demand in the US and Europe. The year-on-year growth rate of retail sales declined from 11.5 per cent in 2007 to (–)2.5 per cent in 2009 globally; it recovered to 10.9 per cent in 2010, but remained below the pre-crisis level (Alpen Capital, 2011). As a result, several European retailers are expanding their presence to new and emerging markets in the Asia Pacific, Africa and South America where there is high growth (Deloitte, 2012). Deloitte (2012) found that European retailers are the most active globally and they have reduced their dependence on their home markets since the global slowdown. Nearly 40 per cent of their sales were generated by their operations outside their home countries. In the past five years, retailers such as Carrefour (France), Tesco (UK) and Metro Group (Germany) saw their revenues in developing countries grow 2.5 times faster than revenues in their home market (AT Kearney, 2012b). Developing country markets such as Brazil, Russia, India and China are attracting a large number of global retailers due to their large and growing consumer base. In 2010, India attracted the largest number of new retailers among emerging and mature markets (CBRE, 2011).

Retail Sector in India

Data on retail trade is available for EU-27 countries, but not for India. The Central Statistical Office in India combines retail with wholesale trade and restaurants and it is difficult to get disaggregated data for the retail sector.

The retail sector in India is characterised by the presence of a large number of small family-owned stores that are low-investment, low-profit outlets that survive on family labour; they are known as traditional/ non-corporate retailers. There is also a small but growing number of modern/corporate retailers. Both Indian and global companies, such as Future Group (Big Bazaar), RPG Group (Spencer's, Spencer's Retail Private Limited), Aditya Birla Group (More, Aditya Birla Retail Limited), Reliance Industries Limited (Reliance Mart, Reliance Retail Limited), Amway (known as Alticor, US), Oriflame (Sweden) and Hindustan Unilever (India), have entered these segments in India. Modern retail formats started developing in India in the past two and a half decades. At present, modern or corporate retail formats are the fastest growing segments of retail and have a lot of untapped potential for foreign retailers. According to the Images Multimedia Private Limited (2014), the share of retail market in India's GDP in 2013–2014 was around 34.3 per cent. This includes the direct and indirect contribution of retail. In 2013–2014, the share of private final consumption expenditure (PFCE) was around 59.5 per cent. In the same year, the retail market was valued at US$648.9 billion grown by an average 16–18 per cent to reach at this value over the last couple of years. It is further expected that by 2017, India's retail market will reach US$1026.06 billion exhibiting a growth of around 16 per cent per annum.

With a share of 9.7 per cent, modern retail is a small but growing component of the overall retail market in India. Modern retail was valued at US$63.5 billion in 2013–2014 and is likely to reach US$150.5 billion in 2017. In 2013–2014, the share of modern retail in the GDP was around 3.35 per cent and 5.63 per cent in PFCE up from 4.3 per cent in 2011–2012 (Images Multimedia Private Limited, 2014). The share of the retail sector in employment in 2009–2010 was around 7.8 per cent, providing employment to around 33.1 million people.[6] This appears to be lower than that of developed and developing countries (10 per cent or higher), but in India, the bulk of the employment in retail is in the traditional/non-corporate segment and is often underreported. The National Skill Development Corporation estimated that the share of the modern/corporate sector in retail would increase to 20–25 per cent by 2022. This will increase the work force requirement from around 0.3 million in 2008 to around 17.3 million in 2022.[7]

Food and grocery is the largest retail segment in India, followed by apparel and clothing. The pattern for modern/corporate retail is the reverse; it has the smallest share in food and grocery retail, and the largest share in apparel and clothing (Figure 10.1).

The growth of the modern/corporate retail sector has led to several changes. Different store and non-store retail formats have evolved: hypermarkets, supermarkets, convenience stores, factory outlets, speciality stores, direct selling, e-tailing, and so on. It has also led to the development of retail infrastructure; the number of shopping malls increased from three in 1999 to 280 in 2007 and is expected to increase at a CAGR of more than 18.9 per cent between 2007 and 2015 (Images Multimedia Private Limited, 2009). The share of revenue of the IT/BPO industry from retail has increased, from 4 per cent in 2001–2002 to 10 per cent in 2011–2012 (NASSCOM, 2013). Thus, the growth of modern retail is propelling the growth of other services sectors.

Modern retail initially started in India in large/metro cities, but is now penetrating into smaller cities where the growth rate is faster than that in large cities. Given that the rural sector accounts for nearly

---

[6] Author's calculations from NSSO.
[7] For details, see: http://www.nsdcindia.org/pdf/Organised-Retail.pdf (accessed on 29 February 2012).

Figure 10.1
Share of Product Categories in Total Retail Market and Modern Retail Segment (2012)

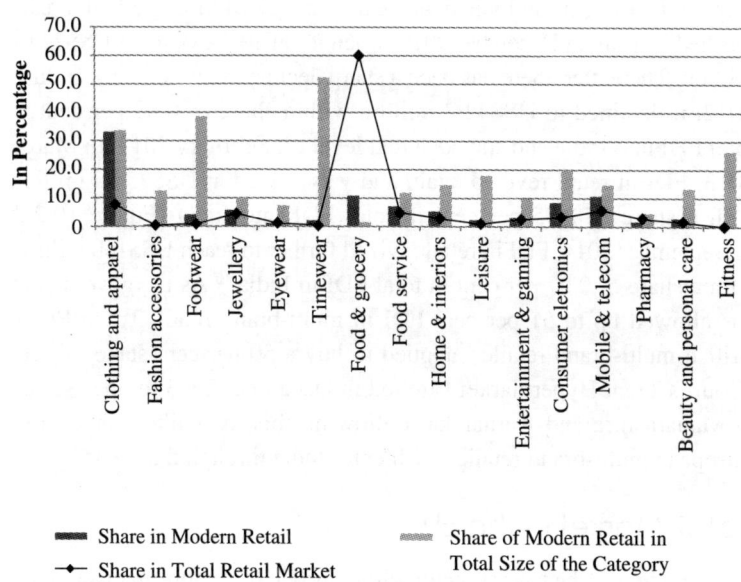

━━ Share in Modern Retail   ▬▬ Share of Modern Retail in
─◆─ Share in Total Retail Market   Total Size of the Category

Source: Compiled from Images Multimedia Private Limited (2013), p. 41.

55 per cent of the retail market and has around 720 million consumers, several modern retailers are venturing into rural markets. These retailers not only offer products but also offer services focusing on the specific requirements of the rural population. For instance, Hariyali Bazaars set up by DCM Sriram for agri-products provides retail banking, credit and other financial services such as insurance. Since food and grocery retailers need to set up supply chains, their rural retail outlets often act as a centre for both sourcing and supplying products. It is estimated that 500 rural towns have the potential to become rural hubs where modern/corporate retailers can set up their base and then cater to around 100 villages each.[8]

[8] Images Multimedia Private Limited (2009) and interviews conducted by ICRIER researchers for the Italian Trade Commission Project in 2010.

The large consumer base and growing Indian market have attracted several foreign retailers to the Indian retail sector. During 2008–2009, when the Western markets were facing a slowdown, there was a huge surge of investments in India in the retail sector. FDI in single-brand retail reached its peak in December 2010, when it touched a value of US$229.1 million. Thereafter, there has been a sharp decline in investments. In June 2012, it declined to US$42.7 million with a share of 0.02 per cent in total FDI into India and stayed at that level till February 2013. In March 2013, FDI in retail revived again and was valued at US$95.36 million with a share of 0.05 per cent in total FDI into India (Figure 10.2).[9] In September 2014, FDI in retail revived further to reach US$160 million with a share of 0.07 per cent in total FDI in India.[10] As the government has allowed up to 51 per cent FDI in multi-brand retail, Tesco Plc, a British multi-brand retailer, applied to buy a 50 per cent stake in Tata Group's Trent Hypermarket Limited in December 2013 to open stores in Maharashtra and Karnataka. Following this, it is likely that more European multi-brand retailers will enter India through this route.

Retail Market in the EU

Retail trade was the largest sector within the EU-27's non-financial business economy in terms of number of enterprises and number of persons employed and the second largest in terms of turnover and value added. In 2009, retail trade accounted for 30 per cent of wholesale and retail trade; repair of motor vehicles and motorcycles.[11] The turnover of the EU-27's retail trade sector was valued at US$3,437.7 billion (€2466.6 billion), from which US$602.1 billion (€432.0 billion)[12] of value added was generated, equivalent to 11.2 per cent and 7.7 per cent, respectively, of the total for the non-financial business economy. There were 3.6 million retail trade enterprises in the EU-27 and they employed 18.5 million persons, equivalent to 17.1 per cent of all enterprises in the non-financial

[9] Compiled from Department of Industrial Policy and Promotion (DIPP), FDI Factsheet, various issues http://dipp.nic.in/English/Publications/FDI_Statistics/FDI_Statistics.aspx (accessed on 28 August 2012).

[10] For details see http://dipp.nic.in/English/Publications/FDI_Statistics/2014/india_FDI_September2014.pdf (accessed on 10 December 2014).

[11] Author's calculation from Eurostat database.

[12] Conversion done using the average exchange rate of US dollar for Euros for the calendar year 2009 (1€ = US$1.3937) using www.oanda.com (accessed on 30 August 2012).

Figure 10.2
Trends in FDI in Single-brand Retail (cumulative in US$ million and percentage share)

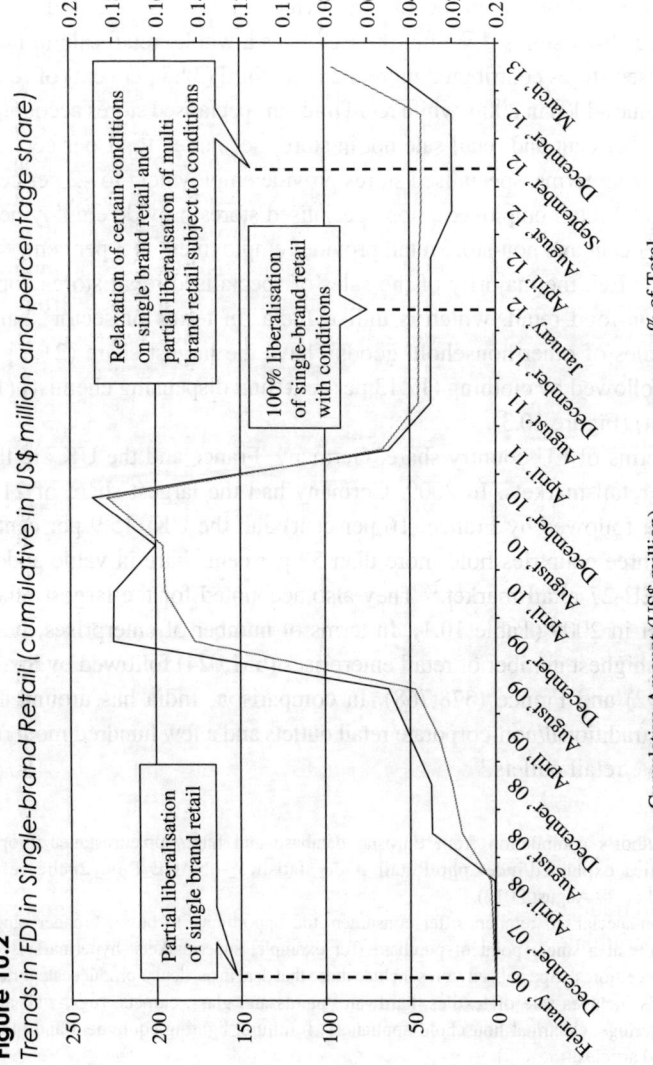

Source: Compiled from DIPP FDI Factsheet, various issues available at http://dipp.nic.in/English/Publications/ FDI_Statistics/FDI_Statistics.aspx (accessed on 18 June 2013).

business economy and 13.8 per cent of the non-financial business economy workforce.[13]

Unlike India, the EU retail sector is characterised by large, corporate retailers. Retail outlets in the EU are divided into non-specialised stores and specialised stores.[14] Within the EU-27 as a whole, retail sale in non-specialised stores contributed more than one-third (34.8 per cent) of retail trade value added in 2009, while retail trade in specialised stores accounted for 60.2 per cent and retail sale not in stores accounted for 1 per cent. In employment terms, specialised stores provide employment to 42 per cent of the total retail employees, non-specialised stores provide employment to 56 per cent and non-store retail provides employment to 3 per cent.

In the EU, the majority of the sales of specialised retail stores comprise non-food retail, which is unlike India. In terms of sector share, retail sales of other household goods[15] have the largest share (21.5 per cent), followed by clothing (17.13 per cent) and dispensing chemists (13 per cent) (Figure 10.3).

In terms of EU country share, Germany, France and the UK are the largest retail markets. In 2009, Germany had the largest share of 21.7 per cent followed by France (16 per cent) and the UK (15.9 per cent). These three countries hold more than 50 per cent share in value added in the EU-27 retail market.[16] They also accounted for the largest retail turnover in 2009 (Table 10.1). In terms of number of enterprises, Italy had the highest number of retail enterprises (651,024) followed by Spain (497,992) and France (378,768). In comparison, India has around 12 million traditional/non-corporate retail outlets and a few hundred modern/corporate retail outlets.[17]

---

[13] Author's compilation from Eurostat database and http://epp.eurostat.ec.europa. eu/statistics_explained/index.php/Retail_trade_statistics_-_NACE_Rev._2#cite_ref-0 (accessed on 29 August 2012).

[14] Non-specialised retailers offer consumers the opportunity to buy a broader range of products at a single point of purchase (for example, supermarkets, hypermarkets or convenience stores). Specialised stores include those that deal in particular product categories.

[15] This includes sale of textiles, hardware, paints and glass, carpets, rugs, wall and floor coverings, electrical household appliances, furniture, lighting equipment and other household articles.

[16] Calculated from Eurostat.

[17] http://csis.org/files/publication/sam_137.pdf and http://www.indiastudychannel. com/attachments/Resources/35680-311746-list%20of%20retail%20company%20in%20 india.txt (accessed on 12 September 2012).

Figure 10.3
Share of Different Product Segments in Specialised Stores in the EU (2009)

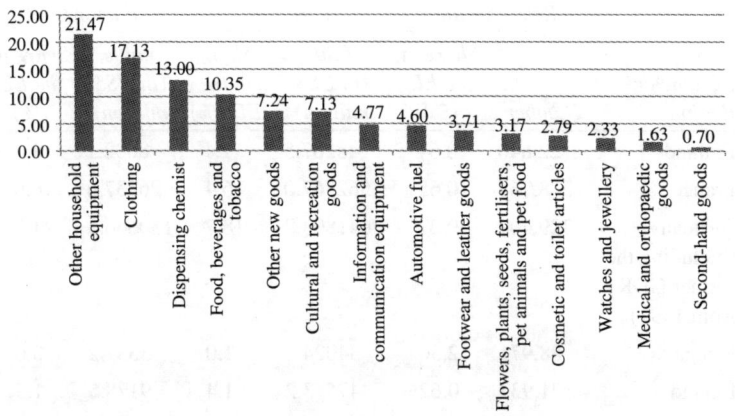

Share in value added in specialsed store in 2009

Source: Compiled and calculated from Eurostat database.

Table 10.1
Size and Share of Different Parameters in Retail Trade by the EU Country

Parameter/ Region	Enterprises in Retail Sector		Turnover		Value Added at Factor Cost	
	Number	Share in the EU (%)	Value (in US$ million)	Share in the EU (%)	Value (in US$ million)	Share in the EU (%)
Austria	40,061	1.13	73989.9	2.2	14456.4	2.4
Belgium	74,260	2.09	110519.3	3.2	17638.8	2.9
Bulgaria	104,850	2.95	13964.6	0.4	1551.6	0.3
Croatia	23,499		17342.9		2698.3	
Cyprus	11,325	0.32	7564.6	0.2	1274.0	0.2
Czech Republic	128,448	3.61	46639.5	1.4	6038.5	1.0
Denmark	21,786	0.61	57278.7	1.7	10112.5	1.7
Estonia	4,484	0.13	6068.4	0.2	638.6	0.1

(Table 10.1 Continued)

(Table 10.1 Continued)

Parameter/ Region	Enterprises in Retail Sector		Turnover		Value Added at Factor Cost	
	Number	Share in the EU (%)	Value (in US$ million)	Share in the EU (%)	Value (in US$ million)	Share in the EU (%)
Finland	22,840	0.64	48267.5	1.4	8002.1	1.3
France	378,768	10.65	562367.0	16.4	96537.6	16.0
Germany (including the former GDR from 1991)	329,409	9.27	641803.7	18.7	130666.3	21.7
Hungary	88,971	2.50	34024.0	1.0	3337.2	0.6
Ireland	21,933	0.62	47553.2	1.4	9178.5	1.5
Italy	651,024	18.31	393699.5	11.5	57646.8	9.6
Latvia	13,566	0.38	7472.2	0.2	917.8	0.2
Lithuania	34,327	0.97	10343.3	0.3	1001.5	0.2
Luxembourg	3,066	0.09	18993.6	0.6	1584.2	0.3
Netherlands	77,879	2.19	145182.0	4.2	28167.7	4.7
Norway	27,006	0.76	62929.7	1.8	10836.2	1.8
Poland	319,039	8.97	120913.5	3.5	15806.4	2.6
Portugal	153,301	4.31	63777.1	1.9	9337.8	1.6
Romania	121,311	3.41	35669.9	1.0	4052.9	0.7
Slovakia	9,764	0.27	13574.1	0.4	2059.7	0.3
Slovenia	6,897	0.19	14704.0	0.4	1879.4	0.3
Spain	497,992	14.01	305943.8	8.9	60513.9	10.1
Sweden	58,487	1.65	78592.0	2.3	13488.5	2.2
Switzerland	18,832	0.53	104972.5	3.1	25521.3	4.2
United Kingdom	187,946	5.29	494219.5	14.4	95495.5	15.9
European Union (27 countries)	3,555,397		3437745.0		602096.6	

Source: Extracted from Eurostat database. Conversion done using the average exchange rate of US$ for euro for the calendar year 2009 (1€ = US$1.3937) using *www.oanda.com* (accessed on 30 August 2012).

European retailers have the most widespread presence globally and some of the top European retailers in the world market are from France, Germany and the UK (Deloitte, 2012). These include non-specialised retailers such as Carrefour S.A. (France, global rank 2nd), Tesco plc (UK, global rank 3rd), Metro AG (Germany, global rank 4th), Schwarz Unternehmens Treuhand KG (Germany, global rank 6th) and Aldi Einkauf GmbH & Co. (Germany, global rank 10th). IKEA, which is a Sweden-based speciality retailer, was ranked 30th on the index.

Regulations in India and the EU

Globally, retail is a highly regulated sector, but most countries now allow foreign investment in retail. Emerging markets started liberalising their retail sectors in the 1990s with China opening its retail sector in 1992, Brazil, Mexico and Argentina in 1994 and Indonesia in 1998 (Mukherjee and Patel, 2005). Several countries have opened up the retail sector in a phased manner, but some impose conditions such as a cap on foreign equity, local partnership conditions and minimum paid-up capital requirements. Some countries have also imposed regulations such as zoning regulations, economic needs tests, labour market tests and local sourcing conditions.[18] While emerging markets mostly resort to FDI restrictions in retail, developed countries impose stringent regulations on retail operations.

Retail Regulations in India

According to the Indian Constitution, the retail sector is under the jurisdiction of the state governments. At the centre, the Department of Consumer Affairs regulates internal trade, while the DIPP, under the Ministry of Commerce and Industry, regulates FDI. Different central government ministries/departments such as the Ministry of Agriculture and the Ministry of Textiles regulate specific products, which has an impact on the retail of these products. The Shops and Establishment Act, under the purview of the state governments, lays down the conditions for establishing and operating retail outlets including shop timings. The state

---

[18] For details, see Goyal and Mukherjee (2012).

governments also regulate sourcing (through Acts such as Agricultural Produce Marketing Committee [APMC] Act)[19] and the entry and movement of goods within the state. Zoning is under the purview of local municipal bodies. Regulations relating to sourcing, packaging, distribution and so on are applicable to retail. The Competition Act, 2002 and its amendments regulate anti-competitive practices involved in the retail of products. From the perspective of consumers, the most important Act is the Consumers Protection Act, 1986 and the Consumer Protection (Amendment) Act, 2002, which became effective from March 2003 and protects consumers of both goods and services from unfair or restrictive trade practices. The number of regulations and extent of restrictions vary across different Indian states and even cities depending on the type of retail format and the commodities traded. On average, a corporate retailer has to obtain 30 licences and clearances, which can go up to 45 for segments such as food and grocery retail (Joseph and Soundararajan, 2009).

After the severe balance of payments and currency crisis in 1991, the Indian government allowed foreign investment in a large number of sectors but excluded the retail sector. In 1997, the government banned FDI in retail. Subsequently, the policy has been relaxed and FDI is allowed through other routes of product distribution, such as wholesale cash-and-carry (100 per cent FDI has been allowed since 2006), franchising and distribution agreements and test marketing.[20] If a foreign company has a wholly-owned subsidiary in manufacturing, it is allowed to retail products.

However, each of these entry routes has drawbacks. For instance, low-priced, multi-brand retailers such as Wal-Mart and Tesco have entered through the wholesale cash-and-carry route, which does not

---

[19] As per the Model APMC Act, 2003, the APMC Act is defined as 'An Act to provide for improved regulation in marketing of agricultural produce, development of efficient marketing system, promotion of agri-processing and agricultural export and the establishment and proper administration of markets for agricultural produce in States.' As per the APMC Act, in each state of India all agricultural products are required to be sold only in government-regulated markets.

[20] Test marketing is the limited introduction of a product or service to test public reaction for a full market strategy. In India, the DIPP has permitted test marketing of items for which a company has approval for manufacture, provided tha the test marketing facility will be for a period of two years and investment in setting up a manufacturing facility commences simultaneously with test marketing.

allow these companies to make direct sales to consumers. Therefore, they cannot reap the benefits of the large and growing Indian consumer market. Moreover, wholesale cash-and-carry is a volume business[21] and may not be suitable for specialised and luxury products that are bought in small quantities. Entry routes such as franchising, licensing and distribution arrangements do not allow foreign retailers to have a share in the profits in India. In addition, foreign luxury brands do not want to give their brand ownership to several distributors, since it reduces the value of the global brand name. Setting up a manufacturing facility requires investment and long-term commitment and is economically viable only if there is sufficient demand for the product. In India, it is not easy to set up a manufacturing facility because companies have to adhere to the labour laws and face infrastructure bottlenecks (such as power shortages). Therefore, most retailers prefer to source from contract manufacturers.

For the purpose of FDI policy, the Indian government has divided the retail sector into single-brand and multi-brand retail trade. In 2006, the government first allowed 51 per cent FDI in single-brand retail subject to certain conditions. In January 2012, 100 per cent FDI was allowed in single-brand retail, and in September 2012, the Indian government liberalised both the single-brand and multi-brand retail policy; thereafter, there have been several amendments to the policy. The highlights of India's FDI regime in the retail sector are given in Figure 10.4.

While the government initiated some reforms with regard to FDI in store-based retail, non-store retail continues to face several regulatory hurdles. For instance, in India, till date, direct selling does not have an overarching regulation and a clear industry definition. Due to the lack of appropriate regulation, it continues to fall under the Prize Chit and Money Circulation (Banning) Scheme, 1978 in India, which is considered to be misapplied. As regards e-commerce, the government is contemplating whether it should allow foreign investments in business-to-consumer e-commerce activity and to this effect, the DIPP released a discussion paper in January 2014 inviting opinion from the stakeholders. However, no progress has been made in both the sectors so far.

---

[21] The route permits business-to-business operations where goods are sold in bulk.

Figure 10.4
India's FDI Policy in Retail Approved by the Cabinet and Notified by the DIPP

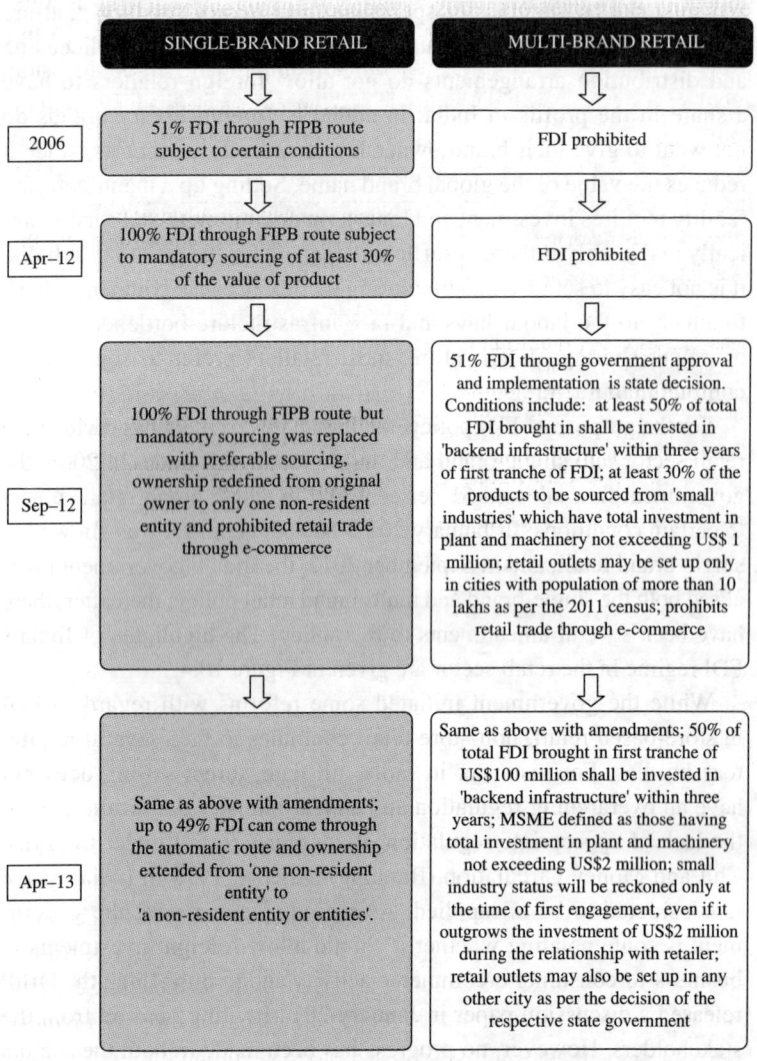

Source: Compiled from http://dipp.nic.in/English/Policies/FDI_Circular_01_ 2012.pdf and http://dipp.nic.in/English/acts_rules/Press_Notes/pn1_ 2012.pdf (accessed on 31 August 2012) and http://pib.nic.in/newsite/ pmreleases.aspx?mincode=61 (accessed on 17 September 2012).

In general, as there were FDI restrictions in the past, India has adopted a restrictive approach in the retail sector in its WTO and free trade negotiations. In the Uruguay Round (1986–1994) of WTO negotiations, India did not undertake commitments in distribution services. In the Doha Round, India offered to undertake commitments in commission agent's services and wholesale trade services for some products. India's commitments in distribution services vary across different bilateral trade agreements. For instance, in the India–Singapore CECA (August 2005), India undertook commitments in franchising services along with wholesale trading and commission agents' services. In the India–Japan CEPA (August 2011), India allowed 51 per cent FDI in single-brand retail, based on the autonomous regime at that time. Thus, India shows some willingness to bind the autonomous regime in trade agreements, but does not offer to undertake forward-looking commitments in this sector. Since India's major trading partners including the EU have a strong interest in this sector, it is likely that the sector will witness more liberalisation in India's multilateral and bilateral trade agreements, especially the India–EU BTIA.

Regulations in the EU

In the EU, there are no retail-specific Directives/regulations applicable to EU Member States. The Services Directive 2006/123/EC in the internal market is applicable to the retail sector and it lays down the general provisions governing this sector.

To ensure freedom of establishment for providers, the Services Directive has conditions governing authorisation and has prohibited certain requirements. Some of these have important implications for the retail sector. The Directive states that Member States shall not make access to or exercise of service activity subject to an authorisation scheme, such as an authorisation required by local authorities to establish operations or sell certain products.[22] Requirements that are prohibited by the Services Directive include discriminatory requirements based directly or indirectly on the nationality of the service provider, prohibition on having an establishment in more than one Member State and case-by-case

---

[22] For details, see Article 9 of the Services Directive.

application of the economic needs test.[23] For instance, an EU Member State cannot impose restrictions on opening retail outlets or branches in more than one Member State.

The Directive also has provisions to ensure free movement of services. These include Articles on the freedom to provide services and related derogations and the rights of recipients of services. The article on freedom to provide services gives the service provider the right to provide services in a Member State other than the one in which they are established. Member States cannot impose requirements on the access to or exercise of services in their territory. As regards the rights of recipients of services, Member States cannot impose requirements on a recipient that restrict the use of a service supplied by a provider established in another Member State. Member States cannot discriminate against a recipient based on his/her nationality or place of residence.

The Directive lays down the conditions applicable to an EU service provider but not those for a foreigner. The treatment of foreign service providers depends on the mode of entry of the foreign company in the EU market. If a foreign company enters through a joint venture or as a wholly-owned subsidiary by making direct investment, it is treated as an EU company. In that case, the company enjoys the same privileges as received by any other EU company and comes under the purview of the Services Directive. Representative offices, branches or distributive offices of foreign companies are not treated as EU companies and, therefore, they do not fall under the provisions of the Services Directive. Such offices have to follow the individual country's regulations governing the sector.

The European Commission has a vision for more efficient and fair retail services in the EU internal market by 2020. In order to achieve this, the Commission encourages Member States to adhere to the provisions under the Services Directive 2006/123/EC. The Commission is now in the process of devising a Retail Action Plan for the EU market that aims to integrate the EU retail market.[24]

There are several regulations applicable to foreign retailers in the EU market. These include economic need tests, zoning regulations, restrictions on the size of the retail outlet and restrictions on the sale of certain

---

[23] For details, see Article 14 of the Services Directive.

[24] For details, see http://ec.europa.eu/internal_market/retail/index_en.htm#maincontentSec1 (accessed on 13 September 2012).

commodities. EU Member States have amended some of their regulations to make them compliant with the EU Services Directive, while other regulations are not compliant with the Service Directive. The table also lists regulations applicable to foreign retailers that are still present in Member States and are not compliant with the Services Directive.

Apart from the Services Directive, EU Directives on consumer protection, employment of people and e-commerce activities are also applicable to EU retailers.

The EU is at the forefront with respect to consumer protection and has several Directives to protect consumers. In 2011, the EC issued Directive 2011/83/EU on consumer rights,[25] which is still under consultation. The Directive merged four existing consumer protection Directives— Directive 85/577/EEC on contracts negotiated away from business premises, Directive 93/13/EEC on unfair terms in consumer contracts, Directive 97/7/EC on distance contracts and Directive 99/44/EC on consumer sales and guarantees—into a single horizontal instrument. The aim was to regulate common aspects relating to consumer protection systematically, by simplifying and updating the existing rules, removing inconsistencies and closing gaps in the four Directives.[26] Directive 98/6/EC of the European Parliament on consumer protection indicates the prices of products to be offered to consumers. Apart from this, Directive 2005/29/EC concerning unfair business-to-consumer commercial practices in the internal market contains basic information requirements that have to be fulfilled by traders before contract conclusion.

Directive 96/71/EC of the European Commission concerning *the posting of workers in the framework of the provision of services* is also applicable to the retail sector. The free movement of workers is one of the fundamental freedoms guaranteed by the Directive. A worker is *a posted worker* when the worker is employed in one EU Member State but sent by the employer on a temporary basis to carry out work in another Member State. The majority of EU Member States have implemented the provisions of this Directive in their domestic regulations concerning labour employment.

[25] For details, see http://eur-lex.europa.eu/LexUriServ/LexUriServ.do?uri=OJ:L:2011:304:0064:0088:EN:PDF (accessed on 24 August 2012).

[26] For details, see http://eur-lex.europa.eu/LexUriServ/LexUriServ.do?uri=COM:2008:0614:FIN:EN:PDF (accessed on 24 August 2012).

As regards online services, EC Directive 2000/31/EC creates the basic legal framework for online services, including electronic commerce in the internal market. The Directive removes obstacles to cross-border online services in the EU and provides legal certainty to businesses and citizens alike. It establishes harmonised rules on issues such as the transparency and information requirements for online service providers, commercial communications, electronic contracts and limitations of liability of intermediary service providers. There is also the EC Directive 2009/136/EC on online cookies, which amends Directive 2002/22/EC on universal service and users' rights relating to electronic communications networks and services; Directive 2002/58/EC concerns the processing of personal data and the protection of privacy in the electronic communications sector and Regulation (EC) No 2006/2004[27] is for cooperation between national authorities responsible for the enforcement of consumer protection laws, which is applicable to retailers involved in electronic commerce.

In its WTO Revised Offer, the European Commission has offered commitments in the retail sector. However, the coverage of retail services and commitments varies across Member States (Table 10.2).

The EC's WTO Revised Offer (WTO, 2005b) in retail services is more liberal than India's offer. While India has not covered retail services at all, the EC has offered commitments in all four Modes. In Mode 1, Austria, the Czech Republic, Estonia, Finland, Hungary, Latvia, Lithuania, Sweden and Slovenia have given full commitments.[28] Cyprus, Malta and Poland have offered no commitment in the sector, while the others have offered to commit only in mail order service. In Mode 2, all Member States have offered full commitments in the sector except Cyprus and Malta. In Mode 3, all Member States except Belgium, Cyprus, Denmark, France, Italy, Malta and Portugal have offered full commitment in retail services. Belgium, Cyprus, Denmark, France, Italy, Malta and Portugal have imposed an economic needs test along with a limit on the number of department stores.[29] Sweden has also

---

[27] For details see http://eur-lex.europa.eu/legal-content/EN/TXT/PDF/?uri=CELEX:32 004R2006&from=EN (accessed on 17 August 2015).

[28] The excluded Member States have given full commitment in mail order service under Mode 1.

[29] The criterion for this is the number and impact on existing stores, population density, geographical spread, impact on traffic conditions and creation of new employment.

Table 10.2
*Coverage of Retail Services by Member States in the EC
Conditional Revised Offer*

CPC	Definition	Member States that have Excluded the Sector
611.1	Sales of motor vehicles	Belgium, Bulgaria, Cyprus, Denmark, France, Germany, Greece, Ireland, Italy, Luxembourg, Malta, the Netherlands, Poland, Portugal, Romania, Slovenia, Spain, Sweden and the UK
611.12	Retail sales of motor vehicles	Poland
611.3	Sales of parts and accessories of motor vehicles	Poland
612.1	Sales of motorcycles and snowmobiles and related parts and accessories	Poland
631	Food retail services	Covered by all Member States
631.07	Retail sales of beverages not consumed on the spot	Poland
631.08	Retail sales of tobacco products	Poland
632	Non-food retail services	Covered by all Member States
632.11	Retail sales of pharmaceutical, medical and orthopaedic goods	Poland and Slovenia
633	Repair services of personal and household goods	Austria, the Czech Republic, Finland, Hungary, Latvia, Lithuania, Poland, the Slovak Republic, Sweden and Slovenia

Source: Compiled from WTO (2005b and 2007).

imposed an economic needs test that sets a limit on temporary trade in clothing, shoes and food that is not consumed at the point of sale.[30] In Estonia, France and Italy, tobacco is a state monopoly and in Ireland the sale of alcoholic beverages is not permitted. Under Mode 4, no EU

---

[30] The main criterion is the impact on existing stores in the geographical area in question.

Member State except Cyprus has offered any commitment for intra-corporate transferees and business visitors. The EU Member States have not offered any commitments for contractual service providers and independent professionals in the retail sector.

Primary Survey

There is a lack of disaggregated data on the retail sector in India. The DIPP and the FIPB give data on foreign investments in India, but there are no studies that highlight the barriers faced by foreign companies in India. Therefore, a primary survey was conducted and the sampling frame is given in Table 10.3.

Presence of Indian and European Retailers in Each Other's Market

Global retailers are growing their store networks in a wide range of international markets (CBRE, 2011). Once the domestic market is saturated, retailers often expand to new and emerging markets to increase their sales. This happened in the case of retailers in the US and the EU after

Table 10.3
Sampling Frame

Respondents	*Number*
EU companies in India	14
Indian companies	4
Industry Associations	3
Embassies of EU Member States in India and EC experts, high commissions	6
Academicians	3
Indian Government	4
Total	34

Source: Primary Survey.

the two markets were affected by the global slowdown in 2008. This section discusses the presence of Indian and European retailers in each other's market.

European Retailers in India

Despite its restrictive FDI policy, India has attracted several European retailers. There has been continuous and significant interest among EU retailers in the Indian market after the economic reforms of 1991. Depending on the prevailing policy, EU retailers have used various routes to enter the Indian market, which include wholly-owned subsidiary through manufacturing, exclusive licensing and distribution arrangement, franchising agreement and wholesale cash-and-carry (Table 10.4).

Table 10.4
Entry Routes of Some EU Retailers in India

Brand	*Mode of Entry*	*Year*	*Country*
Bata	Wholly-owned subsidiary in manufacturing	1936	Czech Republic
Lotto	Exclusive licensing agreement	1989	Italy
United Colors of Benetton	Wholly-owned subsidiary in manufacturing	1991	Italy
Marks & Spencer	Franchising and distribution agreement	2001	UK
Louis Vuitton	Distribution agreement	2003	France
Mango	Franchising and distribution agreement	2003	Spain
Metro	Wholesale cash-and-carry	2003	Germany
Chanel	Distribution agreement	2005	France
Salvatore Ferragamo	Joint venture	2006	Italy
Giorgio Armani	Joint venture	2006	Italy
Tesco	Wholesale cash-and-carry	2010	UK
Pavers England Limited	Single-brand retail	2013	UK
IKEA	Single-brand retail	2013	Sweden

Source: Compiled from the survey.

In clothing and apparel enter through the manufacturing route, because of the lower manufacturing costs in India. Bata Shoes (Netherlands) was an early entrant through this route, and IKEA (Sweden), Marks & Spencer Plc (UK) and Zara (Spain) have been sourcing from India for a decade.

Before 1991, European retailers such as Adidas AG (Germany) and Lotto Sport Italia (Italy) entered the Indian market by giving exclusive distribution rights and licences to Indian distributors. Indian companies such as Genesis Color Private Limited and Blues Clothing Company market and distribute luxury brands in India. European brands such as Canali (Italy), Bottega Veneta (Italy), Paul Smith (UK), Jimmy Choo (UK) and Versace (Italy) entered India through this route. With growing knowledge and exposure to foreign brands in the Indian market, foreign retailers expanded their presence by entering into franchisee agreements with Indian partners; in this arrangement, foreign companies appoint a franchisee that sells the products through their retail outlets by paying a fixed franchisee fee. Today, this is one of the most common entry routes into the Indian market and was used by Marks & Spencer Plc (UK) and Punto Fa, S.L., trading as Mango (Spain).

After India allowed 51 per cent FDI in 2006 through the single-brand retail trade route, several foreign brands, particularly in luxury products, used this route to enter the Indian market. These include Giorgio Armani and Salvatore Ferragamo (Italy). Brands that had already entered the Indian market through other routes changed their mode of presence by collaborating with Indian retailers or other companies. These include Marks & Spencer (UK) and Louis Vuitton (France).

The EU is the largest investor in the retail sector in India with a share of around 55 per cent in the total investment in retail. Of the total investments from the EU, the majority (48 per cent) is in the readymade garment segment. Within the EU, the largest percentage of investments in single-brand retail sector is from the Netherlands. However, in terms of country of origin of the investing brand, Italy is the major investing country, followed by the UK and Germany (Table 10.5). Of the Italian brands that have invested in India, around 45 per cent have routed their investments through the Netherlands with which India has a Double Taxation Avoidance Agreement and Bilateral Investment Promotion Agreement.[31]

---

[31] Calculated from Secretariat for Industrial Assistance (SIA) data.

Table 10.5

Share of Top Investors from EU Member States in India until March 2013 (%)

Investing Country	Share in Investment by Investing Country	Share in Investment by Brand Origin
Netherlands	32.3	9.18
Germany	16.8	17.72
Italy	14.5	30.83
United Kingdom	12.4	26.15
Spain	7.1	7.49
Cyprus	5.8	0.0
Luxembourg	5.3	0.0
British Isles	4.3	0.0
France	1.1	8.05
Belgium	0.6	0.58

Source: Calculated from the Secretariat for Industrial Assistance (SIA) News-letter, various issues http://dipp.nic.in/English/Publications/SIA_News-Letter/SIA_NewsLetter.aspx (accessed on 11 September 2012).

The Indian government has been receptive to foreign investments from European retailers in the retail sector. After receiving several requests from foreign retailers, particularly European retailers, in January 2012, the government extended the foreign investment limit in single-brand retail to allow 100 per cent FDI in the sector, subject to conditions. With this change, IKEA (Sweden) and Pavers England (UK) have entered the Indian market. Since EU retailers have been the largest investors in the retail sector, they have a strong interest in retail liberalisation. Some large EU retailers have been lobbying for retail liberalisation in India (see Box 10.1 for the case of IKEA).

Since multi-brand retail trade was prohibited in India until 2012, EU retailers such as Metro AG (Germany) and Tesco Plc (UK) have entered through the wholesale cash-and-carry route, which permits business-to-business (B2B) operations, but does not allow direct sales to customers. Therefore, the present policy restricts the ability of a foreign retailer to enter through their preferred route and each entry route has drawbacks (discussed later in this chapter).

Box 10.1. IKEA in India: A Tryst with Policy

IKEA is a privately held, international home products company that designs and sells ready-to-assemble furniture like beds, chairs and desks as well as appliances and home accessories. It has around 12,000 products that are sold in product ranges that have separate names. It was founded in Sweden in 1943 and Inter IKEA Systems B.V. was established in 1983 in the Netherlands, when it started to develop the IKEA retail system. The company is the world's largest furniture retailer. In 2012, IKEA had 338 stores in 40 countries providing employment to 154,000 workers. IKEA is expanding its presence in Asia and has recently opened a store in Bangkok. The company has plans to establish a presence in the US$18.5 billion Indian home decor and furniture market, which is expected to grow by 10–12 per cent per annum.

After 100 per cent FDI was permitted in single-brand retail in India in January 2012, IKEA proposed to invest ₹10,500 crore (US$1.9 billion) to set up 25 stores. However, the company had reservations about mandatory sourcing from Indian micro, small and medium enterprises (MSMEs). Based on the company's recommendations along with the recommendations of other foreign retailers, the Indian government tweaked the sourcing norms in India. The latest policy has diluted the previous condition of sourcing 30 per cent of requirements *mandatorily* from Indian MSMEs by stating that sourcing should be done *preferably from MSMEs*. The policy received a positive response from the company and IKEA re-submitted its application to the FIPB in India seeking approval to sell 30 product ranges in India. Since the proposed investment was more than ₹1,200 crore, the company required approval from the Cabinet Committee on Economic Affairs (CCEA).

IKEA received approval from the Indian government to sell its core furniture products, but 18 of the 30 product categories were rejected based on the logic that since IKEA comes under the single-brand retail category, the company cannot be allowed to sell sub-brands. This eliminated home and office solutions, fittings, furnishings, stationery, textile products, consumer electronics, cleaning products, leather products, storage and sorting products and accessories, children's products, safety-related products, travel-related products, cosmetics, recycling solutions and products, lifestyle products, decorative products, gift articles, beach products and accessories, and food and beverages to be served at IKEA restaurants. The FIPB has also recommended that IKEA cannot conduct any activities falling within the purview of activities related to non-banking financial companies, which implies that IKEA cannot offer any finance scheme to its customers. Faced with reluctance from the company to continue with its plan to invest in India, the government finally granted approval to IKEA in May 2013 to bring investments in all the categories to the Indian market. IKEA is now looking for potential locations for investment to go ahead with its investment plans in the Indian market.

Source: Compiled from company website and news articles.

The survey found that European brands have customised their products to cater to the tastes of Indian consumers. For instance, the Indian designer, Manish Arora, has design collaborations with the watch brand, Swatch (Switzerland), and the jewellery brand, Swarovski (UK), to customise their products for the Indian market. Other brands have also altered their pricing strategy for the Indian market.

Indian Retailers in the EU

Compared to the widespread presence of EU retailers in India, very few Indian companies/retailers are present in the EU market. Some Indian retailers are present through standalone outlets in Europe, while others have entered into mergers and acquisitions. Fabindia Overseas Private Limited, an Indian textile retailer, has an outlet in Rome (Italy) and acquired a 62.5 per cent stake in the UK-based women wear retailer EAST in 2011. India's Gitanjali Group, which is world's largest jewellery retailer, has a strong foothold in the European market. The company has acquired Italy's DIT Group's brands, namely Stefan Hafner, Porrati, Nouvelle Bague of Florence and Io Si. Hidesign, which is a leather goods manufacturer and retailer, has stores in Belgium, Germany, Ireland and the UK; it has collaborated with Louis Vuitton Malletier (France) and some of the products are designed by Italian designers. Tata Global Beverages Limited, an Indian multinational non-alcoholic beverages company, is a subsidiary of the Tata Group. In 1992, the company entered into a joint venture with Britain's Tetley Tea Company, and in 2000, it acquired the company. The company has a subsidiary in the Czech Republic and retails its products in almost all European countries. Indian textile manufacturer and retailer Raymond Limited has joint ventures with Belgian and Italian textile and clothing manufacturers. In August 2006, the company entered into a 50:50 joint venture with UCO NV (Belgium) to manufacture and market denim fabric. It also has a joint venture with Cotonificio Honegger S.P.A., (Italy), which produces shirts and fabrics that are retailed in Europe. Haldiram's Private Limited, which is an Indian ready-to-eat food retailer and out-of-home catering chain, has outlets in the UK, Finland, Sweden, Italy, the Netherlands, Germany, Switzerland, Spain, Greece and Romania. The survey found that there are almost 3,000 Indian brands that are trying to enter the EU retail markets. These are not just Indian retailers but branded products in different categories. This implies there is an interest in and opportunity for Indian brands in the EU.

The majority of Indian retailers targeted the large markets of the UK, Germany, France and Italy. When the EU becomes a single market in services, Indian retailers can expand to countries in Eastern Europe such as Hungary and Poland, where there is scope for their products.

Respondents said that Indian retailers have not been able to explore the European market, because modern retail is a new and emerging concept in India and companies are trying to get acquainted with the organised retail market in India before moving to the West. Some companies pointed out that at present there are limited avenues for collaboration in the West, because EU consumers are accustomed to certain brands for food and non-food products and an Indian brand would have to spend enormous resources to create brand recognition in the EU. Indian corporate retailers would need a lot of resources as well as support from the government to explore other markets. Retailers that are already present in the West are large retailers who have the resources to do so at the individual level.

Both the Indian and EU retail sectors have several barriers and opportunities for retailers from each other's market. The gist of the strengths and weaknesses of the Indian and EU retailer sector is given in Figure 10.5.

Barriers Faced by Retailers

The discussion above reflects the importance of the retail sector in India and the EU. Both countries have a dynamic retail market that is expected to grow. India and the EU also have complementarities in the retail sector. At present, retailers from the EU have a vast presence in the Indian market, but given the size and potential of the Indian retail sector, there is a scope for further penetration. The survey found that India lags behind China, particularly in luxury retail. On average, there are around 50 luxury brands in China, while in India there are around 15–20. Indian companies that have established a presence in the local market are expanding their operations and entering foreign markets, particularly EU markets. However, there are several barriers to entry and operations in both India and the EU.

Figure 10.5
SWOT Analysis of the Retail Sector in India and the EU

India

- **Strength:** High economic growth, large retail market size and growing middle class
- **Weakness:** Poor regulatory environment, restrictive FDI conditions, difficult to find local partners, poor technology and infrastructure
- **Opportunities:** Untapped organised retail market, low brand penetration, therefore, scope for more brands, growing brand consciousness, scope for collaboration
- **Threats:** Competition from other emerging markets in the Middle East and Latin America with better regulatory environment and liberal FDI norms

EU

- **Strength:** Availability of high-skilled manpower, efficient supply chain network
- **Weakness:** Not a single market, restrictive country-specific regulations
- **Opportunities:** Services market unification in the EU giving better access to EU Member States, technological collaboration and skill development
- **Threats:** Slowdown in Europe has affected consumer spending

Source: Author's compilation from the survey results.
Disclaimer: This figure has been redrawn by Tanu M. Goyal and is not to scale. It does not represent any authentic national or international boundary and is used for illustrative purpose only.

In India, most of the problems faced by EU retailers are related to the FDI policy in the retail sector. For a long time, one of the main impediments in the Indian retail sector was the prohibition on FDI in the multi-brand retail sector. With the recent liberalisation of multi-brand retail sector, the retail policy has been eased, but the government has imposed conditions that are likely to be restrictive.

European retailers in India pointed out that there are several problems with local sourcing. The conditions seem to be based on the notion that all multi-brand foreign retailers are low-cost volume retailers in the food and grocery segment. High-end, specialised, multi-brand foreign retailers will face the same barriers as single-brand foreign retailers in sourcing from small and medium enterprises. The first concern is related to quality. The revised single-brand policy of 2013 failed to attract major FDI inflows due to the restrictive sourcing conditions. Luxury brands have strict quality standards. Also, most brand names are considered a mark of quality assurance and the products are, therefore, manufactured under close supervision. It is extremely difficult to ensure quality and product consistency if the products are sourced from the small-scale sector. Some luxury retailers pointed out that undertaking domestic manufacturing might jeopardise the global brand name in the long run. Retailers like IKEA that already source 75 per cent of their textiles (carpets) from India said that the company follows strict social and environmental standards in manufacturing their products, which is difficult to replicate in India. It may not be financially possible for small entrepreneurs to get the right technology due to the cost of the technology. One of the oldest operations of Tesco Plc in India is local sourcing. Tesco Plc has US$0.5 billion worth of direct sourcing from India and its indirect sourcing through imports is much higher. India is one of the largest sourcing hubs for textiles and apparel. Interestingly, hard lines such as playground equipment like cycles, stationery and food such as fruits are increasingly being sourced from all over India. Therefore, some retailers pointed out that imposing mandatory sourcing requirements may adversely influence a foreign retailer's decision to enter the Indian market, even if he is sourcing from India.

The multi-brand policy also states that at least 50 per cent of total FDI inflow has to be invested in back-end infrastructure within three years. The first issue is the definition or quantification of back-end investment.

It was pointed out during the survey that if a company has to invest 50 per cent of every dollar invested in the country in back-end infrastructure, it is not very realistic. The back-end cost is usually around 8–9 per cent of the total investment. Investment in back-end operations is difficult for retailers who only deal with front-end retail, that is, they procure products from different sources and sell the products. This condition will discourage foreign retailers that only plan to open retail stores and not set up manufacturing facilities or invest in infrastructure and the supply chain. While all retailers need an efficient supply chain, they do not necessarily invest in it but rely on 3PL service providers, particularly in new markets. Back-end investment also varies by product category. For instance, food and grocery retailers require higher back-end investment than retailers of luxury products, sports goods and furniture. Further, the policy is unclear about whether or not the cost of land and rental for warehousing and cold chains will be considered back-end investment; it states that warehousing is back-end, but land cost and rentals are not. It is also not clear about cases where warehouses are connected to the hypermarket. In addition, these conditions are difficult to monitor and are, therefore, likely to create operational uncertainty.

There are differences across states in the implementation of the policy and, hence, states will have to make some decisions. This has three broad implications. First, consumers are mobile between states with common borders and, therefore, consumers can buy from neighbouring states. Second, retailers can still be present in a state that does not allow FDI in multi-brand retail by entering in a franchisee agreement. Therefore, restriction on FDI is not an entry ban. Using multiple modes of operations leads to operational inefficiencies and ambiguities for a company. Last, this condition may affect the positive impact of other policies such as the GST. Most multi-brand retailers follow a hub-and-spoke model for distribution. At present, the hubs are chosen based on the tax advantage in a particular state and not on logistics benefits. The GST would ensure that such inefficiencies are corrected. However, since some states have not opted for multi-brand retail liberalisation, this may not be possible. Since this is a state-level policy, retailers cannot operate in Gujarat even if it is logistically more efficient than Maharashtra and Andhra Pradesh. So, it becomes difficult to have an efficiently located distribution centre.

Foreign e-commerce companies are at a clear disadvantage with this policy, which prohibits e-tailing companies from undertaking online retail operations in India. The e-retail segment in India has exhibited double-digit growth and has the potential to create one million jobs in the country (Technopak, 2012). In addition, e-retail is an important source of revenue for multi-brand retailers and a prohibition on e-tailing would adversely affect their sales in India.

Another problem in the retail policy is finding the right partner for a joint venture. Very few Indian corporate retailers have the financial ability to collaborate with foreign brands. Companies like Marks & Spencer Plc entered India with a small joint venture partner that led to lower visibility and smaller retail space for the brand. The company later switched to Reliance Retail Limited, which is a larger player.

Apart from investment issues, foreign retailers pointed out barriers related to the movement of people. One of the problems concerned the issuance and renewal of work permits. Indian authorities are inefficient in granting work permit to overseas employees and, in most cases, work permits are issued for only three months; as a result, employees have to keep visiting the authorities. There are also bureaucratic hassles in renewing or applying for work permits.

Apart from these barriers in Modes 3 and 4, foreign retailers in India face several other barriers.

1. *Inadequate Infrastructure:* The present facilities at the airport are inadequate and the retail sector is underdeveloped. Indian airports need to be modernised, particularly to handle luxury products. Extensive paper work and documentation is required to obtain clearances and Indian airport and customs departments lack a centralised system of product clearance. There is also a dearth of 3PL service providers, and in some states an integrated supply network and 3PL services are completely missing. As a result, companies have limited choice, which affects their expansion plans. Warehouses and cold storage facilities in India are insufficient and poorly equipped, which impacts retailers in the food and grocery segment. The warehousing facilities are also not designed to house luxury products. In addition, the available organised retail space is limited. Although several malls are coming up in India,

there are very few high streets where brands can position themselves. Further, 75 per cent of the malls in India have failed due to poor mall management. Since the mall spaces in India are not properly organised, most of the malls are not occupied. There have to be zoning regulations in the cities that include a designated space for retailers.

2. *Regulatory Issues and Policy Uncertainty:* Foreign retailers in India face several regulatory problems. The retail sector is heavily regulated and foreign retailers have to obtain 40–50 licences to set up retail operations. Moreover, the investment promotion board and other authorities take a lot of time to grant approval. Some retailers pointed out that the implementation of rules is a problem. For instance, in IKEA, factory workers have to divide their time between two manufacturing units, which affects their efficiency and productivity. The process of reform is slow and reforms such as the GST have been pending for a long time. Some foreign companies pointed out that they do not have confidence in the Indian policy regime because the government easily rolls back its policies. Referring to September 2012 multi-brand policy, some respondents pointed out that most foreign companies adopted a wait-and-watch strategy on India while waiting for the multi-brand policy to be enacted, which took nearly 10 months to get cabinet clearance. Additionally, non-store retail has problems of missing regulations and industry definition is not clear leading to further regulatory uncertainties.

3. *High Incidence of Corruption:* The high incidence of corruption is another major regulatory problem faced by foreign retailers. Approvals from the government require a lot of informal payments. Importers and distributors of foreign brands pointed out that informal payments are extorted during customs clearance and sample testing. The corruption not only escalates costs to company, but also increases the time involved in getting approvals. One survey participant mentioned that pilferage is a major problem for companies that import products from the EU. When products are sent for testing or customs clearance, they are stolen.

4. *Inadequate Skills:* Lack of skilled personnel, particularly to operate and staff organised retail stores, is a major barrier faced by

foreign retailers. In India, very few people consider retail outlet management as a respectable position compared to other managerial positions. At the shop floor level, most employees lack soft skills and have a lackadaisical attitude; attrition rates are high at this level. The skills at other levels are also inadequate. One garment retailer pointed out that customs officers are not well trained. During sample testing, rather than sending the whole product for testing, they cut off a piece of the garment and send it to the laboratory. This causes a loss to retailers, particularly those selling luxury products.

5. *High Cost of Setting up Operations:* There are several reasons for the high costs of setting up operations in India. Rentals at high streets are very high, so a large proportion of the earnings are spent on fixed costs of operation. In addition, customs duties in India are higher than in other countries like China. The EU companies in India pointed out that they have to pay 30–40 per cent duty on the maximum retail price (MRP) of the product; this is particularly difficult for retailers that operate in luxury product categories because the MRP of their products is very high. Since most international brands harmonise product prices across all countries of operation, the customs duties reduce their margins in India. In India, routine sampling at customs warehouses costs a lot compared to other countries, due to the lack of adequate facilities and shortage of skills among customs staff.

There are very few Indian companies in the EU and the majority of the barriers they face in the EU market pertain to stringent regulatory norms on foreign retailers that vary across countries in the region.

1. *Economic Needs Test (ENT):* An ENT implies that the need for a particular service or service provider should be determined on an economic basis that typically involves demand and supply (Krajewski, 2003). The EU Member States including the Netherlands, Greece, Malta, Austria and Romania impose an economic needs test on foreign retailers. There is no clear definition of an economic needs test as per GATS and, as a result, there is no defined reason for imposing the economic needs test in the EU. This acts as a major entry barrier to the EU market.

2. *Product-specific Regulations:* The UK, Austria, Bulgaria and Hungary have authorisation requirements for product categories such as alcohol, tobacco, gem stones, metals, veterinary products and motor vehicles. Retailers have to apply for licences and get clearances from multiple authorities. This requirement varies across EU Member States, making it difficult for retailers to set up operations.

3. *Labour Market Test:* EU Member States have stringent Mode 4 conditions compared to India. In countries like France, there are labour market tests to hire labourers. In addition, managerial positions can only be offered to French nationals. As a result, there is a restriction on hiring Indians to manage retail outlets in the country.

4. *Differences across Member States:* Unlike the case of goods, the EU market is still not a single market for services. Indian companies interested in entering the EU market have to abide by the specific policies of Member States. There are several regulations pertaining to market access and operations. There are also differences in language, culture and preferences across Europe, which makes it difficult for Indian retailers to establish pan-EU operations.

5. *Restrictions on Ownership of Real Estate:* EU Member States such as Hungary, Latvia, Italy, Poland, Malta and Greece do not permit foreigners to own real estate. As a result, foreign retailers cannot acquire property for setting up retail operations in the EU.

Opportunities and the Way Forward

The discussion above shows that both the Indian and the EU retail markets are large and growing. The retail sector has significant employment potential in both markets. The Indian and EU retail markets are different; while the Indian market is largely unorganised and there is huge potential for modern retail, the EU retail market is largely saturated. There are not many large Indian corporates in the retail sector and there is a need for FDI to bring efficiency in the distribution network in India. The EU can offer efficient supply management technology to India, while India can offer access to a large and growing consumer market. Despite these complementarities, the presence of the EU retailers in India is low compared to their presence in other emerging markets such as China. The presence of Indian retailers in the EU is negligible. Over the past year, India has experienced a decline in retail FDI and the EU saw a fall in the number of European companies among the top retailers in the world market. While this is partly due to the slowdown in the Western markets, some of it can also be attributed to regulatory and other barriers in these markets.

The main barrier is related to the FDI policy in retail. Due to problems with this policy, several foreign retailers are not opting for the direct investment route. As a result, while foreign brands continue to get access to the Indian market through other routes, India is missing out on foreign direct investments. Since the government has already initiated reforms in FDI, there is a need to evaluate the conditions imposed on foreign retailers and make them more realistic. The conditions also have to be clear to avoid operational uncertainties.

Unlike other sectors where reforms are being undertaken, retail sector reforms with respect to store based retail have now slowed down in India. Contrary to this, non-store retail is now in policy focus and, therefore, it is likely that over time, investment opportunities are created in non-store retailing in India.

The survey found that some brands are already sourcing products from the Indian markets and will continue to do so even when they get access to the Indian retail market. Therefore, the sourcing condition needs to be carefully designed to include products in which India has a manufacturing advantage and the skills and capability to produce. In the food and grocery segment, several brands source from farmers and small producers, who do not own a plant or machinery and, hence, are excluded from the definition of SMEs. In addition, no supplier discloses the investments in plant and machinery. It is an investment made over a period. There are several modifications in the entire process. The investment is made, capacity is generated, there is depreciation and, therefore, identification of small and medium enterprises for sourcing products is not easy.

The conditions imposed on foreign retailers are designed from the view that all multi-brand retailers are food and grocery retailers, but some of these conditions may not be applicable to multi-brand retailers in other categories, such as sports goods and electronics. The conditions imposed on foreign retailers should be realistic and should be targeted to support the industry.

If sourcing conditions are imposed, the government has to complement the policy by reducing barriers to trade in goods. Import duties on products like textiles should be removed or reduced, as competing nations such as Bangladesh and China have done. This will make Indian goods cost-competitive in the global markets and foreign retailers will source from India not only for the Indian market, but also for third-country markets.

There is a need for proper zoning regulations particularly for the location of malls in India. At present, there is no Act or regulation that lays down zoning laws. Residential and commercial zones are based on a pre-defined master plan prepared by the Municipal Corporation of that state. The zoning regulation should be delinked from the FDI policy and should be applicable to all retailers. Foreign retailers complain about high rentals, while Indian real estate developers point out that malls are unoccupied. This is due to the lack of proper real estate and mall planning in the country.

As the retail sector modernises, there is a need to train people so that they can get absorbed in the modern retail sector. European retailers have mandatory training programmes for their employees. Large EU retailers can collaborate with management institutes in India to design retail courses and associations like the Retailers Association of India can collaborate to train both modern and traditional retailers and employees in retail outlets. Since Europe has an enormous technological advantage, there should be training programmes for employees to learn to use technology such as bar coding, scanning and online product location systems. In that sense, both India and the EU can gain from each other. The EU gets access to the large Indian retail market, while India can access better technology and receive training from the EU.

The study found that Indian brands are interested in entering the EU market, but their presence in the EU is low. While their brands enter the EU market through channels such as distribution agreements, Indian retailers have not been able to explore the EU market. This is primarily due to the limited financial capacity of Indian retailers; hence, government support is needed in terms of easier access to funds.

The EU has several restrictions on the movement of people, which is a major barrier for Indian retailers planning to set up operations in the EU market. In addition, there are country-specific regulations imposed on foreign retailers. Since India has undertaken substantial reforms in FDI policy, there is a case for securing liberal commitments in the retail sector and pushing to streamline the regulations applicable to foreign retailers across EU Member States. While the EU should aim to get binding commitments as per the existing autonomous regime, India should push for a single market in services in the EU. India may also ask for a more liberal commitment under Mode 4 against liberal commitments that it can now offer under Mode 3.

PART III

11

Trade Agreements and Outcomes: The Way Forward for the India–EU BTIA

Arpita Mukherjee and Tanu M. Goyal

Economic engagement between India and the EU is being facilitated through several forums—multilaterally through the WTO, bilaterally through country-specific bilateral investment promotion agreements (BIPAs) and double taxation avoidance agreements (DTAAs) and through the India–EU BTIA, which is currently under negotiation. In the international space, both India and the EU have signed several agreements that provide evidence of their respective stances with regard to bilateral liberalisation. Due to the political economy constraints, which have slowed down the reform process in India and due to the economic slowdown in the EU region, the negotiations have not progressed since September 2013. However, with the formation of a new government in India in 2014, renewed prospects for economic recovery along with some signs of economic stability in certain EU Member States, the two governments may re-launch the negotiations. This establishes a case to revisit the progress of the India–EU BTIA in light of the ongoing domestic reforms in India and to draw inferences from their respective agreements regarding the likely outcome of this prospective agreement between the two sides.

Globally, recent years have seen a proliferation of regional trade agreements (RTAs). These agreements are defined as groupings of countries which are formed with the objective of reducing barriers to trade between member countries. Contrary to what the name suggests, these groupings or unions may be concluded between countries not necessarily belonging to the same geographical region. India's involvement in regionalism started for geopolitical and strategic reasons. Economics and trade were seen as possible catalysts for improved regional cooperation. The stagnation in the Doha Round and the proliferation of preferential trade agreements (PTAs) among India's major trade partners forced India to embrace regionalism in a major way (Bhagwati, 2008, Hoda, 2011 and Pal, 2005).

Traditionally, India has been a part of the Bangkok Agreement signed in 1976, and it was a member of a South–South PTAs under the Global System of Trade Preferences (GSTP) scheme of UNCTAD signed in 1989. During the 1990s, India mainly focussed on forming RTAs with its geographic neighbours and other developing countries. It formed trade agreements with South Asian countries (South Asian Free Trade Agreement or SAFTA), MERCOSUR (*Mercado Común del Sur*; Argentina, Brazil, Paraguay and Uruguay) and Chile; it also signed four separate agreements with Afghanistan, Bhutan, Sri Lanka, Nepal and Bangladesh. However, since the new millennium, India has started entering into comprehensive trade agreements with several countries and regions. India has signed CEPA with Japan and the Republic of Korea and CECA with Singapore and Malaysia. More recently, India signed an FTA with ASEAN in goods and subsequently signed an agreement in services and investment. In addition, there are several ongoing negotiations on bilateral agreements including a Regional Comprehensive Economic Partnership (RCEP) agreement covering ASEAN plus Republic of Korea, China, Japan, Australia and New Zealand. Among these, the India–EU BTIA is likely to be of immense benefit to the two markets.[1]

Studies show that the benefits of liberalisation under the India–EU BTIA can percolate to several services sectors in India, if the country

---

[1] Indian industry is against any FTA with/including China. There can be domestic repercussions if India signs the RCEP.

can implement a set of complementary reforms. For instance, opening up the retail sector could lead to an improvement in the supply chain and infrastructure. Similarly, opening up the education sector can make foreign education/certification more accessible to Indian students and can improve quality, efficiency and accountability in the educational institutes (CARIS and CUTS, 2007). Competition among a large number of service providers can improve the efficiency of these sectors and also generate employment. The removal of barriers through the bilateral trade agreement will enable companies from the EU to access a large, growing and unsaturated emerging market. The EU, with its ageing population, can benefit from India's high-skilled professionals and skilled workers by easing entry barriers to the movement of people through the trade agreement.

However, till last year, there were grim prospects for conclusion of the India–EU BTIA on both sides. Both Indian and EU policy-makers were less optimistic about concluding the BTIA. More recently, both governments have expressed renewed hopes for starting the negotiations once again.

The previous chapters highlighted that India and the EU have complementarities and trade and investment interests in certain services sectors. Both economies are major proponents of liberalising services trade in the WTO and through FTAs. However, they differ in their sector-wise approach to liberalisation. The discussion throughout this book has highlighted the importance of autonomous liberalisation and reforms in complementing trade agreements to realise the associated benefits. It is observed that countries take different approaches to reforms in the context of trade agreements. Some countries undertake reforms autonomously and then bind these under their trade agreements while others make forward looking commitments to reforms under their trade agreements and, thus, use the latter to provide a basis for reforms. Both India and the EU are characterised by the former approach, as several of the authors in this book point out.

Given this background, we need to examine in further detail India and the EU's approach to liberalisation in multilateral and bilateral agreements and what this would suggest regarding their likely stance in the context of their bilateral India–EU BTIA. The chapter is organised as follows. The first section presents the multilateral engagements of India and the EU by highlighting their stand in the WTO. The second section highlights the bilateral engagement of the two markets by analysing the architecture of their bilateral agreements on services and the level of their services sector commitments under their most recent comprehensive agreements, using the approach of Fink and Molinuevo (2008) and Marchetti and Roy (2008). The third section analyses the bilateral cooperation agreements between India and individual EU Member States. The fourth section provides an overview of the ongoing negotiations of the India–EU BTIA and the progress made. It also provides insights for the negotiations based on the discussions in the previous chapters and analysis of the multilateral and bilateral stance of the two sides as discussed in the earlier sections of this chapter.

Multilateral Engagements of India and the EU

India and the EU are founding members of the WTO and actively participate in the ongoing Doha Round of WTO negotiations. The two economies submitted their Revised Offer in 2005.[2] Both India and the EU are proponents of multilateral liberalisation in services trade. However, their negotiating positions have changed over the years. During the first round of WTO negotiations—the Uruguay Round—the EU had 15 Member States and EU-15 showed interest in liberalising certain services such as transport services. However, they had a defensive position[3] in certain other sectors such as audiovisual services. In sectors such as energy and telecommunications, the autonomous liberalisation process had just begun in individual Member States and, hence, EU Member States were not in a position to undertake commitments. Due to these reasons, the EU made limited commitments. By the year 2000, several EU Member States had undergone autonomous liberalisation, which enabled the EU

---

[2] India submitted its Initial Offer on 12th January, 2004 (WTO 2004) and the Revised Offer on 24th August 2005 (WTO 2005c). The EU submitted its Initial Offer on 10th June 2003 (WTO 2003) and the Revised Offer on 29th June 2005 (WTO 2005b).

[3] Defensive position in a sector means that the country is not willing to undertake commitments because the sector is politically sensitive, or has not yet been liberalised or the regulations are evolving.

to emerge as a major proponent of services liberalisation since the beginning of the Doha Round. Over this same period, with the saturation of domestic markets in some major EU Member States such as France, Germany and the UK, multinational companies from the region also became increasingly interested in exploring investment opportunities in emerging markets.

Although service reforms have been undertaken in individual Member States, the EU's internal market for services is still not fully integrated. There have been attempts at the EU-wide level to integrate the services market across its different Member States through the adoption of various Directives, but this has proven difficult owing to different regulatory structures, issues of standards, linguistic differences and the like which are important in services trade and investment flows. The complexities have only increased with the further expansion of the EU to its membership status of 28 Member States as of August 2015. Given the varying interests, levels of development and extent of regulatory reforms across the EU Member States, regional integration of the services market has proved difficult. Moreover, the regulatory regime in some of the new Member States is still evolving. This is reflected in the EU's WTO Revised Offer (WTO 2005b) where some Member States such as the Germany, the Netherlands, Luxembourg, Spain, Sweden and the UK have been much more forthcoming about undertaking commitments in services, while other Member States such as Cyprus, the Czech Republic, Hungary and Malta have imposed restrictions in sectors such as construction and related services and distribution services. Hence, there is clearly variation within the EU Member States regarding the willingness and preparedness to liberalise services under a trade agreement, a feature which is likely to play a role in the EU's bilateral negotiations with a trade partner like India.

India's stance regarding services liberalisation has changed significantly over time. In the Uruguay Round, India, along with other developing countries like Brazil, protested against the inclusion of services in the multilateral trading system. However, in the 1990s, India embarked on an ambitious internal reform programme including the services sector, although this autonomous liberalisation was not reflected in its WTO commitments at the end of the Uruguay Round. Since the launching of the Doha Round, India has been a major proponent of services liberalisation.

Its WTO Revised Offer was regarded as one of the best Revised Offer submitted to the WTO. In part, this change in stance can be attributed to India's emergence as a leading exporter of knowledge-based services, in particular, IT and IT-enabled services and other professional services given its availability of high-skilled professionals at competitive prices. This change in negotiating stance is also due to India's growing import interests in services as is reflected in its WTO Revised Offer (WTO 2005c) wherein it has offered to undertake commitments in several new sectors such as professional services (architectural services, engineering services, medical and dental services), distribution services and air transport services. India has also improved its commitments in sectors like computer and related services and telecommunication services in its WTO Revised Offer (WTO 2005c), indicating its greater preparedness and willingness to open up a wider range of services multilaterally as these have already undergone autonomous liberalisation.

While both India and the EU have been proponents of liberalising trade in services in the Doha Round, their interests and positions vary across different types of services and modes of services delivery. For instance, India would like liberalisation commitments in knowledge-based services such as computer-related services, particularly in Modes 1 and 4. In Mode 1, India is seeking full liberalisation in a broad range of sectors that would enable Indian IT and business process outsourcing (BPO) companies to provide services to their clients. In Mode 4, it wants commitments from its trading partners for high-skilled professionals in four categories, namely business visitors (BV), intra-corporate transferees (ICT), independent professionals (IP) and contractual service suppliers (CSS).[4] India wants commitments in Modes 1 and 4 to be delinked from the requirement to establish a commercial presence or an office in a foreign country. The EU, on the other hand, is a major proponent of liberalising Mode 3 or FDI in major markets like India and in sectors such as telecommunications, financial services and transport and energy services. Its interest lies not only in securing the autonomously liberalised regime, but also in ensuring regulatory certainty and transparency through binding in the existing policy regime. The EU has a holistic approach to securing commitments. For instance, instead

---

[4] For definitions of each of the category, refer to Chapter 6.

of negotiating transport services, the EU prefers to negotiate logistics services, which along with transport includes the liberalisation of other allied services such as warehousing, transport-related consultancies and postal and courier services (Mukherjee and Goswami, 2011).

Both India and the EU have sensitivities in certain sectors. For instance, India has so far expressed its unwillingness to undertake liberalisation commitments in sectors such as retail, insurance and legal services where it continues to maintain FDI restrictions, while the EU has not taken commitments in sectors such as audiovisual services. There are various reasons, including social, cultural and political sensitivities that underlie such positions in certain services. For instance, in sectors such as postal and courier services, the regulatory regime is still evolving in India; and in retail, liberalisation is politically sensitive; and in sectors such as audiovisual services, the EU has not offered commitments in order to protect and promote local culture.

The differing interests of the two economies in different services sectors are also reflected in their bilateral and plurilateral requests and offers under the Doha Round of the WTO. During the bilateral request-offer process, the EU made requests to India to liberalise sectors such as financial, telecommunications, energy, tourism and travel-related services, distribution services and transport services. India, on the other hand, made requests to the EU in sectors such as professional services (accountancy, architectural engineering and integrated engineering), construction and related engineering services, health and audio-visual services. India and the EU's requests to each other in the plurilateral negotiations are given in Table 11.1. The table shows the different services sectors and modes in which India and the EU have been demandeurs and recipients of plurilateral requests. Only in computer-related services is there evidence of a common interest between India and the EU. In areas where both sides have a strong trade interest, they have been coordinators of the demanding group. The table also shows that while the EU has a strong interest in liberalising infrastructure services such as telecommunications and energy, which in effect implies a primary focus on Mode 3 or commercial presence, India is interested in liberalising Modes 1 and 4. These differences in liberalisation interests across modes and sectors between India and the EU reflect their different sources of comparative advantage, the former in labour-based services and the

Table 11.1
Position of India and the EU in Plurilateral Requests on Different Services Sectors

Sector	India	EU
Air transport services	Recipient	Demandeur
Architectural and engineering services	Recipient	Demandeur
Audiovisual services	Recipient	Recipient
Computer-related services	Demandeur	Demandeur
Construction services	Recipient	Demandeur
Distribution services	Recipient	Demandeur
Education services	Recipient	N.A.
Energy services	Recipient	Co-ordinator
Environmental services	Recipient	Co-ordinator
Financial services	Recipient	Demandeur
Legal services	Recipient	Demandeur
Logistics services	Recipient	Recipient
Maritime transport services	Recipient	Demandeur
Postal/courier services (including express delivery services)	Recipient	Demandeur
Telecommunications services	Recipient	Demandeur
Mode 3 (Commercial Presence)	Recipient	Co-ordinator
Mode 4 (Movement of Natural Persons)	Co-ordinator	Recipient
Mode 1 (Cross-Border Supply)	Co-ordinator	Recipient

Source: Extracted from Chaudhuri (2007), Table 8.1, p. 221; and International Forum on Globalization (IFG), available at http://www.ifg.org/pdf/GATS-table-target-countries-1.pdf (accessed on 19 May 2012).

Notes: 1. Health Services sector is not covered in plurilateral negotiations.
2. NA: Neither recipient nor demanduer.

latter in technology and capital-intensive services and, thus, the inherent complementarities between the two regions in the services sector. But this also suggests the likely quid pro quo negotiating stance that can be expected in the India–EU BTIA discussions and the inherent complexities and sensitivities on both sides in trading concessions between these different modes and sensitive sectors.

Given the slow progress of the Doha Round, there is a proposal in the WTO for a plurilateral services agreement known as the International Services Agreement. WTO Member States have undertaken plurilateral negotiations on several issues; these include the Government Procurement Agreement (GPA) and Information Technology Agreement (ITA). As regards the International Services Agreement, India and the EU hold different positions on plurilateral negotiations in the services sector. The EC proposed to open negotiations on a new international agreement on trade in services. The participants in this initiative are called 'really good friends of services' and include the EU and 20 other WTO Member States. Despite being a proponent of services liberalisation in the WTO and leading coalitions on certain sectors and cross-cutting issues, India has not shown an interest in joining the International Services Agreement. This is because developing countries such as India, China and Brazil first opposed such agreements within the WTO framework as the TISA negates the basic principle of *single-undertaking* under the WTO. Moreover, unlike most of the proponents of services liberalisation, India does not have a strong domestic lobby for services liberalisation. Also, the Indian government has realised that if it wants to join the International Services Agreement, it has to initiate domestic reforms. These domestic reforms are also needed to negotiate comprehensive bilateral trade agreements with trading partners like the EU. Until 2014, the initiation of such reforms was difficult given the coalition government at the centre, which lacked majority and was subject to various political economy constraints that prevented it from taking bold decisions. However, with the emergence of a majority government after the 2014 elections in India, the prospects for reforms are brighter and stakeholder consultations are already underway, which could alter India's position towards the International Services Agreement in future.

Bilateral Engagements of India and the EU

This section discusses the bilateral agreements signed by India and the EU with some select countries. It highlights their negotiating positions and demands from their respective trading partners. This will help to examine their likely demands to each other in the ongoing India–EU BTIA.

We discuss the next three bilateral agreements by India and the EU. The EU–Korea Free Trade Agreement (1 July 2011) is one of the most comprehensive agreements signed by the EU in recent years.[5] For comparison, the India–Korea CEPA (1 January 2010) is selected. The third agreement, between the EU and the Caribbean Forum of Africa, Caribbean and Pacific State, the EU–CARIFORUM Economic Partnership Agreement (EPA),[6] is included because the EU has covered low-skilled persons under this latter agreement, a category that is missing under the EU–Korea FTA.

In all three agreements, both India and the EU have followed the GATS definition (Article I and Article XXVIII)[7] to define services and the different modes of service delivery. All three agreements follow the Provisional United Nations Central Product Classification (UNCPC Prov.) to classify services. Only in the case of spa services and non-therapeutic massages, to the extent that they are provided as relaxation physical well-being services and not for medical or rehabilitation purposes, the UNCPC Version 1.0 is followed (CPC ver. 1.0 97230) in the EU–Korea FTA and the EU–CARIFORUM EPA.

For scheduling its commitments, India has followed GATS' hybrid approach, with a positive list of sectors and a negative list of commitments. India specifies the list of restrictions in terms of national treatment and market access limitations. It has a single schedule of commitments for Modes 1, 2, 3 and 4. The EU does not follow a GATS-style hybrid approach. In both its agreements, it has separate schedules for listing commitments under Modes 1 and 2 (cross-border supply of services), Mode 3 (establishment) and Mode 4 (presence of natural person). For Modes 1, 2 and 3, the EU gives a positive list of sectors and a negative list of commitments, highlighting the reservations in each sector. Although the limitations listed by the EU fall under national treatment and market access limitations, the EU does not specify the two separately. Under Mode 4, the EU follows a negative list, specifying the list of sectors in which the reservations apply and the applicable reservation.

---

[5] Although the EU has completed the negotiations on the EU–Singapore FTA, the text is not available in the public domain and hence the agreement could not be analysed.

[6] This agreement is provisionally applied.

[7] http://www.wto.org/english/docs_e/legal_e/26-gats_01_e.htm#ArticleI (accessed on 25 September 2012).

As regards investment in services, India and the EU follow different approaches. While India has two chapters—one for Mode 3 under the chapter on Trade in Services and one investment chapter in the India–Korea CEPA—the EU has a single chapter for investments and for Mode 3 trade in services, where it lists the coverage and commitments for both investments in goods and services under one schedule.

The EU's FTAs are more comprehensive than those of India. The EU's FTAs generally go beyond the scope of the GATS market access negotiations because the EU wants to ensure regulatory certainty through its FTAs (Horn et al., 2010; Marchetti and Roy, 2008). The EU seeks WTO-plus commitments in areas such as government procurement and subsidies in services. The EU–CARIFORUM EPA includes the liberalisation of skilled and semi-skilled worker mobility, which is not covered in the WTO.

The negotiating positions of India and the EU in services in their FTAs are largely similar to those in the WTO in terms of the sectors covered. There are, however, differences between the two in their positions and in the design of their agreements. While the EU tries to cover the entire value chain, India covers only sectors that are of major export interest. As a result, in general the EU agreements have greater sectoral coverage than the Indian agreements. For instance, in the transport and logistics sector, India has covered only maritime and air transport services, whereas the EU covers all modes of transport including rail transport services covering both passenger (CPC 7111) and freight transport (CPC 7112), road transport services covering passenger and freight transport (CPC 7121, CPC 7122 and CPC 7123) and services auxiliary to rail and road transport and internal waterways, among others. Similarly, in distribution services, India has covered only commission agent's services and wholesale trade services, whereas the EU has included retailing and franchising services. In professional services also, the EU has a wider coverage than India since it includes legal services (CPC 861).

However, India and the EU also exhibit certain similarities. For instance, both India and the EU have a separate chapter on the movement of natural persons. The two countries have listed the different categories of service sellers (suppliers) that are allowed to enter each other's market. However, the definition of the service suppliers differs; India has a broader definition and a longer duration of stay. India divides service suppliers into four categories based on the WTO, namely BVs, IP, ICT and CSS. The EU classifies service suppliers as key personnel including BVs and ICT, graduate trainees, business service sellers, IP and CSS. As shown in Table 11.2, India has given commitments in more categories of service suppliers than the EU in its bilateral agreement with Republic of Korea. India also allows foreign service suppliers a longer duration of stay compared to the EU. In addition, some EU Member States impose economic needs tests and nationality requirements that restrict the movement of professionals.

Both India and the EU have horizontal limitations in their respective agreements, but the EU has imposed a larger number of horizontal limitations on foreign service suppliers under Modes 3 and 4. Under Mode 3 in the India–Korea CEPA, Korean service suppliers are required to get approval from the FIPB in India. In addition, there are national treatment limitations since subsidies are given only to domestic service suppliers. Contracts in collaboration with public sector enterprises are allotted to service suppliers that offer the best terms for technology transfer. In the EU–Korea FTA, several EU Member States such as Austria, Bulgaria, Cyprus, the Czech Republic, Denmark, Estonia and Greece have imposed a restriction on ownership of real estate. The EU also restricts foreign investors from investing in public utilities. There are certain restrictions on the type of establishment—in Bulgaria, authorisation is required for establishing a branch office and in Estonia, Romania, Italy and Finland, there is a nationality requirement for top-level management. Estonia, Bulgaria, France, Finland and Hungary have investment restrictions on ownership share, and there is a minimum capitalisation condition in some EU Member States. There are restrictions on the location of foreign companies in EU Member States such as Finland. Similar restrictions apply in the EU–CARIFORUM EPA.

Under Mode 4, both the EU–Korea FTA and the EU–CARIFORUM EPA contain an economic needs test requirement in EU Member States such as Bulgaria and Hungary. There is a quota restriction on ICT and nationality and residency requirements for managing directors and auditors in Austria, Finland, France, Romania and Sweden. In the India–Korea CEPA, India has imposed a condition that foreign service suppliers must possess the requisite educational and professional qualifications.

Table 11.2
Duration of Stay Permitted by India and the EU for Different Categories of Service Suppliers

Type of Service Supplier	India's Revised Offer	EU's Revised Offer	EU–Korea FTA	India–Korea CEPA	EU–CARIFORUM EPA
BV	180 days	90 days[a]	90 days[b]	180 days[c]	90 days
IP	1 year	6 months[d]	NC	1 year	6 months[e]
CSS	1 year	6 months[f]	NC	1 year	6 months[g]
ICT	5 years (includes managers, specialists and executives)	3 years for managers and specialists; 12 months for graduate trainees[h]	3 years for managers and specialists; 12 months for graduate trainees	1 year; extendable until 5 years	3 years for managers and specialists; 12 months for graduate trainees

Source: Compiled from India and EU's bilateral agreements, available at http://commerce.nic.in/and http://ec.europa.eu/trade/creating-opportunities/bilateral-relations/agreements/ (accessed on 3 October 2012).

Notes: 1. NC means not covered in the agreement.

[a]This is subject to an economic needs test. Entry and temporary stay is permitted for up to 90 days in any 12 months and in the case of Estonia, it is for any 6 months.

[b]In every 12 months.

[c]For a maximum period of 5 years.

[d]In any 12-month period. Commitments are subject to numerical ceiling. Commitments are not subject to numerical ceiling in the case of Denmark, the Netherlands, Poland, Sweden and the UK (other than for computer and related services in the case of the UK, where numerical ceiling apply).

[e]In any 12-month period. In Luxembourg, it is for 25 weeks and in Latvia it is for 3 months. Commitments are subject to numerical ceiling.

[f]In any 12-month period. In Luxembourg, it is for 25 weeks and in Latvia it is for 3 months. Commitments are subject to numerical ceiling.

[g]In any 12-month period. In Luxembourg, it is for 25 weeks and in Latvia it is for 3 months. Commitments are subject to numerical ceiling.

[h]In Estonia, for managers and specialists the period of stay may be extended for up to two additional years for a total term not to exceed five years. In Latvia, for managers the stay may be extended.

In terms of commitments, while India has covered fewer sectors than the EU in its bilateral agreements, India has made more liberal commitments than the EU in some sectors. Under Mode 1, several EU Member States, such as Hungary, France, Austria and Poland, have kept one or more professional services unbound. India, in contrast, has made full commitments in most professional services. However, in services that are of interest to the EU, such as financial services and telecommunication services, India has kept Mode 1 unbound in a large number of sub-sectors. In Mode 2, both India and the EU have given full commitments in most professional services. In computer and related services (CPC 84), India and the EU have made full commitments in Modes 1 and 2. Under distribution services, several EU Member States, such as Austria, Bulgaria, France, Poland, Romania and Italy, have imposed restrictions on the sale of certain products such as tobacco and alcohol. Nearly all EU Member States have restricted the distribution of chemical products and precious metals. Retail services have been left unbound under Modes 1 and 2 by a large number of EU Member States. In contrast to the EU, India has made full commitments in Modes 1 and 2 in distribution services. Similarly, in transport and logistics services, the EU has imposed several country-specific conditions under Modes 1 and 2. In Mode 1, India has kept a large number of maritime auxiliary services unbound, while it has offered full commitments in the majority of services under Mode 2.

Under Mode 3 also, EU Member States have imposed several country-specific requirements in most services. In several countries such as Bulgaria, Hungary, Latvia, Cyprus and Denmark, there is an economic needs test requirement for most professional services. Some countries have also imposed nationality and residency requirements. In India, there is a partnership condition in some sectors, such as architectural services, urban planning and landscape architectural services, medical and dental services and services provided by midwives, nurses, physiotherapists and para-medical personnel. Both India and the EU have made full commitments in computer and related services under Mode 3. There is an economic needs test requirement in some EU Member States for certain services like transport and logistics services. In EU Member States such as Finland and Latvia, foreign service providers need to get an authorisation from the concerned department to set up operations. There is also a nationality requirement in several EU Member States. India has given full commitments in a large number of subsectors within transport and logistics services.

To summarise, while the EU covers a larger number of sectors than India in its bilateral agreements, there are several Member State-specific exceptions. The horizontal conditions imposed by the EU in the EU–Korea FTA and the EU–CARIFORUM EPA are more restrictive than the conditions imposed by India in the India–Korea CEPA under Modes 3 and 4. The EU market is not harmonised and, therefore, even though its coverage is greater, the commitments made by India are more liberal than those by the EU. The aforementioned commitments are indicative of the likely difficulties in arriving at a common position on services commitments within the EU membership and the complexities, this could create in the India–EU bilateral negotiating context.

Bilateral Cooperation and Engagements between India and the EU Member States

India's engagement with the EU is almost five decades old, but it strengthened after the 1990s when both the economies started liberalising. To strengthen their partnership, India and the EU have signed several bilateral agreements. The first agreement, which was a Commercial Co-operation Agreement, was signed in 1974. This comprehensive agreement covers a wide range of areas such as trade, economic cooperation, environment, agriculture, services, tourism and intellectual property rights. In 2001, India and the EU signed a Science and Technology Agreement that was renewed in 2007. The agreement covers sustainable development and also includes a legal framework to safeguard intellectual property rights. Under this agreement, researchers from India and the EU Member States can access each other's research programmes. The EU (and its Member States) has supported various development programmes in India. These include Operation Flood, which helped India become the world's leading milk producer, and the Indian government's District Primary Education Programme (DPEP) and Sarva

Shiksha Abhiyan (SSA) Programme, among others. India is one of the key beneficiaries of the EU Framework Programmes (FP). Under the FP7 programme (2007–2013), around 140 Indian research organisations have been selected for funding in over 90 projects.[8]

To promote cooperation in information technology and the communications sector, India and the EU signed a Joint Vision Statement in 2001. The statement provides a framework for the exchange of views on regulatory practices, mutual cooperation in regulatory and industry initiatives and specific issues/projects of bilateral interest.

In 2003, the EU and India signed a Customs Co-operation Agreement to make customs procedures less complex and facilitate trade in matters pertaining to customs in accordance with international standards. It also sets up mechanisms of mutual administrative assistance for exchanging information and carrying out enquiries, with a view to counter fraud against their respective customs legislation.

India and 27 individual EU Member States (except Estonia) have bilateral air services agreements.[9] In 2008, the two economies signed a Horizontal Aviation Agreement, which represents a significant step forward in strengthening the EU's relations with India. The agreement is expected to restore legal certainty to these bilateral air services agreements and bring them in conformity with EU law. The agreement aims to cover several new provisions including the removal of nationality restrictions in these 26 bilateral air services agreements and allows any EU airline to operate flights between India and the EU Member State.[10] The agreement is also expected to create a sound legal basis for further developing EU–India air transport relations and cooperation in the future. In 2003, two economies also started negotiating a bilateral Maritime Agreement. Although there are certain disagreements on both sides, it is expected that they will reach a consensus and the agreement will be signed.

India and individual EU Member States also have BIPA and DTAA. India has signed BIPAs with 22 Member States and DTAAs with 24 Member States as shown in Table 11.3.

[8] For details, see http://euroindiaresearch.org/fp7_india_indiaFP7.htm (accessed on 27 September 2013).

[9] http://dgca.nic.in/bilateral/Bilateral%20-download.pdf (accessed on 15 May 2012).

[10] http://aerospacediary.blogspot.in/2011/12/exclusive-as-ets-draws-near-india-pulls.html (accessed on 15 May 2012).

Table 11.3
EU Member States that have BIPAs and DTAAs with India (as on August 2012)

EU Member States	BIPA	DTAA
Austria	✓	✓
Belgium	✓	✓
Bulgaria	✓	✓
Croatia	✓	✗
Cyprus	✓	✓
Czech Republic	✓	✓
Denmark	✓	✓
Estonia	✗	✗
Finland	✓	✓
France	✓	✓
Germany	✓	✓
Greece	✗	✓
Hungary	✓	✓
Ireland	✗	✓
Italy	✓	✓
Latvia	✓	✗
Lithuania	✓	✓
Luxembourg	✗	✓
Malta	✗	✓
Netherlands	✓	✓
Poland	✓	✓
Portugal	✓	✓
Romania	✓	✓
Slovakia	✓	✗
Slovenia	✓	✓
Spain	✓	✓

(Table 11.3 Continued)

(Table 11.3 Continued)

EU Member States	BIPA	DTAA
Sweden	✓	✓
UK	✓	✓

Source: Extracted and compiled from different sources: Ministry of Finance, Government of India, available at http://finmin.nic.in/bipa/bipa_index. asp; State Bank of India, http://www.sbi.co.in/webfiles/uploads/ files/1311585986837_DTAA_COUNTRY_LIST.pdf; http://www.lead-thecompetition.in/CA/economy/dtaa.html; http://www.leadthecompeti-tion.in/CA/economy/dtaa2.html (accessed on 30 August 2012).

Notes: ✓ indicates that India has a BIPA and/or DTAA with the EU Member State.

× indicates that India does not have BIPA and/or DTAA with EU Member State.

India–EU BTIA and Beyond: Conclusions and the Way Forward

An analysis of India's and the EU's individual agreements provides several interesting insights: (a) both economies follow different designs for their bilateral agreements, (b) the nature and the level of commitments in each of the agreements are different and (c) the overall expectations from each other are different. While India's comprehensive agreements largely cover issues like goods, services, investment and economic cooperation, the EU has extended its comprehensive agreements to cover several WTO-plus issues like government procurement and sustainable development.

The nature and level of commitments reflect the relative importance of the sectors in each other's economy. For instance, India has a large English-speaking population in the working age group. Therefore, the country has an interest in securing liberal Mode 4 commitments. The EU, in contrast, has a greater Mode 3 interest, as its home markets are saturated and EU companies are looking for lucrative investment opportunities in emerging markets.

The BTIA will be the first bilateral agreement (that encompasses services) negotiated by India with a major trading partner and global player.

It would also be the first agreement negotiated by the EU with a large emerging country. Although India has already signed comprehensive agreements covering services with countries such as Singapore, Republic of Korea, Malaysia and Japan, the India–EU BTIA will set a new precedent in that it will cover issues such as government procurement in services, sustainable development and labour standards, which have not been part of India's earlier agreements. It is likely to be India's most comprehensive agreement and also an agreement that would involve domestic reforms in sectors such as retail and insurance and in areas such as government procurement.

It is important to note that the global economic scenario has changed since India and the EU started negotiating the BTIA. The EU was adversely impacted by the global slowdown and the Eurozone crisis. The growth rate in India has also slowed. The focus of the governments of the two economies is on domestic market revival and GDP growth. During an economic slowdown, countries tend to adopt protectionist measures. This has impacted the India–EU BTIA negotiations. For example, at the beginning of the BTIA negotiations, the EU was willing to liberalise the movement of skilled workers along with easier movement of professionals. However, this position has changed and the focus now is only on the movement of professionals (Mukherjee and Goswami, 2011).

The focus of the India–EU relationship has also changed over the past few years. The role of the EU has changed from that of a donor of aid to that of an economy seeking a competitive partnership. The EU has adopted a *Look East Policy* and both India and the EU have signed a series of agreements with countries in East Asia in the past few years. More recently, the EU has shifted its focus to negotiating a Trans-Pacific Partnership Agreement with the US and India is focusing on the RCEP. Both these agreements are expected to lead to significant market integration and regulatory convergence. Since the two economies have multiple trade agreements, their respective trading partners will request liberalisation similar to that undertaken under the India–EU BTIA. Thus, the BTIA will have implications for their existing economic and strategic relationships.

Both India and the EU have concluded a comprehensive agreement with countries such as Republic of Korea and Singapore. The governments of India and the EU argue that their respective agreements with Republic of Korea can be considered as the starting point for the India–EU BTIA negotiations. The EU–Korea agreement has a much higher level of liberalisation in services than the India–Korea agreement. The two economies have, therefore, started the services negotiations under the BTIA with different levels of expectations. The India–Korea agreement is less comprehensive and, therefore, to begin with, India needs to understand that the EU prefers a more comprehensive agreement than what India usually negotiates. The EU also needs to recognise that India is a developing country with a large number of people below the poverty line; hence, it is not possible for India to undertake commitments in areas that impact livelihood. In addition, India and Republic of Korea are at different stages of domestic reforms. Prior to negotiating a trade agreement with the EU, Republic of Korea had a trade agreement with the US. By negotiating trade agreements with large developed countries like the US and the EU, Republic of Korea has already undertaken many regulatory commitments and steps towards regulatory convergence with its developed country partners, while in India the regulatory regime is still evolving. The EU wants regulatory certainty through its trade agreements, which is difficult for India to offer at this stage.

Given the size of the Indian market, the gains for the EU in the services sector will perhaps be higher than those achieved from the EU–Korea agreement because without the agreement the level of restrictions in India is much higher than that in the Republic of Korea. As a result, the possibilities for removing barriers are also higher and the BTIA agreement can yield greater benefits. In addition, since India is currently not negotiating a trade agreement with the US, the gains from an agreement with India are higher for the EU compared to those from its other trade agreements with countries like Chile, Republic of Korea, Mexico and Singapore, all of which have agreements with the US. If the India–EU BTIA is signed, the EU companies will have a preferential position in the Indian market vis-a-vis companies from countries such as the US. Therefore, it is in the EU's interests to push for liberalisation of services under the BTIA in as many sectors as possible. Even if India were to bind its prevailing autonomous levels of liberalisation in various service sectors, it would ensure operational certainty for EU companies. In fact, India and the EU should explore the possibilities for signing an

India–EU Investment Protection Agreement that will cover services. The EU can design a Mode 4 offer to suit India's demands and follow India's definition of Mode 4 with respect to the duration of stay and coverage. The EU can take steps to streamline the work permit and visa regime across Member States by implementing Directives such as the proposed *Directive on conditions of entry and residence of third-country nationals in the framework of an intra-corporate transfer.*[11] The Directive would remove barriers to the entry and movement of ICT into and within EU Member States and, if implemented, it would generate support for the BTIA in India.

One cannot deny that there are strategic motivations behind trade agreements including the India–EU BTIA. Among the emerging markets, the EU has apprehensions about partnering with China and, therefore, India is seen as a suitable choice for entering into an agreement and a viable counterbalance to China in the Asian region. For India, too, this agreement will integrate two large services markets and help counter competition from China in trade in services. While policy-makers in the two economies understand the strategic importance of the bilateral trade agreement, the political and strategic push for the BTIA is weak. Although the EU is a strategic partner for India, important agendas for the India–EU summits, such as the maritime or horizontal air services agreements, have so far been driven by the EU and India does not see major gains in these areas. Studies such as Allen (2012) have questioned the EU's role as a strategic partner.

Strategic issues are in the domain of both the EU and its Member States and all EU Member States do not have a uniform view. The EU has been slow in its political response to issues like the Mumbai terror attack in the year 2008 or India's entry into the UN Security Council. This has somewhat prompted India to establish strong political ties with individual Western EU member countries such as the UK, France and Germany rather than partnering with the Union. In the Indian Ministry of External Affairs (MEA), different bureaucrats look after select EU Member States and none of them handle the EU. The Indian Ambassador

---

[11] This was proposed under the EC's *Policy plan on Legal Migration (COM(2005) 669).* The text is available at http://eur-lex.europa.eu/LexUriServ/site/en/com/2005/com2005_0669en01.pdf (accessed on 1 June 2015).

to Brussels and the EC is appointed by the Department of Commerce, unlike Indian Ambassadors to other countries who are appointed by the MEA. Moreover, with the enlargement of the EU, while the size of the market has increased, there has been a concomitant increase in the complexities involved in dealing with the EU. Several EU Member States have resource endowments similar to India. Workers from countries like Romania and Poland can compensate for the labour shortage in Western European countries, and this has complicated the relationship between India and the EU. There is a strong push in the Indian bureaucracy to work with Western Europe rather than the EU.

Another factor has affected the India–EU strategic relationship. In India, the EU is viewed as a major donor and the EU's policy of withdrawing aid from India has been criticised. Moreover, India, as a developing country, enjoys Generalized System of Preference (GSP) in the EU, which is likely to be withdrawn after the trade agreement is signed. Several similar issues on both sides have to be resolved before the BTIA agreement can be signed. By identifying areas of trade and investment complementarities and barriers to bilateral trade, this book enables Indian and EU policy-makers to take informed decisions.

Key Takeaways

This book examines the prospects of enhancing trade, investment and collaboration between India and the EU. It also assesses the sector-wise opportunities and constraints in the two markets. The discussion indicates that there are strong trade and investment complementarities between India and the EU. Keeping in view these complementarities and the prospects of entering in a trade agreement, this book makes recommendations on how the BTIA could be strategically leveraged to realise the bilateral trade and investment opportunities to strengthen India–EU economic relations. The book highlights how domestic policy objectives of the EU, its Member States and India can be harnessed through mutual cooperation and collaboration. The recent emphasis on uplifting domestic manufacturing and services sector through the 'Make in India' and the proposed 'Serve from India' campaigns of the Indian government open doors for opportunities to the EU companies to invest in the manufacturing and supply chain sector of India, either directly or through partnership. These initiatives are made robust through commitments under a bilateral trade agreement as they ensure long-term security and policy stability required to leverage for such investment.

In general, the services sector is of importance to both India and the EU. Over the years, both markets have experienced a rise in the share of services in their domestic markets and in their trade baskets. Given the growing significance of services in India and the EU, the sector holds a crucial position in the India–EU BTIA negotiations. However, there are considerable differences in the growth of services at the sub-national level in both India and the EU, leading to differences in the overall approach towards the sector. These differences in approach begin with the very design and architecture of the FTA. The EU prefers to extend the coverage of the agreement to sustainable development, environment and labour standards and government procurement, which so far has not been followed in India's bilateral agreements. Moreover, there are differences in the significance of various services subsectors and modes of trade for the two economies, which aggravate the difficulties in achieving integration in services between the two sides.

The EU wants the High-Level Trade Group report, which emphasises comprehensive sectoral coverage, to be the basis for its services negotiations. India tends to have an incremental approach to liberalisation under trade agreements and so far it has only bound the level of its autonomous liberalisation. However, it becomes difficult to estimate the gains from the trade agreements if only the autonomous regime is committed. This book tries to examine how India and the EU can go beyond the autonomous regime and undertake reform measures that will make the BTIA successful.

In this book, an attempt has been made to examine a few sectors of interest to both India and the EU and their negotiating positions and options. Several recent reforms in these sectors have been highlighted, and it is quite likely that relations between India and the EU will be influenced by these reforms. Considering the wide differences in interests and sensitivities across sectors between the two sides, this book suggests a sector-by-sector approach to the India–EU BTIA, focusing on sectors of interest to the two markets while remaining embedded within an overall negotiating strategy for the India–EU BTIA.

Within each of the four broad clusters of services, namely infrastructure services, business services, social services and other services, this book has focused on certain important sectors of interest to the two markets, namely logistics, energy, IT-ITeS, accountancy, health, environment and retail. The sectors are crucial for both India and the EU and for enabling greater integration of the two markets. However, each of these sectors is unique. While some sectors are relatively liberalised, other sectors require negotiations and reciprocal treatment. In sectors like retail, India has more market access limitations than the EU. These issues need to be addressed through the ongoing BTIA negotiations and also at a bilateral inter-government level between India and individual EU Member States.

The *logistics sector* holds an important position in the India–EU BTIA negotiations. The sector is critical for establishing physical connectivity between the two markets. It is not only a standalone service, but also a facilitator for integrating manufacturing bases, developing production networks and integrating services value chains. While the EU has always emphasised the liberalisation of logistics services under its trade agreements, India has recently given its consent to the WTO's Trade Facilitation Agreement and is in the process of streamlining the logistics sector to increase the *ease of doing business*. Given their common interest in establishment of an efficient logistics network, the sector can witness significant liberalisation under the India–EU BTIA. Chapter 4 highlights that at least India and the EU can bind their fairly liberal domestic regimes under this agreement to give operational certainty to companies in each other's market. The author proposes that India can collaborate with the EU on trade facilitation issues such as the Customs Co-operation Agreement and in the development of better risk management facilities. In order to facilitate trade, there is a need to harmonise port policies. In addition, India and the EU should conclude the Maritime Agreement to provide each other with non-discriminatory access to their port facilities. For sustainable development, India and the EU can collaborate in developing environment-friendly fuel technologies and lighter, safer and cost-effective engines and battery-operated cars. India can seek assistance from the EU in developing its dedicated freight corridors (DFCs) and in minor port development and better sea connectivity. This will also benefit the EU as the country has significant engagement with India through trade and investments. Another recommendation that goes beyond the scope of the BTIA concerns reforming the port community in India and integrating the transport network within the EU to facilitate the operations of Indian service providers.

In the case of *energy services*, both India and the EU are importers of energy resources and, therefore, enhancing production and efficiency are key areas of concern for both markets. Over time, both India and the EU have undertaken domestic reforms to meet the rising demand and to instil efficiency in production. Chapter 5 shows that in energy services although both India and the EU have similar resource endowments, the two economies have different negotiating strategies. While India has a defensive position, the EU has aggressively pushed for liberalising this sector. It points out that there is significant scope for removing barriers in bilateral trade in energy services. Some barriers can be addressed through BTIA negotiations, while others require domestic reforms and greater harmonisation of the EU market. There is scope for greater cooperation through a mutual recognition agreement in scientific research and technical standards for equipment. The two economies can also collaborate in the fields of clean technology, renewable energy and R&D in the energy sector. Due to the cross-cutting nature of energy services, the commitments in the sector should be carefully designed and these should be synchronised with commitments in other sectors as well as other chapters on sustainable development, climate change and government procurement.

Overall, in infrastructure services, the EU wants greater market access in Mode 3, while India has some interest in Mode 4. India seems to have a defensive position in liberalisation of infrastructure services in trade negotiations, but its stance is changing with the country's renewed focus on attracting foreign investment. The EU companies are keen to invest in India. This book shows that there will be investment inflows if India is able to remove the barriers to investments and initiate pending reforms such as the Government Procurement Bill. This is a key demand of the EU, which wants India to undertake commitments in government procurement both at the central and state levels.

IT and ITeS services have enormous potential to generate employment, making it a crucial sector in the India–EU BTIA negotiations. IT and ITeS services are one of India's major exports and India and the EU have strong complementarities in the sector. Both India and EU are keen to enhance trade in this sector, but there are certain regulatory issues. These can be removed through cooperation and inter-governmental negotiations. While most modes of trade are open in the two markets, there are issues related to data security, public procurement and movement of people. The barriers related to data security can be relaxed if the EU accords India Safe Harbor Nation status. In parallel, the Indian government needs to modify the Information Technology Rules, 2011 to include an enforcement clause that ensures that its data protection clause matches international standards. Under Mode 4, the procedures for movement of people have to be stream-lined and there should be easier processes for work permits, visas and movement of foreign nationals within the EU. Chapter 6 shows that data security and the movement of IT/ITeS professionals are the two key issues that India would like to address in the India–EU BTIA. India has a strong offensive interest in this sector.

Accountancy services play an important role in corporate governance, but this sector is also highly regulated in India and the EU. India has significant Mode 1 and 4 interests in the EU market, but in the EU, trade through these modes are conditional on establishment of commercial presence. Foreign investment is not allowed in accountancy services in India. However, that has not deterred foreign accountancy firms from establishing their presence in India through other routes (for example, as a consultancy organisation). Chapter 7 argues that India may consider opening up Mode 3 in exchange for reciprocal access to the EU market through Modes 1 and 4.

If India wants to develop as a knowledge-based economy, it has to upgrade its professional services sectors to international standards and have to allow market access. The country may continue to impose regulations. The book also highlights that regulatory synergies and liberal work permit and visa regimes along with removal of other barriers to movement of people can facilitate greater bilateral trade in business services. Although India is a proponent of liberalising professional services and of Mode 4, it has several domestic market restrictions in professional services, including FDI restrictions. On its part, India has been very defensive in its negotiating stance on professional services under multilateral and bilateral negotiations. Such a stance is affecting the current negotiations with the EU and is delaying the conclusion of the BTIA. The EU has been aggressively seeking market access for its professionals such as accountants, lawyers and architects. A defensive approach by India in these professional categories has weakened India's Mode 4 negotiations under the BTIA.

Health services are unique due to their public good nature. Both India and the EU are sensitive about opening the health sector. In the EU, health services provision is dominated by the public sector, while in India, the majority of healthcare spending is in the private sector. Health services are outside the EU Services Directive and, therefore, there is limited scope for liberalisation under the BTIA. However, there is immense scope for cooperation in this sector. There are several regulatory issues that impede the realisation of the potential for expanding India–EU relations in health services. In the WTO, the EU has exhibited a restrictive approach with respect to Modes 1 and 4, while it has been more liberal with regard to Mode 2. Under Mode 3, the EU has offered to take commitments in specific sectors like hospitals, but it has imposed restrictions like economic needs tests. India has adopted a liberal approach in health services and has offered to make full commitment in Modes 1, 2 and 3. In its bilateral agreement, the EU does provide scope for greater cooperation through the exchange of information, cooperation on standards, technical regulations, confirmatory assessment and mutual recognition of qualifications. India, in contrast, provides greater market access in this sector under its bilateral agreements along with provisions for concluding MRAs. In this respect, India's commitments in health services under its bilateral agreements are more robust than those of the EU. However, the application is limited, as the MRAs have not been signed as yet. It is unlikely that the EU will open the sector substantially, given the resistance from internal stakeholders. One of the wider issues in the sector is related to intellectual property rights in the case of generic drugs. Therefore, as regards the India–EU agreement, priority should be given to negotiating a chapter on cooperation that has a bearing on health services and to promoting greater links between Indian and EU healthcare establishments and providers.

Environmental service is an important sector for the India–EU BTIA, given the growing focus on clean energy and climate change around the world. India is a net importer of environmental equipment and technology from mature EU markets, while a few Indian firms have specialised in segments such as wind energy and labour-intensive sectors such as environmental consulting and management services. While environmental services is a crucial part of the EU's FTAs and environmental standards constitute an important component of the EU's trade agreements under their sustainable development chapter, India does not include separate chapters on environmental services in its FTAs. This is one of the sticky issues in the India–EU BTIA and requires a change in position on one of the two sides in terms of the coverage of the India–EU bilateral agreement.[12] While Indian exporters do meet the EU's environmental (and labour standards), it may be difficult for India to have uniform standards through a trade agreement as the majority of its businesses are in the non-corporate sector and are SMEs. Indian industries have argued that such obligations will increase their operating costs. In terms of sectorwise commitments, the EU market is more restrictive than India's, with entry barriers in Modes 1 and 4, which are of interest to India, while the Indian market is largely open in Mode 3, which is the mode of interest to the EU. Hence, there is clearly a need to resolve these differences through negotiations. Another important issue is supply capacity. While India needs to build its supply capacity in environmental services and for which investments and technology transfer from the EU can play an important role, there is first a need to undertake domestic reforms. So far, the demand for environmental services has been relatively low in India and, hence, the enforcement mechanisms have been weak. There is a need to have a more robust institutional mechanism in India to support the growth of this sector and to take advantage of cooperation mechanisms that may arise under the BTIA. Lastly, since there are clearly mutual interests in both environmental goods and services, care has to be taken while designing the agreement to ensure that the linkages between goods and services are recognised.

While liberalisation of the social sector can be an issue in trade agreements, the trade agreements do not restrict the ability of the government to provide social services. Trade agreements ensure competition in services provided by the private sector if carefully designed trade agreements can help industries to collaborate and leverage their mutual strengths. India has opened up the social sector for private investment.

---

[12] Along with environmental standards, the EU would also like the inclusion of labour standards in the BTIA. The EU would like India to take commitments to prohibit child labour. For India this is difficult, because labour is the joint jurisdiction of the central and state governments and labour regulations vary across states.

The EU companies have technology, knowledge and best management practices in social sectors such as health and environment services which can be beneficial for India. Indian companies too have developed competence in niche areas such as solar and wind energy and IT related to health services. They are exploring the EU market. The India–EU BTIA can set the tone for future investment and collaboration. Indian and EU companies can further collaborate to enter third country markets.

The *retail sector* is one of the most dynamic sectors in the Indian policy sphere. The sector saw a series of reforms at the break of this decade. However, with the new government, while other sectors are liberalising further, expectations as regards retail liberalisation are grim. Nonetheless, due to the large consumer base in India, the EU retailers have a huge interest in the Indian market. Moreover, retail is important for the EU companies interested in establishing a supply chain in India. This makes liberalisation of the retail sector crucial for the EU companies operating in allied services such as the logistics sector. India's negotiating stance in this sector can be a decisive factor in shaping the India–EU BTIA negotiations. The EU's trade interest in retail is through Modes 1 and 3. The Indian government can consider revising the e-commerce policy with respect to foreign retailers as it is of huge interest to the EU companies. Additionally, in Mode 3, while India has opened up the market for both single-brand and multi-brand retailers, it has imposed several restrictive conditions, such as sourcing and back-end investment requirements, which are frequently altered. Considering that, the India–EU BTIA can bind India's existing regime in retail for the EU companies, providing greater operational certainties. The sector can also be used as a tool for cross-bargaining. Indian policy-makers are considering opening e-commerce activities to FDI and by making a full commitment to the EU in Mode 1 of retail services in return for better commitments from the EU in IT services or in Mode 4 in selected professional services.

One key takeaway of this book is that services sectors are interlinked. For example, an efficient value chain or production network cannot be developed if there are restrictions in certain components of the value chain such as the restrictions on FDI in retail. This can deter the most efficient resource allocation. If India wants to develop as a manufacturing and services outsourcing hub, the country has to look at the efficiency across the value chain. While sector-wise reforms are crucial, there is also a need for general services sector reforms in both India and the EU. There is a need to integrate the services sector in both these markets. However, as highlighted in several sector studies, the quasi-federal nature of governance in the service sector makes such integration difficult on both sides. Hence, there is a need for a concerted and comprehensive policy or strategy for services integration in India and also within the EU. Such a focused strategy for services would facilitate progress in the bilateral negotiations. In addition, there is also need for greater knowledge sharing between the two sides, across all sectors. Further, specifically in the Indian context, while lately there has been much focus on market access reforms which are certainly important in the context of any trade agreement, there also needs to be focus on regulatory reforms which are just as important to ensure a conducive business environment and operational ease for foreign companies.

This book highlights that the India–EU BTIA will be a milestone in the India–EU trade and investment relationship. Negotiations on the India–EU BTIA were started in June 2007 but as of date several issues on both sides remain unresolved. These should be addressed before the negotiations can be concluded.

One of the key issues is the pace of domestic reforms in India. Since India wants to undertake reforms first and then bind the regime in the BTIA, domestic reforms are crucial to take the BTIA negotiations forward in sectors such as insurance, retail and banking. The new government, which came into power in the year 2014, has expressed commitment to reforms in sectors such as insurance by bringing out Ordinances. After several years, the government at the centre has a majority in the Lower House of the Parliament which will enable it to push for reforms. The government is committed to implement trade facilitation and ensure ease of doing business. All of these will add a positive impetus to the India–EU BTIA negotiations. However, the government has also declared its apprehension to further liberalise FDI in sectors such as multi-brand retail, which is of significant interest to the EU companies. Thus, while there are positive signals, there are some areas of concerns related to the BTIA. Moreover, the regulatory regime in India is evolving. A study on the EU's PTAs shows that the EU often uses PTAs to transfer its regulatory regimes to its trading partners. Therefore, it is important for trading partners to have a sound regulatory framework in place before negotiating such agreements.

Another issue is that the EU tends to place its demands on its trading partners across different chapters of the trade agreements. For instance, transport may be covered in the services chapter, investment chapter and trade facilitation chapter, among others. Therefore, Indian policy-makers have to carefully match their commitments across different chapters of the BTIA so that there are synergies across chapters and in the offers and demands.

In services, the EU has already scheduled its existing market access liberalisation in the WTO Revised Offer (WTO 2005b), and there is limited scope for improving it further. The adverse effect of the global slowdown is greater on the EU than on India. In the meanwhile, the Indian economy has also faced a slowdown, while the EU has been hit by the Eurozone crisis. Such economic developments have created an environment of protectionism and slowed the process of domestic reforms and trade liberalisation. Therefore, policy-makers in the two economies have to make conscious efforts for trade liberalisation and to proactively push for the realisation of mutual benefits from trade liberalisation under the BTIA.

Overall, this book shows that the India–EU BTIA will facilitate joint ventures, enhance the global competitiveness of both economies and increase investment inflows. It is also expected to provide opportunities to India and the EU to secure autonomous liberalisation in each other's market. However, the likely gains from the agreement depend on the level of opening up or autonomous liberalisation. Even if India binds its autonomous regime, EU companies would have a distinct benefit over companies from other large markets such as the US, since they would get a first-mover advantage. This is particularly true of sectors such as retail where policies in India frequently change. India can use the BTIA negotiations as an opportunity to implement domestic reforms and to develop a services value chain.

There is a need for change in the negotiating approach of both the parties. In the case of India, a lower level of liberalisation than the autonomous regime does not lead to any gains for the other party. Therefore, there is a need to implement reforms in sectors such as insurance and government procurement. There is an urgent need in India to build consensus within India and the EU Member States for reforms. This requires greater inter-ministerial coordination across central government ministries and between the centre and states in India and across Member States in the EU. In the case of India, there should be pan-India stakeholder consultations to understand the concerns and the government should work closely with different lobbying groups to get them on-board. Similarly, the EU should engage with different member NGOs and lobby groups to reach a consensus.

Much of the delay in the negotiations is from the Indian side. The Indian government should set clear timelines and negotiating targets. As of now, unlike the European Commission, India has not done an impact analysis of the existing trade agreements, and there is a lot of apprehension within Indian industry and NGOs about their outcomes. There is need for an independent impact analysis of India's trade agreements so as to inform the negotiations under the BTIA. This can help address the apprehensions and enable a more informed approach to future trade agreements, including the prospective India–EU BTIA.

As a ready reference, this book sets the stage for negotiations and provides a stock-taking of the progress so far. Given the trade and investment complementarities, the two sides should restart the trade negotiations with clear mandate and timelines. This will require support from the highest authorities in India and the EU. In the present situation, a timely completion of the India–EU BTIA will not only help to translate the domestic policy objectives into outcomes but also help to globally deliver the message highlighting the fast paced reform agendas of the new government.

Bibliography

AT Kearney. 2011. 'Offshoring Opportunities Amid Economic Turbulence', Global Services Location Index. Available at http://www.atkearney.com/documents/10192/f062cfd8-ee98-4312-ae4f-0439afc10880 (accessed on 13 August 2013).

———. 2012a. 'Cautious Investors Feed a Tentative Recovery', AT Kearney Foreign Direct Investment Confidence Index 2012.

———. 2012b. 'Global Retail Expansion: Keeps on Moving', AT Kearney Global Retail Development Index 2012, http://www.atkearney.com/images/global/pdf/Global_Retail_Expansion_Keeps_On_Moving.pdf (accessed on 27 August 2012).

Allen, D. 2012. 'The EU and India: Strategic Partners but not a Strategic Partnership', Paper presented at the UACES Annual Conference, Passau, Germany, 3–5 September. Available at http://uaces.org/documents/papers/1201/allen.pdf (accessed on 4 January 2014).

Alpen Capital. 2011. 'GCC Retail Industry', Alpen Capital. Available at http://www.alpencapital.com/downloads/GCC%20Retail%20Industry%20Report%202011_1%20November%202011.pdf (accessed on 27 August 2012).

AMA-IMG Section Governing Council. 2013. 'International Medical Graduates in American Medicine: Contemporary Challenges and Opportunities', Position paper by the AMA-IMG Section Governing Council. Available at http://www.ama-assn.org/resources/doc/img/international-medical-graduates-in-american-medicine.pdf (accessed on 26 April 2013).

Ansari, M.I. 1995. 'Explaining the Service Sector Growth: An Empirical Study of India, Pakistan, and Sri Lanka', *Journal of Asian Economics,* 6(2): 233–246.

Asian Development Bank (ADB). 2012. 'Key Indicators for Asia and the Pacific 2012', Asian Development Bank, Manila, August. Available at http://www.adb.org/publications/key-indicators-asia-and-pacific-2012 (accessed on 14 March 2013).

Asian Tribune. April 2011. 'Sri Lanka-India joint hospital project for cardiac treatment', 5 April. Available at http://www.asiantribune.com/news/2011/04/05/sri-lanka-india-joint-hospital-project-cardiac-treatment (accessed on 13 March 2013).

Baier, S.L. and Jeffrey H. Bergstrand. 2003. 'Economic Determinants of Free Trade Agreements', Working Paper, University of Notre Dame, USA. Available at http://www3.nd.edu/~jbergstr/Working_Papers/Economic_Determinants_of_FTAs.pdf (accessed on 30 December 2013).

Baldwin, R. 1993. 'A Domino Theory of Regionalism', NBER Working Paper 4465, National Bureau of Economic Research, September.

Banga, R. and Bishwanath Goldar. 2004. 'Contribution of Services to Output Growth and Productivity in Indian Manufacturing: Pre and Post Reforms', ICRIER Working Paper No. 139, July.

Banga, R. 2005. 'Critical Issues in India's Service-led Growth', ICRIER Working Paper No. 171, October.

Baroowa, S. 2007. 'The Emerging Strategic Partnership between India and the EU: A Critical Appraisal', *European Law Journal*, 13(6): 732–749.

Battelle. 2012. '2012 Global R&D Funding Forecast, The Business of Innovation', R&D *Magazine*, December 2012. Available at http://battelle.org/docs/default-document-library/2012_global_forecast.pdf (accessed on 13 July 2013).

Beke, J. 2010. 'The Practical Experience of Adapting to the International Accounting Standards'. *Review of International Comparative Management*, 11(1): 110–123. Available at http://www.rmci.ase.ro/no11vol1/Vol11_No1_Article10.pdf (accessed on 28 June 2013).

Bhagwati, J. 2008. *Termites in the Trading System: How Preferential Agreements Undermine Free Trade*. USA: Oxford University Press.

Bhattacharya, B.B. and Arup Mitra. 1990. 'Excess Growth of Tertiary Sector in Indian Economy: Issues and Implications', *Economic and Political Weekly*, 25(44): 2445–2450.

Bjornberg, A. 2012. 'Euro Health Consumer Index Report 2012', Health Consumer Powerhouse, Sweden, May. Available at http://www.healthpowerhouse.com/files/Report-EHCI-2012.pdf (accessed on 3 October 2013).

Bloom, R. and David C. Schirm. 2005. 'Consolidation and Competition in Public Accounting: An Analysis of the GAO Report', *The CPA Journal*, June. Available at http://www.nysscpa.org/cpajournal/2005/605/infocus/p22.htm (accessed on 15 August 2013).

Borchert, I, Batshur Gootiiz and Aditiya Mattoo. 2012. 'Policy Barriers to International Trade in Services: Evidence from a New Database', Policy Research Working Paper No. 6109, World Bank, Washington D.C.

BP. 2008. 'BP Statistical Review of World Energy 2008', June.
———. 2011. 'BP Statistical Review of World Energy 2011', June.
———. 2013. 'BP Statistical Review of World Energy 2013', June.

Brown, A.G. and Robert M. Stern. 2011. 'Free Trade Agreements and Governance of the Global Trading System' Working Paper 614, Research Seminar in International Economics, University of Michigan.

Buchan, D. 2012. 'How to Create a Single European Electricity Market – and Subsidise Renewables'. *Centre for European Reform Policy Brief*. Available at http://www.cer.org.uk/sites/default/files/publications/attachments/pdf/2012/pb_buchan_energy_26apr12-4979.pdf (accessed on 28 June 2013).

Busse, R., Markus Wörz, Thomas Foubister, Elias Mossialos and Philip Berman. 2006. 'Mapping Health Services Access: National and Cross-Border Issues', *Health Access, Final Report*, November.

Busse, R., Matthias Wismar and Philip C. Berman (Eds.). 2002. 'The European Union and Health Services: The Impact of the Single European Market on Member States', The European Health Management Association, IOS Press.

CBRE. 2011. 'How Global is the Business of Retail', CB Richard Ellis, Global Research and Consulting. Available at www.cbre.hr/hr_en/homepage_content/hr_homepage_title/EMEA_FPR_HOW_GLOBAL_2011_EXECUTIVE_SUMMARY.pdf (accessed 24 April 2013).

Cefic (The European Chemical Industry Council). 2012. 'The European Chemical Industry's Priorities in Industrial Policy', October. Available at http://www.cefic.org/Documents/PolicyCentre/Industrial%20Policy/European%20Chemical%20Industry's%20Priorities%20in%20Industrial%20Policy.pdf (accessed on 12 June 2013).

Central Statistical Office (CSO). 2012. 'Economic Survey of India – 2011–12', Central Statistical Organisation, Ministry of Statistics and Programme Implementation, Government of India.

Centre for the Analysis of Regional Integration at Sussex (CARIS) and CUTS. 2007. 'Qualitative Analysis of a Potential Free Trade Agreement between the European Union and India', Centre for the Analysis of Regional Integration at Sussex (CARIS) and Consumer Unity & Trust Society (CUTS), European Commission, Brussels, June.

Chakraborty, D. and Animesh Kumar. 2012. 'EU–India Bilateral Trade and Investment Agreement: Opportunities and Challenges', in Luis Peral and Vijay Sakhuja (Eds.), The EU–India Partnership: Time to Go Strategic. Paris: Indian Institute for Security Studies.

Chanda, R. 2002. *Globalization of Services: India's Opportunities and Constraints*. New Delhi: Oxford University Press.

———. 2007. 'FDI In Hospitals in India: Status and Implications', prepared for the WHO Country Office, India and the Ministry of Health and Family Welfare, New Delhi, September.

———. 2008. 'India–EU Relations in Health Services: Issues and Concerns in an India–EU Trade and Investment Agreement', Report prepared for the Indian Council for Research on International Economic Relations (ICRIER), New Delhi.

———. 2009. 'Trade in IT and IT-Enabled Services: Issues and Concerns in an India–EU Trade and Investment Agreement', ICRIER Report, New Delhi, September, available at http://wtocentre.iift.ac.in/EU%20BTIA/EU%20BTIA/Report%20on%20IT-ITES-%20India-EU%20BTIA.pdf (accessed on 27 November 2012).

Chaudhuri, S. 2007. 'Plurilateral Negotiations in Services', in Suparna Karmakar, Rajiv Kumar and Bibek Debroy (Eds.), 'India's Liberalisation Experience: Hostage to the WTO' (pp. 213–234), New Delhi: Sage Publications.

Commission of the European Communities. 2003. 'Proposal for a Directive of the European Parliament and of the Council Concerning Measures to Safeguard Security of Electricity Supply and Infrastructure Investment'. COM (2003) 740 final, 2003/0301 COD.

———. 2004. 'e-Health – Making Healthcare Better for European Citizens: An Action Plan for a European e-Health Area', Communication from the Commission to the Council, the European Parliament, the European Economic and Social Committee and the Committee of the Regions, 356 Final, Brussels, April. http://eur-lex.europa.eu/LexUriServ/LexUriServ.do?uri=COM:2004:0356:FIN:EN:PDF (accessed on 10 September 2007).

———. 2006. 'Green Paper: A European Strategy for Sustainable, Competitive and Secure Energy.' COM (2006) 105 final {SEC (2006) 317}. March. Available at http://europa.eu/documents/comm/green_papers/pdf/com2006_105_en.pdf (accessed on 27 June 2013).

———. 2007a. White Paper on 'Together for Health: A Strategic Approach for the EU 2008–2013', COM (2007) 630FINAL, Brussels.

———. 2007b. Commission Staff Working Document Accompanying the White Paper on 'Together for Health: A Strategic Approach for the EU 2008–2013', SEC (2007)1376, Brussels.

Consumer Unity Trust Society (CUTS). 2007. 'Barriers to Movement of Healthcare Professionals: A Case Study of India', Prepared for the WTO Cell, Ministry of Health and Family Welfare, New Delhi: Government of India and WHO India Country Office.

Cousins, J., A. Mitchell, and P. Sikka. 2004. 'Race to the Bottom: The Case of the Account-ing Firms'. Basildon, Association for Accountancy and Business Affairs. Available at http://visar.csustan.edu/aaba/publications.htm (accessed on 17 August 2013).

Credit Rating Information Services of India Limited (CRISIL) 2010. 'Skilling India – The Billion People Challenge', CRISIL Centre for Economic Research, November 2010, available at http://www.crisil.com/pdf/corporate/skilling-india_nov10.pdf (accessed on 24 January 2015).

———. 2012. 'CRISIL Customised Research Bulletin'. February. Available at http://crisil.com/pdf/research/CRISIL-Research-cust-bulletin_feb13.pdf (accessed on 20 August 2013).

Das, S.B. 2013. 'RCEP and TPP: Comparisons and Concerns', ISEAS, Singapore, available at http://www.iseas.edu.sg/documents/publication/ISEAS%20Perspective%202013_2.pdf (accessed on 7 July 2013).

Datamonitor. 2012. Datamonitor report on the Global Accountancy Sector 2012, avail-able at http://www.datamonitor.com/store/Product/accountancy_global_industry_guide?productid=ML00004-278 (accessed on 18 August 2013).

Deloitte. 2009. 'Logistics and Infrastructure Exploring Opportunities', August. Avail-able at http://www.deloitte.com/assets/Dcom-India/Local%20Assets/Documents/aLogistics%20and%20infrastructure%206%20Aug.pdf (accessed on 26 June 2013).

———. 2011. "Snapshot of the Status of India's Social Security Agreement with Other Countries and Underlying Comparisons/Implications", Vol. GES/1/2011, available at http://www.deloitte.com/assets/DcomIndia/Local%20Assets/Documents/GES%20alerts/2011/GES-01-2011.pdf (accessed on 14 August 2015).

———. 2012. 'Switching Channels: Global Powers of Retailing 2012', Deloitte Global Services Limited, UK, January. http://www.deloitte.com/assets/Dcom-Global/Local%20Assets/Documents/Consumer%20Business/dtt_CBT_GPRetailing2012.pdf (accessed on 28 August 2012).

———. 2013. 'Global Powers of Retailing 2013: Retail Beyond', Deloitte Touche Tohmatsu Limited, Australia, January. Available at http://www.deloitte.com/assets/Dcom-Australia/Local%20Assets/Documents/Industries/Consumer%20business/Deloitte_Global_Powers_of_Retail_2013.pdf (accessed on 17 June 2013).

Deloitte–ICC. 2012. 'Logistics Sector: Present Situation and Way Forward', January. Available at http://www.deloitte.com/assets/Dcom-India/Local%20Assets/Documents/Thoughtware/Logistics%20Sector-Present%20situation%20and%20way%20forward.pdf (accessed on 28 May 2013).

Demuro, G. 2008. 'European Union: Regulation and Governance', Paper presented at John Marshall Law School, Available at http://unica2.unica.it/giurisprudenza/dispense/costituzionale/EUROPEAN%20UNION%20REGULATION%20AND%20GOVER-NANCE.pdf (accessed on 4 June 2013).

Department of Industrial Policy and Promotion (DIPP). 2010. 'Fact Sheet on Foreign Direct Investment – From April 2000 to February 2010', Department of Industrial Policy and Promotion, Ministry of Commerce and Industries, Government of India. Available at http://dipp.nic.in/English/Publications/FDI_Statistics/FDI_Statistics.aspx (accessed on 10 May 2013).

———. 2011. 'FDI Inflows in India - Annual Issue 2011', Secretariat for Industrial Assis-tance, DIPP, Ministry of Commerce and Industry, Government of India. Available at http://dipp.nic.in/English/Publications/SIA_NewsLetter/AnnualReport2011/main.htm (accessed on 15 June 2013).

Department of Industrial Policy and Promotion (DIPP). 2013a. 'Fact Sheet on Foreign Direct Investment – From April 2000 to April 2013', Department of Industrial Policy and Promotion, Ministry of Commerce and Industries, Government of India. Available at http://dipp.nic.in/English/Publications/FDI_Statistics/2013/india_FDI_April2013.pdf (accessed on 10 May 2013).

———. 2013b. 'Consolidated FDI Policy (Effective from 5 April 2013)'. Circular 1 of 2013, April, Ministry of Commerce and Industry, Government of India.

———. 2013c. 'Review of the FDI – Caps and Routes in Various Sectors', Press Note 6 (2013 series), August 22, Ministry of Commerce and Industry, Government of India.

———. 2014. 'Consolidated FDI Policy (Effective from April 17, 2014)', Government of India. Available at http://dipp.gov.in/English/Policies/FDI_Circular_2014.pdf (accessed on 21 January 2015).

Directorate General for Energy and Transport. 2004. 'European Energy and Transport Scenarios on Key Drivers', European Commission. September.

Directorate General of Hydrocarbons (DGH). 2012. 'Hydrocarbon Exploration and Production Activities 2011–12', Ministry of Petroleum and Natural Gas, Government of India. http://www.dghindia.org/pdf/1DGH%20Annual%20Report%202011-12.pdf (accessed on 18 June 2013).

Dutta, S. 2008. 'Global Information Technology Report: Making Progress', World Economic Forum.

EBI. 2006. 'The Global Environmental Market', Report 3000, Environmental Business International, Inc. San Diego, CA, USA.

ECORYS. 2009. 'FWC Sector Competitiveness Studies – Competitiveness of the EU SMEs in the ICT Services Industry, Framework Contract of Sectoral Competitiveness Studies – ENTR/06/054, Final Report, ECORYS, Netherland, 2009, available at http://ec.europa.eu/enterprise/sectors/ict/files/study_report_ict_services_en.pdf (accessed on 22 January 2015).

———. 'Study on the Competitiveness of the EU Eco-Industry (Final Report)', ECORYS Research and Consulting, Brussels.

ECORYS, CUTS and Centre for Trade and Development (Centad). 2009. 'Trade Sustainability Impact Assessment for the FTA between the EU and Republic of India', TRADE/07/C1/C01 – Lot 1, Study Commissioned by DG Trade, 18 May, Brussels.

Electronics and Computer Software Export Promotion Council. 2010. "Statistical Year Book - 2009-10", New Delhi.

Eur-Lex. 1995. Directive 95/46/EC of the European Parliament and of The Council of 24 October 1995 on the Protection of Individuals with Regard to the Processing of Personal Data and on the Free Movement of Such Data, *Official Journal of the European Union,* L 281/31, Brussels. Available at http://eur-lex.europa.eu/ (accessed on 10 September 2007).

———. 2000. Directive 2000/31/EC of the European Parliament and of the Council of 8 June 2000 on Certain Legal Aspects of Information Society Services, in Particular Electronic Commerce, in the Internal Market (Directive on electronic commerce), *Official Journal of the European Union,* L 178/1, Brussels.

———. 2005. Directive 2005/36/EC of The European Parliament and of The Council of 7 September 2005 on the Recognition of Professional Qualifications, L255/22, *Official Journal of the European Union,* Brussels.

———. 2006. Directive 2006/123/EC of The European Parliament and of The Council of 12 December 2006 on Services in the Internal Market, *Official Journal of the European Union,* L376/36, Brussels.

Eur-Lex. 2007. Council Directive 93/16/EEC of 5 April 1993 to Facilitate the Free Move-
ment of Doctors and the Mutual Recognition of their Diplomas, Certificates and Other
Evidence of Formal Qualifications, 'Medicine: Mutual Recognition of Qualifications',
Official Journal of the European Union, Brussels.

Eurohealth. 2002. 'Promoting E-Health in Europe: Challenges and Opportunities', 8(2),
Spring, London School of Economics, UK.

Europa Press Release. 2007. 'Towards a European Energy Consumers' Charter: Protecting the Consumers' Right to Choose', MEMO/07/278, 5 July, Brussels. Available at
http://europa.eu/rapid/press-release_MEMO-07-278_en.htm (accessed on 12 September
2013).

European Commission. 1995. "White Paper on An Energy Policy for the European Union",
Commission of the European Communities. accessible at http://europa.eu/documenta-
tion/official-docs/white-papers/pdf/energy_white_paper_com_95_682.pdf (accessed
on 13 August 2015).

———. 2001. Report of the High Level Committee on Health: The Internal Market and
Health Services, Brussels, December.

———. 2003. 'High Level Process of Reflection on Patient Mobility and Healthcare
Developments in the European Union: Outcome of the Reflection Process', Brussels,
December.

———. 2005a. 'Doing More with Less: Green Paper on Energy Efficiency'. COM (2005)
265 final, 22 June.

———. 2005b. 'Report on the Work of the High Level Group on Health Services and
Medical Care during 2005', HLG/2005/16, Brussels.

———. 2006a. Special Eurobarometer 258 on 'Energy Issues'. November. Available at
http://ec.europa.eu/public_opinion/archives/ebs/ebs_258_en.pdf (accessed on 28 April
2013).

———. 2006b. 'Fostering the Competitiveness of Europe's ICT Industry', EU ICT Task
Force Report, November. Available at http://ec.europa.eu/information_society/eeu-
rope/i2010/docs/high_level_group/ict_task_force_report_nov2006.pdf (accessed on
12 October 2012).

———. 2006c. 'Global Europe: Competing in the World: A Contribution to the EU's
Growth and Jobs Strategy', Commission Staff Working Document, Commission of the
European Communities, October 2006, Brussels, available at http://trade.ec.europa.eu/
doclib/docs/2006/october/tradoc_130370.pdf (accessed on 4 January 2014).

———. 2006d. 'Report on the Work of the High Level Group on Health and Medical Care
during 2006', HLG/2006/8 FINAL, Brussels.

———. 2007a. 'Accelerating the Development of the E-Health Market in Europe',
E-Health Taskforce Report, Luxembourg Office.

———. 2007b. Communication on 'Services of General Interest, Including Social Services
of General Interest: A New European Commitment', 20 November 2007, COM (2007)
725 Final, Brussels.

———. 2008. 'NACE Rev. 2: Statistical Classification of Economic Activities in the
European Community', ISSN 1977-0375, Luxembourg, available at http://epp.euro-
stat.ec.europa.eu/cache/ITY_OFFPUB/KS-RA-07-015/EN/KS-RA-07-015-EN.PDF
(accessed on 14 March 2013).

———. 2009. 'Challenges for EU Support to Innovation in Services', Commission Staff
Working Document, SEC (2009), 1195, Luxembourg, September.

European Commission. 2010a. 'Communication from the Commission – Europe 2020: A strategy for smart, sustainable and inclusive growth', COM(2010) 2020 final, Brussels, March. Available at http://eur-lex.europa.eu/LexUriServ/LexUriServ. do?uri=COM:2010:2020:FIN:EN:PDF (accessed on 20 March 2013).

———. 2010b. 'Proposal for a Directive on Conditions of Entry and Residence of Third-country Nationals in the Framework of an Intra-Corporate Transfer', COM(2010) 378 final, Brussels, March.

———. 2011a. 'Proposal for a Directive of the European Parliament and of the Council amending Directive 2005/36/EC on the Recognition of Professional Qualifications and Regulation on Administrative Cooperation through the Internal Market Information System', COM(2011) 883 Final, Brussels, 19 December.

———. 2011b. "The 2011 Report on R&D in ICT in the European Union", JRC Scientific and Technical Reports, European Commission, Spain. accessible at http://publications. jrc.ec.europa.eu/repository/bitstream/JRC65175/jrc65175.pdf (accessed on 14 August 2015).

———. 2012a. 'Communication from the Commission to the European Parliament, the Council, the European Economic and Social Committee and the Committee of the Regions on the Implementation of the Services Directive, A partnership for new growth in services 2012–2015', COM(2012) 261 Final, Brusseis, 8 June. Available at http://ec.europa.eu/internal_market/services/docs/services-dir/implementation/report/ COM_2012_261_en.pdf (accessed on 20 March 2013).

———. 2012b. 'Detailed Information on the Implementation of Directive 2006/123/EC on Services in the Internal Market', Commission Staff Working Document, SWD (2012), 148 Final, Brussels, 8 June.

———. 2012c. 'The ICT Sector and R&D&I', Digital Agenda Scoreboard, 2012, available at http://ec.europa.eu/digital-agenda/sites/digital-agenda/files/scoreboard_ict_ sector_and_rdi.pdf (accessed on 28 April 2013).

———. 2013. 'European Economic Forecast: Winter 2013', European Economy 1/2013, Brussels. Available at http://ec.europa.eu/economy_finance/publications/european_ economy/2013/pdf/ee1_en.pdf (accessed on 20 March 2013).

European Commission Statistical Pocketbook. 2012. 'EU Transport in figures', ISBN 978-92-79-21694-7. Available at http://ec.europa.eu/transport/facts-fundings/statistics/ doc/2012/pocketbook2012.pdf (accessed on 19 July 2013).

European Observatory on Health Systems. 2002. 'Healthcare Systems in Eight Countries: Trends and Challenges', Brussels.

European Union Health Policy Forum (EHPH). 2005. 'Recommendations on Health Services and the Internal Market', Brussels.

Eurostat. 2011. 'Europe in Figures – Eurostat Yearbook 2011', Available at http://epp. eurostat.ec.europa.eu/cache/ITY_OFFPUB/CH_10_2011/EN/CH_10_2011-EN.PDF (accessed on 15 April 2013).

Eurostat–EC. 2009. 'The Environmental Goods and Services Sector', Eurostat, European Commission.

EWEA. 2012. 'Creating the Internal Energy Market in Europe: A Report by the European Wind Energy Association', September. http://www.ewea.org/uploads/tx_err/Internal_ energy_market.pdf (accessed on 15 May 2013).

Federation of Indian Chambers of Commerce and Industry (FICCI). 2008. 'Fostering Quality Healthcare for All: Recommendations for the Road Ahead', FICCI, New Delhi.

Fink, C. and Martýn Molinuevo. 2008. 'East Asian Free Trade Agreements in Services: Key Architectural Elements', *Journal of International Economic Law*, 11(2): 263–311.

Francois, J.F., Matthew McQueen and Ganeshan Wignaraja. 2005. 'EU–Developing Country FTAs: Overview and Analysis', *World Development*, 33(10): 1545–1565.

Fukunaga, Y. and Ikumo Isono. 2013. 'Taking ASEAN+1 FTAs towards the RCEP: A Mapping Study', ERIA Discussion Paper Series, ERIA-DP-2013-02, Economic Research Institute for ASEAN and East Asia.

Geden, O., Clemence Marcelis and Andreas Maurer. 2006. 'Perspectives for the European Union's External Energy Policy: Discourse, Ideas and Interests in Germany, the UK, Poland and France', Working Paper FG 1, 2006/1. German Institute for International and Security Affairs, Berlin. December. Available at http://www.swp-berlin.org/fileadmin/contents/products/arbeitspapiere/External_KS_Energy_Policy__Dez_OG_.pdf (accessed on 15 May 2013).

Gerlinger, T. and Rolf Schmucker. 2007. 'Transnational Migration of Health Professionals in the European Union', *Cadernos de Saúde Pública*, 23(2): S184–S192.

Ghemawat, Pankaj. 2011. 'World 3.0: Global Prosperity and How to Achieve It', Cambridge USA: Harvard Business Review Press.

Ghibutiu, A. and Irina Dumitriu. 2008. 'The Effects of Offshoring on Trade in Services: Evidence from Romania', Working Paper, European Trade Study Group.

Global Wind Energy Council. 2007. 'Global Wind 2007 Report', Global Wind Energy Council, Brussels, May 2008. Available at http://gwec.net/wp-content/uploads/2012/06/gwec-08-update_FINAL.pdf (accessed on 21 January 2015).

Gordon, Jim and Poonam Gupta. 2003. 'Understanding India's Services Revolution', Paper prepared for the IMF-NCAER Conference, 'A Tale of Two Giants: India's and China's Experience with Reform', 14–16 November, New Delhi.

Government of India. 2011. 'High Level Expert Group Report on Universal Health Coverage for India', Planning Commission, November, New Delhi.

Goyal, T.M. and Arpita Mukherjee. 2012. 'FDI in Sensitive Sectors: The Case of the Retail Sector in India', in Shahid Ahmed (Ed.), 'Trade, Foreign Direct Investment and Economic Growth: Exploring Challenges and Opportunities Post-Global Financial Crisis', New Delhi: Routledge Taylor & Francis Books India.

———. 2013. 'Movement of Engineers and Architects between India and the EU', Working Paper No. 403, April, Indian Institute of Management, Bangalore.

Greene, W. 2006. 'Growth in Services Outsourcing to India: Propellant or Drain on the U.S. Economy?' Working Paper, US International Trade Commission, Washington, January.

Guru, S. 2002. 'Renewable Energy Sources in India: Is it Viable?' Working Paper, Julian Simon Centre for Policy Research, Liberty Institute, New Delhi. Available at http://www.libertyindia.org/pdfs/renewable_energy_guru_october2002.pdf (accessed on 4 June 2013).

Hansda, S.K. 2001. 'Sustainability of Services-led Growth: An Input-Output Analysis of Indian Economy', RBI Occasional Working Paper, 22, No. 1, 2 and 3.

Havlik, P. 2006. 'Economic Restructuring in the New EU Member States and Selected Newly Independent States: Effects on Growth, Employment and Productivity', February, Vienna Institute for International Economic Studies, Austria. Available at http://indeunis.wiiw.ac.at/index.php?action=content&id=publications (accessed on 12 May 2013).

Hengel, R. van D. 2013. 'The Rise of Mega-FTAs', Fact Sheet, October, EU Centre in Singapore, Singapore, available at http://www.eucentre.sg/wp-content/uploads/2013/10/Fact-Sheet-Mega-FTAs-October-2013.pdf (accessed on 19 May 2013).

Hewitt. 2013. 'Aon Hewitt 17th Annual Salary Increase Survey 2013', available at http://www.aon.com/india/attachments/Aon_Hewitt_SIS_2013_Feb_20_2013_release.pdf (accessed on 15 June 2013).

Hoda, A. 2011. 'Global Developments in International Trade', *Trade Policy and WTO Newsletter*, April. New Delhi: ICRIER.

Horn, Henrik, Petris C. Mavroidis and Andre Sapir. 2010. 'Beyond the WTO? An Anatomy of EU and US Preferential Trade Agreements', *The World Economy,* 33: 1565–1588.

Institute of Chartered Accountants of India (ICAI). 2011. 'Report on Operation of Multinational Network Accounting Firms in India', New Delhi: ICAI.

Images Multimedia Private Limited 2009. 'India Retail Report 2009', New Delhi: Images Multimedia Private Limited.

———. 2011. 'India Retail Report 2011', New Delhi: Images Multimedia Pvt. Ltd.

———. 2013. 'India Retail Report 2013', New Delhi: Images Multimedia Pvt. Ltd.

———. 2014. 'India Retail Report 2014', New Delhi: Images Multimedia Pvt. Ltd.

India Brand Equity Foundation (IBEF). 2011. 'Healthcare', Anarca, November 2011, available at http://www.ibef.org/download/Healthcare50112.pdf (accessed on 5 July 2013).

———. 2013. Report on Healthcare available at http://www.ibef.org/download/Healthcare-March-220313.pdf Innwon P. and Soonchan Park. 2011. 'Regional Liberalisation of Trade in Services', The World Economy, *Wiley Blackwell,* 34: 725–740, 05

International Monetary Fund (IMF). 2012. 'World Economic Outlook: Coping with High Debt and Sluggish Growth', October. Available at http://www.imf.org/external/pubs/ft/weo/2012/02/pdf/text.pdf (accessed on 12 March 2013).

———. 2013. 'World Economic Outlook: Transitions and Tensions', October. Available at http://www.imf.org/external/pubs/ft/weo/2013/02/pdf/text.pdf (accessed on 18 November 2013).

———. 2015. 'Uneven Growth: Short- and Long-Term Factors', World Economic Outlook, International Monetary Fund (IMF), April 2015 accessible at http://www.imf.org/external/pubs/ft/weo/2015/01/pdf/text.pdf (accessed on June 1, 2015).

Invest in France. 2012. 'Doing Business in France 2012 Edition, Invest in France Agency, France, January 2014. Available at http://www.invest-in-france.org/Medias/Publications/862/doing-business-version-anglaise-2012.PDF (accessed on June 1, 2015).

Jain, Sunil and T.N. Ninan. 2010. 'Servicing India's GDP Growth', in Shankar Acharya and Rakesh Mohan (Eds.), 'India's Economy: Performance and Challenges – Essays in Honour of Montek Singh Ahluwalia' (pp. 328–365). New Delhi: Oxford University Press.

Johnson, E. 2007. 'Data Protection Law in the European Union', The Federal Lawyer, pp. 44–48. Available at http://www.fedbar.org/magazine.html (accessed on 14 August 2013).

Joseph, M. and N. Soundararajan. 2009. Retailing in India: A Critical Assessment, New Delhi: Academic Foundation.

Kaeser, T. 2011. 'Trade Facilitation, Logistics Services and Preferential Trade Agreements (PTAs): The Case of the CARIFORUM EPA', World Trade Institute, MILE 11 Thesis, September 2011. Available at http://www.wti.org/fileadmin/user_upload/wti.org/1_master-programme/pdfs/Masters_thesis_Tim_Kaeser.pdf (accessed on 10 May 2013).

Kapur, Davesh and R. Ramamurti. 2001. 'India's Emerging Competitive Advantage in Services', *Academy of Management Executive,* 15(2): 20–33.

Kelemen, D.R. 2006. 'Comment: Shaming the Shameless? The Constitutionalization of the European Union', *Journal of European Policy,* 13(8): 1302–1307.

Kemekleine, G., Heather Connolly, Maarten Keune and Andrew Watt. 2007. 'Services Employment in the Europe: Now and in the Future', Brussels: European Trade Union Institute (ETUI) and Research, Education and Health and Safety (REHS).

Kemekliene, G. and Andrew Watt. 2010. 'GATS and the EU': Impacts on Labour Markets and Regulatory Capacity', Report 116, European Trade Union Institute (ETUI), Brussels.

Keune, M., Janine Leschke and Andrew Watt. 2008. 'Introduction: Liberalisation and the Labour Market', in Maarten Keune, Janine Leschke and Andrew Watt (Eds.), Privatisation and Liberalisation of Public Services in the EU, Brussels: ETUI.

Khandekar, G. and Jayshree Sengupta. 2012. 'EU–India Free Trade: Make or Break', June, FRIDE, Spain, http://www.fride.org/download/PB_10_EU_India_free_trade.pdf (accessed on 17 July 2013).

Khandekar, G. 2013. 'EU–ASIA Trade: in Need of a Strategy', January, FRIDE, Spain, available at http://www.fride.org/download/PB_13_EU_Asia_trade.pdf (accessed on 17 July 2013).

Kochhar, K., Utsav Kumar, Raghuram Rajan, Arvind Subramanian and Ioannis Tokatlidis. 2006. 'India's Pattern of Development: What Happened, What Follows?' Journal of Monetary Economics, 53(5): 981–1019.

KPMG. 2010. 'Logistics in India', Part 1–3. KPMG Business and Industry Issue. November.

———. 2012. 'KBuzz Sector Insights', Issue 16.

Kumar, N.and K.J. Joseph. 2005. 'Export of Software and Business Process Outsourcing from Developed Countries: Lessons from the Indian Experience', Asia-Pacific Trade and Investment Review, 1(1): 91–110.

Krajewski Markus. 2003. 'National Regulation and Trade Liberalization in Services: The Legal Impact of the General Agreement on Trade in Services (GATS) on National Regulatory Autonomy', Kluwer Law International.

Lacity, M.C. and Leslie P. Willcocks. 2001. 'Global Information Technology Outsourcing', Chichester: Wiley.

Liu, S. 2009. 'A Research on the Relationship of Logistics Industry Development and Economic Growth of China', International Business Research, 2(3): 197–200. July. Available at http://ccsenet.org/journal/index.php/ibr/article/download/2897/2688 (accessed on 2 August 2013).

Lunt, N., Richard Smith, Mark Exworthy, Stephen T. Green, Daniel Horsfall and Russell Mannion. 2011. 'Medical Tourism: Treatments, Markets and Health System Implications: A Scoping Review', OECD, Paris. http://www.oecd.org/els/health-systems/48723982.pdf (accessed on 4 August 2013).

Malhotra, D. 2012. 'Study on Government Procurement: Study for Evidence Based Competition Advocacy', January. Available at http://sps.iitd.ac.in/PDF/SGP.pdf (accessed on 6 August 2013).

Mandel, Michael and Diana G. Carew. 2013. 'Regulatory Improvement Commission: A Politically Viable Approach to US Regulatory Reform', Policy Memo, Progressive Policy Institute, May 2013. Available at http://www.progressivepolicy.org/wp-content/uploads/2013/05/05.2013-Mandel-Carew_Regulatory-Improvement-Commission_A-Politically-Viable-Approach-to-US-Regulatory-Reform.pdf (accessed on 21 January 2015).

Marchetti, J.A. and Martin Roy. 2008. 'Opening Markets for Trade in Services – Countries and Sectors in Bilateral and WTO Negotiations', UK: Cambridge University Press.

Menon, J. 2009. 'Dealing with Proliferation of Bilateral Free Trade Agreements', *The World Economy*, 32(10): 1381–1407.

Ministry of Communications and Information Technology. 2011. 'Information Technology, Annual Report 2010–11', Department of Technology, Government of India.

Ministry of Home Affairs. 2011. 'Provisional Population Totals Paper 1 and 2 of 2011 India Series 1 and Paper 2', Census of India, Government of India.

Ministry of Power. 2008. 'Annual Report 2007–08', Government of India. Available at http://www.cea.nic.in/reports/yearly/annual_rep/2007-08/annual_report_07_08.pdf (accessed on 27 August 2013).

Ministry of Statistics and Programme Implementation (MOSPI). 2006. 'Employment and Unemployment Situation among Social Groups in India (2004–05)', Report No. 516(61/10/2), NSS 61st Round (July 2004–June 2005), Government of India, October. Available at http://mospi.gov.in/national_data_bank/pdf/516_final.pdf (accessed on 14 March 2013).

———. 2008. 'National Industrial Classification (All Economic Activities)', Government of India, available at http://mospi.nic.in/Mospi_New/upload/nic_2008_17apr09.pdf (accessed on 14 March 2013).

———. 2010. 'State Domestic Product Series 1999–2000', Government of India, September. Available at http://mospi.nic.in/mospi_new/upload/statewise_sdp1999_2000_9sep10.pdf (accessed on 14 March 2013).

———. 2011. 'Employment and Unemployment Situation in India (2009–10), Report No. NSS 537 (66/10/1), 66th Round (July 2009–June 2010), Government of India, November. Available at http://www.indiaenvironmentportal.org.in/files/file/NSS_Report_employment%20and%20unemployment.pdf (accessed on 14 March 2013).

———. 2013. 'Summary of Macro Economic Aggregates at Constant (2004–05) Prices from 1950–51 to 2012–13', Government of India.

———. 2014. 'Summary of Macro Economic Aggregates at Current Prices, 1950–51 to 2013–14', Government of India, available at http://mospi.nic.in/Mospi_New/site/inner.aspx?status=3&menu_id=82 (accessed on 7 December 2014).

Mukherjee, Arpita and Nitisha Patel. 2005. 'FDI in Retail Sector in India', New Delhi: Academic Foundation.

Mukherjee, Arpita. 2008. 'Services Liberalisation in PTAs and the WTO: The Experiences of India and Singapore', in Juan A. Marchetti and Martin Roy (Eds.), Opening Markets for Trade in Services – Countries and Sectors in Bilateral and WTO Negotiations, (pp. 600–632), UK: Cambridge University Press.

———. 2012. 'Developing the Services Sector as an Engine for Inclusive Growth in Asia', Paper presented at the ADB-PIIE Workshop on Developing the Services Sector as an Engine for Inclusive Growth in Asia, organised by the Asian Development Bank and Peterson Institute for International Economics, 29–30 May, Washington D.C.

———. 2013. 'The Service Sector in India', Working Paper No. 352, Asian Development Bank, Manila. June.

Mukherjee, Arpita and Ramneet Goswami. 2009. 'Trade in Energy Services: GATS and India', ICRIER Working Paper No. 231, New Delhi, January.

———. 2011. 'India–EU BTIA: Implications for Services Sector', *Journal of Indo-European Business Studies*, 1(1): 2–22.

Mukherjee, Arpita and Smita Miglani. 2010. 'Non-Tariff Barriers in the Transport and Logistics Sectors: India'. European Business and Technology Centre Research Report,

August. Available at http://www.ebtc.eu/pdf/Tariff_Barriers_in_the_Transport_and_ Logistics_Sector_India.pdf (accessed on 22 August 2013).

National Association of Software and Services Companies (NASSCOM-Everest Research Institute). 2008. 'NASSCOM-Everest India BPO Study'.

National Association of Software and Services Companies (NASSCOM). 2008. 'The IT-BPO Sector in India', Strategic Review, 2008.

———. 2011. 'Indian IT-BPO Opportunities in the Government Procurement Market Globally'.

———. 2012. 'The IT-BPO Sector in India', Strategic Review, 2012.

———. 2013. 'The IT-BPM Sector in India', Strategic Review, 2013.

———. 2014. 'The IT-BPM Sector in India' Strategic Review, 2014.

Navickas, V., Leila Sujeta and Sergej Vojtovich. 2011. 'Logistics Systems as a Factor of Country's Competitiveness', Economics and Management. ISSN: 1822-6515, No. 16, p. 231–237. Available at http://www.ktu.lt/lt/mokslas/zurnalai/ekovad/16/1822-6515-2011-0231.pdf (accessed on 14 July 2013).

National Skill Development Corporation (NSDC). 2009. 'Human Resource and Skill Requirements in the Transportation, Logistics, Warehousing and Packaging Sector (2022) – A Report'. Available at http://www.nsdcindia.org/pdf/transportation-logistics.pdf (accessed on 17 July 2013).

Organisation for Economic Co-operation and Development (OECD-Eurostat). 2007. OECD Statistics on International Trade in Services, Volume 1, 1996–2005.

Organisation for Economic Co-operation and Development (OECD) and World Trade Organization (WTO). 2013. 'Aid for Trade at a Glance 2013: Connecting to Value Chains', July. http://www.wto.org/english/res_e/booksp_e/aid4trade13_e.pdf (accessed on 13 June 2013).

Organisation for Economic Co-operation and Development (OECD). 2012a. 'National Treatment for Foreign Controlled Enterprises (including adhering country exceptions to National Treatment), Paris.

———. 2012b. 'Health at a Glance: Europe 2012', Paris: OECD Publishing.

Ornelas, E. 2003. 'Rent Dissipation, Political Viability, and the Strategic Adoption of Free Trade Agreements', mimeo.

Pal, P. 2005. 'Regional Trade Agreements in a Multilateral Trade Regime: A Survey of Recent Issues', *Foreign Trade Review* 40(1): 27–48.

Pal, P. and Kristy Tsun-Tzu Hsu. 2013. 'Investment Cooperation between India and Taiwan', in Parthapratim Pal, Arpita Mukherjee and Kristy Tsun-Tzu Hsu (Eds.), 'Enhancing Trade, Investment and Cooperation between India and Taiwan', New Delhi: Academic Foundation.

Palugod, N. and Palugod, P.A. 2011. 'Global Trends in Offshoring and Outsourcing', *International Journal of Business and Social Science,* 2(16): 13–19.

Patel, K. 2012. 'Need for Change in Perspective for Professional Practices', CPE Seminar Organised by the Committee for Capacity Building of CA Firms and Small & Medium Practitioners, 11 August.

Planning Commission. 2002. 'India Vision – 2020', Government of India. Available at http://planningcommission.nic.in/reports/genrep/pl_vsn2020.pdf (accessed on 4 August 2013).

———. 2006. 'Integrated Energy Policy – Report of the Expert Committee', Government of India, August. Available at http://planningcommission.gov.in/reports/genrep/rep_intengy.pdf (accessed on 4 July 2013).

Planning Commission. 2008. 'Report of the High Level Group on Services Sector', Government of India, March.

Planning Commission. 2009. 'Report of the Working Group on Logistics', Government of India, May. Available at http://planningcommission.nic.in/reports/genrep/rep_logis.pdf (accessed on 26 August 2013).

———. 2011. 'Report of Working Group on Warehousing Development and Regulation for the Twelfth Plan Period (2012–17)', Government of India, October. Available at http://planningcommission.nic.in/aboutus/committee/wrkgrp12/pp/wg_ware.pdf (accessed on 2 September 2013).

Polak, G. 2007. 'Labour Mobility of Medical Physicians in EU Countries', Hospital Post Europe, 06/2007, GITVERLAG, Germany, p. 31.

Porter, M.E. 1990. 'The Competitive Advantage of Nations', New York: Free Press, MacMillan.

Quinn, E. 2011. 'Visa Policy as Migration Channel: Ireland', European Migration Network, Ireland, November.

Reddy, B.S. and Hippu Salk Kristle Nathan. 2012. 'Energy in the Development Strategy of Indian Households – The Missing Half', IGIDR WP-2012-003.

REN21. 2012. 'Renewables 2012: Global Status Report', Renewable Energy Policy Network for the 21st Century, REN21 Secretariat, Paris.

Reserve Bank of India (RBI). 2012. 'Monthly Bulletin for October 2012', available at: http://rbidocs.rbi.org.in/rdocs/PressRelease/PDFs/IEPR609B1012.pdf (accessed on 15 June 2013).

Richardson, Ricky. 2002. 'Promoting E-Health in Europe: Challenges and Opportunities', Eurohealth, 8(2): 1–4.

Rubalcaba, L. 2007. 'The New Service Economy: Challenges and Policy Implications for Europe', UK: Edward Elgar Publishing.

Sachdeva, G. 2009. 'India and the European Union: Time to De-bureaucratise Strategic Partnership', Strategic Analysis, 33(2): 202–207.

Sally, R. 2007. 'Looking East: The European Union's New FTA Negotiations in Asia', Jan Tumlir Policy Essays No. 3, European Centre for International Political Economy, Brussels.

Sawhney, A. 2007. 'An Evaluation of Domestic and Trade Policies in Building Environmental Services Capacity in Asia: Balancing Diverse Interests and Priorities', Issue Paper No. 5, International Centre for Trade and Sustainable Development, Geneva.

Singh, Kavaljit. 2009. 'Rethinking Liberalisation of Banking Services under the India–EU Free Trade Agreement' SOMO Paper, Centre for Research on Multinational Corporations, Netherlands.

Supply Chain Management Institute (SMI)-PwC 2010. 'Transportation & Logistics 2030. Volume 3: Emerging Markets – New hubs, new spokes, new industry leaders?' Available at https://www.pwc.ch/user_content/editor/files/publ_trans/pwc_transportation_logistics_2030_vol3.pdf (accessed on 30 July 2013).

South Asia Centre for Policy Studies (SACEPS). 2011. 'Liberalising Health Services under SAARC Agreement on Trade in Services (SATIS): Implications for South Asian Countries', Paper Number 24, Nepal, May 2011. Available at http://www.saceps.org/upload_file/papers_pdf/Paper%20No%2024.pdf (accessed on 22 January 2015).

Stichele, M.V. and Kavaljit Singh. 2009. 'Rethinking Liberalisation of Banking Services under the India-EU Free Trade Agreement', Stichting Onderzoek Multinationale Ondernemingen (Somo), Centre for Research on Multinational Corporations, September.

Technopak. 2007. 'Healthcare Outlook', Quarterly Report, Volume 1.

———. 2012. 'Foreign Direct Investment in Retail: An Objective Assessment of FDI's Impact on the Indian Retail Sector and the Indian Economy', White Paper published by Technopak, October.

United Nations Conference on Trade and Development (UNCTAD). 2004. 'Trade and Development Aspects of Professional Services and Regulatory Frameworks', Note by UNCTAD Secretariat, Document Number TD/B/COM.1/EM.25/2 dated 25 November 2004.

———. 2012. 'World Investment Report 2012: Towards a New Generation of Investment Policies', Geneva.

United Nations Environment Programme (UNEP). 2012. 'Global Trends in Renewable Energy Investment 2012', UNEP Collaborating Centre for Climate & Sustainable Energy Finance, Bloomberg New Energy Finance, Frankfurt School of Finance & Management GmbH.

United States Trade Representative (USTR). 2012. '2012 National Trade Estimate Report on Foreign Trade Barriers', Office of the United States Trade Representative. Available at http://www.ustr.gov/about-us/press-office/reports-and-publications/2012-1 (accessed on 14 May 2013).

———. 2013. '2013 National Trade Estimate Report on Foreign Trade Barriers', Office of the United States Trade Representative. Available at http://www.ustr.gov/sites/default/files/2013%20NTE.pdf (accessed on 13 July 2013).

Upadhya, C. 2006. 'The Global Indian Software Labour Force IT Professionals in Europe', Indo-Dutch Programme on Alternatives in Development, Working paper series 2006, No. 1,

Upadhyay, Dinoj Kumar. 2012. 'India–EU FTA: Building New Synergies', November, New Delhi: Indian Council of World Affairs.

United States Commercial Service (USCS). 2007. 'Doing Business in Europe: A Country Commercial Guide for US Companies', US Commercial Service.

United States International Trade Commission (USITC). 2013. 'Environmental and Related Services', USITC Publication 4389, United States International Trade Commission, Washington D.C.

Veugelers, R. 2012. 'New ICT Sectors: Platforms for European Growth?' Bruegel Policy Contribution, No. 2012/4, Bruegel, Brussels, August.

Woolcock, S. 2007. 'European Union Policy towards Free Trade Agreements', Working Paper No. 3, European Centre for International Political Economy (ECIPE).

World Bank – International Finance Corporation (IFC). 2011. 'Doing Business Report', Washington. Available at http://www.doingbusiness.org/~/media/GIAWB/Doing%20Business/Documents/Annual-Reports/English/DB11-FullReport.pdf (accessed on 25 February 2013).

———. 2012. 'World Development Indicators 2012', World Bank, Washington D.C. Available at http://data.worldbank.org/data-catalog/world-development-indicators/wdi-2012 (accessed on 14 March 2013).

———. 2014. 'World Development Indicators 2014', available at http://data.worldbank.org/products/wdi (accessed on 24 January 2015).

World Nuclear Association. 2008. 'Supply of Uranium', Information Papers, June.

Wouters, J. Idesbald Goddeeris, Bregt Natens and Filip Ciortuz. 2013. 'Some Critical Issues in EU-India Free Trade Agreement Negotiations', Working Paper No. 102, Leuven Centre for Global Governance Studies, Belgium, February. Accessed at

http://www.world-nuclear.org/info/Nuclear-Fuel-Cycle/Uranium-Resources/Supply-of-Uranium/ (accessed on 18 August 2015).

World Trade Organization (WTO). 1994a. Schedule of Specific Commitments for the EC, GATS/SC/31/, Geneva, 15 April.

———. 1994b. Schedule of Specific Commitments for India, GATS/SC/42/, Geneva, 1 April.

———. 1998a. Health and Social Services, Background Note by the Secretariat, Council for Trade in Services, WTO, Geneva, 18 September.

———. 1998b. 'Environmental Services', Background Note by the Secretariat, WTO, S/C/W/46, July.

———. 2003. EC GATS Initial Offer, Geneva, 10 March, available at http://www.gatswatch.org/docs/offreq/EUoffer/EU-draftoffer-2.pdf (accessed on 22 January 2015).

———. 2004. India-GATS Initial Offer, TN/S/O/IND, Geneva, 1 January.

———. 2005a. 'Joint Statement on Liberalisation of Logistics Services', Council for Trade in Services, Special Session, Document Number TN/S/W/34, 18 February, World Trade Organisation, Geneva available at http://trade.ec.europa.eu/doclib/docs/2008/september/tradoc_140506.pdf (accessed on 6 May 2013).

———. 2005b. Communication from the European Communities and its Member States: Conditional Revised Offer, Council for Trade in Services Special Session, TN/S/O/EEC/Rev.1, 29 June. Available at http://trade.ec.europa.eu/doclib/docs/2005/june/tradoc_123488.reduced%20cells%20v2.pdf (accessed on 23 January 2015).

———. 2005c. India–GATS Revised Offer, TN/S/O/IND/Rev.1, Geneva, 24 August, available at http://commerce.nic.in/trade/revised_offer1.pdf (accessed on 23 January 2015).

———. 2007. 'Notification from The European Communities and its Member States Pursuant to Article of the GATS', S/SECRET/11, Council for Trade in Services, World Trade Organization.

———. 2012. 'International Trade Statistics', World Trade Organisation, Geneva. Available at http://www.wto.org/english/res_e/statis_e/its2012_e/its2012_e.pdf (accessed on 15 July 2013).

———. 2013. 'Trade Policy Review: European Union', Report by the Secretariat, May, Geneva.

———. 2014. 'International Trade Statistics', Geneva.

Wunsch-Vincent, S. and J. McIntosh (Eds.). 2004. 'WTO, E-commerce, and Information Technologies: From the Uruguay Round through the Doha Development Agenda', Report for the UN ICT Task Force. Available at http://www.iie.com/publications/papers/wunsch1104.pdf (accessed 12 January 2014).

Yang, Shao. 2010. 'An Application of Spatial – Panel Analysis: Provincial Economic Growth and Logistics in China', *Canadian Social Science*, 6(3): 83–89.

Yang, S. and Zheng J. 2011. 'The Panel Co-integration Analysis between the Logistics Industry and Economics Growth in China', *International Business and Management*, 2(2): 40–46, April.

Yu, L. 2007. 'Impact of Modern Logistics on Industrial Location Choice and Property Markets', Massachusetts Institute of Technology, Department of Urban Studies and Planning, September.

Yuan, H. and Jianmin Kuang. 2010. 'The Relationship between Regional Logistics and Economic Growth Based on Panel Data', Proceedings of the ICLEM, 2010, p. 618–623.

About the Editors
and Contributors

Editors

Arpita Mukherjee is a Professor at the Indian Council for Research on International Economic Relations (ICRIER), New Delhi, with a PhD in Economics from the University of Portsmouth, UK. She has several years of experience in policy-oriented research and works closely with the Government of India and policy-makers in the European Union (EU), the US, Association of Southeast Asian Nations (ASEAN) and East Asian countries. She has conducted studies for international organisations, such as the Asian Development Bank (ADB), Asian Development Bank Institute (ADBI), ASEAN Secretariat, Foreign & Commonwealth Office (FCO, UK), Italian Trade Commission, Konrad–Adenauer–Stiftung (KAS), Organisation for Economic Co-operation and Development (OECD), Taipei Economic and Cultural Centre (TECC), United Nations Conference on Trade and Development (UNCTAD) and the World Trade Organization (WTO). Her research is a key contributor to India's negotiating strategies in the WTO and bilateral agreements. She has written chapters in joint study group reports for the Indian Government and has led research teams that have made pioneering contributions to India's domestic policy reforms in areas, such as logistics, retail and special economic zones.

Rupa Chanda is a Professor of Economics and Social Sciences at the Indian Institute of Management (IIM), Bangalore, with a PhD in Economics from Columbia University, New York. Earlier, she worked as an Economist at the International Monetary Fund (IMF) in Washington, DC.

Her research interests include the WTO, international trade in services, regional integration, health services and migration. She has undertaken research assignments for various international and Indian organisations, including the World Health Organization (WHO), United Nations Development Programme (UNDP), OECD, European Commission, World Bank and ICRIER. She has coordinated a research project on India–EU mobility in collaboration with the European and Indian institutions. Professor Chanda has served on several committees including the Ministry of Commerce's Expert Group on Services, the Ministry of Overseas Indian Affairs' Academic Working Group on India–EU Labour Mobility Partnership and the Planning Commission's High-Level Group on Services. She has written three books and edited one book on India's trade in services and one book on India-EU mobility. She has presented her work in national and international forums.

Tanu M. Goyal is a Consultant at ICRIER, New Delhi, with a Masters in Economics with specialisation in World Economy from Jawaharlal Nehru University, New Delhi. Her research interests include trade in services, analysis of trade agreements, foreign direct investment issues and retail. She has done several projects for the Indian Government and international agencies, such as the British High Commission, ADB and KAS. Some of her projects include study on India–Thailand and India–Indonesia free trade agreement, food supply chain and opportunities for international business, study of bilateral trade and investment collaboration with the European Union and trade and investment collaboration with Germany. She has published policy and trade issues in international journals, book chapters, reports and popular media articles.

Contributors

Ramneet Goswami is a consultant at ICRIER, New Delhi. Earlier, she worked at the National Council of Applied Economic Research (NCAER), New Delhi. She has done post graduation in Economics from Chaudhary Charan Singh University, Uttar Pradesh. Her research areas include trade in services, free trade agreements, foreign direct investment, audiovisual and logistics services. She has worked on various projects sponsored by the Government of India and international organisations, such as the European Commission, KAS and Italian Trade Commission. She has various publications to her name which include a book, various book chapters, articles in referred journals, working papers and media articles.

Smita Miglani is a Research Associate at ICRIER, New Delhi, with an interest in international/domestic trade and investment, energy and infrastructure studies. She has an MPhil degree in economics from Jawaharlal Nehru University, New Delhi and has contributed to studies for the Ministry of Commerce and Industry, the Ministry of External Affairs (MoEA) and organisations, such as the Society of Indian Automobile Manufacturers (SIAM), the European Business and Technology Centre (EBTC) and the American Chamber of Commerce (AmCham) in India. Her work has contributed to India's negotiating strategies in signing bilateral trade and investment agreements and other policy reforms at the domestic level. Her publications include working papers, book chapters and articles in refereed journals.

Parthapratim Pal is a Professor at IIM, Kolkata, with a PhD in Economics from Jawaharlal Nehru University, New Delhi. Before joining IIM, he worked with ICRIER and the Indian Institute of Foreign Trade (IIFT), New Delhi. He has worked on financial markets and international economics. His recent areas of interest are international trade, regional trade agreements, WTO issues and international capital flows. He has several publications in national and international journals and books.

Divya Satija is a Market Research Analyst at Dun & Bradstreet, South Asia Middle East Ltd (SAME), the Kingdom of Bahrain. Previously, she was a trade analyst at the Delegation of the European Union to India and has also worked as a research associate at the ICRIER. She has experience in policy-oriented research across different sectors of interest to the Indian government and governments of Taiwan, the EU and Bahrain. She has worked on projects that analysed the scope for trade, investment and collaboration between India and the EU in the IT–BPO sector and identified trade and investment potential in Taiwan. Divya has done MA in Economics from Jamia Millia Islamia, Delhi. She has several papers in international journals, reports and articles for newspapers, magazines and ICRIER publications to her credit.

Aparna Sawhney is a Professor at the Centre for International Trade and Development, Jawaharlal Nehru University, New Delhi. She completed her PhD from Columbia University, New York. Professor Sawhney teaches courses on international trade, trade and environment and introduction to mathematical statistics and econometrics. Her publications include papers on trans-boundary pollution, the WTO negotiations on environmental services, Indian manufacturing exports and the renewable energy policy in India. She has published a book and written several strategy/policy papers for the Indian Ministry of Commerce and Industry, Ministry of Environment and Forest, ICRIER, TERI, UNCTAD, International Centre for Trade and Sustainable Development (ICTSD) and World Bank.

Index*

---

* Numbers in bold represent the Article number.

RIGHT
TO PASSAGE

Thank you for choosing a SAGE product!
If you have any comment, observation or feedback,
I would like to personally hear from you.
Please write to me at **contactceo@sagepub.in**

Vivek Mehra, Managing Director and CEO, SAGE India.

Bulk Sales

SAGE India offers special discounts
for purchase of books in bulk.
We also make available special imprints
and excerpts from our books on demand.

For orders and enquiries, write to us at

Marketing Department
SAGE Publications India Pvt Ltd
B1/I-1, Mohan Cooperative Industrial Area
Mathura Road, Post Bag 7
New Delhi 110044, India

E-mail us at **marketing@sagepub.in**

Get to know more about SAGE

Be invited to SAGE events, get on our mailing list.
Write today to **marketing@sagepub.in**

This book is also available as an e-book.

RIGHT
TO PASSAGE
Travels Through India, Pakistan and Iran

Zeeshan Khan

Los Angeles | London | New Delhi
Singapore | Washington DC | Melbourne

First published in 2016 by

SAGE Publications India Pvt Ltd
B1/I-1 Mohan Cooperative Industrial Area
Mathura Road, New Delhi 110 044, India
www.sagepub.in

YODA Press
268 AC Vasant Kunj
New Delhi 110070
www.yodapress.co.in

SAGE Publications Inc
2455 Teller Road
Thousand Oaks, California 91320, USA

SAGE Publications Ltd
1 Oliver's Yard, 55 City Road
London EC1Y 1SP, United Kingdom

SAGE Publications Asia-Pacific Pte Ltd
3 Church Street
#10-04 Samsung Hub
Singapore 049483

Published by Vivek Mehra for SAGE Publications India Pvt Ltd, typeset in 11/13 pt Minion by Zaza Eunice, Hosur, Tamil Nadu and printed at Sai Print-o-Pack, New Delhi.

Library of Congress Cataloging-in-Publication Data Available

ISBN: 978-93-515-0894-6 (PB)

SAGE Yoda Team: Nishtha Vadehra, Arpita Das and Neha Sharma

For Sohrab Rahman Khan, whose road was a higher one

__Teertho__, Bangla; __Tīrtha,__ Sanskrit; literally: the shallow part of a body of water that may be easily crossed; used to refer to pilgrimage and travel

---

Once, when the world was less bound up in boundaries, there were no hard lines between here and there, between you and me.

Once, humanity was a flowing river and not small pools, and there was no way to say 'this part of the river is mine', because it kept flowing, as rivers do.

Once, there was no such thing as nationalism and no sharp edges to my identity; no point where it began or ended.

Once, I didn't come from a different kind of people, but was just my own kind of person.

Or maybe later someday it will be so.

Contents

Acknowledgements

It's impossible to do any sort of justice to acknowledgments for this book, since both the book itself and the journey it is about are a result of the incredible support I received from family and friends, and also complete strangers, along the way.

Beginning at home, my parents Shahana and Obaid, and my brother Sohrab were exceptionally supportive, remaining steadfast in their support even when they feared for my safety. My aunt Munia and uncle Kazim were also sources of strength. My dear friend Sadia, who is no longer with us, also gave me a push when it was most needed. I miss her and wish she could have been here to read this.

I'm deeply indebted to precious friends who looked after me on my journey, Disha and Faiz in Delhi, Sobia and her parents in Islamabad as well as to Kazim uncle's entire family in Lahore and Quetta, without whom it would have been impossible to do the Pakistani leg of the trip as easily. I owe thanks to Maham Shah and Basit Khawaja for making my stay in Pakistan feel like home.

I'm glad to have met the people I did along the way, Mr. Arvind Mahajan at Patna Museum; Yves Thieblot, my travelling companion in parts of Iran; Jemimah and Ballal in Yazd; Sana, Marco, Vincent, Jawaad, Somaiyeh, Mahsa, Mohsin, Mahdi, Hodja, and the carpet sellers at Esfahan; Muhammed, Fatimeh, Najmeh, and the family at Shush, and so many others who gave of their time, love and hospitality more generously than I have ever experienced before. The people who run the guest houses I stayed at in Kashan, Yazd and Shiraz also deserve a mention for their warmth and kindness.

I should also thank Azmat Khattak, the visa officer at the Pakistani High Commission in Dhaka, who issued me a Pakistani visa because he liked the idea of the journey, even though the rules required him to tell me it wouldn't be possible to get one from Bangladesh on a British passport.

The book was written all over the place and I would like to acknowledge the help I received from staff at the Sydney University Library, Brisbane Public Library, the Bangladesh Asiatic Society, Library, the Dhaka Club Library, as well as the staff at various hotels and cafes, and backpackers in Byron Bay, Noosa Heads, Adelaide, Darwin, Manali, Leh, Guwahati, Darjeeling and Shillong. The staff on board the Ghan and the Indian-Pacific trains should also be mentioned since a part of the book was written while travelling across the Australian interior. Still in Australia, I owe an enormous debt to Mubin, Nadia, Nafiz, Sadia, Lopa, Binu, Alizeh and Muhib for looking after me like family during my time in Brisbane.

This book might never have happened without the Dhaka Hay Festival 2013 or without Sadaf Siddiqi, Shazia Omar, Saad Hossain, Srabonti Ali and William Dalrymple. A shout out to Zafar Sobhan for letting me take time off from work to write, and to Mahtab Haider, from whom I have borrowed many books and returned none. I am, however, most indebted to Mahrukh Mohiuddin and Sarnath Banerjee for introducing me to Arpita Das, an extraordinary publisher and someone who has since become a close and dear friend. Nishtha Vadehra too deserves thanks for editing my manuscript and putting up with many of my difficult requests.

Finally, much appreciation is owed to friends who gave me feedback and took the time to read and edit my work. My mother, in particular, was most helpful with her criticism, which was often, infuriatingly, sound. My Latu Nani also deserves a mention here for her complete faith in me and her unwavering commitment to flights of fancy.

The credit for everything that is good about this book belongs to the Creative Essence within and around us, but the bad bits are exclusively my own ineptitude.

Prologue

In the Beginning
27 August 2011

The mollah outside my window is howling to his cacophonic heart's content. It's Ramazan and he's been doing this all month with a zeal that reached its tortured crescendo on Lailatul Qadr. So impassioned was he that I thought he would drop stone dead from exhaustion or heart failure. He outdid himself that night, something that I thought he had already done on Shab-e-Barat, but he has clearly saved his best performance for the holiest of nights. He's probably a good sort though. He wakes us up for *sehri*, announces deaths in the area and calls us to prayer. He sings to us sometimes when he's in the mood. All in all, he's become something of a reassuring voice in our little community along Gulshan Lake, reminding me of the presence of God, or at least of His more enthusiastic fans.

The lake is what separates the neighbourhoods of Gulshan and Badda, and the 'haves' from the 'rapidly-getting'. In the last four years, Badda, the poorer side of the equation, has exploded into a concrete catastrophe of low and middle-income housing like so many other parts of Dhaka. Entire areas are now completely overrun by rectangular, precariously positioned buildings that are known to collapse from time to time, and it's impossible to imagine how people living in them do anything with any sort of privacy at all. This is what passes for cities in today's Bangladesh.

I've been restless and sleepless for the last few nights, trying to get organised for an overland journey across Eurasia, but I have no idea what to expect, or how to properly prepare for it. All I know is that it will probably not go according to plan, but whichever way it goes will be the way that it should. I'm due to leave in two days and between trying to factor in the different types of weather I will encounter and the timings of trains along the way, I am buried under a logistical landslide. In the end I decide to err on the side of 'abandon' and leave more than I should to chance.

I
MOHABHAROT

① Full Chakra

Patna, Bodh Gaya

Dhaka to Patna
Day 1

After pissing around for most of the night—a combination of nerves, under-preparedness and procrastination—I manage to get packed and out the door with not enough time to make it to Hazrat Shah Jalal International Airport's Jet Airways counter before it closes. Luckily, an incident with the last remaining 'on time' passenger has kept check-in open long enough for me to slip through. I'm grateful to know that life is looking after its premier fool—a good omen for what lies ahead, but a fraternal telling-off by the check-in clerk also reminds me about all the stacked dominos that won't fall sequentially if the morning's tardiness tells the tone of my *jatra*. I decide to pull up the proverbial socks and to take deadlines a bit more seriously. After a pleasant and casual exchange with the immigration officer, my last 'local' conversation for a while, I am piped through to India.

I've decided to fly to Kolkata and then to Patna to make that my starting point, and console myself about the missed surface miles with the fact that I've travelled from Dhaka to Kolkata by bus

3

before, and between Kolkata and Patna by rail aboard the Rajdhani Express. The flight to Kolkata is ridiculously short and makes an absolute mockery of the 327 kilometres between the two Bengali cities. I stare out the window to catch the transitions that are often missed when flying; but rather than diminish it, the flight in fact encourages the sense of wholeness between our bit of Bengal and the other—a seamless stretch of dark and verdant foliage interrupted by a quilt-like patchwork of fields, small towns and large, winding rivers. From above, it's obvious to see why people have always been drawn to this delta—it's a soft, wet and beautiful land, and there is a graceful sort of stillness about it that can be felt even from 25,000 feet in the air.

Quite perfectly, the in-flight magazine happens to feature an article by an avid overlander about how travelling on foot reveals the continuity of terrestrial space between, say, China and France, in exactly the same way that air travel confounds it. Wonderful. Odd that such an article should appear in a magazine on an aeroplane, but there it is, in my hands, at the beginning of a journey that I hope will teach me exactly that. There are no coincidences in life. 'The Alchemy of Travel' according to the writer Simon Sender, who recounts his journey from Birmingham to Eastern Italy on foot, is this:

If you take faith into your heart and just step outside without expectations, life comes together like a pair of cupped hands to catch you.

More reassuring words couldn't possibly have been penned.

Arriving at Kolkata Airport, I'm pleased to find *dalaals* and opportunists not lurking everywhere. That's not to say they don't exist here, because the first time I came to Kolkata—in 1994, when it was still called Calcutta—the immigration officer shook me down himself. I think I gave him 200 Rupees to stamp my passport after waiting for nearly two hours. The unfortunately named Dum Dum Airport was a seedy place back then, but all that seems to have changed, including the name. Today Netaji Subhas Chandra Bose International Airport is a much slicker place and is consistent with

4

all that India seems to be getting right these days. I step outside before heading to the domestic terminal and breathe in a sense of space that comes from knowing there are no more borders between here and Amritsar.

At the international and domestic terminals I experience a graceful professionalism that is entirely new India. Young, educated, cosmopolitan, polite and exuding possibility, Indians today are a breath of fresh air after the rude and sullen apathy that can often accompany Bangladeshi 'service-holders'. But the staff at the airport is mostly North Indian and their way of uttering certain words always manages to get under my skin. In Bengali we pronounce all our syllables giving our speech a rolling, uninterrupted feel that is conspicuously absent among speakers of languages that developed from Western Prakrit, like Hindi, Urdu, Punjabi or Sindhi, where they drop syllables and then shrink or stretch existing ones disproportionately to create words that, I suppose to some sound posh, but to me just sound lazy and abrupt. For example, the Airport PA system is announcing flights to 'Bhub'nesh'r' instead of to Bhubaneshwar, which means Lord (Eshwar) of the World (Bhuban). It really didn't need to be shortened anymore after it was already whittled down from the ancient 'Tribhubaneshwar'—Lord of the three worlds—another name for Shiva. Pakistani Punjabis do this almost compulsively; beginning with 'Pak'stan' and working their way through 'S'la'la Kum' to *sad'qa*; they invent names like 'Zalf Kali' (Zulfiqar Ali) and then move on to maul English words, turning immigration to 'um'gration', engineer to 'anj'ner' and police to 'puls'. Perhaps our habit of shrinking, say, *darwaza* to *dorja* annoys them just as much, but it doesn't sound nearly as disjointed.

After being pleasantly and professionally processed by Indian customs and the Jet Airways staff, I get on a plane to Patna. It's a small plane with pretty stewardesses speaking smart, *shuddh* Hindi, using words like *'suraksha'* and *'sanmati'*, filling my soul with the wonders of a civilisation that is at once timeless and timely. I'm partial to it, of course, and I can't help but be constantly inspired by the seemingly irreproachable sophistication of Sanskritic culture.

Patna

The plane sets down onto the tarmac and we are asked to walk to the terminal building close by. It's very old fashioned, like the terminal itself, which houses a single, small luggage conveyer with a rubber gill-like belt, and a small airport taxi booth. I make for it, book a taxi and step out into the city of Patna, capital of the venerable old state of Bihar and home to Shomrat Ashoka's ancient metropolis of Pataliputra.

In fact, Ashoka is among the reasons I've come to Pataliputra. The route I am travelling will take me through his empire into Darius's Achaemenid sphere and onwards to Alexander's realm, so I felt it would be fitting to start with his capital. The historical period between approximately 600 and 200 BC which featured these men, all of whom posterity has recorded as 'Great', shaped the cultural landscape of the ancient world in ways that can only be regarded as fundamental. It is the same period that features Socrates, Plato, Aristotle, Buddha, Mahavira, Panini, Valmiki, Kautilya, Vyasa, the Mahabharata, Herodotus, the Roman Republic, the Hebrew Kings, Lao Tsu, Confucius and a host of others who developed a body of knowledge that became what we today know as ethics.

The road from the airport to the centre of town crosses quite a lot of Patna. It all looks like any small town in Bangladesh, somewhere like Dinajpur perhaps. I'm only half surprised by this as I expected the much-neglected state of Bihar to look appropriately run down. Along potholed roads, skinny dogs and desperate people rummage through open garbage bins surrounded by crows, as though they've stepped out of a Jainul Abedin painting of the 1943 Bengal Famine. As we enter town the streets become narrower, and pushing our way through street-side stalls, rickshaws, motorcycles and cars we arrive at an area called Kidwaipuri and pull into Nalini Apartments, to the guest-house I have booked myself into. It's housed in three floors of a residential building in a neighbourhood that looks a lot like Purano Paltan in Dhaka. India has a smell all its own which ambushes your olfactory organs the moment you step out—a sweetish paan masala flavour, mixed with many different kinds of incense, Nagchampa and Chando mostly, and *pata biri*, along with bits of vegetarian body odour and *channa* from the roadside stalls. The smell begins right at the border between Benapol and Haridaspur and ends neatly before Lahore, like a kind of scent marking. Personally, I like it.

Nesh Inn is quite homely, with polite staff that sit around watching TV near the reception desk in their free time. An idol of Ganesh sits in a small niche next to them, looking smug and contented like he usually does. He wears a fresh garland and appears to have been paid sufficient tribute with incense sticks which have since become a pile of ash, their smouldered scent still lingering on. It's a typical three-star place in South Asia, common from Chittagong to Peshawar: a bit tacky yet clean with basically efficient staff, and has hot and sour soup, french fries, chowmein and other 'localised' versions of the originals always available on the room service menu. I love these and order some for dinner. My room is nice and large; there's a complimentary Thums Up cola in the fridge, and cable television, with an assortment of channels both Indian and English. On one of them, a fully clothed woman is provocatively dancing to music coming out of cracked speakers, not Bollywood item-number style—which has its own sort of aesthetic—but very vulgarly. It goes on like this for a song or two until I get bored instead of turned on and change the channel to find a rishi singing hymns off-key, to a large and frenetic crowd. I eventually settle on Star Movies and watch an American action film while enjoying my Indian-Chinese soup.

I fall asleep comfortably reading J.P. Mallory's *In Search of the Indo-Europeans*, a great slab of a book that I brought along to give me an informed sense of the cultures I might encounter on my route, but it was not the smartest of decisions as it adds considerable weight to my bag, and I rarely get through two of its dense pages before dozing off.

Day 2

It's Eid, the day after the month of Ramadan, and I feel remorseful about missing Fajr prayers. Religious discipline during the month of the fast comes easily, and I don't want to lose my form. I've also missed the morning Eid prayers and have to remind myself not to be so sluggish. After a shower and a good Indian breakfast of whole-wheat chapatti, mango chutney, an omelette and *doi* (yoghurt), along with some strong coffee, I'm ready to take on the day. I decide to explore Patna Museum just around the corner before looking for the extant ruins of Pataliputra. The guard, a tall lanky man with a nice moustache and a funny hat hails me a rickshaw and I'm off through the narrow streets that have surprisingly little activity or traffic this morning.

The museum is closed so I go to the nearest tea stall to ask a group of boys standing around it when it might open. They look at me half sympathetically and half suspiciously, as one does most strangers, and tell me the museum is closed for Eid. I suddenly realise why the streets are vacant and almost on cue, a group of white-clad Muslim men glide on by, borne by the waves of their sparkling clean kurtas in the wind. I've seen other Muslim groups around town since I stepped out, carrying the *noor* of the fast in their easy smiles and relieved faces, but I didn't expect it to be a public holiday here. A nearby pharmacy is the only thing that's open so I ask the man there about the ruins of Pataliputra, and he looks at me blankly for a moment as though he's trying to understand what I'm saying and then says,

'Oh *Paat'leputra*, all of this is *Paat'leputra*. But it's in the ground!'

There it is again, that horrible truncated pronunciation. Even here, where Magadhi Prakrit, the ancestor of Nepali, Maithili, Bangla, Oriya and Assamese, was born, our own natural pronunciations are trumped by the Khariboli accent of Suraseni or Western Prakrit languages. The shame of it. But then the linguistic identity of Magadha, today's Bihar, has been altered entirely. Some scant and scattered versions of the original language still survive as second languages, like Maithili and Maghi, but for the most part Standard Bihari is now nearly 80 per cent Hindi, with the rest composed of something that resembles a cousin of Bangla. For example, '*ami*' features more prominently than '*mein*' or '*hum*' so you might hear dialogue like, '*Ami usko bohut bar bolatha, lekin tarporeo wo bola yeh sambhab nei he'*. It varies, of course, depending on whether the speaker's mother tongue is another Magadhan language, and there are differences in Muslim and Hindu vocabulary too, but compared to places further west where it hasn't always been true, in Bihar I am able to get by well enough with my own particular blend of *'Bangdi'*.

I am fascinated by how languages develop, evolve, compete, plunder, devour, survive and then thrive. Some get called prestige languages, others become dialects. Some have scripts, others lift scripts from the ones that do. Some don't ever get written down. All borrow words from one another and most get caught up in the politics of power and class. This happens across the globe and South Asian languages have centuries of politics attached to them. The Aryan–Dravidian divide, for instance, is an old one, so is the tussle between daughters of the Eastern and Western Prakrits; then there's the Hindi versus Urdu issue, the Bangla versus Urdu issue, the Hindi chauvinism issue, the Brahmi versus Farsi script debate, English and its imperialist associations, the various Austro-Asiatic languages of Eastern India, the Tibeto-Burmese groups of the North East have all been stained by the politics of race, religion, class and identity. And it's not in the past either; the issue of language and power still remains potent, sometimes even explosive, in the 21st-century configurations of life here on our own little patch of planetary turf.

To make the most of my time in Bihar, I decide to leave Patna for the time being and go off to Bodh Gaya, about 100 km south of Patna. Bodh Gaya is the most important pilgrimage site in Buddhism—Siddhartha became the Buddha here, bringing in what was to become one of the first, if not the very first, global religion. In fact, all of Bihar is sometimes called the 'Buddhist East' in Indian tourism brochures. I pack my gear, check out and take a rickshaw to the train station. The *rickshawallah* is an old Muslim man, bent over and struggling under my weight. I tell him to stop and take breaks, and consider changing rickshaws but he won't have it. So I chat with him along the way and we arrive at the station just as he's telling me about his children. I pay him, touch his shoulder reas-suringly and head off into the terminal wondering about just how much this kind old man has probably had to endure in his long and difficult life.

At the terminal I find the usual medley of South Asian rail commuters. Villagers with big jute bags strewn across the floor chatter loudly; students with badly faded jeans and strange hair-cuts stand around trying to look modern; paan stains mark the walls and floors; there are some women in burqas others with big bright *shindur* and *teep*; bearded men in turbans feature too, so do labourers with their shovels and jhuris, young professionals, middle class families and occasionally a serviceman. On the wall above the entrance to the platforms, there is a very beautiful mosaic of Gautama Buddha seated and being honoured by a king. It's a very pretty and fitting image for Bihar, which is of course called 'Bihar' because of all the Buddhist Viharas that used to adorn it.

I go to the tourist information booth and find a smallish man there helping a curly-haired Italian woman with her travel plans. He speaks English and is able to advise us about timings and tick-ets. The Italian woman's boyfriend joins her shortly and we chat about our respective journeys. They are on their way to Varanasi and onwards to Delhi, from where they plan to fly home. Other travel-lers are a welcome sight and are also very helpful. These two remind me about the foreign quota tickets that Indian trains have and I rush upstairs to the ticketing office to try and book my passage all the way to Delhi, which, at the moment hangs in the balance. Travelling in Bangladesh during Eid is a nightmare—actually it's almost impos-sible, and I'm sure it's not much better in India where train tickets are famously difficult to get a hold of even during the best of times.

As I'm leaving, I hear snatches of an escalating argument from the next room:

'Where were you? I've been waiting for so long!'

'Just over there, talking to someone, *yaar*!'

'You think I have to wait for you? Why were you not here?'

'*Aree* take it easy! *Itna* rigid *kiu ho rahe ho*?'

'Why do I have to wait for you! WHO are you?'

'Why can't you wait? Who are YOU?'

The ticketing counter is a classic example of Indian bureaucracy. Luckily, it's sparsely populated, with most people having made their travels plans for the Eid break ahead of time. I'm sent from counter number 24 to counter number 6, where a surprisingly helpful man, after much scouring, finds and books me on two trains—one from Patna to Delhi, and another from Amritsar back to Delhi (The Pakistani High Commission declined to give me a land border visa, so I will have to go back to Delhi from Amritsar, and fly to Lahore). From counter 6 I'm sent back to counter 24 to have my documents attested before I can avail of the foreign quota. Just to make it difficult and in spite of the fact that my passport is clearly foreign, I am required to fill out three forms, make two photocopies from a shop across the street, and wait for the lethargic ticketing officer to lazily go through my passport and match it with the photocopies, before scribbling on the ticket—not the attestation, mind you, but a message to the police control room downstairs who, I'm told, will validate it. I rush to the police control room, miss the last bus to Bodh Gaya (but am reassured by the fact that there are frequent trains to nearby Gaya) and wait nervously, hoping the cops won't make a fuss about my Pakistani and Iranian visas. Finally, in a moment that feels as triumphant as squeezing out a turd through constipated bowels, they hand me back my passport and ticket, with the coach and berth numbers assigned. Looking quite ridiculous as I contort my body to face and thank them while running in the opposite direction, I head towards the local train counter to try and get an express train to Gaya, from where I can go to Bodh Gaya.

The express train is non-existent. The platform I've been asked to wait at has no train long after the scheduled time, while the one opposite it does, and to Gaya as well. It is a non-express train. Fed up with waiting, I board it. But so do a lot of other people, and before I know it, I'm squashed up against someone's chest on one side, and the door on the other with nothing at all to hold. I decide to sit on my backpack and spend a considerable part of the journey staring at an assortment of groins while routinely getting kicked as people continue to pour in and fill the space with an efficiency that makes the Tokyo subway's rush hour crunch look almost wasteful. The sour smell of sweat, damp, starched clothes and of the dirt-scraped metal floor is nauseating. My only respite is the music on my iPod, into which I rapidly retreat.

The crowd eventually thins out a little and I am able to find myself a place next to the window beside a Shaivite *shadhu*, to whom I offer some of my recently purchased *jhall moori*. He politely refuses and flashes me the warmest of smiles. I stare out the window and get my first glimpse of the Bihari countryside. It's beautiful, expansive and fertile. There are palm trees, rivers and fields, and I could quite easily be staring out of a train in Bangladesh. It's also similar to the Brahmaputra Valley, and I'm sure if I took the train all the way from Guwahati to Patna I wouldn't have a clue where one state ended and the next one began.

Across the fields I swear I can see them, leaping out of the pages of history books and into my world:

I see the great Jarasandha marching through Mathura. His army is resplendent—hundreds upon hundreds of soldiers, horses and chariots. They wear bronze breastplates and the mighty king sits astride the finest elephant. *Dholoks* march with them, beating a frenzied rhythm. The Pandavas roll it all back, and Bhima is now forging a path towards the capital. Buddha rests under a mango tree there, surrounded by disciples and onlookers. A young Chandragupta Maurya rushes to the edge of the Nanda Empire to catch a glimpse of the Macedonian army. Soon he will make this place his own. Now I see Ashoka charging through with his army, heading south towards Kalinga. He looks fierce, and I can hear hoofs, screams and clashes of swords; here comes the emissary from Taxila. Kautilya is with him and they are headed towards Pataliputra. What elegant clothes they wear and their Punjabi steeds are magnificent. Kautilya is cradling a bundle of manuscripts under his arm; his brow is furrowed and he looks like he doesn't ever stop thinking. Buddhist missionaries are leading a procession out of the city on their way to Central Asia and China. A royal send-off has been arranged; it's fabulous—flowers and sandalwood incense thickly perfume the air.

It all disappears into a blur and the sophisticated Guptas rise out of the ashes. All of India is enriched, but their empire disintegrates amidst squabbles for power. But wait! The Palas are marching from Bengal bearing the Buddhist standard. Now Aatisha has returned from his training in Sumatra and is toying with the idea of going to Tibet. Dharma enjoys a brief reprieve but then it all comes crashing down and its last hurrah is heard pitifully across the land of its birth. It begins to get ugly: the Hindu Sens from Karnataka rule the roost, and there's no love lost between them and the beaten Buddhists. In the midst of it all, Bakhtiyar Khilji pours in from the west, pillaging his way through to Lokkhonaboti, slaughtering Hindus and Buddhists alike. I can hear Farsi and Arabic in the groves and villages; I can see the cultured civilisation of Magadha disappear under an Islamic armoury. It loses everything, even its name. Now Bihar's Afghan warlord Sher Shah Suri conquers Bangala and uses it to beat back the Mughals to become the King of India; his army marches across these fields all the way to Peshawar. It's magnificent—hundreds upon hundreds of soldiers and horses and cannons. They wear chainmail under bronze breastplates, and the mighty king sits astride the finest elephant. Drummers march with them, beating a frenzied rhythm on a duff.

Bodh Gaya

The train reaches Gaya at 6 pm and I hire an autorickshaw to take me to Bodh Gaya, about 45 minutes away. It's dark by the time I reach, and I check into a hotel close to the Mahabodhi temple complex that's full of Sri Lankan pilgrims. There is no restaurant at the hotel and I'm hungry so I walk outside and find a nice open-air place near the temple complex, next to a little bookshop owned by an articulate Muslim gentleman dressed all in white for Eid. The area has a wonderful calm about it, and the various Tibetan shops give it the feel of a Himalayan village, albeit a very humid one. I buy a book on Mauryan India co-authored by Irfan Habib and Vivekananda Jha, and have a dinner of thukpa and tea, before heading back to the hotel for some much needed sleep. Worshippers are still visiting various temples in the area and chanting can be heard. A gentle breeze blows; the halogen streetlights make everything orange and the atmosphere is serene indeed.

I can't sleep so I step out onto the balcony to smoke a cigarette. The town is completely abandoned now; and all I can hear is the rustling of leaves and the battles of bats. It's dark and the wild feels very close even with many urban structures in sight. I try to imagine arriving at this place 2,500 years ago, alone and impoverished, to sit under a tree and spend nights in what must've still been forest, where surely tigers and bears roamed and invisible demons stalked unsuspecting souls. Just the thought of it scares me. How did you do it, Siddhartha? Perhaps it wasn't suffering, poverty or death you were trying to transcend, but only the fear of those things. The enormous courage it takes for people like him to willingly throw themselves into the very things we spend a lifetime shielding ourselves against, humbles me more than their philosophies do.

Day 3

I had wanted to be out by 6 am to watch the morning prayers at the Temple but the constant slamming of doors at the hotel from 4 am onwards rendered me sleepless and I stayed in after everyone had left to get some rest. At 8 am, I groggily venture out of my room in search of food and walk into a small lane behind the Mahabodhi temple to find, surprisingly enough, a Muslim area. Bihar's Islamic history has created a sizeable Muslim population here, and being the day after Eid, they are all out with their families in their best clothes. A fair few also seem interested in their Buddhist heritage and they visit the temple as well as the stores around it, but most carry themselves in a manner that suggests they see themselves as belonging to a different legacy altogether.

I return from breakfast to find a huge *da'waat* tent being set up right outside the temple, with horrid Islamic pop blaring out of large speakers. Young Muslims are gathering inside the tent, where there will be speeches after which they will distribute food in the area. It's all very familiar to me and I'm sure it's being done with the best of intentions, but the way it's being done is obtuse and about as unsubtle as it can possibly get. The quiet and introspective atmosphere is completely shattered by loud and emphatic incantations of *'Allah Hu, Ya Muhammad, Rasul Allah'* to the beat of what sounds like a bad Bon Jovi song. I'm sure the humble monks, here to worship at what is essentially their Mecca, can't appreciate it much but they are either too polite or too intimidated to protest. Peculiar as it is though, I can't deny there is something enjoyable about the audacious optimism of this *da'waat* effort that contrasts sharply with the trying-hard-to-be-sombre worshipper-cum-mendicants who seem to hang around the temple complex just to get some change off more sincere visitors.

Bihar is thoroughly overlaid with Muslim culture and apart from the racket it's making, I'm quite pleased to see it thriving here. I'm sure that's entirely because I'm Muslim too and it makes me feel close to my 'own' atmosphere, but in reality Bihar is a predominantly Hindu place. It has over 69 million Hindus and almost 14 million Muslims, but only about 20,000 Buddhists. In fact, here, at the birthplace of the faith, there are more Sikhs and Christians than Buddhists. It makes one wonder about how viciously the fabric of Magadhan Buddhist civilisation, an entity that stood for over 1,500 years, was systematically uprooted and torn to shreds.

Poor old Magadha. First past the post, it was the most powerful realm in South Asia, for centuries. When Indian civilisation moved with the rains and the rivers east, out of the Indus Valley, a number of *janapadas*, or nation-states, began springing up all over the Ganges basin out of which Magadha became the most prominent. The jury is still out on whether the people of these *janapadas* were the descendants of the Indus Valley people or newcomers from further west. In fact, the jury is still out on virtually all theories about the ethno-linguistic origins of Indian civilisation. We don't know, for instance, if the Dravidian south is the progenitor or the heir of the Indus Civilisation, or whether the Indus Civilisation has nothing at all to do with them, but was in fact built by people related to those who would later go on to call themselves Aryans. Or maybe they had nothing to do with either of them and belong to a race of people now extinct. And India has other layers as well; the *adibashi* Austro-Asiatic Mundas have cousins all across South and South East Asia, possibly even in Australia. Perhaps the Indus Valley culture is their legacy.

But this is taking me off topic—even if it is an interesting tangent. Whatever the anthropology, the political history tells us that 16 *Mahajanapadas* eventually arose in the Gangetic Plain. Some Vedic and Aryan, others non-Vedic. Magadha has been recorded as a non-Vedic kingdom in certain sources although in others its first king is said to be the descendent of a tribe listed as being Aryan. But there were also tribes that 'went native', and departed from the Vedic religion, especially in the Eastern regions, and so it's not impossible that Magadha had an Aryan King who wasn't a follower of the Vedas. And in any case the religions of India eventually melded together, smudging the lines between Vedic and non-Vedic to such a point of irrelevance that Vedic Indra, destroyer of the Dashyu and preserver of the Arya, became a colleague of non-Vedic Shiva who is dark skinned and feral—a deity entirely of Indian origin and possibly in existence since the Harappan Age. They reside together in a pantheon that also includes Manasa, once only an *adibashi* deity.

Over time, a growing rivalry between East and West India becomes full blown. Perhaps Eastern India, dominated by Magadha, had become the bastion of an older, pre-Vedic civilisation, while the Indians of the Vedas, the Aryans as they called themselves, arrived with a determination to dominate the entire Ganges basin. Magadha possibly viewed these Aryan confederacies as nothing more than peculiar upstarts; its most powerful king at the time, Jarasandha, made short work of them, repeatedly scattering them across the western parts of the Indian peninsula every time they encroached on his territory. He sided with Kansa (even marrying off his daughters to him) instead of Krishna in the struggle for the throne of Mathura, and when Krishna killed Kansa, Jarasandha, enraged at seeing his daughters widowed, invaded Mathura, driving Krishna and his tribe of Yadavas to the western edge of India, in Gujarat. He attacked Mathura 17 times, and eventually forced the Yadavas to move their capital to Dwarka. But the jostling for power during those formative years wasn't just between Aryans and non-Aryans. It also happened between the various tribes of Aryans that had fanned out across most of India, forming nations and kingdoms of their own. Among them, the western Indian Kuru tribe, of Mahabharata fame, emerges as one of the strongest.

There are also cosmic interpretations of these battles that raged across, not just India the physical, but India the spiritual as well. They become representative of battles between Suras and Asuras or deities and demons, and between the Devas and the Daityas or gods and devils, all locked in an eternal struggle between good and evil. It's hard to make the distinction between earthly kings and cosmic lords in those epic times and Jarashandha's friend Banasura, for instance, is king of Assam but also a thousand-armed Asura lord. And just to be perfectly contrarian, as is the Indian way, the Asuras are originally the good guys and then become the bad guys when the younger Devas push them out, much like the Titans were pushed out by the Olympians in Greek mythology, leading to a situation where, in Iran, another set of people also calling themselves Aryans worship an Ahura (Asura) Mazda, and demonise a Daeva (Deva). It's all very complicated and also completely useless to our story about Magadha, where the Kuru kingdom is beginning to look quite menacing and a war between the East and the West is imminent.

Krishna grabs an opportunity to get his revenge and destroy Magadha, while also removing the last significant obstacle to a Yadava–Kuru takeover of Upper India. Knowing that Jarasandha was too powerful to be conquered by force of arms but that he was vulnerable in hand-to-hand combat because of a peculiar physical defect at birth, Krishna encourages Bhima to challenge the ageing Jarashanda to a *dondo juddho*, or wrestling duel, where Jarasandha is overcome and his son Sahdeva installed as king of Magadha. It's an early example of regime change and it will prove useful, as

Magadha stays allied with the Pandavas during the Kurukshetra war even when many Eastern kingdoms, including his father's friend Banasura's Assam, and Karna's Anga, opposes them. But the westward power shift will not last long, and after the dust settles, the kingdom of Magadha reasserts itself under the leadership of the Hariyanka dynasty and its most famous King, Bimbisara, to eventually become an empire and once again, the most powerful place in India. This is the realm that Gautama Buddha transforms.

I venture into the Mahabodhi Temple shortly after about 9 am. Leaving my shoes at the entrance I walk towards the main structure where the pink cement fence surrounding it puts me off slightly. There's a small inscription on the wall, shoddily rendered, that gives us an idea about the history of the construction. It tells me Ashoka commissioned the polished sandstone throne that sits where Buddha once sat in 3rd century BC, and that the temple itself was built in the 6th century AD, with major enlargements and restoration work carried out as recently as 1956. It's effectively a 19th-century British Archaeological Society reconstruction of the 6th-century structure, and some of the original parts can be identified by how much better the workmanship is. Otherwise the entire complex is a massive aesthetic letdown; I hadn't expected the very heart of Buddhist civilisation to look this shabby, especially since Buddhist expression is skilful and intricate everywhere else. It possesses none of the finesse that characterises the Gupta or Pala Schools of Art and doesn't measure up to its offshoots either, the ones which produced Borobudur, Angkor Wat or the Bengal Sultanate's monuments. Parts of it are painted badly; most of it is tacky and square-ish and it looks industrial in the way that machine embroidery looks next to the kind done by hand. To be honest, it looks like it was built yesterday by fat-fingered children.

I decide to stop being such a snob and to try and appreciate the atmosphere. Here it was that Siddhartha sat down, I remind myself. Even if I ignore all the myths—like it's the navel of the earth, or that no other place could support the weight of the Buddha's attainment or that when the world is destroyed it will be the last spot to disappear and the first to reappear when it emerges again—it's still an enchanted place. There's a palpable sense of the Sacred even though it's overrun by tourists who strike poses and snap selfies in front of the temple. The complex is large and cluttered with stupas of various sizes added on by devotees from different cultures throughout the ages, yet it possesses a simple sort of sanctity. Myanma monks go through their paces in the garden, and a group of elderly Sri Lankan pilgrims catch their breath under the branches of the Bodhi tree, which are spread out across the garden like outstretched arms. This isn't the original tree but a direct descendant, and there are conflicting stories about when the current one was first planted here, but it's clearly very old, and its enormous limbs are supported by metal beams. The original, legend has it, was killed by Ashoka's wife, Tissarakka, who was jealous about how much time the king spent here. Nothing can escape the wrath of an insecure lover, not even the Buddha's Bodhi tree.

A young monk is walking a line unimaginably slowly, experiencing, as it seems, his every movement along its fullest arc as though it's playing in super-slow motion. Beside him a young woman is praying in a manner that resembles the Muslim *salat*, but with more commitment—she lies face-down and completely flat when she prostrates. Over here a monk is sitting in deep meditation—he hasn't moved in almost an hour; over there, prayer flags are being tied to the railing around the throne. I stop at all the major points in the complex—where the Awakened Gautama stood and stared at the Bodhi tree, where he wrestled with his illusions, where he paced up and down along the Cankamana. It feels current, as though it all happened yesterday, and can't quite understand why—perhaps because pilgrims have replayed it ever since, or perhaps, as the cynic in me cringes, because his energy trail is still warm. But more than anything, being here tells me how human Siddhartha was. I can imagine him as a real person, experimenting with new ways to reach the truth; a wanderer, unsure of what he is doing and ecstatic when he manages to make a breakthrough. He has become very present on the ground.

Engulfed in the tranquillity of the place, I walk around the temple and into it to find a massive and garish statute of Buddha inside. People are thronging to it, praying before it, taking pictures of it. It's nauseating. I leave immediately and do a final round of the gardens, to come across a number of brass plaques with the sayings of Buddha inscribed. Among them are these jewels:

By oneself is evil done, by oneself is one defiled. By oneself is evil left undone, by oneself is one made pure. Purity and Impurity depend on oneself. No one can purify another.

Every gorgeous royal chariot wears out. This body too will wear out. But the Dharma of the Good does not age; thus the Good make it known to the Good.

He who drinks deep the Dharma lives happily with a tranquil mind. The wise man ever delights in the Dharma made known by the Noble One.

I walk out to the main street where a clutch of autorickshaws surrounds me so I board one, and ask to be taken to Buddha's cave. The driver's name is Kalam Khan; we wish each other Eid Mubarak, and head off into the beautiful countryside past small *nullas* and slightly bigger ones, then fields, hills and open spaces. We chat along the way. Kalam plays *qawwali* on his music system, shares some fruit with me and makes me feel very comfortable in his company. He asks me if I've been to Bihar Sharif, and tells me I should visit the Dargah of Makhdoom Yahya Maneri where there is an Urs on; I should also go to Maner Sharif where another saint is buried. When I tell him I'll probably miss both of those, he scowls and says chastisingly that even emperors like Ibrahim Lodi and Akbar didn't skip the Dargah of Makhdoom Shah. The epithet 'Sharif' or 'Hazrat' before a city's name usually lets you know that a powerful and respected Sufi lived or is buried there. It means 'noble' and 'sacred', respectively, but it's very cynical that Bihar the Noble is called such, given that it stands on the ruins of Odantapuri University and on the graves of thousands of murdered monks and scholars. Bihar Sharif, or just Bihar, as it was originally called, was the Pala capital for their province of Magadha until Sher Shah Suri moved it back to Pataliputra and gave Bihar's name to the entire province—probably not in that order, but that's sort of how it went.

We reach the bottom of the hills where the road ends and I walk up to the cave. The view is stunning; it's nearing sunset, and from this elevation I can see the whole horizon, which is flat and lush with elevated interruptions every so many miles. Along the way I see young girls collecting firewood in oversized sacks which they carry on their heads, and a pair of lovers sitting under a tree enjoying the view. The cave complex is tended by Tibetans and is draped in the colours of the Buddhist flag. They rush me to the cave; it's nearly closing time and they want to go home. The cave is tiny and damp, and at the far end, presumably where Buddha used to sit, is a metal statue of an emaciated Siddhartha. He is bearded and his ribs are all visible. His skin hangs on him like cloth stretched out on sticks, yet he wears his characteristic look of contentment and his mouth is gently upturned in a smile. Nothing gets the Buddha down. There are oil lamps, *diyas*, and candles lit in the cave and remnants of offerings—flower petals, pieces of fruit placed at the foot of the statue. The candles make it warm and I begin to sweat, but it's cosy and I imagine Siddhartha probably enjoyed spending the colder nights in this womb-like place.

I want to sit longer but the anxious keeper waves me out so I look at the statue one last time, sitting there in the orange glow of the candle-lit cave, and think about the unwavering dedication of the Buddha to have starved himself half to death in this place. He did have a nice view, though, and hopefully that was of some comfort. There is another cave beside Buddha's, where I'm told his companions stayed, and I discover that he didn't go at it completely alone. Thank God, perhaps with some company it's not as unbearable.

I chat with the Tibetans on the way down; they are a sturdy lot and carry themselves with playfulness and positivity, like almost all the Tibetans I've met do. I ask one of them why Siddhartha would go south from Lumbini and not north into the Himalayas, if it were caves and mountains he was after, to which he replies with a wink,

'But he didn't know what he was after, did he? He just knew he had to seek.'

Buddha spends six years in his cave, putting himself through all sorts of austerities only to find he is just much, much thinner but not much more enlightened. He comes down and stumbles into Uruvela village, today's Bodh Gaya, and nearly collapses from exhaustion—he's at the end of his tether. Shujata, the village head-man's daughter finds him and feeds him *kheer*, saving his life and sending him along the Middle Way by reminding him about strings on a musical instrument.

Too tight and it will snap, too slack and it won't play.

Shujata says the most commonsensical of things, obvious to everyone except Siddhartha, it seems, and triggers the birth of a religion. She should have been credited as its co-founder, yet she has shrunk to near obscurity in the popular narrative as it is a woman's fate to be under-appreciated. The *kheer* gives Buddha power and his strength returns, filling him with an almighty glow that makes him see much more clearly and he abandons his austerities in the cave. Personally, I don't think it was the *kheer* at all, but Shujata's love that did that to him. A woman's tenderness after six harsh years will do wonders for any man's soul—and it can also, evidently, lead to enlightenment. After that he goes to sit under the Bodhi tree and in only seven short weeks receives the Light of Wisdom. The rest, of course, is Buddhism.

It gets dark on the way back and Kalam Bhai goes past his neigh-bourhood, which is not far from the cave. He offers me dinner at his home, and I know that his hospitality is genuine, but it's late, and Bihar is notorious for bandits. He knows this too, because when I say it's probably better that I get back to town, he doesn't insist otherwise. It's too late this evening to take the bus to Rajgir, the next place on my route, so I decide to go back to Bodh Gaya and head out first thing in the morning. Kalam says he knows of a guest-house that's cheap and he takes me there: it's a private house with several rooms for rent. I take one; another one across the balcony is occupied by a couple that sounds French. An Indian man is with them and is trying to teach them how to play a bamboo flute. The owner and his family still live downstairs and his wife cooks me dinner and makes me tea.

Bodh Gaya hosts many monasteries representing the different cultures within which Buddhist thought flourished. There's an array of styles from around the globe—Tibetan, Chinese, Japanese, Thai, Sikkimese, Bhutanese, Korean, Myanma, Vietnamese—each with their own unique aesthetic. They are all pleasant to look at, more so than the Mahabodhi temple itself, and it's clear that Buddhism has become almost exclusively the preserve of East Asian people. Just like Christianity became predominantly European after it got enmeshed in Greek, Roman and Norse mythology and now looks neither Semitic nor Middle Eastern, Buddhism too reflects precious little of the places that cradled its original expression, Bihar and Bengal, where the entire Buddhist world once came to refuel and where teachers like Atisha Dipankar departed from to take the faith to Tibet and beyond. These places no longer influence Buddhist discourse nor add to its colourful cultural landscape.

But that's not all that's changed. There is now a massive 80-feet concrete statue here, commissioned by a Japanese sect, which touches the sky and while impressive, is also very imposing—not quite representative of Buddha's modest, humble spirit. In fact, there is so much deification of Gautama it's easy to forget he was once actually a man. Thousands upon thousands of statues of him adorn temple walls, interiors, homes, diagrams, mandalas and virtually everything else related to Buddhism. Massive ones cut into mountains and tiny ones worn around necks. Buddha has become a fashion accessory, a living room showpiece and a god. He's been incorporated into numerous pantheons, playing a starring role in Hindu mythology as a reincarnation of Vishnu and sharing a stage with the Himalayan thunder gods of lore. In the Chinese pantheon there is an Amitabha, a Buddhist monk turned god. Numerous apologists have explained these away as the Adi-Buddha, a Godhead, and therefore not representative of a living being, but the fact that Buddha's image is an object of worship makes this a tenuous claim. Some schools, like the Theravadins, are much better at separating Buddha the man from the message he brought, but even they endorse a level of veneration that makes me uneasy.

I can't help but wonder if this is how Buddha would have wanted to be remembered. Wasn't he far removed and in fact contemptuous of the sort of tiered edifice, replete with rules, rituals, regimes and ranks, that he's become associated with? Like Christ, he's become immortalised in a pose—the meditating Buddha and the crucified Jesus, anti-establishment mystics who became gods, their images central to the lofty, gilded establishments they spent a lifetime opposing. I quite dislike it. I dislike it as much as I dislike the Muslim obsession with the Sunnah of Prophet Muhammad, which insists that I do everything from cutting my hair to picking my nose exactly the way he did, or worse, the way people say he did.

It's not irreverence for the sake of it. I'm quite aware that my moral and spiritual fibre is at least partly reliant on the stories about these great people, and there's no denying that something of Buddha's peaceful nature gets transmitted in the statues of him. But it's difficult to separate the muck from the material and I often think we end up with as many examples of great people as we do of grand larcenies, loaded with testimonies to fear, ignorance and vainglory. It also bothers me to see people worshipping other people. The statues, the stories, the veneration, the *paramparas*, the claims that Jesus is God, or that Muhammad's name is inscribed on the Throne of God are ideas I can't bring myself to endorse and I find they detract from the unitary and universal nature of Truth. I especially don't like the way we parcel off pieces of these universal teachings and call them our own exclusive religions. But I came here to find Buddha, and will leave with a sense of having met him somewhere between the river and the Peepal tree—a young man stoked by the simplicity of his salvation. I will leave reminded of all the good that he stood for.

Sadly, all that was built on what Buddha stood for collapsed here in India under great waves of imperial ambition. It began to unravel when the Kushan kingdom weakened in northwestern India and the White Huns invaded the area in the 5th century, virtually extinguished the Buddhist city at Taxila, bringing on the beginning of the end. The second Hun ruler adopted Shaivism as his religion and an emboldened Hinduism ran roughshod over the Buddhist sphere. In Central India remnants of the Gupta Empire and Harshavardhana's independent Buddhist kingdom managed to stave it off for a while, but the rise of Hindu Rajput kingdoms in the west hastened the inevitable. By the 8th century, great swathes of Buddhist territory were in the hands of Hindu kings, and in the east only the Pala country of Gour, on the Bengal delta, remained officially Buddhist.

Also known as Goureshwar, or the Lords of Gour, the Palas fielded the religion's last significant challenge to Hindu dominance, conquering much of India all the way up to the Khorasan, in what was Bengal's imperial finest hour. Their first ruler, Gopala, came to power in 750 AD through an electoral process—one of the first of its kind—and began a dynasty that went on to become patrons of art, literature and scholarship. The famous Buddhist universities, where manuals on everything from medicine to philosophy and ethics were written, thrived under their rule, and the Bangla language has its genesis in this period, as does much of Bengali mystic thought. The Palas proselytised far and wide, taking Buddhism into Tibet, Nepal, Bhutan, Myanmar and Malaya, along with their proto-Bangla, which became the language of learning in these places. They also involved themselves in public welfare and social reform, and pursued a policy of tolerance, giving credence to both Hindu and Buddhist views—yet for all their troubles they were usurped by the Hindu Sens who resumed the supplanting of Buddhism with Hinduism with renewed vigour.

After the Hindus were done with it, Muslims came along to pick off the remains. Bakhtiyar Khilji and his band of plundering merry men shot through the Ganges basin on their way to the Sen capital in Bengal, laying to waste the remnants of the Buddhist civilisation, smashing through the universities, beheading the monks, plundering the treasuries and dealing Indian Buddhism its death blows.

And so Gautama's great legacy exited the Indian stage via the Bengali gate, and would never again play a major part in the land that it fertilised for millennia. But I prefer to believe that Buddhism didn't really go anywhere. Instead, its nurturing waters penetrated deep into the cultures of South Asia, and all the way up to Afghanistan, creating a temperament that is uniquely ours and helps us recognise each other as kindred—even if in our modern configurations we're too busy looking for ways to ignore that connection. It was a Buddhist empire, after all, that brought us together under a single banner and gave us identities larger than our tribes, nations, totems and gods—our first international experience, fashioned in the mould of Ashoka's 'Empire of Virtue'. I'd like to believe that its imprint remains with us, and the fact that India adopted the Chakra as its national symbol and the Ashokan lion as its emblem, says something about how deeply ingrained the Buddhist years are.

It's unusual to talk about it in those terms, but Ashoka's Empire of Virtue, or his *Dhamma* project, is actually an early example of a theocratic state. It may have also been among the more ambitious ones as his empire was vast, diverse and religiously heterogenous. Just like the neighbouring Zoroastrian Achaemenid Empire, which preceded it slightly, and the much older Jewish kingdom of Israel, religiously defined ethical standards were at the heart of the Ashokan polity and determined its role in the life of its citizens. Perhaps it's no wonder then that in the modern world, Israel, Iran, Afghanistan and Pakistan are also basically theocratic, and India's Hindutva agenda contains trace elements of it too. Gandhiji's ahimsa movement was certainly somewhat Ashokan. Several Mesopotamian kingdoms in ancient times were similarly oriented, but few were able to fuse statecraft with faith as deeply or as effectively as that.

Ashoka wasn't always interested in benevolent governance, though; in fact he was originally known as the rapacious Chandashoka or Ashoka the merciless. It was only after the pyrrhic victory against Kalinga, today's Odisha, that he realised he had caused tremendous misery and was consumed by remorse, that he began to turn towards Buddhism and the principles of Dharma—a story that may be fabricated as it serves to reinforce the transformative appeal of religion. Perhaps it was guilt and a desire to atone for his crimes or perhaps it was genuine conviction, but Ashoka took to his faith with such passion that he became, according to at least one historian, more monk than monarch, and for nearly 40 years, ruled his kingdom like it was a seminary. He didn't see *Dhamma* as simply piety or formal religious practices but as 'conformity to a social ethic,' according to historian Romila Thapar, and used Buddhism to develop moral laws while attempting to create a new sort of mind, one that would ensure ethical behaviour between his subjects and respect the dignity of sentient life. He says this quite candidly in one of his edicts:

> *On the roads I have had banyan trees planted, which will give shade to beasts and men. I have had mango groves planted and I have had wells dug and rest houses built every nine miles.... And I have had many watering places made everywhere for the use of beast of men.... I have done these things in order that my people might conform to Dhamma.*

He also did his best to frame his Dharmic mission in universalist tones, hoping to appeal evenly to all the ethnic and religious groups that lived within his realm. This had to have been a very revolutionary idea for the times and also sensitive as it was essentially state proselytism, but Ashoka was convinced of the benefits of his creed for all mankind and had edicts issued to that effect, saying,

> *Ten years [of reign] having been completed by He who is the Beloved of the Gods and who regards everyone amiably, has made known the doctrine of Piety to men; and from this moment he has made men more pious, and everything thrives throughout the whole world. And the king abstains from killing living beings, and other men and those who are huntsmen and fishermen of the king have desisted from hunting. And if some were intemperate, they have ceased from their intemperance as was in their power; and obedient to their father and mother and to the elders, in opposition to the past also in the future, by so acting on every occasion, they will live better and more happily.*

In line with this, he also downplayed traditionally Vedic distinctions of *varna* or caste and *jati*, race—words which don't feature in his public edicts and are replaced with words like family, clan and sect. This may have been a conscious moving away from the older Brahmanical order as Ashoka's empire of virtue was, like most theocratic movements, a reaction to something that went before it—in this case, Vedic Brahmanism, which was seen as no longer relevant as a moral force.

Ashoka's empire also shared some other features with theocratic movements, past and present. For one, he was sometimes intolerant of different opinions on the definition of an ethical society and had monks and nuns who disagreed with him expelled from the *Sangha*, the community of spiritual guides. He may have even been fanatical about his faith and according to a set of legends called the 'Ashokavadana', had 18,000 Ajivikas (followers of a religion similar to Buddhism, now extinct) executed because one of them drew an unflattering picture of the Buddha. In another instance, he supposedly had a blasphemer burnt alive in his house along with his family, but both these legends have been dismissed as sectarian propaganda and the fact that he was probably not a bigot is evidenced in another of his edicts where he says,

All religions should reside everywhere, for all of them desire self-control and purity of heart.

What is true, though, is that Ashoka believed in exporting the Revolution beyond his borders and sent preachers all across the world—to Egypt, Tajikistan, Greece, Anatolia, Central Asia, Myanmar and Sri Lanka—claiming that everyone had been converted to the *Dhamma*. He may have overestimated the appeal of his system, but there were certainly some who were interested, especially in Sri Lanka and Myanmar, and many parts of Central Asia where Buddhism managed to take a firm hold. And finally, he created a special category of officer in his bureaucracy called the *dhamma-mahamattas*, who were responsible for safeguarding the righteousness of his subjects and their society—the very definition of Saudi Arabia's religious police or Iran's Basij guards, if I ever heard one.

Ashoka's experiment in creating a just and moral empire didn't succeed, of course. He may have had too much faith in people's ability, or indeed desire, to be better than they are, and they didn't eventually set aside prejudice, hatred, violence or crime, no matter how much he encouraged them to do so. But he tried, and that counts for a lot. Romila Thapar, a leading authority on Ashoka and the Mauryas, puts it succinctly in her book about early India and says,

Nevertheless Ashoka deserves admiration, not only for recognising the need for a social ethic, but for attempting to both define and implement such an ethic in his capacity as emperor.

This was unique in Indian history and rare in the histories of other societies.

❷
East is East

Rajgir, Nalanda, back to Patna

Rajgir and Nalanda
Day 4

I wake up early after having slept badly because of a wasp that was buzzing around in the room. I was afraid it would sting me, so kept waking up to see where it was most of the night. People like Buddha might be able to brave tigers, but the humble wasp is all it takes to keep me up. I sit outside my room sipping a cup of coffee and watch the daybreak; it rained overnight and the air is infused with the lovely smell of moist earth. Mr. Jyoti Gupta, the owner of the house, brings me the bill, which I clear and wait for Kalam Khan, the autowallah, to come and take me to the bus station. Mr. Gupta is a polite and pleasant man who sounds well-travelled and looks like he spends time in Goa when he gets a chance. He's a local so I ask him about why so little of the original architecture remains in Bodh Gaya.

'But that's simple, thousands of years of plunder and very little excavating.'

He points to a big empty space that's been put aside by the Archaeological Survey of India beneath which a temple might sit, and says,

'Personally, I prefer it stays underground for now, it's safer that way.'

I've been planning to take the bus to Rajgir when Kalam suggests we 'auto' it all the way instead. He will stay with me, take me to all the sights and even to nearby Nalanda before putting me on a bus or train to Patna. It sounds right so we haggle on the price and then set off on what turns out to be a great ride as the openness of an autorickshaw lets me experience the environment in a way that buses just can't.

The horizon pushes further out as the land becomes more expansive, and palm trees stand around matter-of-factly among rice and wheat fields. We pass a river that's drying into the sand with *kashphool* along its original banks and a full one, the Phalgu, which is sacred to Hindus as yet another embodiment of Vishnu. We go through little towns where the traffic gets stuck in unnecessary knots; a backpacker on an Enfield motorbike goes whizzing by; precariously piled produce on rickshaw vans bob about as semiclothed kids play on the side of the road with homemade toys, running around with broad, toothy smiles lighting up their faces. I see the carcass of a cow being picked at by crows—it's bloody and all bones. Hills and rocky outcrops begin to appear and become more frequent as we go along. The terrain unflattens.

We go past a funeral procession. The women are wailing and slapping their chests as the menfolk take the body away to the sound of beating drums—in almost a festive rhythm. One woman is wailing louder than the others; she crumples to the floor as if the very life in her is carried away with the shrouded corpse. All along the way, mosques, mandirs, mazaars and murtis feature, woven together as a single plait. Towns and villages hug these structures, making them look more like place markers or street art than anything religious. Most of the people I see along the way are very dark-skinned. They don't look Indo-European, nor do they look quite like Dravidians. They resemble the Shaotals and Mundas, mostly, and in fact some of them probably are. The women wear brightly coloured saris— reds, magentas, saffrons, blues, which stand out stunningly against their dark, glistening skin. Young Muslim women with their faces covered like ninjas can also be seen along the road. You can tell their age by the way they walk.

A set of hills appear on the horizon and we drive into it on a road that seems to appear out of nowhere. The paddy fields disappear and I've forgotten they were ever there as we climb to find ourselves in a temperate climate with taller, deciduous trees. While ascending, it feels like being ushered in at a slow and ceremonial pace towards the remains of massive imperial gates. The gates are long gone but the hills look like huge walls, and on top of them are actual walls, running the length of them on either side as far as the eye can see. Dry stonewalls the type you might expect to find in the Alps or Devon, or even in Kashmir, but not here among the bamboo belt of the Ganges basin. It's all quite dramatic and feels a little mythical— a fitting approach to the legendary city of 'Raja Griho', the Abode of Kings.

Raja Griho, or Rajgir as it's been irreverently shortened to, is picturesque. Here, surrounded by what seems like an impregnable fortress of seven hills is the first capital of the Magadha tribe, a people who are as old as at least the 'Atharva Bidda', one of the four Biddas (or Vedas, or Wisdoms, depending on your language) that form the foundations of Sanskritic or Vedic civilisation. The sacred mantras mention them along with other nations of eastern India, including my own, the Banga. This, their original capital city, was established by Brihadratha, who is said to have descended from Bharat, the eponymous ancestor who conquered all of upper India in the Vedic Period, and established Bharat Barsha—'Bharat's Realm'—before realising that he would never be all-powerful nor would he be the only world conqueror, and went off with a *shadhu* to find spiritual peace—a quintessentially Indian story as old, it would seem, as Bharat himself.

Rajgir was the centre of the South Asian universe once. The Jain prophet, Sri Mahavira delivered his first sermon here and Ashoka breathed his last here. The cave at Vulture's Peak was Buddha's favourite place, and it is from here that he set out towards his Pari-Nirvana, or death. The First Buddhist Council, where the structures and strictures of the religion were set down, was convened here; it's here that Buddha's arch-nemesis Ajatashatru imprisoned his father and even the Mahabharata's got it, calling it Grhirviraja, where Krishna came to seek revenge for the destruction of Mathura. There's a pair of deep grooves cut into the rock near the entrance of Rajgir, which, the story goes, were created when Krishna descended on the city in his chariot drawn by the steeds of heaven. The grooves run on for about 50 feet and are flanked on one side by a wall bearing shell-shaped inscriptions in some indecipherable language. Some say it's the code to opening the *'Swarna Bhandar'*, the Treasury of Magadha.

There's more. In the Buddhist records that talk about Ajatashatru's treachery, there is mention of a prison in Rajgir where his father, the good king Bimbisara, was tortured and kept. The cell's location was determined by descriptions of the view from inside it and by the remains of thick walls. British archaeologists excavated the site and found, to their surprise— but not to the locals', presumably—a pair of iron shackles and other prison objects. You can still see the clasps today, embedded in the floor. It's hard to know what to believe about Rajgir. All of Indian history seems to be connected to it. Even the Muslims have put in their bid—one of the hot springs here is supposed to have been formed when the Sufi Makhdoom Saheb threw pebbles at a rock face to scare off a tiger. He used to like to spend time here alongside Hindu and Buddhist ascetics.

There are 12 hot springs in Rajgir which, apart from their therapeutic value, have spiritual significance for Hindus and Jains. Eleven of these used to be off-limits to Muslims because of a court order that was issued in 1934 forbidding them from entering the water, lest they pollute it. There was a signboard until 2009 to remind visitors of this rule but I didn't check to see if was still there. Not that it would make much of a difference if it wasn't—it's bad enough that a bigoted law written during a time when dogs and Indians weren't allowed to enter certain colonial establishments was still being applied until as recently as a few years ago, and besides, prejudice rarely needs a law to give it licence. Rajgir is both a real place as well as a place 'a long time ago, far, far away'. It's teeming with tourists, drawn by the cooler climate of the hills, taking rides on tongas and the famous cable car. Many are here for the hot springs, though I suspect not too many are Muslims. Very few are here because of its centrality to India's past.

But Buddhist pilgrims come too and they do possess a sense of Rajgir's history. The city features very prominently in their literature as well as in Jain texts, with both religions claiming King Bimibisara as an adherent. Buddha's teachings confronted the political and religious establishment of the time, but also got caught up in a rivalry with the other great Shramana religion, the teachings of Mahavira. The Shramana traditions are decidedly non-Vedic and are also different from the cultures of the more Shaivite south. They are the products of lands and people beyond Arya Varta who, by about the 6th century BC, were deeply entrenched in the search for meaning, like their counterparts in Greece and China. Great minds were firing off everywhere during the Age of the Thinkers and the world was pregnant with philosophy. In India two great schools arose—the *astika* and the *nastika*, and a period of tumultuous debate followed between the theists and the 'un-theists', creating fertile ground for numerous religions and cults. Not all *nastiks* were the atheists their name suggests they were—many believed in neither negating nor affirming the Vedas' claims to being divinely inspired, but considered it a moot point and simply put it aside. They became more concerned with self-improvement and spiritual attainment for its own sake. They became the Shramanas: the Buddhists, Ajivikas and the Jains.

Both Buddha and Mahavira played vital roles in the history of Magadha and ultimately, of India. Chandragupta was a Jain and his grandson Ashoka a Buddhist and both became emperors before becoming ascetics. Mahavira's severe austerities earned him the name '*Maha Veer*', the Great Rebel, and his true followers have always been similarly determined. Chandragupta starved himself to death after giving up his throne. Buddha's gentler Middle Way was possibly an affront to the Jains, so they competed for influence here in Rajgir, and tried to discredit him. They failed, of course, and Buddhism went on to win not just in Rajgir but all across India. Other religious contestations happened here too: Devadutta, a student and cousin of Gautama, challenged him for the leadership of the fold or *Shango*, and when he failed, split from the Buddha to create his own flock. People have always had very strong positions about how they define their faith, it seems, or perhaps about how they define their influence.

Virtually nothing is left of Rajgir today. All that seems to have survived are walls and outlines of structures that were built in stone. I visit some of these, but miss out on seeing Jarashanda's Akra, the remains of a *kusti* wrestling gym named in honour of the mythical matches fought between Bhima and Jarashanda. Instead, I go to where the first Buddhist Council was convened, and to the hospital where Buddha got his regular check-ups with his personal physician, Jivak, one of the founders of the Ayurvedic tradition as we know it today. But like everything else in Rajgir, there's nearly nothing left of it to help conjure up a sense of the times, so we speed off to Nalanda, about 10 kilometres down the road, to make the most of what's left of the day. The hills disappear almost as quickly as they appeared, and we are back on the flat paddy plains of the Ganges basin. It's an odd sensation—as though the whole place is an encapsulated drop of time, high on those hills in another, almost imaginary, world altogether.

I'm stoked to be going to Nalanda. It's been a place of wonder for me ever since I first read about it as a child. Its university was the oldest in a chain of Buddhist institutions that hung around Bihar and Bengal's neck like a string of pearls, and had three massive libraries, the Ratnasagara, Ratnabodhi and Ratnaranjaka. One of them was nine storeys high and is supposed to have burned for six months when the Turkic invader Bakhtiyar Khilji set fire to it. Nalanda University was an exceptional establishment. Called one of the 'first great universities in recorded history', it formally commenced in the 3rd century, during the reign of the Gupta king Kumaragupta, although some believe it belongs to a much older establishment, which was around during the life of Buddha himself. Its libraries have been compared to the great library in Alexandria, but while the one in Egypt was destroyed slowly over a period of time, the ones at Nalanda were set upon with such viciousness that in an instant, centuries of learning were turned to smoke and dust. Thousands of monks were beheaded or burned alive along with volumes upon volumes of manuscripts. In an instant, an entire civilisation was reduced to intellectual poverty.

But Bakhtiyar Khilji may not have been solely responsible for the destruction of Nalanda's libraries, though he, along with Muslims in general, have had to bear the blame of it for centuries now. A politically inconvenient and lesser-known tradition says Hindus, in fact, set the thing ablaze. Tibetan pilgrim Sharmasvamin, who visited Nalanda less than 30 years after it was destroyed, had this to say about it:

They (Hindus) performed a Yajna, a fire sacrifice, and threw living embers and ashes from the sacrifice into the Buddhist temples. This produced a great conflagration which consumed Ratnabodhi, the nine-storied library of the Nalanda University.

I walk up to the old university where a plaque at the entrance gives us a concise history of Nalanda's legacy. It also has a list of the university's impressive luminaries. It tells me that Nalanda was established during the Gupta age and grew under the patronage of the Palas to become one of the world's leading institutes—one in a set of five—offering subjects like philosophy, ethics, medicine, astronomy, governance, history, logic, grammar, metaphysics and a range of other disciplines found in a classical education. People from around the world, from Japan, Korea, China, Turkey, Greece and Persia came here to learn from some of the greatest minds of the time. The 'string of pearls', as the group of universities were sometimes called, also included Somapura Bihara, today's Paharpur in Bangladesh and Jaggadala Bihara, which has been lost to time (though mounds in North Bengal suggest it stood somewhere near today's ancient city of Gour). In Bihar there is Vikramashila, a stone's throw from the Bengal–Bihar border, and Odantapuri, which was, of course, crushed under the weight of Muslim Bihar Sharif. They were collectively known as the *Maha Biharas*, or great monasteries.

A book called *Buddhist Monks and Monasteries in India* by Sukumar Dutt has the following information about these institutions:

... all of them were under state supervision [and there existed] *a system of co-ordination among them ... it seems from the evidence that the different seats of Buddhist learning that functioned in eastern India under the Pāla were regarded together as forming a network, an inter-linked group of institutions.*

Nalanda was the oldest among them, but on the northwestern frontier, Taxila, many centuries older, illuminated the outer regions of India's cultural and physical domain and also belonged to this network. Pandit Kautilya, the genius in Chandragupta Maurya's cabinet, studied and taught at Taxila before returning to the court at Pataliputra, and the five universities in the east remained academically linked with the one in the west throughout.

In his book, *Universities of Ancient India*, D.G. Apte, of the Faculty of Education and Psychology at the University of Baroda says,

It is stated that at one time there were 10,000 monks staying at Nalanda. Of these, 1,510 were teachers and the remaining 8,500 were students belonging to various levels of attainments and studying

various subjects. It has been pointed out that there were on an average a hundred lectures or discussions every day. On an average the number of students per teacher was seven or eight and it must have been very convenient to give individual attention to students.

Massive brick walls greet you as you enter the complex. Red brick, with horizontal stone beams—a look that immediately reminds me of Bengali Sultanate Mosques. The tiered bases, the decorative engraving, the windows and the door frames are all familiar, but the ones here are much larger. The scale is staggering; it sprawls out in an area of over one square kilometre and the buildings are neatly clustered according to their purpose—educational, residential or religious. Many open courtyards feature; each of the 11 monasteries has an open space in the middle, with stone and marble-columned cloisters. The terracotta decorations, the niches in the walls, the patterns of the trims, the mix of stone and brick, and the designs on the columns, all share stylistic features with both Adina Mosque in Pandua and the citadel entrance at Gour along with numerous other Bengali Muslim structures which were influenced by the Pala school of art. There are massive staircases (which remind me of our affectionately named 'thinking steps' at my University in Australia), and moss-covered groves surrounded by stupas.

Chinese traveller Hiuen Tsang, who spent two years at Nalanda between 637 and 639 AD, wrote this in his journal:

... richly adorned towers, fairy-like turrets appearing like pointed hill-tops, and observatories lost in the mist of morning. The upper rooms towered above the clouds and from their windows one could see the winds and clouds producing ever new forms and from the soaring eaves the sunset splendours and the moonlit glories. All the outside courts in which were the priests' chambers were of four stages. The stages had dragon-projections and coloured eaves, pearl-red pillars, carved and ornamented, richly adorned balustrades while the roofs were covered with tiles that reflected the light in a thousand shades.

The few surviving buildings have extensive drainage systems running all through, along with verandas, open spaces, water tanks and beautiful decorative trims. I try to imagine students and teachers in maroon and saffron robes languidly discussing philosophy by those steps beside the water, while another group assembles to collect plants to use in Ayur Bidda formulas. Here astronomers are discussing the mathematics of trajectories and there, the fundamentals of ethical governance are being debated. It's a beautiful, spacious place, lovingly adorned. There are stone-carved glyphs of superb quality that seem to be a sort of Potochitro-like storytelling along the base of the walls.

Hieun Tsang continues,

... azure pool winds around the monasteries, adorned with the full-blown cups of the blue lotus; the dazzling red flowers of the lovely kanaka hang here and there, and outside groves of mango trees offer the inhabitants their dense and protective shade.

While walking around I hear a man speaking on the phone in Bangla, so I go up to him and say,

'*Koto shundor jinishtake ekdom noshto kore dilo.*' (They ruined such a beautiful thing.)

To which the Kolkata-accented man says, without missing a beat,

'*Ar ki korbe dada? Manusher to bhalota sojjo hoi na.*' (What else can they do, people can't stand good things.)

A Buddhist package-tour of pilgrims arrives on the site and groups of the faithful—in maroon, saffron and white—pour out into the complex to create the impression of a living Buddhist university. They are soon followed by a school tour, with uniformed children who complete the illusion.

Today there are plans to create a new Nalanda International University near the original, and intellectuals like the late Indian President A.P.J. Abdul Kalam, Nobel Laureate Amartya Sen, and celebrated historian Sugata Bose (Netaji's grandnephew) have been involved with the project, with funding being arranged from a number of Buddhist countries including Japan and Singapore. It opened its doors in 2014, and intends to remain true to the legacy of its name. I hope it's just as magnificent.

I stand on the leftover walls of temples and look across at what was once a triumphant testament to human consciousness. It's heart-breaking to imagine how much was lost. Stocked libraries, a chain of Mahaviharas, philosophers, scientists, teachers and political strategists—Eastern Indian Civilisation, wherever its roots are, was at its zenith. It was Indian Buddhism's final flowering and the last days of Mighty Magadha. I try to absorb what's left of its embers, and to imagine living in a world where the Ratnabodhi still exists, a world where at least libraries are spared the ravages of an unrelenting human charge.

When the Muslim civilisation rolled out of Afghanistan and into the Ganges basin, many ancient scenes were replayed. A new Central Asian wave sought to superimpose its worldview upon Central India, borne by a people as convinced of their superior place in the universe as the Vedic Aryans were before them. They were following a migratory pattern that is as old as time, and were driven by motives that were equally primordial. On top of that, they were being pushed eastwards by Mongol waves sweeping west, and soon after the destruction of Nalanda, Hulagu's hordes were setting fire to the Bait al-Hikmah, or House of Wisdom (some 400 years younger, but kindred to the Buddhist institution) and all the libraries in Baghdad. In a span of about 50 years two great lights went out in the world, and centuries of painstaking research went up in smoke.

Many great minds were extinguished in both of these horrendous events but in Central Asia the Mongols became Muslims themselves and tried—though never successfully—to replenish the civilisation they had destroyed. In India, the invaders didn't become Buddhists, nor did they try to restore the civilisation they had conquered, although for a time some people thought they might. According to an 11th-century work called the *Shunya Purana* by Ramai Pandit, Buddhist persecution at the hands of a resurgent Brahmanism in

Bengal is halted by the arrival of the Muslims, who are portrayed as the revival of Dharma:

In Jajapur and Maldah, sixteen hundred families of Vedic Brahmins mustered strong. Being assembled in groups of ten or twelve they killed the Sat-Dharmis (Buddhists) who would not pay the religious fees, but uttering incantations and curses. They uttered mantras from the Vedas and fire came out of their mouths as they did. The followers of Sat Dharma trembled with fear at the sight thereof and prayed to Dharma; for who else could help them in that crisis? The Brahmins began to destroy the creation in the above manner and acts of great violence were perpetrated on the earth. Dharma who resided in Baikuntha was grieved to see this. He came to the world as a Mohammedan. In his head he wore a black cap and in hand he held a cross-bow. He mounted a horse and was called Khoda. Niranjana incarnated himself in Behest (Heaven). All the gods being of one mind wore trousers.

Muslims were expected to weigh in on the side of the Buddhists and though they didn't exactly do that, their arrival shifted the balance of power decisively away from Brahmanism. It also gave Buddhism in Bengal a renewed lease of life, and 200 years after they had conquered the country, Bengali Sultans were sending Buddhist monks to China to propagate their religion. The Sultans were generally tolerant of both Hinduism and Buddhism, culturally at least, and eventually absorbed much of their art and mysticism, grafting chunks of the older culture onto their own one to carry it into the present.

I'm curious about whether Bihari Muslims have a similar relationship with Bihar's extensive history since in Bangladesh we think of Biharis as only Muslims and of the Pakistani kind, often ignoring the fact that Bihar is right next to Bengal and has a cultural legacy not unlike our own. I had hoped that they might see themselves as heirs to that culture as we see ourselves as heirs of Bengal's, but in very general terms, they belong to an Indo-Muslim civilisation that lends credence to the two-nation theory everyone was obsessing over in the 1940s.

Muslim culture in India has a uniformity about it that reaches into regions you might not automatically expect it to. Friends of mine from Hyderabad, for instance, have an Urdu cultural orientation that's strongly present in Bihar as well. Of course, that's not to say that they don't absorb local cultures and languages—they do, particularly in the south—and even though it's not a very stark contrast anymore, they share a cultural context that is evident even among non-Bengali Muslims in Bengal—in their food, customs, mannerisms, and etiquette and in the way they fit themselves into mores that aren't exactly 'indigenous', for lack of a better word.

Many well-to-do Muslim families in urban Bengal were originally Urdu-speaking; the Nawabs and Zamindars anywhere from Jolpaiguri to Joydevpur, were of course usually so, but so were many ordinary citizens in the Mughal cities of Chittagong, Murshidabad and Dhaka. In Kolkata and Malda an Urdu-speaking Muslim gentry still exists, though it is much smaller in number now. These are the Suhrawardys and Mohammed Alis of Bogra. They belong to the Aligarh-Lucknow-UP-centric classical Indo-Muslim culture with strong Mughal leanings. There is also an ethnic component, though this is thoroughly diluted and absurdly racist.

All across India, Muslim culture has developed a similar look and feel, incubated almost in an island that has kept it apart from its surroundings. Folk stories narrated by Muslims are often about Middle Eastern people, are of Middle Eastern events and places, and even include pre-Muslim parables from other now-Muslim lands, like the story of Rustam, which is actually Zoroastrian. They are rarely connected to the legends and stories of the place—and those are often relegated as 'Hindu' stories. Muslim moral and intellectual inspiration is usually sought outside of the Indian reference, and if they are Indian, they are usually Muslims Sufis and saints; never, for instance, Kautilya or Sri Choitonno Mohaprobhu, the enigmatic 15th-century preacher. In 'twilight zone'-like surrealism, Muslim India removes itself from India's history and puts itself in an India that is part-Persia, part-Afghanistan part-Arabia, sometimes even part-Turkey. We share these stories and this sense of common space, to give us a social cohesion that is too many parts fantasy to be taken seriously anymore.

But identity is a complex phenomenon. In India, Muslims were always the minority even when they were rulers and so an isolationist attitude was perhaps somewhat inevitable. What made assimilation even more complicated are the clearly defined ethno-religious lines in Indian society itself so that when Muslims arrived on the Indian scene, immigrant and convert alike, they tended to stay outside, rather than be able to sink into these formations even if they wanted to, and most often they didn't. There were various permutations of caste, region, languages, deities—too complex a configuration for outsiders to be accommodated into, resulting in the creation of a different context altogether. Ethno-religious nationhood is not so bizarre when you consider that in Malaysia today, you qualify as a '*bumiputra*', if you are both Malay and Muslim. By this definition, a Chinese Muslim Malaysian who has lived there for four generations is never an insider. But more oddly, neither is the Malay Christian or Malay Buddhist, whose family has been there since the beginning of time and is probably as *bumiputra* as it gets.

Imagined communities can have high walls.

But in spite of these, assimilation managed to take place in Bengal in a way that it didn't in many other places in India. A little over a hundred years after the Delhi Sultanate took Bengal from the Hindu Sens—during which time numerous attempts at independence were fielded—the 'Sultanatiya-i-Bangala', or the Sultanate of Bengal began, in 1352, as a sovereign Muslim kingdom. One of the first things they did as an independent country was to build the largest mosque in South Asia at the time, the Adina Mosque in West Bengal, using a blended style of Pala, Sena, Islamic and pre-Islamic Persian influences. It was probably intended as a statement of distinction from their co-religionists in Delhi, a decisive split from the homogenous Indian Islamic fold, by endorsing both Islam and multiculturalism or more specifically, Bengali multiculturalism. It was also a ploy for support, of course—by connecting themselves to the Pala and Sena dynasties, they were carving a place for themselves in the natural progression of Bengali politics. This must've worked; it's inconceivable how they would've had the man-power to resist repeated attempts by Delhi to recapture it otherwise. Richard Eaton, in his phenomenal book, *The Rise of Islam and the Bengal Frontier*, writes:

.... Stylistic motifs in the mosque's prayer niches reveal the build-ers' successful adaptation, and even appreciation, of late Pala-Sena art. The imposing monument is also likely to have been a statement directed at Sikandar's more distant Muslim audience, his former overlords in Delhi, now bitter rivals. Having successfully defended his kingdom from Sultan Firuz's armies, Sikandar projected his claims of power and inde-pendence by erecting a monument greater in size than any edifice built by his North Indian rivals....

... these kings yielded so much to Bengali conceptions of form and medium that, as the art historian Percy Brown observes, 'the country, originally possessed by the invaders, now possessed them.'

Then there were the Sufis. The Chishti Sufis first came to Bengal in 1296 and Shayekh Akhi Sirajuddin, the third saint of this order, arrived in 1357 on the instructions of his spiritual guide, Nizamuddin Awliya in Delhi. Sirajuddin left behind a line of spiri-tual successors who strove to bring Islamic mysticism to the Delta, but during the course of it, the Sufis were also changed by the place. They incorporated the practices and philosophies of Bengali yogis into their own spiritual paths, hoping to be able to experi-ence higher, or at least different, states of consciousness and became comfortable with Bengali to a degree that it became their own first language. Similarly, Hindu mysticism, after coming in contact with an Islamic worldview began rearranging itself according to a Sufi appreciation of the Divine as love. Beneath both these layers surged a Buddhist orientation, which dominated Bengali spirituality for over a thousand years. The confluence of these three mystical traditions in Bengal, encouraged by Sri Choitonno, resulted in

Boishnobism, a creed focused on the love of God, manifested, in this case, as Krishna. The Boishnobis would later join forces with the Sufis themselves to spawn the Baul tradition, an integral component of Bangladeshi culture and arguably the most relevant vehicle for spiritual enrichment in my country.

And so, eventually this Bengali milieu—pluralistic, multi-faithed and multi-ethnic in its composition, fused into a nation some time in the 15th century, after all the necessary blood had been shed, of course. But did the Sultanate create a Bengali nation or did a self-aware Bengali nation already exist since at least the time of the Buddhist Charjapadas? Did it run through the Pala and Sena kingdoms of Gaur-Bongo, to the Vangaladesa of the Dravidian Cholas—to be reborn in the Muslim State of Bangala? Or has it been conscious of itself since the mythical eastern kingdoms of Anga, Banga, Kalinga, Pundra and Sumha grew and prospered on the most fertile delta in the world? Whatever the sequence, the result was an identity that was both new and ancient and one that the Sultanate inherited as its own. Eaton writes,

In reality, the emergence of the independent Ilyas Shahi dynasty represented the political expression of a long-present cultural autonomy. In the late thirteenth century, Marco Polo made mention of 'Bangala,' a place he had apparently heard of from his Muslim informants, and which he understood as being a region distinct from India....

... balancing the Persian symbols that pervaded their private audiences, the later sultans observed explicitly Indian rites during their coronations, events that were very public and symbolically charged. Contemporary poetic references to these kings as raja or isvara should not, then, be dismissed as mere hyperbole. They had become Bengali kings.

Parallel to the cultural transformation of the Sultanate, a political transformation also seems to have taken place, allowing the attribute of a modern state, like institutions and budget bi-lines, to emerge. It was enough of an anomaly in the medieval age of empires to prompt Babur the Mughal to remark about it in the *Baburnama,*

> *There is an amazing custom in Bengal: rule is seldom achieved by hereditary succession. Instead, there is a specific royal throne, and each of the amirs, viziers or officer holders has an established place. It is the throne that is of importance for the people of Bengal.... The people of Bengal say, 'we are the legal property of the throne, and we obey anyone who is on it.'... Whoever becomes king, must accumulate a new treasury, which is a source of pride for the people. In addition, the salaries and stipends of all the institutions of the rulers, treasury, military and civilian are absolutely fixed from long ago and cannot be spent anywhere else.*

Bengal remained outside the Mughal sphere until 1576 and only after years of fierce resistance by the remnants of Sultanate authority and the 12 Bhuiyans did it finally succumb to Akbar's expansionist policy to became a *subah,* or province. The fault lines that arose between the identities 'Bengali' and 'Muslim', encouraged by Ashraf, or non-Bengali, Muslims and Hindu puritans alike, following the Mughal conquest and long after the Sultanate's sublime social experiment had been violently arrested, were exploited by All-India Muslim League politicians during Partition, and took us away to Pakistan just as a united, independent Bengal came within kissing distance in 1947. But the Pakistani administration's ethno-linguistic chauvinism, along with its economic exploitation, led to Bengal's final detachment, several centuries in the making, from the monolithic Muslim culture that had attempted to assert itself over all of Muslim India, and we left behind both nations of the ill-fitted two-nation theory, preferring instead to belong to a Bengali legacy that stretches deep into the past, to the Vedas and beyond, and carries with it all the influences that have shaped it since.

But none of this seems to have happened in Bihar.

The day has ended and I say goodbye to my companion Kalam Khan before boarding a bus to Bihar Sharif, to change for Patna.

The ride is pleasant even though there's a horrendous Hindi film on at full volume. It's a local bus, the type that have 'conductors' hanging out the side slap-navigating, and are filled to capacity with whatever can go—crates, chickens, cycles. Across the aisle there is a very attractive Muslim girl speaking loudly on the phone. She's done up in a 'sequence' *kameez* and gaudy nail polish, but has lots of sex appeal.

I change buses at Bihar Sharif and board the one to Patna, another local one, equally shabby, but slightly larger. Hawkers drift in and out periodically as the countryside disappears into a messy semi-urbanisation and we reach Patna just after evening. The shiny buildings we pass on the way tell me that Patna does have a newer part with modern infrastructure, not unlike modern Dhaka. The bus stops to let me out and I hail an autorickshaw; the driver has only one leg, and a friend with him for company. The pair seems prone to bouts of panic and overreact like cartoon characters as they try to overcharge me or suggest seedy hotels that provide female 'companionship'. They finally accept my price and destination, but they don't know where it is, so after going up the wrong way on one-way roads, dodging cops and experiencing more animated exasperation, they manage to find Nesh Inn, where I've decided to stay another night. Say what you want, but after dirty buses, autorickshaws and budget guesthouses with wasps, a decent place with hot water and clean sheets is worth as much as it costs.

Patna
Day 5

My train to Delhi is at 6 pm, which gives me time to finally explore Patna Museum and the remains of Ancient Pataliputra. Patna Museum is housed in a flamboyant building that looks slightly Mughal, slightly Rajput, slightly British and slightly awful. But the structure, opened in 1917, has charm, and looks every bit as fantastical as anything that's called a *jadu ghor* should. I lose myself among the exhibits that take me through the various ages of India:

from the Indus Valley to the glory that was Mauryan Magadha, into the Buddhist Gupta and Pala era, through to the Muslim Sultanate periods, the Mughal era and finally to the British age. Artefacts from each period are displayed haphazardly, and the labelling could be much better—but it's all there. Relics from the Bronze Age, inscriptions from mosques in Arabic, swords, shields, British guns, carved pillars, scrolls, thankas, portraits, and lots of statues. I love the sensuality of their poses and the intricacy of the motifs they are set in. But mostly I love the expressions—a knowing serenity—usually with closed eyes and gentle smiles.

There is an art gallery as well, with both old and contemporary art and a 'Relics of the Buddha' chamber, which is guarded by a set of heavy wooden doors and a metal cage-like structure. I opt not to see the relics; I'm already put off by the level of veneration being lavished onto Siddhartha's physical form, but more than that, after having felt the living presence of the Buddha in Bodh Gaya, I don't want see him as a pile of ashes encased in gold. A massive petrified tree trunk, some 200 million years old, is on display as well, as is the museum's *'pièce de résistance'*: a sandstone statue of an extremely busty woman, identified as the goddess Yakshi—a veritable Indian Venus de Milo. She's from the Mauryan age and may have been made around the same time as her Greek counterpart; they were found nearly 100 years apart—Venus in 1820 and Yakshi in 1918—both by farmers. But she's better endowed than Venus, and not ruggedly masculine like her either. With very wide hips and a bit of a tummy, she smiles as she exudes a sexuality all her Indian own—more playful and less *femme fatale* than her European cousins. But she lacks the realism that is so characteristic of the Greek tradition—a realism that can make stone look like velvet, hard marble look like soft skin and our own sculptures look like theme park mascots.

I wander around the hallways, looking for someone in charge, an historian or a curator who can tell me a little more about Magadha and Pataliputra and am directed to Dr. Arvind Mahajan, Assistant Curator and Lecturer, who is in his office attending to a colleague. He sees me and asks me to have a seat; I am given tea while

Dr. Mahajan finishes his conversation and then, most graciously, apologises for the delay before asking me what my business with him is—it's a deeply appreciated gesture. Dr. Mahajan is a jovial man and he seems quite passionate about his work—when I walked in he was talking about a dig being conducted somewhere nearby and he was perceptibly excited about it. I tell him I'm from Bangladesh and am curious about the history of Magadha as it might hold clues to the origins of the Bengali language, but he shoots me down,

'You won't find the roots of Bangla in Magadha, my friend. It's a completely different history.'

'But I've read that Bangla is one of the languages that came out of Magadha Prakrit. Surely there is some link, considering that we were almost one half of the kingdom that created the language.'

'You are not the heirs of Magadha,' he tells me mockingly. 'Bengal was incorporated into the Magadhan kingdom, yes, but Bengali culture, as you know, is from the Aryan traditions and Magadha was not Aryan.'

His colleague, who has been listening intently, jumps in.

'No, no, he's right, Bengali is not really an Aryan culture. It has borrowed elements from the Aryans, but Eastern Bengal, especially, is outside Arya Barta.'

'*Aree*, Aryan culture diffused beyond the borders of Arya Barta between the Vedic and the Imperial ages,' says Dr. Mahajan. 'You can say that Bengali was influenced by Magadha Prakrit, but it belongs to the settlements on the North Bank of the Ganges, and came into the Delta through the Barind Tract.'

I've never heard any of this before but it sounds right and the realisation that there is so much more to learn excites me quite a bit.

'North Bank cultures differ from South Bank cultures?' I ask, sheepishly, feeling considerably out of my depth.

'The Aryans settled on the north of the Ganges; moving eastward from their homes near the Indus, they occupied the narrow stretch of land between the Himalayas, the Ganges and the Indus. They were Republics—tribal and democratic, like the Liccivites who were often at war with Magadha.'

'They moved south along tributaries like the Ravi and Sutlej, in the west, but in the east, the Non-Aryan kingdoms that held the regions south of the Ganges obstructed them.'

'This includes part of Bengal too.'

'Yes, parts.'

'These south bank tribes were oligarchic. Kingdoms, focused on the central authority of an individual or a dynasty. They had urban complexes and held territories and were very different in orientation from the Republics.'

'Who were these people?'

'Not were, are. They became the dominant form of government in India and eventually absorbed the eastward expansion of the Aryans. This is the Indian history that doesn't get told. The myth of Aryan dominance has been propagated because it was politically convenient for the British, but too much evidence suggests otherwise. I have a theory I'm working on that looks at this.'

I ask him if he believes a cultural superiority led to Magadha's pre-eminence during the Mahajanapada period as well as its success as an empire, but he puts it down to geo-strategic factors instead,

'Pataliputra sits at the junction of four major rivers and so could command the inland trade better than many of the other kingdoms. This is what made Magadha great. It became rich and could build, attract talent, have a strong army and concentrate on developing more sophisticated aspects of life.'

Dr. Mahajan has been very accommodating but I sense he has more pressing matters to attend to so I ask him one final question about the Mauryans and Ashoka.

'Ah Ashoka. India loves the Mauryans because they were glamorous. They had what you might call "Bollywood appeal", and so India uses them as their standard, its glorious beginning. The truth is the Mauryans were not the beginning. They were heirs of the Nanda dynasty; in fact Chandragupta usurped the kingdom.'

'Were they Aryans?'

'They belong to the period after the Kurukshetra war, so there might have been Aryan influences, but no, essentially they were not.'

I leave the museum thinking about the many folds and nuances of Indian history that have been simplistically glossed over by British interpretations and then confidently handed down to us as conclusive fact. I suppose it wasn't intentional; they were, after all, looking for their own 'Aryan' place in the story and could only observe it through their Eurocentric lens. But I'm thoroughly pleased to have been re-schooled by Dr. Mahajan, and head towards the extant remains of Pataliputra to look for more clues.

But there's nothing there—nothing at all, except a few bases that testify to the existence of an 80-pillared audience hall, where the third Buddhist Council is said to have been convened. No recent excavation has been done, and the place is just a large park. There is nothing here that can speak for the metropolis of Pataliputra, once called the 'greatest city on earth' by Megathenes, the Greek ambassador to Chandragupta's court, and writer of the famous *Indica*. It's incredible that there should be absolutely nothing left of it—all the kings, merchants and scholars from places between China and Greece that once graced the courts here, all the power and magnificence it possessed, all the influence it had on the affairs of the ancient world, are gone without any trace at all. Eastern India, once the heart of Indian civilisation, is a completely forgotten story. The centres of power have moved so decisively westward that the great Ashoka survives only as a symbol while his capital, one of the oldest constantly inhabited places in the world, lies unloved and neglected under today's equally unloved Patna. It's almost malicious. So much has happened in India since then that it's probably unrealistic to expect any better, but surely a tad more deference can be shown to a place that is as vital to India's civilisation as Athens is to Europe's.

3

Golden Temples, Iron Walls

Delhi, Amritsar, Harmandir Sahib and the Sikhs, Wagah and entering Pakistan, back to Delhi

Delhi

The train ride to Delhi was easy, but very cold as the air-conditioning was on far too high. I took a second-class sleeper, a very comfortable way to travel, with four bunks per section, curtains, meals and fresh sheets. The Indian Railways is so overworked, that most days you are lucky to find a seat outright and are usually put on a wait-list, which means you come to the platform before the scheduled departure time and feel like you've conquered the world if you see your name neatly typed on a computer-generated list stuck to the side of the carriage. But this time, having confirmed my seat courtesy the foreign quota system, I stroll confidently in while others huddle around the list. I feel positively regal.

The difference in wealth, attitude and confidence between the average Bihari and Delhiite passenger is instantly apparent. There is also an obvious ethnic difference—Delhiwallahs have more angular features and are generally larger. My cabin mates are a young Punjabi couple with a small child, who look and talk like the India that is shining, but the atmosphere feels shallower than the one I'm leaving behind and the tone of the voices more bellicose. I sleep through the entire journey and arrive at Delhi early in the morning and head to Paharganj, an old familiar haunt from backpacking trips in my teens. I have breakfast at a cosy Nepali-run cafe in one of the narrow side streets—baked beans, sausages and an egg—and have a pleasant chat with a sunny lady from New Zealand, who keeps returning to India and to Paharganj for spiritual replenishment. After breakfast I sit outside for a smoke and borrow a light from the owner of the cafe, who lives in Australia for parts of the year, and has a home and a family there. Naturally, we talk about Australia and how lovely it is, but also about how it lacks the sort of energy that makes India, and South Asia, magnetic.

After we've shared our mutual dislike for Indian hegemony, his more than mine because of Nepal's near total dominion status, I head off to the metro station to go to Gurgaon where friends of mine live. The station has a metal detector and a bag-check counter, and as I'm going through the paces, a large Rajasthani guard in a smart khaki outfit says, *'ektu taratari korun dada,'* to my great and pleasant surprise. I ask him how he knew I'm Bengali and he says he's lived in Kolkata for a few years and can, very impressively, recognise us by our bearing.

The Delhi Metro is an impressive piece of work. It has many stops and many lines; the stations are large and chaotic with people darting about, and like any self-respecting metro, it successfully confounds you. Luckily, good maps and assistants are never far. It's still being built, and is the first metro system in the world to be awarded carbon credits for weaning people away from cars and autorickshaws. There's even a separate bogey exclusively for women. On the metro I notice the strong Punjabi element in Delhi and how Indians from the North East, with their East Asian faces and more reticent demeanour, feel slightly intimidated by the robust and jovial Indo-Aryans that dominate their shared capital city. Alongside the tree-lined lanes and the colonial architecture of Connaught place and India's Parliament House, winding its way past the grandeur of the Mughal imperial capital, speeding by the remains of the old Sultanate and possibly even the Pandava city of Indraprastha, New Delhi is starting to look every bit the centre of the emergent new powerhouse that is India. 'New', of course, is a relative term. The inimitable Shashi Tharoor, begins his *The Great Indian Novel* by saying,

I tell them they have no knowledge of history and even less of their own heritage. I tell them that if they would only read ... they would realise that India is not an underdeveloped country but a highly developed one in the advanced stages of decay.

He goes on,

They laugh at me pityingly ... and I tell them that, in fact everything about India is overdeveloped, particularly the social structure, the bureaucracy, the political process....

India's Commerce Minister Anand Sharma added to this during a Davos Summit, when asked what he thought about the 'new' positions of China and India in the global economy. He quite poignantly stated that for most of recorded history India and China had commanded a lion's share of the world GDP and so there was really nothing new about it, but simply a 'restoration of the natural order of things'.

Smug as it might be, it's also spot on.

Delhi has been silent witness to many layers of India's past: Indus Valley settlements have been found near the area, and it is said that nine (or eight, depending on how you classify them) capital cities have been built here, most in quick succession. But a telling 1,000-year gap between the first and the second cities speaks of Pataliputra's supremacy during this time. Delhi oozes history and it's one of my favourite places in the world. On an earlier trip I went to the now ruined Tughlaqabad—the fifth Delhi—to pay a visit to the Tughlaq Sultans, Sultanate Bengal's old adversaries. It was built by Ghiyasuddin Tughlaq, who, in the process, invoked the ire of Nizamuddin Auliya, the Chishti saint who then cursed the city, leading to its ruin. It stood for just six years and the dynasty was eventually destroyed by Timur the Mongol, who invaded and sacked Delhi in 1398, killing over 100,000 people. Ghiyas's mausoleum is still there at Tughlaqabad, a single-domed square tomb where both he and his son are buried, along with the enormous stonewalls that surrounded the city—mute testimony to the power they once commanded.

If you take the yellow line on the metro to HUDA City Centre in Gurgaon, you will cross swathes of empty scrubland, but also country clubs, huge mansions, acres of tended gardens, burgeoning satellite towns that look similar to parts of Malaysia or the UAE. I am going to Gurgaon to stay with friends I went to university with in Australia, Faiz and Disha, who moved back to Delhi a few years ago and live in a new purpose-built suburb, in a large three-storeyed house with a rooftop jacuzzi. They pay just 25,000 Indian Rupees a month for it, which is less than you would pay for a 2,000-square-foot flat in Dhaka. Faiz also tells me that the houses I saw along the way—bigger than most places in Dhaka—are just upper-middle class houses and that the rich live on properties several times as large. It's a completely different ballgame.

But there are two modern Indias—one that is racing ahead into the future, driving Indian-assembled BMWs and the other that is still wrestling with conditions inherited from its cataclysmic colonial past. There's a severe imbalance in the way this new progress is being enjoyed—many, if not most cities, like Patna and Guwahati, are worse off than Dhaka, and Indian slums are famously unbearable. There are still power shortages, water shortages, poor sanitation, insufficient job opportunities, corrupt government and state-capturing powerful elites all across the country. But there is change, especially among the middle classes, that is bringing India up to speed with the developed world in a way that is less pronounced in many other parts of the region.

Young Indians are switched on, conscientious and active. The brimming and educated Indian middle class ensures a constant supply of commentary in print, on television, online and—to the delight of anglophiles like myself—in good English. Important and often controversial topics ranging from politics and governance to religion and gay rights are discussed on networks across the country. These provide a crucial alternative to an all-too-worrying obsession with film stars, skin whitening products, cricket players and scandals—epic Indian myth and drama re-cast for today's less-than-epic world. Good, well-designed newspapers and news channels like NDTV keep sensitive issues in the public domain and debates rage on, on air, in all the national languages of India, with a sensationalism and hype that's as Indian as turmeric.

India has other things going for it as well. It has a competitive and meritocratic bureaucracy; there are civil society actors, promoters of civic sense, human rights defenders, environmental activists, watchdogs, gatekeepers, checks, balances and all sorts of enthusiastic efforts to inject ideals into a world that attempts to avoid having any every chance it gets. This, of course, happens everywhere in South Asia; our social consciences sit in stark contrast to the social injustices that plague our region, and remain vigilant even when they are somewhat impotent. And let's also not forget that the largest exercise of democratic principles in human history took place in India's last general elections.

My friend Faiz is determined to play his part in this new Indian story and when I leave Delhi for Amritsar, he goes to attend a BJP Eid Milan, the right-wing Hindu party's nascent attempt at cultivating a Muslim wing, as oxymoronic as that might sound. Faiz belongs to a political landowning family from Muslim UP, and also descends from a number of Sufi pirs. His family has a *kursi*, which literally means 'throne', but in a Sufi context means something between a pulpit and a station. Faiz's uncle currently occupies the *kursi*, and there are good reasons to believe that it will fall to Faiz to succeed him, though he dreads the thought and intends to discontinue the tradition if he's ever in a position to do so. He's also got political ambitions, and so he should, as his thirst for leadership is almost instinctive.

Faiz married his university sweetheart, Disha Bole, a Gujarati Hindu girl with Rajput origins, and their inter-faith marriage was not without storms. Issues were made about her name, which she wouldn't, and indeed shouldn't, change, and Faiz agreed, defending her the way any man should defend his wife and her principles. She became Muslim, causing upsets within her own Hindu community as well, but they stuck it out, and now live together in Delhi, at the heart of one of the most ethnically, linguistically and religiously diverse countries on earth. Faiz is trying to become useful to movers and shakers in Delhi and makes it clear that his heart is all-Indian. His disdain for narrow Muslim interpretations of identity as well as his abhorrence for Islamism is well known and he categorically refuses to be classified as a Muslim instead of as an Indian. He mingles in political circles trying to find his niche, and attends, among other things, BJP Eid Milans. But he's disappointed by what he finds there.

'Dude, what a bunch of clowns, these "Muslim" groups are, fussing about protocol and falling over themselves to appear important. Not the slightest bit of earnestness anywhere in the room. No plan or political strategy in sight.'

He becomes indignant,

'They thought all I was there for was to be a functionary or a volunteer or something … just there to usher people in or heap biryani onto their plates.'

I interject, tying to be fair to the clowns who have clearly provided Faiz with no laughs at all.

'Well it was a Milan, so I suppose it was mostly about entertaining, no?'

'I had a number of side conversations with other members there and no one had a shred of political consciousness. They were just going on about the guests, about this person, or that person, who they were, what they do, etc., like a bunch of lackeys. There were a few foreign embassy people there too and when I started speaking to one of them these lackeys hovered around suspiciously, wondering who I am and why this *ferang* should give me any attention. Meanwhile we were just talking about football!'

Faiz goes on about all the pseudo-pomp and the sycophantic behaviour, about how he finally, against his preferred approach, had to drop names to be taken seriously and I begin to visualise these characters as incarnations of Bangladeshi politicians. I can see their faces—their all too familiar faces on Bangladeshi television ... why yes, it's the same bunch of clowns.

'This is not the leadership the Muslims here need. We need people who will bring us into the mainstream of Indian politics. Not just Muslim politics, but Indian politics. I'm an Indian; I belong to this entire nation and this entire nation belongs to me. Our community needs to come out of this rut it is in—relegated to low paying jobs, being shat on by other communities. But the leadership is so shabby and self-centred that all they can manage are some concessions—scraps off the table. Not that they would know what to do with even those, if they ever got anything bigger.'

Faiz gets excited, his speech quickens as he begins to sound like a man with a mission. As I listen to him I can hear the political voice of Muslim India—the voice of men like Syed Ameer Ali, Maulana Abul Kalam Azad, Sher-e-Bangla Fazlul Haq, Hussain Suhrawardy, Khan Abdul Ghaffar Khan and even Muhammad Ali Jinnah, before it all tragically disintegrated into myopic religious nationalism in 1947. These men were Indian nationalists once, but somewhere between serving their nation and protecting their kind, they managed to split the whole thing into two. Of course the events leading up to Partition are much more complicated than that, but Partition has everything to do with why that brazenly confident voice has been systematically 'shushed' to a whisper, if not a whimper, in an India that, in spite of itself, remains uneasy with both its own Muslims and with its Muslim neighbours. Faiz, for one, would like to hear it clear its throat and return to form. I'm sure I would too, but perhaps not the way the people at the Eid Milan are envisaging it.

'"When we are back in power, then you will see," they kept saying, these puffed up parasites, with a nostalgia that would make you think they are Akbar himself. When we are in power. Who is "we", and what will they do with this elusive power they can't seem to find?'

The 'we' and the 'us' and the 'them' that led to the colossal cock-up that was 1947, has its roots, partly, in the British census of 1871, which classified people according to their religious orientation. 'Majorities' and 'minorities' emerged following this, along with an assumed understanding of distribution and concentration patterns. An 18th-century English obsession with the imperfect science of statistical analysis meant that the one-dimensional findings of the census affected policy decisions in a significant way—decisions that either antagonised Hindus or Muslims, or both.

For example, shaken by the 1857 Anglo-Indian war (incidentally, the greatest struggle against European imperialism anywhere in the world) and the second Anglo-Afghan war, the British, in the form of Lord Curzon, became eager to appease Muslims and economically develop Muslim majority areas, for fear of an attack by disadvantaged and marginalised Muslims. This thinking directly informed the first partitioning of Bengal in 1905 and the establishment of Aligarh Muslim University, running contrary to previously Hindu-centric polices that were designed to contain an imperial Muslim presence which had resulted in—surprise, surprise—disadvantaged and marginalised Muslims. Suddenly the Muslims were the loyalists, led by anglophiles like Sir Syed Ahmed Khan, and the Hindus, previously patronised by the British establishment, made up the bulk of the revolutionaries.

The census also made Hindus nervous for political reasons. They had to contend with the fact that there were certain areas where Muslims had an electoral upper hand, causing groups like the Arya

Samaj, for example, to actively encourage 'reconversions' and 'allow' Muslims to return to the Hindu fold in an attempt to nullify demographic discrepancies. This, of course, accelerated Muslim fears of being overwhelmed in a Hindu-majority India after the British left. Another all-India census in 1931 further cemented the idea that India was a country divided by religions and languages, with uncomfortable concentrations of majorities and minorities. The idea of cohesion was ruled out as impossible because it was presumed, or rather proposed, that a resurgent, majoritarian Vedism wouldn't rest until it held the fort and succeeded in alienating others, especially Muslims, and relegated them to 'outsider' status.

These questions of culpability have never properly been answered in the partitioning of British-occupied India. It was never 'British India', of course, no matter what the old schoolbooks say or what those splashes of pink on old maps suggest—we never stopped trying to shrug them off our backs throughout the 190 years that they were busy leeching off us and we certainly didn't hand our freedom over to them with a bow and a smile. Any attempt to pass off British imperialism in India as welcomed benevolence is nothing but self-serving drivel of the most laughable kind. Incidental and accidental benefits like the railway, this language I'm writing in and parliamentary democracy, while useful indeed, were not delivered munificently as many apologists might have us believe. Quite the opposite, they were done to service the Empire's needs. English education in India, for example, was initiated by a certain Lord Tomas Babington Macaulay, a babbling fool who was flagrantly contemptuous about Indian culture and said in 1835,

All the historical information which has been collected from all the books written in Sanskrit language is less valuable than what may be found in the most paltry abridgements used at preparatory schools in England.

A more fitting testament to the deficiencies of those same preparatory schools where Lord Macaulay was so insufficiently educated

60

is hard to find. That a man so ignorant should go on to be regarded as an authoritative historian and then also become a government minister is further proof of the British Empire's glaring intellectual inadequacies. Macaulay goes on to assert,

> *It is impossible for us, with our limited means, to attempt to educate the body of the people. We must at present do our best to form a class who may be interpreters between us and the millions whom we govern, a class of persons Indian in blood and colour, but English in tastes, in opinions, in morals and in intellect.*

And that's how mutts like me were created.

On the question of political traditions, Amartya Sen comes in to strip the British of their haughty assumption that they bequeathed democracy to India although it's true that they may have catalysed the modern version of it. In his brilliant book *The Argumentative Indian*, Dr. Sen points out,

> *The historical roots of democracy in India are well worth considering if only because the connection with public argument is often missed through the temptation to attribute the Indian commitment to democracy simply to the impact of British influence.... In the history of public reasoning in India, considerable credit must be given to the early Indian Buddhists, who had a great commitment to discussion as means of social progress. That commitment produced, among other results, some of the earliest open general meetings in the world. The so-called 'Buddhist councils', which aimed at settling disputes between different points of view drew delegates from different places and from different schools of thought.*

In fact, some of the earliest instances of democracy have been found in the Mahajanapadas of ancient India, with one of them, Vaishali, being regarded by some as the world's first republic. Their democratic Sangha, Gana and Panchayat systems are still being used in Indian villages. Historians of Alexander the Great also commented on this when they encountered territories in Pakistan and Afghanistan, whose 'form of government was democratic and not regal'—possibly a reference to the Jirga system still in use among the Pashtuns. And of course more recently, the first Pala ruler of Bengal came to power through a democratic process in the 8th century AD, as documented by the Tibetan historian, Taranath.

But fun as it might be to dress the British down, none of this excuses our own actions in the lead-up to Partition, nor does it justify the inexplicable communal tensions that erupted into utter madness. The truth of it is, while the British may have been anything but honest brokers, the hate and prejudice that exploded bloodily onto the scene in 1947 was wholly an Indian phenomenon, albeit precipitated by the wounds of subjugation borne by both Hindus and Muslims during nearly two centuries of British domination.

The Indian Republic, and indeed the popular narrative, puts the blame squarely at our, that is, the Indian Muslim's feet. We are the traitors, the separatists, the ones who rent the sacred tapestry of India asunder with our narrow, selfish ambitions. We, the outsiders, people of a different legacy, not Indian really but at best 'Indianised', shattered the great Indian dream and abused *mataram's* hospitality. It's a convenient narrative, but one without much substance, because, while it's true that the two communities had different religions and different versions of a shared Indian culture, there was no question of creating different countries until threats and fears, both real and perceived, developed a political currency that became too strong to ignore. And perhaps Muslims overreacted to this a great deal, in fact they most certainly did, but the fact that there was something there to overreact to is the part that always gets left out.

Days 7–8

I did little else in Delhi except smoke up and hang around Paharganj reading an English version of the Rig Veda picked up in Patna. I also had stimulating conversations with Faiz and Disha about social and political issues, and about how to improve our respective countries. It made me realise how different our situations are. Their ministers resign when faced with public pressure; their media is strong and prolific; they have an impartial judiciary, a meritocratic bureaucracy; they've never lived under martial law; and while Disha and Faiz listened to my stories about the Bangladeshi scene with dread, I felt that they had no real way of relating to it—proof of how far governance has come in their country. India feels like a functional place, yes with many fractures along caste, class, race, language and communal lines, yet one that is trying to pull together, patiently, towards a common future. I observed with envy the positivity with which Indians engage with their country and their city. I watched people give up their seats for elders on the metro, watched young Indians look and sound like their counterparts in Malaysia or Australia, noticed the wide streets and developed suburbs, the orderly traffic and the respect for rules. Truly, India looks poised for take-off.

After lounging around for the better part of two days I hop onto a night bus bound for Amritsar. It's the cheap kind, a sleeper and a really bad, bad choice. For one, it's filthy and the moment I get into my bunk, which is above the seats and close to the roof, I realise that there is very little chance of not falling out of it and onto the hard steel floor. If that wasn't enough fun, there are protruding panels of rusty metal around the frame, and the whole thing smells like sweat. You get what you pay for.

As the bus fills up I get the strange sensation that I might have stepped into a Punjabi satire, replete with Bhangra music (the British kind, exported back to its roots, remixed) playing out of mobile phones, and words like *o pain de* and *e puttar o*, being shouted out in strained, nasal tones by big, turbaned men sharing bread with each other. I expect someone to break out into a shoulder shiver and a *chak de!* any moment now. Punjabis are very Punjabi as I'm discovering and can become stereotypical versions of themselves in the blink of an eye. I'm sure they think Bengalis are a peculiar bunch too. I certainly do. At any rate, they seem to have great humour about them and hectic as they are, their high spirits are lots of fun. Maybe the straight faces they pull when they aren't being their most exaggerated selves are just survival tools.

A hawker comes in to sell something, some passengers engage him, it all sounds cordial enough but then he gets off, and starts shouting *'Madar chod, behn ke laure!'* from outside while kicking and slapping at the bus.

Amritsar

I arrive in Amritsar tired and cranky. The bus ride was from hell. The driver sped and swerved the whole night through, as I held on for dear life. I'm from Dhaka and am used to rough driving, but this was on another level altogether. I got no sleep at all, expecting to either fall out of the bunk or for the bus to crash into something and deliver me up a very bloody ending. Death on the Grand Trunk Road or India's NH-1, exotic as it might sound, isn't something I'm really looking forward to at the moment. We enter Amritsar at 6 am, and they let me out near the central roundabout, beside the Mughalesque Lahori Gate. A *rickshawallah* spots the tourist and hovers around, but I'm too tired to protest or look for my own accommodation, so I get on and tell him to take me to the place that gives him a commission for bringing people from the terminal.

The receptionist at the motel is a pink-faced, rather rude Hindu Kashmiri (I asked him), who seems mistrustful and demands that I pay in full up front. I get the feeling he might be a bit uncomfortable serving my darker skinned Muslim self.

'Is this your idea of customer service, brother? This is my introduction to Amritsar?'

'Sorry, there are many frauds who try to stay without paying, so I'm a little suspicious and was just making sure that you are a serious customer. Please excuse me. It's also early morning, and I've been here all night.'

So it's not the colour of my skin or my religion after all. It's my own prejudice that has gotten the better of me this morning.

I rest for an hour and around 8 am, set off towards the Golden Temple. I have just half a day to explore the Temple and make it to Wagah by dusk to watch the flag lowering ceremony. Tomorrow morning I'm on a train back to Delhi to catch a flight to Lahore in the evening, since the Pakistani High Commission wouldn't give me a land route entry, in which case I could've casually strolled into Pakistan and taken a taxi there. All this rush is in anticipation of a train from Quetta in Pakistan, to Zahedan in Iran, which only runs twice a month, and if I miss the one on 15 September, I won't have enough days on my Pakistani visa (they only gave me 20) to make it to the next one on 1 October. So it's all a bit of a carefully choreographed blitz through India and Pakistan.

I walk through an Amritsar that's just waking up. Some shops are still closed and rickshaw vans are delivering stock to the ones that are open. A low hanging dust cloud is slowly settling around the edges of the streets, having been violently roused by the street sweeper's *jharu*. Sunlight passes through it, and the suspended particles take on a hallowed look far above their station as humble fragments of dirt. The city has a cosy feel to it, numerous old buildings—Mughal, Sikh and British—enjoy a slow demise along the narrow roads, their faces blackened by the carbon discharge of motor vehicles. They are bound and gagged by the crisscrossing of telephone and cable TV wires and banners advertising everything from political candidates to English medium schools—a cityscape like many old towns across South Asia.

I stop for breakfast at a mandir *langar khana*. These are free kitchens run by temples for the benefit of pilgrims, passers-by and poor people, which get the occasional charlatan like myself stepping in and abusing their hospitality. The people handing out the meal tickets seem a bit short tempered, and I feel self-conscious, as though there are specific rituals or a certain type of behaviour that I'm supposed to be displaying to deserve a smile. Or maybe they can spot the freeloader. Amritsar is a religious city. It's plain to see from the number of stalls selling religious paraphernalia—posters, amulets, idols, rosaries and all sorts of other little trinkets.

I walk past them, and also past a dead pigeon, which disturbs me considerably. Pigeons frequent religious sites, God knows why, but they do, and this is the first time I've seen a dead one at a place like this. I think it's a sign, of course, but it probably isn't and I continue walking.

The most noticeably visual feature in Amritsar is of course the turbans. Almost everyone is wearing one, and they are beautiful for the colour they add to the scenery. Various loud and bright hues scream shamelessly off the heads of otherwise stern look-ing individuals. They wear them with a pride that makes them look quite dignified though, which, if I didn't see it, I would never believe could be pulled off in colours like electric blue, baby pink, neon yellow or scarlet red. The women look lovely too, in *shalwar-kameezes* of various pastel tones like mauve, peach and light blue, with thin chiffon *oornas*. Punjabis have beautiful faces, men and women alike, and they carry themselves with a sort of conceit that is sometimes appealing but often also arrogant. I also see, as I have in Bihar and Delhi, plenty of women driving motorbikes and scooters. Muslim ones too, with their faces wrapped except for their eyes that are covered by sunglasses. Or maybe they aren't Muslims, just women trying to protect their faces from the dust and the fumes. Others just wear the sunglasses. Not enough of them wear helmets.

I duck into a tea stall before entering the Temple area to scribble a few thoughts in my journal, and smoke a cigarette away from the disapproving glare of Sikh puritans who find tobacco anathema, as well everyone should. A very mystical looking man comes and sits next to me and seems to enjoy watching me write since he's staring intensely at the pen in my hand. It's odd, but not odd enough to make me want to move away from him. I offer him tea; he politely declines and keeps staring, amusedly, at the words on my page. He has a gentleness about him, and a kind smile. I finish my cigarette, we shake hands warmly, and I walk off, but before I reach the Temple, I come across the site of the Jallianwala Bagh massacre, an infamous event that changed the course of Indian history.

The horrendous violence that was wrought upon unarmed villagers on 13 April 1919, assembled at the Bagh mainly for Baishakhi and quite unaware of the curfew in place, isn't the actual crime though. The killing and injuring of hundreds, even thousands of men, women and children; the firing without warning straight into the crowd and then into the thickest part of it when it broke up and people ran in a complete panic towards absent exits, to be crushed underfoot or against walls; the continuous shooting until they ran out of ammunition, executing people wholesale and then leaving them there in piles of bodies, to die, if they weren't dead already, of their injuries; the utter and deliberate disregard for human life and for humanity itself—these aren't the real crimes. The real horror is in the way that this act of terrorism, by Winston Churchill's own admission, was applauded by large sections of British society, both in India and in the UK. In the clubs across India, including our own Dhaka and Chittagong Clubs, and in the homes, barracks, and offices, prim, polite Englishmen and Englishwomen were sipping drinks served by their 'native servants' and celebrating the temporarily ranked Brigadier-General Dyer's firmhandedness in dealing with these local upstarts, who had had the cheek to confront British authority or worse, challenge the white man's unquestionable right to bear his 'burden'. I can only imagine the conversations.

'I say, jolly good show by that Dyer chap, wouldn't you say? Taught that filthy lot a good and proper lesson.'

'Oh, yes! Charming fellow too, and very handsome, I had the pleasure of meeting him at the Gymkhana in Lahore, you know.'

'I hear he's the man to get the job done ... put down this ab-suuuurd talk of "home-rule" and send the little bastards back to where they belong. I mean, honestly, Indians, running this place? What a laugh. Hey Salim, you there *chokra*, come here! You people think you can run things? You ... servants? No, of course you can't. Now take your black, ugly face away, and bring me another of the same. *Joldi*! All you can run is the bar, and you don't even do that very well. Go!'

'Yes, but I hear they've called him into an inquiry, Harry. Something about excessive force. He might even be relieved of command ....'

'Rubbish! Stuff and nonsense! They probably want to give him a medal, but have to be discreet about it, what with all the ruffled feathers among the likes of Gandhi and Tagore, you know, those pretentious native "gentlemen" types—as if there could ever be such a thing! No, no, Dyer is a hero. He's put the very fear of Christ into these godless, unfortunate creatures.'

'Hear, hear. If they thought they could shake our Empire with their Hindoo hocus-pocus and their fakirs, I'm sure they're thinking again, now that they've had a taste of the old Lee-Enfield. Eh, eh?'

We certainly were thinking again. Thinking again why 43,000 Indians died fighting for Britain in the First World War, why Indian politicians remained loyal to the UK, assuaging fears that we would use this opportunity to revolt while they were committed militarily in Europe. We were also thinking again about why nearly 1.25 million Indian soldiers and labourers served the war effort, and why our autonomous princes sent food, money, and ammunition of their own accord, to help Britain in her time of need. But mostly we were thinking again about why we ever expected the British to honour their agreement and give Indians more legislative liberty once the war was over.

But what happened here, in Amritsar, was something that no one quite expected. Not even the British. In a 1920 speech to the House of Commons, Winston Churchill, then Secretary of State for War showed uncharacteristic sympathy for Indians and answered questions about whether it would be 'un-English' to punish Dyer for simply doing his part to protect the Empire. Instead of suggesting it would be, Churchill went on to assert,

It is an extraordinary event, a monstrous event, an event which stands in singular and sinister isolation.

.... An unarmed crowd stands in a totally different position from an armed crowd. At Amritsar the crowd was neither armed nor attacking.

I carefully said that when I used the word 'armed' I meant armed with lethal weapons, or with firearms. There is no dispute between us on that point. 'I was confronted,' says General Dyer, 'by a revolutionary army.' What is the chief characteristic of an army? Surely it is that it is armed. This crowd was unarmed. These are simple tests, which it is not too much to expect officers in these difficult situations to apply.

.... There is surely one general prohibition which we can make. I mean a prohibition against what is called 'frightfulness.' What I mean by frightfulness is the inflicting of great slaughter or massacre upon a particular crowd of people, with the intention of terrorising not merely the rest of the crowd, but the whole district or the whole country.

.... Such ideas are absolutely foreign to the British way of doing things.

.... The British way of doing things, as my right hon. Friend the Secretary of State for India, who feels intensely upon this subject, has pointed out, has always meant and implied close and effectual co-operation with the people of the country. In every part of the British Empire that has been our aim, and in no part have we arrived at such success as in India, whose princes spent their treasure in our cause, whose brave soldiers fought side by side with our own men, whose intelligent and gifted people are co-operating at the present moment with us in every sphere of government and of industry.

Dyer was relieved of command and forced to retire, but he was never punished and enjoyed the support of many higher officials, including the Army Council and the Deputy-Governor of Punjab, Michael O' Dwyer, who formally congratulated him. In fact, nothing at all might have happened to him had it not been for Lord William Hunter, who relied on his conscience and not on popular sentiment to deliver his judgement, sentiment that was echoed in the House of Lords, and even, sadly, by Rudyard Kipling who started a fund for General Dyer to compensate him for his loss of pension.

Churchill may have thought the 'British way' was infallibly honourable—in the supercilious, super-silliness of the age I suppose he had to, a bit like the Americans have to today. But in reality, the British Empire in India was a particularly ignoble endeavour, and there was nothing at all isolated about that sinister, monstrous event on 13 April. In fact just two days later another gathering at Gujaranwala, protesting the massacre at Amritsar, was set upon by the British, this time with aeroplanes and machine guns, killing 12 more people, including children.

Indians were routinely subjected to all manner of violence, from being publicly flogged, to being tied to the mouths of cannons and blown to bits. Summary executions were common, so was torture and exile. And of course apart from the physical violence, there was psychological and economic violence as well. In 1943, up to 5 million Bengalis died slowly of starvation, because Churchill didn't think it worth his while to send food to them. In fact, the frequency and intensity of famines during British rule in India was consistently higher on both counts than it had ever been in years prior, or has been since. So callous was Britain's attitude towards the loss of life in India that when Florence Nightingale put out a series of publications during the late 1800s with the hope of educating the British public about the human cost of their luxuriant Empire, it had little effect.

Before the British arrived, famines occurred mostly in drier parts around Delhi and Sindh, not in fertile and agriculturally endowed areas like Bengal or South India. Yet in British times these are exactly where they happened, resulting in extermination on a scale that makes the Nazis look like sloppy amateurs. A staggering number of people were allowed to die. Each famine killed millions—over 7 million in the Great Famine of 1876–78, and 10 years before that, in 1866, over 4 million, including a third of the population of Orissa at the time. Various theories exist about why this was the case, but the general consensus includes the following: land usage for industrial crops like indigo, jute and cotton at the expense of food grain and livestock, the commoditisation of grain, export agriculture for foreign revenue with little thought about domestic subsistence, inadequate transportation, heavy taxation, ridiculously low wages, a redirection of resources towards military spending and British upkeep, a conspicuous absence of any accountability or system of representation for Indians and, more tellingly, an absolute lack of care for Indian life.

Even when decent men like writer William Digby who witnessed the tragedy of 1876 first-hand, insisted that there be a policy change or some sort of famine relief, he was defeated by the Viceroy's pompous assumption that it would only make the Indian workers lazy—'demoralisation', I think is what he called it. Around the same time that Indians were experiencing an agonising and skeletal demise, this celebrated and Right Honourable Earl of a diplomat held a banquet for almost 60,000 guests, while exporting tons of rice and grain to the UK and the USA as part of a policy of non-interference with free trade—England's lifeblood, siphoned off from the varicose veins of an atrophying India.

No one sums it up better than American scholar Mike Davis, who calls the famines 'late Victorian Holocausts', and says,

Millions died, not outside the 'modern world system', but in the very process of being forcibly incorporated into its economic and political structures. They died in the golden age of Liberal Capitalism; indeed, many were murdered ... by the theological application of the sacred principles of Smith, Bentham and Mill.

Far from being a well-ordered example of British administrative prowess, and without much of a 'civilising mission' anywhere in sight, the Raj was, in fact, a shabby and mismanaged disgrace, excelling only at dispassionate plunder cleverly disguised as government. Bengal, for instance, with its wealth and abundance, and whose people had never before experienced such acute want, was robbed to the point of being beggared, copping it badly on both ends—at the start of British occupation and at the finish. In 1770, only 13 years after the British orchestrated a regime change in Murshidabad, the richest province of the Mughal realm experienced a famine so severe that a third of the population, possibly 10 million people, perished in only 10 months. It's been called the worst genocide in history by some because when the deaths began, the East India Company increased the land tax to 60 per cent so that they could compensate themselves for the loss of revenue fewer peasants, producing fewer crops, would result in. In other words, Bengali deaths were seen as a liability and the ones who didn't die were required to pay double the tax so that the British treasury could continue to swell. And swell it did; the East India Company made more money in 1771, at the height of the famine, than it did in 1768, when things were relatively normal. And of course, no relief was provided for the victims; none was even thought of.

Then, as a parting gift, just four years before they left India for good, while Hitler was putting into place his 'final solution' for the Jews, Churchill cut off supplies of rice and other staples to Bengal to deprive the Japanese army of sustenance, should they break through the Eastern gate after the fall of Myanmar. This 'scorched earth' policy was among other disastrous strategies concocted by the British government to protect all sorts of priorities in India, none of which were the lives of Indians, who were instead slaughtered by the millions at the altar of administrative oversight.

But rather than show any sort of remorse over this presumably unintended consequence, Churchill jeered at the starving people dying all across Bengal saying,

I hate Indians. They are a beastly people with a beastly religion. The famine was their own fault for breeding like rabbits.

Of course it wasn't, as confirmed by the findings of Britain's own Inquiry Commission, which concluded that inaction and mismanagement of an entirely preventable sort were the real reasons. In fact in 1943 there wasn't even a particularly severe crop failure. Churchill didn't stop there, and when British officials in India begged him to do something, he flat out refused and diverted the medical supplies and food that had been allocated for the victims of the famine to soldiers in Europe. An online reader on social and economic history at the Open University has compiled various reports and eye witness accounts to present a picture of the famine, which includes this very poignant observation by an unnamed source:

I still remember as a young boy seeing those starving men and women and children in the streets. They lay there and they died. As easy and simple and weird as that. They died.

And then this most incredible one,

Three million Bengalis died all over the state. Many on Calcutta's streets. Not a single loaf of bread was reported stolen from the bakeries and confectioner's shops that ... and the new market. And I wonder then what was this [sic].

Since the British left, there hasn't been another famine of such unconscionable proportions anywhere in Bangladesh, India or Pakistan. Ever. If that really isn't the last word on all that I don't know what is.

The 1878 famine had, as one might expect, a profound and permanent impact on Indian affairs. In fact, it can be said to have led to the end of the Raj. British civil servants in India like William Wedderburn and A.O. Hume, distraught by how the government in India regarded Indians as little more than disposable labour— to be kept alive only as long as every ounce of their strength could be harnessed—and Indian's first political leader, the formidable Bal Gangadhar Tilak as well as Gopal Krishna Gokhale joined forces to form the Indian National Congress, less than a decade later in 1885. The rest, as they say, is history.

In 1919, Amritsar proved to be the very tipping point in the struggle for freedom. Kobiguru Robindronath returned his knighthood, the slogans gradually changed from 'Home Rule' to 'Quit India', and Gandhiji was finally incensed enough to see the futility of believing there could ever be a relationship of two adults between the UK and India. The cord was cut. Dominion status would no longer do and only full independence was acceptable. Britain would have to be forced to stand entirely on its own feet; it would have to be weaned completely off the fulsome Indian teat on which it had grown so very fat.

I walk around the premises at Jalianawala Bagh. It's a museum now, with an eternal flame, and a minar-like monument at the spot where the shooting was most heavily concentrated. The surrounding buildings are pock-marked, and places where the soldiers set their guns and took aim, are signposted. The well that people jumped in to avoid being shot, an enormous cavern of a thing, is still there, now housed in a shed and made safe for visitors. The place is fittingly somber, and the entire atrocity can be followed step by step by using the signs and markers. It's quite an upsetting thing to experience, and the indignation rises through my body to sit heavily on my chest. Some European travellers stroll about the grounds; I glare at them sideways hoping they'll hang their heads in shame for the contempt their forefathers showed mine but they don't, of course, and probably aren't British to begin with.

There is a small picture gallery with portraits of people attached to the freedom struggle and to this place. One of them is dear Udham Singh who, 21 years later, exacted his revenge, not on Dyer, but on O'Dwyer whom he believed was ultimately responsible for the carnage. He shot him twice, in London, at Caxton Hall, in full view of everyone during a meeting where the British Minister Cabinet for India, Laurance Dundas of Zetland was also present. In fact he shot Zetland too, for good measure, but didn't manage to kill him.

'Is Zetland dead?' he asked later, and pointing to his stomach, said, 'He ought to be. I put two into him right there.' He then lamented, 'Only one dead, eh? I thought I could get more. I must have been too slow. There were a lot of women about, you know.'

Udham Singh, who renamed himself Ram Mohammad Singh Azad to reflect his religious universalism, didn't for a minute resist arrest and went happily to the gallows, saying simply,

'I did it because I had a grudge against him. He deserved it.'

He certainly did, and worse. And Ram Mohammad Singh Azadji deserves an international award.

After looking at some more exhibits, among which was a picture of an old Indian man being made to crawl, while British soldiers stood around and jeered, across the street where an English schoolteacher was being assaulted during the uprising, I leave the museum full of utter disgust for the Empire. As I walk the short distance between the Harmandir Sahib or Golden Temple and the Jallianwala Bagh memorial, I think about how cynical it is that the inelegant, brutish and brutal materialism of Imperialism should have collided so forcefully with India's spirit, right here in Amritsar, one of her holier places.

The streets around the Temple complex are full of daily commuters all bowing and folding their hands (along with a few other gestures that I don't recognise) as they go past the gates, wearing as grave an expression as they can muster and making pretzels of themselves to avoid having their backs to the sacred space. People almost fall off rickshaws doing this. There is something in their eyes that looks like fear, not fear *per se*, but perhaps a fear of offending. Offending what, I wonder, the temple? God? Is God offended if we don't bow and curtsy or fall out of rickshaws trying? Wouldn't that be a bit petty of Him?

I approach the temple gates, and a man with oversized everything—beard, spear, turban, hands—summons me, and quite gruffly asks me to dispose of any tobacco products I might have in my pockets, to wash my hands, and to surrender to him all weapons I may be carrying. These are the famous temple guards, who carry long spears and impressive daggers and have done so for centuries. I wonder if it's frequent that someone casually pulls out their Kalashnikov, or their pistol, or perhaps even their sword and hands it over to them while stepping into the small trough of water between this spot and the temple, washing their feet and purifying their journey into the presence of the Divine, leaving cigarettes, weapons and other cumbersome worldly artefacts behind.

It's a common feature, ablution—for a lot of us, no matter what our faiths, water manages to, in our minds at least, wash more than just our bodies. But the presence of water at this particular holy site is significantly greater than it is at any other I've been to. The temple stands stately and shimmering in an enormous pool called the *sarovar*, which is said to contain *amrit*, or the nectar of immortality after which Amritsar takes its name. People ritualistically bathe in it, and hymns fill the air with song as people stream into the complex and into the water. The atmosphere resembles a social function like a community picnic rather than anything overtly religious. I watch a very dark-skinned man, one of the temple guards, conduct his ablutions in the *sarovar* and put on his clothes, carefully wrapping his bright orange turban around his head. The contrast between his skin and turban is striking.

People walk briskly around the pool, along a path with elegant white structures, stopping at significant points to perform rituals. All the while the hymns keep going and in the Langar Khana, the food (and the diners) keeps coming—mountains of *chapatis* stacked in rows. People take turns washing dishes and handing out water to visitors—all part of the *shaeba* done by pilgrims who dedicate their time and energy to serve other worshippers, as part of their own worship. Grim old ladies, smiling bearded men, young boys and little girls are all doing tours of duty at a self-governing, self-perpetuating commune that even has sleeping arrangements.

The hymns being sung form the *Guru Granth Sahib*, a holy book that is a living person to the Sikhs. There is a causeway linking the temple to the path around the pool, and it is thronging with pilgrims on their way to catch a glimpse of the Book that is housed in the temple, and from where the hymns are being read. I pass on it, it will take me too long to get there and back. The Guru Granth Sahib is the eleventh and perpetual guru of the Sikh religion. It was composed between 1469 and 1708 and was declared a Guru by the Patna-born Guru Gobind Singh, thereby becoming an elevated and actual personality, perhaps the first and only book to have managed to do so. It's a wonderful amalgamation of religious and philosophical traditions written in Sant Bhasha, a coalescing of various languages including Khariboli, Sanskrit, Punjabi, Farsi and Arabic, and containing teachings of various Gurus, even Prophet Muhammad and Lord Krishna. It uses Gurmukhi, a script that was designed specifically for the Adi Granth (what the Guru Granth Sahib was called before it 'came to life' as it were), and is now also the script for Punjabi this side of the Wagah Border.

Sikhism is possibly the most prominent syncretic tradition in South Asia, though not the only one. It is also the world's fifth largest religion and growing fast. It was born in the 15th century, when Guru Nanak, the first guru, shared his insights with the world. It's a beautiful creed, and encourages us to achieve, through a personal connection with God and though rigours and meditations, an enlightened and moral state of being. Similar to Sufi thought, Bliss is described as union with the *Waheguru*, the Sikh rendition of God, and damnation as being cut off from this Eternal Source of Love and Grace. Sikhs aspire to be *Sant-Sipahi* or 'Saintly Soldiers' and espouse both martial and mystical ideals. Similarities between the word 'Sant' and 'Saint', or for that matter with Santa, San, Sanitary, Sanitation, Sanity, Sante, Sanitorium and the rest of the family, are not coincidental. They all share a common Proto-Indo-European ancestor, which must've been a word for a state that combines peace, wellbeing and purity—what a lovely state it must be too.

The Sikhs place truth and justice above all else, and Plato's utopian Philosopher-Kings are very real role models in the Sikhi way of life. In fact, a *Sant-Sipahi* (Saint-Soldier), when he is a king, attempts to be just that. But it didn't begin that way. Guru Nanak's teachings were mostly esoteric and concerned, overwhelmingly, with the Divine and the Soul, and far less with earthly duties like governance or defence. These became enshrined in the Sikhi code after Muslims forced their hand by attacking their temple and killing the fifth Guru. It's quite tragic, actually. Sikhs and Muslims were kindred once, and Muslim teachings, including those by Sufis both in India and Persia, are still a significant part of the Sikhi way. Sikhism, while ostensibly standing as a midpoint between

Hinduism and Islam, seems actually closer to Islam to me but then it's quite absurd to position Islam and Hinduism as polar opposites to begin with. At the core, they promote almost the same values and so Sikhism is perhaps more of a return to the essence of both, rather than a 'third way'. For example, the Vedic *Yamas* and *Niyamas* are remarkably similar to Islamic ethics and also to the Sikh principles that promote modesty, charity and patience, and discourage materialism, unfaithfulness and intoxication. All three faiths also share a similar understanding of who, or what God is. Sikhs believe,

God is One. His name is True. He is the Creator. His is without fear. He is inimical to none. His existence is unlimited by time.

This is not entirely unlike the Quran's 'Surah Ikhlas', which says

Say: He is Allah, the One and Only; Allah, the Eternal, Absolute; He begets not, nor is He begotten; And there is none like unto Him.

Both are a bit similar to the Rig Vedic prayer that goes,

They call Him Indra, Mitra, Varuna, Agni, and He is heavenly nobly-winged Garutmān. To what is One, sages give many a title—they call it Agni, Yama, Mātariśvan.

But there are areas of difference, at least in dogmatic matters. Sikhs consider the Islamic 'halal' form of slaughtering animals cruel, and won't eat halal meat. They prefer the Hindu *boli* method, arguing that there is no such thing as a sanctified slaughter anyway, and that *boli* is more humane. Who knows, maybe it is. They also don't believe in fasting or pilgrimages or of any other sort of austerities, and in this they differ from Hindus too. Being casteless and non-hierarchal, they differ from Hinduism's institutionalised structures. I could go on about the intersections between Islam, Hinduism and Sikhism, but standing here, at the last city before Pakistan, these feelings seem sadly redundant.

Sikh literally means 'study' or, as you might expect, 'seek', and adherents originally studied from a panoply of religious sources, preserving the best of many faiths and managing to separate their truths from their superstructures, to produce a code which states quite simply that,

> *Only those who selflessly love everyone, they alone shall find God. Realisation of Truth is higher than all else. Higher still is truthful living.*

It's a refreshing approach; Sikhism is all heart, a mystical one at that, and it's consciously universalist. But that's not to say that it hasn't been a physical force as well. The Sikhs had a powerful kingdom and contended with the Mughals for control over Punjab and beyond. Maharajah Ranjit Singh extended his sway all the way up to Peshawar, and down to Multan, encompassing more than half of today's Pakistan, creating a realm that, by many accounts, was a bastion of secular, tolerant ideals. True to the nature of Sikhism, the *Sarkar Khalsaji*, or the Khalsa Government, had generals and ministers from a variety of faiths. All of this was a reaction to late Mughal chauvinism, where many instruments of authority and power were denied to Sikhs after turbulence between them and the Muslims in North India became an irreversible reality.

Mughals and Sikhs fell out in a terrible way soon after Emperor Akbar's reign. Akbar, to his credit, was very accommodating of Sikhism and the third Mughal had a good relationship with the third Guru, Amar Das, whose Langar impressed the Emperor enough to make him bequeath land for its expansion—land on which Amritsar now stands. Akbar, of course, respected all religions and was particularly fond of Sikhism, but the Mughals were always slightly more wedded to power than to principles, and when the fifth Guru, Guru Arjan Dev sided with Jahangir's son Khusrau Mirza in the succession battles after Akbar's death, he was executed. Khusrau didn't fare much better himself, and was also executed, by his brother Shah Jahan.

The affront of having their Guru murdered turned the Sikhs militant and they established the Akal Takht or Eternal Throne, a symbol of Sikh sovereignty, while pushing for a split from the Mughal Empire. Both Shah Jahan and Aurangazeb suppressed this nationalism aggressively, and Aurangazeb went the extra mile of giving the ninth Guru, Guru Tegh Bahadur a choice between converting to Islam and being put to death. He chose death, and the gulf between the two communities became permanently unbridgeable. The tenth and last human Guru (the eleventh being the Granth Sahib), Guru Gobind Singh was ambushed on his way to meet Aurangazeb's successor Bahadur Shah, and sustained wounds that eventually led to his death. But during his life he formalised many of the Sikh tenets, the Khalsa, and turned Sikhism into the religion we recognise today. The Sikhs became a fighting force, with territory and a military, laying the foundations for what would become Ranjit Singh's empire 90 years later. His commands include the following:

You will love the weapons of war, be excellent horsemen, marksmen and wielders of the sword, the discus and the spear. Physical prowess will be as sacred to you as spiritual sensitivity. And, between the Hindus and Muslims, you will act as a bridge, and serve the poor without distinction of caste, colour, country or creed. My Khalsa shall always defend the poor, and 'Deg', or community kitchen, will be as much an essential part of your order as Teg, the sword.

The Sikhs never really had their triumphant moment in the sun, though. Not for long anyway. The formative years of their empire were tough—they had to contend with marauding Afghans, the Marathas and Punjabi Muslims still allied to remnants of Mughal power. They managed to field a formidable polity in the end, but it was subsumed by the British Empire only 50 years after it was established. Sikhs and Muslims were at each other's throats again during Partition, and in the 1980s the Khalistan movement, which attempted to create a Sikh State, was violently crushed by the Indian government in Operation Blue Star which saw Indian soldiers enter the Golden Temple and fire rounds inside the complex, killing hundreds of civilians and damaging the Akal Takht, the very symbol of Sikh nationalism.

Ironically, the man leading the operation was Sikh himself and one of the men he went in to get was Major General Shabeg Singh, a veteran of Bangladesh's War of Liberation, who trained countless Mukti Bahinis or freedom fighters during our nine-month campaign. He fought hard, but the man who helped us create our country was killed trying to establish his own. Indira Gandhi, also a friend to Bangladesh, was assassinated in the aftermath by her Sikh bodyguard and the 1984 anti-Sikh riots that followed claimed thousands of Sikh lives. Sikh nationalism has been dormant, maybe even dead, ever since.

As I stroll around the Harmandir Sahib complex, I admire the architecture and observe how it looks a little like Mughal architecture, but not quite. I suppose the Sikhs, as successors and competitors to the Mughals, tried, somewhat in vain, to imitate their style as well. But the whitewashed 17th-century buildings and the Golden Temple in the middle of the pool certainly paint a tranquil picture. I enjoy the atmosphere, and sit for long periods against the wall along the cloisters. I'm sure the water has a lot to do with the sense of peace I experience, as does the music, but it also has to do with the mood of the visitors. Everyone is welcome in this place and one can sense it. Sikhs and non-Sikhs alike seem genuinely happy to be here—I certainly am. There is a large LCD screen displaying messages and slogans in Hindi, Punjabi and English. I catch one, it says,

O wise friend, ever think thou of thy Lord in thy mind.

Beautiful. But I have to tear myself away from this serene place if I'm going to make it to the Wagah Border in time for the ceremonies.

Wagah

I wait at a teashop for the shared taxi to fill up with passengers and take me to the border. In the meanwhile, I indulge in some people watching and observe how many Punjabis look a lot like Persians or Central Asians, even a bit like southern Europeans. They have angular features, some with blue or green eyes and are sometimes quite light-skinned, all of which lends credence to the notion of a Caucasian migration into North India. Historical and religious literature like the Vedas and the Gathas in Iran identify a people who consciously refer to themselves as Aryans, living on both sides of the Indus River and in the mountains of Afghanistan but nothing tells us what their physical characteristics were. There are also no clear references to a lost homeland somewhere beyond this region, although, in his book, *Arctic Home of the Vedas*, Indian political leader and writer Bal Gangadhar Tilak points towards numerous clues in Vedic and Iranian Avestani hymns that place Aryan origins near the North Pole, before the last Ice Age. But these are vague and implied and difficult to confirm. The alternative is that they were always here—perhaps this is where they spread from, rather than spread to.

In fact, a school of thought in anthropology called the 'Out of India Theory' or the OIT proposes just this. They use a number of variables to establish their claim including language, mythology, historic literature, place names, geological phenomena, climate patterns and a range of other things that give us clues about human migration during the Copper and Bronze Age. In a bizarre narrative twist, OIT proposes that the Aryans have prior claim to North India, and that others arrived from elsewhere. They support this by pointing out that the Dravidians are linguistically related to the Middle Eastern (Iranian) Elamite people and may have settled in South India after arriving by sea, and that the Eastern Austro-Asiatic Mundas have cousins across South East Asia and Australia, and might have simply moved west into Bengal and Bihar, and then beyond. They also argue that biological anthropology shows no significant physical differences between the people of the Indus Valley Civilisation and the Vedic

Aryans. Of course other theories argue just the opposite and with as much conviction, so in the end it's a moot point. Besides, there have also been plenty of later migrations from Central Asia and Anatolia, even from Greece through this part of India so it's safe to say that the gene pool here is particularly diverse. But that there are ethnological differences between them and me is as clear as the fact that there are ethnological differences between me and the Garo tribes of Meghalaya.

Finally, after waiting for the last passengers and amidst a flurry of unnecessary hyperactivity over the assigning of seats, we set off towards the border, to the other end of India, that other line in the sand, the pair of which made us all fractions of ourselves. I'm sharing a taxi with two students from Madhya Pradesh, a Pakistani traveller and a family of Sikh Punjabis. The Sikhs are either very shy or very rude, and do not acknowledge the other passengers in the car. But the rest of us have a fun enough time on the way as we share stories, experience each other's languages, talk about how similar they all are, and about how wonderful it would be if we could all get SAARC visas.

The city of Amritsar slowly fades into a messy suburban sprawl and then disappears altogether, to be replaced by fields of grain. Ahead in the distance, littered with buses, trucks, people, signposts and check-posts, is Wagah Border. To my right I see a barbed wire fence slicing through the greenery and running on into the horizon. A short walk away is a monument 'dedicated to the 10 Lakh Punjabis that died unsung in 1947', in the shape of a handshake.

Wagah is spectacular and is the most exciting border I've ever experienced. All borders should be like this—if we have to have fences, we might as well be theatrical about it. Considering the seriousness with which the 'Berlin Wall of Asia' was erected, it's amazing how, every afternoon since 1959, India and Pakistan have put on this melodramatic display that seems almost to make a conscious mockery of it. But it's not, of course. They take it very seriously, as they do their nationalism, but perhaps the histrionics reflect an underlying recognition of the juvenility of it all. Or maybe that's just the way I'd rather see it.

83

The atmosphere is carnival-like. Huge crowds sit in galleries, waving flags, shouting patriotic slogans, dancing, and singing along to popular Bollywood tunes playing out of large and bellowing speakers. A.R. Rahman's 'Jai Ho' features, predictably. An MC coordinates this overflowing nationalism, shouting slogans into the air, which the crowds repeat. A massive party is happening at the highly sensitive India-Pakistan border, complete with cheerleaders and vuvuzelas! It's surreal.

It all begins with bugles. Then very tall soldiers in starched khaki outfits and *sindoor* (vermillion) *pagris* with enormous crest-like attachments march towards gates that look much like the ones leading to large houses in South Asia. There's even a small lawn and some landscaping around them. They open these gates and begin performing a high-testosterone martial dance that includes, posturing, gesturing, strutting, snorting, stomping, eye-balling, huffing, puffing, pacing, flexing, and virtually all and any sort of mock-aggression that can be mustered. Both sides do this, and they mirror each other perfectly. It's quite a sight. Legs fly up in the air and land with thundering crashes as the soldiers stomp along the border fence, signalling limits and challenging intrusions. As the soldiers get high on these feats of masculinity, they grunt and snort and shake their heads the way bulls or horses do. I've never seen a more vivid display of human territoriality and pride. It's actually quite charming and reminds me of the complex mating rituals that certain types of birds go through. Traveller extraordinaire Michael Palin eloquently calls it 'carefully choreographed contempt; chauvinism at its most camp', and comedian Sanjeev Bhaskar thinks they must've needed approval from Monty Python's Ministry of Silly Walks. A writer for the *Sydney Morning Herald* calls it South Asia's Hakka.

It all ends with the lowering of the flags, which happens in perfect unison lest one nation gets the better of the other by having their flag fly higher than the other's even for a second. In a final show of bellicosity, a soldier from each side stomps dangerously close to his counterpart, squaring up aggressively before simply shaking hands with him and smiling, a perfect finish that draws loud claps and howling cheers from the crowd. And with that, the gates are literally slammed shut on the other nation's face. I find it all unabashedly honest and very endearing, with plenty of love flowing across the border. There are none of the jagged edges I expected to find here. The atmosphere is mostly like an Indian wedding characterised by what is basically extravagant banter of a most South Asian kind. It's something that all of us are familiar with, and beneath the faux-friction, it feels full of affection. Perhaps Jinnah's hoped-for 'divorce before marriage' isn't as absurd as it sounds—there is a great energy about the place, which fills you up with hope. It's a sibling-like competitiveness, a very Punjabi one at that, and I can't help but wonder if the whole matter is just an overblown case of an Aryan obsession with one-upmanship and symbols—my tribe is better than yours; my flag is brighter than yours.

But there are also elements in the display that makes unnatural splits and unnecessary associations. For instance, I didn't like it very much when '*Vande Mataram*' and '*Sura Ya Sin*' were pitted against each other, nor did I particularly like seeing the Ashokan Lion Capital and an '*Allah Hu*' design 'facing-off', on the sides of the gates. It seemed to suggest that you could like one or the other, that you could be only one or the other, but not both. As a Bengali Muslim, wedded quite happily to both Islam and Indian civilisation, this is an absurd proposition. I found it very disturbing to hear '*La ilaha Il Allah*' being chanted like a nationalistic slogan from the Pakistani side, in response to '*Jai Hind*' or '*Hindustan Zindabad*,' only to be jeered by the Indians. In fact, I didn't like it at all that Pakistani nationalism seems to be so heavily reliant on Islam. It seems to do a disservice to the religion by embroiling it in our petty turf battles. It's as though they've turned Islam into a totem or a kind of superhero to combat India's own superhero nationalism—as though the countries wear costumes and a have a big Dharma chakra, or a star and a crescent emblazoned across their chests like Superman's 'S'.

That's all nationalism is, really. A sort of hero-worship, where countries become superhuman defenders, complete with colours and special powers, flying off into the sky wearing embarrassingly fitted spandex suits. It's all very unnatural and imaginary. But what I find most awkward about Pakistan's religious nationalism versus India's cultural nationalism is how India's antagonism towards Pakistan inevitably carries anti-Islamic overtones while Pakistani antagonism towards India trashes Sanskritic civilisation. The configurations they have created almost necessitate this, even if that isn't the intention. Hindustan is Pakistan's evil other and vice-versa. Never mind that the Dharma Charkra and the Lion Capital are Mauryan and Buddhist, and that the people immediately on this side of the border are predominantly Sikh; 'Hindustan' embodies all that Pakistan rejects, just as Pakistanis feel rejected by an Indian identity that became uncomfortable with their Islamic bend.

They are possibly both right, of course, and I will explore it more as I travel in Pakistan, but for now I feel concerned that mutual appreciation cannot thrive in this climate and in spite of the '*mrido*' or mock nature of the hostility, the crowd may be getting the impression that *Sura Ya Sin* and *La Ilaha Il Allah* belong on 'that' side of the gates, and that Indian civilisation ends on 'this' side (outside as well, from the Pakistani point of view), both of which are simply not true. But maybe I'm paranoid and can't appreciate the '*mazaaq*' of it all. I am Bengali, after all; we're not particularly good at *mazaaq*.

We arrive back in town at night. I go to a teashop and make change to pay my fare but return to see that the Pakistani traveller has already paid for me and won't let me pay him back. He just counters my insistence with '*Meherbani*' and a smile. I am humbled, and get my first introduction to the large-heartedness that will feature prominently in my travels through this man's land. I weave my way across a festive Amritsar and, along the way, hear two elderly gentlemen speaking Kolkata Bangla. They sound like an island to me, in this unintelligible sea of unknown languages. I stop for some tea, duck around a corner to smoke a cigarette, buy some toothpaste and shampoo, and head to the hotel for a good night's sleep.

To Pakistan

A small miracle waits for me at 5 am as I walk towards the station to catch my early morning train back to Delhi. Late and walking the wrong way, I come across a lone rickshaw parked at the end of the road, as though it has been called to collect me. There isn't a single other person or form of transport, public or otherwise, on the streets this morning and if I had kept walking, I would never have found the station. Even if I had, I would've certainly missed the train, leaving my chances of catching the evening flight from Delhi to Lahore hanging in the balance.

Five hours later I arrive at a Delhi in a state of high alert. A briefcase bomb has just gone off near gate 5 of the High Court building where people gather daily to attend court cases. Some have been killed and injured. Police barricades are in place everywhere. There are men in khaki stopping and searching vehicles and rifling through the shops in Paharganj, where one of the attackers allegedly hid. I exit the train station and go straight into the commotion. The blast happened only moments ago and the anxiety in the air is all too thick. I'm angry and saddened by the loss of life, but have no time to process this as I have to get out of the area as quickly as possible. I catch a taxi to Disha's place; the driver already has the radio on and is listening to updates. The news is being read out in exasperated tones and details of the attack are at this point, still unclear.

I find myself wondering about what might happen if I'm stopped and questioned. It looks quite bad, actually. I, a Muslim, flew in from Dhaka on a British passport, avoiding the police registration that all Bangladeshis, Pakistanis and Afghanis have to go through. I arrive in Bihar, a notoriously ungovernable state with a significant Muslim population. I could have picked up contacts, expertise or even explosive devices there, before travelling by train to Delhi. That, too, while Manmohan Singh is in Bangladesh. Surely the police officers who approved my foreign quota seat in Patna will remember, when questioned, that they had seen Pakistani and Iranian visas in my passport and I did seem a little anxious, now that they think about it.

He had a beard, sir. We knew he was up to no good when we saw him. He did what, sir? Went to the Pakistan border, in the cover of night, disguised as a local? God knows what he got up to there, probably passing messages to masterminds on the other side, or collecting codes and coordinates, maybe even getting people across. There's no telling what he might be plotting, sir, his name being Khan and all. We wanted to detain him, but you know how these Muslims are, na, he would have accused me of being prejudiced or something. Wo log to bohut sensitive *hain na?*

It's all too suspicious. I have a flight to Pakistan on the day of the blasts, and was at the border just the evening before. The border officials have a record of my being there as they checked my passport before letting me into the gallery. The hotel at Amritsar has a record, too. I'm going to Iran at some point. The only people I visited in Delhi are Muslims, and politically active ones. I have 'journalist' stamped on my visa, but no news organisation currently has me on its payroll, and when the visa officer in Dhaka asked me where I was going in India, I said, 'oh just West Bengal', to avoid a long conversation. Surely he'll remember that too, and the fact that there was no Pakistani visa in my passport when he issued me the Indian one. I even hung out in Paharganj when I came to Delhi. I begin to worry quite a lot.

Luckily, I don't get stopped and after a brief pause at Disha's place, where I learn that no one has claimed responsibility for the attack yet and that 12 people have died, with more than 70 injured, I head off to the airport with tremendous trepidation. With many major roads barricaded, the traffic is terrible and I become very anxious about missing my flight. The next one is in a week. We reach in time but, as expected, there are armed guards patrolling the airport and an armed soldier checking passports on the way in. 'I'm finished,' I think to myself, 'this is impassable.' I walk the walk of dread towards him and just as I'm about to hand him the passport, a guard at the next entrance calls out agitatedly. The two then consult each other about this other passenger's status or visa. He then looks over my passport, but is distracted, and is still mumbling to himself, so I decide some small talk might be useful.

'Some problem over there?' I say to distract him even more.

'Some people just don't understand the formalities, sir. You know these types, workers, flying for the first time. He doesn't understand that we are trying to help him. His work visa was ....'

He continues talking but I've stopped listening since all I can notice is that he has idly flicked through my documents and is handing them back to me with a smile. Relieved, I add some sugar-coating,

'I think it's very nice that you are trying to help the poor fellow. I mean it's not their fault you know, it's difficult for them and they are such an important part of the economy.'

He does the Indian head wobble, obviously pleased with my sympathy for the working man, and tells me to have a good flight before waving me in. I'm through, and it took another miracle. I feel terrible for thinking the worst of those people in Bihar and Dhaka who didn't harass me for a moment; in fact, they made it easier for me. Fear does horrible things to our minds. Indian immigration is also event-free, but getting to Pakistan continues to be fraught with other hiccups. From the very start it's been difficult. The visa took ages, and was expensive; they were reluctant to issue it on a British passport in Bangladesh, flatly refused a few times until a kindly visa officer called Azmat Khattak decided to let me get through the space he guards between the Radcliffe and Durand lines, but not, as I would've liked, via Wagah Border.

Now the flight is delayed. Initially they say two hours, but that becomes three, then four, and then no one knows for sure anymore. It's all quite a bungle, *yaar*. Passengers argue with PIA staff—they lambast them, actually—and the whole waiting lounge becomes a fretting, moaning mess. No one knows what the hold-up is; mechanical issues in Lahore, I overhear. Impromptu unions are formed, a leader rises and voices the people's frustrations then fades away, another takes his place—passengers demand answers. A pair of Pathans in *shalwar-kameezes* sit in a corner smirking, an elderly anglophile in suspenders shakes his head, gaudily made-up ladies gossip, kids run around here and there, a few Europeans, keeping their peace, read books or play with their electronic devices. Red-eyed and moustached individuals stand around menacingly, and a very good-looking family sits together in a circle, keeping their spirits high by joking and laughing. They speak a language I can't recognise but it sounds like Farsi or Turkish. It turns out to be Kashmiri, and I remember the softness of both their tongue and their hearts from an earlier visit to Srinagar, in the Indian-controlled part of their land.

After eight hours, during which I wonder if the delay is because Indian authorities are going to sweep the lounge and arrest me, the plane finally arrives and we board. I'm seated next to an extremely talkative Pakistani-Punjabi man, who insists on telling me about his contacts and connections in Pakistan and about what he does, which is actually quite fascinating—he runs leadership seminars, to try and breed a culture of good governance in Pakistani Punjab. He tells me about Pakistan's woes, about his other businesses, and about the time he was invited by the EU to give a talk about the issues facing Pakistani politics. He is interesting company in the end, although a bit too much company for my liking and I wish he would stop at some point. The plane is in quite a state; the tray in front of me is broken and fastened with duct tape, the window is almost completely scratched, and when I hear the stewardess carry on in her heavily accented and archaic English, I can't decide whether its Bangladesh Biman or PIA that takes the cake for shoddiness.

We arrive at Lahore around 12 am. The airport is seedy and much smaller than I expected. Almost instantly the sycophancy endemic in developing countries reveals itself when a group of people and then two other individuals are ushered through immigration by separate sets of suited and suitably small sycophants. The bigwigs carry themselves with appropriate amounts of pomp and immigration officials bend over as far backwards as necessary for them. 'Salaams' fly all around the place, and everything else has to wait until their highnesses are suitably serviced. It's an all too familiar scenario.

The immigration officer who attends to me is a sullen and unfriendly lady who hardly looks up at me and doesn't reciprocate when I wish her a good evening. She seems bothered, generally, and becomes even more irate when she sees that my disembarkation card has no address on it.

'Where are you staying in Pakistan?'

'With family.'

'I can't process "with family". I need an address!'

'I don't have one, but people are here to pick me up, maybe I can go ask them?'

'I can't let you through until everything is entered in the system. Phone them.'

'My phone is dead. Can I use yours?'

'(Disturbed) Use his—Akbar Bhai, let him use your phone for a minute (in Urdu).'

'Oh no! The number is in my diary, in my backpack!'

'You are a difficult person.'

'I'm sorry. But it's the truth.'

'Akbar Bhai, accompany this gentleman to his luggage, but bring him straight back after he makes the phone call.'

Akbar Bhai is a serious young man, with a slight stubble and pink cheeks. He doesn't smile and, like many of the other guards in the airport, I get a sense that he can access great reserves of cruelty when required. It's a feeling I will get from many, if not all Pakistani security personnel, and to a smaller extent, Pakistani men in general, especially the ones in Lahore and Islamabad. That's not to say they aren't kind and exceptionally warm—they are, but they also seem capable of releasing a beast if the occasion calls for it. I'm not sure if that's strength, tyranny or just my pre-conceived notions of Pakistanis. It's possibly a combination of all three, but whatever it is, it's intimidating.

I call Mujeeb Uncle, my *Khalu's* brother-in-law, and my host in Lahore. He doesn't answer, maybe because he doesn't recognise the number, and I'm beginning to get nervous. Akbar Bhai makes an independent decision (impressive, as his counterparts in Bangladesh would never have had the courage without official approval) and takes me outside to find my man. But I've never seen him before and have no idea who I'm looking for. It's all very odd and I hope he sees me before things start to get sticky. Just then a tall, thin man pushes through the crowd and asks, 'Are you Zeeshan?'

Reprieve. I'm saved.

I get my bag and get out of the airport just as the teasing begins. The guards have found this whole episode very amusing and are having a go at me. I get in the car, apologise profusely to my host for the delay, and then discover that he's a sharp, polite and soft-natured man with a healthy appetite for good conversation.

There is a very heavy feeling in the air here, which I can feel almost immediately and which doesn't dissipate much during my travels in this country. It's palpably and quite pervasively tense. On the way home from the airport we are stopped at a check-post, where the officer, armed with a machine gun which he clutches tightly, looks over Mujeeb Uncle's papers. The power dynamic is stacked significantly in his favour and his expression and gestures insist that we remain keenly aware of this. As we drive away Mujeeb Uncle tells me it's because the Pakistani Taliban have declared war on all security personnel in Pakistan and so a state of high alert is constantly in play. I am clearly quite far from the temperate tones of India already.

Their double-storeyed house is in a neighbourhood called Gulberg, which reminds me of Baridhara in Dhaka—meaning it's posh, exclusive and clean. After a good night's rest I wake up at noon and have lunch with many members of my uncle's family, among whom are a number of beautiful and passionate girls determined to live lives less ordinary. They are adventurous, and at least two of them have spent time alone in China doing research in anthropology. We have very enjoyable conversations at the table before Mujeeb Uncle gives me the use of a car and his driver, Ismail Bhai, to go and explore the city. I decide to go to Wagah Border, to see it from the Pakistani side, and cover the full 50 kilometres or so, between Amritsar and Lahore.

Along the way I catch my first glimpses of Pakistani street life. Lahore looks like most South Asian cities, the noticeable differences being the way people dress and the script used in signs and banners. There is a conspicuous absence of women, except a few veiled ones who scamper hurriedly to their destination with their eyes down, almost apologetically. Virtually everyone I see is male and in *shalwar-kameezes* that come in a range of unimaginative colours like white, light blue, dark green, black and light brown. And they are all in monotone—no mixing and matching, just one shade per person. Gone are the vibrant, brilliant colours that characterise most of South Asia and much of Southeast Asia, and I'm beginning to think that these are possibly the least colourful people in the entire region. It feels as though there is some sort of mandatory and enforced dullness that informs their national dress sense. If they are feeling a little tickled, they might cheekily don a brightly decorated prayer cap in what is surely an act of rebellion against the gods of gloom, but otherwise they are all in their standard issue uniforms. Very few people appear to be in western wear.

The other thing that stands out as strikingly different is the Shahmukhi script. Shahmukhi, meaning 'from the King's mouth', is a subset of the Persian Nastaleeq script that was derived in Tabriz from the Arabic script sometime around the 9th century, and in which Urdu is written. Shahmukhi is used to write Punjabi this side of the International Boundary, as opposed to Gurmukhi in India. I can't help but wonder what would've happened to Gurmukhi if all of Punjab had gone to Pakistan. Surely it would have ceased to exist as a living script. This makes me realise just how important it was for us to refuse to write Bangla using the Nastaleeq script in East Pakistan, because it's not just about scripts really—it's about civilisations.

All Indian languages, including Bangla, Sanskrit, Gurmukhi and even Tamil are written in derivatives of the Brahmi or Indic script, which also spawned the Tibetan script and scripts for languages of an area known as *Shubornobhumi* in Indian Literature. These are the Thai, Burmese, Lao, Cambodian, Mon, Javanese, Balinese and many other now extinct Southeast Asian scripts. It's a huge family and it's ours and it used to go right up to the Indus River and into parts of Afghanistan. In contrast, Iranian languages were influenced by cultures to their west and were written in the Sumerian Cuneiform script as well as the Aramaic script, borrowed from Mesopotamian civilisations.

Arabic script replaced the Mesopotamian ones after the Arabs invaded Persia and Farsi came to be written in a stylised version of their coloniser's script as a result of nearly 400 years of forced 'Arabisation'. The Persians carried this script, Nastaleeq, with them, when they themselves expanded to reclaim some of their historic *Iranzamin* or the 'Iranian Cultural Continent', including parts of Central Asia and Pakistan. But *Iranzamin*, both in its Zoroastrian and its Islamic incarnations ended, at best, at the Indus. Beyond that was 'Hind', and everyone, all the way from the Ancient Greeks to the mediaeval Arabs, knew this well. Even today, Balochi and Pashto speakers from the western bank of the Indus River refer to Punjabi, Sindhi and Urdu as Hindustani languages. But the Delhi Sultanate and the Mughal Empire were both ruled by people who had Persian influences and used Farsi in their courts, giving Iranzamin a partial toehold in Bharatbarsha. Now it has carried away chunks of it entirely.

I can't pretend that I didn't feel sad to see Persian writing completely take over parts of what used to be Brahmi territory. Even though this began happening many centuries before 1947 it was never so absolute. Partition separated the two scripts and then pushed them up against each other in a way that makes it a painfully obvious and potentially irreversible fact. What's worse is that it happened in the very parts of Punjab where both sources of Indian civilisation, the Harappan and the Vedic, had their genesis and where Indian Aryans began the chronicles that would later become the foundation for Sanskritic literature. It's also where Sanskrit grammar, syntax and semantics was formulated by Panini, the great grammarian in his treatise, the *Ashtadhyayi*, or the 'Eight Chapters' in the 6th century BC. In other words, Indic writing was born almost exactly in a place where it now no longer exists. What a treat you are, Partition.

We get to Wagah in time for the ceremony. As I enter the gallery, a giant, fair-skinned man asks to see my passport. He's easily 7 feet tall or more, dressed in the military attire of the Pakistani Rangers at Wagah, which is a black *shalwar-kameez* and a black turban with black crest-fans attached to them, making him appear even taller. He asks me where I'm originally from, as my British passport doesn't tell him anything about my ethnicity, and I say, audaciously, 'Bangladesh', to which he replies, *'Kemon achen?'* and my face lights up. He smiles, says welcome to Pakistan and shows me to my seat. I watch the whole thing again from the Pakistani side. They certainly do it all with much more bluster, and their greater zeal is matched by their larger size. They are taller and hardier looking, and far more arrogant than the Indians, which, given the occasion, seems more appropriate. The galleries are segregated here; single men sit on one side, and families on the other. The architecture is much nicer on this side, but a massive picture of Jinnah adorning the gate does it a disservice. It's less festive, but then there are fewer people as well. Still, they do their best to match India's revelry and do a pretty good job of it too.

On the way back, I stop to say Maghrib prayers at a small mosque near the border and see some of Pakistan's famous decorated trucks parked outside. They are elaborately done up with colourful patterns, beautiful calligraphy and dangling ornaments, and easily display the best examples of South Asian truck art I've seen so far. I experience serenity praying together with people I don't know, but with whom I feel an instinctive connection. The sun sets, white-clad individuals alight from the mosque and go their own way in silent contemplation, and in the reddish glow of the evening I notice that Pakistan has a sober, almost philosophical calm about it that's very becoming.

4

The Shoulders of Giants

Lahore, Taxila

Lahore

The next morning I wake up to the sound of birds and ferrywallahs. The exaggerated musical callout, which lets you know that '*doooodh*' or '*taaaaaath*' or some other ware and service is being hawked on the streets outside, creates a familiar atmosphere and reminds me of both home and of a simpler, cosier time when South Asian cities had *paras* that were strung together by travelling salesmen. It's hot and humid in Lahore, and if it wasn't for the absence of the dark, tropical foliage, I might easily think I'm still in Dhaka. But Lahore is green as well and Punjab is a very fertile place, with many rivers and plenty of rain. After lunch I decide to go with Mujeeb uncle's son, Omer and Ismail Bhai to the mosque for Jumma prayers. In Pakistan even mosques can be terrorist targets, and there is a rifle-toting guard at the entrance, which is reassuring but depressing at the same time. Afterwards, I want to go and explore the city, so Ismail Bhai takes me to the Shahi Qilla in Old Lahore.

Through an area very reminiscent of Old Delhi, and a little bit like Old Dhaka, we negotiate thick traffic to arrive at the massive white columns of Alamgiri Gate at the Fort or Qilla of the walled

'Androon Shehr' or Inner City. Old Lahore is a collection of Mughal-era buildings, and is a beautiful example of 16th-century urban Hindustan, with a fort, a walled city (most of the walls were destroyed by the British and no longer exist), the splendid Badshahi Mosque, gardens, mausoleums and lots of breathtaking architecture. I enjoy looking at the fine latticework designs in marble, the precious stone inlaid motifs (now long plundered) the tiled facades, the cupolas, the scale of the buildings, heavy and carved Burma teak doors, frescos, and mirror-covered walls in rooms that light up like diamonds when the sun hits them at the right angle. I am pleased when I see a Bengali 'chauchal' design adorning a roof, and outraged when I discover that the British converted one of the structures into a pub (almost as outraged as I felt when I discovered they had demolished large sections of the Red Fort in Delhi to build army barracks). There's also a temple dedicated to Lav, one of Lord Rama's sons, who, so the story goes, was the original founder of Lahore some 4,000 years ago. It's only an indistinguishable ruin now, but is protected and preserved by Pakistani authorities.

There are a number of gates and divans, darbars and pleasure palaces, and each courtyard, turret and room has a story or a legend attached to it: a fable filled with intrigue and glamour. The Mughals lived here, after all, and lived large. Lahore was their Punjabi capital and along with Kabul, Delhi and Agra, one of the grand imperial cities of their realm. It contributed significantly to the flowering of Indo-Persian art and architecture during the 15th century, and was also among its chief beneficiaries. By the time the British took possession of it, it was a shadow of its former self yet still enticing enough to prompt Rudyard Kipling to write 'On the City Wall', in which he describes an atmosphere that must've seemed both glamorous and hedonistic to 19th-century European colonialists like himself.

The floor of the room was of polished chunam, white as curds. A latticed window of carved wood was set in one wall; there was a profusion of squabby pluffy cushions and fat carpets everywhere, and Lalun's silver huqa, studded with turquoises, had a special little carpet all to its shining self....

In the long hot nights of latter April and May all the city seemed to assemble in Lalun's little white room to smoke and to talk. Shiahs of the grimmest and most uncompromising persuasion; Sufis who had lost all belief in the Prophet and retained but little in God; wandering Hindu priests passing southward on their way to the Central India fairs and other affairs; Pundits in black gowns, with spectacles on their noses and undigested wisdom in their insides; bearded headmen of the wards; Sikhs with all the details of the latest ecclesiastical scandal in the Golden Temple....

Lahore is still a beautiful city, and has retained much of its good taste to become the cultural capital of Pakistan. It still has some of the best parks in the country, and the highest number of educational institutes per capita. It also has quite a few good murals on the walls, with political and patriotic messages—sometimes in English. The upscale areas are awash with boutiques, restaurants, galleries and cafes, all very tastefully, and expensively, decorated. There is plenty of wealth on display, but it seems, as it does in Dhaka, to be confined to a few streets and neighbourhoods. The old town is being partially restored, with areas set aside for a car-free zone and al fresco dining. Leading in this urban renewal project is Cooco's Den and Cafe, an old haveli-turned-restaurant and art gallery.

Located in Heera Mandi, the famous 'courtesan street' or red light district where nautch girls have been entertaining men for centuries, Cooco's was created by the famous artist, Iqbal Hussain, who paints portraits of prostitutes and was also born to a prostitute mother, right here in this 300-year-old brothel. Along with a few living quarters, the building houses the gallery and a rooftop restaurant that has an incredible view. It overlooks the Badshahi Mosque, which is less than two minutes away, and the contrast of mosque and bordello rubbing up so closely against each other is only an apt reflection of the Mughal Age, when religion, hedonism, art, cruelty, philosophy and ambition, all seemed to coexist as a single indivisible whole. Iqbal Hussain advocates for the women of Heera Mandi. He calls them 'holy' as they give up so much of themselves, and feels they are unjustly marginalised by a society that simultaneously exploits and condemns them. He's absolutely right.

The British contributions to the city are also quite impressive and are designed to fit right in. The Raj attempted to entrench itself in India by engaging in a vigorous 'indigenous' building campaign towards the end of the 1800s, and perhaps they were driven by a competitive urge to match up to the Mughals. They created a new style, which they dubbed 'Mughal-Gothic', and added their distinctive flavour to the city, which, in all fairness, isn't altogether ungainly. But unlike the Mughal structures, which are fluid and have elegant pillars, gentle arches and large open spaces, the British ones are monolithically stiff, imposing and closed. They lack flair or gaiety and while attempting to look stoic and business-like, manage to end up looking quite dour. If it weren't for the red brickwork, the window designs, the slight decoration on the doorjambs and the domed tops, they might have looked very ordinary indeed.

The Lahore General Post Office, the High Court, the railway station and the museum are all built in Mughal-Gothic style, but the enormous Anglican Church, built around the same time and in the same area, isn't. It's built in a firmly European Neo-Gothic style, carefully omitting even the slightest hint of anything Oriental. Given Lahore's tiny Protestant population, the church could only ever have been intended as an expression of cultural dominance, or as the edification of extreme optimism. Its Catholic cousin, the Sacred Heart Cathedral, also huge and built even later, is an absolute anachronism and goes a step further by using the entirely out of place Roman-Byzantine style. Clearly a chauvinistic use of religious architecture is something the British and the Mughals both had a taste for. Mughal-Gothic or Indo-Saracenic (as they fancifully called it) architecture was later seen in other parts of the Empire as well, like Curzon Hall in Dhaka, and the Victoria Memorial in Kolkata— Britain's Mughal-Gothic masterpiece that was intended to rival the Taj Mahal, but is really only about as similar to the Taj as a Peanuts comic strip is to the ceiling of the Sistine Chapel.

Before leaving the old city, I spend some time at the larger-than-life Badshahi Mosque. 'Larger than life' is actually an understatement. It is a behemoth and was the largest mosque in the world from the 16th century until 1986, when it was overtaken by its fellow Pakistani Faisal Mosque in Islamabad. The old giant has suffered many blows and insults over the years, and has even had some of its innards ripped out in an attempt to render it harmless to invaders, after it was briefly used as a garrison by the Sikhs. Several restorations later, it can hold its head up again the way it must've done in its youth.

I leave my shoes at the entrance and walk in with a crazed man in tow, going on about my camera and about photography being *haram*. I want to challenge him, but consider it a waste of time so just look at him and smile as if to say 'fuck off'. To my right is a room displaying verses of the Quran embroidered in gold and silver thread. People treat it like a shrine; they kiss the glass of the display counters, run their fingers along it and seem to believe that they are in the presence of Holiness. I don't much like all the theatrics and so leave as soon as I enter, but not before being stopped by the 'curator', who, in his most earnest of rehearsed performances, tells me I have to pay, literally, for the pleasure of having enjoyed this enchanted experience. I've seen these characters many times before at shrines, mosques and temples, and if I were Jesus, I would've kicked over their tables and sent them all packing, along with the money-changers. There is a relic chamber in the Mosque as well, containing a turban each of Prophet Muhammad and Imam Ali, which were brought to India by Amir Timur (Tamerlane), but I learn about this only after I've left.

I say Maghrib prayers at the mosque and make my way out. The sun's dying rays bounce off clouds and diffuse picturesquely into various shades of pink and red, right above the central dome of the red sandstone mosque. Streams of people in white or pale-coloured *shalwar-kameezes* pour out and scatter across the massive courtyard. Their plain, monochromatic outfits add to the serenity of the moment and I'm beginning to warm to this concept of simple, noise-free clothing.

On the way out of the compound I pass by the tomb of Allama Mohammad Iqbal, but purposely don't go inside—perhaps because of a resentment I feel towards him, for his role in the partitioning of India. I know it's probably not my place to feel this way about such a towering and brilliant man, but nonetheless, I can't bring my legs to walk towards it. I keep thinking about how things might have turned out had he had less of an influence on Jinnah, who was always slightly more committed to an undivided Indian future. Allama Iqbal, who wrote praises of his beloved Hindustan, was a Cambridge-educated descendent of Kashmiri Hindu Pandits and a follower of Jalaluddin Rumi. But he is often credited as being the intellectual inspiration for the Pakistan Movement, a movement based on notions of exclusivity and separation, rather than on the principles of universality that Rumi espoused. The contradictions in that bother me too much, so I simply nod in his direction to pay my respects, and walk away.

So far, my time in Pakistan has been fairly family-oriented. My hosts are very accommodating and independent travel is, for the moment, on hold. It's not unlike what we do in Dhaka when we have 'foreign' guests; we feel protective about them, and swaddle them with cars and chaperones. I'm not complaining. It's a very pleasant experience, and has also allowed me to get an inside look at Pakistani life. They're not a typical Pakistani family, though, and are similar to the sort of family I'm from myself, adding to the impressions of likeness I've been getting since I got here. Increasingly, I'm finding Pakistan familiar, more so than India in certain ways. It has plenty to do with the uniformity of Indo-Muslim culture of course, which, much as we'd like to feign indifference about it, is woven into our national fabric, influencing everything from our folk music to our sense of both *adab* and *qaeda*. But it also has to do with Islam itself and the sort of personal fortitude it encourages along with an openness of spirit, called *udharota* in Bangla, which eschews snideness and being hard-hearted. These and other things make Pakistan quite recognisable.

There are more obvious reasons too. For the nearly 25 years that Bangladesh was East Pakistan, both wings of the country probably had a similar sort of socialisation and maybe that's why—in ways I can't exactly put my finger on—Pakistan reminds me of the Bangladesh I knew when I was younger. After all, my father and his generation were Pakistani for all of their childhood and parts of their adulthood. When they were in thrall to the euphoric patriotism of youth, it was a Pakistani flag they waved and wrapped themselves in. Our grandparents must have worn that badge with a lot of dignity once—being Pakistani wasn't a de facto identity, it was a deliberate one, and one with profound significance. It was their sacred deliverance from the domination they had endured in a Hindu-administered British Raj.

They gave birth to Pakistan; they wished it into existence and then bled heavily to push it out of the womb. Many, including my mother's family, left everything they had to move there, believing that it was their promised land, a land of new beginnings, of restorations, of safety, of singing songs around a campfire and shouting 'free at last'. They must have been immensely proud of it. It was like no other country on earth: the first modern nation to have been created as a homeland for a religious community (followed shortly by Israel). Pakistan was the embodiment of conviction and of will, and was fashioned by people who could congratulate themselves for being able to resolutely answer the compelling call of destiny. They were people of the hour, a chosen people. What a high it must've been, what a triumph, and how rude an awakening the events that followed must have been for them.

But Pakistan didn't veer violently off course only in the eastern wing. The country today is quite a different animal than the one conceived of by its founders, not least by Jinnah himself. Just as Bangladesh has moved away from where it was when it, and I, were younger, so too has Pakistan, but in a different direction entirely and I'm not convinced that either extreme is really the answer. Bangladesh, in principle at least, has tried to move towards progressive liberalism (even if certain sections have become more illiberal as a reaction), and while I'm all for it, there's no point being naive about the social laxity that has also followed. Pakistan, on the other hand, seems to be steadily going towards a strict, religious conservatism, one that is beginning to resemble the joylessness that overcame its northern and western neighbours in the recent past, and brought with it a set of moral deficiencies of an altogether more dangerous kind. Already, Pakistani public life feels contaminated by that edgy sort of severity and I find myself feeling quite worried for this place but grateful that we are no longer tied to its fortunes.

Day 11

I arrive at the Daewoo bus counter while it's still dark to catch the 5:30am bus to Rawalpindi. It will get me there at 10am and I'll taxi it to Taxila, which is 30 minutes away, giving me just enough time to explore the site and get back to Lahore by evening.

Daewoo buses are the best mode of surface travel in Pakistan. Given the dismal state of Pakistan's trains, they are often also the only one. Although the South Korean corporation went bankrupt in 1999, its logo survives here, and a fleet of Daewoo-made buses owned by the Sammi Corporation provides luxury travel to virtually every city in the country. They are head and shoulders above the Volvo buses in Bangladesh and are similarly priced. They are also driven properly and at a pleasant speed, which is something I'd pay any amount of money to be able to have back home. These buses are spacious, air-conditioned and clean, and come in two classes, although the difference is minimal. They have good reclining seats, foot rests, televisions, large windows and even stewardesses on board, who come around and pour you soft drinks every so often. A snack box also comes with the seat, and usually has a sandwich, a bag of crisps and a piece of cake or pastry. All in all the Daewoo bus experience is a very enjoyable one and I use the service frequently while I am in Pakistan.

I find myself seated next to one Captain Nausher, a young, unassuming man who is not in uniform and is on his way back to his base in Bajaur, after having spent the Eid holidays at home. Bajaur is in the Federally Administered Tribal Areas on the border with

Afghanistan and on the frontline in the war against the Taliban. My estimation of him increases upon hearing this and to be perfectly honest, I begin to feel a bit like jelly next to him. We chat in broken Urdu and English and when I tell him I'm from Bangladesh he nods in a way that signals an apologetic acknowledgement of the troubled history our countries share. Then he says,

'Bohut badi ghalti ho gayi aap logon ka saath, bhai.'

It catches me by surprise, but I decide it would be ungracious of me to say 'damn straight', and so just smile and tell him that the past is in the past, and neither of us was there at the time. We talk some more. Captain Nausher is a very gentle, soft-spoken man, quite unlike what I had expected a Pakistani soldier to be. I'm very curious about the situation on the border so steer the conversation towards the topic of the Taliban and his job, and begin to ask him some cheeky questions, like if he feels afraid, to which he says, 'After six years on the front, and with all the training I have received, I am no longer afraid. I consider it my privilege to serve the motherland, and anyway, my fate is in Allah's hands.'

Is there regular conflict? Do they shoot at him every day?

'Yes, every day. And there are mines on the road to the base. We always have to be vigilant. Our enemies created them, you know, the Taliban, created to destroy us.'

I want to tell him that the army he serves might have also had a hand in their creation but realise that this would be impossible for him to believe, and also very cruel of me to point out, considering that the same army has now wagered his life to fight against them.

'Who are your enemies?'

'India, our traditional enemy, and also America. Don't be fooled, America is not a friend to Pakistan.'

'But America assists you, no? Didn't they recently provide Pakistan with …?'

'*Yaar*, they are using us. We are not stupid, we know this very well. But we let them think what they want, because we are using them too, in fact. We are playing a double game with them. We kill a few terrorists, and they give us more money, more weapons. Ultimately, we will turn on them. They know this too, but at the moment neither of us can do anything about it, so we just play the game.'

What a dangerous game. And such a careless conversation I'm having about it, with a Captain in the Pakistani Army no less.

'What about the drone attacks? Don't they kill civilians? Is this a part of the "game" too?'

'Yes, in fact, it is', he counters, quite unruffled. Drone attacks don't happen without our permission. We are the ones who tell them when and where to attack.

'You use American drones to kill your own civilians? Are you serious?'

'Don't believe everything you hear on the news. We can't tell the public a lot of things. It's a strategic move to label them as collateral damage, because, you see, in fact many of the civilians are also combatants. What I mean to say is that combatants don't always declare themselves, and they also get support from the local population, especially in the Tribal Areas, where loyalty is to the warlords who might have a brother or cousin who is Taliban. The Pakistani Army is seen as an outsider in these areas so we use the Americans to take out obstacles to Pakistan's authority.

'But that's not the point; the point is, if we were to declare openly that civilians are involved, there would be indiscriminate aggression against all civilians. It's a very delicate situation. We are fighting the Taliban, but also the warlords and their people, while trying to protect innocents at the same time. Innocents do get killed and we regret it, but we are at war and it happens. It's not a habit.'

'It's not a habit' were his exact words.

'And what about Osama Bin Laden? Was he really living in Abbotabad? Didn't you guys know he was there?'

'We didn't know about it. It's a big mystery. It's a big intelligence failure on our part, but it's true, he was there.'

Well there it is, from the horse's mouth, but I don't buy it. I think he's covering or just doesn't know. I change the subject.

'Is this war winnable, do you think?'

'We have to win. Our existence is at stake. If Sri Lanka, a weaker army than ours, can win against the Tamil Tigers—a stronger enemy than the Taliban who even had air defence—then we surely can. Even if it takes us 25 years like it did them, we have to do it. By the way I have trained with Bangladeshi officers too. We do joint exercises. They have been here, and our officers have gone there. Good fighters!'

I take this as an indication that he doesn't want to talk about Pakistan's vulnerabilities any more, and so stop interrogating him.

But that's the truth of it. Pakistan really is fighting for its survival. The country is engaged in an existentialist struggle while being hit by many forces and tugged at from all sides. It's embroiled in America's and Al Qaeda's Great Game in Central Asia, is being attacked by the Taliban, is receiving mounting international scorn, is still uneasy about India's growing power and its territorial claims, has rouge fiefdoms within its borders, has a Saudi-funded Wahhabi movement growing inside it like a tumour, and, as I will find out later, also has deep and violent fractures along ethno-linguistic lines with separatist undertones. On top of that, there is sectarian tension in Balochistan and inter-party political violence in Sindh, not to mention the usual South Asian ailments of corruption, nepotism, poverty, illiteracy and bigmanship. Pakistan is truly at a very difficult time in its life. It is struggling to keep standing in a tough neighbourhood, straddling the ancient crossroads of conquest and right next door to Afghanistan's unconquerable 'graveyard of empires'. From here, 1971 seems like a distant memory and just another small chapter in the complex story that is Pakistan.

Captain Nausher has a smile on his face as he naps, and looks just like a sleeping child. He's a good-looking man, younger than me, and I feel very worried for him. I pray that he won't be behind the next headline that reads: *Taliban attack Pakistani armed forces on the border: 20 killed*, but it's possible, and I will never know. I feel worried for Pakistan in general, and sad that these people whom I have begun to like quite a lot, should have to contend with such heavy odds. I also feel disappointed that we—SAARC, India and the rest of South Asia—seem to have abandoned them to their fate, disowned them as though they are not a part of us when, in fact, they most certainly are.

The motorway between Lahore and Rawalpindi is first class, perhaps even better than the roads I encountered in Gurgaon. Quite a lot of Pakistan and India's more recent infrastructure in and around their capital cities is high in quality: six lanes, flyovers and great carpeting. The bus doesn't use the N-5 highway, which is part of the Old Grand Trunk Road, but the newly built M-2, which runs slightly to the south of it. The scenery is stunning; the road goes through passes in the hills and across wide, rugged plains, green and dark brown, fringed by mountains. Punjab is a beautiful country. I romanticise that these are the places vividly described in the Rig Veda, marked with sacred spaces and littered with ceremonial sites no longer visited. Buried beneath those are the cities of the Indus Valley Civilisation and some of our oldest roots.

The bus station is along a dusty stretch of highway outside Rawalpindi. There's an armed guard letting people in and out of the terminal and I'm beginning to get less and less surprised by how many people in uniform—any uniform—carry weapons in this country. Even simple security guards are packing. I go to the nearest *dhaba* to get something to eat, and have a two-egg omelette with two large *parathas* and some tea. Then I go and haggle with some taxi-wallahs to take me to the ruins. Both the dhabawallah and the taxiwallah don't appreciate the attitude of entitlement I initially approach them with, an attitude that is almost essential in Dhaka sometimes. People here speak to and expect to be spoken to with a degree of respect; there's an egalitarianism about the way they interact with each other and a basic amount of courtesy seems to be built into most conversations, regardless of rank or station. I like this very much, and will notice it throughout my stay in Pakistan. People aren't as servile here, and there is far less bowing and scraping going around. It could be pride, or maybe they're over-sensitive about being slighted, but it's pleasant nonetheless.

I fix a taxi and a price and head off towards Taxila, getting almost run off the road by an SUV that overtakes us and vents its frustration at having to be stuck behind us for all of three minutes. *'Sala behnchod Pathan, kutte!'* yells the taxi driver out the window as they pass us by. So much for courtesy.

Taxila

Taxila was originally called 'Takshashila' after Taksha, Lord Rama's brother, and sits astride the boundary between Punjab and Khyber Pakhtunkhwa. It is nestled in hills and valleys and at first glance looks topographically similar to Rajgir, but spread across a larger expanse. In fact the hills roll on to become the western edge of the Himalayan Range and the eastern extent of the Iranian Plateau. Surrounded by the great rivers that created the Indus Valley, Taxila was one of the most important ancient cities in South Asia. It's the place where South, West and Central Asia meet, and has, at various times, belonged to empires coming out of all of three. It was even a Hellenistic possession for a while. Taxila has traded hands so many times that its long and illustrious past is a catalogue of the cultures that poured through the region and were eventually absorbed by it.

It all begins in prehistory. Some 30,000 years ago, settlements arose around the confluence of the Kabul and Indus rivers near Attock, traces of which have come to us as stone-age tools and implements, and a few bones. Nothing else remains of it, or if it does, we haven't found it yet. The next time we hear about the people living here, they are called the Gandhari, and they have founded a kingdom called Gandhara, one of the 16 Mahajanapadas of Epic India, with Taxila at its centre. Puranic literature tells us that they are the descendants of a king who was also called Gandhara, of the Dhruyu line, one of the several dynasties mentioned in the Rig Veda.

Hindu literature is scathing in its opinion of the Gandhari, calling them *'mleccha'* or impure, beyond the pale of civilisation—in other words, savages. The Vedic Aryans used *mleccha* as an all-encompassing term to describe a host of characteristics and often populations that were considered undesirable or unfit for social and marital contact. This included eating habits, customs, values, religious orientation, language and speech, build, facial features, hygiene, and virtually anything else that we might describe using the words 'crude and uncouth' in today's version of Brahmanical snobbery. The Aryans had enormous contempt for these people and often went on pogroms against them, or tried to convert them, showing early signs of a propensity for ethnic cleansing and missionary zeal. It wasn't a racial classification; it could include people of 'mixed-ancestry' and other races, but also Aryan tribes who had abandoned the Vedic way of life. The word was used the way that Ionian Greeks used 'barbaros', but in this case, the Ionians, or Yavanas in Sanskrit, were themselves also *mleccha*. So were we—the Bangas, and the Angas of Eastern India, as well as Muslims, in a later application of the term.

The Gandhara kingdom grew in that grey area between the Indian and the Iranian cultural continents. They used an Indic language but the Kharoshti script, which came from West Asian languages, while their immediate neighbours, the Kamboja (also dismissed as *mleccha*s) spoke an Iranic language but were considered part of Bharatbarsha. They were also consistently called 'Kamboja' throughout Indian history, from the time they had a Mahajanapada, some time in the 8th century BC, all the way to the 10th century AD and even into the present. There is still a Kamboj clan living somewhere in Punjab.

But this isn't their story, fascinating as they might be. It's the story of Gandhara, and a very good one too. We can catch up with it in the Mahabharata.

Act 3, Scene 1. Taxila. Indoor. Day

Prince Shakuni is in a state. He has just been released from prison in Hastinapur and has had to watch his family die just to keep him alive. His sister, Queen Gandhari, who has blindfolded herself in solidarity with her blind husband King Dhritarashtra, manages to get him out of the Kuru Kingdom, and he has lodged himself in the nearest Gandharan city, Takshashila, to plan his next move.

Shakuni: The bloody Kurus, and that little bastard Duryodhona! I knew Gandhari should never have married that blind, weak man. They've always had their eye on Gandhara, you know, ever since that albino Pandu conquered the eastern kingdoms to create his United States of Kuru. Greedy Aryas! And what a family of freaks, look at them: blind, pale, diseased, a hundred test-tube babies ... they had to 'outsource' fatherhood to even have a king at all!

Shakuni's Minister: Freaks or not, they have killed the king of Gandhara, sir. You are the king now. You must restore our honour, sir, and avenge you father. It's your duty!

Shakuni: Shut up, you fool! I know this all too well. We were trying to save Dhritarashtra's life! But Duryodhona is as blind as his father, and filled with the vilest of qualities—jealousy, pride, lust, ambition, and most of all, vanity. It will be his undoing ... yes, his undoing, and I shall be the one to undo him ... and his whole world. Here, make yourself useful, call my advisers and tell them we must have an emergency meeting to plan our course of action.

Minister: We could make an alliance with Jarasandha, the Magadhan king who hates the Kuru. We could attack their Federation from both sides and ....

Shakuni: You are thinking far too small, Ramchandra. The kind of revenge I have in mind will take time—an incubation period— and a series of well thought out moves, like a game of Chaturanga. It will be felt across Bharatbarsha and by all the descendants of Bharat! Oh yes, Ram, I intend to make even their ancestors pay. When the last piece falls, we will be at the beginning of a new world order. They will be talking about it for thousands of years. Now get lost, and tell the cook to prepare dinner. Oh, and get the boy to run a bath as well, won't you? That's a good minister.

Act 3, Scene 2. Hastinapur. Evening

Shakuni plots the end of Kurustan. He returns to Hastinapur in the guise of a friend pretending that all is forgotten and becomes one of Duryodhona's closest confidantes. He embeds himself in the Kuru court, and when Dhritarashtra honours the ancient rite of primogeniture by choosing Yudhishthira, Pandu's first born, to succeed him, Shakuni seizes upon the opportunity.

Shakuni: Duryodhona, there you are, my strapping young nephew. Listen, I've been meaning to ask you, are you really going to let this go without a fight? You, the finest member of the House of Kuru? I mean the Pandavas aren't even entitled to the throne by birthright. It's not like they've sprung from the loins of anyone in this family, right? They aren't Pandu's children, everyone knows that. You're the real firstborn of this House, the actual bearer of the royal Kuru blood.

Duryodhona: I'll be damned if I do! It's a travesty. It's bad enough that we've had to live in this kingdom with those illegitimate children of Kunti's—virgin births and sons of gods ... hah! We've tolerated it long enough. They have no claim to this throne whatsoever, and if I have to, I will very happily send them back to their fathers in the sky, if that's even where they come from.

Shakuni: I'm glad you say that, because, well, I've sort of thought of something, something that will rid you of your troubles, and won't soil your lovely, manicured hands in the process. But far be it for me to tell you how to run your affairs in Kurustan ....

Duryodhona: Stop being coy and just come out with it, you weaselly old man. What's this plan of yours?

Shakuni: Okay, listen closely ....

Shakuni unveils an elaborate plot to assassinate Yudhishthira and his brothers by secretly immolating them in a purpose-built wax palace where they are to be made to stay during an orchestrated ambassadorial visit to Varnavata. The plan is implemented but they are saved, following warnings by their uncle, Vidur. Dhritarashtra, recognising that this sibling rivalry is becoming deadly, partitions his kingdom, and gives each set of cousins their own separate realms. The second capital of Indraprastha is established and Shakuni wrings his hands in delight.

Act 3, Scene 3. Hastinapur. Night

Duryodhona is pacing up and down his bedchambers. He's troubled; Indraprashta is thriving and his own subjects hold Yudhishthira in higher regard than they do the Kauravas. Duryodhona seethes with envy.

There is a knock on the door. Shakuni slithers in and sits by the bed.

Duryodhona: I just don't understand. We gave them the worst part of the realm, very little resources and there are only five of them. We are a hundred, we hold the capital, yet their city is the most beautiful thing I have ever seen. I bet that blasted Krishna has something to do with it. He's become their adviser, you know, and he has … these powers. But you are mine, and this is your fault. Your 'great' idea has cost me half my kingdom!

Shakuni: No, my glorious King, it has gained you half, but never mind that. I have a better plan this time. This one can't fail. Yudhishthira is a gambler; he has a terrible weakness for games and can't resist a chance to test his skills. Invite him to Hastinapur for a game of Chowka Bhara. Call it a reconciliation game. Keep it friendly, let him win a few rounds but goad him on. Get him to stake their kingdom on it and when that happens, slam! You will have them out of your country and out of your hair for good.

Duryodhona: But it's a game of chance; it could go either way. I could lose my throne too! How is this a good plan? Are you senile, old man, or are you secretly trying to ruin me?

Shakuni: Heavens no, my dear, what a horrible thought. You see, the truth is, I have a pair of these magical dice ….

The die is, well, cast. Yudhishthira gambles and loses it all, including, ever so symbolically, himself. As per the conditions of defeat, the Pandavas spend 13 years in exile and return to find Duryodhona intoxicated by his absolute power and unwilling to return Indraprastha to them. Naked aggression now replaces the previously veiled variety, and even after Krishna asks, for the sake of peace, for just five villages, Duryodhona flatly refuses to share even an inch of his kingdom. The only options open to the Pandavas are to slink back into the forest, which they briefly consider, or going to war. But they are vastly outgunned and have no appetite for bloodshed.

Kunti, their mother, steels her heart and tells them to hold their ground,

'A bad king is a disease. He perverts his Age. If you live with the fear of death, why were you given life? Burn like a torch, even if it is only for a moment.'

Krishna, too, urges them to fight, but just before battle is joined, Arjuna, the most skilled of the Pandavas, can't bring himself to fight his own family—his cousins, nephews, uncles and teachers—knowing how much suffering it will cause on both sides. He becomes philosophical and withdrawn. Krishna tells him that victory and defeat are the same, and that he should fight with no attachment, and no desire of an outcome. He must become an instrument of fate, nothing else. He tells him to go beyond illusion, of which even filial affection is a part, and into the place where all things are alike.

But Arjuna is not convinced. Unable to reason with him, Krishna becomes Vishnu and reveals to Arjuna the universe as it exists on every dimension. He shows him the cosmic continuity that results from doing one's duty, and the need to fight so that virtue can triumph over treachery and courage can dispel fear. He shows him eternity and sings the Bhagavad Gita to him. Arjuna relents and begins the Kurukshetra War, which rages for 18 days. Emotional and physical torment follows—many rules are broken, many vows abandoned and a stack of Dharma discarded. The Kauravas are completely destroyed and all hundred brothers are killed. The Pandavas also suffer great losses but the brothers survive, their morality in tatters. It's the most pyrrhic of victories as all of Bharat has been set ablaze—kingdoms are ruined, kings and their successors are dead or scattered, armies are shattered, divine favours have been exhausted; peace, prosperity and integrity have all been very badly battered.

Shakuni has exacted his revenge, and how frightfully accurate his calculations have turned out to be. Bharatbarsha will never be the same again. The Mahajanapada system has effectively been extinguished and the Age of Empires will soon be upon them. Kali Juga is on its way.

Shakuni, whose name translates, aptly, to 'vulture-like' in English, doesn't survive the war—he must not have wanted to, as he fought on the side of the Kauravas and was expecting them to lose all along. Gandhara is incorporated into the new Hastinapuri kingdom with Yudhishthira as king, and perhaps that's what Shakuni had hoped for since he knew, like everyone else, that the Pandavas were the better crop of Kurus. Takshashila becomes a major city in this kingdom, and Parikshit, the sole surviving descendent of the house of Kuru (though, considering that neither Arjuna nor his 'father', Pandu, was actually biologically related to Kuru, this is a bit of a lie) is coronated here after he succeeds Yudhishthira.

Parikshit's life ends by snakebite and his son Janamajaya, believing it to be no accident, attempts to exterminate the Naga race (liminal beings associated with serpents, perhaps like shape-shifters or composite creatures like the Greek centaur) which has taken up residence at Takshashila. It is during one such purge that the Mahabharata, the greatest story ever told, (incidentally also the longest piece of literature in existence), is recited for the first time— right here at Taxila.

An aside: The greatest story ever told

It's a big claim—the greatest story ever told—but it's true. The Mahabharata has such depth and breadth of perspective when observing the subtleties of human circumstance that it's almost impossible not to consider it so. British director Peter Brook called it 'a poetic history of mankind', and then directed quite a poetic adaptation of it himself. The Mahabharata covers history, philosophy, anthropology, sociology, cosmology, geography, mysticism, spirituality, wisdom, magic, romance, sex, drama, jealousy, rivalry, treachery, tragedy, devotion, heroism, humour, humanity, compassion, respect, loyalty, sport, politics, economics, war, art, religion, responsibility, ethics, duty, family—I could go on and on. The conversations in it are profound and ponderable. Virtually every sort of question, crisis of conscience and contradiction is captured effortlessly, so much so that it makes me wonder if our collective consciousness hasn't travelled backwards since those times, rather than forward—like sitting against the direction of travel on a train, looking at, but moving away from a time when we had a better grasp on the fullest meaning of being.

The tally of one's good actions reaches heaven and spreads over the earth. As long as that lasts, so long a person, to whom the agreeable and the disagreeable, weal and woe, the past and the future are the same, is said to possess every kind of wealth.

When a sentient person ceases to see different identities because of different material bodies and he sees how beings are expanded everywhere, he attains to the Brahma conception.

Death cannot devour a man who has shaken off his dust; it is powerless against Eternity. Life flows from the infinite. The wise man soars between the worlds; when his body is dissolved, death itself is dissolved, and he contemplates infinity.

The story is set at the end of the Dvapara Juga, when Dharma is a biped and men are only half as good as they are capable of being. Virtue is slipping away and the age of destruction, the Kali Juga, is snapping at its heels. The characters in the story represent this moral crisis, and all of them, the gods as well, are fabulously flawed. They are simultaneously petty and profound, and are hurtling towards a terrible conflict, which is raging both in and outside of them. There are no absolute heroes or outright villains. All of them are recognisably vulnerable, with injustice, fear and doubt plaguing them all evenly. The whole thing is a statement on the condition of souls. It's a tale of consequences and of mankind's station in the cosmos—wavering between divinity and damnation—and faithfully reflects the absence of absolute certainty captured in this brilliant hymn from the Rig Veda,

But, after all, who knows, and who can say where it all came from, and how creation happened? The gods themselves are later than creation, so who knows truly where it arose from? Where does all creation have its origins? He, whether he fashioned it or whether He did not, He, who surveys it all from highest heaven, He knows—or maybe even He does not.

They are tested; there are ascetics, madmen, mystics, magicians and demons. It shows you the heart of people standing at the precipice of the end of their world. You feel for them, feel their torments and their struggles and are given the backstory explaining why they are the way they are, as if to ask you not to judge them. It attempts to give you both sides of an argument and holds firm to the eternal doctrine of Love as the source of virtue. You won't cheer or boo anyone particularly loudly, and will probably end up being fair in your opinion, which will include some disdain for nearly everyone.

The story doesn't lie to you or give you unreasonable expectations about a 'happily ever after' but teaches you a great deal about the way things are when they are at their best or at their worst, or somewhere in between. It's an exceptionally elegant approach. There is an ocean of wisdom in the story—about the strength of Dharma, the nature of goodness, the ugliness of avarice, the hatefulness of war (as well as one of the earliest examples of ground rules for it), the pre-eminence of the Spirit, the inescapable balance of Karma, the power of Truth, the Maya (illusion) of being, and plenty more, but I would be kidding myself if I thought I could summarise the worth of the Mahabharata in a few short paragraphs so will give up trying now, and get us back on the road at Taxila.

The on-site Taxila Museum is a real treat. It's Sir John Hubert Marshall's baby, that extraordinary British archaeologist who excavated Taxila, as well as Mohenjodaro and Harappa, and a large portrait of him still hangs at the entrance. It's one of the best site museums I've come across in South Asia, with a large, well-labelled collection from many different eras, but mostly from the Buddhist and Hellenistic periods. It specialises in Gandharan Art, a style of

Graeco-Buddhist sculpture notable for the clearly Greek influence on the postures and features of figures. There are many stucco reliefs depicting various stories from the Jataka Tales along with other quintessential Buddhist iconography and various sized stone statues and busts, all with a greater amount of realism than similar ones elsewhere. They're all very well preserved too. Taxila's artists were noted in the past for their superior stonework and some of these skills seem to have been handed down the ages. On my way up to the site, I stop at a workshop to admire well-crafted stone sarcophagi decorated in complicated floral patterns and Urdu calligraphy. Quite a few small workshops are busy making them, and my taxi driver tells me that well-to-do people across the country place orders here for these rather macabre pieces of art.

The museum also has coins and jewellery and a section on household appliances from the 5th century BC, including something that looks like an ancient water purifier. Being well maintained and so close to the capital, Taxila is the most visited archaeological site in Pakistan and there are also a few foreigners here. It's the single largest gathering of foreigners I will see on the Pakistani leg of my route, and there are only about 10 of them. Tourism here has taken quite a battering since it all went belly up with the terrifying war on terror.

The site is spread out over a large area and contains the ruins of a number of cities, built by different civilisations and empires during different times. One of them might be the city of the Mahabharata, but it's very difficult to know that for sure. The earliest city to have been dug up is from the 6th century BC, at the Bihr Mound, by which time Taxila was already being included in Persian records as a part of Darius the Great's Achaemenid sphere of influence. But the absence of cuneiform markers or tablets to signal territoriality, a usual Achaemenid practice, suggests that Gandhara was an autonomous vassal state, and so the urban landscape uncovered at Bihr is not Persian-built, though some of the structures have Achaemenid influence, but older—very possibly the remains of the same city where the Mahabharata was first recited. Gandhara's, and more specifically Taxila's, independence is also supported by the fact that it was a known centre of Sanskrit scholarship before it became a Persian possession, and remained so all the way through, until it reverted to Indian hands. Enter the Maurya.

The Maurya belonged to a Magadhan expansionist movement that began 300 years earlier when, Bimbisara Haryanka, whom we stumbled upon in Rajgir as a disciple of Buddha (and possibly also Mahavira), restored Magadha's position on the Gangetic plain following the devastating effects of the Kurukeshetra war. It pushed westward, right up to the old Kuru kingdom, which had by now begun fading into obscurity. This was later consolidated by the Nanda Empire, generally recognised as India's first experiment with imperialism. The new and fledgling religions of Jainism and Buddhism bubbled away within these realms and began pushing the older Vedic system into the background. A new world order was indeed in the offing, and was brushing up against another great force from the west, the Zoroastrian Achaemenid Empire. Taxila fell squarely in the middle of both.

The Persians took it first—or at least claimed to have—and Alexander the Great took it off them in 326 BC. Chandragupta Maurya, perhaps in his early teens, and a student of the great strategist Kautilya, is said to have met Alexander, but of course this could be myth. Taxila's king Ambhi was a bit of a collaborator, or perhaps just a survivor, and assisted the Greeks against his neighbour Purusha, or Porus, the Punjabi king who gave Alexander a run for his money and killed his famous horse Bucephalus at the Battle of Jhelum. In fact the battle took so much out of the Greeks that they had no heart to go further, into the lands of the Prasoi and Gangaridai (almost certainly Bihar and Bengal, respectively) whose armies were larger and fiercer than Purusha's. Perhaps the loss of Bucephalus had something to do with it too. After all, Alexander had owned him since he was a 13-year-old boy and rode him into battle all the way to India.

Taxila went on to become the Oxford of the ancient world after it was wrested from the Greeks by the Mauryas, along with the other Greek satrapies in the region, around 316 BC. Takshashila

University is sometimes called the oldest university in the world, and, along with the ones in the East like Nalanda and Somapura, nourished the intellectual and spiritual life of India and indeed the world for many centuries. It produced some of the finest minds in history and its faculty included the likes of Panini, the grammarian, and Kautilya, or Chanakya, the political scientist who wrote the Arthashastra, the definitive text on political economy and statecraft, which became the blueprint upon which the Mauryan Empire was built. It could also boast Vishnu Sharma, the professor of ethics and possible compiler of the Panchatantra (although this is sometimes attributed to Kautilya); Charaka, the health scientist who wrote the Charaka Samhita, and added to existing medical knowledge to create the Ayurveda as we know it today; Jivak, Buddha's personal physician who ran the hospital in Rajgir, and a galaxy of others whose names have been washed away by the tides of time. Its students included Chandragupta, of course, but also his grandson Ashoka, as well as at least one king of Kosala, today's Ayodhya.

Students at Takshashila University could study more than 64 disciplines, including grammar, etymology, philosophy, logic, ethics, law, ayurveda, surgery, history, agriculture, politics, international relations, archery, warfare, astronomy, accounting, commerce, music, dance, poetry, numerology, futurology, the Vedas, the epics, the Puranas, the Buddhist canons, the study of encrypting and decrypting messages, languages, including even Greek. The education system didn't include awards or examinations and students only 'graduated' when they were thought to have reached the limits of their understanding of a particular subject. There was no government regulation or a government approved syllabus and Pandits were free to set their own curriculum, form their own 'colleges' and have complete autonomy in both their research and their teaching methodologies.

In his book, *Universities of Ancient India*, D.G. Apte explains in detail the way this education was paid for.

All the necessary financial assistance was supplied by the society to teachers who as a general rule provided free boarding and lodging to all the students. No student was required to pay any fees on a compulsory basis. The non-payment of fees never resulted in expulsion from the institution nor in any differential treatment. In fact, stipulation that fees should be paid was vehemently condemned. Knowledge was considered too sacred to be bartered for money and Hindu scriptures contain specific injunctions against those who charge money to students.

He goes on to tell us,

The community ... was conscious of its duty to the cause of education. Moneyed people very often used to make arrangements for the food of the students all throughout their courses of education ... students after finishing their education approached kings for money to be offered to the guru and their requests were always granted by kings.... Failure to help a student in need of money for paying the teacher's honorarium was regarded as the greatest slur on a king's reputation.

And here's the best part,

What the pupil learnt at the university was based on the dictum 'Knowledge for knowledge's sake'. The accomplishment had not to be used as an instrument for earning one's livelihood.... Admission never became a problem for those who had the requisite qualifications, namely, freedom from jealousy, straightforwardness and self-control.

I try to find the site of this incredible old institution and end up at Jaulian, a little further away from the main sites at Bihr and Sirkap. On a hill from where I can get a great view as well as a sense of perspective (the caretaker there points out the direction of Afghanistan, Delhi and China), sits the remains of an old monastery as well as some decorated stupas and a dormitory. The Pakistani Government notice board calls it Jaulian University, but it seems a bit too small to be the fabled one. Perhaps the rest of it is still buried or was turned to rubble. The stupas, which are protected by a shed built around them, are covered in statues and statuettes of Buddha, almost all of them with their heads smashed in. The caretaker tells me the White Huns did this and all the other pillaging in Taxila, in the 5th century, when their king, Mihirakula, a convert to the cult of Shiva, made known his hatred for Buddhism by smashing up Taxila, and effectively killing it off forever. It never recovered, and was never again the place of knowledge it had been for over a thousand years.

The caretaker, a bearded, toupee-wearing man, asks me to take a closer look at the stupa designs. He shows me the seven celestial realms, and says with a great deal of reverence,

'Like the seven heavens in Islam, no?'

Yes, just like them. He tells me more things that he's learnt over the years about Buddhism and why he thinks it has many similarities to Islam and I enjoy listening to him, encouraged by the knowledge that in spite of all the divisions and prejudices we get bombarded with daily, the plain truth can be obvious to anyone, if they would just think about it.

I head off to see more ruins, some by the Central Asian Kushans and others by the Indo-Greeks from Bactria, reflecting the panoply of influences—Zoroastrian, Hellenistic, Buddhist, Jain, Shaivite, Shamanistic—that washed over the cultures of this area at different times. 'Guides' hang around them and try to sell you rare coins found in the surrounding fields. The locals here are nicer than the people in Lahore and I find myself wondering if it's just an urban–rural thing or if their Buddhist history has something to do with it since there is a softness about them that reminds me of more eastern cultures.

Taxila has the most heavyset Buddhist expression I have yet encountered. The stupas are massive stone structures, covering large areas and standing a few storeys high. Everything is very robust and fort-like, and not at all like the more delicate brick-and-terracotta structures of Eastern India. There's also something unique about the way structures are put together here—they are made of large stones placed regular intervals apart, with the space between them filled with smaller slate stones instead of mortar. It looks neater and more patterned than lots of other stone structures I've seen in other parts of the world.

I'm running out of time so decide to skip the colossal Dharmarajika stupa, which was built by Ashoka and is said to contain the ashes of the Buddha. Instead, I make a stop at Sirkap, which has remains of the Indo-Greek city and a Jain temple, but once again all I see are lots of stones piled on top of each other in the shape of a city grid, only slightly more full than Rajgir or Pataliputra, and like both, overgrown and overrun by pastoralists and their grazing animals. But to Pakistan's credit, they've done a good job of preserving the ruins at Taxila, which many in this country probably consider a '*jahiliya*', pre-Muslim remnant of their past.

It's become dark so I take a taxi back to the Rawalpindi bus counter, where I make it just in time for the last bus, and sleep all the way back to Lahore. Mujeeb Uncle picks me up at the station, and I wake up from dreams of epic times to be transported, in an instant, back to the present tense.

I spend a couple of more days in Lahore and catch up with my friend Maham, who is a lawyer, and studying for exams she'll be taking in a few months. She's an empowered, progressive woman made in the mould of women like Asma Jahangir, and refuses to let the 'new' Pakistani climate affect her lifestyle. She drives, works, talks boldly and doesn't dress to hide herself away. She has refused to get married at least twice and continues to hold her ground, even, at times, against her own family. She's also quite religious, won't drink alcohol and says her prayers regularly. She does these completely out of choice and asserts that she loves being a Muslim woman. We have breakfast together and she tells me about how things are changing in Pakistan, with people becoming haughtier on the one hand and more fanatical on the other. She has to battle daily with chauvinism and with people casting aspersions on her character, simply because she refuses to be reticent.

That's the real tragedy of this impending Pakistani story. Moderate Pakistanis were already quite conservative to begin with— Pakistani society is naturally so, and religiosity is quite prominent in everyone's lives. A lot of my liberal Pakistani friends won't drink alcohol and many of them try to be regular with their religious duties. Quite a few of them will only eat halal meat. 'Liberated' Pakistani women are sometimes more modest and often more religious than their counterparts from other Muslim environments and they don't feel particularly conflicted by this in any way. Ordinary Pakistanis tend to remain constantly aware of God's pre-eminence, even in the most secular of contexts, and are imbued with an Islamic sensibility that is not particularly overt or self-conscious but governs their sense of *tameez, mehmannawazi* and *adab* or their decency, hospitality and manners.

I'm not trying to suggest that Pakistanis are paragons of Islamic virtue—far from it—but I am saying that the liberal ones are often more so than their 'Islamist' counterparts, whose penchant for things like honour killings and sectarian murder keep them very far from any sort of virtue at all. But secular Pakistanis, like Maham and Mujeeb Uncle's family, will never be able to 'appear' pious enough to Islamists without making a big show of it all, something they shouldn't have to do.

They feel threatened, and worried that their lifestyles, no matter how moral, will never be good enough for the extremists until they are all in burqas and beards, and perhaps even killing a 'kaffir' or two for good measure. I suppose that's pretty obvious—extremists have no time for moderates and vice-versa, but the trouble is the extremists seem to be on their way to setting the agenda here. It seems to all be a train going in the wrong direction and fast, and the thought of yet another organically Muslim culture being imposed upon by the Islamists' cerebral and hyper-paranoid construction is heart-breaking. It's also telling—all of our countries are susceptible to this disease and there is enough reason to believe that it won't end with Pakistan.

Over one of our dinner table conversations, Mujeeb Uncle, whose family migrated from India during Partition, tells me how the Indian Muslim civilisation he belongs to, the one that sprung up in Uttar Pradesh and Hyderabad and revolved around Delhi, Agra and Lucknow, has been trodden underfoot in Pakistan, where they had arrived out of the fear, ironically, that it would be trodden on in India. To give his story context, he begins by telling me about the sociology of Partition and how by 1947 Indian Muslims had become fearful and insular, and were struggling to preserve their culture in an environment that was increasing dominated by what they perceived as Vedic nationalism. This might not have been a problem if it weren't for the paranoid conclusion that it would invariably lead to the persecution of minorities.

The truth is, Indian leaders were recalling Sanskritic civilisation as a cultural force, to recover a sense of dignity and self-worth after nearly two centuries of subjugation. They were trying to reconnect an emergent India with its extensive and elaborate history and counter a colonial conditioning that gave invaders, both the Muslims and the British, an entirely unsubstantiated civilisational superiority complex. It wasn't an attempt to stifle pluralism, since India's character has always been pluralistic, and there has always been, even within Hinduism itself, plenty of room for differences. In fact the practice of calling Hinduism a single religion rather than a collection of different and often opposing religious traditions, is a fairly modern concept.

Muslim India might have noticed that, had it not sat pompously on top of Sanskritic civilisation, rather than within it. Even though there was considerable syncretism, by the 1940s Indian Muslim civilisation saw itself as an alternative to rather than an extension of Indian culture, and this didn't go down well with anyone. So while Muslims grew worried about what effect Vedic rhetoric would have on their unique identity, others grew tired of their assumption that it was any more unique than the plethora of identities India already sustained.

Indian Muslim civilisation *was*, in fact, very Indian. It came out of the blending of different traditions and cultures, just like Urdu did, midwifed by India's accommodating embrace. This culture was now sitting 'outside' India—dislocated and distanced from the roots that helped it to flower into an exceedingly cultivated one, with its leanings towards classical music, poetry, literature and art. Now, amidst the arid acrimony of Balochistan, the rugged realism of Pakhtunkhwa, the sardonic strong-arming of Sindh and the patronising pomposity of Punjab, this flower, denied the soul-feeding nutrients of the Ganges flood plain, has begun to wilt. Mujeeb Uncle blames the crassness of these 'rougher' people for crowding out a better quality of Pakistan, and their belligerent overconfidence for not letting them know the difference between the two. He also resents that they try to dominate the instruments of state. It all sounds so familiar.

'I know it does,' he says. 'We were always aware of the under-currents in 1971. Bengalis are smart, cultured and more politically astute than most of "them", and this they couldn't tolerate. They knew that no amount of feudal bellicosity would beat that, so they turned their guns on you. They demonised and then attacked you.'

I'm flattered and incensed at the same time, but then think about Bangladesh and wonder what we're doing, exactly, with all this 'smart, cultured and politically astute' stuff that we're supposed to be made of. But I know what he means and also why we could no longer stay in a country that possesses a military-industrial complex on steroids.

This issue of dominance is rife in Pakistan. Even ordinary, everyday encounters carry with them a subtle attempt to establish it. People here, especially in Punjab, seem very conscious about making sure they are on top, or at least of giving the impression that they are. It's uncomfortable, and on a national level, catastrophic. Pakistan is, after all, not a whole country but a collection of halves, cleaved out of territories with a memory of being an independent *mulk*, some time in their recent history. It is made up of parts of Kashmir, parts of Punjab, parts of Balochistan, parts of Sindh and parts of Pakhtunistan. Bangladesh is a half of something as well, but half of a single thing (the Chittagong Hill Tracts notwithstanding, which should never have been included within our borders in the first place), and is far less contradictory than many halves put together and expected to act as a whole.

The question of a provincial pecking order has been an issue in Pakistan from the very beginning, but with Punjab pulling away as the clear winner, other provinces are growing increasingly militant in their reaction to it, leading to bloodshed. Punjabis and Balochis are virtually at war with each other, and in 1967 Sindh considered the possibility of breaking away from Pakistan to create Sindhudesh. The Sindhu Desh Liberation Army and a Balochistan Liberation Army are both still active in their respective provinces. Pieces of the Pakhtun sphere are virtually independent, and old Kashmir (now Azad Kashmir and Gilgit-Baltistan) is mired by complications too well known to require re-telling. Migration between provinces is dangerous, and minorities like the Muhajirs in Sindh and the Punjabis in Balochistan are subject to attacks. It's a complete mess. The pre-1947 Indian Muslim community's fears of persecution and destruction have turned into reality, not in India but in Pakistan, and religion has nothing at all to do with it. Two nations, my eye.

5

Crosshairs across Worlds

Back in Lahore, Islamabad, Peshawar, Multan, Quetta

11 September is Muhammad Ali Jinnah's death anniversary and is known as Jinnah Day here in Pakistan. The irony of that, considering how Bin Laden's dramatic story ended right here in Pakistan, and only this year, seems to have escaped everyone else but me. The headlines carry next to nothing about the 10th anniversary of the terror attacks in the US or the Bin Laden raid, giving it a half-column mention somewhere on the back page. The front page is decidedly more local and suited to the context of Jinnah Day, but in the op-ed section, there's a piece about the war on terror in relation to Pakistani statehood, and as expected, the Americans aren't the heroes but the villains. The op-ed outlines the numerous violations of international law and states' sovereignty committed during this period and devotes considerable space to the humanitarian crisis precipitated by the invasion of Afghanistan. It goes on to mention the illegality of drone attacks and the countless innocent civilian lives that have been lost on both sides of the international border. It laments Pakistan's loss of control over its own territory and armed

forces and considers what Jinnah would have made of this insult to the people and the nation he dedicated his life to protect.

There's another piece that talks about Jinnah's legacy in regards to the Balochi insurgency where we, erstwhile East Pakistan, get an honourable mention too. Pakistan's struggles with defining its statehood and well as its standard response to any sort of dissidence, which is usually just to throw more lead at it, seems not to have worked, and 1971 comes up as an example of what could go wrong if the state doesn't demonstrate more tact in dealing with the Balochi. It talks about Jinnah's vision for a pluralistic, multicultural Pakistan where the sort of treatment being meted out to the various provinces would be completely unacceptable. I enjoy the article but am surprised by how even the liberal voices here can't look at 1971 without insisting it was an Indian-orchestrated conspiracy to weaken Pakistan. It certainly was that also, but Pakistan left itself wide open to being severed by not being able to find the formula for cohesion, and one language, one religion was certainly not it.

I'm booked on a shared taxi bound for Quetta, in Balochistan, which will take me closer to the Iranian border on my way out of Pakistan. I've been advised to avoid taking a bus from Punjab, since Balochi tribesmen often ambush buses to murder Punjabi passengers, and given the chance, could also kidnap foreigners to hold the government to ransom. The trains are unreliable and don't run on time, sometimes not at all (and can also be attacked), and I'm not willing to fly since it defeats my purpose, so a shared taxi is the only option open to me. It's a 16-hour ride in a Toyota Corolla—I've booked the 'VIP' seat, the front passenger's one, in the hope that it makes the journey at least partially bearable. We show up at the pick-up point at the designated time (8 am), but there is no taxi. We call the company but there is no answer. After waiting for an hour, we try again and a just-roused-from-sleep kind of voice answers to tell us that there is no taxi going today. I tell him I have a booking and he says, 'a booking on a non-existent taxi can't really mean anything, now, can it?' I lose my temper but he seems completely nonplussed, and when I ask him how I'm supposed to get to Quetta, he says, 'walk', and hangs up.

Defeated, we go to the Lahore Museum to avoid wasting the day completely. Built in the Mughal-Gothic style, it seems quite run down. It has a large collection of items stretching as far back as the Harappan Age; a badly labelled and dusty gallery of items collected from Maharajah Ranjit Singh's court; a gallery of Islamic art, and many pieces of sculpture from the Buddhist and Hindu periods, including ornate doorjambs, deities, wall decorations and Ashokan pillars. These are some of the best pieces I've seen anywhere in South Asia, but sadly the museum is in a horrid state of disrepair. It's haphazard and dirty, and looks completely unloved. There seems to be no conscious or creative energy running through it, and at best there might be someone that comes in to dusts everything off, but doesn't do that too diligently either. I remember getting a similar impression at the Indian Museum in Kolkata, the largest one in India, and our National Museum of Bangladesh is quite the joke.

Considering how much we rest on the laurels of our historicity, it's surprising how little we actually do to search for or preserve records of it. South Asia has all the ingredients for the best museums on earth—a history as old as time, Palaeolithic remains, clues to mankind's journey into civilisation, ancient cities, great empires, cross-currents of cultures, international trade, brilliant art, mythology, epic dramas, languages, ethnic diversity, enigmatic personalities, founders of religions, science, technology, discovery— anything at all that one might need to weave a wonderful tale and then put in on display in an inspired and entertaining way.

It did stir the British quite a bit though. Much of the archaeological work and almost all the museums are remnants of the work they initiated to establish the field of 'Indology'. Scattered clues of our past were dug up and then stitched together by men like Jones, Prinsep and Marshall to create something of a consistent and presentable story. Of course, the story hasn't always held up to educated scrutiny, and their own socio-cultural contexts may have also influenced their perspective, but considering they were studying a foreign culture's history, often in several dead foreign languages, they didn't do too shabbily at all.

That's not to say that we didn't have a sense of our own antiquity before the British 'bestowed' it upon us, far from it, we've had historical writing throughout, from at least the time of the epics, Ramayana and Mahabharata, which are also called *itihasha*, literally, history. There are the Puranas, the Vedas themselves, the Buddhist chronicles, and later Muslim contributions by the likes of Abu'l Fazl and Minhaj al-Siraj; a smattering of travel writing and the auto-biographical works of the Mughals kings, the *namas*, all of which inform our sense of history and give us an idea about the political geography of those times. But there's no real guarantee that any of them is more accurate than the British versions, since history is anything but an exact science; it's quite possibly the most inexact one— it's speculative, deals with assumptions and is tainted by vainglory, politics, power, false testaments, embellishment, errors in interpretation, an incorrect premise, inaccurate chronologies, hearsay and just about everything else that can invalidate a position or a point of view.

But that's not the point. The point is that somewhere along the way we lost our curiosity for the past, for cultures and for how things fit together. These days we're more interested in glittering, glamorous futures. Wealth, prestige and power are all the rage and I don't know too many people who study curation sciences or would consider running a museum for a living. It's just not sexy enough and it hardly pays. In fact I doubt these subjects are even widely offered at our universities. But perhaps I'm being too dismissive. There are some glaring socio-economic realities that have to be factored into the equation too. British archaeologists had the resources of the empire to draw upon and didn't have third-world dysfunction or desperation to contend with. People obsess about money and power here because they need these in substantial quantities for even the most basic of conveniences—ill-provided by our most inconvenient governments. But even after we make all our excuses, it's still true that a lack of passion lies at the root of this decline, especially since there are plenty of very well-to-do individuals and institutions around, and gross amounts of wealth being tackily tossed about.

Day 14

Reluctant to try again for a seat on the next shared taxi, I do the unimaginable—I buy a ticket for the train. Mujeeb Uncle decries it, everyone else *tsks* disapprovingly, but I have no choice and have decided to rely on the power of positive thinking to get me there without incident. Others say, 'let him learn the hard way,' but I'm undeterred. I believe that I will be able to get to Quetta on the rails, even if it means having to put up with a few delays. How bad could it be? Mujeeb Uncle explains that Pakistan Railways has a shortage of engines, so they have to send the same ones all over the country to be attached to different carriages on different routes and schedules are slightly less accurate than a bookie's spread but I decide to do it anyway. We get to the station two hours early, and sure enough there is a three-hour delay. 'That's nothing, I'll just go away and come back later,' I tell myself. I ask Mujeeb Uncle to leave me at the station in fate's hands and not to worry.

I go wandering through old Lahore again to pass the time and end up at the Data Darbar complex, the tomb of Baba Ganj Baksh, or Abul Hasan Ali Hujwiri, one of the first Sufis to come to South Asia, from Afghanistan, in the 11th century. Ali Hujwiri also wrote one of the first Persian books on Sufi thought, and was called the perfect guide by none other than Moinuddin Chishti, who frequented this place before going on to establish his own dargah at Ajmer. I arrive at the complex and am overjoyed to see light-hearted smiling Sufis, with their followers in tow, playing music, singing, talking to themselves and spreading love to passers-by in the shape of garlands, which they randomly hand out. They appear completely, exquisitely insane.

The smell of channa masala wafts out of the *langar khana* (free kitchen), which feeds the hungry every day, all day. Qawwali music plays from roadside stalls that sell amulets, prayer caps, CDs and books, and soothsayers line the pavement with their parrots and pigeons, ready to read your fortune using their beaks. Taking the bitter with the sweet means having to tolerate frauds preying on the superstitions of simple people, and in any case, I'm not a complete sceptic so can't outright dismiss 'divining tools' to begin with. Suicide bombers blew themselves up at the shrine in 2010, killing 50 people, so now there's a security check and lots of police presence at the entrance.

They don't allow me into the tomb complex with my camera and I have nowhere to leave it, so I have to just hang around outside. I don't mind it as it gives me a chance to people-watch. Dreadlocked and bead-wearing brothers flash broad grins at me and then strike comical poses when I try to photograph them. In corners, pairs of individuals sit facing each other, talking in hushed tones like they're sharing secrets. They nod and smile the way people do when enjoying a delicious meal, and a sort of light engulfs them, turning their white clothes extraordinarily bright. They all greet each other with warm, lingering hugs, express themselves lucidly and honour each other with soft, soulful gestures. There is a fragrance of incense and flowers in the air. I'm in an atmosphere I relish, an atmosphere that drips with tenderness and an abundance of the feminine principal.

Back at the station, I wait for the train to arrive. The schedule still shows a three-hour delay and I'm feeling optimistic. The station is grand, built by the British with turrets that make it look bold and martial. It witnessed some of the worst moments of 1947 when Sikh and Hindu fanatics slaughtered trainloads of Muslims on their way to the new nation of Pakistan. The Muslims retaliated, sending death and putrefaction over to India as well. The horror must have been unimaginable—trains arrived drenched in blood carrying only corpses while families waited on the platform to receive their loved ones coming across the border. Almost everyone on board would have been dead, brutally murdered as they left their lives behind in search of a new one in this 'sanctified' space. So many people suffered because of Partition that history shouldn't record it as anything more than the savage dismemberment that it was. There is nothing good about it at all. The lines it drew up sliced through hearts and bodies, tore into pregnant women, tore apart unborn babies, ensnared and decapitated elderly people, cut off women's breasts, men's genitals, children's heads, leaving gaping gashes in our souls, our consciences and our memories. No amount of spin can turn that into a noble and necessary sacrifice for a greater good.

I walk down to the platforms and look for a place to wait. They are spacious, with kiosks and bookstalls every so many metres along the length of them. They only have Urdu titles, though, which is quite different from bookstalls at Indian stations, which stock many English books as well. This place must have been lovely when it was brand new. Its high arched ceilings, solid pillars and iron staircases speak of the sense of purpose with which it was built. I imagine well-dressed men and women with parasols and porters embarking and disembarking from wood-panelled carriages as station masters dutifully record journey timings and signal track clearances. It would have boasted tended, clean premises with potted plants and drinking fountains, where soldiers with big canvas bags and smart uniforms would stand together in small groups waiting for 'all aboard!' to be called out. Everyone would be smiling, including the coolies, straining there under the weight of white men's burdensome baggage. I think I can even hear songbirds.

But it's a sepia-tinted, utopian scene of course, plagiarised from films and books, but perhaps reality wouldn't have been very different and it would certainly have contrasted severely with the dismal dereliction that has descended upon the station these days. Now there are people sleeping on dirty floors wrapped in the melancholy of disenfranchisement, bad lighting, the pungent smell of stale urine, unfriendly glances, soot-stained walls, broken doors and benches and every other general symptom of extreme neglect, including some that aren't general at all, but particular to this place, like the sinister man at the only tuck shop who looks like he's plotting a murder. Unlike India (and Malaysia for that matter), both Pakistan and Bangladesh seem to prefer, for the most part, to let their colonial heritage fall apart. Perhaps it's a kind of dismissive disdain for the humiliation it represents.

I find a room called the 'Upper-Class Gentlemen's Waiting Area'. The sign on the door is the hand painted original, which must've been here since it was indeed such an esteemed place, as no one, not even someone with the most acrobatic of imaginations, could believe it warrants such an eminent appellation any longer. Fading away furniture from the early part of the last century populates the room; items like parlour mirrors, barber's chairs, tables, sofas and glass-topped coffee tables built in heavy wood wear a dark varnish and a thick coat of dust as they stand around like poorly displayed collectors' items in an antique shop. They look as though they've been here, exactly as they are, since they were first put in a hundred years ago. Nothing seems to have been changed, fixed or added and like a yellowing old photograph, preserves the picture of an older atmosphere that's still hanging around, decades past its era but well before its expiry date.

This must have been quite the place once. 'Upper class gentlemen' during the Raj would have been an unusually pampered lot. Obliging *'napits'* would have groomed them on the barber's chair in front of the parlour mirror and an army of bearers would have serviced the room, bringing tea, meals, drinks and whatever else their *sahibs* required. Perhaps there was a massage table somewhere as well. The conversations would have carried sufficient weight and their aristocratic accents would have been amply obnoxious. The bathroom, which is now completely vomit-worthy and made even worse by the unflushable load left behind by the last 'gentleman', is covered in blue tiles and is very large, with three washbasins and a wide, continuous counter. It would've been spotlessly clean once, with flunkies standing in a corner holding out muslin towels to patrons after they washed their hands, but before they used the complimentary *eau de toilette* that might have been kept by the basin. There's even a shower room.

I wait in this area; the chairs are still useable and it's quite a lot better than the rest of the platform. A guard comes to check my ticket, and in an act that is perhaps the epitome of officiousness, makes sure that I do, in fact, have a first class berth before being content to let me sit here in this rarefied rubbish heap. But I'm glad to see him. It's become dark and I don't feel completely safe in the dowdy station anymore. I check my watch; the estimated departure time has come and gone. A three-hour delay has now become four, and no one is able to tell me how much longer it might be. In fact there is no one here anymore except other passengers, a few guards and the shopkeeper at the kiosk. The other passengers seem resigned to the fact that it will come when it comes, so I decide to adopt this particularly sagacious attitude as well and settle in for the wait.

Eleven hours later, the train arrives on the platform.

I board the train to find that there is no first class but just a very hot and smelly sleeper class with plastic bunks. I'm not a stickler for class and I would have taken the thing, except it has decided not to move and remains at a complete halt on the platform. There is one other person in the room, and he's fast asleep. The door doesn't lock and the window doesn't have shutters—features that might be vital (or in fact completely useless) in the event of a motivated Balochi assault. Sticky, humid heat and mosquitoes are pouring in to colonise the cabin. The train remains at the platform for what feels like forever and nothing at all seems to be happening. I try to secure my things but am haunted by the memory of a stolen carpet during a similarly unsecured train journey in Morocco. Still, I'm determined to go to Quetta on this train; I've waited 11 hours for it, damn it.

But I keep waiting. Two more hours pass, and the train shows no signs at all of moving. It's nearly 5 am and I'm desperate for some sleep, but can't find a way to get comfortable in this stagnant sauna of a cabin, with mosquitoes buzzing around my ears and attacking every bit of exposed flesh. At this point I have more to fear from the dengue-carrying insects (causing an epidemic in Lahore, incidentally), than I do from Balochi bandits. Another hour passes; I contemplate the journey—it could take up to 28 hours and will bring me to Quetta with hardly eight hours to spare before the Zahedan Express to Iran, a 40-hour journey on upright wooden benches through the desert. I can't do it; I'm low on sleep and morale and the train is not moving, giving me too much time to think about getting off. I get off.

I head out of the station and scowl at some guards sitting by the exit. They ask me what my problem is and I tell them Pakistan Railways, frankly. They shrug, offer no excuses or sympathy and look at me deadpan, as if to say 'what do you want, an apology?' I do, I suppose, but mostly I want an acknowledgement of the faith I had in their remorselessly dysfunctional system. I go outside and get into an autorickshaw. I'm tired, bothered and have no idea where I should go. I don't want to go back to Mujeeb Uncle's house since I'm already in the frame of mind to move on so I go to the Daewoo bus counter instead and buy a ticket to Islamabad. It's the capital; perhaps things will be more straightforward from there.

I will later discover that the Zahedan Express to Iran no longer runs, following Balochi separatist activity near the Pakistan–Iran border, and getting to Quetta by 15 September would have been quite pointless. If I had stayed on that train, I would have missed spending a few more wonderful days exploring Pakistan, so the delay now seems quite fortuitous. It also means that all my well-laid plans to get across South Asia in time have come to no use but I'm actually quite relieved to be off the clock.

A police check-post stops my autorickshaw on the way to the Daewoo counter. It's not yet twilight and four officers with torch-lights surround the rickshaw. They are all armed, of course, but this time they are also pointing their guns at me. I'm instantly nervous. The lead officer, a bearded and large individual, orders me out of the vehicle and asks to see some papers. His manner is rough and intimidating, and the other officers are looking at me askew, down their gun barrels. I look perfectly suspicious too. I'm tired, dishevelled, a little lost, a little angry, a little anxious and much more than a little afraid, considering I've never had so many guns pointed at me before. They check my bag, pull out the books and CDs that are sitting on top and rummage through my clothes. The lead officer speaks to me in Urdu, but I decide that this would be a good time to become completely foreign. I reply to him in English, and pretend not to understand his language. This annoys him, as he doesn't speak English very well and can do a better job of talking down to me in Urdu. I can sense stirrings; the others are talking among themselves and looking at me with scorn. The man looks through my passport. He notices that I have come in from India. He asks me if I'm Indian and I tell him I'm British, as my passport states. I don't know why I thought that was safer than saying Bangladeshi, but it isn't and his tone changes from sternness to contempt when he hears me call myself British.

'Zeeshaaan Reh'man Kghhan ... Bertish,' he says mockingly, and smiles at his colleagues who have, by now, thankfully, lowered their weapons. He looks at my Pakistani visa and notices that the 'Exempt from Police Registration' stamp is slightly off the edge of the visa rather than flush on it.

'Did you register with the police?'

'I'm not required to sir, it says so right th ....'

'Why, who are you, *koi min'ster, shin'ster hai, tum, Bertish?*'

He is baiting me, of course, and delights in being able to cut me off to say that. I keep my cool and tell him I'm nothing at all except a simple traveller, but I can already hear *'Usko thana le jaiye'* being suggested by his hyena-like colleagues. I tell him again, that his government, the High Commission in Dhaka, exempted me from registration so it's something I didn't bother with. He tells me the stamp is fake and that it was stamped before the visa was attached, but then he realises that it makes more sense to accuse me of stamping it after the visa was attached, and then realises that I could just as easily have stamped it flush, if I had such a rubberstamp to begin with. He gets tangled up, embarrassed and goes quiet, like he's going to erupt.

I quickly cut through the tension that's building up and ask if he would like me to go with them to the station now, to get this registration business out of the way. It works. Volunteering to go to the *thana* turns the tables as it ceases to be a threat they can use, and becomes a way for me to get them off my back. They would be able to check with the High Commission in Dhaka and see that everything was on the level but that, of course, isn't what they want to do; they probably just want a bribe. I suspected it the minute he chose to accuse me of fraud, but decided against playing the game since I could have been wrong, and a miscalculation with aggressive, armed Pakistani police men on a lonely road in the dark isn't something worth chancing. He tells me the *thana* isn't operational this early in the morning—a dubious statement—and lets me go, but before he does he tells me fraternally,

'It's for your own safety, police registration. Do it later, but do it. Pakistan is not safe; it's better if you tell us you are here.'

No, it certainly isn't safe, but I wonder if it isn't less so because of police officers like him. He manages a smile and pats me on the shoulder as I get back into the autorickshaw. Perhaps he *was* just trying to do his job after all, but surely he would have taken me to the *thana* if that were really the case. Perhaps he's only half good.

Islamabad

Islamabad is a well-developed, purpose-built city surrounded by the beautiful Margalla Hills. It is laid out in a perfect grid and features broad roads, orderly traffic and easily navigable streets. It was designed by the Greek architect Doxiadis (interestingly enough, considering its proximity to the Indo-Greek Gandharan civilisation of Taxila) and it's the third time a city in South Asia has been named Islamabad. The first was Chittagong in the 17th century. It goes on for miles and, like Putra Jaya in Malaysia, was built as an administrative city for an anticipated population rather than an actual one. It might be the most developed city in South Asia and looks a bit like Abu Dhabi did about 12 years ago. But even with its perfect freeways, its neat design, its tunnels and underpasses, its whitewashed walls and its large squares, it doesn't yet have a metro system.

It doesn't have much of a soul either and is every bit the capital of Clerk-istan, where government housing and diplomatic mansions dominate city blocks. There are no chatty crowds or eccentric autorickshaws on the streets, only metered taxis that dutifully follow the speed limit. It's not unappealing; in fact it has nice landscaping, good parks, a few decent neighbourhoods, interesting architecture (including the very unusual and attractive Faisal Mosque) and a professional atmosphere that inspires a sense of confidence in its systems. It also seems like quite a safe city, but sadly has all the charm of a piece of toast. It's atypically South Asian and hints at what the future might look like, after we've been drained of our colour and forced to walk in perfectly straight lines.

Islamabad was built in the 1960s, when arguments over disproportionate government spending between East and West Pakistan reached a crescendo. Much of the revenue that went into building Islamabad came from the lucrative jute trade in East Bengal and people there were incensed that so little of it was being spent in the province itself. The 'second capital' in Dhaka was built to allay these tensions, which is our Shongshod Bhobon complex and a few surrounding streets but when you compare the difference in scale between the two capitals you can't help but think that they were either seriously taking the piss, or took us for complete fools. But this 'diminutisation' is nothing new, of course. If you compare the scale of Mughal architecture in Lahore, Delhi and Agra with the almost miniaturist versions in Bengal, you get a sense of how infrastructure can be used to illustrate an imperial ranking system.

I check into a reasonably priced guesthouse in sector F-6, which is run by a moustachioed man from Abbotabad, whom I have to ask about Bin Laden, naturally.

'*Bakwas*. Complete nonsense! I lived there all my life and everyone knows who is there and what is going on. People talk about everything. If Bin Laden were there, in that house, everyone would know about it and—believe you me—people would have tried to capture him for the reward. It's a lie, *pura jhoot baat hay*.'

That's a pretty good point, actually. Well there you have it again, from the horse's mouth and this one even had an important moustache.

After a much needed nap I go for a little wander about and meet a friend for coffee at Kohsar Market. It's in a very nice, tree-shaded upscale enclave that looks a little like Bangsar Village in Kuala Lumpur or Khan Market in Delhi. A few foreigners come and do their groceries from modern supermarkets—the sort of place where you might be forgiven for not knowing that the processed and packaged meat in your trolley comes from an animal, and where all fruits are always in season. The shops, cafes and restaurants are posh and cater to expatriates as well as a cosmopolitan set of better-off Pakistanis. There are a few bookstores, a pizza place, the Starbucks has outdoor seating, birds call out in the trees: it's all nice and polite.

Imagine my surprise when my friend points to the spot where, just nine months earlier, the governor of Punjab, Salman Taseer was brutally gunned down by his bodyguard, Mumtaz Qadri, for defending a Christian woman's right to blaspheme, if indeed she had—which she hadn't. The idyllic atmosphere disappears with the sort of squealing abruptness that music playing from an audio cassette does when the tape gets chewed up. I imagine a blood-stained pavement, the sound of machine gun fire, a bullet-ridden Mr. Taseer falling to the ground with 27 holes in him, people screaming and running, children crying; the birdsong changes to the cawing of a hundred crows as the yellow, sunny day turns red and black, and a horrific, evil laugh fills the air as Qadri's wild eyes stare right at me, as if to say,

'What? What are you looking at, kaffir?'

Salman Taseer became part of an unenviable list of Pakistani politicians who have lost their lives at the hands of violent religious extremists, when he was killed for trying to defend Asia Bibi, a Christian woman sentenced to death under Pakistan's absurd blasphemy laws. A clear fracture in Pakistani society became visible following Taseer's killing on 5 January 2011, but so did the numbers in either camp. Only a small group of liberals condemned the killing while a vast number of people actually celebrated it. Mumtaz Qadri was applauded as a hero; rose petals were thrown at him as he went to trial, religious clerics from various sects forbade the mourning of Mr. Taseer and the Imam of Badshahi Mosque became suddenly 'unavailable' to lead the funeral prayers. The Pakistani Taliban also kidnapped Salman Taseer's son in Lahore a few months later.

Secular, cosmopolitan Pakistan is completely exposed and dangerously vulnerable. The Pakistan that makes enchanting Sufi music at Coke Studio sessions and bold films like *Bol* and *Khuda Ke Liye*; the Pakistan of the mystics and shrines, of the Ismailis up in the Hunza Valley, of *Dawn* newspaper, the one that promised to treat their minorities with the respect of an *amanat*, a trust, to be protected and cared for, the Pakistan that Jinnah said would cease to distinguish people by their religion, and could have represented the very best of an enlightened Indo-Muslim culture—that Pakistan is under attack everywhere, even at places like Kohsar Market where it might have once felt safe.

I get back to the guesthouse in the evening and settle in to watch some TV. I'm hungry and feel like having the standard french fries, hot and sour soup and chowmein that all South Asian guesthouses make exactly the same way, so I call the reception to place my order. The man on the other side quotes me the bill and I tell him it's more than the amount stated on the menu, to which he says, 'Tax, bhaisaab, for the charitable Asif Ali Zardari Fund. We have to help the poor man, na?" It makes me smile. Jovial wit and a light-hearted playfulness about serious issues is Pakistan's strong suit. It makes their edges soft and gives their words a litheness that makes them quite endearing. I watch American programming on Indian networks again, along with local channels like GEO, and enjoy thinking about how we're all watching the same television across the region, even the same advertisements, and though it may seem trite, it actually helps us remain similar. That, and the shared experience of loadshedding. But take a bow, India; your media industry might just help to preserve our extended family yet.

Day 16

There are fewer beggars in Pakistan. Some cities have more than others but generally speaking, there aren't too many. They are also less persistent and a simple 'sorry' tends to send them on their own way. Streets and public spaces in cities like Lahore and Islamabad are less grimy than major ones in India and Bangladesh. Currency notes aren't as worn or stained, and on the whole, Pakistan is cleaner— its lower population density and drier climate sees to it. So does, perhaps, a certain degree of conscientiousness. There is far less litter or rubbish on street corners and there are no cyclerickshaws in the major cities.

I've been wandering around 'Jinnah Super', a large open-air shopping area with a food court that has incredibly good fruit juice and some of the best grilled chicken I've ever had. Stalls call out for customers and the combined smell of meat and charcoal seasons the air. It's a pleasant atmosphere and I spend time taking it in. Families come here for an outing of juice and ice-cream; school students hang out after class, livening up the place with a rowdy ebullience; laughing ladies with too much makeup go shopping together, carrying expensive-looking handbags; a group of people go off for their Zuhr prayers in a designated area at the end of the square and life in Pakistan's capital carries on at an easy and unhurried pace. There are all sorts of faces here—from the very fair to the fairly dark, European faces with cold, grey eyes, Middle Eastern faces with piercing eyes, Indian faces with playful eyes and Mongoloid faces with almond eyes—Pakistan's diverse and sometimes uncomfortable ethnic mix coming together in a city where tribal and territorial boundaries don't mean anything, in a country where they often mean everything.

I find a great second-hand bookshop at the Super and spend a few hours browsing through its collection. The slightly effeminate Pathan shopkeeper chats with me for a while and gives me his card in case I want to have books delivered to Dhaka. I pick up a small publication called *A Letter to Pakistan* by Karen Armstrong in which Armstrong is writing to Pakistan asking it to find its way back to the Islamic compassion preached in the Quran and practised by the Prophets before it's too late and a violent bent consumes it. It's a heartfelt appeal full of sisterly and motherly affection, and is a very good effort, but she's being a bit patronising and seems to 'talk at' rather than 'talk to' Pakistan. If I were Pakistani I think I would find it a bit offensive and probably wouldn't bother getting the message. It's also in English, which sort of makes it absurd and talks to the wrong section of society.

Even if they did understand it, I doubt the average Pakistani would like to be told how to be proper Muslims by Karen Armstrong, even if a lot of what she says about forgiveness and love is true. This place has a very masculine culture; it contains barrels of bravado and is hardy like the land itself. I get the feeling that softness and compassion might be perceived as feminine or weak. It's a strange sort of dynamic—their overly butch demeanour hides a rather obvious homoerotic tendency, and I think they 'feminise' other ways of being men, to give vent to it. Either way, it's all a bit peculiar and not exclusively a Pakistani problem, but Karen Armstrong's approach may be a little ill-conceived.

Casual conversations on Pakistani streets can be quite different from those in India. From the eavesdropping that I habitually do I know that Pakistanis tend to talk a lot about international relations, power, politics and Islam. Spirituality is present but thin on the ground, while religiosity, almost a precondition for being Pakistani, is thick. None of the philosophical debates elemental to Indian culture seem to feature here, but then again they didn't seem to feature much in India either. Indians these days talk about the economy and stock markets, and the trappings of success; they are up on their corporate jargon and frequently use words like 'value addition', and 'key performance indicators'. They love being sexy, measure themselves and others by their pocketbooks, and are all set to conquer the world of high finance, fashion and fine living. It's another case of the 'Singapore Syndrome', an aspiring middle-income country's perennial social climbing condition, replete with a Wall-Street-in-Monaco attitude.

Pakistanis are more conservative than Indians in almost everything except their opinions. People here state their positions and prejudices candidly, no matter how controversial or contrary, and don't seem too concerned about niggling things like political correctness. They will quite happily say, for instance, that the Taliban are non-Muslim, that Americans are imperialist pigs, that the War on Terror is a war on Islam. They'll tell you quite confidently Pakistanis are better-looking than Indians, that Israel is single-handedly destroying the world, that Al Qaeda is not responsible for September 11 and that Muslims are all going to go to heaven anyway. They are natural and forthright with their comments, which belong mostly to the alternative stream of thought, unlike the opinions in India, that are more aligned with a globally sanctioned narrative which tells us American imperialism is a force for good, and expects us to believe everything we hear on the news without being offered the smallest shred of evidence.

A collection drive is driving, literally, around Jinnah Super. Two microbuses are slowly making their way through the square, 'mic-ing' an appeal to everyone to give generously in Allah's name. Torrential rains have been hitting Sindh over the last few weeks, and have now evolved into major floods. Over 300 people have been killed, many homes have been lost, and people are stranded and starving. The ancient Sindhu-Saraswati, or Indus, Valley ruins at Mohenjodaro have also been damaged. For many, it's bringing back bad memories of the floods in 2010, which also started, inoffensively enough, as heavy rain, but ended with more than one-fifth of Pakistan submerged. It's tragic and yet another bit of misfortune for this nation, yet another way for people to die in a country where they are already spoilt for choice. That might sound facetious, but consider the following headlines gleaned from newspapers over the last few days:

Four shot dead over marriage dispute; Suicide Strike in Lower Dir kills 26; 5 more fall prey to dengue in Lahore; Drone strikes kill 6; 15 killed in Khyber clashes; Bomb attack in Peshawar claims 5; 8 killed in Karachi explosion; Pro-government tribal elder killed in Bajaur; 342 killed in Sindh flooding; Taliban attack school bus, kill 4 children.

144

But let's be fair. You could pick up a newspaper in Bangladesh, Nepal, India or Sri Lanka and find a similar body count. Journalists in South Asia are married to the age old maxim that bad news sells newspapers, and South Asian people seem committed to age old practices like kill thy neighbour, thy lover, thy children, thy cousins, thy rivals. Our inept governments and the poor living standards don't help much either, so the news of horrible, unnecessary deaths is as much a staple on our breakfast table as our standard cup of sweet tea.

Basit Khawaja, a friend of Sobia's, my Pakistani friend from Switzerland, meets me at the square and takes me to Sobia's parents' house where she has insisted I stay for the remainder of my time in Islamabad. Pakistani hospitality is spontaneous and reflexive, but Sobia's offer to put me up at her parents' is much more than just a formality; it's most genuine and lets me feel like I have family here, which is what she intended. Hospitality is fundamental to Asian cultures and we all take it quite seriously. The Persians call it *mehmannawazi*, Indians call it *atithisatkara* and in traditional Arab hospitality it's rude to even ask your guest about their journey until you have looked after them for at least three days.

Basit is very enjoyable company. He's a man of strong convictions and of action, and talks mostly about peace, charity and development. He's soft-hearted and lives by exactly those Islamic principles of compassion that Karen Armstrong is self-righteously trying to bestow upon him. He works for the Taleem Foundation, an organisation that endeavours to bring education to the blighted regions of Balochistan, and speaks fluent NGO-speak. It's very pleasant to hear, so we walk and talk all the way to the tent-like and Turkic Faisal Mosque (designed by a Turkish Architect), about politics, the story of the Taliban, the damage Zia-ul-Haq did to Pakistani culture, 1971, Islam, women and anything at all we feel like trading views on. Basit is organising a cycle tour from Islamabad to Lahore as part of an initiative called 'Pedal for Peace' to raise awareness about the need for a peaceful solution to Pakistan's problems, and to generally scatter about some good vibrations. People like him, if they are given a chance, could bring in a positive future for this country but how much space he'll ever get is the biggest question.

After a criminally carnivorous meal at an Afghani kabab place, we part ways and I head off to sleep in the warm home that Sobia has provided me with.

Peshawar

You can tell a lot about the average height of a country by how well you can scale the urinals in public toilets. In Malaysia I'm well above the average, but in Pakistan I can barely make it into the bowl. I manage, however, and come out of the public toilets at the Rawalpindi Daewoo bus counter just as they are making the boarding announcements for the bus to Peshawar.

Peshawar—that fabled frontier city on the old Silk Route to China and on the supply route for America's Afghanistan adventure. I've wondered about this place for years. Long before it made headlines as a dangerous den of crazed Pathan extremists, it was known for its urbanity and for its culture. The artisans and craftsmen of Peshawar were famous the world over, and being as much a Central Asian as it is a South Asian city, Peshawar was a grand emporium of goods from everywhere in the known world. It was a multicultural, international city and a hub on the overland trading circuits—the original vehicles of globalisation. It's one of the oldest continuously inhabited places in the world, the oldest in South Asia, and also somewhere a part of my paternal ancestry may have flowed through during its slow, 300-year migration from Kabul to Dhaka.

The bus travels along the Grand Trunk Road and I'm on it for the third time on this journey. The first was from Delhi to Wagah and the second was from Wagah to Lahore. But these short little segments do no justice to this infrastructural marvel that was the superhighway of its time. It was re-built four times in four different ages. The Mauryas are said to have laid the foundations when they built the Uttarapatha linking Pataliputra to Taxila, along which many a great man, including Kautilya and Ashoka himself travelled.

The second version was built by Sher Shar Suri in the 1500s and was called the Sarak-e-Azam. This one began at Shonargaon in the kingdom of Bangala, Sher Shah's base, ran through Sasaram, his birthplace, to Agra and then onwards to Multan, the western extent of his empire. It was lined with trees and serviced by caravanserais, which provided shelter for travellers, tradesmen and soldiers. The Mughals then extended it to Kabul in the west and Chittagong in the east—its greatest extent—before the British rerouted it from Kolkata and ended it in Peshawar.

Some distance into the journey the road begins to look as legendary as it sounds. Tall hills are thrown up followed by short mountains. Rivers wind their way around these features, one of which is the Indus, the grand old mother of Indian civilisation, and I keep my eyes peeled so as not to miss her. I spot an old, ochre house around a courtyard, labelled 'Bahram's Pavilion', and just as I'm wishing I could get out and explore it a little, an enormous fort comes into sight, straddling a hill that ends in the bluest river I've ever seen—blue like coral seas. The scene is epic. On one side of the river, the sprawling fort cascades down the hill until it almost touches the water and on the other, much taller hills stand sentinel-like, announcing a frontier. The fort, which looks like it was built to compensate for the smaller hills on the eastern bank, is the Attock Fort, built by Emperor Akbar to 'attock' or 'arrest' Afghan invasions from the west, and the river is none other than the Indus herself, her aquamarine waters marking the cultural fault line between Iranzamin and India. She will run for miles before she reaches the Arabian Sea, and won't be blue anymore when she arrives, but here, near the source, she looks as icy as the Tibetan glaciers that birthed her.

The road to Peshawar is of obvious military significance. We pass quite a few outposts and fenced off areas featuring barbed wire, observation towers and worried looking men with powerful-looking guns. The 'frontier province' takes its old name quite seriously, but I'm having trouble taking the many Disney-like gates that frame the road too seriously at all. They start as we approach Nowshera and carry on all the way to Peshawar, looking a bit like a bad film set made of papier mâché. But other than that, this end of Khyber-Pakhtunkhwa is quite tame. Most of the road after the Indus runs through small towns, little villages and pastoral land with grazing livestock. There's nothing particularly rugged about it and as we enter Peshawar city, the crowded, chaotic streets with virtually everything—from car repairs to carpentry—being done along their sides, remind me of mild old Dhaka.

I have lunch near the bus stand—half a chicken kadhai, served right in the kadhai and hot off the fire, with some Peshawari naan. It's far too much for me but when I try to tell the waiter I'm full, he says in heavily accented Urdu,

'Are you a man? My little boy eats more than this!'

Maybe *that's* why Peshawar was called Purushapura once, the 'city of men'. There's a playfulness about the people here; they seem lighter than the people in Punjab and more laid back. Urdu has effectively evaporated, and everyone speaks Pashto on the streets—lots of it. Unlike the self-conscious and somewhat terse atmosphere in Lahore and Islamabad, here the streets are loud and raucous. Something about it all just says 'bolder'. As I pay my bill, I ask about places to see in Peshawar and a very regal looking man speaking good English comes over to answer the question. He looks like an Indian Prince, very tall, with a thin moustache and dark skin. I ask him if he's Pashtun and he says yes, and then just as a retort, says, 'why, are you one too?' I say, 'no, but I'm a Khan', hoping to throw him off a little. He smiles and says, quite seriously, 'oh but then you are one!' and I tell him I'm not, actually, but it's possible that some of my genes come from here. He nods and says,

'So you are here because of your forefathers? This is very good, but tell me why don't you speak the language?'

I laugh, thinking he's joking, but then realise it's a real question.

'I'm from Bangladesh, brother, why would I speak Pashto?'

'So you've forgotten your roots. Khans are Pashtuns, wherever they live.'

A gallery of Khans—Aamir Khan, Ustad Amjad Ali Khan, Allauddin Khan, Nusrat Fateh Ali Khan, Saif Ali Khan, Zaheer

Khan, Alivardi Khan, the Aga Khan, even Kublai Khan, all appear before my mind's eye, looking quite puzzled.

'I haven't forgotten anything. *My* roots are Bengali. Maybe I should speak Mongolian too; I'm a Khan, right, like Changez?'

He laughs and shakes my hand to say, 'touche', and then adds, 'You should learn Pashto. It's a nice language.'

'I probably should, but tell me something, is it dangerous in Peshawar?'

'Peshawar is not safer or more dangerous than anywhere else. You just have to know your way around it, like any city.'

I ask him about the violence, and about the Taliban, the war in Afghanistan, the bombs that go off in his city, all the other things that, sadly, this fabulously ancient place has become known for. He rotates his hands to throw his palms open in that very South Asian gesture of futility and says,

'What is there to do? It's part of our lives now.'

'It's part of our lives now'—those words stay with me a long time, long after he's hailed me a '*raksha*', haggled with the driver and told me, with much hospitality, that I'll be safe and looked after.

I can't decide which is sadder—the fact that this charming city, with its beautiful, smiling faces and cheerful energy should have to suffer violent tears in its otherwise harmonious tapestry, or the fact that it happens frequently enough for them to have accepted it as a part of life, like blackouts and loadshedding.

A huge adobe fortress, rising up at least 25 metres from the ground, greets you as you enter Old Peshawar. It sits on a slightly elevated plinth and has a number of flags on it, one for each Unit of the Frontier Corps, which has called this their home base since 1949. It's called Bala Hissar and is very old. The fort was renovated by the Sikhs in the 1800s and more recently by the British. No one knows for sure quite how old it is, but it might be the place mentioned by the famous Chinese traveller Hiuen Tsang in his accounts of 630 AD. It's been destroyed by invaders and rebuilt to be used again as a fort—and is still being used as one. The sight of ancient earthen turrets sporting shiny modern machine guns is something you don't encounter often. Contemporary soldiers wearing fatigues stand on the clay walls of an ancient fort, the type you'd expect to visit as a ruin, carrying semi-automatic, state-of-the-art weaponry instead of swords and bows and arrows. I like it a lot, a fully functional and very solid looking mud fort that seems to be from the past and the present at the very same time.

In fact that's how I would describe the rest of Peshawar as well. So far I've visited ancient cities that are little more than rock gardens or new cities that have been built on top of them, but Peshawar is a new city built *into* the old one. It has a sort of seamlessness that can make you forget what era it is, a feeling that gets all the more pronounced once you step into the bazaars. Old Dhaka, Old Delhi and Old Lahore can do that to you too, but Old Peshawar seems to do it just a bit better.

The *raksha*, or autorickshaw, brings me to a narrow street surrounded by shops—small ones, similar to the ones on 'Gold Street' in Shakhari Bazaar at Old Dhaka. I get down and walk, but suddenly there's a lot of commotion as I see some people running towards me, frantically waving everyone off the road. Almost immediately I hear a loud and continuous 'Crackatakakakakakakaaakak!' accompanied by the smell of gunpowder. I cower, convinced that rounds are being fired. 'This is it!' I tell myself, 'I'm in Peshawar at the wrong place and at the wrong time. I'm dead!' I close my eyes and wait for the inevitable but soon after, hear happy voices and look around to find people pointing in my direction laughing. Firecrackers! Just then, a crowd appears out of one of the alleys with a man being carried on another's shoulders, as the market erupts in cheers. The person being paraded is a shop owner who has just won a local council election. Wearing a pink paper garland, he waves at his supporters, as they shower him with confetti and glitter. Everyone is cheering and clapping and I feel quite silly but try to act like I was just playing it up, before quickly disappearing along a pathway flanked by shawl shops.

I'm gradually absorbed into the nebulous network of narrow streets. There's very little traffic; in fact, there's none, apart from the occasional motorcycle or *raksha*, giving me plenty of space to take it all in. Deeper inside, the automotive sounds of the surrounding streets disappear entirely and the sensation of timelessness is made complete. The shawls, turban material, prayer mats and carpets hanging out of shops insulate the area and create a kind of sound-proofing. It becomes very cosy, like a padded room, and people talk softly since their voices carry well enough without having to be raised. I find myself at a *chourasta*, a narrow crossroads, where each corner has an old wooden building with latticed balconies, facing the X. The facades are decoratively carved and it all looks very elegant. I keep walking straight, entranced and unable to stop myself from going deeper into this wondrous maze. The smell of herbs, spices and incense fill my nostrils. It's absolutely exquisite—not overpowering but just enough to make me feel light-headed. Various coloured piles sit in squat baskets beside neatly laid out rows of leaves, bark, twigs and other assorted parts of plants. Some shops have big and small bottles of perfumed oils, *attar*, golden and dark brown, looking like an elixir or an ale. Cloth merchants call out to me asking me to feel the quality of their wares; shawl-wallahs tell me winter is coming and that there is nothing in the world quite as warm as a Peshawari *chador*; sandal sellers tell me that the Peshawar *chappal* has no equal, but no one is particularly pushy. Instead, they try and sing you in, speaking to you sweetly using tones that plead, entice and dare. All sorts of everyday things are also available like groceries, pots, pans, creams, cosmetics and cheap plastic toys made in China.

But I'm not just a potential customer, I'm also a curiosity and people seem more interested in discovering what I am, than pitching to me.

'Irani? Hindustani? Aah Bangladesh! *Mera bhai. Kya naam he aapka? Iddar kyu aye hain? Accha* tourist. *Bilkul. Mussulman? Bas mashAllah. Chai piyo? Wo kya?* Camera? Camera *he tumhara pas?*'

I had tried to conceal my camera, since many conservative Muslim societies have an issue with photography, and hearing the surprise in his voice I prepare myself for immediate censure, when one of the shopkeepers says,

'*Mera tasweer pakro!*'

'*Mera bhi, mera bhi! Mera tasweer bhi pakro! Ei ei, mera! Mera bhi pakro!*' I've been outed. News travels fast and swarms of kids surround me almost everywhere I go just like the kids in Bangladesh do when they see foreign people—laughing, talking, shouting, bubbling over, shoving, pushing and climbing on top of each other while trying to climb onto me. They want their pictures taken, they want to be boisterous, they want to shout, they are just generally excitable, and a stranger is something new and exciting. I show them their pictures, they grab the camera, laugh at each other, chatter like birds then want more pictures, they pose, they push their friends out of the frame, they laugh loudly, they are like so many little balls of energy, a mini riot, and my face begins to hurt from smiling too much.

Soon enough some curious adults come and surround me—they also want their pictures taken. I enjoy a brief and furious career as the portrait-maker of Peshawar, before having to almost run to get away from requests. They follow me, of course, so I try to distract them by asking them about buildings, neighbourhoods, history, but it's difficult to do as we have only one language, Urdu, between us, and we all speak it quite badly. It's not just the camera; I'm an oddity and they are friendly and this is their turf—they aren't going to just let me wander around as if it's uninhabited, or worse, a theme park, and when I accept this, I begin to appreciate their *melmestia*—hospitality, Pakhtunwali style.

Like I was telling the Indian Prince, I'm a Khan. I'm not Pakhtun, but our family tree tells me that we descend from a man who probably was, and might have lived in Kabul, 10 generations ago. My maternal grandmother was also a Khan before she got married, and my maternal grandfather comes from a community of people called the Shershabadi, descendants of Sher Shah's soldiers in northwestern Bengal, most of whom were Afghans. But all of these might be myths since Muslims in India often tried to fasten their ancestry to an Ashrafi, that is to a Pakhtun, Turkish, Mughal or Persian bloodline, as part of a naked and absurd form of racism against Atrafis, or Muslims of darker, Indian heritage. But there's some truth in it. Droves of Pakhtuns (Pathans) settled in India after the 13th century, enough to make a demographic dent, and many kept moving east until they arrived in Bengal. They settled there, eventually intermarried and became part of the local fabric. When Babur, the Mughal, overthrew the Delhi Sultanate, another influx of Afghans, chased out by the Mughals from Kabul and Delhi, headed east and joined the Bihari Afghan, Farid Khan's (Sher Shah Suri) ranks.

In the racially charged atmospheres of both Mughal India and the British Raj, descendants of these waves of Afghans probably asserted their 'Central Asian-ness' to escape the insults that flew at Indians of Indian origin, and so myths like the Shershabadi colony began to circulate. It was essentially Brahmanical Aryanism all over again; people rarely tried to claim an Arabic ancestry, since Arabs were essentially dark skinned *mlecchas* too. Unless, of course, it was a Syed ancestry, which was the trump card. It meant you belonged to the blood of Muhammad, and propelled you to a place in society reserved for the elect, a nobility of the purest race. It's all so hilariously primeval and, in fact, counter-Islamic that it can't be rubbished fast enough. However, for a very long time people took this nonsense quite seriously. At any rate, I'm a Khan and this is part of where Khans come from, so, real or not, I have something of a preternatural interest in this atmosphere.

Pakhtuns were a distinct people long before they got mixed up with Middle Eastern Muslims and with Islam. The Rig Veda refers to a people called the 'Pakhta' living near Aryana in today's Afghanistan, who went to war against the Tritsu—Bharata's people, in the Battle of the Ten Kings. They also feature in Ancient Greek literature where they are called 'Pactyan' and are described as having characteristics that are not too different from those of the

Pakhtuns today. They were divided into clan-groupings that are still recognisable, with a clear reference to a people called the Afrit—possibly the Afridi clan. Today most of them live in Pakistan within a complicated network, featuring hundreds of clans, tribes and kin groups—the largest segmentary lineage system of its kind in the world that is either a very sophisticated form of social organisation, or a very primitive one. Pakhtuns live and die by these lines, and by the code that unites them—the Pakhtunwali or Pashtunwali, which I'll tell you all about in just a minute.

Although it's rare to isolate Pakhtun culture from its Islamic context, it's not entirely incongruous. It's also not that odd to differentiate between the many ways of being Pakhtun. The Taliban are Pakhtun, but so is Hamid Karzai, and so was 'frontier Gandhi' Khan Abdul Gaffar Khan, as well as the Sufi Rahman Baba. With 50 million people calling themselves Pashtun, Pakhtun, Afghan or Pathan, spread across at least four countries and among various ethnic groups, it would be quite surprising, actually, if they were all the same. In Peshawar they live with the urbanised Hindko, consisting of a few different ethnicities, including settled Pakhtuns, who are referred to as '*kharay*' or 'city-folk' by tribal Pakhtuns. The Hindko, as their name suggests, are more Indic than Iranian, and speak a language that's derived from Prakrit but with plenty of loan words from Pashto. Peshawaris are indeed city slickers, urbane and artistic, and even seem slighter-built to me, than the famously robust people of the Swat Valley and the caves of Afghanistan. They are also different from their fierce southern cousins near Balochistan, who use 'sh' instead of 'kh', rendering 'Pakhtun' into the more familiar 'Pashtun'.

Pakhtun ethnicity is complicated. Like all people in South Asia, they have different phenotypes. There's a tendency towards fair skin and light eyes, though dark-skinned Pakhtuns abound as well. Some have rust-red hair. They share quite a lot of genetic material with North Indians and Persians and more recently with Turkic people from Central Asia (Indo-European ones), and their roots are in the original Aryan tribes that went on to become the nationalities of India, Persia, Anatolia and possibly even Southern Europe, depending on which Indo-European migration theory you prefer to subscribe to. It's possible that plenty of other DNA also floats around in Pakhtun blood, including remnants of the Indo-Greek kingdoms that inherited Alexander's legacy and were eventually absorbed into Afghanistan and Pakistan's bloodstream. So too were the Arabs, who came with Islam and whose genealogy is more traceable. There's even a slim chance that Hebrew tribes, fleeing persecution in Central Asia, found themselves at the eastern extremity of the Persian Empire and bequeathed some of their customs and genes to the Pashtuns, but this is completely unrelated to the much-touted notion that Pashtuns are entirely Hebrew and come from one of the Lost Tribes of Israel.

But it's not blood or language or place or colour or even tribe that really creates 'Pashtunness'. That distinction belongs to Pashtunwali, the chivalric code I alluded to earlier, which enters a Pashtun's constitution almost by osmosis. It's taught by example and is, as a Pashtun friend once eloquently told me,

Something you can't describe, but you know what it is when it is not there.

Pashtunwali is ancient and its origins are lost somewhere in the mountain passes of the Hindu Kush range. It's transmitted automatically like languages are, and there's never been a textbook that tells a Pashtun how to be a Pashtun, although the famous Pashto poet Khushal Khan Khattak did attempt one in the 17th century. For those of us who didn't grow up with it, Lutz Rzehak of the Afghanistan Analysts Network has a paper called 'Doing Pashto', which gives a clinical yet accurate explanation of what it's all about. The title itself—which is what Pashtunwali literally means—says plenty about its place in Pashtun life. Pashtun author Abdullah Bakhtani goes as far as to say that 'a person who speaks Pashto but has no Pashtunwali is not a Pashtun….'

According to Rzehak, the nomadic history of Pashtun culture necessitated an honour code that could travel with them, unlike legal systems that are reliant on institutions, jurisdictions and establishments. It rests, fundamentally, on this statement:

A Pashtun is he who disgraces neither himself nor others.

But the details of how that's achieved is complicated and structured around a number of absolute principles, which are: honour (of the individual and the group), courage, combat-readiness, equality, respect for elders, democratic decision-making, willpower, sincerity, patience, justice, retaliation, generosity, hospitality, protection, modesty, dignity and passion (or audacity). A person demonstrating a high level of all of these attributes is considered *ghairatman*—dignified. Many of them have specific formulas, such as the rules for retaliation, *badal*, which, in the Pashtun worldview, isn't just an eye for an eye (taken quite literally in Pashtunwali) but can also include escalation, leading to blood feuds that engulf entire tribes and entire invading armies too. But it's not all gore and violence; peaceful and amicable solutions are always sought first, and *badal* also includes the meticulous repaying of debts, as a Pashtun's freedom demands that nothing is owed to anyone.

The Pashtun political process is inclusive: consultative decision-making and judicial rulings are all done through the mechanism of the *jirga*, which will convene for as long as it takes to reach an unopposed decision—unlike virtually every other democratic tradition on earth where numbers rule the day. Other principles are also similar in their espousal of 'all or nothing'. Hospitality includes laying down one's life to defend a guest; willpower means trying until death to overcome odds; sincerity, *merana*, is understood through phrases like 'speaking Pashto and keeping one's promises are synoynms'.

Pashtunwali, with the possible exception of Bushido, enshrines perhaps the most uncompromising set of ideals ever devised, which are of course aspirational, and not always realistic. I don't like some, like the seclusion of women, but then that's dictated by the principles of protection, which I do like. Others I absolutely love, like equality, *musawat*, which states that every Pashtun weighs one man; there are no half men among them. They believe in this enough to not have dignified rank consciousness with vocabulary and the Pashto language has no native words for 'slave', 'servant' or 'master'. That's not to say they don't have a hierarchy, they do, but it's one of respect and reverence—for elders, chiefs, sufis, mollahs, householders, etc. In other words, they carry whomever they wish on their shoulders, under no force or duress.

When Pashtunwali met the similarly uncompromising idealism of Islam, Pashtuns became entirely unconquerable in both body and spirit. The Persians, the Mughals, the British and the Russians have all tried to dominate them, and while all have made considerable territorial gains and inflicted tremendous damage, no one has ever been able to completely subdue the Pashtuns. The Americans are trying, and failing mostly, managing to control only a few streets in Kabul at the best of times. But *dulce et decorum est* aside, all these battles have left indelible scars on the Pakhtun psyche. The energetic tribesman, once colourful and ebullient, with music and poetry sitting comfortably alongside chivalry in a large, friendly heart, has spawned a severe and disturbed child that seems determined to drag us all by our collars to our reckoning one way or another. Enter the Taliban and their unshakable vision for a 'perfect' world.

But let's not think about them or the horrors they've unleashed upon Afghanistan and Pakistan; it's all too common knowledge these days, and our helplessness in being able to stop them is both terrifying and heart-breaking. So much suffering has been caused by the Taliban's violence and by the violence directed against them, that it's hard to see any good at all in any of it. But to think that they are an anomaly, or even an isolated phenomenon, is naive. They belong to a strict and literalist school of Islamic thought that's been missing the point since perhaps the 10th century and certainly since the 16th, when Abdal Wahhab came onto the scene in Arabia. Since then it's been spreading across the globe like a plague, with no end in sight. In Afghanistan, less than 40 kilometres from Peshawar, Wahhab's ideological descendants have succeeded in replacing tempered civility with a melancholic and maniacal world order, while proceeding determinedly to wipe away all memory of their ever having being any other way. Now they want to do that in Pakistan—bombing Sufi mazaars, misusing misinformed Hadith, killing Shias, stoning people to death, forbidding music, burning blasphemers, frowning on celebrations and preventing every sort of expression of exuberance and joy. It's predictably standard and perfectly sickening.

I keep walking though the bazaars, past piles of fruits, vegetables and spices. Everyone is friendly, slightly eccentric and full of a natural joy. People offer me tea and nibbles as an expression of courtesy. It's a heart-warming gesture and as it will turn out, quite consistently Pakistani. Sometimes it's mint tea, sometimes tea so milky it's white. I see a turbaned Sikh, not Punjabi but Pakhtun, living comfortably with his non-Sikh counterparts. I meet a large, red Scotsman of a Khan, who has been to Bangladesh by sea when he worked on ships. 'Chittagong *gesi ami*,' he tells me in Bangla. We chat a little, he says he felt very at home in Bangladesh and tells me we are the same country but I hasten to remind him that we aren't. He nods a forlorn acknowledgement but then I tell him about the Pathan soldiers who refused to fire at fellow Muslims in Dhaka, and our bond is restored.

I walk past the clock tower that was built by the British and is completely inconsistent with the surrounding bazaar; watch a mad man rant in the opening under a large sprawling tree, with people cheering him and clapping; nearby a craftsman is carving decorations onto a chest of drawers. I carry on towards a fortress gate, and then through it to where there is an old Shiva temple. A massive archaeological dig, confirming Peshawar as the oldest city in South Asia, also lives here. It starts to become evening and I stroll around the grounds of the Gorkhatri caravanserai, where the Emperor Kanishka's great stupa was said to have stood when Peshawar was the capital of the Kushan Empire. I chat with friendly locals who call themselves 'citizens'—a translation of '*kharay*'—but which sounds like a dystopian Orwellian reference to me. I catch a *raksha* to the Daewoo bus counter to head back to Islamabad, am searched by police on the bus as we cross into Punjab (for hashish or bombs, presumably) and pull into town around 9:30 pm, ending the surreality of a day trip to the frontiers of my imagination.

Multan
Day 18

Call me stubborn, but I decide to try for the train to Quetta again. After all, it's why I came to Islamabad in the first place and I'm not willing to give up on the idea of covering my entire route overland until I've exhausted all possible avenues. Sobia's father gives me the use of a car and driver and I'm taken to their family travel agency, where the lady at the desk looks a bit like Nusrat Fateh Ali Khan, though not quite as large. I tell her about my earlier experience, she listens with sympathy and tells me there's no guarantee it won't happen again, but the Jaffar Express is more reliable than the train from Lahore. Yup, good enough for me, I'll take it, one sleeper bunk please. The train leaves later in the day so I decide to kill time at one of those 'Supers' they have in Islamabad, after I do my Friday prayers at the small mosque in the lovely residential area where Sobia lives, amidst parks and green spaces.

As I approach the Super, I see considerable police presence and a small crowd gathered there, so I move closer to get a better look. A number of activists with placards, microphones and banners have assembled at the square, and are saying lots of things quite angrily, mostly in Urdu. A look at an English poster tells me a hunger strike is underway with an Anna Hazare-like character at the centre. His name is Jahangir Akhtar and he's a local businessman, who, inspired by India's Hazare, is fasting unto death to protest the corruption in Pakistan's administration. I can't make out if Mr. Akhtar is actually here or not, of if these are just his supporters. Civil society here seems to have a bit of muscle, but in their posturing, the cops are making it abundantly clear that theirs are the bigger ones. I hesitate to take out my camera, and decide against lingering there too much longer.

After leisurely waifing around the shopping complex expecting the train to be delayed, I go to the station 40 minutes after the scheduled time, only to find that the train has actually been and gone this time! It's unbelievable. In one of the rarest moments in Pakistan's recent locomotive history, a train arrived within an hour of its scheduled departure time and is now heading to Quetta where I need to go, and I had a ticket for it! It would almost be poetic if it wasn't so painful. I run to the stationmaster; he tells me I can catch it from Lahore or Multan, or get the next one in a day.

I decide to go back to Lahore, but not to catch the train as I won't make it in time anyway, but to find out about that other train to Iran from overland travellers staying at Regale Internet Inn, one of the better known budget accommodations in Lahore, and where information about overland routes can be found. I arrive in Lahore at night and head straight for Regale, where I meet a Frenchman and a Spaniard who are also traveling to Quetta in a few days. I ask them about the train to Iran and they confirm that it has stopped running (they asked a German motorcyclist who came from Iran), but there are buses that regularly do the crossing, as well as a flight from Quetta to Zahedan, as the very last option. I'm relieved: I wouldn't have made it to Quetta in time anyway, and now I can visit Multan too, from where I can try and catch the train again.

The next day, I take a bus to Multan and along the way notice that Multanis are darker and smaller-built than their mountainous northern countrymen. They also seem more humorous. The countryside is green and flat, and after some kilometres of industrial sprawl outside Lahore, it becomes reminiscent of the agrarian landscape of the Ganges basin, but with more wheat than paddy. Here, near the geographical centre of Pakistan, the contrasting forces of fertility and sterility face off against each other—the barren Thar Desert stretches from Cholistan eastward into Rajasthan past Jaisalmer and Amer, while the western part is the Sutlej and Indus river system. It's also where Harappa, the pre-Vedic Indus Valley city once flourished some 4,000 years ago. We pass the site on our way, but I don't manage a visit.

As we enter the Saraiki belt, south of Punjab proper, people begin to dress differently. They wear colourful kurtas and *shalwar-kameezes* that aren't monochromatic while some even have—wait for it—decorative *noksha*. They wear *lungis*, both checked and plain white, and also the straight white Aligarhi or Delhi-style pyjamas which are quite uncommon in the north. Women wear large white bangles and colourful, printed *oornas*, not unlike their Rajasthani counterparts further into the Thar. They walk boldly and don't shrink in public as women in some other parts of Pakistan do, nor do they always cover their hair. Their rich, dark skin glistens and reminds me more of India than Pakistan.

I get a *raksha* to take me to a guest house and along the way the driver tells me about Multan and about the numerous dargahs and shrines here. His tone and manner of communication is humble and *antorik*, or 'intimate', for lack of a better English equivalent, and quite a bit less haughty than what's typical of Lahore or Islamabad. I'm taken to a place that appears to be a combination of a wedding hall, a guesthouse and an NGO office, and as I go towards what surely is the reception but could also be the place where you drop off gifts at weddings, I am met by a very beautiful woman who looks Bengali with her large eyes and '*paan*' shaped face. She looks at me confidently with nothing over her head except her Sahasrara Chakra and gives me a room but charges me far too much so we bargain it down. She's a good sport and a good flirt and in the end she wins but it's a good room. The manager hears me speaking in English and very politely makes the host in him available to me. He's well educated and when he hears me say 'Bangladesh', he says

'Ah, but so cultured the Bengalis are, we lost a lot of intellectual substance when we lost Bengal.'

This rumour is very popular in Pakistan, it seems. I don't think they've met too many of us lately.

It's evening, and I go out to get something to eat at a roadside restaurant where I order some chicken kadhai and naan, which, like in Peshawar, is served piping hot in the kadhai itself. I speak with my family on the phone and enjoy being in a place that feels markedly less intimidating or aggressive than other places I've been to in Pakistan, even less so than Peshawar. I return to the guesthouse. There's been a conference on another floor, and many of the participants are staying the night. I notice that they are mostly disabled people. I ask the receptionist about it and she tells me that an NGO that works with people with disabilities is having a three-day event in Multan for people from the surrounding villages. It's a nice atmosphere, kind and hopeful, and I fall asleep to the sounds of people talking in the hallway, chattering excitably like schoolgirls.

Day 20

I'm up early and while having my room-serviced breakfast, spend some time watching Multani television. I find a news channel in English called Express 24/7, and listen intently to the stories of the world I've been missing:

.... There's been a 6.5 magnitude earthquake in North East India, Nepal and Bangladesh have also been affected (I worry about my family and friends).... *The Delhi bomber is Indian and not Pakistani.... Iran and Pakistan are trying to establish a gas pipeline through Balochistan.... The US is accusing the Pakistani administration of having ties to the Haqqani network ... Libya: Gaddafi is unrelenting, more people brutalised ... 20 people killed in anti-Saleh demonstrations in Yemen.... Floods worsening in Sindh.... Palestine seeks UN recognition.... Greece in Eurozone crisis.... The two Koreas hold nuclear talks.*

I keep flicking through the channels and find Khyber TV, an all Pashto channel featuring comedy and music. I enjoyed it without understanding a word, for the insight it gives me into Pashto pop culture and wonder if there might have been a Bangla channel that a Pakhtun would have enjoyed, had things turned out differently in pre-1971 Pakistan. I also find a few Saraiki language ones, and notice that it sounds nothing at all like Punjabi. The intonations are completely different, and they speak with a musical lilt. In fact it's different enough for the Saraiki belt to want to be recognised as a separate province along linguistic lines, recalling a time when Saraikistan was part of the princely state of Bhawalpur—an independent entity that acceded to Pakistan during Partition and was merged, against its wishes, with Punjab.

I head out to see about the Jaffar Express, (not the one I missed but the next one) which should be in Multan today on its way to Quetta. I take a *raksha* to Multan train station, which is easily among the prettiest train stations I've seen anywhere, featuring cupolas and blue decorative tiles, and buy myself a ticket for the 8 pm train—my third ticket on as many trains to Quetta. There's plenty of time until departure, so I head off to explore this very crowded and colourful city.

We come to a walled old quarter from where I decide to go on foot. I ask the *rakshawallah* to wait at one of the large gates and carry on down the ring road which runs along the walls. Multan is very old and like Peshawar, has a lived-in charm with attractive yet decrepit buildings. But what sets Multan apart entirely from other Pakistani cities I've visited so far, or, any other South Asian city in fact, is its generous use of decorative tiles. These are called *kashi*, glazed ceramic tiles decorated with complicated geometric or floral patterns and vibrant colours, set around an entrance or on the facade of a building as a mosaic. Entire structures can be covered in them and they are usually blue. They get their name from Kashgar, in Eastern Turkistan, now a part of China's Xinjiang province, where they are believed to have originated. I'm not convinced that's true, though, considering tile mosaics were used in Iranian Elamite structures as well, and Iran, in fact, is where the usage is full blown, covering complete urban landscapes like gorgeous Persian carpets. Here in Multan, they are evidenced mostly on Sufi mazaars, but not exclusively—they can even appear on old buildings that are hidden away from sight, in an alley somewhere, falling apart but still fabulous for their tile work.

Multan's got a great story. For starters it's one of the places where the Rig Veda may have been composed, although the fact that there is no way of knowing where or when the Vedas were composed nearly nullifies this claim. A less flattering version has it as the place where Satan landed on earth after falling from grace. Some say the arch was perfected here and that the first book on architecture was also written here, but I'm quite sure Vitruvius, the acknowledged inventor of the arch, would have something to say about that. It begins to get clearer after 326 BC when Alexander the Great, on his return home, decides to do a bit more plundering in Asia and attacks Multan. He was wounded very seriously here and his soldiers, believing Alexander to be dead, slaughtered the city's inhabitants with genocidal intent. The Khuni Burj or Bloody Tower in the walled city is where it all happened.

Multan became the first major South Asian city to be incorporated into the Muslim realm, when the teenaged Muhammad bin Qasim defeated Raja Dahir around 712 AD and added Sindh to the Ummayad Empire. Many people died then too, but the Aditya Sun Temple, said to have been built by Krishna's wayward son Samba, was left unmolested, as was the population's faith. The altogether more brutish Mahmud of Ghazni was far less considerate, and he smashed the temple in 1026, killing thousands of people and forcing the rest to convert. He also ransacked Mathura, Krishna's city and a sort of Medina for Hindus, destroying most of it and making off with all the loot. Ghazni's heavy-handedness and his belief that he was on a holy war against Kaffirs sullied, almost permanently, Islam's arrival into India and made it far less appealing to Indians than it naturally might have been (adding insult to injury, Pakistan pompously named its nuclear-capable ballistic missile 'Ghaznavi' in honour of the Afghan warrior, something that even the cultural minister of Afghanistan at the time took exception to). About 300 years later, Ghiyasuddin Tughaq launched his imperial ambitions here and went on to rule all of North India.

I walk around the old city taking pictures. People here are less eager to be photographed than they are in Peshawar, and I'm able to take in the place at my own pace. They aren't any less polite though, and people offer me tea and call me in to their shops to satisfy their curiosity about the obvious out-of-towner. I stumble upon an abandoned temple that's being used to store grain, walk down really lovely alleys with rows of garishly painted townhouses, and follow winding mazes that open out to courtyards of Sufi mazaars. The atmosphere is gentle and sublime and people carry themselves with a dignified modesty, keeping their voices low but their esteem high.

It's remarkably different from the testosterone-driven schoolboy complex in Lahore and Islamabad, and I'm able to let my guard down without feeling like I'm being sized up or set up to become the butt of a joke. An impromptu 'guide' gives me a tour of the mazaar, pointing out the graves of magnificent men whose names I can't remember, their tombs lovingly decorated with tiles, fragranced by incense and adorned with flowers. Some of the smaller graves in the outer courtyards have earthen water urns placed by their feet. People come—most in some emotional state or another—and sing, wail, pray or just sit in complete stillness next to the sarcophagi. I'm not sure I understand why they feel these great but dead men can take the weight off their hearts as they perhaps could have done while they were still alive, but they come to them anyway and it seems to work.

I'm intrigued by this need, this reliance on stations, symbols and ceremonies to prop us up and give our invisible faith some sort of corporeal shape. It's as though we need to have tangible anchors which we can throw into the terrifying vastness of an intangible eternity, allowing us to make believe we can halt a while and hold off this inexorable tide that steadily drags us out. Or perhaps, as I was thinking in Bodh Gaya, these places have some sort of residual spiritual energy. The pigeons certainly seem to think so; there are always loads of them at all of these religious places, but I suspect the feed that's scattered by the caretakers every day biases them just slightly.

While wandering I find myself on the outskirts of the city, on a slightly elevated plain, looking out over low-rise rooftops. In the distance a big green dome catches the sunlight and dominates the skyline. Multanis say it's the tomb of Shams-i-Tabrizi, the great mystic

165

who taught Jalaluddin Rumi the religion of Love, but it probably isn't. There are legends about Shams everywhere; he was a *qalandar*, a wanderer, originally from Tabriz, but spent most of his life moving from city to city in search of minds that would inspire him, being finally satisfied with Maulana Jalaluddin Rumi, in Konya. He disappeared after the Maulana's disciples plotted to kill him for what they perceived as an unhealthy relationship between the two men, and because they felt jealous of their closeness. Some say he came to Multan, and when people here refused to give him fire to cook his fish, he called the sun closer to help him do the job, turning Multan into the furnace it can become by the middle of summer. All fantastical and absurd, but with *qalandars* and the like, you can never be sure.

What *is* certain is that the tomb beside me belongs to the Sufi Shah Rukn-e-Alam, and it stands firm in all its solidity, wearing, according to some, the world's second largest dome on its tiled and decorated head. It's squat but massive, and the single white hemisphere contrasts nicely with the mostly aquamarine and yellow ochre building. Ghiyasuddin Tughlaq had it built for himself between 1320 and 1324, but his son Muhammad bin Tughlaq gave it to Shah Rukn-e-Alam's family in 1330 and interred his father in the very simple tomb at Tughlaqabad Fort instead. This splendid structure now contains many graves (73, by some accounts) belonging to the Sufi and his descendants. By the entrance, a hawker sells *pani puri* and I gorge on about 20 of them, the tamarind water lubricating my parched mouth, while watching a colourfully dressed family glide by looking like a flock of rainbow lorikeets. They step and speak lightly, and from certain angles, appear to be moving along on a conveyor belt.

I enter the complex and notice it's nearly time for afternoon prayers so head towards the domeless mosque inside the grounds, which is dwarfed by the mazaar beside it. I pray and then make my way into the mazaar through large, beautifully carved wooden doors where incense and perfumed oil lamps produce an almost overpowering olfactory experience. A very blissful looking man in a green cap sits against a wall participating in what looks like *sohbet*, a spiritual discourse, with another man whose back is towards me. I want to capture the moment with my camera but the man in the green cap wags a finger at me forbiddingly. I gesture a 'why not?', but he just shakes his head politely, offering no reasons.

I go further inside and see numerous graves surrounding Shah Rukn-e-Alam's fenced off and draped sarcophagus, which sits directly under the large dome. It's adorned, like most mazaars are, with a *chador* bearing gold lettering in Thuluth script, lots of tinsel, streamers, flags and something that looks like tiny paper pom-poms on a string. The area is crowded with graves made of plaster and arranged in rows like pews, all running north-south across the east-west orientation of the room, faithful to an Islamic interpretation of Feng Shui. There's a very beautiful mirhab in the western wall as well, made of blue tiles and elaborate woodwork. It's the first time I've seen a mirhab in a mazaar, and wonder why it's there. The room is dark, and slightly dismal, and there are people wailing and singing over the saint's grave. I don't particularly enjoy the atmosphere so leave in a hurry. It's much nicer outside and I wander around the courtyard for a bit before heading towards the other white-domed structure, further ahead.

This smaller dome covers the tomb of Bahauddin Zakariya, Shah Rukn-e-Alam's grandfather. Bahauddin Zakariya was a heavyweight Sufi of the Suhrawardiyya order, a tradition that was founded in Baghdad by an Iranian mystic in the 12th century. He was a disciple of the founder's nephew and wandered for 15 years before settling in Multan to spread his teachings across South Asia. The Suhrawardys depart drastically from established Sufi principles like detachment and reclusiveness, and promote social and political involvement on an international scale. They aren't particularly allergic to wealth either. Throughout the ages, they've been involved with diplomacy, education and government, and a present-day descendent of Bahauddin Zakariya, Shah Mehmood Qureshi, also the custodian of this tomb, became the Foreign Minister of Pakistan in 2008. Hussain Syed Suhrawardy, that giant of Bengali politics, was also a member of this order.

Bahauddin Zakariya died in 1268, and a mausoleum was erected over his grave but the one I'm looking at isn't the original; that was destroyed by the British in 1848. It's a restored and reconstructed version but stunning nevertheless. As I approach the entrance, an armed officer wearing the black and khaki uniform of the Pakistani police force barks, '*No K'maera!*' in as unfriendly a manner as he can. His behaviour undermines the serenity of the place and I'm annoyed by his presence here. There's also a metal detector and a cordon around the complex, just as there was at the Data Darbar in Lahore. It's utterly insolent that extremist Muslims can think of attacking the graves of men like these, but it's happening across the globe and people who liken the veneration of graves to idol-worship violently pick on the practice, completely impervious to the good, like feeding the poor, that these places do. I can understand how it may appear like people are worshipping a dead man and some-times they do go a little overboard. People are, after all, just people and need to believe in the power of intercession—someone to put in a good word—especially if they grew up in nepotistic environ-ments where even getting a telephone line can sometimes require an influential intercessor. But that's no reason to attack them.

I show the officer some of my pictures from Shah Rukn-e-Alam's tomb and tell him I'm a photographer and simply want other people to appreciate the beauty of Pakistan. It works—appealing to vanity nearly always does—and he lets me through *avec k'maera*. The spa-cious tomb area, unlike Bahauddin's grandson's, is not stuffy or closed but endowed with enough sunlight to require bamboo blinds over the openings to keep some of it out. It's much more inviting, and in fact quite a lot more attractive. The pillared cloister makes it feel like a house, and fresh flower petals are strewn over the tile-covered graves in the courtyard as well as over the saint's grave in the main room. Shah Rukn-e-Alam was originally buried here too, but was later transferred to his own tomb—a very unusual thing for a Muslim community to do.

I leave as it becomes evening and realise that I will never be able to find my way back to the gate where I left the *rakshawallah* waiting. I feel remorseful as I hadn't paid him yet and head to the train station I set off from, hoping he's there. Naturally he isn't, but some of the porters suggest I give the amount to a mosque as a *sadaqah* donation, and maybe Allah will forgive me. That's great, but the *rickshawallah* still doesn't get his money, which is what I'm more concerned about. I do it anyway, hoping that a karmic cycle will somehow compensate the poor man, and then head to the guesthouse to pick up my bag. Brilliantly, the *rakshawallah's* older brother is waiting for me there—how he knew where I was staying is still a mystery, but I don't care as I'm overjoyed to see him. I pay him what's owed, apologise profusely, and rush upstairs to grab my gear.

After a modest (by Pakistani standards) delay of four hours, the train arrives in Multan and sets off for Quetta. The route will take us south into Sindh, and then west across the Indus, through the desert and to the eastern edge of the Iranian plateau. I'm completely thrilled—after all the delays and missteps, I am finally on my way to Persia.

I board my cabin, which I'm sharing with Tauqir, a Punjabi who's traveling to Quetta for the first time. He's also travelling by train for the same reason that I am, just for the experience of it, and I instantly take a liking to him. We chat for a while, in the language I use as an excuse for Urdu, but manage to get quite a lot of communication in somehow. I learn that he has a small daughter, is a businessman, is 31, has some relatives in Quetta and is looking to expand his business there. I manage to tell him about my journey, a little bit about India (which all Pakistanis are curious about but most can't visit, and vice-versa) and about the book I hope to be able to write. He's a kind and gentle sort, and buys me tea and cakes at Rohri, where we pull in for a halt before crossing the Indus.

Pakistani trains aren't like Indian trains. In India, even second-class berths come with two meals, tea, a pillow, fresh sheets and a quilt. In Pakistan, first class is a cabin with an en suite bathroom and nothing else—they basically just give you a berth and forget about you. They also drive the trains very fast and stop suddenly. At times it feels like the train will come right off the rails, or buckle forward. But I'm not complaining, really. As trains in South Asia go this one is not as bad as it gets. It's a clean air-conditioned cabin with a good loo and a door that locks. We hold at Rohri for a long time where I fall asleep and miss, much to my disappointment, the Indus crossing.

I wake up when we are leaving Sukkur district as morning turns to day, to see that it's abundantly fecund outside, with rice, wheat and mustard fields, and tall grass growing around swamps and marshes. The trees are thick and dark and a delicate paddy green dominates the landscape, soothing my eyes. It's the Indus flood plain, and I'm tempted to say that it's even more fertile than the Ganges plain. There are miles of lushness in every direction, palm trees, wetlands, bright fields, birds, flowers, farmers and even smiling children who wave at us from their mud hut villages. There isn't the slightest hint of a desert, yet the desert is only a few hundred kilometres away on either side of this hyper-productive tract. It's no wonder that the Indus, or Sindhu River was elevated to supernatural status in Vedic literature—it's quite spectacular for its ability to irrigate a desert.

Tauqir, Hussein (a friend we've made) and I stand near the open door between carriages, smoking cigarettes and feeling the warm air on our faces. The Indus basin is now behind us and the land has become slightly drier. We arrive at Jacobabad, named after its founder John Jacob, and I notice that the station buildings are in Mughal-Gothic style, but more Gothic than Mughal. I'm impressed by how determined the British were to totally possess India. They even remade, in their own image, this edge-of-empire dusty little town, which is one of the hottest places in South Asia. We are at the frontiers of Balochistan and the flat, dry land is a world apart from the rivers and mountains of a place once called Aryavarta, the Aryan lands of upper India. From here, the sophistication of Sanskrit civilisation will fade into a rugged tribal fraternity that will, in turn, become an elegant Avestani atmosphere. The stretches of emptiness between all three insulate one from the other, keeping their distinctions intact.

It's also become tenser, as we enter a territory that has an antagonistic relationship with the rest of Pakistan. Balochis harbour a resentment that their language and culture are being purposely subverted by provinces from across the Indus and don't like that the Hindustani—Punjabi, Sindhi—dominated country they are part of treads noisily over Balochistan's integrity, exploiting its resources and giving little back to its inhabitants—an old familiar tune to a Bengali like me. Armed guards board the train with Kalashnikovs and automatic rifles as we cross into the province of Balochistan. They are very large men with bronzed, leathery skin, and wear black *shalwar-kameezes* with their bullet straps slung across their chests like hunters. I'm told they are the Pashtun frontier corps, a paramilitary force made up of people from the province. They patrol the corridors of the train, intimidating passengers and potential perpetrators alike and it's the first time since my escape to mild-mannered Multan that I've seen such an incontestable reliance on weaponry. I had forgotten just how heavily armed Pakistan really is. The militiamen also create a safe passage for us by standing vigilantly in the desert every so many metres along the length of the track, as the train slips by behind this human wall of wild and weather-beaten warriors.

It's not an exercise in paranoia; the threat of a Balochi attack is very real. We could be attacked for any number of reasons: it could be a straightforward train robbery or a reprisal attack for Pakistani military strikes in Balochistan. It could be tribal vendetta against someone associated with Pakistan Railways; we could become a Taliban target or a means for Balochi separatists to send a message to the Pakistani government; or, they could board the train looking for Punjabis to kill. This has happened in the past—buses, trains even taxis have been stopped, the Punjabi passengers pulled off, lined up and executed, just for being Punjabi in Balochistan. It's very depressing and my mind immediately goes to Tauqir, who's quite worried and has already locked the cabin door. He tells me about the stories he's heard, people he used to know who were killed in this way, and I feel sad and angry at the same time. I think about his gentleness and his generosity, his baby daughter, his humour, and feel almost physically sick thinking that someone might just discover he is Punjabi and shoot him, without any of those things mattering to them for a moment. My Khalu's family in Quetta is Punjabi too and has been living there for ages. Why should they be unwelcome where they live and raise their children?

The parallels between Bengal and Balochistan have the same two sides, and the aggression against Urdu-speaking settlers and West Pakistani businessmen was equally indiscriminate in 1971. We were just as defensive when it came to accepting people from different cultures and just as obstructive in allowing them to have free reign in what was essentially their own country. I'm not trying to excuse the horrors that were perpetrated against Bengalis during the war—not at all—but I'm not blind to the horrors that were perpetrated by Bengalis as well. There's an old Bangla adage that fits here and never seems to fail: it takes two hands to clap, meaning, roughly, that all conflicts have two culprits.

Tauqir and I talk about the situation. He makes the very good point that everyone is welcome in Punjab and that Punjabis don't go around killing non-Punjabis. He then makes light of it by saying,

'Let them take Balochistan and go. Let them all go, no problem, we will call our country Punjabistan and be very happy with it!'

I wonder if that isn't what Punjabis would like to be able to do with the whole place anyway. After all, we did that, didn't we? The name 'Bangladesh' proudly proclaims that all non-Bengalis in our population are out of place and alien squatters in my *Lebensraum*, giving no consideration whatsoever to the nearly two million people of the Chittagong hill tribes who have always lived where they live. Tauqir plays music on his mobile phone. He loves '*Dil to baccha hai, thora kaccha hai*' and sings along, then he plays '*Kabhi kabhi mere dil mein*' and we try to forget about the tensions outside our cabin. I teach him a few words in Bangla so that he can pose as a Bangali should anything go wrong, and advise him to congratulate any separatist he meets by saying, '*Shabash bhai, chalai jao, tomrao parba*'. He tries to say it, butchers it, and we laugh together as if all were right with the world.

Fourteen hours have gone by and the land is now almost entirely dry. It's not the sort of desert I had expected, though, with sand and dunes, but a sort of scrubland, mingled with infrequent patches of complete barrenness. Quite a lot of vegetation occurs here, which seems to be sustained by small rivulets and the occasional rainfall. There's also groundwater and a random oasis every now and then. The terrain is flat as a board for miles upon miles as the horizon spreads far out into the distance, and I've never seen so much uninterrupted space before in my life. It's very beautiful in its sparseness and I stare out at the light brown landscape for long periods of time. It's amazing that a train goes through here at all, and it needs mentioning, grudgingly, that the British are exceptionally good at laying railway tracks even in the remotest of places, under the harshest of conditions. Or perhaps I should say they were very good at having them laid; locals did the actual laying of course. When I'm being completely honest I'm actually quite impressed by many things the British were able to achieve in South Asia, often against considerable odds, and this fantastic track is easily one of them.

It becomes mid-afternoon and an orange light adds to the already mythical quality of my experience in the wastelands of the Pakistani interior. Mud huts and entirely adobe villages appear from time to time, populated by very brightly dressed desert gypsies. Their children run at the train excitedly, like coloured balls of bubbling life against a dead, dry background. Women carry urns on their heads and walk long distances to collect water, and little boys struggle to find firewood in this place of treelessness which yields no tinder. Their lives' battles are told in the trenches that run, from their eyes to their ears, across their temples. A highway goes alongside us sometimes, where decorated trucks and SUVs zoom past, creating mini-dust storms in their wake. Sometimes a gas pipeline snakes its way through the desert. The sun is blotted out by the sand in the air but I can see it set behind the distant peaks of the Iranian Plateau, creating craggy silhouettes. It's very peaceful and from where I'm looking at it, there seems to be nothing at all threatening about the province of Balochistan.

And then it comes home in a God-awful way. During one of the longer stops, Tauqir and I leave the station to get some freshly made naan and come back to find that a mournful pall has fallen over the crowds on the platform. There are furtive glances, a lot of murmuring and a general sense of discomfiture in the atmosphere. Something's not right. Tauqir goes to find out what, while I go to the 'tea and snakes' stall and order us a couple of cups of chai. He comes back shaken; his face is pale and wears an expression of sorror—equal parts sorrow and horror. Twenty-six Hazara Shias have been pulled off a Taftan-bound bus and shot dead at a place called Mastung, near Quetta. They were on their way to Iran for a pilgrimage. We stare at each other in disbelief for what seems like an age, until the silence becomes pregnant with our feelings of helplessness and delivers up an unnatural dread. And then we remember Hussein, the man we had met on the train. He is travelling to Quetta with his family to catch a bus to Taftan, for a pilgrimage. They are Shia.

We find him at the end of the platform, smoking like he's gasping for air, inhaling entire cigarettes in seconds. His eyes are wide open with worry.

'They will kill us. Kill me, kill my wife, kill my children. They are killing Shias like dogs. Worse than dogs, no one hunts dogs. If they don't kill us on the train they will kill us on the bus. We have no chance. Look what they did.... How could they do it ... how could they? They were going to *ziyarat*, like me. It could have been me.'

He breaks down and buries his head in his hands. I'm gripped by grief for him and for the 26 men I never knew. My heart aches for their families, for their mothers and their wives and children; I worry for all the Shias of Pakistan. How can prejudice so easily turn to murder? Which religion teaches them this? We try to console Hussein, who has decided to try and fly to Iran from Quetta or just go back to Rawalpindi. There must be many others doing the same—people with modest means who may have saved up for ages to make this trip. I try to imagine those poor Hazaras, lying dead somewhere on the ground, all their hopes and dreams spilling out with their blood onto the dry desert. For the first time, I'm worried about going to Iran by land.

Quetta

We reach Quetta after midnight, nearly 10 hours later than scheduled. The last leg of the journey took us up into the mountains as we ascended the Iranian plateau in the dark—these were tense hours since the train climbed slowly through narrow gorges, making it an easy target for bandits or terrorists. There was every reason to believe we might be attacked—in fact, we were all bracing for it the whole time. After we got through the mountains and into semi-urban spaces, we neared the terminal and I texted Hassan Uncle, my Khalu's brother in Quetta, to let him know I'm alright. At the station, the relief is almost tangible; people hug their loved ones with an intensity that tells you no one was really sure that we would make it here at all.

Hassan Uncle picks me out in the crowd and comes towards me. He's a short, stocky man, with an optimism that devours gloom anywhere around him and it's almost impossible not to take an instant liking to him. We talk about the attack at Mastung and he tells me about the 12 people who were killed in another attack on Shias during Eid prayers, just a few weeks ago. If it weren't so tragic it would be hilarious that people who kill Muslims during Eid prayers, after Ramazan, can call themselves Muslim. We drive through town and I can see that Quetta becomes completely deserted after dark. There's also a light mist, and it's several degrees cooler here than the places we've come through. Hassan Uncle points out the landmarks; one of them is a beautiful hotel made to resemble an adobe fortress, where most of the expats stay. Along the road I see an unexpected street sign in English and Urdu that reads,

Please drive carefully. We love our children.

We pull into the 'Awan Qilla', a rarefied, walled complex that the Awans, my uncle's family, built decades ago when they moved to Quetta. It's a huge area, with houses, fields, livestock, peacocks, flowers, fruit trees, streams, gardens and swimming pools. Behind the solid steel gates that keep the dry, dusty and dangerous city out, Awan Qilla is a green and plentiful place where one family's interpretation of the good life flourishes. It's quite a perfect one too.

Hassan Uncle's home is lovely. Parts of it are decorated like a Pashtun house, with carpets and kilims and low seating around a central table. His family looks after me like one of their own, and his mother—a warm, strong, trooper of a woman who reminds me of my own dear grandmother—tells me stories about my Khala and Khalu, from before I was born. After breakfast, Hassan Uncle and I go into town to see about getting me to Iran safely over-land and to his office to make phone calls. It is apparent that he is something of a don on his turf; people gather around him like an entourage but it doesn't seem to have gone to his head at all and he remains absolutely modest, treating everyone, including me, as equals. It's an incredible quality, and very humbling.

We make a few inquiries about flights and buses. Hassan Uncle is uncomfortable about letting me take the bus but won't stand in my way if it's really what I want to do. He still wants to book a flight, just in case—and it's tricky because flights from Quetta to Zahedan are going full, presumably because Shia pilgrims have given up the idea of travelling by land, and there are only two or three seats left on one that can get me out before my visa expires in less than a week. I'm also being difficult about it and don't want to take a flight to anywhere further west in Iran. Hassan Uncle's dedicated team of friends-cum-colleagues-cum-fans is busily calling their contacts to see what can be arranged by way of favours. In the meantime, another set is looking into shared taxis and buses. Tea arrives as all this goes on, and a storm of activity accompanied by loud, exaggerated conversation and thunderous table-slapping has manifested around an odd stranger's stranger odyssey. I feel guilty until I realise that they're actually enjoying it.

We get something, and with the heightened urgency that has characterised the atmosphere since morning, speed off into town to the travel agent as Hassan Uncle delegates his actual work to colleagues in preparation for a wasted day with me. Like everyone else, he wears a plain, camouflaging *shalwar-kameez* and I'm beginning to wish I had one too. While sitting in his office, a number of people come in, among them drivers and workers—all dressed in basic *shalwar* sets, and it is hard to discern any sort of rank because of these clothes. But mostly it's the attitudes of the people—there is an absence of the sort of social insecurity that requires a demonstrated superiority, or inferiority, and this Pakistani, or more appropriately, Pashtun egalitarianism is particularly pronounced in Quetta.

There are large numbers of Pashtuns in Quetta—a majority, in fact. It's always been a Pashtun city, and was originally called 'Kuwatah', a variant of the word 'Kot'— Pashto for 'fort'—since it sits ensconced in mountains guarding the Bolan Pass. It should actually be a part of Afghanistan and indeed it was, until it was given to the British as a peace offering at the end of the Anglo-Afghan wars of the 19th century. Its links to anything 'Hindustani' are tenuous—the languages are Iranic, the air is less humid, the faces more crimson and many heads sport the distinctive grey-green Pashto turbans. They're quite different from the Pakhtuns in Peshawar, who seem to be attached, albeit in a semi-detached sort of way, to an Indian zone. Being close to Kandahar, Afghani refugees stream into Quetta as well and push it further beyond the Indian cultural continent, wherever that ends.

While we are on the subject, it's worth mentioning that some 63 per cent of all refugees out of Afghanistan live in Pakistan, amounting to over a million people. At its peak the number was closer to 3.5 million and Pakistan took in more refugees than any other country in the world. It's one of the great, untold humanitarian tales: a single developing country accommodates more displaced people than nearly all the developed countries put together. It's no wonder we don't hear much about it—it's shameful, and gives Pakistan an inconvenient upperhand that's entirely incongruous with its role as designated villain. Just imagine how it might look if they were seen to be helping people that are being harmed by their liberators? Why, we can't have that now can we, Harry?

The Pashtuns and the Baloch seem to get along fine and I ask Hassan Uncle about this, considering the Baloch are so famously territorial. He tells me that in Quetta at least, the Baloch and the Pashtun have become similar over the years and recognise each other as kindred. They both live in democratic, tribal federations that acknowledge the other's territorial claims (Quetta actually belongs to the Pashtuns if it comes to that), are both notoriously independent, have always had a problem with authority and are allied in their mistrust of eastern Pakistanis.

We go over to 'BIG Travels' and meet its very accommodating agent, a lanky, dark-skinned Sindhi who offers us tea and patties while looking over the logistics of issuing me a plane ticket. It seems in Pakistan nothing is simple, and I will have to buy a return ticket, even to make a one-way journey, something that for the life of me I can't understand. I explain that I won't be returning, that my visa expires in a few days, and that I'm travelling onwards to Europe. He asks me if I have any documents to prove that, which I don't, and he tells me this is the only way to do it then, if I want to leave Pakistan by air. We leave his office to mull it over, and go outside to enquire about alternatives. The shared taxi people want far too much money since they don't have enough passengers to go full, and candidly admit that they can't be sure it's completely safe. The buses are on strike indefinitely, following the Mastung incident.

Hassan Uncle is visibly relieved, and I'm beginning to see that I might have to accept the ground realities, literally. As we walk, people greet him on the streets and stand around talking about their lives or catching up on local news, in the way that people from close, small communities do. People who live in higher altitudes tend to have positive attitudes and that seems to be true of the people here as well. They also enjoy dressing well—many wear smart waistcoats with their as-baggy-as-can-be *patiali shalwars*, elaborate turbans and fitted *kameezes*. Some decorate their eyes with *surma*. It's certainly a boy's town—there are virtually no women in public anywhere, but it's not the combative atmosphere you find in some other all-male environments. This is a different air; it's weighty and calm and would smell like flint if it didn't smell like strong, spicy *attar*. I look closely but can't see where they are hiding that ugly part of themselves, the part that kills people during Eid prayers.

While trying to decide what to do we get the news that Iran has closed the land border for a week, following the killings at Mastung. That's that then. My visa will expire before it reopens, so I don't have a choice anymore. The thought that fate may have intervened to save my life crosses my mind, but I don't have time to entertain it as I rush to buy the plane ticket before the price changes, but only after being assured that the return part can be refunded afterwards. Ticket secured, it's now just a matter of waiting, and appreciating the presence of guardians in the ether.

I end up spending five days in Quetta and enjoy them immensely. It's a simple, bare place with beautiful views made most worthwhile by the people I meet. I feel included here by Hassan Uncle's friends and colleagues, and a sort of camaraderie develops between us, sustained by feeling of brotherhood across our mutually unintelligible languages. I enjoy watching them engage in Punjabi vs. Pashto banter; sit around the office like it's a darbar; talk politics; pray together in the garden and tell tall tales about their adventures. I'm quite certain the all-male atmosphere contributes to this sort of bonding, though some paranoid homophobes might find that discomfiting and suspect. I spend the evenings at home with Hassan Uncle's family having lively discussions and watching the news. Hassan Uncle is a great conversationalist and speaks a number of languages, gliding in and out of Punjabi, Pashto, Urdu and English, effortlessly, and often in the same breath. His wife is a kind, loving lady from a Pashtun noble family who is slightly shy and retiring. Their son Hurrairah, who is nursing a broken foot from falling off the roof stargazing, is about to take his O-level exams.

One evening, I ask about the Balochi insurgency, and though it's a complicated and sensitive topic, Hassan Uncle ventures a telling. He says it began as early as 1948 when the Khan of Kalat, one of the three princely states that make up today's Balochistan, opted for independence instead of joining India or Pakistan. But he was forced to accede to Pakistan and the gradual dissolution of provincial autonomy, starting with the One Unit policy, caused stirrings. Pakistan responded with characteristic force, and crushed the rebellion by killing its leader and his sons. In the 1960s and 1970s disputes over the distribution of natural gas revenues from Balochistan's fields escalated into armed struggle and once again, rather that attempt to address the issues, Pakistan pounded its way in and imposed marital law. The Murri and the Bugti tribes emerged as the main opposition to the Pakistani state, and remain so today.

In 2005, leaders of the Bugti and Murri tribes placed a demand before the Pakistan government for greater control over the natural resources within their own tribal territories and for a halt to the militarisation of Balochistan. Rather than consider the proposal, Pakistan responded with an increased military presence, causing the Bugti and the Murri tribes to give up on the idea of peace and go back to armed resistance. In 2006, the elderly and much respected Nawab Akbar Khan Bugti was assassinated on Pervez Musharraf's orders, causing the Balochi insurgency to spin completely out of control. The demands for autonomy have now turned into a struggle for independence, which shows no signs of slowing down. It has, since, also deteriorated into an ethnic struggle between Balochis and Punjabis, who have generally been the more industrious people in the province and so are viewed as exploiters. It's become doubly complicated with the arrival of a terrorist organisation called Jundullah, an Iranian Sunni group that has made Pakistani Balochistan their base to fight for the rights of the Sunnis in Iran, mostly in the Iranian province of Sistan va Baluchistan. This group is funded and supported by Saudi Arabia, to attack Iran in a localised version of the regional Sunni-Shia conflict and allegations have been made, not surprisingly, about Israel and the US as well.

Hassan Uncle takes me on drives out of the city along dirt tracks that run past dusty military compounds at the base of rocky desert mountains. He tells me that the US army flies missions out of these into Afghanistan and Pakistan's tribal belt, and shows me their attack aircrafts—F-15s, F-18s, Blackhawks and other abominations, parked alongside Pakistani ones, which are also US-made and supplied. Tellingly, the Pakistani aircrafts are smaller and less powerful. He shows me the barracks where US Marines live and they look just like the ones in war movies, basketball court and all. They also look a little like American college campuses. Hassan Uncle is well known in the area and the guards greet him with smiles as we drive through the various check-posts.

I hear a sound—*whop, whop, whop, whop*—which becomes progressively faster until I'm able to recognise it as the slicing sound of helicopters overhead. I get a terrible feeling in my stomach; I've never seen an invading army on mission before and the menacing sight of attack helicopters hovering, like birds of prey, over the mountains is extremely unnerving. The whole base is intimidating and there's an overwhelming presence of force— tanks, fighter planes, firing ranges, bunkers—quite unlike the much tamer cantonment areas I've seen in other countries. It all spells 'domination' and makes me feel about as small as an ant.

Hassan Uncle and I talk about this, and like every other Pakistani, he's completely incensed by the humiliating presence of foreign troops in his country, especially ones this powerful. His voice goes up by several decibels and his arms flail about as he describes the derision his country is being doused in, with ample contempt. He tells me how the Pakistani army and government are being held hostage by the US, how the Taliban was created by the CIA and how they had anticipated this 'Islamic blowback' as early as the 1980s. He goes on to to tell me how many innocent people have been killed in both Afghanistan and Pakistan and how US troops carry out their depredations with impunity, expressing their lusts and vices on the population as they please. He paints an awful picture, which includes everything except a tower of skulls, and as he talks I look for a drone or two among the aircrafts, but don't spot any.

When we get back to town I go to an ATM to withdraw some money for the onward journey but the machine eats my card, and I have a small panic attack. A very calm bank official opens the machine, retrieves it and then asks me into his office to fill out a form for their records. Relieved, I ask him why the machine did that and he says with a smile, 'I don't know, maybe it liked the taste.' He hands me the form and lends me his pen, then discovers that I'm left-handed and says, 'You're a lefty. We're the smart ones, they say ... but I bet I'm smarter.' I laugh, a group of elderly turbaned Pashtuns sitting in his office also laugh and I nod at them to show my respect. They nod back and ask me where I'm from.

'*Oh Bangali! Tom log to hamara aage chala giya. Ha ha ha!*'

He talks in a heavily Pashto-accented Urdu, which sounds a bit like the way the British speak it, making an obvious reference to Balochi secession. I laugh along nervously, unsure about whether I should be seen agreeing with them or not. They ask me general questions about my journey and about Dhaka until they get bored of me and go back to talking among themselves.

We leave the bank and head to a different one to exchange my Rupees for Riyals. The man behind the counter knows Hassan Uncle well and they catch up. As we wait for someone to bring the Riyals they talk about the horrible killings at Mastung. In fact, everyone we meet in town talks about it—clearly it has shocked the entire community. The Riyals arrive and it's the first time I've seen Iranian money. The notes are large and colourful with the ever-present image of Ayatollah Khomeini on every denomination, looking his severest, as he always seems in pictures. Riyals are in units of 1,000s and 10,000s, making it very confusing to convert. To add to the confusion, one can drop a zero and call it a Toman. So, for example, 10,000 Riyals is 1,000 Tomans and 1,000 Riyals is 100 Toman. I finally get the hang of it, and count up several stacks of the stuff.

On the way home I ask Hassan Uncle about the Brahui, another ethnic group in Balochistan, and a very curious one at that as they speak a Dravidian language. He points them out; they are completely conspicuous and are known for their flamboyance and very colourful clothes. The ones he shows me have long matted hair with flowers in them, and wear bright red patchwork tunics. They look delightfully mad, and smile as though they know things that the rest of us don't. Their Dravidian language and culture is an anomaly in an Indo-Iranian cultural zone, and is the only member of the predominantly South Indian family this far northwest. I'd like to believe it proves that Dravidian, and indeed Elamite culture, if the two are related, once spanned the entire area between Babylon and India, before an Indo-European migration through Central Asia and Anatolia displaced them.

But the going theory doesn't confirm this; instead it posits the Brahui as later migrants who moved north some time between the 10th and 14th centuries AD from Central India. This is because no linguistic influences from older Indo-European languages in the area, like Avestani or Sanskrit, is evidenced in their language, but they do seem to have borrowed prolifically afterwards, with the Brahui absorbing very many Balochi and Pashto words and enough Indo-European genes to make them virtually indistinguishable from anyone else in the area. But I'm not convinced of that theory—it's quite unlikely that Dravidians would move north into the desert, when they don't seem to have migrated anywhere else more easily accessible.

Today the nearly 2.5 million Brahui are classified as 'Balochi' and are Sunni Muslims. The original Khan of Kalat, the princely state which acceded to Pakistan and effectively created the province of Balochistan, was Brahui. Not enough research has been done on the origins of these unusual people; it's not impossible that they began in Mehrgarh, the pre-Aryan Indus Valley city that is very close, in fact, to the traditional Brahui heartland around Quetta. I wanted to visit Mehrgarh—it's the oldest site in South Asia, dated to about 7000 BC, and the one furthest away from the Indus system—but it sits on territory that is contested by two feuding tribes and is now a dangerous place to visit. I'm told that it's been damaged in this conflict and is lying in a state of neglect and disrepair.

We pull into Hassan Uncle's driveway as the afternoon's colours begin to drain into evening's grey and US fighter planes fly noisily overhead, just as they do every morning and afternoon, piercing

183

through the peace, and the sky, on their way to a feud, leaving Afghanistan lying in a state of neglect and disrepair.

On another day we go for a drive along a different route, through scenery that's stark and severe, and especially beautiful for it. Dry mountains that look like all vegetation has been singed off them on purpose rise up from a rocky dust bowl that spreads out forever in every direction. Various shades of sandy brown and grey dominate the picture. We drive along Urak Valley towards Hanna Lake, witnessing mountain streams that sustain fruit trees, sometimes entire orchards, along the way. Quetta produces quite a lot of very good fruit, which seems peculiar for a place this dry, but they have incredible quality and their cantaloupe is particularly sweet and delicious. There are public swimming pools on the route as well, which are part of a dam and irrigation system, where we see picnickers revelling in the generous reprieve of cool waters on a hot, dry day.

A massive British-built dam creates Hanna Lake, which is, for once, a piece of British infrastructure that blends beautifully into its surroundings. It looks like a Muslim citadel and is built to fit both the climate and the culture of Balochistan. Channelled snow-melt also feeds this reservoir, which is the only place in the entire province of Balochistan—some 44 per cent of Pakistan's total land area—where there is enough water for a water sports academy. It's quite magnificent and the sight of the silken blue water relieves my eyes of the scorched-mountain view. On the way back we stop at a small mosque along a tranquil stretch of the road surrounded by mountains and caves that resemble giant anthills. Hassan Uncle's family sponsors this mosque, and it's a lovely, rustic little place. It's so quiet that all I can hear is the sound of mountain streams running through natural stone troughs where worshippers perform their ablutions. I do the same, and wash the sun-charged cells of my limbs and head with the invigorating water of this cold, clear stream before standing in silent remembrance of our Generous Sustainer. Bliss comes unannounced and bounteously.

In the evening, Hassan Uncle takes me to an older part of Quetta, to his tailor, to get me the *shalwar* set I've been hankering for. First we stop at the fabric place and pick out the cloth. Hassan decides I should have two so I choose black and brown after being told that the maroon fabric I was originally eyeing is too feminine by Pakistani standards. We go to the tailor, who is an old Punjabi man and a good friend of Hassan Uncle's, and they spend a few minutes talking in their common tongue about the *'zuloom'* of violent extremists, in particular about the killings at Mastung. I suspect they also talk about their own positions as Punjabis in Balochistan without actually having to say it. It's easy to know when Punjabi is being spoken—they lean towards sounds like *'tha'*, *'thi'* and *'otthe'* and talk a lot faster than Pashto speakers. It's also cosier and relies heavily on tones, like most Indic languages.

Then I'm introduced to the wonderful world of *shalwar-kameez* tribalism, expressed in cuts, corners, collars and cuffs. Balochi *shalwars* are the baggiest, with enough material to fit three entire people in them, but also look the nicest to me for their drapes and folds. They are modelled after the *shalwars* of Patiala, in Indian Punjab, but ironically the Punjabis here don't use this style. They wear something more conservative, borrowed from the Pashtun outfit, which is a bit confused about whether it's a straight leg or a *patiala* and ends up looking like an old, stretched sock. It also lends itself to that awful above-the-ankles' Salafist invention. The Punjabi *kameez* is, by contrast, longer and baggier than the Balochi one and tends to have a western-style shirt collar (although not exclusively), western cuffs and rounded edges. The Balochi *kameez* can have both western collars and eastern (band) ones, is more fitted and much shorter, with straight ends instead of rounded ones. I like the Balochi style better, and ask for my suits to be rendered such.

We then go to Hassan Uncle's favourite Afghan restaurant for dinner, and this much I can tell you—it is perhaps the greatest ceremony of meat that I have ever attended. We sit on the floor Afghan style, with the table in front of us. A soup of meat stock is presented to us, along with mint sauce and freshly baked naan, to whet our appetites. Then it begins—out come skewers of succulent lamb, beef and chicken, charred black at the edges and tender enough for jets of juice to be sprayed into my mouth as I bite into the perfectly seasoned morsels. The wood-smoked flavours create a sensory experience that is nothing short of an orgasm on my tongue. Much gorging follows and by the end of it, I can barely move and feel as though a solid mass has been shoved down my gullet, pulling me to the ground like a stone. Nearly comatose, I stagger to the car as digestion commences but doesn't conclude until I'm well beyond Kerman, in Iran.

On my last day in Quetta, Hassan Uncle takes me to their family coal mines, high up in the grey mountains that gird the city. He tells me the story of mining in Quetta and of his family's involvement in the coal business, which goes back nearly a hundred years. When we go back to the office, he tries to get some work done, sorting out the insurance for a car of theirs that was recently stolen. I'm wearing one of my new *shalwar* sets, which was produced, amazingly, in just a day, and feel freed from self-consciousness as I sit there looking just like everyone else. Rahim Khan, one of Hassan Uncle's workers, keeps me company and tells me, predictably, that if I'm a Khan I must be Pashtun. I tell him, 'I've heard it all before, and I'm not one, sorry to disappoint you'. We chat and he asks me how many brothers I have, I tell him just one, and he says, 'Just two sons?! You're right, you're not Pashtun. If you were, there would have been 22 sons!'

We talk more, he tells me I should marry an Afghan woman and return to the fold, so to speak, and that he can arrange it straightaway, soon enough, it seems, for me to be able to put her in my backpack and carry on along my way. I tell him it's very generous of him, assuming it's a cousin of his that he has in mind, but politely decline the offer to be re-Pashtunised. He delivers one last pitch, clearly the one he's been saving for stubbornness like mine and tells me, 'Bangali girls are too dark, your children will be black. You marry an Afghan girl, lovely white skin, so good to look at!'

I think of replying with, 'beauty is in the eye of the beholder', or with Dr. King's loftier 'not the colour of their skin but the content of their character' speech, or even perhaps by going all the way across and saying, 'darker the berry, sweeter the juice', but decide against using any of them, knowing that they will probably make no sense at all to him, and might at best give him a mild headache. So I just grin ambiguously until he gets bored of me.

We end the day watching YouTube videos. He asks me to show him videos of Bangladesh and gets terrified when I show him pictures of the sea and the rivers. He can't swim and says the only thing that can scare a Pashtun is the sight of so much water. He loves all the green though. Then it becomes decidedly Afghan. Rahim wants to show us videos he likes watching, and lo and behold, it's all about guns. I watch with horror as he plays videos of machine guns, anti-aircraft guns, rocket launchers and other military hardware being fired clamorously from cliffs, in villages, up in the air and into rocks while children stand around, close enough to get killed, clapping excitedly. It's like a fireworks show gone horribly wrong. I cringe as I watch shells and casements go flying in the air, centimetres from the face of a laughing child who is as oblivious to the damage that it can do as his father is, shooting off his rounds like an idiot on drugs. Water, perhaps, but Pashtuns don't seem the slightest bit afraid of fire.

Night falls, and I sleep for one last time in Pakistan. Beyond this, there will be no more Star TV, no more 'Hindustani' and no more friends or family until I reach Turkey. This is the end of any place that I might sentimentally call my 'known world'.

II
IRANZAMIN

6

New Familiar Faces

Quetta Airport, Zahedan to Kerman,
Rayen, Mashhad

At Quetta Airport
Day 25

The small and nondescript international airport at Quetta isn't exactly teeming with activity, so the immigrations and customs people have the time to be extra diligent. A stern looking man with a moustache asks me to empty the contents of my backpack. I tell him it's a real pain to put it all back in again, but if it makes him happy, it's my pleasure. He smirks and says he'll buy me tea for my troubles. The equal and opposite retort is impossible to escape in Pakistan. He looks over my books and CDs and says, 'you have to leave them here, you can't take them into Iran'. I can't see why but say it's no problem, and ask him to please make sure the gentleman over there, pointing to Hassan Uncle, receives them. I'm not pleading enough for him to suggest that a 'small fee' might make it possible, so he changes his mind and just says, *'koi baat nei, le jao tumhara saath'*. The elderly gentleman next to him with very dark skin and a mehndi-red beard, checks my passport and says, 'Khan *hai tum? Qaum kya tera?'* (Are you a Khan? What's your tribe?)

It's the 'Khan is Pathan' conversation again. I tell him I have none, I'm afraid, I'm not Pathan but look, if it means that much to you, you can have the name back, I promise it's only slightly used.

'You are not Pashtun if you have no tribe.'

You don't say. Why, you're absolutely right. Now can I go? No perhaps not, he's seems to want to make a point here.

'All Pashtuns have a tribe. I'm from the Mansoor tribe. You are nothing without your tribe. Your ancestors, like so many others, lost their way in Hindustan and now have no place. There is no tribe called Khan, it's a title. So you have no place in the world because tribes have a territory.'

I had really hoped that I wouldn't take that bait, but the 'you are nothing' really gets under my skin, and I find myself having to have a conversation with a total stranger about identity instead of boarding a crucial flight to Iran.

'Look, I'm Bangali, we don't have tribes. Our place is Bangladesh and we are not lost. This business of tribes gets all of you killed anyway. Why do you need it, why can't you just be Pakistani? We're all just people in the end.'

'We are all people in the end, of course. But does Pakistan or your Bangladesh have a mother and a father? Are you connected to it by blood? Did it exist 100 years ago and will it exist 100 years from now? Will it always defend you and will you always belong to it? Can't you be denied entry to it? *Mere bhai*, these ideas—flags, countries and nationalities—come and go. They are artificial, life-less things; you belong to them because of pieces of paper, records that can be erased. But your tribe is an extended family. You share characteristics with them, like you do with your immediate family, and your ties to it can't be erased. It has feelings for you—a state can never have that.'

I want to get into the more complex conversation about the difference between states and nations, about linguistic and cultural communities, about temperaments, about how a nation is really just a large tribe and that *janapadas* grew from small bands or interrelated people originally anyway, but realise that it's all quite academic and what he's alluding to will remain true even after that. He's absolutely right—states and nations are impersonal. They almost have to be because of their sheer sizes and are, as he points out, imagined communities and not kin groups.

I begin to think about whether its genetic material or shared values and experiences that creates belonging, but do it silently as I can't afford to debate this any longer, and also because I don't really think it's as clearly an 'either-or' answer as we'd like it to be. I concede the point and gesture that I have to go, when he shares some trivia, which, true or not, has become part of Pashtun folklore. He tells me the word 'Pathan' is a corruption of '*Fatah'n*', from the Arabic root '*fatah*' which means to open. Many centuries ago, when Khalid bin Waleed was 'opening' the world to Islam, the Pakhtun were among his front-line soldiers and so were called Fatahn—the openers. He then proceeds to tell me with glee about the martial prowess of Pashtun warriors and how they pillaged and plundered their way through 'infidelistan'—a narrative that too often reflects Pakistan's disturbing perspective of its place in history. At any rate, he is kindly and before I go tells me—leaning in close like it's a secret—that all Pashtuns descend from two main branches, the Durrani and the Khilji, and that's its crucial I know which one my family comes from. I nod to allow an old man his convictions, and keep the knowledge of how completely irrelevant that distinction is in my world, to myself.

I head towards immigration and see two foreigners involved in some sort of row with the officials. One of them is being a bit belligerent, so the officials are being reciprocally officious. The other one, in a long beard and spectacles, is standing around, looking quite zen—he's clearly used to hurdles like these. I'm dressed in my brand new black *shalwar-kameez* and feel wonderfully inconspicuous as I approach the counter. I check in and then queue up behind the bearded sage, but the immigration officer waves me forward and says she'll do mine first, as these '*betameez goras*' are making her very annoyed and it

could take a while to process them. I quite enjoy being considered a
'local' and smile at her to say, 'ah well, what can you do?' But wait, I
recognise these goras; they're the two I saw in Lahore at Regal Internet
Inn. They're also flying, under compulsion, after coming to Pakistan
overland from China hoping to carry on to Europe. So it's true, the
land crossing really is impossible at the moment; I feel vindicated, and
a little less like a coward for flying.

I chat with the bearded Frenchman, Yves, while Carlos the
Spaniard checks his email as we wait to board the flight. Yves has
been travelling for 16 months and spent a year in Australia before
that. He's good company and we compare notes about Pakistan. He
tells me how most Pakistanis only seem interested in talking with
you after they have established if you are Muslim or not, something
I noticed too by the sequence of their questions. Invariably, the
second one after 'how are you' is 'Are you Muslim?' He also felt
they just fire off a barrage of set questions, designed to measure him
up and find him wanting, so that they could feel superior to him—
superiorly Muslim.

It's time to go and after we take off, the plane flies low enough
to get a good view of the 600 or so kilometres of open desert that
we're forfeiting on our overland route to Europe. Yves feels equally
dejected, and we tell each other that we'll return to make it up some
day, 'inshAllah'. We fly past the grey mountains and some patches of
agricultural and pastoral land, before coming over complete and utter
desolation. Even from the air, the place is hauntingly forbidding,
with faint outlines of tracks disappearing into patterns in the sand
made by the wind. The great slate mountains of the Iranian Plateau
carry on through the desert but their valleys widen, creating vast dusty
expanses where certain and agonising death will be all too happy to
visit you, if you happen to run out of water or lose your way.

Alexander the Great learnt this the hard way; he lost over 12,000
soldiers and thousands of others members of his expedition when,
further south, he crossed this desert on his way back home. It was
the biggest mistake he made in his whole glorious, glittering campaign from Macedonia to the Indus River and reduced his army,

by some accounts, to one third of its total size. The place looks like it belongs on another planet. Entire mountains have been worn down by wind and sand, creating semicircular craters that look like the mouths of Martian volcanoes. Inside them, dust swirls around giving the impression of steam rising out of a cauldron. Occasionally I spot what looks like a salt lake, bluish with white edges, looking radioactively bright against the matte surroundings, like something from a science project. There's absolutely no sign of life anywhere and it's all beautifully eerie.

Greater Balochistan straddles both sides of the international border between Iran and Pakistan. To the west it becomes the Iranian province of Sistan va Baluchestan. The northern part is Sistan—a bastardisation of the word Sakastan, the southernmost extent of the realm of the Scythians, who were called Saka in Iranic and Indic languages. The territory claimed by the Baloch lies to the south, and separatist struggles rage on, on either side, with the aim to integrate both parts and a third from the southern part of Afghanistan into a single country. It would certainly be a thirsty place, and they could quite easily call it the Lunar Republic of Sandpitistan without anyone being the slightest bit surprised.

But it's romantic enough: I imagine Zarathustra, the Persian prophet, roaming these deserts in search of a flock, and nearby in Zabul, the great Rustam experiences the second of his seven tests, where he nearly dies of dehydration. The Indus Valley would look like pure heaven to anyone going east across this terrible place and if the Aryans did come this way, it's easy to understand why they associated rivers with gods—they must've been gushing with gratitude to have made it to water. But they probably didn't come this way; they'd have to be mad to. Most routes into India from Western Asia went via the north, through the more accommodating Afghanistan, and this place was always an impenetrable barrier between the eastern and western lands of the Arya.

The aeroplane begins its descent and a city of boxy, legoland structures huddled together like a Soviet ghetto comes into sight. It is an eyesore and seems to appear out of nowhere to rudely interrupt the extravagant endlessness of the desert. The landscape is similar to Quetta's—the same dry mountains stand at attention around a dusty, desert town. The airport is similarly small, but much cleaner and more modern. Everything is neat and my very first impression is that this is a tidy place. There's also a stillness in the air which is both peaceful and unsettling, but my perceptions are tainted by my preconceptions about Iran, and I expect officialdom here to be strict, impatient and aggressive. I become self-conscious and presume that all of us are being assessed according to how sombre we can look and so do my best impression of a humourless person. All the signs and instructions are in Farsi only, and there is absolutely no way of knowing what the words on the walls say. This will prove to be a serious problem throughout Iran; it's already become a problem for Carlos who walks into the women's toilet and straight out again when he can't find the urinals. Luckily for him, it was empty at the time. I shudder to think what happens to a Western man in Iran when he walks in on Muslim women while their modesty is compromised.

The immigration officer is a delicate-looking young man and wears a plain white shirt instead of a uniform. It's disarming and pleasant, like his demeanour, and he addresses us courteously. Then he amuses himself by calling out our nationalities in loud exaggerated tones.

'Francaise! Welcome! Espana! Welcome! Britannia ... Khan? Britannia? *Saalom berader*, welcome!'

Through. To be honest, I was slightly nervous about crossing Iranian immigration as a British national, but already I'm beginning to notice a considerable difference between the real Iran and the Iran we've been sold. The customs officers are similarly casual in their attire, and also polite. There's definitely something different about these people—they aren't imposing, and don't seem to project themselves in an obtuse way. I'm asked to empty my backpack, but he realises it's a hassle so just has a quick look at some of my things and waves me through. He stares at me for a bit as I'm leaving as if to try and determine something, and then asks, 'Pakistan?'

I say no, Bangladesh actually. He doesn't seem to know where that is. 'Hindustani?' Sure, why not. He smiles warmly and asks me if I'm Muslim.

'Shia or Sunni?'

It's the first of many times I'll encounter that question in Iran. I've also just realised that I'm a minority here.

'I'm just Muslim.'

'*Elhamdolillah*, we are all Muslim, but what kind?'

'Does it matter?'

'Yes of course it matters. If it didn't matter it wouldn't exist.'

'Well in that case I'm Sunni. I like lots of things about the Shia version too, but in all honesty I don't know enough about it.'

'In Iran we're Shia so you will learn a lot about it now.'

'I know, and I hope so.'

'You should convert. Become Shia, it's better.'

He says this with a smile and with good intentions, but it's a first for me. I've never had anyone say anything so evangelical to me before and I'm slightly at a loss, so just smile awkwardly and say, 'Maybe I will'.

Yves, Carlos, a Pakistani gentleman we met at the airport and I share a taxi to the bus terminal. We don't intend to hang around in Zahedan; it's quite an unattractive town, and is also dangerous for foreigners since the Baluchi insurrection employs kidnapping as a bargaining strategy. Just like in Pakistan, the Baluchi—they spell it with a 'u' and not an 'o' in Iran—are viewed with suspicion here, but with an added element of mistrust. They're predominantly Sunni, and Iran is uncomfortable with this 'other' in their midst. The city looks like a shabbier suburb of Geneva—it looks distinctly unlike South Asia and a lot more like Europe. We arrive at the terminal to find a market-like atmosphere with agents for different bus services loudly calling out to passengers, advertising their rates and sometimes nearly dragging them to their respective counters. Now this is more South Asian! The competition is intense and it's all in Farsi— all the voices, all the signs, everything is uttering only Farsi. I have absolutely no way of navigating intelligently in this environment.

We hear someone say 'Kerman' and run straight to the man, who takes us straight to his counter. In stuttered English we try to ask about prices, timings and durations but it's no use. No one understands us, and we don't understand them. A green-eyed, light-skinned man speaks to us in Farsi, saying, presumably, 'Well, do you want seats to Kerman or not?', but we can't be sure so we say, in a combination of Urdu, English, Bangla, French and Spanish, hoping that an Indo-European ancestor will come to our rescue, 'Well, do you have seats to Kerman or not? It's still no use. Finally, an interpreter happens by—a Pakistani who speaks poor Farsi but is able to translate my even poorer Urdu into a shabby sort of communication. We're away. We manage to get across that we'd like three tickets to Kerman, but suddenly Carlos decides that he wants to go all the way to Tehran instead, and goes off to look for a ticket. So it's two—two tickets to Kerman please on the next available bus.

'How much is that? *Kitna chaiye?*... Is that a reasonable price?... It is?... Okay, thank you so much. *Bohut shukriah, bhaisaab.* Can I offer you something? Tea? Cigarette? Have you had lunch?... What's that? You have to go? Do you really? Okay thank you.... Yes God bless you too.'

He's gone, and we're deaf and dumb again. Carlos comes back with a ticket for Tehran—God knows how he got it—says goodbye and disappears into the crowd. It's the last I see of him. Yves and I wait for our bus, which leaves at 5 pm, or at least that's what we've been told. Our tickets are also in Farsi and Yves is trying to match the numbers with the ones in his phrase book. He seems to have got it—yes, there's no mistaking it, that's the Arabic *'khamsah'* or *panj* in Farsi. Five it is.

We've got some time to kill so I decide it's a good idea to go and say my prayers. I ask around for a prayer room using the only word I know that might work—namaaz—and am directed to one. I'd forgotten that I'm wearing a Baluchi *shalwar-kameez*, and can't understand why people look at me strangely when I sound illiterate, instead of speaking in Farsi or Baluchi. I study faces as I make my way to the prayer room; theirs are like ours but different. The darker

Baluchis look just like Indians, but even Persian faces resemble ones you might see in South Asia, with slight differences—just in their expressions perhaps. It's obvious we share a lot more than just common words. The women are quite beautiful, and there are many more of them around than in Pakistani public places. The prayer room isn't like the ones I'm used to—the carpet isn't segmented into rows and columns but is a large Persian rug with beautiful patterns on it. Near the entrance, there's a shelf of *turbahs*, the clay tablet Shias use to rest their foreheads on during prostration. I'm tempted to use one, but don't and I pray silently before joining Yves in the waiting room.

Close to 5 pm we go out to the platforms to board our bus. The people at the counter manage to convey that we should go to bay number 7, and wait for it there. We struggle to identify the number 7 and manage—thanks again to the phrase book—but no bus shows up so we worry about whether we've got it right. We haven't. The bays are numbered from right to left and not left to right, so it says '7' in front of the bay that I logically assume is the next bay, i.e., bay 8, while we've been waiting at bay 6. A small panic follows but soon subsides as we realise that the bus is waiting for other passengers as well and is in no mood to move just yet. We have a few cigarettes and talk about our travels, again about Pakistan mostly. Both of us agree that Pakistan and its egalitarian *shalwar-kameez* are very likeable. Yves also has two of them—one white and the other blue. About an hour later we're on our way.

Seating is assigned but not enforced and people can sit wherever they want. The only conditions are that women sit with women and men sit with men unless they are travelling together. It's a nice bus, large like the Daewoo ones in Pakistan, with comfortable seats. A group of young Baluchi boys sitting in the row in front of us pull out a bag of nuts and sunflower seeds and offer it to everyone around them, including us. It's a warm and inclusive gesture and something, as I will discover, very Iranian. The journey is expected to take about seven to eight hours, and will include numerous checks—the only place in Iran that I encounter this. It's because of the Baluchi separatism, of course, but also because of the province's proximity to Afghanistan and Pakistan, from where both Sunni extremists and refugees are likely to come. There are women on the bus, and they all draw a cloth over their heads like the women at the terminal did but not tightly, and it seems to be more about form rather than function. Yves and I settle in and start talking about nationalities, identities, religions and cultures, as you do, and inevitably get to the topic of France and its discomfort with the hijab. But first it's the evening prayers.

The bus stops at a basic little mosque along the highway as sunset approaches. We're on an empty stretch of desert and there is nothing anywhere around us, except this mosque. It's quite atmospheric. We use water bottles to do our ablutions and pray in the courtyard since the main building is closed. My first evening in Iran and it's a good start. The silence is absolute; there are no sounds at all, not of trees or birds or even of the wind. It's completely still and all I can see are the silhouettes of worshippers, and a fading blue-orange glow behind the darkening outline of mountains in the foreground.

We carry on and Yves seems bothered by this little pause, perhaps because he felt excluded, so he uses it to try and illustrate the point about France and Muslims.

'A bus would never stop for a prayer break in France. How absurd. It would run according to its schedule. These things are just not French!'

I feel slightly sorry for the French if their identity so crucially depends on things like bus schedules, but relish the prospect of a meaty argument which Yves seems to also want to have.

'But you have provisions for religion too, no? Christmas holidays, Easter, Sundays?'

'But that's different, you won't have this five times a day, it's too much of a distraction.'

'Distraction from what?'

'From life!'

'Some might argue that life is the distraction.'

'That's my point. It's a different lifestyle.'

'Sure, but why does it have to make France uncomfortable with Muslims?'

'Because they might ask people to stop the bus to let them pray.'

'But if enough people wanted to pray, including the driver, then it would be fine.'

'But here, even if the majority doesn't get out to pray it will stop.'

He's got a good point there, so I try an evasive manoeuvre.

'Well that's not the same as creating a national dress code.'

Evasion unsuccessful. He's coming straight at it.

'Besides, the fact that one day it might be the case that a bus stops because the majority in it want to pray, is exactly what we worry about. When you are a minority in your own country, it's something to worry about!'

'But they would be French Muslims perhaps. It's not foreign, just a different faith, but the same people, same culture.'

'It's not the same culture. Islam brings certain cultures with it and this influences the convert. They stop being French; they even change their names.'

It's a genuine concern. I listen as Yves explains how French culture has unique sensibilities and its own set of values. He boasts about how they honed it over the centuries, producing sophisticated art and enlightened philosophy, and managed to protect it distinctiveness even from other European influences. Now, with Salafist views taking hold among French Muslims, he fears it will lead to an existential clash. I can relate—in Bangladesh too, we wrestle with the influence of Salafi-inspired Arabic mores which attempt to supplant our own unique culture with something the Salafists believe resembles Prophet Muhammad's lifestyle. The French just haven't been confronted by such impertinence before.

'Alright, well, even if we leave that aside for now, I'm still trying to understand what business it is of the French government's, to tell Muslim women what they can wear.'

'It's about security.'

'What about the headscarves? There have been issues about that too.'

'It's not just the headscarf; any religious expression, by any faith, isn't allowed in France.'

'It's not expression—though banning that is pretty fascist too—it's a religious requirement for some people. I bet no one questions the Sikhs about their turbans (they do, in fact, but at the time I didn't know this).'

Okay, yes, we don't like the scarf or that whole way of thinking—of covering women up. Look at our lifestyles, at our women. The veil and the scarf are a complete affront to it.'

It's out of the bag.

'Why should it be? And even if it is, pluralism requires you to accept it. No one should tell non-Muslim women to wear veils and no one should tell Muslim women they can't. That's how this works.'

'Here all women are required to wear scarves, Muslim or not. If they can decide what sort of public environment they prefer, why can't we?'

'I'm assuming you know that you're not helping your case by making this comparison. But okay, tell me about minars in Switzerland, and restrictions on the call to prayer, and things like that. Isn't it actually true that Europe is allergic to Islam, and that everything else is just pretence?'

'Not at all, but the Muslim world, especially Saudi Arabia, may have an allergy to Europeans and Christians. You can't build a church there, you know!'

'References to Saudi Arabia isn't making your point; it's making mine.'

'Come to Paris and you will see a wonderful Mujedar-style Mosque built in the 1900s. We are proud of this, and of our association with Muslims.'

'Your "association" with Muslims was one of master and subject.'

'Oh come on! We were driven out of Algeria, a part of our country. And you know, people still resent that, yet we get along with Algerians.'

'You had occupied Algeria! Yves, you don't actually believe that you had a legitimate right to be there.'

'Why not? Algeria used to be part of the Roman Empire. The Berbers might be of European origin. You could say the Arabs are the occupiers.'

I'm shocked, but have to accept that there are contending points of views for every occasion, as far-fetched as some might seem, and that everyone has their blind spots. But wait, Yves has a caveat,

'Yes, we behaved awfully in Algeria and maybe that carries some scars. It's part of our national guilt and we have an exaggerated fear of North African Muslims because of it.'

He's honest, but I realise that we're going all over the place with this and are not likely to come to any clear conclusions. I'm also worried that it may strain our fledgling friendship so I decide to tone it down a little.

'Well, on the issue of religion versus culture, all I can say, from our own experience, is that cultures can absorb new dimensions without being eroded.'

'Much of French culture is based on Christian thought. Even if we have moved away from it, it's still a part of the bedrock. You can't expect France, one of the oldest Christian countries, to suddenly have a new religion. These things take time. Even if France were ever to become a Muslim majority country, it would be soon its own terms and in its own time.'

You can't argue with that. In fact, you can't help but respect that. It is Europe, after all. It's not going to just roll over for anyone, and why should it? Why should any place? We leave it at that, and Yves tries to take a nap while I listen to music on my iPod.

A little later, the bus stops again. A fellow passenger, who speaks a bit of English, tells us it's a check-point and that we need to get down. I wake Yves up and we stand in a queue with our bags. Yves lights a cigarette, and almost immediately, one of the guards yells out something in Farsi. He then bounds up to Yves and says it again. Yves looks at him dismissively and carries on smoking. The guard becomes visibly aggravated and stands right in front of Yves, almost nose to nose, staring him down. His posture suggests he might get physical at any moment. But Yves isn't intimated and arrogantly says,

'Quoi? Je ne comprends pas votre langue.'

It's a bad scene. Everything else has stopped and all attention falls on this intensifying standoff which Yves can only lose. More guards gather around, other passengers are saying things to them in Farsi, *'ajnabi… mehmaun… Farsi nisht…'*. I tug at Yves's arm and tell him he has to let it go because it will get much worse for him if he doesn't.

'It's about the cigarette. It's bugging him. Just toss it, otherwise we're both going to end up in jail, and this is Iran, and we have European passports.'

He does it, and the guard disengages instantly, as though a magnetic charge was reversed, and goes back to his post. It's a most bizarre reaction. They search our bags along with everyone else's and we're on our way again. Two hours later the bus is checked again, and this time by a Basij Guard—the Revolution's watchdogs. You know them by the white *kiffaya* they wear around their necks. He is slightly more polite, but still quite gruff.

Some time after 2 am, I notice that the street signs (which are also in English, luckily enough) say that Rafsanjan is about 70 kilometres away. They were pointing towards Kerman about an hour ago, but now there's no mention of it. I quickly pull out my guidebook and, sure enough, Rafsanjan comes after Kerman. We've gone past it. We shout at the driver to stop but without any language to do it in, probably make no sense to him whatsoever. We manage to explain that he must let us out but he says the bus won't stop until it reaches Rafsanjan, over a 100 kilometres west of Kerman. At around 2.40 am the bus finally stops near a roundabout on the highway, far away from any real town and we get out. A few taxis wait to pick up passengers but apart from them, there is absolutely nothing around.

There's no way of getting to Kerman tonight, so we share a taxi into town and look for a place to stay. It's all very difficult without a common language, and I'm beginning to wish I spoke better Urdu, as the overlaps would have been useful. Some of the other passengers suggest a dormitory boarding house, but no one knows where to find one, not even the taxi driver. In town, most of the places are closed and it's now after 3 am. We walk around for a while and then Yves suggests we go to the bus station and wait there. It will be light in a few hours anyway and we can make our way to Kerman then. It seems like the only option available to us, so we take a taxi there. Luckily there are always taxis.

The bus station is completely empty. All the shops and terminals are closed but there are benches, and we have cigarettes and music, so we make ourselves comfortable. It's a bit cool, and we pull out our sleeping bags to wrap ourselves in. We're a sight—tired, dishevelled, smelling quite foul and sitting on benches smoking cigarettes with sleeping bags over our heads. Thankfully there's no one here to see it. And thank God we have each other; I don't think I'd really have the heart to do it alone. A couple of cats come along to keep us company and Yves plays with them tenderly. There's a toilet and a public drinking fountain so we're quite well, actually, all things considered, and also quite safe.

Just before dawn, a bus pulls into the terminal and Yves runs towards it to see if it might give us a ride to Kerman. But it's an army transport and a lot of sturdy cadets wearing olive green uniforms pour out of it to use the toilet and stretch their legs. They are friendly and apologetic, and tell us they might have taken us if they had space. As they leave, I say 'Salaam', and one of them, a young, tall man with another one of those beamingly confident Iranian smiles, tells me,

'Salaam is hello. When you want to say goodbye, say Khoda Hafez.'

Of course! This is the birthplace of 'Khoda Hafez'. How could I forget? I liked hearing him say that very much; all throughout Pakistan, people say 'Allah Hafez' and it's rapidly becoming the standard greeting in Bangladesh too. But I grew up with Khoda Hafez, and the other thing just sounds spliced and inelegant to me.

Finally, at around 5:30 am, a bus that can take us to Kerman arrives. The ticketing office and the coffee shop open, more passengers come to the terminal and the place begins to come alive.

Smartly dressed, freshly washed people look at us with a curiosity that's a few parts surprise and some parts disgust, but we're so past caring that all we can think of is a seat on a bus going the right way. The people wear western clothes, don't look particularly ethnic— it's a lot of jeans and fitted Dolce & Gabbana T-shirts for the men. The older women have black chadors wrapped around them while the younger ones just wear a long coat and a loose headscarf, which shows more hair than it covers. Some passengers address me brusquely in Farsi assuming I'm a local, but when they discover I'm not, they become much friendlier. We dismantle our little camp and board the bus heading east, as the sun comes up over stark mountains and blesses this Islamic Republic with a picturesque, technicolour morning.

Kerman

We arrive at Kerman as the day steps up to full swing. The city is quite nicely laid out and surprisingly modern. It looks quite a lot like Europe to me, France in particular, but maybe that's because of all the Peugeot cars on the streets—old ones, from the 1970s and 80s—adding to Iran's somewhat timeless appeal. The urban design is slightly plain but there are parks and green spaces and everything seems well tended and clean. It's not a chaotic, messy place at all and has none of the squalor of South Asia. There are lots of women on the streets, young and old alike. In fact it's possible that there are more women out than men. Many of them look like students, and carry books and bags. There are black chadors and full hooded hijabs, but these are outnumbered by blue jeans and manteaus, and entirely outdone by a strong showing of heavy makeup and puffed up hair, albeit under rather non-committal wraps. They all smile easily, and don't cut nearly as subdued and forlorn a figure as their Pakistani counterparts do.

We get out of the bus and walk for a bit before taking a taxi to Hotel Akhavan, which is recommended in the guidebook as a mid-range option. It has a horribly gaudy exterior, but inside it's cosy and almost exactly like those small hotels near Victoria Station in London. We haggle over the price of a double room, manage to bring it down to 40 US dollars, which is exorbitant in Iran for something in this range, but we're tired and since it comes to 20 dollars each, we decide to take it. The room is very comfortable and has an old-fashioned radiator heater in the corner, increasing the London vibe. We take turns showering and freshening up and then watch a bit of Iranian TV. There are a few channels, all in Farsi of course, and there seems to be plenty of revolutionary propaganda on display. Numerous images of martyrs are shown. I try to follow a talk show with a former revolutionary but he's not a revolutionary; he's a soldier from the Iran–Iraq War. There are scenes of battlefields, flags, the impression of blood, pictures of victory and smiling faces, all set to thumping marching band music—Persian style.

It appears Iran's fascination with its war with Iraq is as current and alive in the public consciousness as Bangladesh's war with Pakistan is. They seem to play it up like we do and engage in the sort of vulgar chest thumping we've taken such a liking to these days too. Maybe there's some significant date around the corner, like a Victory Day or something. It's tedious so I switch channels and find, bizarrely, an international Kabaddi tournament being broadcast. There are teams from many countries participating and at the moment we're watching Iran take on Sri Lanka. The Iranians are quite a bit larger than the Lankans, but they don't seem to be getting the better of them. From the excited tones in the commentary I can easily tell that Iranians like a chance to demonstrate their physical prowess, and to take advantage of that universal connection between sports and nationalism. Don't we all?

After sleeping for a few hours we make our way to the Bazaar-e Bozorg (Grand Bazaar) area, Kerman's equivalent of an old town. The bazaar is sprawling, and as we approach it we see a domed adobe structure with decorative patterns carved into its walls and an ingenious earthen air-conditioning system called *badgir*. *Badgirs* appear over the roofs of buildings and use the Coanda Effect to cool the interiors of houses—as they have done for thousands of years.

It all begins to look quite old and rather like the Persia of legends. The new city seems to blend in with the old—modern walls are built along 16th-century ones, and the two run together for a while until the contemporary yields entirely to the ancient and we enter a Sassanian city that the British knew as Carmania.

Actually, that's not entirely true. The Sassanian city that was built here in the 3rd century AD by Ardeshir I, the Sassanian Zoroastrian king, was called Behdesir and is all but archaeologically lost to us. The city that was known as Carmania is from the Middle Ages, and is a combination of Seljuk, Muzaffarid, Safavid and Qajar influences. It has both a terrific and a terrible past, as all places that straddle trade routes do. It is mentioned in Achaemenid records as a satrapy but not as a city, which suggests that the overland trade between South Asia and West Asia happened exclusively along the northern routes at the time. From the 3rd century onwards, however, Kerman became an emporium city and a hub on the routes across the region. Sections of the Grand Bazaar are said to be from that time, but there's no way of knowing which ones. The newer structures are connected to the 15th-century Safavid-era Ganj Ali Khan Square, an open courtyard surrounded by shops, similar to its much larger cousin, the Naqsh-e Jahan in Esfahan. Kerman was conquered by the invading Arab Muslims along with the rest of Persia in the 7th century, but the Rashedun Caliphate's grip over eastern Iran was tenuous and it managed to support a Zoroastrian presence for a few centuries longer, until that brute Mahmud of Ghazni had his way with it in 1027. It saw more horrors later too; the Qajars, when they took the city in the 17th century, killed or blinded all the men and had a pile of 20,000 detached eyeballs poured out in front of the king for his ghoulish pleasure.

Kerman's relative independence also made it attractive to the outlawed Kharijites, the very first Muslim extremists and the people who popularised the practice of calling other Muslims kaffirs if they didn't like their stripes. It was a Khariji assassin that killed Hazrat Ali Ibn Talib, last of the Rashedun Caliphs and the first of the Shia Imams, during what is known as the 'Muslim civil war'. The

Khariji, which means 'the ones that left', are a confusing lot. All my instincts tell me that I should despise them for their hard lines and for killing Ali but there are things about their beliefs that are interesting, if not admirable. For instance, they were convinced that political leadership should be based on merit and not blood ties, and that rulers could only be considered legitimate if they relied on a consultative process to govern justly. If rulers deviated from these principles it became a duty to confront them. They also insisted that Islamic jurisprudence be based on the Quran alone and eschewed many subsidiary sources like the Hadith. They were well ahead of their time with ideas like these, but none as exceedingly progressive as their belief that a woman could be an Imam and lead the faithful if she had the right qualifications. In the dichotomous world we live in they are a complete absurdity, yet there they were, representing that most unusual combination.

Kerman was the capital of Iran at different times in its history. The Muzzafarids, who defeated the Mongols in the 1300s and began the Persian *Reconquista* of Iran, had their capital here and built the splendid Jameh Mosque, which lies at one end of the Bazaar-e Bozorg. Subsequent dynasties, most notably the Safavids, later added their own touches to it. Its enormous *iwan* (portal) is a thing to behold; it rises some 20 metres into the sky and is one of Iran's largest and most beautiful *iwans*. This is also my first glimpse of Persia's fabled mosaic tile work and it's spectacular. I stare unblinkingly at it, mesmerised by the geometrical patterns, the arabesque designs, the calligraphy, the floral and vegetal motifs, the honeycombed endings and the balance of light and shade, all done using just four colours—white, yellow, aquamarine and royal blue. It has three other smaller *iwans*, equally if not more beautiful (using many more colours), and the four face each other across an open courtyard in an archetypal Persian mosque plan. The eastern *iwan* opens out to the street, while the other three are closed prayer halls. The mirhab is in the western one. It's hard to properly describe the intricacy and subtlety of the tilework, and how perfectly symmetrical everything is, but it gives me a wonderful feeling of harmony.

The only thing that jars is the enormous clock above the eastern *iwan*. It's square, modern and horrible, and the neon sign of an 'Allahu' in Arabic letters above it is unforgivably ugly.

The covered bazaar has openings in its multi-domed roof and flower-like panels around them; their lit petals diffuse the light to illuminate a larger area. Shops sell virtually anything from clothes, to trinkets to music, to electronics, to spices, to nuts, olives, gold jewellery, copper pots and pans, food, fruit juice, fabrics, bedsheets, beds. It's an ancient mall essentially, with beautiful decorated ceilings, that carries on forever on either side, and throngs with shoppers who have been using it for centuries. I say my prayers in the mosque and notice that most people praying alongside me are doing it the Sunni way. Quite a few Baluchis come around as well, wearing the *shalwar-kameez*. There is a strong Baluchi presence here, preserving a sense of contiguity with the world I come from, but it's the last place, going west, that I will see people, in any significant number, wearing this familiar outfit.

We stroll across the roundabout bustling with late afternoon shoppers, dating couples, taxis, buses, people returning from work, mothers with children, hawkers and vendors. It's a lively scene of ordinary life in Iran set against dry mountains, ancient earthen bazaars, modern yellow public telephones, the brilliant blue dome of a martyr's tomb and lots of young, attractive people dressed smartly in contemporary clothing—sporting hip hairdos and trendy shoes. It's certainly not the sort picture of Iran a popular narrative would have you imagine; it's not even as sinister looking as London's East End.

We step into a *chaikhaneh*—a teahouse, and find mostly elderly men sitting on cushioned and carpeted benches along the walls, sipping tea and sucking on *hukkas*—water pipes. The place is scented with flavoured tobacco and the conversations are animated and lively. The gurgling sound of water bubbling on as smoke and air is drawn through it scores the lull. We ask for some chai and a *sheesha*, but the waiter looks at me with horror, as if I've asked him for illegal narcotics. It turns out I have, since in Iran the word '*sheesha*' can mean anything from a sheet of glass to a hit of crystal meth, but never a water pipe. The proper word for that is *qalyan*, and after some laughter, one is brought out for us along with black tea and a pile of sugar cubes. This pipe-o-many-names is actually an Indian invention that swept across Persia before being adopted by the Arabs who made it entirely their own. It's called a *nargile* in Syria and Lebanon, after the Sanskrit word for coconut, which in Bangla is *narkel*, and the very stuff that a traditional villager's water pipe is made of in Bangladesh. We spend an hour or so in the *chaikhaneh*, smoking, relaxing and soaking in the unhurried atmosphere before getting some sandwiches and heading for a walk through the old quarter on our way back to the hotel.

Day 27

We check out early from Akhavan and move into Reza Guest House, a much cheaper alternative, just off the bazaar. It's a good move—the rooms are spartan but with a great view of the mountains and closer to the parts of Kerman that are more interesting. I manage to change the last of my Rupees and we head off into the labyrinth of passages that make up the wonderful old market. It's much less crowded at midday and many shops are closed. I soon discover why: commercial life in Iran comes to a halt between 12:30 pm and 3 pm, when the heat is most intense, and people go home to have lunch and take naps—*siestas* basically. This relaxed pace of life is extremely agreeable to me and I wander around the maze getting strong sensations of familiarity. It feels a little like New Market and Chandi Chawk in Dhaka, but about a few hundred times bigger. I lose Yves as he wanders off on his own but expect to see him later at the guesthouse if not sooner.

As I walk around, I get asked, '*Koja has'ti?*' or, '*Kodam keshvar? Paw-kistan, Hendustan?*' frequently, until I'm able to work out that *koja* must mean 'where', *has'ti* means 'from' and *Kodam keshvar* means 'which country'. The people here are very curious and seem to love engaging you in that childish and playful manner in which they also speak. There's no reticence in their approach nor is there an imposing quality about it, not even when they are stopping you in your tracks to interrogate you! It's all very light-hearted and jovial, like they're perpetually amused. They also have impeccable manners.

I wander into Santoori, an 18th-century hamaam that's been converted into a restaurant and perhaps the most beautiful teahouse in the world. It has domes with lightwells for roofs and ornately decorated walls, pillars and arches. On them hang lamps, paintings and prints. The lighting is low and colourful and I'm transported to the sort of Persia that fables will help you conjure up in your imagination. In the centre of the room hypnotic folk music is being played on a santoor accompanied by a duff. Tables, divans, cushion and carpets are spread around the stage in a circular fashion, conforming to the design of the building, which also has great acoustics. The smoke from the *qalyans* creates a haze and slows the air down. It's an enigmatic experience.

I find Yves here. He's sitting with Mohsin, a calligrapher, who greets me as I enter and we immediately start chatting. Mohsin is a self-declared *'Majnoon'* and his wide, luminous eyes testify to it. We're instantly plunged into a deeper dialogue and start talking about how to live blissfully in the knowledge that death is always only one breath, one heartbeat away. For fun, he writes my name in Farsi and I write his in Bangla, and then he tells me that there must be absolutely no application of mind, no thinking in any truly honest attempt at natural being. I bring up names like Hafez and Khayyam and he dismisses them all as thinkers.

'No thinking. There isn't freedom in thinking, only more constraints. Constraints of language, of logic, of rhetoric, of conclusions, of alternatives, of reason, of information—all sorts of things that have fences and edges. It's not the same as "being", which has no edges, nothing finite, no endings. Not even death.'

But I have to ask him about things like livelihoods. How does one just be, given that life requires bread?

'Bread will run after me, not I after it. If you do, you will be like that dog that chases its own tail, going around in circles and never getting your bread. God has ordained your Rizk, so trust Him and live every moment free. Free of the thought of bread.'

Seeing my furrowed brow he realises that he's oversimplified the matter and caveats it by saying,

'It's training, *Agha*, it's not that you just say "tomorrow I'll be free". You train yourself for austerity, for simplicity, for freedom from all things, including your mind. It's not easy, but as you do it, your soul will become stronger and it will be easier.'

Many hours pass in the absorbing atmosphere of Santoori. It's almost impossible to leave. We have lunch here, and then go back to smoking, drinking tea and listening to music. I do plenty of people-watching. Groups come and go, mainly young and mixed groups of boys and girls, perfectly comfortable to be hanging out together. No one finds it strange and apart from the loosely fitted headscarf, there's nothing sequestering about the way people carry themselves. They seem comfortable in their bodies and no one seems to be interested in making them feel otherwise, unlike in parts of South Asia, where such a casual attitude to 'free mixing' would be given a pornographic spin. Jealous and lecherous eyes might have made the women recoil there, but Iranians seems to forgo these baser indulgences, revealing the enduring urbanity of Persian civilisation. They also have a gentle, courteous nature, which is completely genuine.

Young Iranian men sometimes look a little effeminate—they wear skin-tight clothing and are noticeably concerned about their appearance—quite unlike the rugged and more overtly masculine Pakistanis. Their manners and mannerisms are 'Asiatic', for lack of a better word, reminiscent of an East Asian kind of humility, which is familiar to me as a Bangladeshi. They seem to like each other's company very much and a natural, almost childlike joy radiates from them; their edges are very smooth. The women are pretty but all have similar faces and dress very alike—blue jeans, black tops and single, solid-coloured scarves. It seems to be a conscious sort of conformity.

Yves meets a man who owns a travel agency and talks with him about places to visit while Mohsin goes and catches up with some people he knows. He seems to have gone off us slightly and when he sends a pot of tea over to us before he leaves, I find the Bangla calligraphy I had given him, torn to shreds and strategically placed under the teapot. I'm hurt by this, and can't seem to recall what I might have done to cause him the offence that he has gone to creative lengths to make apparent. I ask the travel agent about it, and he tells me not to worry, *majnoonis* like Mohsin wear their hearts on their sleeves and can find even the slightest of turning-away devastatingly rude,

'It's almost impossible not to upset them since they only understand absolute love. If you prefer to measure out your love, like most people do, they will find you miserly. Besides, Iranian manners are very nuanced; if you aren't Iranian it's easy to accidentally offend someone. Don't worry about it.'

We leave the teahouse with the travel agent, who takes us to his office and lays out a number of tour options for us. Like many Iranians, he makes it a point not to be overbearing. We take his phone number and tell him we'll mull it over, and then head off to see the 12th-century Emam mosque, the oldest and largest in Kerman.

In the evening, we go looking for an Internet café and take a walk through the newer part of the city. We still aren't able to communicate with people on the streets properly, so find our way mostly by following a map and landmarks. There are lots of people out, mostly young, walking around and shopping. The most popular places seem to be shoe shops and ice-cream joints. Persian house music blares from many of the outlets along the road.

While walking we see, through a door left ajar, a strange wrestling gym that has an octagonal floor with rings like a dart board. Percussionists perched high above the floor in a decorated gallery are keeping a steady rhythm on massive traditional drums. The rhythm quickens and with it my pulse, and now a hypnotic chanting can also be heard. A man entering the gym sees us standing in the doorway and invites us in. We sit in the stands and watch the wrestlers in embroidered Indonesian batik-like shorts, as they go through a series of calisthenics and chant along with the drummers in a ritual that's clearly more than just a physical exercise. I recognise the scene from a clip I once saw on the news in Dhaka, when a tournament for the sport was being held there. We're watching a session of *varzesh-e bastani* wind down at a *zoorkhaneh*.

Zoorkhaneh, which translates into the more recognisable '*zaur khana*' in Urdu, means 'the place of strength' and is really just another way of saying fitness centre—but with a difference. It's not just about the fitness of the body, but also of the mind and spirit—not entirely unlike yoga, actually, or the East Asian martial arts, or even Brazil's capoeira. There are contending theories about its origins. Some say it began after the Arab invasion as a way for the Persians to defend themselves and their heritage; others believe that it began between the 1st and 4th centuries AD and yet others take it to as far back as the beginning of the Zoroastrian civilisation. But all agree that the practice was developed as a way of preserving the physical, philosophical and spiritual integrity of Persian life. The present form dates to the 14th century and to a poet-*pahlevan* called Pouryay-ye-Vali, who revived it and established its present structure. The aim is to produce *bastanikars*, who embody martial skill as well as moral principles like kindness and virtue, entwined with Sufi ideals of Dervishism. Like many things Persian, *varzesh-e bastani* attempts to combine all of Iran's inherited values, Islamic and pre-Islamic, to produce a code that brings out the best in a person's character.

The highest form of a *bastanikar* is a *Pahlevan*, and its similarity to the Hindustani '*pahalwan*' isn't a coincidence. It shares a number of features with the Indian *malla-juddha* wrestling style, and the oblong, aubergine-shaped wooden clubs used by *bastanikars* are acknowledged to be of Indian origin. The names of various exercises are recognisable to speakers of Indic languages—names like *sheena* exercises (push-ups), *greiftan* (a sort of clean and jerk), *narmesh*, ('soft' excercises like stretching) and *charkhidan* (whirling, a practice that also mimics the dervish). The culmination of a session is *kusti*, the wrestling match between pairs of *pahlevans*. It's all very '*deshi*', and in fact so kindred are India and Iran in this respect that in rural Punjab a champion *pahalwan* will be conferred the title of *Rustam-i-Punjab* or *Rustam-i-Hind*, invoking that legendary Iranian strong-man. Sessions at the *zoorkhaneh* include a *dhikr*-like chanting as well as recitations from Persian epics, encouraging athletes to aspire to both spiritual and heroic heights. It's Sufism in jockstraps, and is

215

also, as some have suggested, the reason why Iran has such a good wrestling record at the Olympic Games.

Traditional Persian wrestling is considered Iran's national sport but it nearly disappeared altogether in the 1930s when people forsook it for being unfashionably un-modern. Luckily, though, it didn't, and is being practised with gusto here in Kerman where the *bastanikars*, some quite elderly, shake hands with us enthusiastically after they finish, their eyes and bodies bathed in a contented, adrenalin glow. Some also wear the Zoroastrian Faravahar symbol around their necks, along with their '*Allahu*' pendants.

We carry on towards the Internet café and come across another gym. This one's a kickboxing arena that has younger, leaner Rustams vigorously going through their paces. There are no numinous undertones here, just heavy metal music blaring and explosive, loud, punishing action. The 'slap-thud' of leg meeting punching bag calls to mind a dull pain as these energetic boys go at it again and again. Kerman is clearly battle-ready. We watch them for a while and then head to the Internet café around the corner, which is manned by Jawaad, a cherubic medical student who's as pleasant as the colours of spring, and works at his brother's Internet shop in the evenings.

We pick Jawaad's brain for a while about places to see in Kerman and then check our email. After about 45 minutes he comes over to us and says, 'Okay, we are closing, my shift is over, but come with me if you please'. We go out and get some ice-cream together, which Jawaad won't let us pay for, and then he announces that he will give us a short tour of Kerman by night—a most unexpected offer which we immediately decline. This sends us through the motions of Iranian etiquette where offers are declined, insisted upon, declined again and insisted upon again, declined again, insisted upon again and finally accepted. They call this gracious little dance '*tawrouf*' and everyone here knows the steps. Now Jawaad has taught us too and tells us that it's good we refused his offer initially (because we genuinely didn't want to put him out) as it would have been rude to deny him the chance to insist. It's all convoluted and superfluous but extremely charming, and a permanent feature of virtually every interaction with Iranians.

Jawaad takes us first to the Kerman Library, a stately old building with beautiful arches that, oddly enough, began life as a textile factory, and then to the parks around the *yakhchal* or icehouse. *Yakhchals* are a staggering feat of ancient engineering. So staggering in fact, that you can't help wondering how far ahead of everyone else the Persians were in 400 BC, when they managed to keep large quantities of ice frozen in the middle of summer, in a blistering desert. They could make ice in winter using *qanats* (another brilliant innovation) to channel groundwater into the *yakhchal* where it would freeze, shielded from the sun by enormous walls made out of a material called *sarooj*, a composition of clay, egg white, lime, animal hair, ash and sand that is heat-resistant and waterproof. The structure is a massive inverted cone attached to walls, with landscaping and gardens around it. People have put out blankets and are sitting on the grass, smoking *qalyan* and enjoying the night sky.

Jawaad tells us a little about his life and dreams. He wants to be a General Practitioner, loves Iran but seems to have reservations about the government. He has a girlfriend and is your regular, polite *bhodro ghorer chele*. But in Iran *bhodro* often means going beyond what would be enough in other places. For instance, his sense of *mehmannawazi* has him spending the evening with strangers whom he regards as guests in his city instead of with his now undoubtedly disgruntled girlfriend. He also won't let us pay for a thing, and gives generously of his attention, his enthusiasm and his good nature, well into the late hours of what has possibly been a long day for him.

We compare vocabulary and look for common words between French, English, Farsi and Bangla (where I discover that Bangla has less in common with other Aryan languages than I had previously thought) and I see that Jawaad is as excited as I am about our shared ancestry. He tells us how his father was killed in the Iran-Iraq War, after I complain, rather indelicately, about the stuff on TV, which, it turns out, is on there because September is the month of the 'Holy Defence'. He doesn't seem offended, though, and tells me how Shias see martyrdom as a matter of immeasurable pride. I'm sure they do, but I don't believe for a second that death isn't as devastating for them as it is for everyone else. We talk about Iran and the US, about the recent fuss that's being kicked up by Israel, and Jawaad asks, with an endearing earnestness,

Why? Why do they all hate us so much?'

We talk until it gets late and then start walking towards the main road. A convoy of cars passes us tooting their horns in unison and Jawaad tells us it's a wedding party. Balloons and ribbons are tied to some of the cars, and girls hang out the window waving their arms in the air like orchestra conductors. We decide to take a taxi back to the guest house, which Jawaad won't let us pay for, of course. The music being played by the driver is lovely, so I say so, and when he drops us off, he pops out the cassette tape and says, 'Take it, *Agha*, it's yours'. I decline, he offers again, I tell him its not *tawrouf*, I simply don't own a cassette player. He accepts this reason and laments that if only he could take the player out of his car, he would give that to me too. What peculiar people.

Rayen

'Saalom. *Rayen Buru? Deux nefari, sil vu plait. Sirf rafta … bargesh nisht. Na, na!* Reserve *nisht, dui sandali … aree na shudhu duijon,* no no, not the whole taxi! What do you mean we can't? Just take us to the bus station please. *Istgah otobus?*'

It's infuriating and not just because we can't speak a proper sentence in Farsi between the two of us. We're trying to take a Savari—a shared taxi—to visit the adobe Arg-e Rayen fortress 85 kilometres from Kerman, but the taxi drivers want to scam us into taking the whole thing instead of just two seats. We tell them to forget it and to just take us to a bus station but they say there are no buses that go to Rayen, and say it forcefully. They're lying, of course. If there's one thing you know as a traveller it's that there are, in the very least, rickety local buses that go almost anywhere. We get to the station and sure enough there's a small bus leaving for Rayen in 30 minutes or when it fills up, whichever is earlier. We buy some water, pistachio *gaz* and salted dry sunflower seeds to snack on along the way. Iranians eat these seeds by the hundreds and the sound of their shell being cracked open is an integral part of the soundtrack here. Iranian *gaz* is without doubt the best nougat in the world.

It's a sandy, surreal landscape. The desert and scrublands run on for miles in either direction, interrupted by bizarre rock formations and craggy mountains. Settlements and townships have sprung up at the foot of these mountains, drawn to them by the springs and the snowmelt—a riverless region's frugal substitute. The rock formations are massive C-shaped craters like the ones I saw from the air in Balochistan. They look like a cross between a volcano and something that happens when an asteroid hits a mountain and takes out a large chunk of it. It's all very epic and mystical. I spy caves and wonder if a wandering holy man ever made one of them his home. The sheer, windswept emptiness of it is unusually evocative.

In the middle of all this blankness stands the town of Rayen, and in the middle of that, Arg-e Rayen, currently the best example of a fortress-city, built entirely out of mud and straw. A similar Arg, or fort, at nearby Bam was previously the largest adobe structure in the world but was destroyed by an earthquake in 2003, taking with it more than 26,000 people, or nearly half the population of Bam at the time. It was possibly built during the Parthian Age which, if true, means that it had stood for well over 2,000 years. Rayen has one as well, albeit younger.

Speculation has it that the Sassanians originally built Arg-e Rayen and subsequent empires added to it while remaining true to its structural character. The Sassanian Empire was the last Zoroastrian empire ever to exist, and the last time that Iran was an entirely indigenous polity, or at least as indigenous as it had been since the Aryans took it from the Elamites. In fact, the name 'Iran' comes from what the Sassanians called their realm—Eranshahr. They were phenomenal builders and the entirely earthen 20,000-square-metre complex is the result of structural mastery at an extraordinary level. It's like a life-size model one might build out of clay for a science fair.

Sections of it are marvellously intact. We walk through its lanes, climb into its turrets, scramble along its huge outer walls and go into the houses—the experience is like being on a film set for *Prince of Persia: The Sands of Time*. A *zoorkhaneh* and a mosque can clearly be made out among the buildings.

Arg-e Rayen is maintained by the provincial authority of Kerman, but the governor of Kerman province, clearly not as aesthetically astute as the custodians who went before him, has built himself a modern little residential office right in the middle of it, inside the old citadel. Still, a lot of reconstruction work is being carried out and it's clear that keeping the Arg-e Rayen in its original form is very much part of their agenda. The hay used in the construction of the enormous walls created soundproofing, which, coupled with the already silent desert, makes for a very serene place. It's also cool, as the building materials are designed to absorb the heat. It's exciting to think that the town within its walls was inhabited until just over a century ago when it was completely abandoned, for reasons unknown. I perch myself on one of the walls overlooking the desert and take it all in.

No sooner have I drifted off into the romance of the shifting colours and sands do I see a petite East Asian woman and a red-skinned, red-haired man coming towards my lookout. She's carrying a big camera, and has sensed, rightly, that I have a great view. I help them onto the ledge, and we start chatting. She's Indonesian and he's English, they met in Kerman and are doing this day trip together. I'm duly impressed to meet a Muslim Indonesian woman backpacking alone—in Iran, no less—and doing it with an abundance of enthusiasm. The English 'lad', on the other hand, is sullen and predictably awkward. He whinges a lot and looks uncomfortable in his own skin, which turns redder by the minute. His stiff and stern demeanour makes him look constipated instead of unruffled as he gracelessly tries to sit cross-legged on the floor. We stay there for a little while longer, admiring the Hezar Mountains that appear to shimmer translucently in the yellow desert heat, before heading back towards the bus stop.

On the way back to Kerman I spot a new mosque under construction which is using the *iwan* and dome design of classical Iranian structures. They're even using mosaic tiles on the facade. Persian aesthetics still inform the architects and designers of today's Iran, quite unlike in Bangladesh, where our classical Sultanate-era style has given way to a confused kitsch that faithfully represents nothing more than our expanding identity crisis.

In the evening we go to the grounds of Kerman Library and use their free WiFi to check our email on Yves's laptop. Then we walk around the city until late, appreciating the clean public squares, the well-laid streets and the manicured gardens that justify Kerman's inclusion in a list of the 100 cleanest cities in the world. I also feel perfectly safe here. Nothing and no one feels threatening—in fact, quite the opposite—they all seem helpful and protective. There are also public telephones and water fountains all over the city.

Yves and I spend another day in Kerman, before parting ways. He wants to carry on to Yazd, and I have a date with Omar Khayyam's tomb in Neyshapur which, in spite of Yves' insistence, I don't intend to miss. It will take me way off course, up to the north-eastern corner of Iran to Mashhad, but Khayyam's is one of my favourite minds, and I can't be so discourteous as to come to Iran, and not pay him a visit. We meet Jawaad for one last time, and when he learns I'm leaving that afternoon, drops everything and takes me in a cab (which, of course, I'm not allowed to pay for) to the bus station where he tells the man at the counter to look after me and make sure I board properly. He then apologises vigorously for not being able to see me off, but only because his brother's shop needs tending and if it were his own he would surely have shut it and stayed until I was on my way. What beautiful, peculiar people.

As the bus pulls out of the bay, people chant a prayer in unison. I make out the names 'Ali' and 'Muhammad' and realise that this is a bus full of pilgrims on their way to the tomb of Ali ar-Ridha, or Imam Reza, the seventh descendent of Prophet Muhammad and the only one of the Shia Imams to be buried in Iran. This is the Great *Ziyarat* at Mashhad.

Mashhad

After a 14-hour bus ride through two deserts, Dasht-e Loot and Dasht-e Kavir—Dasht-e Loot had the hottest temperature recorded on earth in 2009—I arrive at Mashhad. The ride was comfortable although I grew tired of the constant teasing by other passengers, for whom I had become something of an amusement on a long and empty desert road. They would speak to me in Farsi and then burst into fits of laughter as I inevitably said something ridiculous and stepped into a neatly laid linguistic trap.

On the way and as dawn approached, we stopped at a place called Ferdows alongside some ruins and an uncharacteristically unadorned structure with bare *iwans*. The sun gets there after us, and comes up behind the mountains to flood the place with a pinkish hue. I'm told that the austere looking building is a religious school from the Safavid era and the ruins scattered around it are the Kushk Historical Complex. Adobe structures form chambers both inside the ground and above it, which are adapted so perfectly to their surroundings that you might not know that they were there at all. They look just like natural mounds of clay, and the only things that give them away are their perfect contours and the smoothed, sloping domes. Ferdows, or Tun, as it was originally called, was once a major city in the Khorasan until the Mongol invasion swept it away in 1239. It recovered to become a thriving city by the time Marco Polo passed through the area, but ultimately succumbed to an earthquake in 1968. If I didn't know any better I could be convinced that I am at Luke Skywalker's home in Tatouine.

Iran's highways are very well developed and ensure connectivity. Towers carry cables deep into the landscape and I don't experience a single blackout or anything resembling South Asian loadshedding the entire time I am there. It's no small matter to be able to network such a vast and unyielding place and the economic sanctions imposed on Iran certainly haven't had any effect on its infrastructure. As a Bangladeshi I feel ashamed at our inability to manage our tiny country, even with so many hands to do the work.

But more than that I feet indignant, on Iran's behalf, for the disdain that it's being dealt by the US and its friends. The fact that there's even talk of attacking this well-managed, orderly country and potentially demolishing years of progress, not to mention centuries of history and culture, makes me very sad indeed, and I find myself wondering if Iraq was similarly intact before the invasion pulled it back to near third-world conditions. It reminds me of those boys in school who could only win a race by tripping up their opponents.

Iran's modernity flies in the face of Western ethnocentricity and challenges the colonial perception of the East which, in the words of Edward Said, is seen as 'separate, eccentric, backward, silently different, sensual and passive', able only to progress if it has been seeded with Western mores and ways. In Professor Said's seminal book, *Orientalism*, he comments on how the East is popularly narrated through Western eyes and can only be understood as a departure from the norm which inevitably is European civilisation, but only after it (European civilisation) has been shorn of its Afro-Asian antecedents. The Age of Imperialism required a re-branding of the East as irrational, weak and 'feminised' to contrast it with the rational, strong and masculine West and justify a paternalistic approach to its people. This selfsame claptrap also informs US attitudes about Iraq today and is reflected in phrases we often hear like, 'when Iraq is able to govern itself—as though Iraq, the place where laws and governance quite possibly began, were some irresponsible adolescent only just coming to terms with adulthood, oh just some 4,000 years after Mesopotamia gave birth to the Hammurabi Code.

Professor Said said it best when he wrote,

So far as the United States seems to be concerned, it is only a slight overstatement to say that Muslims and Arabs are essentially seen as either oil suppliers of potential terrorists. Very little of the detail, the human density, the passion of Arab-Muslim life has entered the awareness of even those people whose profession it is to report the Arab world. What we have instead is a series of crude, essentialised caricatures of the Islamic world presented in such a way as to make that world vulnerable to military aggression.

An aggression that has visited countries on two sides of Iran, but the less thought about that the better.

Mashhad is Iran's second largest city, and its holiest one. Imam Ali ar-Ridha or Imam Reza, the eighth of the Shia Imams, was buried here after Caliph al-Mamun, feeling threatened by the Imam's growing political influence, allegedly had him murdered in 818 AD—although many other accounts suggest his death was natural. Al-Mamun's father was the famous Caliph Harun-al-Rashid, known to the West as Aaron the Upright, and is widely regarded as one of the most cultured caliphs to have ever ruled the Muslim world. His reign is replete with all the trappings of a learned and curious society: scientific scrutiny, philosophical inquiry, cultural expressiveness, art, music, literature, social reform and, most remarkable of all, the creation in Baghdad of a 'Bait al Hikmat' (House of Wisdom), which became the epicentre of intellectual activity during Islam's Golden Age. Bait al Hikmat was a library and a translation centre, where reams of knowledge from across the globe were laboriously preserved and propagated by having them translated into Arabic—the *lingua franca* of progress at the time, and, as the saying goes, the language of science for nearly a thousand years. Works by Greek, Persian and Indian thinkers like Plato, Aristotle, Brahmagupta, Shushruta, Charaka, Pythagoras and many others were brought here to be studied, translated and meticulously catalogued for reference.

On these foundations, Muslim thinkers of the age built their own intellectual and philosophical traditions. For instance, the health sciences taught by Hippocrates, Shushruta and Charaka informed the writings of Ibn Sina, while Pythagoras and the Indian Aryabhatta influenced the mathematician Al-Khwarizmi, who lent his name to the Algorithm (*Al khwarithm*) and developed Algebra. A few centuries later, the translated works of Plato and Aristotle taught the Spaniard Ibn Rushd about the possible and active intellect, and a few more centuries after that, his own philosophy, Averroism, became one of the pillars of secularism. And that's not all. The Syrian astronomer Ibn al-Shatir inspired Copernicus's heliocentric model of the solar system and the zoologist Al-Jahith developed his own theory of natural selection nearly a millennium before Darwin was even a twinkle in his parents' eyes. It was all happening then, in the age that Europe calls 'dark'.

It was a monumental service to civilisation, and its importance as the prism through which the many strands of ancient wisdom, which might have been lost otherwise, came together to become the white light that was beamed into the future, to our time and possibly even further—can't ever be overstated. But the Bait al Hikmat wasn't a novel idea. It was borrowed from the Sassanian Persians who couldn't get enough of the information coming to them from around their empire and engaged armies of scholars in translation and knowledge management enterprises. They too built research centres, and libraries—prototypical universities—to keep the light of learning alive. Harun al Rashid was born in Iran, near Tehran, and he was heavily influenced by Persian culture. This is the point where 'Islam al Ajam', the Islam of non-Arabs, begins to compete with Islam al Arab as the main vehicle of cultural and political expression.

Harun al Rashid is also buried in Mashhad; in fact, Imam Reza is buried next to him, and their tombs face each other's inside the complex. The Caliph's tomb was here first, but he's been swallowed whole by the Imam's posthumous enormity, and you can miss it if you aren't looking, as I did. It's surprising that Harun al Rashid still has a tomb here at all since, depending on which side of the sectarian fence you're looking at him from, Harun, as well as his son Al Mamun, are either villains or heroes. Shias dislike both of them as treacherous usurpers and Imam killers—the seventh and eighth, respectively—and in the contest between the 'Ahle Bait', the bloodline of Muhammad, and other Muslims about who has legitimate authority over the *Ummah*, they're regarded as among the very worst of sports. The more mainstream historical narrative, however, sees them as Renaissance men who began the process that took Islamic minds to new and enlightened heights.

Al-Mamun and his successors belonged to the rationalist Mu'tazila school of thought, which, like all good things, came to its inevitable, unseemly end. In fact, it may have even become a bad thing before it did, causing a reaction that was quite a bit worse. It came in the shape of the *Mihna*, literally 'test', initiated by al-Mamun, which was a sort of inquisition where scholars and clerics were tormented and even killed for not accepting the state-sanctioned, rationalist doctrine. It lasted for 15 years and caused irreparable damage to the classical Islamic tradition of judicial plurality, where multiple interpretations and schools of jurisprudences, *madhhabs*, could happily co-exist in the same realm, even if they were completely opposed to each other.

The Mu'tazili Caliphs were the first to try and establish an 'official' position on faith, and they did this by stamping the authority of their own over everyone else's. Nothing unusual, of course, except that it was the rational, and by today's classifications, liberal, school that was forcefully imposing itself upon the more theocratic ones. To be fair, they were up against a virulent opposition, which called them everything from heretics to unbelievers, and a clergy that had set itself up as the last word on all things scriptural, using a newly-minted yet unsubstantiated body of work called the Hadith. But the Mu'tazila response was authoritarian and over the top, and cut the lines of communication between independent thought and unquestioning obedience, perhaps for good. It eventually resulted in a backlash against them and they fell out of favour not just with the theologians, but also with ordinary citizens, philosophers, non-Muslims and even with atheists, all of whom felt that their *Mihna* left everyone else with very little room to manoeuvre.

Al-Mutawakkil, the last significant Abbasid Caliph, finally discontinued the *Mihna*, much to the relief of many Muslims at the time, but unfortunately his disgust for the overconfident absolutism of his predecessors led him to develop contempt for the Bait al Hikmat, and in particular for Greek philosophy, seen as an insidious 'western' corrosive, which had, no doubt, led them away from true Islam. Caliphal patronage of the institute dwindled and with this came a process of turning towards dogma on the one hand, and towards mysticism on the other. The Mu'tazila school was unfairly blamed for the excesses of its overzealous adherents who just happened to also be kings, and though it still managed to influence Islamic intellectual life for a few centuries more—producing proponents of liberalism, humanism, secularism, ethics and logic as well as of a range of other disciplines like medicine, science and politics—it eventually lost ground completely to the contending Ash'arites, and their insistence that the 'the gates of *ijtihad*', or reasoning, be forever closed.

But back to Imam Reza and Caliph al-Mamun, who were never enemies to begin with, nor was Reza's death a result of the *Mihna*. They were colleagues; even worse, al-Mamun may have even been Reza's father-in-law. Al-Mamun had appointed Reza governor of the Khorasan province, with the aim of appeasing Shias in his realm who, believing that the Caliphate could only belong to members of the House of Muhammad, had demonstrated a willingness to challenge him during contestations for the throne following Harun al Rashid's death. Al-Mamun even insinuated that Reza might succeed him as Caliph, but this proved to be a very bad move since the Sunni Abbasid dynasty, to whom al-Mamun belonged, saw this as treasonous and readied to move against him. But al-Mamun refused to dismiss Reza as governor, possibly for fear that he would appear weak in the face of resistance and also because it might have caused the Shias to revolt. He may have also genuinely believed that Reza was the right man for the job. Instead, Imam Reza mysteriously died in the middle of all this controversy, conveniently ridding al-Mamun of his problem altogether, and leading to suspicions that he had something to do with it.

Al-Mamun did try to prove his innocence, though, and insisted Imam Reza's body be examined for evidence of foul play. He was also genuinely overcome with grief at his passing, spending days in mourning, and so there is no doubt that he was very fond of Reza, but his tears may have also been some parts guilt, as the narrative suggests. Innocent or not, the doubts cast over al-Mamun's involvement in Imam Reza's death have never been lifted and continue to taint the Caliph's name here in Iran, more than a thousand years later. I can't help but feel sorry for him.

I only came to Mashhad to be able to get to Neyshabur, which is about two hours from here by bus. But since I'm here it would be silly not to visit the tomb complex that makes this the most important pilgrimage site in Iran. So I check into Pars Hotel, a dilapidated but pleasant establishment owned by a gentleman who lived in England once and speaks fluent English. He helps me get my bearings and after a short rest, I decide to get some food and walk through the city towards the complex. I eat at a nearby restaurant, some *'chelow kebab'—kebab* and buttered rice with fried tomato—and have to sprinkle tablespoons of anything I can find on the table (chicken salt and a sad excuse for chilli powder) to try and give the meal some zing, but it's hopeless. It's just too polite and like a lot of Iranian cooking, so delicate it almost disappears.

Mashhad, which means 'the place of martyrdom', is modest for being the country's second largest city; most buildings are low-rises and of the 1980s variety, with some glass-and-steel buildings bringing it a bit of novelty. It has narrow car-free brick lanes lined with shops and restaurants, and wide pavements with kiosks and newsstands on them, reminiscent of New York City. It also has lovely gardens in the middle of the city. It's an interesting blend of Western urban design with Perso-Islamic architecture, more pronounced here than in Kerman. Quite a lot of Iran is laid out like this and if it weren't for the Farsi writing and the women in chadors, you could easily be forgiven for thinking you are somewhere else. Even the faces might confuse you, since similar ones are found in France, Italy, Greece or Spain. There are even one or two that look Teutonic. But mixed in with those is an abundance—a majority in fact—of Middle Eastern and South Asian faces, mostly of the North Indian variety, and some that could comfortably pass as Bangladeshi. It's easy to understand where the term 'Indo-European' comes from when you're in Iran. This place has bits and pieces of an ethnolinguistic spectrum that features India on one end and Europe on the other.

I walk past a few government buildings where temporary shrines made up of sandbags, keffiyehs, flags and helmets have been erected.

The Holy Defence, or the war with Iraq, began in September and ended, eight years later, in August, so plenty of nationalistic paraphernalia is scattered around the country at this time of year. Massive billboards of martyrs are also out in force. People are friendly and unlike parts of Pakistan, Iran doesn't feel anything like a garrison or a military-run enterprise. Security personnel are scarce, and you don't see semi-automatic weapons at every turn. This is a settled, civilian environment, more akin to India than Pakistan. Pakistanis and Iranians are similar in other ways, though—they both employ a lot of courtesy in their interactions with people, making the casual off-handedness one experiences in India and Bangladesh feel like a harsh and hostile approach.

I arrive at the shrine complex, which is decorated with fairy lights and looks, at first glance, like a Sufi mazaar, only several hundred times larger. It dominates the horizon and appears to hover over the city, an illusion reinforced by the fact that the main arterial route that leads to the area dives into a tunnel under it and comes out on the other side. The facade is decorated in Persian tile mosaic, and consists of a series of gates, *iwans* and arches. It's festive, and seems to have been done up specially for an occasion, or what we would call an *urs* in South Asia—which literally means 'wedding' in Arabic and is marked on the day that the Sufi was wedded to eternity, i.e., died. It turns out that it *is* a special occasion—the beginning of the Days of Dignity, the 10 days between the birth anniversary of Imam Reza's sister Fatimah and his own. So it's not an *urs* then but a separation.

I hesitate to enter. I don't feel completely comfortable since I'm not Shia and wonder if I might end up offending someone. It's a religious occasion at a very important religious site, and I'm just a tourist really. It feels a bit irreverent. I go away to contemplate it and walk around in the market where I have some tea, smoke a couple of cigarettes and then decide I should experience the occasion, even if it's only as a tourist.

I go through the gates and there's a bag check where I'm required to leave my camera. I'm relieved, actually, because I would have had trouble resisting photographing the beautiful compound and that would have made me extremely conspicuous. As I walk towards it I imagine the man at the counter asking me if I'm Shia or Sunni, discovering that I'm Sunni and then going into hysterics before pulling out some Shia scripture to thump me with while the authorities drag me away by the collar. Or perhaps I'll lie and say I'm Shia and he'll glance askance at me and say 'What's the password?' for which I'll have no answer and then he'll pull out the Shia scripture, thump me with it, before calling the authorities to lead me away as they taunt me with, 'password Sunni, what's the password?'

I approach the counter, the man checks my bag, says *'Saalom'*, smiles at me, and hands me a token. To my enormous relief, neither an awkward question nor a voluminous book makes any appearance.

The place is immense. It's easily the largest decorated space I've ever seen and it's done up dazzlingly. Every inch of the 6,443,890 square foot complex is covered in glazed, painted tiles and the seven courtyards that surround the shrine are massive offerings to the gods of colour and design. It's enormous and is sometimes called the largest mosque in the world by area, but the presence of the large shrine in the middle, which would have to be discounted from the total, makes it a complicated equation. It's not just the floor space that's large, the structures built on it are towering and muscular, but decorated all over in delicate, intricate patterns. It's awesome, in the very literal sense of the word.

The seven courtyards look similar to each other, and before long I've lost all sense of direction and just wander around in this wonderland with gilded domes, a network of 21 chambers each with cavernous *iwans* and a number of halls, all designed to draw you in through what is akin to a psychedelic experience, towards the tomb. I walk through one splendid chamber into another, each more stunning than the last, where people are praying, bowing, kissing the doors and walls, and are generally experiencing a sort of contained rapture, which becomes less and less contained as we move closer to the burial chamber. Multicoloured lighting adds to the surreal feel of the absorption.

All of a sudden a crush of people files through the doors chanting prayers and gesturing wildly with their arms. I'm swept up in the current and before I know it, I'm chanting and beating my chest as well, having become a part of this wailing, flailing multipede that's moving towards the engraved, gilded cage ahead of it. We enter the burial chamber which is so overpowering in its splendour that no superlative can do it justice. The interior is covered in a serrated, mirror-like material and huge chandeliers send light towards it that bounces around in every direction, shooting off this corner to that one, that angle to the other, until the entire chamber shimmers and glows with a brilliance that's blinding. Coming in from the dark outside, it feels as though I'm looking upon the *noor* of heaven itself, which is, of course the desired effect. It's impossible not to be overwhelmed by it and tears stream out of my eyes along with everyone else's, and all I can think of is touching the Imam's grave. I must manage a little touch. I lunge towards it desperately as though my very life depends on it, my heart a few paces ahead of my body, in what is a most bizarre loss of self. People are touching, stroking, caressing, kissing, cleaning and clinging to the cage-like structure, lavishing it with bales of affection. In my turn, I do the same and can't get away from this overwhelming emotion. A pane of glass separates the women from the men, but there's nothing between them in terms of passion.

Guards armed with multicoloured feather dusters like the ones we use to clean cars in Bangladesh, gently tap pilgrims and urge them to move on. All the guards in the complex carry these, which they use to keep things flowing and staying between the lines. It's a civilised alternative to sticks and whistles, and another example of Iran's 'softly, softly' approach, which also manifests in their manners. *'Agha'*, meaning 'Sir', always accompanies every tap, followed quickly by *'bebakshi'* meaning 'excuse me' and *'mikhonam'*, 'please.' I hear these words a lot, everywhere in Iran. It's a far cry from many other similar places where people are herded and prodded like cattle while being shouted at—places like Medina, I've been told, though I've never been myself. Different strokes for different folks indeed.

I move on, still caught in the human sea that pours me out into another courtyard where people are prostrating on carpets that have been spread out for them. They pray fervently, the women clasp their hands at their chest, and press them to it tightly. Rows rise and fall in unison, solitary figures drop to their knees, Qurans are out on laps. The weather has become cooler, cold almost, but the warmth of bodies keeps the courtyard temperature-controlled while a tranquil atmosphere reigns. I want to pray, but feel unsure about formats and other silly things, so don't. I hang around for a long time soaking in the vibe, then slowly make my way towards the exit, but very slowly.

The atmosphere of *ziyarat* isn't unique. I've seen all of these emotions before, on this very journey, in fact. It was there in Bodh Gaya, when pilgrims kissed the frame around the Bodhi Tree. I saw it in Amritsar when they touched the sacred spots and stood in solemn prayer facing the Golden Temple. Again in Lahore, when people kissed the Quran written with gold thread at the Badshahi Mosque. It followed me to Multan, where there was a grave in a cage just like this one. I have seen it at Shah Jalal's mazaar in Bangladesh, and in mandirs and churches everywhere. I've seen it on television when Jews rock on their heels in front of a wall in Jerusalem, and people have seen it at the Kaa'bah in Mecca and at Prophet Muhammad's grave in Medina. They only differ in intensity and that too, not by very much. It's always the objects that receive all of their affection. Doors, curtains, shrouds, drapery, walls, graves, buildings, caves, stones, symbols, idols, cages, pots, pans, bowls, footprints, strands of hair, cremation ash. It makes very little difference which religion it is; the sentiments are always the same. They always want to touch something, to kiss something, to hold on to something.

Maybe we need a place to hang our hearts, which are so laden with all of life's joys and sorrows that perhaps some sort of brace becomes necessary. Or maybe we need to unload our love, our despair, our gratitude, our pain, our guilt, our fears and our hopes to empty ourselves of life, and we need to do it out loud, out here, in the world of things. But it all feels strangely limiting to me. I wonder what God makes of all this—does it amuse Him or annoy Him? And what does He make of me, this judgemental rationalist who, like Mu'tazila fascists, seems to have little patience for irrational, explosive expressions of faith? And yet I believe in the absolutely unreasonable proposition that an angel spoke to a man who recited what he heard in rhyme and produced a transcription of God's words. It's positively absurd.

Life-sized black bags with women in them flap around the compound, stopping only to kiss a door or two. My mind goes back to those poor Hazara pilgrims who might have been trying to do their *ziyarat* during the Days of Dignity and I feel deeply sad about how it turned out for them. Here I am, a sceptic, tramping around on their sacred ground and having conversations with myself about the worth of the very rites they lost their lives to try and perform; and there they are, dead before they got past their doorsteps. I pray for them, and offer my *ziyarat* as theirs, hoping that it might be accepted as some sort of substitute.

As I walk back to the guesthouse I think about the fact that there are such things as Pilgrim Visas which were dreamt up by the 'sensible' world of public policy, and that countries with loads of contempt for each other, countries like Iran, Iraq, Pakistan and India, can cooperate long enough to create safe passages for pilgrims of one country to get to their sacred spaces in another. Sikhs and Hindus have sites in Pakistan and are allowed to travel to them from India, circumventing the complex visa regime that divides the two countries. Hindus, Muslims and Sikhs from Pakistan also go to India with similar ease. Shias from Iran, Pakistan and India go to Iraq, to Karbala, their holiest site. Shias from Iraq and Pakistan go to Iran to Imam Reza's place, and so on. In a region where little love is lost between neighbours and where religious prejudice has led to frontiers and conflicts, these most religious of travellers receive international exemptions and are facilitated in their movements by things as entirely unreligious as government bureaucracies. How perfectly unreasonable.

Day 30

My backpack has become heavy with things collected along the way so I've put the excess into a separate box to send them off to Dhaka. But by the time I get to the *Poste Markezi*, the Central Post Office, it's closed. *'Tawteel, Tawteel!'* the man at the gate repeats a few times, wondering why I don't seem to get it and get lost. Finally a postal worker on his way out understands that I'm not Irani and interprets for me.

I didn't make it during working hours because, earlier, I spent far too long at the smaller post office near my hotel where I had gone to inquire about sending my parcel, but where they don't have an international service. The friendly employees there sat me down to have a cup of tea and to satisfy their curiosity about me—someone that looks a bit like their ducks, but doesn't quite sound like one.

'Hindustan and Iran are both Aryan countries, you know? We are cousins!'

They are, but I quickly tell them I'm Bangladeshi and want to tell them about Bangladesh's non-Aryan, or as Iranians say 'Anaryan' roots, but realise that it would only sound to them like I'm trying to distance myself, so I don't. Then they find something more current to bind us together with.

'Oh Bangladeshi! You know Iranian football player Hejazi? He used to be the coach for Mohammedan Sporting, in Bangladesh. You know this team? Mohammedan? Hejazi has died, you know, only a few months ago.'

They all say something mournful together under their breath, a prayer for the great footballer perhaps, and then return to their otherwise unassailably enthusiastic selves.

Of course I know Nasser Hejazi. Anyone who loves football knows 'Ostureh', the Legend, who was Iran's goalkeeper during its greatest footballing years and is often considered the best Asian goalkeeper of his times. He was so good that Manchester United wanted to sign him but the Iranian Revolution got in the way and it never came to pass. He later became Mohammedan's coach and then manager and did such a good job that he was made manager of our national team in 1989. Nasser Hejazi was one of the best things that ever happened to Bangladeshi football, and the fact that I'm getting a chance to talk about him in Iran is extremely enjoyable.

Drawn in, I carry on for a while and tell them that Mohammadan SC is still one of the most successful clubs in Bangladesh with an arch rival in the younger Abahani Limited. They tell me about the Tehran Derby between Estheglal FC, Hejazi's old club, and Persepolis FC, and how it's the most watched football match in Iran. We drink more tea and then they tell me, apologetically, that they can't process the parcel here, since it's the central post office that deals with overseas deliveries. I thank them for the tea and conversation, and head off towards the *Poste Markezi*, but it's too late.

But every mishap is an opportunity to be exposed to grace, which arrives in the shape of one Mr. Abbas and a bus driver. Mr. Abbas is the postal worker who helps me understand what is being said and when he sees me walking away with my cumbersome box, he offers me a lift. I accept, relieved that I won't have to walk around looking for a taxi, but he insists on dropping me all the way to my hotel. The trouble is, there are two Pars Hotels in Mashhad and when we get on to the expressway, I realise that we're getting further away from the one I'm staying at so I tell him he's very kind, but we're going the wrong way. He apologises and then turns around to take me to the closest bus terminal. He has already gone considerably out of his way, and now goes even further to bring me back towards town. Then, after all that, he expresses regret at not being able to drop me at my destination, and hands me over to a bus driver, telling him in Farsi I'm a foreigner and lost and that he should make sure I get to my hotel safely. The bus driver accepts this responsibility with no qualms at all and asks me to sit next to him so that when we come close to the hotel he can tell me to get off. I try to pay but he shakes his head and smiles that large Iranian smile that looks like sunlight. People like these make mishaps worth wishing for.

7

Nothing in my Cloak but God

Neyshabur, Tus

Neyshabur

The kindly gentleman at Pars Hotel lets me leave most of my luggage in his storeroom so I pack a day-bag and hop onto a bus for Neyshabur. The landscape is grassy and more like plains than arid mountains—this is the Khorasan, a name that features prominently in legends about Central Asian kings and sages and captures all the romance of a frontier land. Stretches of green are interspersed with craggy escarpments and the horizon is far and expansive. We pass farmlands, gently sloping hills and a forest of white wind turbines with massive blades that turn lethargically in a paltry breeze.

It's evening by the time we reach Neyshabur, so I settle into a reasonably priced hotel before going out to get some food. I find myself on a charmless street, which looks just like other charmless streets in other Iranian cities. The more recent urban development here lacks imagination. Buildings are square and uniform, and the boxy structures seem to be filled with the same things everywhere—the same shoe shop, scarf shop, clothes shop, corner shop and sandwich shop appears again and again, along virtually every street. There is something very mediocre about it, but it's not like this just in Iran, of course. A mass-produced world seems to revel in this sort of sameness everywhere. Young Iranians tend to all look fairly similar as well and all of them look like imitations of their Mediterranean counterparts further west—wet and styled hair, fitted, partially unbuttoned shirts, chains, pendants, white pumps, tight jeans, rings, ear studs and shiny belts. The women wear too much makeup and puff their hair up under their scarves.

I buy a generic Iranian sandwich, which is a chopped sausage in French bread with cheese, onions and a choice of sauce; a few supplies from the generic corner shop where I have a fun and playful conversation with the storekeeper who is from Turkmenistan, just north of Khorasan, and then head back to my room.

The revolution is being televised again and public broadcasting here is an endless assortment of Iran's totems—The Holy Defence, martyrdom, the Ahle Bait version of Islam, Iranian sporting greatness, the Revolution, Ayatollahs past and present, and occasionally a cooking show. On one of the channels I watch a video of a devotional song about Imam Reza that sounds a lot like German death metal, with someone who sounds like he's in considerable pain shouting the song out in low-pitched, guttural tones. This is certainly not Iran the elegant, but it's an Iran all the same.

Some words in Farsi do, in fact, sound quite Germanic. The negative '*nisht*' sounds like '*nicht*'; '*dokhtar*', for 'daughter' is exactly the same as the Dutch '*dochter*', and remarkably similar to the German '*tochter*'; the word for 'eight', '*hasht*' isn't too different from '*acht*'; 'is' becomes '*ast*' in Farsi and '*ist*' in German; 'thunder' is '*tondar*' in Farsi and '*donnar*' in German. It has many similarities with English, Hindi and Bangla as well, though it seems to share the more throaty and angular sounds with the Germanic branch of our extended linguistic family. I find Farsi very pleasing to the ear. It's not so much the language, because to a Bangla speaker it can seem slightly simplistic in its construction, and their pronunciation of our shared words can sound a little contrived, but it's the affectionate intonations, the almost coy *taan* and the youthful pattern of their speech that are most attractive.

That said, I can't understand why Farsi was considered the language of sophistication in India for hundreds of years when several Indian languages are much more complex and intricate. It's grudgingly acceptable that it had pride of place in Hindustan as the language of the court and of the conquerors, but what's baffling is why families in far-flung Bengal, for instance, would speak Farsi if they wanted to acquire for themselves an air of refinement, when the cultural and linguistic environment they were living in was sufficiently sophisticated, if not more so.

I'm just about to bunk down for the night, when I hear a knock on my door. I don't expect it, but vaguely remember the Turkmen shopkeeper asking me which hotel I'm staying at. Sure enough, it's him, along with the receptionist who's come to make sure I know this man. Mahdi, as he says his name is, wants to invite me to hang out with his friends—'*mehmannawazi*', he says, among a collection of Persian words I don't understand. I find it odd, and become a little concerned that there might be some sort of hidden agenda, like there usually is in Bangladesh when people cosy up to you and do you lots of favours out of thin air. I thank him for his offer, but tell him that I'm tired. He insists, and tells me it will just be for a little while. I don't know why, but in spite of an unabated feeling of suspicion, I agree—something in me wants to know where this will lead and I want to trust him. We go downstairs and there's a fairly large man waiting at the reception named Hodja who shakes my hand and kisses my cheeks, which is normal in Iran but usually among people who know each other better. There's another person waiting by the car. I'm beginning to get slightly worried since they are talking in Farsi and laughing eerily.

We pull up in front of a house on a small street and Mahdi starts calling someone down. I'm convinced now that this is going to get very ugly for me. I'm going to get robbed, or kidnapped, perhaps even killed. Maybe there are sexual depredations that repressed subjects of the Islamic Republic want to indulge in. A hapless tourist with no ties or contacts in Neyshabur is perfect for all of the above. A fourth person gets in the car, they speak among themselves in Farsi and then tell me to sit in the front seat where I'll be more 'comfortable'. 'This must be it,' I think to myself, 'they're setting me up for the kill.' I'm quite scared at this point and chastising myself for having been this stupid. What was I thinking? That the world is made of people who just want to take you out and show you their town? Or did I think they would ask me for something later and I could make all sorts of noncommittal statements to wriggle myself free? Gosh you're dumb Zeeshan, and now you'll probably be dead.

Hodja, sitting in the driver's seat beside me, seems to have read my mind. He looks over at me and makes the gesture of a person putting his head between his forearms, like a boxer does, to show me that he can see I'm cowering, and then shakes his head to say, 'don't'.

'Na, na naters, khushali!'

He runs his thumb and index finger upwards along his face when he says the word '*khushali*' and a smile blooms, as though the edges of his mouth were attached to his two fingers by an invisible thread. He then slaps his chest and says in broken English, 'heart... open'. I have no idea why but I trust him and immediately relax. I've been going on faith all along anyway, and now feel it being reinforced by Hodja's astute sensitivity.

Sure enough, the moment I stopped being afraid and 'open my heart', it stops looking ominous, nobody looks like a rapist and it all becomes a lot of fun. We get on the highway and drive all the way out of Neyshabur, to the neighbouring town of Firoze, talking constantly even though communication should have been impossible—they speak perhaps 20 words of English, and I speak about five and a half words of Farsi, but together with Bangla, Urdu and, surprisingly, even Turkmeni Turkish, we manage to get a conversation going. We turn onto a small road, and then along an incline behind a military base, up to an old house where someone opens the

239

gate to let us in and looks around furtively before closing it again. You could easily think you were in one of those movie scenes where a drug deal or a sting operation is about to unfold, but it's nothing of the sort; it's a party!

Smartly dressed boys and girls hang around chatting and laughing, and have taken up corners in the large house where they sit together on raised divans. Good music is playing out of large speakers. Upon closer inspection, I discover that it's an after-hours *chaikhaneh*, and that people are paying at a counter for tea and *qalyan*, which is being served to them in their circles. The secrecy is required because of the presence of women and the fact that it's operating late at night, probably without a business permit. I look around for alcohol and hash, but don't spy any. People who know the group I'm with come over to kiss and hug them; there's never a dearth of affection among Persians.

We virtually mime through conversations about girls, relationships, sex, politics, countries, races, *tawrouf*, hospitality, our shared heritage, our mutual disdain for 'Arabisation' and other things we have in common. It's surprising how much you can talk about without actually having any medium to do it in. They have no agenda for bringing me here and are just a bunch of guys enjoying the chance to exchange notes with someone from a different cultural context, who is recognisable enough to be similar but strange enough to be worth examining. I express my admiration for Persian culture and Hodja, delighted that I brought it up, plays some Persian music on his phone. He boasts that Persian music is the best because no one can vibrate their voices like Persians can, and I want to tell him that it's almost as good as the warm-up exercises of an average Hindustani classical vocalist, but don't.

We talk about Islam, and about how it should always be felt and never forced, an understanding quite common in Iran even if it sits in complete contrast to many of their government's authoritarian policies. I enjoy the atmosphere thoroughly, which has no trace at all of cynicism or meanness, and I feel distinctly ashamed for thinking the worst of these boys who have been nothing but exceptionally kind to me. It's not common in my world for this sort of thing to happen but it absolutely should be, and when I tell Mahdi that on the way back to the car he simply says,

'You are alone in my city, so you are my guest.'

Like Jawaad in Kerman, Mahdi's sense of hospitality is so far above what normally passes as good enough it's unquantifiable, and it won't be the last time I experience this either.

On the drive back we listen to Persian pop from different regions of the country, each with their own distinct sound. The car becomes an impromptu club and we all start dancing in our seats when Hodja throws on some house music and tells me that Iran has many clubs, but they're mostly underground and usually just for men who go there to drop ecstasy pills together. I'm quite sure I'm not missing anything if I never go to one.

When they drop me off, Hodja says, 'The car of Hodja is for Mister Zeeshan. Tomorrow I can drive you around anywhere.' It was *tawrouf* but I refuse to play this time since I feel embarrassed enough already and don't want to accidentally end up accepting any more of his generosity. After they leave, I reflect on the magic of what just happened—complete strangers, in a foreign land, treating me like a good friend and with no motive at all. Too often we don't allow ourselves to open up to this sort of experience because, sadly, these things can also go horribly wrong. But maybe for every one time that it does there are five times that it doesn't, though we never hear about those since bad news has better legs. And maybe if we did, and we experienced it often enough, we would be able keep our faith in humanity, and pass it on too—I now feel more inclined to be generous with my time and hospitality.

Great Minds
Day 31

The next morning, I head off to Aramgah-e Omar Khayyam. A friendly taxi driver drops me off and gives me an apple because he happens to have an extra one and I haven't had any breakfast yet, so it's perfect. There's an Omar Khayyam Science and Cultural Institute under construction nearby, which, considering Khayyam was as much a scientist as he was a poet, is quite fitting. Like Leonardo Da Vinci many centuries later or Aristotle over a millennia earlier, he was not conflicted by this dichotomy, nor did it prevent him from excelling in both areas—polymaths were less uncommon before clever penmanship infected us all with an enduring paranoia of becoming 'masters of none'.

Omar Khayyam was the master of plenty. Minds like his rarely grace any civilisation, but even in a civilisation that can boast so much brilliance he stands out as being especially exceptional. Apart from having written the *Rubaiyat*, perhaps the most forthright piece of spiritual literature there is, he formulated the Jalali calendar which is among the most accurate calendars in the world, more accurate than the Gregorian one that we use, and about 500 years older. He helped to evolve mathematics by bringing the disciplines of algebra and geometry into better harmonisation—a debt mathematicians still acknowledge. Astronomers, astrologers and even space explorers hold him in high regard, naming a lunar crater and a small planet after him. Lovers adore him, writers revere him, sceptics quote him, and hedonists, atheists, theologians and mystics alike all call him their own.

He's as famous in the West as he is in the East and Edward Fitzgerald's translation of the *Rubaiyat* was the most celebrated book of poetry in 19th-century England, so much so that Omar Khayyam Clubs sprung up all over the place for budding orientalists to demonstrate their love for all things exotic. He was even able to keep his own name when he went across the divide, and escaped the indignity that Ibn Rushd, Al Ghazali, Ibn Sina and Al Biruni had to suffer when they became 'Averroes', 'Algazel', 'Avicenna' and the entirely odious 'Alberonius'. For me, Omar Khayyam is inspiring for the bold, almost blasphemous nature of his religious commentary. He didn't seem to be held back by anything or have any sort of conditioning corralling his mind—his thoughts were, in the truest sense, free. He could and did, say just about anything. Things like:

On every path I take, Your snares are spread
To entrap me should I walk without due care
Utter extremes acknowledge Your vast sway
You order all things, yet You call me a rebel?

Or

Ordaining every cause for life or death,
Gaurding this tattered robe we call the sky
Say, am I sinful? Are you not my Master?
Who sins then, when you alone created me?

When bending low, God moulded me from clay,
Incontrovertibly my life was ordered,
Without his order I abstain from crime,
Why should I burn then, on His Judgement Day?

Audacious words from a man absorbed in *obhiman*, the bittersweet taste of true love. And why not? He spoke for all of us when he said that. But he also said other, more straightforwardly adoring things like,

You have said that You will torment me, but I shall not fear such a
warning.
For where You are, there can be no torment, and where You are
not...
... How can such a place exist?

It's hard to tell if Khayyam was a Sufi or not. Contemporary Sufis have called his *Rubaiyat* a mystical masterpiece, yet he belonged to no order, had no disciples and no sheikh. His writing has a terrestrial quality that is different from the more ethereal appeal of Jalaluddin Rumi or his fellow Neyshaburi, Fariduddin Attar. In fact, Omar Khayyam speaks about the Sufis glowingly but doesn't seem to include himself among them,

They cleanse the rational soul of the impurities of nature and bodily form, until it becomes pure substance ... whatever man lacks is due to the impurity of his nature. If the veil be lifted and the screen and obstacle removed, the truth of things as they are will become manifest and known ... tell the 'reasoners' that for the lovers of God, intuition is guide, not discursive thought.

Like Imam Ghazali, who was his contemporary and friend, Khayyam places the mysticism of the Sufis above the reason of the philosophers, which makes his scientific bent of mind all the more peculiar to the proponents of today's bifurcated beliefs.

But some of Khayyam's opinions and his repeated references to an allegorical or actual 'wine' rendered him heretical to many of the Islamic orthodoxy of his time, and ever since, and have also led to him being called a licentious drunk. If he were alive today the likes of Hizb-ut-Tahrir would have derogatorily called him a liberal, given over to 'western' immorality, and surely some Taliban or another would have tried to assassinate him. Ayatollah Khomeini might have even called for a massive bonfire of the *Rubaiyat* and put fatwas on his head, to which Khayyam would no doubt have said,

And do you think that unto such as you, a maggot-minded, starved, fanatic bunch
God gave the secret, and denied it to me? Well, well, what does it matter—believe that, too!

In actual fact, Omar Khayyam's soul was sublimely God-conscious; you might even say it was too conscious. He wasn't content to simply bow his head in operatic obedience, and chose instead to approach his relationship with God as an adult might, with both scepticism and faith. Personally, I think a God that doesn't appreciate that sort of boldness isn't worthy of the name. The *Rubaiyat* looks melancholic nihilism in the eye and wrestles from it an ecstatic joy that comes from a full-hearted embrace of the moment. It's simply brilliant writing and allows you to imbibe the carefully blended bittersweetness of life, without burning your mouth.

Ah, my Beloved, fill the cup
That clears Today of past regrets and future fears
Tomorrow? Why, tomorrow I may be
Myself with yesterday's seven thousand years

And if the wine you drink, the lip you press,
End in the nothing that all things end in, Yes
For fancy as you are, you are but what
You shall be—Nothing—you shall not be less.

Leave the wise to wrangle, and with me
The quarrel of the Universe let be:
And, in some corner of the Hubbub couched,
Make game of that which makes as much of Thee.

Omar Khayyam didn't exist in a vacuum; his Neyshabur was one of the intellectual centres of the Islamic world at the time and also one of its largest cities. The Hadith compiler Muslim ibn Hajjaj was born and lived here in the 9th century and his teacher, Muhammad Bukhari, also settled here for a while. They were contemporaries of two other great and completely different sorts of Iranian Muslims, Mansur al-Hallaj and Bayazid Bastami—and it's no small irony that the ideological split between Sufis and Salafis can be traced to the differences between these same four men. Hallaj and Bastami are regarded as teachers in many Sufi traditions and heretics by the *Alhe Hadith*, or the People of the Hadiths. Many great minds lived and travelled between cities like Cordoba, Cairo, Baghdad Neyshabur and Samarkand, teaching and studying at various institutions, among which were the *nizamiyyahs*, theological schools that were begun by Nizam al-Mulk, Khayyam's friend and author of the *Siyastanama*, an 11th-century treatise on governance.

The pair was also friends with Hassan-i Sabbah, the founder of the extremist Ismaili order, the Hashashins, and the story of their lives, friendship and falling out is creatively fictionalised in Amin Maalouf's 1988 novel, *Samarkand*. The fact that they lived at the same time and were once good friends is an almost poetic embodiment of the internal struggles that plague the Muslim family today. These theological forces, which represented three very different sides of the same thing, repelled each other, and their irreconcilability is the very same stuff that still divides the House of Islam against itself. It's reductionist to say that their spiritual descendants are the mollahs, the mystics and the terrorists, but there may be grains of truth in it.

It's exactly a month since I started out from Dhaka and Omar Khayyam's tomb is just the sort of destination I had hoped to arrive at on this journey. Set in a beautiful garden beside the mausoleum of an Imam, Khayyam's tomb is a simple, open structure that shoots upward like a tower. It's meant to resemble a Central Asian tent since 'Khayyam' means 'tentmaker', and is adorned with calligraphic pieces of his poetry set in glazed *kashi* tiles. The ceiling and the inside of the walls are made of aquamarine tiles with floral patterns looking decidedly celestial. It's beautiful. There are bright red roses in a garden that is lush and plays host to a variety of singing birds, perhaps the way Khayyam envisaged a perfect patch of forest. I sit on the veranda around the garden smoking apple *qalyan*, and drinking zafran tea, while Khayyam's *Rubaiyat*, set to music, plays out of the gift shop nearby, creating the perfect atmosphere. Visitors flock to his grave; they touch it lovingly and pray for him. Hardy and smiling old ladies ask me to take their picture and a beautiful young woman smiles at me and speaks to me in English. Everyone is buoyed by an easy sort of happiness. A bust of the great man, long bearded and pensive, greets us as we enter the garden; he looks away from us—staunch and intense.

Accept my respects, Khayyam of Neyshabur; like every other bee here, I have come drawn by your irresistible nectar. You are long gone and but your essence still brings people here. All kinds of people have come. You would be pleased to see them. Scientists are here, doctors too. Women in chadors, clerics, men in suits, a little boy sits on your head and dangles his feet, he's adorable. They've been coming to you for a thousand years, and will keep coming for a thousand more. You are very loved, here in the land of your birth and across the world, and in spite of the allegations of heresy, the Islamic Republic of Iran can't but show you the respect you so richly deserve.

A road connects Khayyam's *aramgah* to Fariduddin Attar's, who was also from Neyshabur and is buried about a kilometre away. All along it, between the hills and the plains, people picnic on the grass, the concrete, the tarmac, and virtually everywhere they find a bit of space. Families grill food on public barbecues, people smoke *qalyan*, drink chai. Children play football, cushions and blankets have been set around, and it's a lively, domestic atmosphere, right there by the road. This is the first glimpse I catch of the Persian penchant for picnicking. They simply love it, and do it anywhere and everywhere. They seem to be permanently prepared for it as well, as blankets and teapots are always at the ready, along with an endless supply of tea, tobacco, dried seeds and other necessary ingredients.

Attar's tomb is more tomb-like than Khayyam's—it's a closed chamber and has the decorated dome you might expect an Iranian tomb to have. A stylised bust of him draped by birds sits at the entrance of a compound which also contains the tomb of Kamal al-Mulk, a 20th-century artist, though its far less ornate. Picnickers smile at me as I enter, and now its Attar's poetry to music that plays out of a similar gift shop. The interior of the tomb is a small space which can hold only a few people at a time and we remove our shoes to enter. It has cushions along the walls for visitors to sit and reflect and one of the walls bears a beautiful ink etching of a scene from *The Conference of the Birds*, his best known work. An older tombstone, said to be from the 15th century, is also kept next to the new one. I watch as a middle-aged man dressed in a shirt and trousers, kneels by the grave and caresses it as thought it belongs to a precious relative. He lingers there with his hand on the marble for a long time as his eyes well up. Later, I see him walking around the grounds reading a book, presumably by Attar, with his hand to his heart, shaking his head softly as he's moved by the words before him.

Attar of Neyshabur is the Sufi's Sufi. In some ways he's the fountainhead of the sort of poetry that flowed though Jalaluddin Rumi's pen. They even met once, when Rumi was 18 and his family was on the move from Afghanistan to Turkey, fleeing an impending Mongol attack. It may have been Attar who uttered the famous line,

'Here comes a sea followed by an ocean', when he saw Rumi's father, a theologian, walking ahead of Rumi as the family passed through the Khorasan. It's also been said that he gave Rumi the *Asrarnama*, the Book of Secrets, which deals with the soul's entanglement in the material world. Rumi called him 'the spirit', and said of him,

'Attar roamed the seven cities of love—We are still just in one alley'

He was a perfumer by trade, or came from a family involved with perfumes, and so cleverly used 'Attar' as his pen name, along with Fariduddin, both of which have become the names we know him by today. His real name was Abu Hamid bin Abu Bakr Ibrahim and he was born some time between 1120 and 1157. He may have lived long enough to witness Central and West Asia being turned inside out by Genghis Khan and his Mongol hordes when they depopulated entire cities, to the last soul, and may have even lost his own life in this genocidal butchery, but there are contending views about that.

Not much is known about Attar, except that he travelled for a while and is believed to have visited Iraq, the Arabian Peninsula, the Caucasus, Turkistan and India before returning to his native Neyshabur to teach Sufism. About 30 of his works have survived, among them, the *Asrarnama*, the *Illahinama* (The Book of God) and, of course, the *Mantiq at-Tayr*, better known as *The Conference of the Birds*, in which he uses allegory to describe a search for Divinity, which ends up being the essential, enlightened self, or as Attar might have preferred I say, the Presence that's left after the 'self' is shed.

It isn't easy to get our heads around the concept of 'annihilation', and even when we can, cognitively at least, we don't often properly understand how deep it actually goes. People like the 9th-century mystic, Mansur al-Hallaj did, though—he lost himself so completely that he couldn't see anything anymore except Essence, and in the exuberance of those moments, ran around saying '*Ana'l Haqq*', 'I am Truth', or, in fact, 'I am God'. It cost him his head and he was savagely put to death on the recommendations of a clergy that didn't quite have the depth to grasp what he meant when he said,

248

There is nothing in my cloak but God.

Al-Hallaj explained comments like this in his book *Kitab al-Tawasin*, but it probably made matters worse for him since it also contained a defence of the Devil's refusal to bow to Adam. He does this to set up a brilliant argument: Satan's refusal to bow to Adam and his subsequent sending to hell, is nothing other than an expression of his absolute commitment to *Tawhid*—God's singular and unique Majesty. To al-Hallaj, his refusal to bow is the purest expression of love, since even when confronted with the prospect of exile and distance from his Beloved, Satan, or Iblis, refuses to show devotion to anyone but Allah. Hell then, is nothing but the pains of separation. God banished Satan for not being able to recognise Him under veils, as a true lover might have, and so we arrive at *Ana'l Haqq*, because angels and jinns can't be asked to bow to a created being unless, perhaps, there is something of the Divine in it, something perhaps, like the *ruh* of Allah—His own Spirit?

Al-Hallaj was called everything from a crypto-Christian to a polytheist, and finally a heretic. Even other Sufis, including his old teacher Junayd Baghdadi, creator of the 'sober' school of Sufi thought, wasn't shocked to see the end of him. He believed that al-Hallaj had broken the code of mystical secrecy, which required controversial insights to be shared exclusively among the elect and the initiated, and not shouted from the rooftops as al-Hallaj had preferred to do. But al-Hallaj wasn't the only one doing this—he was following in the footsteps of Bayazid Bastami, the Sufi who began the 'intoxicated' or ecstatic Sufi school, a tradition to which both Rumi and Attar belonged. It may have been Bastami who coined the now well-known term '*fana*', to describe the state of being dissolved, through complete union, in Allah. The ecstatic Sufis believed in expressing their love for Allah publicly and without regard for consequences, which were very often dire, but what a poorer world it would have been if they had all agreed with Junayd's shrouded approach and didn't, for instance, give us this, by Attar:

How long will you persist in blasphemy?
Escape your self-hood's vicious tyranny
Whoever can evade the Self transcends
This world,
And as a lover he ascends.

Set free your soul; impatient of delay,
Step out along our sovereign's royal Way

But you must empty this first glass;
The wine that follows it is love's devoted sign.
If petty problems keep you back, or none
How will you seek the treasures of the sun?

In drops you lose yourselves, yet you must dive
Through untold fathoms and remain alive.
This is no journey for the indolent
Our quest is Truth itself, not just its scent!

If you become that substance I propound,
You are not God, though in God you are drowned;
Those lost in Him are not the Deity—
This problem can be argued endlessly.

You are His shadow
And cannot be moved by thoughts of life or death
Once this is proved.

When neither Blasphemy nor Faith remain,
The body and the Self have both been slain;
Then the fierce fortitude that the Way will ask
Is yours,
And you are worthy of our task.
Begin the journey without fear; be calm;
Forget what is and what is not Islam.

Neyshabur's life ended very badly. The city called Neyshabur today isn't a continuation of the original Silk Road city, but is a new one built near the ruins of the one that was completely destroyed by the Mongols in 1221, in reprisal for the murder of Genghis Khan's son-in-law. It is said that its inhabitants—all 1.7 million of them—were put to death, and towers of skulls made from their heads. According to the plaque at his tomb complex, Fariduddin Attar was among them. Given Neyshabur's cultural heritage, it's painful to think about how many other illuminated minds might have been extinguished in the Mongol conquests, which have been described as the worst destruction experienced by mankind until the 20th century. Just 15 years earlier, Bakhtiyar Khilji had wreaked similar havoc in India, and thousands of Buddhist scholars, students and monks from Nalanda and Odantapur were executed wholesale. When you consider that many Sufis travelled to India for inspiration, and that students at the Bait al Hikmat, which was smashed by the Mongols, studied texts found in India, possibly at Nalanda, you can see just how much of the East's spiritual heritage was obliterated in almost a single fell swoop.

I head back towards Khayyam's tomb to catch a bus into town and get something to eat. There are food stalls in a slightly touristy market and the gardens here draw as many people as the tombs do. I feel like praying and it's early afternoon, so I put out my *gamcha* and say a few *rakats* in the garden after washing up in the cool water of a large ablution tank outside the mausoleum. It's very hot, and the water provides a lot of much needed relief. I step into one of the ubiquitous sandwich shops on the roadside, and have the same French bread and sausage sandwich I've had since I arrived in Iran. I'm sure proper Persian cuisine is sufficiently varied and sophisticated, but the regular fare is irritatingly ordinary. After eating I catch a bus back to the hotel. A few teenage boys get on soon after and talk loudly among themselves. They look like urban roughs and at first I think they're ill-mannered but then notice them giving up their seats for older people and gesturing towards them with respect.

Tus

The next morning the receptionist, who has since become my Facebook friend, helps me buy a ticket for a sleeper berth on a train from Mashhad to Yazd. I catch a bus back to Mashhad and get there with lots of time to spare, so decide to check out Tus, only 45 minutes away, and really just a part of the greater metropolis. The local bus is crowded and I ask the man sitting next to me to let me know when we get to Tus but it turns out to be unnecessary since the route ends at Tus, in front of Ferdowsi's tomb—Iran's most respected poet.

Ferdowsi belonged to a family that was part of the old Sassanian aristocracy, the Daghans, who emerged from the Arab conquest in the 7th century as champions of all things Persian. The Arabs had gone to great lengths to try and eradicate every trace of Persian nationhood, from their religion and culture to their language, for nearly 400 years, and were doing pretty well, too, until their power in Eastern Iran and Central Asia waned and the Samanids, ex-Zoroastrian Persians, managed to reclaim chunks of territory for Iranzamin, including the Khorasan and Tus, where Ferdowsi lived. The Samanids restored Afghanistan, Uzbekistan and Tajikistan to Persian authority but it was a shortlived revival as a Turkic presence from the Altai Mountains in Inner Asia was already making itself felt in the region, and by the 10th century had imperially arrived in the form of the Ghaznavids.

But luckily enough, the Ghaznavids were Persianised Turks with a strong interest in Persian culture, and in fact it may have been our old friend Mahmud of Ghazni who commissioned Ferdowsi to write the *Shahnameh*, the Book of Kings. Ferdowsi's 30-year magnus opus, written in pure Farsi and purged of most Arabic loan words, puts to poetry the collected stories of Iran's historical and mythological dynasties as well as its creation myth. It serves as a historiography, an encyclopaedia, a dictionary and much, much more, and is monumental really, quite beyond the abilities of ordinary mortals.

I'm pressed for time so skip visiting the great poet who almost single-handedly restored the Persian language as well as Persia's heritage following the cataclysmic Arab invasion. Besides, I'm not in Tus for Ferdowsi; I've come here to see Imam Ghazali, who is one of the more problematic gods in my theological pantheon. He was, in effect, the death of the Mu'tazila school, and his international, cross-generational literary conversation with Ibn Rushd, the last great Mu'tazila, is one of the great intellectual battles of all time. He has often been held responsible for the eclipse of rationalist, scientific thought in the Muslim world, and as proof of the superiority of the Ash'arite position, which continues to inform mainstream Sunni Islam today. But that's probably a little unfair, since the trend had already begun well before his arrival on the scene, and his positions differ quite significantly from the more orthodox Ash'arite ones. His most ardent fans consider him the most influential Muslim after the Prophet and he is applauded for his efforts in reviving Islam after its fanciful sojourn into the 'mire' of intellectual inquiry.

But none of these fans of his do him any sort of justice. It's redundant to try and parcel his work off and use it as proof of how one way is better than another, because Imam Ghazali's writings had one of the broadest spectra of his times. He wrote about a range of subjects related to social and personal morality—from theology and Sufism to philosophy and jurisprudence—and tried to create a much-needed bridge between many of these contending traditions. Ghazali was personally perhaps somewhere between a Sufi and a theologian. His father was a Sufi and he was certainly exposed to Sufism as a child, but his own road took him towards *fiqh*, or jurisprudence, and when he was 28 he travelled to Neyshabur where he caught the attention of Nizam al Mulk and was made head teacher at the very important Baghdad *nizamiyyah*, in 1091. Ghazali also knew Omar Khayyam and the two would discuss spiritual exegesis to refine their respective understandings of the Divine. But unlike Khayyam, Ghazali's jurisprudential writings as well as his position as a teacher threw him into public debates and made his voice a popular one among those being raised by the *mutakallimun*, scholars of *kalam* or theology, during their dialectic conversations about, on the one hand, *qadar*, power (will) and *jabar*, obligation; and on the other, reason versus revelation.

Imam Ghazali wrote a book called the *Incoherence of the Philosophers* in which he tore into the Mu'tazila position through an argument that demonstrates how reason and rationalism falls short in a number of areas and can't, for example, satisfactorily prove the existence of a single God without simultaneously allowing for the existence of many gods, or no God at all. He then sets up the notion of occasionalism where he argues that created substances themselves are not the cause of events, but God is, and so, for instance, fire can be cold if God wills it to be (as mentioned in the Quran regarding the trials of Prophet Abraham)—something that would be difficult to explain using reason alone. Ghazali explains that while the universe acts, for the most part, according to predicable patterns, miracles can, and do, occur when God instructs phenomena to behave differently. He sums it up like this:

The laws of phenomena must be constant, or there could be no such thing as science; but it is a great error to mistake the slaves for the master.

A number of other metaphysical constructs are discussed in the book, setting off a chain reaction of philosophical writing beginning, a generation later, with *The Incoherence of the Incoherence* by the last great Mu'tazila scholar, the Spanish Ibn Rushd who quite successfully refuted Ghazali's positions point by point. This was followed up by a similarly themed book from his student Ibn Tufail, which was in turn refuted by Ibn al Nafis, and finally, in the 15th century, the Turkish scholar Khawajah Zada wrote a refutation of Ibn Rushd, bringing to an end a rather useless and speculative 400-year-long discussion on things that no one can really know about for sure.

The real, pertinent debate between rationalists and others was over the crucial question of law and ethics. The Mu'tazili refused to simply accept what religious authorities designated as absolute moral law, but believed instead that one must apply reasoned thinking to interpret and apply the words of the Quran. This was necessary, they argued, to prevent the clergy or political elites from furthering a partisan agenda in the guise of absolute truth, i.e., without the freedom to reason, argue and debate the intended meaning of God's message, it could be hijacked or distorted by those claiming to have a righteous sanction. The judge of truth for the Mu'tazili was ultimately human reason and not a religious authority, combined with revelation and spiritual intuition, which they acknowledged as deeper truths that cannot be known through reasoning.

They further argued that the Quran itself stresses on human intellect and urges people to use that gift from God to its fullest capacity to try and understand the wisdom of revealed laws. Nowhere does it encourage a blind acceptance of moral precepts, they argued; instead, it emphasises the fact that human beings are capable of 'knowing the names of things' or the essential nature of reality, and by extension, the logic behind moral precepts, if they sincerely apply their minds to it.

They were challenged by the Ash'arites who, while conceding that certain vital truths could be known by reason alone, argued that most could not be, and this necessitated a strict obedience to God's commands and prohibitions. The Ash'arites argued that the reasons for certain instructions are not immediately apparent and that only through divine guidance, incorporated in religious authorities, can moral behaviour be achieved. They drew on verses in the Quran that speak about confused individuals being brought to guidance after surrendering their personal opinions and insisted that the Quran emphasises blind obedience, evident in the verse that says,

And it may be that you dislike a thing which is good for you and that you like a thing which is bad for you. Allah knows but you do not know.

To the Ash'arites, the designation of an act as either good or evil is not measured by anything intrinsic but is understood as the obedience or disobedience of God's laws, i.e., goodness simply means to obey them and evil means to not.

Al Ghazali was not strictly of this opinion; his criticism of the rational method focused mostly on its inability to grasp the significance of prophetic revelation or the divine mysteries, as these lay beyond the scope of the intellect and were not accessible via the senses or the faculties of reason—a position not vastly different from the Mu'tazila one itself. He did, in fact, believe that reason could provide sound and consistent judgement in the areas of knowledge that were open to our perceptual and intellectual abilities, and was clear about the fact that he had no problem with the other branches of philosophy like physics, logic, mathematics and even certain readings of ethics. His main quarrel was with the rational approach to metaphysics.

Imam Ghazali experienced an existential crisis while he was teaching jurisprudence, causing him to withdraw from the world for 11 years and live the life of an ascetic. In his later writings he affirms the mystic route as the only real path to Truth, above both *kalam*, or *fiqh*, and defines moral and spiritual elevation as the desire to attain a nearness to God for its own sake, and not as an obsession with intellectual or ethical veracity. He believed seekers would hold firmly to two pillars to achieve this, *Ishq* and the *Shariah*—their actions would be governed by the recommendations of *Al-Shar*, or divine duty, as they appear in the Quran and the Hadith, and the centre of their hearts would be dominated by feelings for God. Al-Ghazali explains these feelings as genuine humility, adoration, remorse and gratitude, born of an experiential awareness of both the beauty and majesty of God and expressed as rapturous love, or *Ishq*.

In his book *The Alchemy of Happiness*, he outlines the sources of true joy, asserting that it is only found in possessing four types of wisdom: knowledge of the Self, knowledge of God, a true understanding of the limits and of this world and a full-souled yearning for the limitlessness of the next. It contains passages like these:

If a man knows not his own soul, which is the nearest thing to him, what is the use of his claiming to know others? It is as if a beggar who has not the wherewithal for a meal should claim to be able to feed a town.

...

The highest function of the soul of man is the perception of truth; in this, accordingly, it finds its special delight.... The higher the subject-matter of the knowledge obtained the greater the delight. A man would be pleased at being admitted into the confidence of a prime minister, but how much more if the king makes an intimate of him and discloses state secrets!

And this:

... if his love is really strong, he will love all men, for all are God's servants, no, his love will embrace the whole of creation, for he who loves any one loves the works he composes and his handwriting.

This is precisely why Ghazali is problematic for me. On the one hand he says beautifully liberating things like these, and on the other he advocates for an end to deliberative reasoning. And though these two things don't contradict each other (in fact they may even be complementary), it makes it difficult for people like me who can appreciate both the mystic and the Muta'zila approaches to understanding God. But my bigger gripe is not with Ghazali particularly but with the unintended consequences of his writings, which encouraged a climate of anti-intellectualism and aggressive hostility towards philosophical curiosity. It didn't help either that he said things like this:

I have seen a group who, believing themselves in possession of a distinctiveness from companion and peer by virtue of a superior quick wit and intelligence, have rejected the Islamic duties regarding acts of worship ... they have entirely cast off the reins of religion through multifarious beliefs, following therein a troop 'who repel away from God's way, intending to make it crooked, who are indeed disbelievers in the hereafter'.

It's a most misinformed position considering the aim of the philosophers, *falasifa* in Arabic, was entirely spiritual and that the Mu'tazila were among the strongest defenders of Islam during the early years of contact with others religions and materialists. The polymath Al-Farabi, often called the first Muslim philosopher, explained the desired outcome of their speculative inquiries as this:

... the end towards which one should tend in studying philosophy is the knowledge of the Creator, exhaled is He above all: that He is one and unmoved and that He is the efficient cause of all things and that He organises this world by means of His generosity, wisdom and justice.

Imam Ghazali was not fond of Al Farabi's writings, but he also expressed unhappiness with the strictly doctrinal approach to religion followed by traditionalists and believed it missed the very point, which is an experiential faith unique to every individual—the *dhawq*, a Sufi expression that literally means 'taste'. He wrote,

In other words, if we are to arrive at pure spiritual truth, we must put away, for the time being, knowledge which has been acquired by external processes and which too often hardens into dogmatic prejudice.

Ghazali's work helped to find common grounds between Sufism and the orthodoxy, but it did the opposite for philosophical rationalism, making it appear foreign, heretical and destructive, and when lesser men inherited these ideas they understood them to mean independent reasoning should no longer be allowed in Muslim heads and summarily shut it out.

There's a large red-brick building here called the Haruniyah, named after Harun-al-Rashid and Imam Ghazali's memorial stone (not his tomb, which has never been discovered) is said to be inside it but it is closed by the time I get there. I walk around the place for a while. There's a big park in front of it where I offer my evening prayers and watch the sun go down over the city of Tus. After finishing, I stay seated on the ground for a while thinking about Tus, Mashhad and Neyshabur and about how so many heavyweights of Islam's Golden Age lived or passed through these cities. Conquerors did too, sadly, including Nader Shah, the man sometimes called the last Asian conqueror and someone who idolised Genghis Khan and Tamerlane.

Nader Shah was as cruel as his idols and the Turkic general arrived on the scene when the Mughal Empire in India and the Safavid Empire in Persia, allies for over 200 years, were both in an irreversible state of decline. By 1736 he had deposed the last Safavid King, had succeeded in driving Afghan aspirants out of the picture and had managed to secure a border with the encroaching Ottomans in the west. He then looked eastward and like any good opportunist, made a play for the Mughal territories, as its king tottered on his embattled throne. He defeated Mohammad Shah in 1739, killed over 30,000 of Delhi's inhabitants in a single day, and plundered the Mughal treasury so thoroughly that he apparently didn't need any taxes to run his empire for about three years afterwards.

He made off with, among plenty of other things, the Peacock Throne, the very seat of Mughal authority, and the Koh-i-Noor, one of the largest diamonds in the world, which has since made its way into the Crown Jewels of the UK. It's fitting really, since the pair of them unwittingly colluded to impoverish and enslave a country that was among the wealthiest in the world at the time. Nader Shah defeated the Mughals but didn't incorporate India into his empire. British academic Michael Axworthy, in his biography of Nader Shah, credits him with opening India up for the British and goes as far as to say that had he not attacked Delhi, the British may not have noticed how weak the Mughals had become and might never have tried to replace them. I don't know about that—it's not likely that the British wouldn't have ever tried; they would have surely looked for gaps to exploit on their own, but Nader Shah gave them every reason to do it sooner. He is, of course, a national hero in Iran for halting the disintegration and colonisation of Persia—as surely as he hastened it for India—and is buried in Mashhad, in a splendid modern mausoleum.

The train from Mashhad to Yazd is very impressive. It's clean, carpeted and the compartment has a built-in television, with English news on it too. The interior is head and shoulders above any train I've taken in India, Bangladesh or Pakistan and perhaps even better than the one I took from Paris to Madrid. The bunks are soft and nicely upholstered, like a sofa, and nothing like those god-awful rubber-coated ones you get in South Asia. The windows are large, there's good lighting and the sheets they provide smell like fabric softener.

The whole experience of train travel in Iran is very enjoyable and unlike the buses, which have hectic counters and late departures, the rails are professional and timely, with large, tidy terminals that have check-in counters, metal detectors and the equivalent of immigration officers who check your documents, register you if you a foreigner, and let you through. The standard is fairly high.

I go through the whole process of boarding as though I'm blind, basically, and experience, for the first time, what it must be like to be illiterate. I feel just like the migrant workers I've seen at the airport in Bangladesh who struggle with the embarkation form and ask people for help to fill it. I can't read the language on my ticket, can't read the signs in the terminal, don't know what the formalities here are, don't know which platform to be on, don't know which gate leads to the platform; I don't where I am. I can't make out a single thing. I'm moved forward through the slightest of nudges by people I accost for information and assistance, until I reach the train, and then carry on doing that inside to find my room and berth. It's really a miracle that people are able to work or migrate to a completely different language environment and go on to even thrive in it.

My travelling companions are a family of three—a young bearded man, his wife in chador who never looks directly at me, or I at her, and their daughter. They are warm and talkative, though I can tell that there's some wariness about the presence of a single male in the compartment. I try to diffuse it by being as unobtrusive as I can, and after the customary exchange of pleasantries, I disappear behind my iPod and book, leaving most of the cabin to them. I also use the opportunity to gather some of my impressions on the prejudices about Iranian life and society, especially about the place of women.

So far, none of the stereotypes I had heard about Iran have been true, apart from the fact that women have to cover their hair and there's a tendency towards national propaganda, but from an eastern or Asiatic point of view, neither of these is particularly odd. What's more striking is the confidence with which women conduct themselves here. Unlike their Pakistani counterparts and a bit more like their Bengali ones, Iranian women are bold and assertive, and seem to be able to command the sort of respect they need. Unlike their Bangladeshi counterparts, however, and more like their Indian and Pakistani ones this time, many more Iranian women drive and run establishments.

The incidence of full-faced veiling is much lower than it is in both Pakistan and India. In fact it is non-existent. Instead some women try to cover their faces with the cumbersome black chador; they grip it with their teeth and hands while also grabbing bags and children. It's more common among older women, but some younger ones do it as well and it looks quite awkward generally. It's also black and thick so possibly hot. That, along with the standard issue rigid and restrictive manteau that almost all of them wear, probably doesn't do anyone any favours in the body odour department.

None of the florid, fluid sensuality of soft Hindustani clothes, like the *shalwar-kameez* or the sari, draping lightly over the contours of a beautiful body, feature here. I suppose that's the point, though, but it's a shame really, because the women here are very alluring and would look so much nicer in freer, more flattering clothes. Still, for all the fables about exotic Persian beauty, I'm not convinced that South Asian women aren't more seductive with their rich, darker skin, their softer slopes, their sultrier sway, their larger eyes, larger lips and, well, larger assets, generally. They are just more feminine, and dress like women instead of this fairly androgynous business of jeans and stiff shirts. Speaking of androgyny, there's a lot of 'dandy' in the men, and it ranges from the metrosexual to homosexual.

There also seems to be less of a gender gap between men and women—they don't seem to stand too far apart on any sort of hierarchy that might exist between the sexes, and tend to talk with each other as equals. Of course I could be wrong since it's only the impression of an outsider, but I also don't see anything that resembles scenes we were made to imagine as children, of Basij guards standing around with whips or tar or something else wicked, tormenting all the colourful creatures of the land and sea. In fact it's nothing at all, on any count, like the dystopian non-civilisation we were told about.

But this is all 30 or more years after the Revolution so it's difficult to form an accurate opinion about Iran without taking that into account. It's hard to know, for instance, where it was headed pre-Revolution or what the Revolution's dynamics threw up and threw out. This is a post-Revolution country, and to its credit, seems to list things like social welfare and civic amenities among its priorities—which is a lot better than can be said about many other countries, especially my own. Thugs and extortionists also appear to have less of a free hand here than they do in South Asia, and the sight of prostitutes and junkies on street kerbs is completely out of the question. Even local television seems more sanitised—I've hardly seen bloodshed or senseless violence on screen and there is nothing even close to explicitly sexual content. There's a flowery, child-friendly wholesomeness about its public persona.

Maybe Iranian society was like this anyway and an essentially Persian sense of *tameez* or decency governs their public behaviour more than the Islamic Revolution does. At any rate, the absence of sleaze is quite a welcome change. An implicit and actual purdah, reinforced by the mandatory hijab, keeps the social decorum between men and women cleaner, and prevents excessive perving. In the train compartment, in India, when I woke up and stared right at the man's sleeping wife, my gaze lingered on the shape of her neck, an image altogether unavailable to me in Iran, where the man built his wife a little shelter with sheets, safe from the wandering eyes of one *Agha* Zeeshan Rahman Khan, fellow passenger in cabin *chahar*, *sandali beesht-o-panj*.

8

Rise and Rise Again

Yazd, Esfahan, Kashan

Yazd

I wake up early and look out the window at the complete desert outside. Unlike the one in Pakistan, this is the sort of desert any self-respecting desert would want to be. Cavernous valleys of sand, occasionally ridged with grey rocky peaks, but mostly white-yellow sand and towering dunes. We're going through the Dasht-e Kavir, or the 'Great Desert', which certainly lives up to its name in distance and desertness.

I get myself an Iranian breakfast, which is good cottage cheese, a bit like feta, with naan, honey or jam, butter, some olives, olive oil and very, very sweet tea. The absence of meat and eggs takes some getting used to, but when you do it's a pretty good meal. In better places, they even give you eggs with it. The journey is about 15 hours in, and nearing the end, and it's been a hell of a lot of sand with the occasional industrial activity—possibly mining—spotted quite frequently along the way. The man in the family I'm sharing the cabin with is an engineer, and in the morning we chat about work an pay in Bangladesh. He seems to think that the monthly salary for someone in his position is better in Dhaka than in Iran, but of course I never ask him how much that is. He's the same age as me but has a daughter who is possibly eight or even nine, a home and a career. I think about how much I haven't yet got and feel a bit sad.

Yazd is almost at the geographic centre of Iran and nearly the mid-point between Greece and Bangladesh, along the old trade routes. It's a desert town, much of which was built in adobe as a covered city, with miles of roofed passages running through the old quarter to shield people from the unbearable midday heat in summer. It also has two enormous towers of silence, the sky burial chambers or dakhmas of Zoroastrian funerals. The fire worshippers, as they're inaccurately called, leave the bodies of their dead for the vultures and other birds of prey to pick apart and eat, and consider both earth burial and cremation an abomination—a poisoning of the earth or the ether. Sky burial is also practised by various Tibetan and Mongolian people, who, conforming to Vajrayana Buddhist traditions, consider it the most generous way of disposing of a body. They also encourage a gruesome *shadhona* or meditation, where devotees sit at a burial chamber and watch corpses being consumed, so that they can overcome an aversion to death and decay and are reminded of the impermanence of bodies.

Arriving at the historic city, I head straight for the Silk Road Hotel, a traditional old clay residence that has been converted into a guesthouse, and where to my delight, I find a scene which is perhaps as old as the house itself. In a tranquil open courtyard shaded by flower trees, a company of ragged travellers sit on old traditional furniture around a long table, laughing, smoking and drinking chai—just as they have probably done along this route, for hundreds of years. Among them is my new-old friend Yves. With him also is the red-faced English boy we met at Rayen, a dreadlocked Dutchman, a couple of Germans, a young French woman and a Turkish lady. The old converted house in the centre of old Yazd is a bastion of bohemianism and it suddenly feels like an international overland backpacking hub. There are traditional decorated divans strewn around the courtyard and next to the house, the 12th-century Jameh Masjid is getting its most recent facelift.

I get a bed in the 14-share dorm in the basement and park myself on the table to smoke a cigarette and share in the conversations. Different people have come by different means, along different routes; some have brought their motorcycles, others have taken the train. Some have bussed it, some drove while others hitched. A French Canadian couple cycling around the world came in from Central Asia to escape the approaching winter. All sorts of experiences are shared, from scuffles with Turks on the ferry, to camping out along the desert in Iran. There are also Pakistani stories and Indian stories, Senegalese stories and Indonesian stories.

A girl with the bluest eyes, covering her hair, like all women, locals and travellers alike, have to do in public, comes in from outside looking like the very postcard of beautiful, her green headscarf bringing out the colour in her cheeks and eyes. Everyone turns to stare at her; she has the most amazing smile too. Sana, who I'm sure has been told by every Iranian boy who's flirted with her or every Iranian person that stopped her to get to know her, about how Persian her name is, sits down among us and starts talking about the horrible injustices in the world and how it's all just a lot of rot. She's Dutch with dark hair and light eyes and her peach-pink skin is nicely bronzed. She's lovely and very interesting.

A German motorcyclist, who was an IT engineer in a former life, is travelling east from Germany, cruising about leisurely for months on end without an itinerary or a deadline. He'd like to make it to Australia. He's currently waiting in Iran for his visa to Turkmenistan, where he fancies a bit of a spin on the Steppes. Sana is thinking of heading to Jordan. A real *shadhu* of a British hippie walks about barefoot, his skin leathered through many years of travel. The deep ridges running along his temples catch the sun when he smiles and they glisten with all the gathered joys and sorrows of what looks like a fulfilling 48-year lifetime. Martin, the Dutch boy with dreadlocks, says he's escaping the great depression of his life in spiritually underdeveloped Europe. People share conversations, philosophies, reflections, impressions, prejudices, book titles; names of great travellers like Marco Polo and Ibn Battuta come into the description of routes and it carries on until about four in the afternoon when the day begins to wane, and some of us decide to visit the Towers of Silence to avoid making a complete cauliflower of the day.

Yazd has the largest (and largely resurgent) Zoroastrian community in Iran, supported internationally by a few countries, especially India. The teachings of Zarathustra runs in Iran's veins, and their hearts never seem too far from a religion which, as Iranians like to point out, was the first monotheistic religion in the world. It wasn't, of course, since the ageless religions of Indian tribes like the Khasi or the Munda or even of Australian aboriginals and Native Americans are essentially monotheistic. But in the context they mean—in relation to the Semitic challengers of Judaism, Christianity and Islam—it just might have dibs. Yazd is still a pilgrimage site for adherents of the faith and has become something of a 'return to roots' centre for people of the Parsi diaspora. It has a famous *Atash Kadeh*, a fire temple and remains one of the last places in Iran where Ahura Mazda is still worshipped as the God of Wisdom and Light. The similarity between the word *Ahura* and the Hindu *Asura* isn't—as it never is—accidental: the *Asuras* in the Rig Veda are the older gods with a moral and social jurisdiction while the *Devas* are the younger gods of natural and physical phenomenon. In Iran, too, in the Gathas, the oldest of the Zoroastrian texts, both sets of supernatural beings are featured but the *Daevas* are the bad ones.

We arrive just at sunset with enough time to get a great view of Yazd from a distance and see how it is utterly dwarfed by the desert, which submerges the city in its bare, blank expanse. It's a sombre feeling. The towers, which are not towers actually but hills, come into sight ahead of us, standing quite silently indeed. They are large and the ascent is steep—it must've been hell on the pall-bearers. At the base, a group of cheerful young Yazdis sit smoking *qalyan*, while the girls among them dance to music playing out of smartphones. We climb up and into the very pit of the thing, where the body was to be tied as an offering to the vultures, which is a massive circle hewn out of the top of the hill. There are channels for the blood to run through and a small bone yard, which no doubt some poor wretch, responsible for maintenance, had to clean out periodically. I think it smells of rot; of course it probably doesn't since the last time anyone ate at Chez Dakhma was the 1970s, but I'll bet you could find a finger bone or two if you looked hard enough.

The German biker and I sit off the edge dangling our legs and look at the city as the blue of the evening replaces the afternoon's red before fading away. I bring up the fact that Iranians and Indians called themselves Aryans long before Germans did and he tells me some Germans actually come to Iran looking for connections to that Aryan past. We start talking about Hitler and he tells me that everything is ultimately good, even the existence of Hitler, because nature creates balance and Hitler's life has given humankind a solid reason to produce better people.

Now we know where we went wrong and how to be better so that we never create another one like him. We are aware now of how depraved men can be and can remain more vigilant about ourselves.

We talk until we become silhouettes and then three people, a woman and two men, whom we had seen fiddling with a camera and sound equipment earlier, position themselves against a good backdrop of the city as the woman, in deliberate silhouette, begins playing something that sounds like a brass instrument. It's a clarinet and the tune is haunting and woeful. They film this and we all experience it in silence, transfixed by the perfect symmetry between the music, the dakhma and the dying light in the sky. Fade to black as the girl plays on in the complete darkness and it's hard to imagine a more cinematic ending to a perfect day. We return to Silk Road in a taxi, I manage to stitch together a conversation with the cabbie as we drive back to the ancient city, which can convincingly live up to its claim of being one of the oldest constantly inhabited places on earth—and I've seen quite a few claimants already.

Back at the hotel we bump, or rather collide into Jemimah, a refreshing but obnoxiously Australian layabout who's been hanging around Iran for seven months, working here and there, and at Silk Road at times. She carries herself with some authority and it becomes clear why soon enough—she's married to Ballal, a relative of one of the owners. Ballal comes off as an unlikable sort at first—cynical, sarcastic and quite rude—but in the end seems to have his heart in the right place. He's lanky with big, curly hair and a dry sense of humour. Jemimah explains how she could get no respect as a girlfriend, and couldn't have any sex really, so a *muta'a* wedding was the only way to go and it changed everything. *Muta'a* is an Iranian Shia invention, which doesn't seem to exist in other Shia traditions and it certainly doesn't exist in a Sunni context. It allows for marriages that can be set for a fixed term, for a fixed sum, for the sole purpose of temporary companionship. It's an odd way around the issue of pre and post-marital sex, and is a great way for everyone to get laid without anyone getting stoned to death.

I spend a few days at Yazd lazily, mostly in the courtyard of Silk Road, or walking through the endless passages of the old city. Occasionally, I pop my head into the back of *shonpapri* shops to see the stuff existing in its preparatory candyfloss-like state, or pause at *chaikhanehs* for a smoke and some tea. An entire city lies inside these passages, briefly coming out into gardens and squares, before going into the shade again. It's sparsely populated and like most of Iran, almost completely shuts down between 12:30 pm and 3:30 pm, the hottest hours of the day. I have lots of great conversations in Yazd. Once, Sana and I go out to have lunch and talk about religions, coming to the inevitable conclusion that they are all fervently, and fundamentally alike. Sana says she's suspicious of religions and I try to decide whether I'm for them or not, and then she adds this,

But this much is certainly true about religion—it reminds people about the fact that there is a great cosmos around them, in which they are just a tiny speck, which is a valuable truth to carry around, and also about the endless nature of consequence from all actions, good and bad. Whether it's called Karma or Heaven is irrelevant; what's important is that it alludes to infinity and consequence. These can't be bad things.

Sana calls herself agnostic, but I doubt even an Imam could have made a more convincing case for religion. For such a beautiful girl, Sana is remarkably down to earth. She could easily have been a delicate diva, but instead she's rugged and road-hungry, and delights in dreaming of places she might go to if she doesn't go to Jordan. She says her grandfather once told her that we need no more material than our undershirts and should live just as lightly. So she does, not quite as lightly, but she's giving it a go.

I also finally discover Persian cuisine and it's quite good actually. It has subtle flavours, very different from the hard-hitting Indian ones and is more delicate overall. Silk Road Hotel has a great kitchen, so one night I enjoy a barley, bean and chicken stew. Another day I have a camel and potato curry, and then there's *fesenjun*—meat balls cooked with a paste of pomegranate and walnuts. It has a sweet and bitter aftertaste with a grainy texture. Quite delicious. Their breads are nice too.

I sleep in the dorm, which is below ground level, and wake up to the sound of people talking around and above me. It's an ensconcing feeling and I enjoy the energy that fills the courtyard everyday as backpackers, tourists, businessmen, archaeology enthusiasts and a range of other travelling sorts come in for chai, some food, or some *qalyan*, sitting on a colourful divan under the shade of bougainvillea trees. After breakfast together, Yves and Martin the Dutch Rastafarian head off, literally on the spur of the moment, to intercept a bus at an intersection on the highway and take it into the desert where they will be able to meditate, or, if they feel like it, go to a desert rave that kids from Tehran put together annually. I decide to stick around in Yazd and promise to catch up with Yves again in Esfahan a few days later, but we never meet again in Iran.

I hang around with other guests at Silk Road, on rooftops in old Yazd, taking in amazing views of the plateau and the domed houses that look baked and fired in the scorching sun. The *badgirs*, tile-worked *iwans* and alleys of the city all squash up along the mountains, as though looking for shelter. During a lunch at a local restaurant in Amir Chakhmaq Square, I notice that Iranians don't eat as much meat as Pakistanis or Afghanis, or at least don't eat it by itself as much. I later discover that it's because of a Persian nutritional science that recommends combining food groups classified either as hot or cold, but not the way we are used to thinking of them. For example, animal fat, poultry, wheat, sugar, certain fresh fruits and vegetables and all dried ones are considered hot. Beef, fish, rice, dairy products, certain other fresh fruits and vegetables are cold. So a dish like say *fesenjun* containing walnuts, a hot food, will also contain pomegranate, a cold food. Taken to its perfection, a properly planned meal will account for the nature of the people consuming it, the season and even ailments, when combining the two types of foods. To say this is a uniquely Persian science is a bit incorrect. It was adapted in Persia by, among others, the brilliant polymath Ibn Sina, from Greek writings which attributed illness to an imbalance in the body between opposing qualities, like heat and cold or wetness and dryness.

Yazd is a safe, secluded little town that has unbroken ways of living stretching back at least 5,000 years, to the Median city called Issatis. It's a rare phenomenon in a country that has witnessed numerous interruptions to its indigenous trajectory, but being in the desert, it managed to weather both a western wave from Arabia and an eastern wave from Mongolia, to become something of a haven for people fleeing both. Marco Polo described it as being 'seven days from Kerman by horse and out of the way of everything'. Its isolation also made it ideal for Zoroastrians, who managed to protect their religion here, and for a tax, were allowed to continue to practise it freely even after the Arabs had Islamised most of Iran. To a lesser extent this was true of Kerman as well, but Yazd became the centre for the faith and Zoroastrians from other provinces moved here to be able to retain their way of life. Its Fire Temple, though built in the 1930s with money from the Indian Parsi community, holds a flame that has been kept alight continuously since 470 AD, but not continuously at this location, of course.

The influence of Zoroastrianism on the religions of the Middle East is one of theology's great untold stories. Some consider it to be the first of the world's Prophet-driven, monotheistic religions and the original ancestor of the Abrahamic faiths—concepts such as a cosmic struggle between right and wrong, the superiority of ethical choice, monotheism itself, the judgement of every individual after death and the final triumph of good at the end of time, are all supposed to have been first introduced to mankind through Zoroastrianism. The British scholar Mary Boyce, a leading authority on the faith is quoted as saying,

Zoroastrianism is the oldest of the revealed world-religions, and it has probably had more influence on mankind, directly and indirectly, than any other single faith.

The problem is, it's difficult to ascertain when that was exactly. Just like Hinduism, its origins are lost in time and the slightly eccentric if not utterly insane Annie Besant suggested that Zoroaster, along with the Hindu prophet Manu, belonged to some Great Lodge and were taught by the primordial Sons of Fire, more than tens of thousands of years ago. The more sober options include 6350 BC according to the Greeks, between 1767 BC and 600 BC according to Persian writings, and between 1500 and 1200 BC according to more modern scholars. Like many Hindu characters, Zoroaster has become both a mythical as well as an historical figure and the whereabouts of his birthplace are also subject to speculation and controversy.

According to the Avesta, Zoroastrianism's holy book, Zoroaster or Zarthosht as he's called in Farsi, received a vision from Ahura Mazda or God, and was instructed to preach the truth, which is that man must choose sides in the cosmic battle between Ahura Mazda, the God of Light, and Ahriman, the principle of evil. It's a forgone conclusion that Light will win, mankind just has to choose correctly or suffer as a result of being far from God. This choice is manifested as the promotion of truth, *asa*, over lies, *druj*, and is made by thinking good thoughts, saying good words, and doing good deeds. By increasing this divine force of truth in the world and in ourselves we assist in the restoration of the world to its perfect state called *frashokereti*.

The law of Asa, or Asha, is 'rightness', the virtues by which all things become what they should be, and the daily Zoroastrian prayer, called the Ashem Vohu, is basically this,

Righteousness is the highest virtue. Happiness to him who is righteous for the sake of righteousness.

It's beautiful and simple and just about the best approach to truthfulness there is, and even though Zoroastrianism has a complex cosmology, with several larger and smaller deities serving Ahura Mazda as well as book-loads of rituals, it revolves around these three very simple principles: *Humata*, good thoughts, *Hukahta*, good words, and *Hvarshta*, good deeds. Expanding on that in the Mumbai-based publication the *Parsi Times*, a certain Dr. Ramiyar P. Karanjia explains what this means as a faith.

Humata should not be perceived as a stray good thought practiced at will and convenience. It has to be a permanent state of mind. Hukahta is the goodness and sweetness of tongue which should be a life long companion and not just to be used at one's convenience. Hvarshta is a uniform attitude of goodness and benevolence to all, and not an isolated act.

Zoroaster is said to have composed the *Yasna Haptanghaiti* and the *Gathas*, liturgical hymns familiarly named mantras, which form the oldest parts of the Avesta and are in a language remarkably similar to Sanskrit. In fact, according to Mary Boyce, Zoroaster may have created a rift regarding two sets of deities and driven a wedge between people who had once considered themselves a single community. The event is mentioned in both the Avesta and the Rig Veda, as a religious war between supporters of the *Devas*, or *Daevas*, and supporters of the *Asuras*, or *Ahuras*, resulting in a permanent split between the Vedic-Aryans of northern India and the Avestani-Aryans of Iran. The two sets of gods were originally colleagues and both Devas and Ahuras were worshipped by everyone, perhaps all the way from the kingdom of Mitanni, between Turkey and Syria, in the west to the countries of Airyana Vaeja and Arya Varta (which might have been the same place referred to in different dialects) in the east. But over time these gods began to fight, caused sometimes by deception, other times by jealousy, until they weren't friends anymore but enemies with genocidal intent.

When Zoroaster arrives on the scene, the *Daevas* are in the ascendant, spreading dishonesty, greed and lawlessness among their followers, prompting the Prophet to declare,

All you Daeva are the progeny of wicked thoughts.

One Daeva in particular, Indra, is singled out for rebuke in the Avesta while in the Rig Veda he is lauded as a hero, as are all the Devas, illustrating the irreconcilable differences in perspective between the Indian and the Iranian telling of the same story. Zoroaster attempts to restore virtue and righteousness and in the process starts a war that leads to one group leaving the community and migrating out to new lands. It's not clear which group won so it's hard to tell if the Indians left Iran or the Iranians left India, or if they both left some place in Afghanistan and moved east and west. It seems likelier that the Indians won, since the Battle of the Ten Kings in the Rig Veda talks about how the Bharatas, with the help of Indra, triumphed over his opponents, one of whom were the Parsu, or Persians. No corresponding tale exists in the Avesta, however, to corroborate this. Either way, the people of the *Ahuras* and the people of the *Devas* no longer lived together after this point and formed separate societies based on their respective, inverted convictions about what is good and what is evil.

A significant difference between the Iranian and Indian versions of the Aryan fallout is Zoroaster's adherence to an uncompromising monotheism. He announces that all other deities that claim to be omnipotent beings are liars and counterfeit gods and that the unseen, non-anthropomorphic, all-powerful Mazda, who created everything by just thinking of it is God, and He alone is God. Mazda, which mean's 'wisdom' in old Persian is most likely *medha* in Sanskrit, a word we still use in Bangla to mean 'intelligent'.

Zoroaster's campaign against polytheism is mentioned in the *Shahnameh* as well and the chapter opens with the following lines,

> *I've said preceding sovereigns worshipped God*
> *By whom their crowns were given*
> *To protect the people from oppressors.*
> *God they served, acknowledging God's goodness—*
> *For to God, the pure, unchangeable, the Holy One!*
> *They owed their greatness and their earthly power.*
> *But after times,*
> *Worship of God gave way to idolatry and pagan faith,*
> *And then Mazda's name was lost*
> *In adoration of created things.*

Sana and I visit the fire temple at Yazd one afternoon. It's quite nondescript until you go through the gates where you discover a large pool of water in the centre of the compound. Behind it, a single-storeyed building with elegant columns sports a large Faravahar on its forehead along with a plaque that tells me it was paid for by Indian Parsis. Zoroastrianism is experiencing something of a revival in Iran and, more and more, Parsis around the world are coming back to visit or are sending money to support their co-religionists here, whose numbers are slowly growing. It's very encouraging. The temple, or Atesh Kadeh as it is called for the fire, or *atesh*, it houses, is empty except for the 1,500-year old flame that's burning in a large chalice-shaped burner behind glass. It feels like a living presence and I almost want to greet it as I enter.

Zoroastrians are mistakenly called fire worshippers but fire only serves a symbolic purpose in their faith, representing the creative energy of Mazda. In Zoroastrian scriptures, God is described as 'full of lustre, full of glory', and things like fire, the sun, and the stars are regarded as proof of the divine and of the inner light. That light is also the divine spark within each of us—what we might call *noor* in Islam. It also stands for illumination, for an enlightened mind. Iranians have an affinity to fire in general, and their Nowruz celebrations involve a ceremony called Chaharshanbeh Surior Red Wednesday, where people jump over fires singing '*zardiye man az toh, sorkhiye toh az man—my yellow is yours, your red is mine*', to mean they desire the vitality and the redness of the fire and to be relieved of their pallor and sickness. Chaharshanbeh, Wednesday, literally means Day Four because Iranian names for the days of the week are just numbers. The week starts with Shanbeh, which is Saturday, and then Yek-Shanbeh, Do-Shanbeh, Se-Shanbeh, Chahar-Shanbeh, Panj-Shanbeh and the entirely out of place Jomeh, for Friday, taken from the Arabic Jummah. Arabs are similarly unimaginative with their day names and also simply number them. It makes me laugh every time I hear it.

There are framed posters in English and Farsi on the walls of the Atesh Kadeh with the sayings of Zoroaster from the Avesta and I read through some of them before leaving.

O God of life and creation, may we be sincere servants of yours like those who make the world renewed. May we enjoy your help through Asha, so that whenever our minds waver in doubt, our hearts and thoughts may turn to you.

The pure minded and the righteous man, O Ahura Mazda, whose soul is in harmony with Truth, thinks of You alone and dedicated his good actions to You. O Ahura Mazda, may we approach You, praising You and singing Your songs.

The wise man, through love and faith towards God, shall teach evil doers and those who have gone astray, good action and Love. Ultimately all wicked people, by learning the Truth, shall come towards you, O Mazda Ahura.

And this prayer:

Upto the end of my life, I will adhere in my mind to good thoughts, I will adhere in my speech to good words, I will adhere in my actions to good deeds; I will adhere to a good God-worshipping religion. I agree to be one with all righteous deeds. I agree to be opposed to all sinful deeds. I will be grateful for all the good I receive and I will remain contented in the midst of all trouble that may come to me.

One night, I meet an interesting person called Vincent, a very short German manboy, with delicate features and fine hair. He's a museum curator, and has taken his annual leave to try and see Iran and Pakistan by land. He wants to know about the border and I tell him what I've seen and what I've heard but he's decided he's going to do it anyway. We talk about a number of other things this very refined and highly cultured man appreciates, and he teaches me things about the history of the German people, about languages and art, and about Central Asia, which is his area of study. I take a great liking to Vincent; we talk into the evening, and I try to impress upon him the importance of putting his safety first, if he is indeed going to take the bus into Pakistan. He leaves for Kerman the next morning and I've never heard from him since. Another night, Jemimah and Ballal invite me to smoke hash with them. I go to their apartment and smoke bucket bongs of some very good Afghan Black, then stagger back to the hotel under dim streetlights singing Baul songs loudly and off-key with made-up lyrics.

During one of the afternoons at Silk Road, I get into a very engaging conversation with Sami the Afghan. Sami hangs around the hotel often; he's friends with Ballal and so comes for the company, and possibly also for work. He looks South Asian and at first I'm sure he's Indian but then we start talking and he tells me about Afghanistan and how his family fled from the Taliban to live in Iran. He's a masseuse, a Sunni and a refugee, and says that the authorities here persecute him on all three counts. He's part of a growing refugee concern for Iran, exacerbated by the US colonial enterprises on either side of it, which causes a demographic imprint and puts economic strains on the country. Add to that your garden-variety xenophobia and you get profiling, marginalisation, racism—the works.

Sami attests to being mistreated regularly, and has even had his hopes of leaving to study in Germany dashed by bureaucratic hurdles that won't allow him a travel permit. All in all, I feel very sad for him and it suspends my appreciation of an Iran that I had thought would have put a premium on social justice. But Sami lays it on thick too. He likes to conjure up stories about being manhandled by the police because they think he's gay for being a masseuse, and other scandalous, sensational stories until Jemimah tells me that he's a compulsive storyteller, i.e., a fibber. But there must be grains of truth in what he's experienced and the fact that he's clearly quite a disturbed individual must have plenty to do with what he's had to go through in life. I like him; he reminds me of home for some reason.

Sana leaves for Shiraz. I feel sad, because we became close and I spent much of my time in Yazd with her. Managing this heavy emotion, which occurs repeatedly in this sort of living, is another part of the Jedi training of travel. It hurts slightly, and leaves you with an empty feeling of loss after the fullness of spontaneous bonding with complete strangers. Those bonds also nourish a mutual need for family and familiarity, something that becomes very valuable when you are on the road alone. With Yves and Sana both gone, I feel like it's time to move on.

As I ready my bag, I see a dreadlocked, bearded person at the next bunk doing the same, so we start talking. He's Italian and called Marco, but I refrain from asking the inevitable 'Polo?' as he must've heard it a sickening number of times, travelling as he is, in Iran. He works in West Africa for an NGO dealing with indigenous rights and is just going to spend a couple of weeks here, before heading back to work. He loves Iran, especially its women, and is in complete bliss when he talks about them. We have breakfast together and he tells me how his fascination with Ancient Persia and its relationship to Ancient Rome brought him here. He's come from Esfahan and tells me, in a thick Italian accent, two very contradictory stories about the place—one involves him kissing an Iranian woman under a bridge, and another involves a Basij guard and a lewd comment.

Two girls are walking by, right, and this guy comes out of the shadows and up to one of the girls, and whispers something in her ear. I was walking around nearby, and hear the girl scream something in

277

Farsi, suddenly a man comes out of the crowd grabs the startled boy, and identifies himself as a Basij guard. First a slap, then questions. He asks the girl what happened she says something, he looks at the boy, he nods to confirm, another slap. He asks her if she wants to press charges, she appears to say no, and then he takes the boy up to the girl and makes him apologise, and then he tells the women to carry on, while he keeps talking with the boy.

In the afternoon, we head to the bus station together to try and go to Shiraz, but find that all the buses are going full; it's a long weekend and lots of people are catching the evening trips. We can't get two seats to Shiraz on any of them. The best they can offer us are two inverted buckets in the aisles, which Marco considers taking but I refuse to. After a while Marco gets a proper seat and takes it and I decide I'll go to Esfahan instead since I haven't been there yet and there are seats available on the 2 am bus, so we part ways. I wait in the lounge for four hours and drink perhaps five cups of coffee to stay awake, then board the bus.

Esfahan

It's dawn when I arrive at Esfahan, and it's colder here than it was at Yazd. I get out and fumble with the Lonely Planet guide to try to use the map and get a sense of where I am in relation to the Imam Square, which is where I want to be. I'm half asleep, need to pee and need a coffee. A cute girl with a nice smile comes up to me and says,

'Excuse me mister, are you in Esfahan for the first time? I can help you. I saw you get on in Yazd. Where do you want to go?'

This is an odd moment because I don't know if I'm supposed to receive help, as a single male, from a single Iranian female. In fact, I don't know if I'm even allowed to talk to her and become slightly dumbfounded. This must have been written on my face because she quickly mentions her brother, whom she's travelling with. Somayeh, who wears a black headscarf and speaks decent English, asks me to follow her and to do as she does. First we meet the brother, who's in the Iranian army, and then we work out where I should stay near the Square. We go to a bus counter, where she buys me a 'touch and go' card, and before I can even offer to pay her back we are in the queue getting into a bus and then are on our way. In the bus I ask her how much I owe her but she tips her head back while simultaneously throwing her right hand up, palm out and fingers pointing upwards, so that her head and hand are tilting together, almost at the same angle. This is Iranian body language for 'don't worry about it'.

I chat with her brother and he tells me about the mandatory military service all young men here have to do, which lasts for 18 months. He did it too before deciding to join the regular army and tells me about his job and his base. He speaks little English but we can understand each other. Somayeh is a graphic designer who works freelance for foreign clients as well. I think perhaps they are going this way too and will tell me when to get off so I don't ask any more questions about where we are and just enjoy their very pleasant company. We travel for about 30 minutes before I ask Somayeh if this is the way to her home and she laughs quietly before telling me they're taking me to my hotel! I'm mortified and insist that they stop this nonsense immediately and let me feel no more obligated than I already do, to which she just gesticulates 'relax, it's no problem at all', and almost forbids me to protest. Iranians are impossible, but this is over the top.

We get to the Si-o-Se Pol Bridge over Zayandeh-Rood, which literally means the 'River of Life' and get off at the roundabout there. On the way I notice a lot of side streets with cobbled floors and small arched bridges, a bit like the ones over dykes in Amsterdam. The area is old, and has a Middle Ages urban-space-set-in-stone sort of charm to it. The Si-o-Se Pol (or Thirty-Three Pole, meaning arches) Bridge is also made of solid stonemasonry and bestrides Central Iran's only river to speak of, and you wouldn't be able to speak much of it since it's nearly dry and quite narrow to begin with. Still, it's enough to support one of the grandest settlements in West Asia, a city vain enough to call a part of itself the world's beauty spot, or the Naqsh-e Jahan and Iran's most celebrated place.

Somayeh and her brother take me to the hotel. She tells the receptionist in Farsi to look after me and then hands me her card and asks me to call her if I need anything. She works around the corner, she says, and I feel a bit relieved so I ask her if she'll go to work from here, but she says she would have gone home to get ready first, but there isn't time for that anymore, so she might go after lunch. I'm at a total loss—maybe there's some secret way that Persians know who's been shown hospitality before, and then try to outdo the last person that showed it.

I don't like the receptionist; he smiles little and the hotel is old, but it's within my budget and has a nice breakfast hall, overlooking the roundabout. I have some chai and take a shower before heading off towards the Naqsh-e Jahan, or Imam Square, stoked by the fact that I'm staying so close to it. I walk away from the bridge and along an old tree-lined, park-benched boulevard, called the Chahar Bagh. The road is divided by a wide central reservation, which doubles as a small park. There are water fountains and public toilets on it. This is standard in all Iranian cities—good parks, public toilets and drinking fountains. I walk past a walled space with a beautiful dome over it and then find myself in a large park with walking tracks running through it. I follow these tracks past a number of old structures, variously labelled as part of the Safavid palace until I see the Square in front of me.

Perhaps I was expecting it to hover slightly above the ground shimmering, and like a model in 3D Studio Max, swivel around to show off its best bits. I think I also thought there would be Persian Opera playing, while a 15th-century Safavid counterpart of Mughal Emperor Akbar or Henry IV of France danced in the middle of the square in utter abandon, attended by effete sycophants. Maybe they would be holding a durbar somewhere in the open air maidan—jugglers, jesters and performers would be on hand to keep the place lively. Safavid splendour would require the place to be fully carpeted and gold inlays in the doors and arches would glimmer. After all the glamour and hype that's been lavished upon it, I had imagined it to look entirely out of this world.

But it doesn't. It's very much in this world and in the present, with all the signs of 21st-century living. Initially, you don't really know when you're in the Square because it's massive and the shops don't look very different from an old market anywhere else in Iran. But then you look around a little and you see a pool and fountain in the middle, some more shops across the yard, and then you see that the yard seems to carry on forever—you see street lights on what looks like walking paths but are actually three-lane city roads and far in the distance an *iwan* can be spied, then you realise that the entire area is a single, enclosed complex which is about as large as a small neighbourhood. After that, it becomes quite super.

The Naqsh-e-Jahan Square is 86,000 square metres in area, but isn't a square at all and is very much a rectangle, nearly five times as long as it is wide. The Safavid Shah Abbas had it built when he moved his capital to Esfahan during the early 1600s. It's truly an enormous space unlike any I've seen before. There are two-storeyed rows of shops along the boundary where all the goods of the entire Silk Road used to end up and in perfect Persian symmetry there are four structures set in the middle of each side, facing each other. Two are mosques, one is a palace and the other is a gate. It was designed by Baha al-Din al-Amili, another Persian polymath who is also one of the founders of the Esfahani School of Islamic thought, a philosophy cultivated by the Safavids to try and bring about a cultural revival in the post-Mongol Islamic world, but which didn't flourish as well as they might have hoped it would.

The Safavids were game-changers in many other ways; in fact the building of Esfahan was essentially a statement of power before they dissolved provincial authority and limited the reach of the military. They also established Shia Islam as the state religion of a previously Sunni Iran, a legacy that defines Iran's character as much as the Farsi language does. The dynasty occupied the throne during an especially productive period in global imperialism and it might not be too much of a stretch to say that the world we live in today began exactly then. Mongol supremacy was receding and new international configurations were in the offing. The Turkish Ottoman

Empire, already well established by the 1500s, was on the ascendant. The Mughal Empire had captured India. A fledgling British Empire was finding its feet in the New World. The Spanish and Portuguese Empires were colonising the Americas and the Ming Dynasty in China was in bloom, having shaken off Yuan overlordship a century earlier. In Iran, the Safavids managed to create the country's most robust domestic empire since before the Arab invasion, and their greatest ruler, Shah Abbas, created this city as a testament to both his power and to the considerable heights of his taste.

I walk in through the western entrance and head towards the Imam or Shah Mosque to my right. Like many other structures around the country, it's being restored and the *iwan* is covered with blue tarpaulin sheets as well as scaffolding. But even with its bandages I can see just how spectacular it is. The mosaic work is absolute— every inch of surface of the *iwan* and the semi-circular portal it sits in is decorated with tiles and calligraphy and is more colourful than others I've seen like it elsewhere. The design uses larger, seven-colour tiles, which is considered less elegant than the more painstaking method of creating mosaics with bits of single-coloured ones but it's quicker and the Shah wanted it to be completed during his lifetime. I think it looks splendid enough. There are two large minars on either side of the *iwan* and stalactite or honeycombing tilework on the ceiling. The mosque behind it sits at an angle to face Mecca as the square isn't set on the East-West axis but on the North-South one, probably a deliberate design, to allow the smaller inner courtyard, with a four-*iwan* layout, to be visible from the palace and the maidan. It also gives it more dimensions, since you can see the mosque from its side, making it look less ordinary. Only the main structures are decorated, with much of the compound still brown and earthen. Even the mosque looks like it's made of mud-brick, as just the facade and dome are colourfully tiled. I'm not sure if this unfinished look is deliberate or if it was simply a question of funds, but it makes for a striking contrast. Personally, I think a coat of blue all around would have done wonders for it, but then I'm no Baha al-Din al-Amili.

There is a set of stairs in front of the *iwan*, which sits on a raised platform, and I climb onto it to look across the maidan. People are sitting on the grass in various places; some are on benches, others on the walls of the elevated walkway. Gardeners tend to the bushes and horse-drawn carriages clip-clop along the bitumen track that runs around the square, taking tourists and lovers on rides. There's an old marble goalpost at the end of the maidan for times when polo was played here, usually during special occasions like Nowruz, the Persian New Year. At other times the square would be abuzz with markets and food stalls during the day, and with mystics and courtesans in the evening. It must've been a fabulous place back then and is still quite special, even if it's more PG-13 these days. I decide to stroll through the markets along the boundary (not the bazaar at the northern end of the square) where I find shops selling items like carpets, paintings, carvings, metalwork, furniture, tiles, photographs, wall hangings and an assortment of other articles intended as gifts.

At one of the carpet shops, I meet Mahdi, a young man perhaps in his mid-20s, who tries to convince me to step in and have a look at his wares. I tell him I haven't come to shop today but will certainly come back another time. Like most Iranians, he's not pushy at all and nods graciously before offering me some tea. I accept, and we go outside to drink it. Mahdi speaks perfect English and is used to foreigners; he tells me most of Esfahan is, since it's a tourist destination and it's also the only place in Iran where you can still use a credit card. US sanctions make its virtually impossible for international financial institutions to operate here but other than that, they don't seem to matter much. Still, Iran's isolation, which both the Islamic regime and the international community go to great lengths to maintain, makes the people here desperate for external contact as well as a chance to be understood. People always want to engage you to speak a bit of English and to tell you about Iran and its culture. It's very lovely but a bit heartbreaking at the same time.

There's a poster of Ayatollah Khomeini in the square and Mahdi points towards it to ask me if I know who it is. I tell him I do and he says,

'But do you know that he's our father?'

Sure, why not, Father of the Nation, I suppose. But Mahdi protests, clearly that's not what he meant and I think perhaps he's even more devoted to the old man than I'm being able to appreciate.

'No, no he is our real father! Do you know why?'

'Why?'

'Because in just one night, he fucked all our mothers.'

We go on to talk about how the 'Mullah Regime' is choking the life out of a Persian society that is naturally playful and progressive and entirely unlike the sombre edifice that the Ayatollahs would like it to become. He seems particularly upset by how the women have suffered in the process, and brings up the issue of *mut'aa* marriages.

'Do you want an Iranian woman to keep you company while you travel? Beautiful women, so sexy, so lovely. It's so easy—an Iranian woman has no honour, she only has a price. You can buy her, just give her family some money and then when you are finished, return her. Some people do *mut'aa* for a week, for a day, even for a night. It's legalised prostitution and you don't even have to be prostitute to play. Every woman is available. This, my brother, this is the Islam Way, didn't you know?'

We're joined by his friend Salman, who also has lots to say about the regime and begins by telling us that it's like an old-fashioned telephone stuck up Iran's arse—painful on the way in and impossible to take out. We have lively discussions about the differences between religion and culture and about how this harsh version of Islam is unlike the natural Persian temperament, which is softer and more accommodating. I tell them we have similar problems in Bangladesh, as Salman laments about how the government is more interested in religion than the economy. We continue talking and I become pleasantly surprised to discover that Iranians struggle with questions of identity too, especially since, in South Asia, we're used to thinking of Iranian society as being perfectly wedded to its Islamic orientation. Not so, evidently.

At some point I begin to feel hungry and there's a very interesting looking restaurant in the market, so I decide to grab a meal there.

It's a traditional Iranian restaurant called Bastani and the décor, music and furniture keep perfect pace with the historical sophistication of Naqsh-e Jahan. It also has a retractable roof, which is very high-tech but doesn't look as out of place as you might expect. I ask for a Coke and some olives and am going through the menu when I see an exceptionally beautiful woman walk up to the dining area, and then I can't seem to do anything else but stare at her. She stares back and comes towards me, sending my heart completely aflutter.

'Hello! Are you being looked after? How was your meal? Is there anything we can do for you?'

Oh, she works here and I'm just a customer. Slightly deflated, I tell her I haven't ordered yet, but maybe she could suggest something as I'm a little out of my depth. She sits beside me on the divan and starts listing off items, but I can hardly hear anything because she smells amazing and her light-brown skin glows, most distractingly, in the sunlight. I manage to order something in between asking her questions about herself; it's her father's restaurant, she's a dentist, she speaks more French than English, she studied in Ukraine, she's applying for post-graduate studies in America, she's gorgeous. Our cosy conversation becomes conspicuous and the waiters begin to whisper, so she gets up and excuses herself to attend to other patrons. My meal comes, I thoroughly enjoy it and when I call for the bill, she intercepts the waiter to bring it over herself. I ask her if she's married; she isn't, she tells me with a suggestive smile. I tell her a little about myself and once again the whispers begin so we break it off and as I'm leaving she tells me, looking me dead in the eyes, 'be sure to take the bill with you'. I do and when I look at it I find her name, number and email address scribbled on the back. Nicely played, Mahsa Maksabi.

I wander around the square for a bit. It's late afternoon going on evening, and the families are out in full force. People walk around the track, sit in the gardens, picnic, smoke, shop, talk, play football and volleyball and populate the place with their leisurely selves. A group of students from an art or architecture class are sitting in front of the *iwan* with their sketch pads out, as their teacher instructs them to copy the structure and pay attention to its vaulting. Most exciting are the cycle gangs—groups of boys on BMXes doing stunts like jumping off staircases, climbing onto structures, spinning around on their front wheels and pulling extreme wheelies. They're very impressive and if they had access to a skate park they could quite easily be contenders at the X games. In fact, I'm quite sure it's only a matter of time before they are. There are skaters too—rollerbladers and skateboarders—doing their own set of stunts in front of the mosque as the sun sets in Esfahan and throws an orange hue over the blue tiles.

I'm busily trying to photograph all this when a group of slightly nerdy looking schoolboys come up to me and start talking with me in English. They want to practise their language skills, they say, so I oblige them and we find a park bench to sit on and chat. They're history buffs too, like me, and tell me interesting things about Iran's pre-Islamic period, things like how it was a matriarchal society before the Arabs appeared. Like many others, they resent the Arabs for 'enslaving' Persia, as they put it, but seem to also thank them for introducing Islam into Iran. Just to be difficult I ask them if Zoroastrianism wasn't fine anyway, and that perhaps Persia didn't need another religion. They've clearly pondered this themselves, and bring up the Cyrus Cylinder—an edict issued by the great Cyrus, or Kurosh, the legendary Achaemenid King, which is widely recognised as the world's first Declaration of Human Rights. Kurosh was probably not Zoroastrian though, as Prophet Zarathustra may have existed after his time, but he was Iranian and that's the more relevant point.

I decide to be even more controversial and ask them why Shias worship the blood of Prophet Muhammad, thinking it safe to ask schoolboys this, as they probably won't try to assassinate me immediately after I do. I learn that they don't, in fact, but simply believe that spiritual leadership of the *Ummah* ought to be given by people who possess secret wisdom, passed down in the family from generation to generation, beginning with Imam Ali. They list the 12 descendent Imams for me and tell me how they were all persecuted and about why they differ from the Ismailis, popularly known as Aga Khanis, who follow a related but slightly different line of succession. I ask them about Imam Mahdi, the twelfth Imam who is said to have disappeared and gone into 'occultation' in the year 872 AD without dying, to return at the end of days. I ask how they believe it's possible that he is still alive, to which they confidently reply,

'You believe in Quran, yes? In the Quran Noah lived for nearly a thousand years, Abraham for much longer. Why can't an Imam live just as long if God wills it? They are all just mortal men after all.'

Compelling, but I don't fully buy it, and considering its 2011 now, he's lived a fair bit longer than Noah did, so I change the subject and ask them if they like the Islamic regime. They have mixed feelings about it, but remind me that autocratic government in Iran didn't begin with Khomeini because the Shah banned the hijab as passionately as the Ayatollahs enforce it, and that perhaps it's just an equal and opposite reaction. For a bunch of 16 year olds, they're incredibly switched on.

We talk about tons of other things until it gets dark and it's time to head back to the hotel. On the way I spot two girls I saw at the bus station in Yazd walking along the same road. They must've noticed me there too because they point at me so I wave at them. They wave back and we talk as we walk together towards our hotels, which are in the same direction. I enjoy their company and when we arrive at their hotel, I ask them if they would like to join me for tea somewhere. They agree and the three of us, Fatimeh, Najmeh and myself, head to the Si-o-Se Pol Bridge, to a charming little hangout under the bridge inside one of its 33 arches. It's bustling with young people and travellers and has a platform out over the water, though at the moment there's absolutely no water under it. Music plays, various little stalls serve food, drinks, tea and *qalyan*, and if this wasn't Iran it would be exactly the sort of place you'd come to get a cold beer or a nice glass of wine. I can't help but wonder if this is where Marco made out with that girl 'under the bridge'. It's likely because there are lots of dark little corners.

Najmeh and Fatimeh are Yazdis. They come to Esfahan twice a week to attend University and stay at a hotel when they are here. They're both studying to be nurses. We stay at the bridge for about an hour, and on the way back talk about Sufism, especially about the poet Hafez and how his writing is popular all over the world, including in Bangladesh. But Hafez means something entirely different to Iranians. They keep a collection of his poems beside their Qurans and turn to it for answers when life becomes existentially complex—and find them there too, apparently. Hafez is no ordinary poet here; he's a Seer and Najmeh decides that I must experience his incredible power, so when we get to their hotel, she goes up and gets her copy of his *Divan*, and we sit in a park on the Chahar Bagh to witness the magic.

Just as we're about to begin, two couples show up looking harrowed, with sleeping bags and blankets in their hands. They speak to the girls in Farsi and then leave, but I'm too curious and have to know what it was all about. Najmeh tells me they are from Shiraz (Hafez's town, coincidentally—or is it?) and are on holiday here but can't get a room, probably because no hotel trusts them not to criminally fornicate when everyone's asleep. They've decided to camp out somewhere and were asking Najmeh and Fatimeh if they know of a safe place in the area. They're quite young, in their early 20s or late teens, and look a lot like the kind of person I was and the kind of people I would have hung out with at that age. They also look stoned, just like I was for much of my 20s.

But back to Hafez. Najmeh says some sort of prayer and blows into the book, waves it around, and then puts it to her chest as she asks me to think about something that's troubling me. I can't think of much at the moment, but decide to settle on family and stability, and the question of whether I'll ever have either. She says another little prayer, blows into it again and then opens the book to a random page and begins reading. She recites the verse thunderously, heaping on generous helpings of gravitas but I understand none of it. The intonations stir me, but the words mean nothing at all. Najmeh is quite struck by their perfect resonance, though, because she's shaking her head as if to express utter disbelief at how accurate Hafez's diagnosis has been.

'You see? It's just amazing, isn't it?' she says, forgetting that it made about as much sense to me as a whale song does, but realises it when she sees the blank expression on my face.

'Ah, of course, you need English. But it's not the same. He's saying ....'

Something quite generic about happiness and companionship and a lot of other things that might make an appearance in a self-help book. It's not particularly profound or relevant, but the girls are convinced and so I play along and do my best awestruck look. Then Najmeh gives me a crash course in Farsi. She pulls out a page from her notebook and begins writing down words:

Tree = *Derakht;* Star = *Setara;* Generous = *Khasis;* Dirty = *Kasif;* Beautiful = *Zibalghashang;* Road = *Khiyoban;* Cold = *Sard;* Hot = *Garm*

We carry on until midnight and there's almost no one left on the streets. I walk them back to their hotel and they tell me that they have a bit of time tomorrow before they catch the bus back to Yazd, in case I want to hang out again. I'm not sure if that's *tawrouf* or a genuine offer, but I could use the company so do the courteous pillow-passing until it's my turn to accept it.

Day 39

Najmeh and Fatimaeh meet me outside my hotel and we head off on a walking tour of Esfahan. We pass through the old neighbourhoods around the Square where people are curious about my *Keshvar* and when I tell them to guess they list off 'Arabistan' and 'Pakistan' with traces of hostility but beam with delight when I say it's Bangladesh, which is, of course, understood as Hindustan—'Ah, Hindustan!' they say, with unconcealed relief. They like India in Iran, but don't particularly like Afghanistan or Pakistan, and think of them as outlying rogue territories. India, on the other hand, is a complete civilisation as far as they're concerned, or that's what my female companions tell me anyway. We go into the square to explore the Ali Qapu Palace, a multistoreyed pavilion where Safavid monarchs would entertain their guests in reception rooms and banquet halls. The rooms are themed according to their usage; decorations in the banquet hall resemble vessels and cups while the walls and ceiling of the music room feature motifs of musical instruments. From the wide, pillared upper galleries, the Safavid rulers watched horse races, army manoeuvres, Nowruz celebrations and public executions carried out in the Square below.

It's ferociously hot so we take refuge under the shade of trees in the garden, with the cool grass providing added relief. It's Friday and I can hear the congregation assembling inside the Imam Mosque. I want to join them but feel unsure about praying in *Jamaat* with people who will surely do it differently from the way I'm used to. Fatimeh notices this and says we should pray together in the garden instead. A blanket appears out of one of their bags, and we go to do our ablutions in the large fountain. Fatimeh asks me to watch her as she washes up the Shia way and tells me, quite confidently, that theirs is the proper way of doing it. She says that the Caliph Omar bin Khattab, reviled in Iran, changed the format for everything, including ablutions and prayer, and essentially buggered up Islam. She could be right because I have my own suspicions about Islamic formats, though I can't conclusively say who did the buggering. Her face scrunches up in contempt when she utters Omar's name, and I think she even washed her mouth a second time after saying it. She then gives me her *Mohr*, and says I should use it to pray since physical contact with clay has beneficial properties. I'm moved by the gesture, even if it is an attempt to convert me.

After prayers the girls leave, and I spend the rest of the afternoon exploring the gardens around the Hasht Behesht and the Chehel Sotoun—buildings that were once part of the Safavid Estate. All the gardens are full of people enjoying the open spaces with their families, something that has become a permanent fixture in my impressions of Iran, along with the sound of sunflower seeds being cracked open in mouths. In one of these gardens, a few elderly men sit on a bench harmonising with each other as they chant a prayer or a song, completely unfazed by the presence of passersby like myself. It's an uplifting sight. Flowerbeds line all the walking paths, and fountains full of water become illuminated with coloured lights after the sun goes down.

I go back to the Square and to Bastani Restaurant hoping to meet Mahsa again, but she isn't there so I go to the *chaikhaneh* nearby and smoke some *qalyan* as I write my journal. A tall, pretty girl comes and sits next to me and asks me what I'm doing. There's distress in her eyes and she also looks high on amphetamines. I offer her some *qalyan* and she tells me about a fashion business she has, and how she will be going to Pakistan soon to pick up fabrics. It sounds like a lie, and she looks like a made-up person. I can't quite understand why she's talking with me, but she seems to be asking for help somehow. That or she's trying to get me to take her to bed, for money. She asks for a piece of paper and draws a picture of the sun with a face on it, and tears rolling down its cheeks. She writes her name—Marjan—in both English and Farsi, and then 'Friends', 'Love me', 'Boy' and three telephone numbers. It smacks of an invitation for sex, but somehow I don't think it was. She looks troubled, generally, and a bit like someone trapped. She shakes my hand firmly for a long time, and then leaves. I never call any of those numbers, but I can't forget Marjan, and I hope she found what she was looking for.

I spend one more day in Esfahan and make arrangements to leave in the evening. I want to go to Shiraz but there isn't a train going until a couple of days later so I decide to go to Kashan in the meantime, four hours west of Esfahan, also by train. But before that I spend the day exploring the Chehel Sotoun, 'the 40 Columned', a Safavid reception hall or durbar where diplomats and foreign leaders were received before being taken to the Palace to meet with the Shah. Twenty massive wooden columns, looking as tall as the surrounding deciduous trees, dominate the front of the building, but unlike Mughal architecture, which occurs simultaneously, this design looks as though it wants to blend in rather than extend itself out of its environment and is far more organic in its orientation and construction material. Its aesthetic embellishments, however, are a world apart.

The walls are decorated with wallpaper-like arabesque designs and the ceiling of the veranda is covered in geometric patterns. The doorway to the main hall is done up with mirrors and the curved surface lets light reflect and bounce off every side, dazzling anyone who passes through it. Inside, lashings of gold paint gleam in the afternoon sun and gild the huge frescos that ornately depict Safavid foreign policy. Once again it's hard to tell European and Persian sensibilities apart—such an interior wouldn't look completely out of place in the Palace of Versailles during the 15th century, but the style of the artwork is entirely Iranian. In a hall with high ceilings and large, curtained windows, giant miniatures ('maxitures', really) tell the tales of Safavid martial exploits and their benevolent overlordship of surrounding nations—an extension of the age-old Achaemenid and Sassanian hegemonic worldview.

There's even, to my great discomfort, a mural of hateful old Nader Shah, who wasn't Safavid at all and perhaps had it commissioned after he returned victorious from India. It shows Nader Shah slashing his way through a teeming thicket of Mughal soldiers, his eyes fixated on Babur's descendant Muhammad Shah astride his white elephant—quite a contrast to the other one which shows Badshah Humayun, son of Babur the Mughal, sitting with Shah Tahmasp I receiving a royal welcome and refuge after being chased out of Indian by Sher Shah Suri, the Sultan of Bangala. Humayun is shown looking gaunt and forlorn, his arms limp and fallen helplessly by his side with palms turned up as he is fed and entertained by Tahmasp's entourage. He is dark-skinned and decisively Indian looking, and a rotund and rosy-cheeked Tahmasp sits beside him looking quite pleased with himself. The modern-day plaque describing the fresco tries to put a contemporary Shia-Sunni spin on Humayun's plight, suggesting that the Sunni Sher Shah was after Humayun because he was Shia. This is fanciful and probably rubbish since Humayun was Sunni until he was asked to become Shia during his time at Tahmsap's court.

The Safavids and the Mughals were allies and together with the Ottomans (with whom they weren't), formed the Gunpowder Empires, since they were among the first to use this powerful new substance as a weapon of war. In fact the Mughal Empire may never have even survived its second king if the Safavids hadn't come to their rescue. In the mid-1500s, when he was driven out of India altogether by Sher Shah Suri, the Afghan chieftain from Bihar, Humayun asked his rival the following question:

What justice is there in this? I have left you the whole of Hindustan. Leave Lahore alone, and let Sirhind, where you are, be a boundary between you and me.

To which Sher Shah very sarcastically replied,

I have left you Kabul. You should go there.

It was a Safavid-bolstered Mughal army with, according to some estimates, 12,000 of Shah Tahmsap's finest cavalrymen that returned to India and put Humayun back on his throne. It also brought with it a large contingent of Persian noblemen who changed the character of the Mughal court by infusing Central Asian Turkic culture with Persian influences, evident in the new styles of art and architecture, but most significantly in the new court language, which changed from Chagatai Turkic to Farsi. This 'Persianisation' was also accelerated by the fact that Humayun himself was deeply enamoured with all things Persian; the splendour of the Safavid realm had made a lasting impression on him and he was eager to emulate it.

There are other murals in the Chehel Sotoun of Uzbek and Turkish kings expressing obeisance or being overcome by a re-emerging Iranzamin, and in all fairness, the Safavids could quite legitimately claim to be the resurrection of Persian glory. They were beautiful builders, discerning patrons and effective rulers who were fond of the finer things in life, many of which are on display on the walls of their buildings. While looking at the murals I meet a Syrian gentleman who tells me a little about the rich history and archaeology of Syria. He's a doctor, a soft-spoken, polite man, and we talk about the conflict in his country, which has just begun. He believes it will die down soon and tells me it's not a natural experience for Syrian society where, according to him, more than 70 per cent of the people are educated professionals or agricultural-ists, and most are cultured and liberal. On my way out, I walk past the large pool outside the entrance where, reflected in the waters, the 20 pillars look like 40, giving the building its name.

I get some corn in a cup mixed with spices, pepper and mayon-naise, and walk around the neat and nicely laid out city. There's abundant greenery and nice pavements with drinking fountains every so many kilometres. Out of all the Iranian cites I've visited so far, this is certainly the prettiest. I walk past a government building and see yellow signs attached to its walls. I had seen similar signs on buildings in Yazd but hadn't read them there, so get a closer look. They're quotes from the Quran in both Farsi and English, which isn't unusual except there are many of them all around the structure and they look almost like large post-it notes. And like post-it notes, they carry short, vital reminders.

And be good and kind to the people as Allah has been Good
And do not be inquisitive about people's lives and do not backbite about one another
Oh mankind! What has made you so rude and arrogant towards your Creator, the Supremely Bounteous?
Give full measure and do not cause loss to the buyer by diminishing the weight of their goods
And this Quran that We reveal is a healing and grace
Speak nicely with people

I return to the Naqsh-e Jahan one last time where I meet a British couple from London and we chat about Iran, my journey, their lives in England, Empire, South Asia and some other things we have in common. They go away and I find a *chaikhaneh* to sit and drink something sweet and smoke something flavoured until its time to catch the train to Kashan.

Kashan

The train arrives at Kashan in the middle of the night, at about 2 am, and I feel a bit bothered by the thought of finding a bed at this hour since most places will probably be shut. The station is small and there is a waiting area with a guard and an attendant but hardly any passengers. The guard approaches me and speaks Farsi, presumably asking me where I'm going, and I manage to say I'm looking for a hotel, cheapish. He asks me to call a taxi, I tell him I have no way to, he tells me that I can use the yellow public phone, which is free for any local number in Iran. The taxi arrives and takes me to the nearest hotel where the receptionist has to be woken up before I can check in.

In the morning, I set off towards the centre of town to check out the 'historic houses' that Kashan is famous for. It looks like there's a school field trip underway at a building I walk past, called the 'Scientific Institute', and I stop to take in the excitable early morning chatter of children. Motorcycles, some named 'Simorgh', presumably after the character in Attar's *Conference of the Birds*, ply the streets or are left parked by the pavement. They are all under 200cc, since Iran, like Bangladesh and Pakistan, puts a limit on engine sizes. I've never understood why, but the logic seems to be that it allows the police to catch crooks on bikes. Things like these don't bother India, though, and you can quite comfortably find powerful 500cc Royal Enfields virtually everywhere and even 1200cc Harley Davidsons in major cities. Young Iranians like to ride their bikes fast and recklessly, and pulling a little wheelie before setting off is almost standard practice.

Unable to find them on foot, I stop a taxi and ask to be taken to the '*khun tarik*', or 'house history', which is terrible Farsi but it seems to work because he doesn't look puzzled at all and nods an acknowledgement. In the wonderful world of languages the word '*khun*' means three weirdly related things in three different tongues. In Farsi it's 'house', in Urdu it's 'blood' and in Bangla it's 'murder'. Similarly, '*tarik*' means 'history' in Farsi and a calendar date in Bangla. We drive past a very odd-looking tomb with a silly conical top that looks like Merlin's cap in the Disney cartoon, and the driver tells me its Pirouz Nahavandi's tomb. I later find out that Pirouz or Firoz Nahavandi is none other than the Persian who stabbed Omar bin Khattab, the second Caliph of Islam, to death, during dawn prayers in Medina. Pirouz killed Omar for not presiding over a wages dispute he was having with someone else, but it has often been suggested that the actual reason for his murderous contempt was Omar's conquest of Sassanid Persia. In the standard story, Pirouz stabs the Caliph and tries to flee but never manages to get anywhere near Kashan, killing himself shortly after killing Omar; however, an alternate ending has him evading his would-be captors and escaping to Iran where he is welcomed as a national hero. Many argue that this isn't Pirouz's tomb, but it doesn't matter very much since, regardless of where he's buried, Shia Iran will always be indebted to Pirouz for disposing of the much reviled Omar: usurper of the Caliphate, co-opter of Islam and enemy of Persia.

We ring a few roundabouts and reach a nondescript neighbourhood where I see a sign for Ehsan Guest House. The sign says it's a historic house and so I decide it's a good place to stop the cab. It's located opposite the Agha Bozorg Mosque or the 'Mr. Big' Mosque, which is unusually plain, with only selected parts decorated with ceramic tilework. Bits of Kashan resemble Yazd, particularly the desert architecture and feel. I walk into Ehsan Guest House and find a beautiful courtyard that has a large central pool with a fountain in it and divans spread out along the edges. There is shade and awnings made of thatch and wood; near them flowering trees play host to impatient birds that stop briefly on their way across an otherwise treeless landscape. It's not unlike Silk Road Hotel in Yazd, but larger and more open. I'm drawn to a lovely little shaded corner and park myself on the divan to listen to the sound that grumbling leaves make when they're being bullied by the breeze, a sound like rainsticks. I ask for some tea and relax; it's just after 12:30 pm and most of Iran will probably be doing the same.

Kashan's historic houses aren't very historic, and considering how ancient most of Iran is, it's a bit misleading. They were built in traditional Persian design during the Qajar period, for 18th- and 19th-century aristocratic families, and look both modern and classic instead of historic. Kashan was where the older Safavid aristocrats built their villas as well, but an earthquake in the 1700s destroyed much of their legacy. It's also, according to some people, where the three wise men of Bible fame set off from, on their way to meet a famously articulate baby. I go up to the receptionist at Ehsan Guest House to get some travel tips and find a beautiful dusky woman on duty. She suggests the Fin Garden and the Elamite ziggurat but those are in different parts of the town and it's unlikely I'll be able to see both in one afternoon. I choose the Elamite ziggurat and she calls a taxi to take me there. She has the sweetest way of saying '*baleh*' or 'yes' in Farsi and I can never get enough of these adorable Persian intonations.

Long before the Aryans—the Persians and the Medes—arrived and essentially colonised Iran, the kingdom of Elam flourished in southwestern Iran alongside the Mesopotamian states of Sumer and Akkadia. They called their country Haltamti and others sometimes called it Sushiana after their capital Susa—a name still used for the city under which it stood. A lot of conjecture exists about Elam and its cultural orientation—it might have been a Semitic civilisation but neighbouring Sumer wasn't and it's possible that Elam may not have been either. Some say it was related to India's Dravidian civilisation, others that it developed independently out of a yet undecipherable culture near Jiroft in Kerman. Whatever its origins, Elam exerted its influence over the Indo-European waves that swept through Iran long enough for Elamite to still be in use as an official language of Parsa, or Persepolis, during the peak of Achaemenid power—many centuries after the Aryans had already established themselves as the dominant people. They clearly mattered, and were part of an urbanised international order that included the Indus Valley Civilisation to its east and Pharaonic Egypt to its west.

I reach the outskirts of Kashan, to Sialk, where a set of steel gates open to reveal what looks like an enormous, oddly shaped pile of clay. A man on a white BMW motorcycle is preparing to leave and has just put his helmet on. His bike has an EU registration with the letters GR written next to it, telling me he's from Greece and has ridden from there. There's a small museum at the site too. The first thing I learn about the Sialk *tepe*, or mound, is that it may not be Elamite at all but something slightly older. I'm told it's over 9,000 years old, which means it's from the Stone Age and possibly part of the earliest version of a settled, agricultural community in the region. It was built by people who might have belonged to the hypothetical Zayandeh-Rood Civilisation, said to have sprung up around the river I saw in Esfahan, but since nothing has been found to prove this, it's only speculation so far. Either way it's very old, perhaps the oldest man-made structure I've ever seen.

Quite a bit of excavation has been done here so far and a wooden walkway has been laid out to prevent visitors from stomping all over the delicate and protected site. I clamber up to take in the stunning view from the top. It's late afternoon and like paint being washed off an artist's brush, the sky lets all the colours of the day run to create enormous abstract masterpieces splattered above the wind-swept desert. From here I can make out an outline of the structure I'm standing on. It was probably step pyramidal, similar to a zig-gurat, and had solid, defined walls that are still discernible. It was built in brick and covered with clay—unless the clay was deposited over the centuries. No one knows yet what it was used for or how long it was in use. The artefacts collected from it include the usual medley of things: pottery, bowls, animal bones, flints, tools, sculp-tures, household appliances—the lot. There are a few graves, too, which have been opened and preserved under glass, and when I peer into one of them I'm startled by the grisly sight of an ancient child's tiny skeleton, curled up in a foetal position.

The site museum has a range of items that give us a sense of who these people were. They certainly had aesthetic inclinations as everything is decorated and a number of beautiful terracotta reliefs have been uncovered, telling the story of their lives and times. Sculptures and busts of animals make an appearance too. The style and colours are reminiscent of African and Mycenaean art, and most things are dated to about 5000–6000 BC, meaning the site was used or inhabited for well over a thousand years. For people who lived thousands of years ago, their lives seem quite recognisable to me. The things they drew and used and, more importantly, the way they expressed themselves are not drastically different from our contemporary expression and I wonder if I would have found these people perfectly familiar had I met them on the street, somewhere in the Twilight Zone.

I head back to Ehsan Guest House, and back to the beautiful receptionist who tells me that they have free rooms in case I'm interested in staying. We haggle over the price until both of us are happy and after she hands me the key I tell her I'll have to go and get my stuff from the other place. A friend of hers, sitting with her at the reception, volunteers to take me there and back on his motorcycle. Spontaneous Iranian helpfulness to the rescue, and we're off on his bike through the narrow and crowded streets of Kashan, which remind me of many old neighbourhoods in Dhaka. I notice a festive atmosphere's in force tonight and fairy lights adorn homes and shrines together with coloured banners and flags. It feels a lot like Shab-e-Barat or Durga Puja in Bangladesh; people are out on the streets and the traffic has become impassably thick. I ask my companion what this is all about and he tells me it's the end of the Ten Days of Karam or Dignity that I learnt about in Mashhad, and also Imam Reza's birthday. A group of boys with broad grins come rushing towards us to distribute juice and cakes, and the occupants of vehicles in now standstill traffic beam back at them, just as pleased, honking their horns in celebration. Others are literally dancing on the streets. Glitter confetti is released into the air and falls over everything, giving the streets and the cars a colourful glossy shine.

My companion parks his bike to get a cup of juice and some cake for the two of us. He insists we eat it since it's good luck, and by his exulted tones I can tell that the carnival atmosphere has seeped into him—he's only a foot tap away from breaking into dance himself. I share in his joy, honoured to be included in it, and when the road becomes fluid again we're on our way. We return to Ehsan Guest House with my backpack. My room is on the second floor, over-looking the courtyard. It's a lovely little room with old furniture and a *badgir* for air-conditioning. There's a common balcony just out-side, and a Belgian man from the adjoining room is sitting there in his boots reading a guidebook. I take a shower and freshen up before going downstairs for dinner, and then wander around the house in the moonlight, serenaded by the sound of water rising and falling from a fountain into the pool in the centre of the courtyard.

Dasht-e Kavir

I want to experience the desert in full so put my departure to Shiraz back by a day and look for a way to spend the night in the Dasht-e Kavir, just outside Kashan. I enquire about a service that takes people out to the caravanserai there, but it turns out to be too expensive for just one night, as most of the trips are priced expect-ing a group going for a few days. I settle on a day trip that will take me into the desert and to the caravanserai before bringing me back in the evening. Reza the driver arrives shortly after noon and we drink some tea together before setting off. We take a straight road though town to a crossroads just outside the city, where Reza takes a left and we're on a stretch of bitumen flanked by arid plains and scattered shrubbery. There are no buildings anymore, just an ancient, abandoned fire temple standing solemnly at the edge of the approaching desert.

Dasht-e Kavir spreads out in front of us in every direction, unblemished by anything resembling a fence or some other instru-ment of ownership. There might be parcelled off bits that belong to various mining companies, but thankfully, their pernicious grip isn't flagrantly signposted, allowing the illusion of infinity to remain intact as we drive out towards an ever-expanding horizon. A deep ochre dominates the palette. Sandy cliffs and cavernous canyons appear and then melt into flat plains that support large salt lakes. The horizon pushes out ever further, and silhouetted rows of hills stand almost translucently against it, like a delicate Japanese watercolour. We pass the enormous Namak Lake which, as its name suggests, is more salt than lake, and looks like a shallow crater caked with a crusty white lining that's been shattered into a million parched panels. There seems to be enough water in and around it to support a frugal ecosystem though, and quite a few saltbushes abound. Birds are also drawn to this place.

I step out of the car and a loud, bellowing silence envelops me instantly. It's total and nothing interrupts it; just an occasional sifting as windswept dunes plead for more silence with a demure and drawn out '*shhhhhhhhhh*'. I head towards them, the great piles of sand sitting on the rugged floor inviting me into their voluptuous curves. I run up, roll down and lie in their warm, cushioned embrace. All around, the arid desert looks disapprovingly on, reminding me that a brief respite on the softness of sand dunes is no match for the feelings of terror that will accompany getting lost in this place. I pray a rakat or two; it's a long, deep prayer and I emerge to find that the late afternoon sun has turned all the dunes into a brilliant gold. It begins to set and we drive towards the caravanserai as the orange glow mingles with the white light of the rising moon to produce an enigmatic evening. The desert seems to shimmer as the fading light is reflected back in its sand and the scattered stones.

We stop at Namak Lake and I walk on its brittle surface. The crackling sound of salt underfoot doesn't reverberate but just hangs in the air in abrupt disjointed sequences. I instinctively feel thirsty. We drive on as evening passes and pitch-blackness puts every speck of moonlight to flight. They retreat to become the brightest spot in a spangled sky where billions of sparkling stars assail the non-luminous matter and challenge its presumed nocturnal supremacy. Reza turns on the radio and fiddles with the channels. I hear something that sounds vaguely familiar—it's probably an English broadcast, since I hear words I can understand. I try to tune into it, and as it gets clearer I hear the words '*Quraner alo*' along with a few others that are unmistakably Bangla. I manage to catch the station and sure enough, I'm listening to a Bangla radio programme about the virtues of the Quran, in the middle of the Dasht-e-Kavir in Iran. I slap Reza on the shoulder repeatedly while bouncing on my seat saying,

'Bangla, Bangla! This is my language!'

He tells me there are a lot of Bangladeshi workers in Iran, especially in Bandar Abbas which is a hop away from the UAE, and that this broadcast out of Tehran is probably for them. We listen to it all the way to the caravanserai. In complete darkness, with the smell of salt and earth clinging to the air and the open, barren spaces amplifying the crunching sound of our tires, it pours melodiously into the picture like a gurgling brook, bringing with it the suppleness of a faraway, fertile land. Recited Bangla is an elegant, soothing sound, but it is the fact that it reinforces the very thing I have set out to experience, that moves me the most. Here, in the middle of nowhere, in an alien linguistic landscape, my own language has found me, as though to remind me of the continuity of territorial space and of the cultures that sit on it. I listen to the rest of the religious programme, then the world news, Bangladeshi news, Iranian propaganda and a few advertisements, all in Bangla, until the 400-year-old restored caravanserai comes into sight, standing in its baked clay glory in the middle of one the driest deserts in the world, and I realise that I'm nowhere near wet and green Bangladesh anymore.

The Maranjab Caravenserai was built by the Safavids and is a huge fortress-like structure with solid walls and imposing bastions. It belongs to a network of inns and rest stops that were set up for travellers and traders on the overland route across the country before our noisy age of mechanised transportation put it out of commission. It's a tourist attraction now but still lives out its purpose as a place of respite. There are rooms, bunks, a kitchen and restaurant, and guests are welcome throughout the year. The walls enclose a large square space, with benches attached to the inside face. I conjure up the wicker lamps that must've sat where the electric ones do now. It's dark and there seems to be no one living here at the moment, although the smell of a recent wood fire attests to the presence of current visitors. As we're leaving, two busloads of civil servants and servicemen pull up near the entrance. They troop out and into the caravanserai; bedding and furnishings follow, borne by an army of flunkies. Important looking men in suits lead the caravan; their buses hiss and grumble as they put down for the night, getting a good scrub before bed.

On the drive back, Reza and I chat about the government and the economy, and he tells me that since Ahmadinejad has been in charge the cost of living has risen sharply. He blames the sanctions too and tells me a kilogram of chicken used to cost less than a dollar but it's over four dollars now. He doesn't like the religious excesses and the disparities between men and women. We talk about cars, petrol versus CNG, politics, girls, sex and all the things two people can find to talk about on a lonely desert road in the dark. When we enter town he asks me to come to his house and have a cup of tea, where I can also see some samples of his wife's carpets which, he assures me, are among the finest in Kashan. Subtle salesmanship, but I'm in no hurry and it can't hurt to have a look.

I meet his elderly father, his adorable little daughter and his wife and sister-in-law, who are weaving a carpet. His wife tells me a good 12-metre carpet can take up to a year to make and is painstakingly laborious. They give me watermelon and tea and I sit on the carpeted floor of their large living room with Reza's father, who has just been woken up from his nap. He lives with Reza since his wife passed away six months ago, and also occasionally with his other children. I feel sad for him; he seems distant, somewhere in his memories, perhaps. Reza speaks to him softly and helps him sit up, giving him a kiss on his forehead as he hands him a cup of tea. Affectionate gestures are never far away in Iran. After tea, I politely explain that I would not be able to carry a carpet with me on my continuing travels and Reza nods understandingly.

Back at the guesthouse, I browse through the bookshelf at the reception where travellers past and present have left books they no longer want to carry with them. There's a good collection, with many titles in languages I don't understand, but I spot something in there that excites me a great deal. It's a copy of the *Divan-e-Hafez* in English, pocket-sized and with an elaborately decorated cover. I pull it out hastily and proceed to flick through it with an uncontainable enthusiasm. The receptionist sees this and says,

'You like Hafez? In Iran he is like gold.'

'Yes, I like Hafez very much. He is well loved all over the world. I'm actually thrilled to find a copy of his *Divan* in English. Can I borrow it for a little bit?'

'No. But you can have it. A gift from the land of Hafez!'

'I couldn't possibly.'

'Why not?'

'No, no, I can ... I mean ... I'm honoured. Thank you!'

Tawrouf be damned. This is gold.

After a dinner of Iranian mutton *dhansak* (not unlike Indian *dhansak*) and naan, I sit in the courtyard and smoke a cigarette trying to eavesdrop on the conversation underway at the next table. From their expressions it looks interesting and I want to know what they are talking about. But they're Germans, speaking German, so it's futile and I decide that a front-door approach will probably serve me better. A polite knock won't do; I decide to kick it in with an obnoxious opening line, and ask,

'I noticed you're Germans. Are you here looking for your roots? You don't actually believe that you're Aryans, do you? I mean, you manufactured that identity using ours, right?'

It works; they enjoy the audacity and switch to English to include me. I pull out a bag of sunflower seeds to share with them and we get stuck in some very interesting conversations about culture, societies, spirituality and ethics. I'm not quite sure if it's the road or if it's Iran that produces them, but I seem to be having a lot of these here. The Germans have been travelling in Pakistan and Iran and seem fond of the absence of absolute order they've witnessed along the way. They tell me the flexible, almost organic approach to public life in these countries is more appealing to them than their organised obsession with efficiency, and I want to tell them that a trip to Bangladesh might convince them otherwise but don't, especially since I've just heard them have a go at the Italians for being too chaotic.

They're a well-read bunch, and the conversation leads into another one about material versus spiritual indices of success, and to the differences between societies that prioritise one over another. We arrive at the junction where rational materialism and intuitive mysticism go their separate ways, and are unanimous in our opinion that much has been lost because of the industrial revolution and the commoditisation of our lives and our time. This leads us to the question of how nations are governed and we talk about different systems and ideals and about Islamic ones too, but a sense of unease permeates at the mention of this last kind of system.

'The Islamic version of an ideal world is Shariah law, though, and this is problematic,' Says one of them, with typically German academism. I feel temporarily undermined but regain my poise and attempt to show him that he may have an ill-informed opinion on the subject.

'But that's not the Islamic ideal. Perhaps you know something about the social and intellectual history of Cordoba in Spain?'

'Of course, and high Islamic civilisation like that had a profound influence on the world but that's not what you see with Muslim culture today. In fact we have a lot of problems with Muslims in Europe, in Germany with the Turks. They are very anti-social.'

I'm surprised to hear a traveller, and an educated one at that, speak with such unabashed prejudice about an entire set of people. I wonder if he can hear himself sound like a bigot.

'I'm quite sure they've had to face plenty of anti-social attitudes as well. Have you never thought it could be reciprocal?'

'Yes, Germany is not good with helping people assimilate, it's true.'

'That's not quite what I meant but since we're on it, why should anyone have to assimilate at all? Why isn't German society flexible enough to accommodate different kinds of people?'

'It's not about that, it's about mentalities. It's difficult to accommodate a mentality that looks down on you and believes that everything about your culture is immoral and rotten.'

'I'm quite sure it's the other way around.'

'Sure, Germans and Europeans in general have a superiority complex. It's nothing new, but we're trying to grow out of that, and when we see this in the immigrants, it worries us.'

'Probably because it's like a mirror?'

'I don't know anything about that; I just know that we are worried about what will happen to European civilisation if this keeps up.'

'Maybe it will change for the better.'

'But maybe not. You talked about the great heights that Islamic civilisation reached in the past, and it's true, it did. We know about it well, we even know that Europe has a lot to be grateful to it for, but where has it gone? Why don't we see it anymore? If Muslims can kill off their own civilisation, what will they do to ours?'

9

A Gate for All Nations

Shiraz, Takht-e Jamshid

Shiraz

I check out of Ehsan Guest House at noon and book myself onto an afternoon bus back to Esfahan from where I will take the train to Shiraz. I've been reading a collection of Kazi Nazrul Islam's poems in Bangla and when I set the book down on the counter to settle the bill one of the girls who work there sees it and traces the Bangla letters on the cover with her finger.

'So beautiful, this is your language?'

'Yes, it's our alphabet.'

'India?'

'Bangladesh.'

'Like *nagsh*—you understand *nagsh*?

'Yes, I understand *noksha*, and your Farsi script is also beautiful.'

'But it's not Farsi, its Arabic. We lost the Farsi writing. If you go there, you will see it in Persepolis, on the walls.'

'Well you're welcome to use ours if you like.'

'Hahaha! Who knows, maybe someday.'

I want to leave a memorabilia of some sort but have nothing from Bangladesh with me. I do, however, have an Indian Rupee note in my wallet and since I've been representing all of Hind anyway, I hand it to the receptionist who pins it on the bulletin board behind her. It has a picture of Gandhiji on it, and she touches it reverently,

'Ah! Gandhi. The world needs more people like him.'

'He was a great man. Have you been to India?'

'No, but it's my dream. I love India!'

'Why do you love India?'

'Because it's the land of all religions.'

I pass the remaining time exploring some of the other historical houses. One of them features an enormous and multi-chambered *badgir*, another a large central courtyard surrounded by decorated buildings. A group of pretty girls are doing the same rounds and I bump into them at each of the houses where they smile to acknowledge me, but keep a dignified reserve about them that makes them all the more attractive. In the afternoon I catch a bus to Esfahan and am shown a great movie onboard, in Farsi with no subtitles, but I'm able to follow it. I later discover it's called *A Separation*, and I'm reminded of just how very good Iranian cinema is—their films often have a very natural treatment and pay great attention to emotional detail so that you end up feeling them rather than watching them. Meanwhile, I've eaten a fair few of those salted sunflower seeds and my bladder is exploding. I'm desperate to take a leak and there's no sign of the bus slowing down or any question of asking it to stop without becoming a laughing stock for the rest of the journey. It's torture but the film keeps my mind off it, until it ends—then it's just anxiety all the way and that horrible feeling of wanting to pee in my pants. My tribulation ends ahead of schedule when, to my inexpressible glee, we arrive at the bus station a full 20 minutes early and I make a mad dash for the loo, nearly knocking over a pair of portly women as I go.

I take a taxi across Esfahan to the train station, where I will have to wait for several hours before the train arrives, but have no other option since the city will shut down soon and I have nowhere else to wait. I grab a quick bite before I go—a stew that, judging by the denuded skulls beside the cauldron, is made from goats' face—and then pass through a slick, modern city across Si-o-Se Pol Bridge, markedly different from the old part of the city I had stayed in earlier. The station is a large, well-maintained modern building; police officers come towards me as I enter and tell me there are no more trains until 2 am, which is the one I'm taking, and I tell them I'm happy to wait at the station if that's allowed since I haven't got anywhere else to go. They ask me to register with them, ask me questions about Bangladesh and my journey. They are friendly, warm and like every Iranian I've met so far, exceedingly upbeat.

I spend the hours listening to music, reading and thinking about how skewed and incomplete an impression most of the world has about Iran. Far from revealing anything about the country, the stigma that gets slapped onto it actually reveals more about the redundancy of Western rhetoric, and tells you how little politicians really know about anything. There's no denying that the Islamic Revolution brought with it many horrors and impinged upon things that people in many other countries enjoy as fundamental rights and civil liberties, but for the most part Iran is like any other functional country; in fact, in some ways it's better. It could even be argued that things might not have been this good without the Islamic Revolution, considering the Shah's excesses and the political repression he presided over.

Most people forget that 98 per cent of Iran's voting population at the time voted, by national referendum, to become an Islamic Republic and to adhere to a theocratic constitution. The Iranian Revolution began decades before it actually happened and was the result of a series of events that started during the the reign of Reza Khan, the first Pahlavi Shah, which left the Iranian people disenfranchised and disillusioned with the instruments of a western-oriented global system. In 1941, Reza Shah was forced, by Britain and the USSR, to hand over power to his son Mohammad Reza, who was seen as more pliable. But Iran had a constitutional monarchy and elected representatives ran the state, more or less, so in 1951, when the fiercely independent and far-sighted lawyer Dr. Mohammad Mosaddegh became the democratically elected Prime Minister of Iran, he rapidly brought in things like social security, rent control, a dole system, benefits for sick and injured workers and land reforms, causing considerable discomfort to the landed aristocracy. But his boldest move was the nationalisation of Iran's oil assets—under British control since 1913—and also the cause of his downfall. He made this statement when he did it,

With the oil revenues we could meet our entire budget and combat poverty, disease, and backwardness among our people. Another important consideration is that by the elimination of the power of the British company, we would also eliminate corruption and intrigue, by means of which the internal affairs of our country have been influenced.

Britain, of course, wouldn't have it and used subterfuge, with the help of America and the CIA, to orchestrate a revolt and have Mossadegh removed. They also made the puppet Shah appropriate more powers to himself, so that no subsequent representative of the people could pull a stunt like that in the future and helped him set up the SAVAK, a brutal secret police notorious for cracking down on political opponents, particularly the Left, and clerics. The SAVAK was given extraordinary powers to spy on, torture and kill anyone deemed a threat to the monarchy or the state and so the denial of civil liberties to Iranian citizens began long before the Islamic Revolution; in fact, some were probably returned to them as a result of it.

The Shah's regime became increasing oppressive, especially against the clerics, who were seen as agitators, and any sort of political dissent, making censorship of the press, of art and literature commonplace, along with surveillance. He was supported in this by the CIA and the American government, who gave him weapons and trained SAVAK operatives in exchange for the lion's share of Iran's oil assets. But ironically, it was the Shah's attempt at bringing in economic and political reforms, in the shape of the White Revolution, that proved to be the last straw. His land reform programmes angered the feudal landlords; his attempts at making political office accessible to women and minorities angered the Ayatollahs; his one-party system, his unchecked extravagance at a time of mass inflation and the forced westernisation of the country—'westoxification' as they called it—angered the Left. A perfect storm was brewing.

The revolution that was to become the Islamic Revolution was originally led by writers, thinkers, poets and academics and was decidedly left-leaning. But it contained Islamic elements as well, in the writings of men like Ali Shariati who advocated for a Socialist Islamic state. Both of these groups, the Socialists and the Islamists, represented rural and working-class Iranians and so found common cause in their opposition to the elite, but they didn't remain allied for long, and the Islamists muscled their liberal colleagues out with a vengeance once the Shah had been deposed. To his credit the Shah made numerous conciliatory concessions, restructuring the SAVAK, relaxing censorship and promising elections, and seemed genuinely to be trying to get on the right side of history, but it was too little too late. The popular imagination was already fired with the promise of social and economic emancipation delivered through the wonders of the holy revolt.

Iran's Revolution was far from emancipatory and it moved violently against anyone who deviated from Ayatollah Khomeini's austere, absolutist vision. But it did free Iran from America's manipulative grasp and from its stranglehold over Iranian oil. It was caused, ultimately, by American-led policies of control and may have righted some of the wrongs of the past in the process, though there are probably thousands of people—women, political opponents, religious minorities and people accused of espionage—who will strongly disagree. But the more distorting factor is the way certain patterns of thought, especially Western and Islamic ones, can only understand the evolution of societies after they've placed their own at the most advanced stage of a linear trajectory they assume all of us are travelling along. Every other society has to aspire to be like theirs or fall short of the ideal and it's never easy to alert them to the reality of alternate trajectories or to the fact that *they* themselves might be the ones stumbling along some earlier evolutionary stage.

The train arrives shortly after 2 am and I enter a cabin where all the occupants are fast asleep. I try to make as little noise as possible as I climb into my bunk and settle in for the night. I'm tired and sleep comes easily, but not before I displace a young man from the Alborz region who belongs to the next cabin and snuck into ours to escape a snoring bunkmate. I wake up at daybreak as the sun begins to shoot streaks of light through our large cabin window. I meet the boy from Alborz in the line for the toilet. He asks me if I slept well but I don't ask him the same and try to sound apologetic when I tell him that I did. Afterwards, I meet a train operator who bursts into mock-Bollywood dancing when I tell him I'm not Arab but east of Hindustani. I go to the dining car and have my Iranian breakfast of cheese, jam, bread and tea, looking out the window as the train pulls into suburbs and then into Shiraz proper—the capital of Fars Province and the heartland of Persian civilisation.

The British hippie I met in Yazd had told me to stay at Niayesh Guest House if I was ever in Shiraz so I stop a taxi and ask to be taken there. It's a long way from the station but I'm glad since I get a chance to see quite a lot of the city on the way. It looks lived-in and busy, and a little more like South Asia than most of the other cities I've seen in Iran so far. It also has a lot of street art and the large mod-art murals give it an air of urban chic that's particularly appealing. I like it enough already and when a jaywalking girl shouts expletives back at a honking car, I'm completely sold.

We come to an older part of the city built around a large medieval fortress, which I'm told is the Arg-e-Karim Khan, the seat of Persian power when Karim Khan, one of Nader Shah's generals, established the Zand dynasty, whose rulers, quite unusually, called themselves *Vakilol Ro'aya* or the 'Advocate of the People', instead of Shahs. We take a side road off Shohada Square and go past an old school, then an old mosque, until we arrive at narrow alleys being upturned by road works and impossible to traverse by car. I get out and walk and find the guesthouse just around the corner. It has a wonderfully old feel to it, decorated using traditional Iranian art and carpentry, and as I wait to check in, I read up a little about the history of this

19th-century house. It began its public life as Mostafavi's House of Publishing, when a certain Mahmud Mostafavi invited a group of scholars to his home and created the Literature Association of Shiraz. This went on to become the city's first publishing house, counting the *Divan-e Hafez* as one of its titles. Shiraz's first newspaper is thought to have begun here, too.

I check into a room since there aren't any dorm beds left and am led through a central courtyard where a buffet lunch is being laid out for guests. It's a cosy space, smaller than the one in Kashan but more elaborately done up. My room on the second floor is accessed through the narrowest of staircases, and ascending it with a backpack requires considerable dexterity. It looks out onto the courtyard, with stained-glass windows that render it yellow, orange and blue in the late morning sun. After a short nap and some lunch, I set off towards Hafez's tomb.

Persian poetry in the park

It's impossible to get away from Hafez if you love mystical poetry. You wouldn't want to either, in fact you would do your very best to become as wrapped up in him as possible. Kobiguru Robindronath Thakur was a fan as well and visited his tomb in 1932, following which he wrote:

Sitting near the tomb, a signal flashed through my mind, a signal from the bright and smiling eyes of the poet on a long past spring day—akin to the springtime sunshine of today. We were, as it were, companions in the same tavern savouring together many cups of many flavours. I had the distinct feeling that after a lapse of many centuries, across the span of many deaths and births, sitting near this tomb was another wayfarer who had bound a bond with Hafez.

The Bengali poet came to Iran as Shah Reza Pahlavi's guest—a grand king showing his appreciation for a great mind. Five centuries earlier a Bengali Shah, Ghiyasuddin Azam, did the Iranian poet a

313

similar honour by inviting him to his country for precisely the same reason. Hafez never left Iran in all his life and declined the invitation, but to show his gratitude he sent Ghiyasuddin a *ghazal* which is said to have been included in the *Divan* later. The two may have even co-authored the *ghazal*—a story has it that Ghiyasuddin sent incomplete lines to Hafez, which Hafez finished and sent back. It read:

Vin bahas ba salase ghasaleh mi ravad
Shekar shekan shavand hamah totiane hind
Zin qande parsi keh beh bangaleh mi ravad.

Meaning,

This debate continues over three cups of wine
And all the parrots of Hindustan have become sugar greedy
At the thought of this Persian candy going to Bengal.

The notion that this was co-authored is quite possibly a bit of wishful thinking by later historians, but it underlines how prominently Hafez features in the cultural context of his Age, not least among the kings of my country.

I had expected to be alone with him, or perhaps with a few other people. As I approach the tomb complex, I notice a huddle of chadors standing beneath a large banner that says '*Hafez Day 12.10.2011*'. They look like an outing of schoolgirls and seem very excited about being here. Many more people, all in their good clothes, push past me as they go towards the tomb. Some are carrying flowers. A man in a suit is making announcements over a microphone and rows of chairs have been laid out facing a lectern in front of Hafez's grave. Television film crews are filing in. I seem to have managed to arrive, quite by coincidence if there is such a thing (and there isn't), at Hafez's tomb on Hafez Day—the day that Iran sets aside to venerate the poet—and just in time to be part of the official celebrations at his tomb. I muse about the many ways that this might never have happened. If Marco and I had managed to get seats on the bus from Yazd I would have arrived here days ago and left. Or maybe I wouldn't have delayed my trip from Kashan to go into the desert, again, I would have been gone by now. Even earlier, when Sana left for Shiraz I had thought about going with her, but didn't because I decided to smoke hash with Jemima and Balal instead. And finally, today before I left the guesthouse, I had briefly considered doing something else and coming here tomorrow.

But here I am at this august occasion, like very many others. Some people seem to be here out of a sense of tradition, maybe even obligation, others appear to be here to be seen and to mingle among members of a cultural class they probably aspire to belong to. In front rows, people, especially women, fiddle with their clothes and compare their bags to see if they look sufficiently sophisticated and put on their best affected face. The presence of photographers and television cameras doesn't help much either as the posing carries on unabashedly. But for the most part, there is a genuine reverence of the great poet, and oratory tributes are being flung from the lectern to any and every one that will have them. Behind it sits Hafez's column-ringed grave, covered in elegant marble and calligraphy.

In 1390, Khawaja Shamsuddin Muhammad Hafez gave up the ghost and became an immortal. He almost became a god and, not unlike the Bengali Thakur that loved him, went on to become the measure of a civilisation's soul. But very little is known about Hafez the historical character. It's supposed that he was born between 1315 and 1317 and spent the last years of his life in a Persia firmly under Amir Timur's hold. According to at least one legend he may even have met the conqueror, who chastised him for a poem in which he wrote that he would happily trade the cities of Samarkand and Bukhara for a mole on a beautiful Shirazi's cheek. Timur took particular offence at this, since he was from Samarkand and ruled both of those cities.

How can you give away so cheaply cities that are so glorious that I have subjugated the whole world to set them on top of it?

315

He asked, and the poet replied,

It's just the sort of extravagance that keeps me in poverty, my Lord.

Hafez had an exceptional memory, which of course is why he was called Hafez, and memorised tomes, like the works of Rumi, Attar, fellow Shirazi Saadi and the Quran. He began public life as a theological scholar, but quickly moved towards mysticism, causing an upset in the conservative court of Mubariz Muzaffar which promptly threw him out. He returned to royal patronage under the rule of Mubariz's son Shah Shuja who was a poet himself and allowed him to flourish as both an artist and a mystic. Hafez grew enormously during this period and exploited the Persian poetic tradition of mystical lyricism to become one of its greatest proponents.

More and more people arrive as the ceremony continues; nearly all of them carry a copy of the *Divan* and read it silently or out loud, wherever they are in the tomb complex. The *Hafezieh*, as it's called, is a large enclosure with the tomb in the centre of it and landscaped gardens all around. It has a paved area and places to sit and eat; there are *chaikhanehs* as well and an art gallery at one end, with an exhibition on. A single cloister runs perpendicular to a long walkway. The grave itself is housed in what looks like a tall gazebo with slender columns and a blue-green dome, the inside of which is covered with exquisite tile-work arranged in kaleidoscopic patterns. People fill the small space underneath the dome. Prayers are pronounced over the marble grave, flowers are laid, tears shed. The emotions are raw, as though he was just interred, and as evening approaches people stand in a sort of silent remembrance interspersed with occasional chants. Maghrib prayers are held in congregation shortly after.

Then it really begins. As night falls, coloured lights are turned on to produce a mystical atmosphere, which complements the recitations that are being dramatically delivered by writers and poets from the podium in front of the grave. There are loudspeakers and musical interludes. The audience hoots, whistles and cheers, and a chorus of

'Bah! Bah!' bellows across the park. Others sit or stand next to lights so that they can keep reading the *Diwan*; many have their hands over their hearts and are absolutely still, as though stunned into solemnity by the power of the words they ingest. Expressions of intense adoration adorn their young faces; most of them look younger than me. A calligrapher sits against a wall along the edges and creates intricate masterpieces using a bamboo pen. He's absorbed in his work and a girl sits next to him holding his cup of tea as she watches him. Every so often his hand flourishes off the page leaving behind elegant black strokes that stride boldly across the paper.

People talk softly like they're telling secrets and flash full-faced smiles at each other. There's a bohemian feel to the whole occasion and several times I feel like I am at *Bokultola*, at Art College in Dhaka, listening to a Baul musician pour out his soul under an evening sky in Spring. 'This is Persianness at its most native self,' I think to myself, but can only experience it vicariously as the language barrier keeps me out, and entirely unable to dive into this churning ocean of inspiration. But the emotions don't escape me; I can experience them by what they're doing to the audience: they sway, and cry—entire families together—and hold each other as the profundity of the poetic panacea passes through them. It's deeply moving and I can only guess what's being said, but perhaps it's this:

I have a thousand brilliant lies
For the question:
How are you?

I have a thousand brilliant lies
For the question:
What is God?

If you think that the Truth can be known
From words,

If you think that the Sun and the Ocean

Can pass through that tiny opening
Called the mouth

O someone should start laughing!
Someone should start wildly laughing now!

Or this:

I have come into this world to experience this:

men so true to love they would rather die before speaking
an unkind word. Men so true their lives are His covenant—
the promise of hope.

I have come into this world to see this:

the sword drop from men's hands even at the height of
their rage because we have finally realised
there is just one flesh we can wound.

Hafez, like Khayyam, ran into trouble with the orthodoxy to the extent that he was almost denied a Muslim burial, but he was too loved and too popular for that to have ever become a reality, and even now, more than 600 years later, he occupies an incontrovertible station in Iranian life as the Seer of Shiraz. No one else, not Khayyam, not Rumi, not Saadi nor Attar is held in such high regard, though I'm not sure why, since any one of them seems equally deserving. But then I'm not Persian and I'm sure there's something in the language that doesn't quite translate.

The ceremony continues well into the night and shows no sign of slowing down, but I'm tired and it's after 1am so I gradually make my way towards the exit. On the way out, the smell of charred corn cooking over open coals at a food cart tempts me, so I stop to indulge in one. A lot of others are doing the same and while standing in line I watch children play between their parents' legs, quietly, as though they are being careful not to shatter the serenity of the evening. The sound of poetry and music continues in the background as people come out to go home bearing blissful expressions. They are almost lucid, having imbibed the wine that Hafez has pressed for them, and wear their intoxication in the form of a luminous, velvety afterglow.

Takht-e Jamshid
Day 44

The 8am tour service to Persepolis leaving from Niayesh Guest House has been and gone when I show up at the reception an hour later, inquiring about alternatives. Yves, who I've been keeping up with on Facebook, has already passed through Shiraz and given me a few suggestions about how to get to Persepolis on my own so I ask the receptionist about those. Mehsooba, the receptionist, assures me that it's possible to do it Yves's way and calls me a taxi to take me to the depot from where I can take a bus to Marvdasht, close to the ancient site. While waiting, I strike up a very candid conversation with Mehsooba about permissiveness, freedoms and relationships, or rather she strikes one up with me, when she asks me if people date freely in Bangladesh. Her English is good and she's only 20 years old, but she has a self-assured manner about her, which I'm sure will take her quite far. We talk about the regulations in Iran and about how young people, both here and in Bangladesh, find their own ways of being able enjoy intimacy and she says,

'It's not like the police can actually stop people from screwing. If they really want to do it, there's always a way.'

She doesn't feel the slightest bit bashful talking about things that leave me a little turned on, frankly, and looks me dead in the eye when she says it, but it's too early in the day to be able to interpret insinuations, and besides, the taxi is here.

I reach the bus depot and, as expected, the usual shouting matches between agents from competing services are well underway. I ask about the bus to Marvdasht but it's nearly empty and could take ages to fill up, so I opt for a shared taxi instead. While waiting for the last spot to be filled, the drivers, predictably, start entertaining themselves at my expense and I provide them with ample ammunition by trying to speak Farsi. When I get tired of being a joke I start speaking to them in English and when they get tired of that, one of them says, pointing towards the ground,

'No English. Farsi. This is Fars!'

Well it is now, and has been ever since it came into contact with an Arabian inability to pronounce the letter 'P', but it was originally called Pars—homeland of a people calling themselves the Parsu, or Persians. Originally one of a number of different nomadic tribes, they may have settled on the Iranian plateau around 1000 BC and created the equivalent of the Indian *janapadas*, or early nation-states, giving their names to the territories they claimed. History has recorded these people as the Persians, the Medes, the Scythians, the Bactrians and the Parthians and they collectively called themselves Ariya, or Aryan.

The Rig Veda has an extensive list of Indo-Aryan tribes as well, which mentions a tribe called the Parsu and another one called the Parthava—possibly early historical references to the Persians and the Parthians. The Pakhta are also mentioned, and Bactria, which comes from the Farsi word Bakhtar, corresponds to the Pakhtun word Pakhtar. Later Indian records also talk about a people called the Saka, who are possibly the Scythians. If those are true, then they are chronicles of the ancestors of people who later became the populations of Khorasan, Afghanistan, Sistan and Persia, and may originally have gone out from India, but where they came to India from, if they came from anywhere at all, is a different question altogether. The Medes settled in the west of Iran and the Persians near the centre, but the indigenous Elamites in Haltamti, to the southwest, who flourished here for over 2,000 years before the Aryans arrived, were the powerhouse in the area until they were overthrown by the Semitic Assyrians from Mesopotamia, in today's Iraq. In the shake-up, the Persians and Medes managed to put in their own bid to bring down the Assyrians and by the 6th century BC, the Aryans had emerged as the new power in Iran.

The Persians were originally junior partners in this new Aryan alliance, and the Medes, from their capital in Ecbatana, created a kingdom called Media, which stretched from Anatolia to Afghanistan and became one of the four major powers in the region, alongside Egypt and Babylonia. We first hear about the Persians in Assyrian records where they are again called the Parsu and live in places called Parsua, Parsumash and Pashiru next to Anshan, the eastern half of what was once the Elamite realm.

History comes to us as disjointed pieces of recorded information, often embellished, sometimes contradictory. It's difficult to tell if Anshan was culturally Elamite or Persian or both, but inscriptions on a cliff in Behistun, Iran, states that a Persian ruler named Shishpish conquered the Elamite country of Anshan and began a new dynasty, to which Cyrus the Great belongs. It's possible that Anshan had become a part of Parsu territory by then, and Shishpish's two sons, Kurush I, (not Cyrus the Great who is his grandson) and Ariaramna inherit two separate regions of his kingdom, Anshan and Parsa, respectively. The trouble is the Cyrus Cylinder, composed in 539 BC, documents Cyrus's lineage as the kings of the city of Anshan, with no reference to a Persian takeover.

These territories were administratively independent of Media, but subject to it, and with the Medes and Persians being kindred people the lines between them were often blurry. A marriage takes place in the 5th century BC between the daughter of a King of Media and the King of Anshan, Kambojie, which changes regional and indeed international relations forever. Kambojie has a son called Kurosh, who accedes to the throne of Anshan in 559 BC and in 553 BC rebels against his imperial grandfather, the King of Media. Greek sources tell us the ironic tale of how the King of Anshan gets the better of the King of Media, along with the gory backstory of why the Median general Harpagus sides with Kurosh and goes against his own king, effectively determining the outcome of the conflict.

According to Herodotus, the Greek chronicler, the King of Media, Astyages, has a premonition that his grandson will challenge him for his throne and orders Harpagus to kill the newborn child when the family comes to Ecbatana. Harpagus doesn't have the heart to kill a baby, and when Astyages discovers that baby Kurosh is still alive, he kills Harpagus's son instead, cooks him and serves him to his father as a dish during a banquet. Harpagus swallows this, no pun intended, but bides his time for revenge. Some years later, when Kurosh is a young adult, he tells him the story and the two plot a revolt against the King of Media, their common enemy. Harpagus will feign loyalty to Astyages until the time is right to turn on him.

Kurosh enlists some of the neighbouring Persian tribes to support him in his revolt, identified by Herodotus as the Pasargadai, the Achaemenidai, the Panthaliaians, the Derusiaians and the Germanians, who are all settled farmers, and others that are still nomadic, such as the Daoi, Mardians, Dropicans and Sagartians, all of whom are disgruntled with Median rule. During the battle between Kurosh and Astyages, Harpagus, who is still Astyages's general and is leading the Median army, defects with his troops and tips the balance in favour of Kurosh, who wins and conquers Media. Astyages is spared and lives out his days as a subject of the king of Ahsan, ruler of Media and leader of the Persians. Kurosh is, of course, none other than Cyrus the Great, the ruler who presided over the genesis of Fars's place at the centre of one of the world's earliest empires.

The road to Marvdasht is dusty but among the dry plains and mountains are cultivated patches of grain, wheat and vegetables. I'm baffled by how these plants thrive in such a hard place with no major source of water anywhere in sight. We drive past the Quran Gate, and along the highway towards Persepolis, which is locally called the Takht-e Jamshid, or the Throne of Jamshid, after a legendary Zoroastrian king. It was originally believed that Jamshid, the fourth ruler of the semi-mythical Pishdadian dynasty, built Persepolis some time in the untraceable past as the fact that it's actually Achaemenid surfaced much later, but the name stuck and now the Pishdadians, called the first dynasty of Aryans in the *Shahnameh*, share in the Achaemenids' immortality.

We ascend up to barren valleys and come into a street that ends in a cul de sac. A walkway begins where the street ends, lined with souvenir shops and horse-drawn carriages to take passengers to the nearby Necropolis, or Nagsh-e-Rustam, the burial chambers of the Achaemenid Shahenshahs. At the end of the walkway on a 125,000-square-metre terrace shielded on one side by a mountain, sit the remains of the palace complex and the extraordinary citadel of Persepolis.

Dariyush or Darius the Great, the third ruler of the Persian Empire, commissioned the building of Parsa—as Persepolis was originally called—which was also the name of their empire. By the time the city was built in 518 BC, imperial Parsa had grown from being an obscure collection of Persian territories to the largest realm in the world in just over 35 short years. It inherited the Median territories and included most of West and Central Asia, Anatolia, the Caucusus, as well as today's Iraq, Syria, Jordan, Lebanon, Israel, Palestine, western Pakistan and the Greek Aegean Islands. Parsa was the third imperial capital, after Pasargadae and Susa, and was mostly a ceremonial city, designed to flaunt the glory and grandeur of the Achaemenid kings, who could at the time justifiably call themselves the greatest, and possibly the richest, kings on earth.

Instead of a single long staircase running down the centre, four separate but inter-connected staircases wind their way to the top in what feels like a considerably easy ascent. A series of small two-dimensional step-pyramids act as a sort of railing. Along the shallow stairs there are recesses for *coopi*s or oil lamps, still black from use centuries ago when lighting was provided for the royal guests who made their way up the to the Gate of All Nations, doorway to the heart of Parsa. Nearly 2,500 years after it was built, the gate is still phenomenal though it's not much of a gate anymore since the walls it was attached to no longer exist. It must've been simply awesome when it was new. Massive bull sculptures, representing wealth and strength, and embedded into the remains of the jambs look outward from the palace both prosperously and protectively. These were probably gilded or, at the very least, glazed, painted and decorated when they were newly made. They've lost their heads over the years but it takes nothing away from their stature. The workmanship is incredible and details like tendons and hair bring the stone statues to life, denuded and defaced, literally, as they might be. I walk through the portal slowly, closely examining the colossal structures, which bear vandalous inscriptions by conquerors and explorers who have passed through them over thousands of years. The official inscription is an *utshorgo*, a dedication, to God by the king who commissioned it and reads,

A great God is Ahuramazda, who created this earth, who created heaven, who created man, who created happiness for man, who made Xerxes king, king of many kings, commander of many commanders.

I am Xerxes, the great king, the king of kings, the king of all countries and many men, the king in this great earth far and wide, the son of Darius, an Achaemenid.

King Xerxes says: by the favour of Ahuramazda I built this Gate of All Nations. Much else that is beautiful was built in this Persepolis (Pârsâ), which I built and my father built. Whatever has been built and seems beautiful—all that we built by the favour of Ahuramazda.

King Xerxes says: may Ahuramazda preserve me, my kingdom, what has been built by me, and what has been built by my father. That, indeed, may Ahuramazda preserve.

It's Old Persian written in cuneiform script and repeated in Elamite and Babylonian. I have the transliteration in a booklet I bought on the way in. Some of the old language is recognisable for Sanskrit's proximity to Avestani, words like *asmanam, pita, kartam,* and *duar* are all still in use and the last line, 'Indeed, may Ahura Mazda [preserve]'—*Avaschiy Auramazda [patov]*—sounds to me a little like, '*Obboshoi Auramazda [palon]*' in Bangla. The tone of the inscription is interesting. It's partly boastful but mostly reverential and I can hear the voice of a man who sounds appreciative rather than arrogant, aesthetic rather than vain. Parsa was the emblem of Zoroastrianism's triumph and the worldly manifestation of Ahura Mazda's glory; there were moral and mystical connotations to it.

On the opposite side, as you enter what would have been the courtyard before the Hall of a Hundred Columns are a pair of lamassus guarding the other end of the portal, as large as the bulls you leave behind. Their heads and faces are intact and fantastically their wings as well, which are detailed to the feather and seem to glisten in the sunlight. They seem to be welcoming you in, which isn't too unusual, as lamassus were originally ushering deities associated with service and femininity, but while transitioning from a Semitic Assyrian to an Aryan Persian deity they became male beings on a protection detail. Like its cousin the sphinx, it's a hybrid creature—part human, part eagle and part bull. Statues of lamassus guarding buildings used to feature all over Anatolia, the Middle East and Persia, a bit like the European gargoyle or the Chinese guardian lion still does in their respective cultures.

After the enormous gate there's an empty area that was once the Council Hall, followed by the Unfinished Gate, which was still under construction when Parsa met its untimely end at the hands of the Macedonian army. Alexander the Great and his men did considerable damage to the complex and over the centuries it's been reduced to virtual rubble, but the structures that have survived are complete enough to give us a pretty good sense of who the Achaemenids were and what they stood for. Luckily they were very good at leaving records in the form of inscriptions, tablets, letters, administrative correspondence as well as glyph-storytelling on their walls, and were keen to promote themselves and their philosophies in larger-than-life ways.

Dariyush was Kurosh's son-in-law and might have been related to him through Shishpish as well. But there are conflicting theories about Kurosh's ancestry; he may not have been Persian at all but Elamite, though Dariyush appropriated his legacy and turned him into an Achaemenid to further his claim as the rightful heir to his empire. There's an inscription in Pasargadae, Kurosh's capital, which identifies him as a Persian and an Achaemenid; however, it's possible Dariyush had that engraved posthumously as evidence. Personally,

I think he *was* Persian, but perhaps not from the Achaemenid line, though it doesn't matter since the Achaemenids ultimately triumphed and the vast territory of imperial Parsa became known as the Achaemenid Empire with Darius the Great as its chief architect.

But he inherited an empire in revolt with nearly every territory either asserting its independence or refusing to acknowledge Dariyush as king. With the help of allies and nobles, he put them down in just a year and slew, in his own words, 'eight lying kings' to achieve cohesion and overlordship. He did the unforgivable thing of killing an ally and his entire family too, when he lost his mind and couldn't trust anyone, but he eventually regained his footing and conquered Egypt, the last of the four great regional powers to succumb to Parsa. He then looked east and invaded the Indus Valley, capturing Sindh entirely, along with parts of Punjab and Khyber Pakhtunkhwa including Taxila. He expanded west by taking Bulgaria and Macedonia, but met stiff resistance from the independent Greek city-states. Fuelled by a desire to punish them for supporting their cousins, the Ionian Greeks of Anatolia, in their bid to secede, Dariyush went to war with Athens and Sparta but didn't succeed in overcoming either.

He withdrew to Asia Minor, having captured a number of Greek islands, but the Persian charge had effectively been halted. It was a defining moment in history; the Greeks had, for the first time, defeated the seemingly unstoppable Persian Empire and had managed to go from a collection of feuding city-states to a united federation that was capable of establishing a cultural frontier and catalysing a different kind of civilisation—European Civilisation. A second, more pounding assault on the Greeks came 10 years later from Xayarsha (Xerxes), Darius's son, who succeeded in taking virtually all of Greece in spite of a valiant last stand by Leonidas, the King of Sparta, and his 300 Spartans at the Battle of Thermopylae. Athens was captured and the Acropolis was set on fire, leading eventually to the entire city being burned. The Greek narrative holds Xerxes responsible for this; however, it might have also been the Greeks themselves who did it, accidentally or as a scorched earth tactic. But the vastly outnumbered Greeks regrouped and beat the Persians back, managing to stop the Achaemenid Empire from ever expanding towards the Adriatic Sea. In fact, it did more than that— it began a Greek counter-offensive, which ended, over a century later, with Alexander's conquest of Persia.

I walk into the remains of the Hall of a Hundred Columns, past another large bull sculpture that's mostly fallen away. The surviving gates have bas-relief characters and epics chiselled in them. None of its columns have survived. However, tall ones shooting out of the floor of the nearby Great Palace of Xerxes are capped with the remains of griffins and double-headed bull capitals. Some of the capitals have tumbled to the ground and are kept behind glass for preservation. From shadowy corners, Achaemenid 'Immortals', the palace guards, observe me as I traipse about in their domain, their images come out of the walls all over Parsa. Their spears are primed and their identical bearded faces are turned towards an ancient assembly of royal ghosts. Their expressions are the most impressive bits; they look stoic without looking severe and a steely concentration fortifies their fawn-like eyes. There is something *gentil* about all the faces I see on the walls. They all look calm and unruffled, even when they do ruffling things like single-handedly slaying lions, as Xerxes is shown doing in one of the reliefs. He's also shown slaying something that looks like a lamassu or a winged horse, which seems like a strange thing to do considering they're thought of as good deities.

A group of Iranian girls are enthusiastically taking pictures. They have good cameras and look like they could be photographers. I watch them at work and enjoy the neon-coloured laces on their sneakers, which stand out against the dusty, monochromatic ruins. Some Europeans are with them and I think they're all speaking French together. Behind them another European tourist, a great oak of a man with longish brown hair comes striding triumphantly into the fallen-down hall, looking as though he's channelling an ancient Macedon or two.

They certainly left their mark here, the Macedonians—many of the walls have scars and gashes where Alexander's soldiers ran their blades over them. Reliefs of Xerxes seem to have been given the special treatment and are particularly damaged. Persepolis was the richest city in the world at the time, and its treasury had the largest store of wealth under the sun. Plundering it gave Alexander and Macedonia unprecedented power not just in Asia but also in Europe, so after four months of enjoying it, Alexander and his troops thoroughly looted Persepolis, carrying off its treasures on 20,000 mules and 5,000 camels. They also did the dastardly thing of destroying the city and killing all its male inhabitants, even though it had been won without any fight from them at all.

In May 330 BC, Alexander ordered that the palaces and audience halls be burned as he left to find Darius III, the last Achaemenid king, who was still alive but on the run. He did it, ostensibly, in reprisal for the razing of the Acropolis 120 years earlier but I don't really buy that tenuous attempt at validating what was essentially the drunken thrill of being able to destroy something beautiful and grand, and give vent to the envy it inspired. It's curious why he waited four months to destroy it, but the most plausible reason is that he wanted to be recognised as a legitimate king of Parsa and so perhaps planned to keep Persepolis as his own city, his elegant Persian mistress. It would have been hard to resist such a fabulous place, and given his tendencies to 'go native', it's not unlikely that he would have wanted to live here like an Achaemenid. But when he realised that the Persians regarded him not as their king but as a rogue and still called Darius III their leader, he turned on them and on the city like a jilted lover, desecrating the object of his desire so that no one else could have it.

But Persepolis has retained her dignity and remains a testament in stone to Persian good taste. It also signals Parsa's desire to be remembered as the multicultural entity that it was. Many things mark it out as being tolerant, even appreciative, of other nations, even if accepting Persian supremacy was a necessary prerequisite. Dariyush made Semitic Aramaic an official language of the Empire, alongside other non-Persian languages like Elamite and Babylonian, and Kurosh has left behind his famous Cylinder, which is one of the earliest attempts in known political history at a bill of rights. It was written in the 6th century BC, in Akkadian, another popularly spoken Semitic language, and enshrines principles like religious equality, a right of return for deported people and the restoration of desecrated temples—all of which are very progressive even by today's standards. It contains lines like this,

My vast troops were marching peaceably in Babylon, and the whole of [Sumer] and Akkad had nothing to fear. I sought the safety of the city of Babylon and all its sanctuaries. As for the population of Babylon who, as if without divine intention, had endured a yoke not decreed for them, I soothed their weariness; I freed them from their bonds....

.... I sent back to their places, to the city of Ashur and Susa, Akkad, the land of Eshnunna, the city of Zamban, the city of Meturnu, Der, as far as the border of the land of Guti—the sanctuaries across the river Tigris—whose shrines had earlier become dilapidated, the gods who lived therein, and made permanent sanctuaries for them.

I collected together all of their people and returned them to their settlements, and the gods of the land of Sumer and Akkad.... I returned them unharmed to their cells, in the sanctuaries that make them happy. I have enabled all the lands to live in peace.

Among the people Kurosh freed from bondage were the Jews, who had been brought to Babylon as slaves following the destruction of the kingdom of Judah in 597 BC, and among the sanctuaries he restored was the Temple of Jerusalem. Both of these acts are corroborated in the Hebrew Book of Ezra.

.... The Lord aroused the Spirit of Cyrus, king of Persia, and he spread a proclamation throughout his kingdom, and also in writing, saying: 'So said Cyrus, the king of Persia; All the kingdoms of the earth gave to me, the Lord, God of heaven, and He commanded me to build Him a House in Jerusalem, which is in Judea. Whomever is amongst you of all His people, God be with him, and he should ascend to Jerusalem, which is in Judea.

There are Faravahars everywhere in Persepolis, hovering protectively over images of some Darius or Xerxes or another seated on his throne with fan-bearers in tow, while companies of Median and Persian noblemen assemble in front of him. You can tell their nationality by their clothes and their implements. Great emphasis is placed on depicting their hair and beards, which are very thick and curly, in tight rings and always well tended. They look oiled and combed and fall in neat buns and long manes around the whole head, usually under a cap or with a headband. They all wear earrings.

Literally hundreds if not thousands of these figures adorn the walls, staircases, jambs and tombs, and anything else that still remains of these once magnificent structures. Symbols of the Persian New Year, Nowruz, which is the image of a ravenous lion trying to overpower an unyielding bull, also feature repeatedly. The lion's musculature is prominent, just like its claws, perhaps to suggest *carpe diem* (or *carpe annum* in this case), and might have been intended as an affirmation of renewed vigour. There are also images of wheat stalks as tall as people, signalling abundance or fertility. Along with the *Apadana*, there is a palace of Xerxes, a palace of Darius, a harem of Xerxes, two separate halls of audience, a treasury, but most curiously, no remains of an Atesh Kadeh or any other sort of temple, or at least nothing that's identified as one. The whole place is the colour of brown sandstone.

A group of Indian Zoroastrians or Parsis are being given a guided tour by an Iranian man who looks a little like Aamir Khan, the Bollywood actor, and I listen in every now and then to catch a bit of his commentary. He's telling the group about the stories carved into the walls of the *Apadana* and interpreting the inscriptions and edicts for them. The *Apadana*, or 'arrival place', is the next structure after the Hall of a Hundred Columns, and is among the oldest buildings at Persepolis. It once had enormous verandahs on three sides where, presumably, the Shahenshahs would receive guests from across their Empire. The Persian love for architectural open spaces, evidenced in their later buildings, including their mosques and squares, seems to have begun here. The walls of the *Apadana* are decorated with bas-reliefs of the 23 nations that were vassals to the Persians. They are seen bringing tributes to their emperor, carved along the staircase that actual delegates would have had to climb to perform the same act. Depicted in their traditional costumes and carrying gifts from their respective realms, the reliefs record the world as it was in the middle of the 1st millennium BC, when Parsa was the reigning superpower of its day. You can even see subtle ethnological differences.

And over here we have the Indians. See, they look like Indians!

Says the guide who looks quite like an Indian himself, as he points out the delegation from Sindh to his Indian tour group. I go closer and see that they do in fact look like Indians and have straight hair and beards, unlike all of the other nationalities, even the ones from Afghanistan, who are shown with woolly hair. The Egyptians might have also had hair like ours, but the relief depicting them is badly damaged and it's impossible to tell. We're also the only ones going barefoot and bare-bodied, with just a short *lungi* falling around the thighs. Only the man leading the delegation is wearing sandals and a robe, draping it like Buddhist monks still do, over one shoulder. They all wear headbands. He looks exactly like the 3,500-year-old sculpture of a priest-king that was unearthed in Mohenjo-daro, which is of course in Sindh. Their gifts include a mule and—surprise, surprise—spices, carried in two woven-grass baskets hanging off the ends of a long stick slung over one of their shoulders, the way things are still carried in almost every village across South Asia.

The 23 nations are: the Medes, colleagues and co-founders of the empire; the Sarmatians; the Thracians; the Ionian Greeks, the Anatolian Lydians; the Egyptians; the Parthians; Libyans; Ethiopians; Indians from Sindh; Aryan tribes from the Khorasan; the Elamites, whose language was an official one across Parsa; Babylonians; Assyrians; Arabs; Armenians; Phoenicians; Scythian tribes; Jews; the Pakhta; Gandharians; Sogdians and Arachosians, from

Balochistan—an unprecedented diversity of peoples, representing various races, languages, religions and cultures. It's quite likely that Parsa was the first international empire of its kind but there isn't any evidence of it trying to impose religious or linguistic uniformity, aimed at assimilation, over the entire realm. I dare say there was something particularly enlightened about the way it was run and perhaps they really did believe in amity—there are reliefs in Persepolis showing people of different nationalities walking together holding hands.

The Indian-looking guide says, with considerable esteem, that Persian subjects were never slaves, but free people who saw the wisdom in belonging to *Pax Achaemenica* and were received honourably as guests to Persepolis. It's probably true, in a relative sense; however, the thought that it might have been unwise to confront a powerful and expanding Parsa would surely have crossed the minds of many.

I wander around the complex as afternoon sets in, and the orange light turns the place a dark shade of pink. The endless rows of identical immortals look almost alive as the shadows around them dance and deepen. There are reliefs showing people walking around with parasols and others depicting noblemen in everyday scenes of mirth and merriment—they touch each other affectionately, a hand on a shoulder here, holding hands there. There's nothing homoerotic about the images; they look like typical male companionship gestures anywhere from Turkey to Bangladesh, even today. Among these are several insciptions, usually in three languages, Old Persian, Elamite and Babylonian, but none, surprisingly, in Median.

I hear the guide telling his Parsi group that Old Persian was written from left to right in the 'nails script', i.e., cuneiform, which looks a bit like a spilt box of nails, hence the name. Then he says something that blows my mind. He tells them that the alphabet used to begin with the letter K, pronounced as the sound '*Ka*'. No way. I pull out my little brochure remembering that there was a *bornomala*, an alphabet key, in there somewhere and hope that what I'm thinking is true. It surely is. There in front of me, in nails script, is the Old Persian alphabet and it's arranged like this:

Ka [Ku] Kha Ga [Gu] Gha Ja [Ji] Jha Da Di Du Ta [Tu] Tha ....

It's an uncanny and unmistakable resemblance! There's just no doubt about it—Persian writing in the past followed a pattern that Indic languages have used throughout the ages, and conformed to a unique, almost emblematically South Asian arrangement of letters.

The site is closing for the day so I make my way to the *chaikhanehs* and gift shops below. I have some tea and a smoke and am looking at the books on display when I see the Parsi group come into sight. They're led by an elderly gentleman with a white cloth wrapped around his head in an unusual way. He's quite rotund, and wears a white half-sleeved shirt. His followers walk beside him, reverentially cutting their pace to let the old man stay ahead of them.

The Parsis have an interesting story and finding them here, from 'whence they come', is a fun coincidence. When Arab invaders began spreading across Persia in the 7th and 8th centuries, Zoroastrians were given the choice of becoming Muslim or paying a *jizya* tax, something they must've found both inconvenient and offensive, considering this was their own land. Many did neither and settled near the Hormuz Straits before leaving Persia completely, setting sail for India. I remember an old story I heard once about how the Zoroastrian Persians came to our shores. They landed up in Gujarat and encountered Jadi Rana, king of Gujarat, who, when asked for shelter, bought them a jar of milk filled to the brim, to imply that his kingdom was full. A Zoroastrian priest added some sugar to it, which dissolved in the milk without causing it to overflow, helping him elegantly make the point that they would dissolve into Gujarati society harmoniously, only making the lives of its people sweeter.

Jadi Rana was won over and granted them asylum, but on four conditions—they were to speak the local language, Gujarati; dress like locals; agree to not bear arms; and perform their marriages in the evening, like Indians do. He then asked them to tell him about their faith and the Parsi rendition of the story says he found it to be a very peaceful one. So peaceful, in fact, that Indians have never had any trouble with Zoroastrians in nearly 1,400 years. The Parsis have also kept their promise of making the lives of Gujaratis, and Indians, better. They are represented in every sphere of Indian life: doctors, intellectuals, generals, including Sam Manekshaw to whom Bangladeshis owe a national debt, entertainers, industrialists, and politicians—a full range. They are also famously philanthropic, spending a great deal of their considerable wealth on public service and development.

I catch up with the group and introduce myself. I tell them about my book and my route and ask them if they wouldn't mind answering some questions about their customs, so they take me to their high priest, who is very conversant and an absolute pleasure to talk with. I ask him about the relationship between Avestani and Sanskrit, which he says are so similar to one another that they could have easily been dialects of the same thing. He then tells me how the Vendidad, a part of the Avesta, and the Vedas contain similar characters and references, and that *Hapta Hindu* in the *Vendidad* is *Sapta Sindhu* in the *Vedas* or the Indus Valley river system to us. The priest tells me the Parsis chose India because of these similarities and called themselves Parsi after the language they once spoke, which was still being called Parsi when they left Iran. I ask him about the word *Arya*, and he tells me that their legends say North Indians and Iranians belonged to a federation of Aryan tribes that migrated from the Arctic region to settle in the lands between the Tigris and the Indus, over 9,000 years ago—throwing everything that I've read in modern history books completely out of sync.

The 100,000 or so Parsis in India and Pakistan have since shed all traces of their Iranian culture and are now more or less assimilated into their local settings. Their holy books are transcribed in the Gujarati script and they are accepted as part of India's diverse religious landscape. But they are proudly Persian and have attempted to preserve both the race and the religion of their ancestors, marrying mostly within their own community. So the heritage of Parsa has become shared between the Iranians and Parsis—Persians kept their language but lost the religion and the Parsis lost the language to keep their religion.

I walk with the group for a while; they will stick around for the light and sound show, but I don't have a ticket and the counter has already closed. Before leaving, I hear the tour guide tell the Parsis about Alexander and how Parsa was eventually destroyed, adding

'*Agha*, Europeans think the Romans were the height of civilisation, but the Romans were feeding people to lions and gathering in stadiums to watch this with their families. So how will they appreciate something as fine as Persepolis?'

Persian vainglory, certainly, but perhaps not too far off the mark.

Niayesh Guest House is an exceedingly easy place to get used to. I spend a large part of the morning drinking tea, checking emails and writing my journal sprawled out on a divan in the sunny courtyard. The unhurried Iranian pace of life makes it almost the obvious thing to do. I gave up my room and checked into the dorms the night before, where I met a Japanese couple, the only other occupants. They've been travelling together for a few months, and met in Central Asia. He's been drifting for nearly a year and is otherwise a lawyer in Tokyo. I asked him how he ended up in Iran and he told me he was unemployed, and Japan is expensive so he took a ferry across to Korea, to travel. It was the first time he'd ever left Japan. After that he thought he might as well just go west since there was so much west to go, and kept travelling through Asia—Mongolia, China, Kazakhstan, Tajikistan and now Iran. Like most Japanese, he's unassuming and self-censuring; you'd never guess by seeing him that he's trodden so many terrific trails.

Not content to just laze around, I head off towards Pasargadae, Kurosh's old capital. It's along the same road as the one to Persepolis, which now feels familiar and recognisable. We take a small left off it, and arrive at a dry, shrubby place bound by equally shrubby rolling hills in different shades of light green and ochre—the Morgab plains. My taxi driver is a friendly, chatty man who parks the car and walks up to the gate with me, before deciding that he should stay by his vehicle. In front of me stands a massive rectangular structure on a plinth, in brown limestone. It's a sarcophagus-style tomb with a gabled roof, like many other tombs across South Asia and

Iran, except its much, much bigger. It's presumed to be the tomb of Kurosh, Cyrus the Great, though it's called Prophet Solomon's mother's tomb, because a clever caretaker 1,400 years ago had the presence of mind to call it that, and spare it from the carnage unleashed by invading Muslim conquerers. Prophets' mothers are, after all, entitled to their dignity.

It's a good thing he did too, because virtually all of Pasargadae is invisible. Unlike Persepolis, nothing at all of the structures, sculptures or steps remain here. It's just a huge open space with scattered bits of monuments that were once part of grand palaces. There's nothing to suggest a city, much less a capital, stood here, far less the capital of a major empire. A few pillar bases and a solitary wall, with some visible bas-reliefs is mostly what's left of it. In the distance a large rectangular structure with strange, irregularly shaped windows stands several storeys tall. It's called the 'Prison of Solomon' but might also be the remains of Cyrus's son's tomb. Still further in the distance are parts of a fortress on a hill.

I walk up to Cyrus's tomb to get a closer look. It's completely intact and has an Arabic inscription—a verse from the Quran— near the entrance, carved over the original epitaph. It's an imposing structure, 36 feet high, and in remarkably good shape, perhaps because it's a base-isolated structure—the very first of its kind in the world, making it resistant to seismic activity. According to Arrian the Greek historian who wrote the *The Anabasis of Alexander*, the original epitaph read,

Mortal! I am Kurosh, who gave the Persians an empire, and was king of Asia.
Grudge me not therefore this monument.

Other historians have said it was probably more like:

O mortal, whoever you are and wherever you come from, for I know you will come, I am Kurosh, who gave the Persians their Empire. Grudge me not, therefore, this little earth that covers my body.

336

Alexander certainly didn't; instead, he had the interior of the sepulchral chamber decorated and had the entire structure restored after it was broken into during the chaos that was the Macedonian invasion. He was reportedly horrified by that act of vandalism, and by the disrespect shown to a man he greatly admired. He wasn't alone in this; Cyrus was respected far and wide during his lifetime as well as after it, not least by the Greeks and by Xenophon, a student of Socrates who wrote the *Cyropaedia*, which Alexander read at an early age. Cyrus was also deeply respected by the Jews and was called a Messiah in the Tanakh, the only Gentile ever to be given the honour. It's possible that the Quran also mentions him, as Dhul-Qarnayn, and regards him as one of God's chosen ones. In 1971 the Pahlavi Dynasty marked 2,500 years of Iranian monarchy here, where Mohammad Reza Pahlavi is quoted as saying, 'Rest in peace Cyrus, for we are awake', and in 2003, during her Nobel Peace Prize acceptance speech, celebrated Iranian lawyer Shirin Ebadi said,

I am an Iranian, a descendant of Cyrus the Great. This emperor proclaimed at the pinnacle of power, 2,500 years ago, that he 'would not reign over the people if they did not wish it'. He promised not to force any person to change his religion and faith and guaranteed freedom for all.

I'm taking pictures when a young man, maybe in his early 30s, comes up to me and hands me his camera to take a picture of him with the tomb in the background. He grumbles about the Arabic inscription and speaks to me in Farsi, but I understand him. He's here alone, and possesses himself with characteristic Iranian ebullience. There's also a tour on, with a pretty middle-aged woman leading it, speaking Farsi. I want to know what she's saying but haven't got a clue.

Junayd, as he tells me his name is—in English when he realises I'm *ajnabi*—is originally from Ahvaz, a city close to the Iraqi border with a large Arabic population. He's on a road trip and has driven here from Esfahan, where he now lives, in search of Persian history.

He's handsome, with a nice smile, and wears blue jeans with sandals. Pictures taken, we start chatting and he asks me if I'm Muslim. Expecting 'Shia or Sunni?' to be the obvious next question and to be berated for being Sunni, I somewhat trepidatiously say yes, Muslim. To my surprise, he nods a disinterested sort of acknowledgement, which either means he's not one for details or that he finds me unimaginative and dull. I feel brushed off and suddenly long to be berated for being Sunni. 'Why, aren't you?' I ask him, confident that a Junayd has to be.

'No, I'm Zoroastrian.'

'Oh.'

'My parents are Muslim.'

I do a double take and think to myself, 'is that even allowed in Iran?' It's always unusual to hear about Muslims going the other way, but especially so in Iran, where Islam seems to be as much a *fait accompli* as can, well, be *accompli*. He spots my bewilderment, and adds, almost as a passing shot,

'Islam is killers, sorry.'

And then he walks on, as if uninterested in getting into what he probably assumes will be a long, entangling conversation.

I'm happy he did as well, as it gives me time to think up a counter-argument, and I look for examples from Hafez's poetry but then think he might tell me what Jemimah told me in Yazd, that Hafez was Persian and it was Persian pre-Islamic devotion to Love that enriched his poetry, not Islam. But he's nowhere in sight anymore so I walk towards the second monument and am intercepted by a group of young Iranians, a pretty woman and two guys, offering me drugs. They gesture 'chasing the dragon' and I immediately recognise it as either speed or heroin. They have a car and are telling me to go for a ride with them. The girl is trying to seduce me into it and I'm tempted to go along. My driver comes towards us to try and extricate me, but before he can reach, Junayd skids up beside me in his car and, lion-like, shoos away the hyenas with an outstretched arm. They slither back, and he opens his door to let me in.

Junayd drives an old two-seater Mazda RX, which feels lived-in and includes the assorted paraphernalia of a road trip: chips packets, chocolate wrappers, cigarette butts and sunflower seed shells. As soon as I step in, he offers me some string candy, sticky and pink in long strips. Iranians always offer you things when they meet you and they always have something to offer too. Seeds, fruit, candy, lifts in cars, protection from a drug-fuelled robbery or death—it's a boundlessly warm and generous culture.

In the car, Junayd seems to open up and feels comfortable expanding on why he's not Muslim anymore.

'*Be bakshi Agha*, I like Zarthosht religion, because it is Love. There is just you and God. No Hassan, Hossein, Imam, Ali, Muhammad.'

I want to tell him Islam is too, but recognise his angle and the Shia climate that has brought him to his dismissive conclusions. Still, I can't help but wonder if all versions of Islam aren't equally convoluted, what with their over-reliance on practices and personalities, hadiths and 'experts', creating a row of hurdles between people and their spiritual destinations. Like all religions eventually do— also, in fact, Zoroastrianism. But there he is, Junayd, the young Persian computer scientist who prefers the teachings of Zarathustra, doesn't like the Arabic inscription on Cyrus's tomb (neither do I, incidentally) and has managed to find a way back to his roots, guided by a luminosity that reached out to him across millennia, piercing thousands of years of Islamic Iran and even Khomeini's Islamic Revolution. A well-travelled man who has been to India and Indonesia, Junayd disappeared as suddenly as he showed up, leaving me to wonder if a similar overhauling of my own religious orientation is not in the offing, somewhere on my spiritual horizon.

Because the truth is, I find religious institutions, and the formats they prescribe, often have arbitrary, artificial premises that confound followers with a combination of cultural imperialism and mythological superstition, leading them to accept as truth almost everything else except the things that really are. And the things that really matter usually remain unchanged even without the institutional superstructures that religions rely on. Like Junayd, would I too need to shed these redundant layers to return to a more honest perspective on God and virtue? My own deconstruction would probably lead to a Vedic foundation, and I would most likely arrive at the inevitable conclusion that all the faith one needs is preserved in the Sanskritic understanding of Dharma.

Trouble is, Vedic, or Sanskritic religions are also afflicted with the same institutional *rigor mortis* as any other, and contain moral inconsistencies that make them a difficult alternative to Semitic ones. Then, of course, there are the pre-Vedic strands of my spiritual DNA, things carried forward from a time before the 'Aryanisation' of Indian beliefs. But these are all about 'being' and what I'm really interested in is 'essence'. My essence is at peace with, in fact, it's sustained by, Islamic, Shonatan Dharmic, pre-Vedic, post-Vedic, Buddhist, Shinto, Zoroastrian, Jewish, Christian even Australian aboriginal beliefs. Everything under the sun that speaks sense to my soul informs my spiritual orientation, and to be perfectly honest, all the religion I really need is the poem *Desiderata* by Max Ehrmann.

My essence is at peace with all of them, and their essences are at peace with each other. But I consciously chose to follow the Muslim road because it seemed uncluttered enough for me once, and still does, but perhaps that's because I have preferred to ignore the vast swathes of non-prophetically uttered, doctrinal literature which cause most of the confusion. And perhaps that's the only way to be religious anymore, if searching for a truer connection between being and its Essence is really your bag.

I catch up with the tour and try to learn things, but it's no use because the guide is speaking Farsi. When they move on I try to steal snippets of conversation from her, asking her a few questions in English, which she obligingly answers. If there's anything the Iranians are, it's abundantly accommodating. I learn that the tomb of Cyrus may not be where Cyrus was actually buried, but a cenotaph, though she acknowledges that the Greek writings mention the existence of a coffin. She also confirms that Cyrus wasn't

Zoroastrian, but worshipped the Babylonian god Marduk, who is mentioned in several of his edicts, including the Cyrus Cylinder. Apparently Zarathustra came along after Cyrus died, but mythological time competes with the official chronology to confound the issue. Kurosh's ethno-cultural orientation is indecipherable. He seems to belong more to the older Mesopotamian world of the Elamites than the newer Indo-Aryan one to which Dariyush firmly does. It's a bit ironic then, that Parsis across the world are often called Cyrus. As I'm leaving I tell the tour guide that I'll be going to Alexander's city on my route, and playfully ask her if she has a message for him from Parsa.

'Tell him Iran wishes him good luck in hell,' she says, with a wink.

There's still some of the afternoon left so I decide to check out the Necropolis, or the Naqsh-e Rustam—burial grounds of the Achaemenid kings of Persia. It's located close to Persepolis amid sudden cliffs that obtrusively stand up over the flat fields around them. Naqsh-e Rustam, or the 'engravings of Rustam', is more than just a burial site, though; it's also an encyclopaedia of imperial exploits preserved in the form of bas-reliefs, *naqsh*, carved into the rock faces. At the foot of enormous dry sandstone cliffs, which look like they're made of fired clay, centuries-old pictorial representations cut into the cliffs showing later Iranian rulers, the Sassanians, gaining victory in battle against other world powers. In one of them the captured Roman Emperor Valerian is seen begging for his life at the feet of Shapur the Great, the second Sassanian Emperor, while in another his father Ardashir is seen receiving a heavenly mandate from Ahura Mazda, God of the Zoroastrians.

High above those, great plus sign-like openings are carved into the cliff, creating caves where the Achaemenid kings have been interred. There are four of them, but only one, Darius's, is clearly marked. The others are thought to be for Xerxes, Artaxerxes and Darius II, and there's an unfinished one as well, possibly for Darius III, whose reign was also unfinished, being interrupted by Alexander's invasion. The entrances to the tombs look like entrances to a mansion, with pillars, and are decorated with typically Achaemenid iconography: Faravahars, representations of seated Shahenshahs, and 23 figures representing the nations of the realm, holding up a platform that supports the royal derriere. The tombs are all stupendous for their scale, for the height at which they are built and for their detailed embellishments.

There is an intact cuboid building opposite the cliffs, called the Ka'ba-ye Zartosht, or Zoroaster's Kaaba, a name almost certainly given to it by Islamic invaders, that might have been anything from a safe to a tomb, or even a fire temple. Ancient metal clasps hold the stone blocks together in lieu of mortar and it's inscribed, in three languages, with a declaration by Kartir, the Sassanid-era high priest and Grand Vizir, whose religious efforts in the 3rd century AD resulted in the triumph of Mazdaism over Zurvanism— a popular, if somewhat heretical belief in eternity, or time, itself as God. But his declaration is boastful and vulgarly self-promoting, quite unbecoming of a high priest, let alone the one that rescued Zoroastrianism from the clutches of heresy. He gloats about how he exterminated followers of others cults and religions, killing their prophets and driving them out of the kingdom. All in all, he doesn't sound particularly enlightened or enlightening, and it reads more like the claims of an arrogant politician, or worse, a religious supremacist, and reminds me of what's wrong with many sorts of Muslim 'priests' these days.

A few hundred metres away are another set of engravings and inscriptions called the Naqsh-e Rajab, and here too there is a declaration by Kartir, with a bust of his profile carved into the rock. It's as haughty as the first one and goes as far as to say that Kartir has 'decided' that there will be a heaven and a hell and that religion, morality, even the afterlife, will be what he says it is, since apparently God himself takes his orders from Kartir. The Naqsh-e Rajab also has some impressive Parthian and Sassanian reliefs, which are larger and deeper than the one at the Naqsh-e Rostam, and are almost like sculptures. Two French women are the only other visitors at the site, and since I've let my taxi go, I ask them for a lift back to Persepolis, from where I can catch public transport to Shiraz.

Arriving in the evening, I'm led by the nostrils to the Shirazi street food being served up in huddled stalls around the Arg-e-Karim Khan. For the first time since arriving in Iran, I encounter a wide selection of snacks, from boiled peanuts to skewers of meat with naan and beans mixed up with vegetables, resembling something like *chotpoti*. Even the spices and flavours are recognisable. Smoke from charcoal grills float across the black sky and diffuse to cover the place in a mist-like haze. Hawkers and vendors call out to people passing by; one in particular is shouting, 'shish, kofta, kebab' in a rhythm that makes the place feel festive. I gorge on the delectable delights while engaging in banter with a group of Uzbek refugee boys who wear baseball caps backwards and pose like gangster rappers when I try to take pictures of them. They are quite poor in pocket, but very rich in laughter.

I spend the evening in the guesthouse courtyard drinking chai and reading, while the kind staff look after me with the attentiveness of family members. Across on the next table, I hear an Iranian woman speaking with a French group, in French, about the realities of life in Iran. She looks and sounds like someone raised in an environment like my own, and the little French that I know lets me listen in as she describes social circumstances that I can understand and even relate to. She tells her very inquisitive friends about what it's like being an Iranian woman and counters their patronising presumptuousness with stories about her experiences in France, where she says she felt less empowered and less respected as a woman. I like the matter-of-fact way she is dealing with what are clearly intended as insults to her culture and country.

They switch topics and talk about the economy. She tells them about how costs of living are hard to meet on most Iranian salaries and how people aspire to be doctors or engineers, not because they want to be, but because it improves their position in society and their prospects for marriage, especially for the men. If I didn't know any better, I could have sworn she was talking about Bangladesh. A little girl runs around the courtyard playing Angry Birds on an iPad, while her parents, a posh looking couple, fuss and grumble about nothing in particular while having their dinner.

Tired, I make my way to the reception area to check my email before going to bed. There I meet Mr. Jaffar, the night receptionist and a polite, personable gentleman. I tell him I've been to Pasargadae and he says,

'Ah, to see Kurosh. He was Iran's best ever king, you know. It should have always been like that. Darius was also good.'

This leads us into a conversation about Zoroastrianism, which Mr. Jaffar insists was moral and decent and in no need of being replaced by the Islam of the Arabs, for whom he appears to have very little respect.

'Islam is not a problem; the problem is that it was conveyed in the rough tongue of a rough people.'

The perspective I've gained on Iran's relationship with Islam since I've been here is intriguing. This, the *ajam* half of Islamic civilisation and a vital engine of its growth for nearly all of its existence, seems to still be at odds with its Islamic inheritance. But perhaps retrofitted Persian ethnocentrism, designed to accommodate an ageless Iranian belief in the superioriority of their way of life requires this unease. It's not unlike South Asian superiority complexes where everything was invented by Indians and Sanskritic civilisation is the bee's knees. Islam and Arabs are the villains in that story, too, but I find this scapegoating dishonest and distasteful. Islam hardly deserves this much scorn; it arrived on the scene as a vigorous moral force, necessary and able to breathe new life into the degenerating societies of grand old India, Egypt and Persia; and the Arabs were not brutes but conscientious and adventurous people who were courageous enough to earn their own place among the great civilisers of the world.

We talk about other things. Mr. Jaffar tells me how Shirazis are the most laid back of Iranians, wizened as they are, by a long and affluent past which affords them the luxury of having nothing much to prove. He tells me they have a reputation for revelry, entertaining and camping outdoors in groups, which before 'mullah rule' impinged on their celebrations, included alcohol—wine, obviously, music and merriment. Shirazis enjoy the good life and appreciate art, he says, and many of the richer ones have villas by the sea or out in the desert which are as full of art as museums. I can believe it. There is old world, old money sophistication in the atmosphere, and like most old places, Shiraz has many hustlers and messy traffic along with an un-shininess that makes it all the more appealing.

It has crass people as well, of course. There are versions of that Bangladeshi sort of shallow snobbery here, where suddenly 'arrived' people looking at you with contempt when you happen to look like the unkempt scruff-ball I've turned into lately. It's ironic that I should get these stares here in Shiraz, where the mystic Musleuddin Saadi lived, and whose famous parable addresses this very matter so very eloquently. Actually, I'm not sure it really is a Saadi story, but it was attributed to him when I first heard it on the streets of Dhaka many years ago. It goes like this:

Once upon a time, the wandering dervish Saadi Shirazi was invited to a banquet at the home of a respected and refined noble-man, where various local and foreign dignitaries were also to be in attendance. Accustomed to the ways of the poor, Saadi, like many Sufis might have, showed up in his patchwork clothing, but was promptly turned away by the guards at the gate, who mistook him for a beggar. He went away and returned wearing an elegant tunic, which he had received as a gift, and was given a proper welcome this time, bows and all. The meal was served and the dervish was invited to sit at the head table with the host. During the course of the ban-quet, Saadi began stuffing his various pockets with morsels of food and continued doing this until his host, red with embarrassment, finally said,

'Master, why are you behaving so strangely? If you wish to take some of this food home you need only ask and I shall arrange for it immediately.'

Saadi carried on filling his pockets without looking up at his host, but casually replied,

'No, no, your Excellency, that won't be necessary. However, I felt it would be rude if your guest was not properly entertained. You see, when I came to accept your invitation the first time, I was turned away at the door because of my shabby appearance. I returned wearing this tunic and was graciously welcomed in, so that can only mean that my tunic is the real guest at your table and therefore it should eat well.'

My conversation with Mr. Jaffar ends with him telling me I should live in Iran and teach English, since they desperately want to learn the language and prefer not to bring European 'heathens' in to do the job. He tells me I will make good money, but more importantly, will be coveted by beautiful Iranian women who, on account of my religion and my British passport, will marry me and keep me very happy so long as I promise to take them out of Iran at some point. So a blissful life is available to me courtesy Britain's controversially acquired international edge and my command over this, our coloniser's tongue.

The Japanese couple have checked out, so I have the dorm to myself and I watch a bit of TV before going to bed. While flipping through channels, I come across an English news bulletin where I learn that President Obama has decide to increase sanctions against Iran for its nuclear ambitions. His language and tone suggests that he is talking about a delinquent juvenile, and not the mature, cultured country I've been travelling in, and it's blatantly apparent how large the gap between the sensationalism we're fed on TV and the actual world really is. Amused but infuriated, hearing Obama go on about Iran with pompous, unfounded authority, I turn him off and turn in.

⑩

Never Too Old

Ahvaz, Chogha Zanbil, Shush, Tehran, Tabriz

Ahvaz

Shiraz has many murals and on my last day here I spend some time going around looking at them. I also enjoy walking through crowds listening to people speaking in Farsi, which has many words ending in the sound 'am'—*nadaram, biram, mutsakaram*—that makes them sound similar to words in Vedic hymns. People smile and gesture amiably as I pass them on the street. Most Persians have a soft, kindly nature and it's easy to appeal to their sense of compassion, which reminds me of something Mr. Jaffar had told me the night before. He said, while having a go at the Arabs, that

'Arabs are hard; they look at people ferociously. They are not peaceful, but we are basically peaceful. I wish we could have been left in peace and not invaded so often. Arabs, Turks, Mongols … peace has been hard to preserve in Persia.'

I wanted to remind him about the number of times an Imperial Persia didn't let its neighbours live in peace either, especially India, but was not in the mood for a long discussion, which it would inevitably have become since Iranians have numerous blind spots about their own faults. I head to the station in the evening to take a bus to Ahvaz, in search of the greatest surviving Elamite ruin in Iran, the Chogha Zanbil ziggurat. As I wait for my night bus, I take in the array of faces at the station: white faces, brown faces, women in chador and no makeup, women with scarves and lots of makeup, Balochis in *shalwar* suits, people in jeans, old distinguished men, young posers, tall people, short people. Some look very European, others very Indian. Iran's ethnic fabric is a tapestry as diverse as South Asia's, but with a tendency towards lighter rather than darker skin. My own face is, as usual, a 'middling' face but I can more or less get by undetected anywhere between Bangladesh and Turkey.

On advice from a fellow passenger I decide to take the 'VIP' bus, which is only slightly more expensive but considerably more comfortable than the normal ones. There are fewer seats, and they become completely flat, like business class seats in an aeroplane, perfect for a nine-hour overnight ride. We arrive at Ahvaz at dawn when it is already quite bright, and I'm woken up by the light streaming in through the large bus windows. Ahvaz, or Ahwaz, is the capital of Khuzestan province, which is less arid than Pars, as a river, the Karun River, runs through it. Karun isn't a large or raging river, but it's enough of one to let Ahvaz and its surroundings support what looks like a range of crops on its flat, featureless expanse. In fact it's quite lush in places and it's humid, much like home and unlike the parts of Iran I've travelled through to get here. Unfortunately, it's also very polluted, and the blue sky is almost permanently besmirched by black smoke being belched out of ugly industrial complexes that have aggressively imposed themselves upon the riverbanks. They're quite an eyesore, and interrupt the otherwise pleasant proliferation of green in this dry and dusty part of the world. But Khuzestan borders the ancient Fertile Crescent, and the Karun River empties into the Shatt al-Arab or the 'Stream of the Arabs', which runs towards the Persian Gulf from the confluence of the Euphrates and the Tigris near Basra, to form the southern international boundary between Iraq and Iran.

Chogha Zanbil is well off the beaten path and I have to frequently change modes of transport before I can get to it. At Ahvaz station I wait for a local bus to Shush, which is another three hours away, but I can stay the night there and explore Achaemenid ruins once I'm done visiting the Elamite ziggurat. Besides, I'm well rested, so the prospect of onward travel doesn't seem tedious. I have a cup of tea and use the loo before going to the counter to buy my ticket, where the usual ensues:

'*Koja hastid? Keshwar? Pawkistan?* (suspicious), *Hendustan?* (amusing), *Bangladesh?... Koja Bangladesh?* (oblivious)'

Some rare people know where it is though, since they've known Bangladeshis from their time as migrant workers in Gulf Arab countries, and tell me we're a happy, friendly bunch who speak fast and write funny. I buy my ticket and wait for the bus to fill up (local buses run when they are full rather than according to a schedule). A group of ticketing officers sip tea and laugh together at the counter in front of me; their joy is contagious and I feel happy just watching them. The Arabic influence on Khuzestan province is very apparent; in fact, parts of it adjoining the Iraqi border were officially known as Arabistan once and are still called that in popular speech. Nearly half of the province is effectively Arabic, and separatist movements have also sprung up here from time to time, though mostly benign ones. Iran is hardly a homogenous place. Only the central provinces are Persian in the truest sense and nearly all the edges contain large populations that are associated with neighbouring cultures, some related to Persians, like the Kurds, and others not, like the Azeris, who are Turkic. Khuzestan is particularly not Persian, and the half that is not Arabic is Luri, a people related to both the Persians and the Kurds but distinct enough to self-identify as something else.

Arab-Iranians greet each other with '*Salaamalaik*', instead of the more familiar '*Saalom*', and say '*Shukran*' instead of '*Merci*' or '*Mamnoon*'. Some speak Arabic fully, but most speak a Farsi interspersed with Arabic. A prevalence of the *dishdasha,* or thobe, the tunic that Arabs everywhere from Morocco to Iraq enjoy wearing, also gives this place an added Arabian feel. I haven't seen these since I left Bangladesh where, oddly enough, they feature quite a bit. To their credit, Pakistanis don't imitate Arabs in their dress sense and prefer their own South Asian *shalwar-kameez* style. Nor do Iranians, who wear the 'Shalwar Shirazi' if they aren't wearing western gear, but they don't wear it often enough; it's a very smart pair of trousers and I'm keen to get one myself.

The minibus takes ages to fill up and I'm wishing I had opted for a Savari instead, but we're finally away and I'm taken through fields and vegetation reminiscent of a tropical place, with palm trees and thick, humid air—a world apart from the dry desert heat of Pars. It's also completely flat, unlike anywhere else I've been in Iran, where mountains are a permanent feature on the horizon. Instead, miles and miles of wheat, as tall as a person, are spread out in every direction, only interrupted by date trees and a few other varieties of palm. It's certainly a very fertile place. We arrive at Shush, where I have a sandwich and notice that my shoes have absolutely had it. The soles have come undone so I look for a *moochi,* a cobbler who can sort me out. I find one, who promptly asks me, 'Pakistani?' No, I'm Bangladeshi ... for God's sake, can't I just be myself for once?' This pleases him as he says, beamingly, in broken Urdu,

'Hum Afghani, Urdu samajta he. Bangladesh accha hae lekin Pakistan bohat Shaitan!'

I'm as pleased to meet another South Asian as he is, and through all the smiling and bowing, I feel compelled to defend our embattled cousins, the Pakistanis, and tell him there are good and bad elements in all countries, to which he says,

'Kyun, tum logo pe zuloom nahi kiya un logo nai?'
'Ha kiya, lekin ....'
'Afghani ko bhi kartay hai.'

'Accha, accha theek hai bhai, kartay hai. Abhi mera juta theek kar do na please?'

At Shush bus station I'm told I have to take a bus to Haft Tepe, a town and an archeological site, 20 kilometres south, to get within reach of Chogha Zanbil. Haft Tepe, which means 'Seven Hills' for the seven mounds that have grown over the ruins, was an Elamite settlement, possibly Kabnak, and one of humanity's original cities. The area around Shush and Ahvaz, bordering Mesopotamia, was the headland of the Elamite world, and Chogha Zanbil belongs to this legacy as well. I opt not to explore Haft Tepe though it contains archeological treasures that stretch back to the agricultural revolution and the dawn of settled communities, and satisfy myself with the search for the largest surviving temple from that period— the Chogha Zanbil ziggurat. Before I board the bus, an Arabic-speaking man I smoke a cigarette with notices that I'm foreign and without any hesitation says, 'Bangali?' Amazing! It's the first and only time I'm identified correctly in Iran, but how? Ships and Chittagong, of course—like the man in Peshawar, this gentleman has also been to Bangladesh.

The small bus is full of very pleasant village folk, some with their produce, others with livestock, chickens mostly. It's a rural route and the bus stops frequently for passengers and their assorted luggage. School children get on and off at various points. The driver struggles to accommodate everyone and everything, strapping a bicycle to the side of the bus once and rearranging the boot more than twice. Much debate and deliberation accompany all of these efforts. The route takes us through sugarcane plantations, and reminds me of scenes from my childhood in Mauritius, where we lived briefly. My fellow passengers are friendly and enjoy watching me take pictures through the window. They smile at me with the warmth and simplicity of most rural people anywhere. We arrive at Haft Tepe where everyone alights, but it's a suburb and not the main town so the only place I can go to get directions is the cluster of village shops standing sleepily by the side of the road.

Chogha Zanbil

After uttering the words 'Chogha Zanbil' at random people a number of times, I find a person who knows another person who can take me there, so we walk to his house around the corner where we find him washing his car. He's Arab-Iranian and everything about him, from his body language to the way he speaks, tells the difference between Persians and Arabs. For one he is more overbearing than many of his Persian countrymen and has less regard for etiquette. He is distinctly less courteous but also less shy, and carries himself in a bold, almost domineering manner. I am slightly intimidated by him, and find myself having to shrink to accommodate his rather large presence. But he's a friendly person and his brash approach is also honest and cheery. There's a wild sort of spontaneity about him that is very Arab, and very enjoyable.

We drive past several un-excavated sites and buy some slices of watermelon from a farmer along the way—my driver swears the best watermelon in the world grows here. It's very good, actually, and perfect for the weather. Then I'm given a brief history of the region in broken English and Farsi, which he insists is a Semitic history as the Elamites were Semites, according to him, and therefore closer to Arabs than Persians. The telling of history is replete with claims to originality and this is no different. We arrive at the site and go to the guard-house to register and pay the entry fee but there is nothing else here to indicate any sort of tourist activity at all. It's literally in the middle of nowhere. The ziggurat is enormous and towers above the surrounding landscape as a rectangular block of baked ochre bricks. There are other smaller sites nearby but I only have time to explore the main one and an on-site guide comes along with me to tell me its tales.

Chogha Zanbil ziggurat is the central instalment of a city that was originally called Dur Untash after the Elamite king Untash-Napirisha, who built a new city here, sometime in the 13th or 14th century BC. '*Dur*' means 'place' in Elamite and a similarity with the Arabic word '*dar*' for 'abode' is probably not coincidental, lending credence to my taxi driver's claims of a Semitic subtext to Iran's original civilisation. King Untash-Napirisha is known to us through a letter written by a later Elamite king to a Babylonian ruler in the 12th century BC, popularly known as the 'Berlin Letter' (because it resides there), which catalogues the political dynasty of Elam and it's connection, through marriage, to Babylonian courts. The letter discusses trade, territories, honour and alliances, giving us a sense of the power dynamics at the time and Elam's not inconsiderable position in an emerging, urban-based world order, physically manifested as a mountainous temple at the centre of a city that would never be completed.

Elam existed as a powerful Iranian civilisation alongside Mesopotamian ones from as early as the 3rd millennium BC, until it was invaded by Sargon the Akkadian, from what is now Iraq, as part of the first ever empire-building project in the region, which subjugated all the Fertile Crescent peoples. The Elamite cities Anshan and Awan, were completely overrun, along with Susa, to the point where Akkadian language and culture were forcefully imposed— an almost exact precursor to what happened when another wave of Iraqis, the Arabs, did very much the same about 3,000 years later. It's possible that Elamite culture took on Semitic elements during this time (even abandoning its original script for the Semitic cuneiform of the Akkadians) since the general scholarly consensus is that they were not Semites but were, like the Sumerians, Egyptians, Minoans and Harappans, bearers of a culture that was gradually replaced by both Semites and Indo-Europeans over a staggered period of time.

From the look of it, Dur Untash was a ceremonial city, a sort of pilgrimage site—like Elam's Mecca. A city wall once enclosed an area of about 100 hectares that had two sections—the ziggurat and the royal quarter. The rest of the land inside the city wall was never built up substantially, meaning that Untash-Napirisha either never intended it as a permanent settlement or never got around to making it one, as he died before the city was finished. His capital was in Susa (Sush), the seat of Elamite power for centuries, which is only 40 kilometres or so from here so it's unlikely that he would need another residential city this close to it. Perhaps a change in Elam's political orientation, from the plains to the hills, had something to do with it, because the ziggurat sits near the main route into the Zagros highlands and belongs to the Middle Elamite period.

During the Middle Elamite period, when Chogha Zanbil was built, the Elamites were shaking off vestiges of their colonisation by 're-Elamising' their culture and language, and engaging in monumental architecture. It was a renaissance of sorts following the end of Akkadian rule and Elam's return to independence, which was facilitated by attacks on Akkad by a highland people called the Gutians. The Gutians are a very interesting element in this story as they belong to none of the classical and competing civilisations of Mesopotamia or Iran. They have been recorded as uncouth, crude and lacking in any sort of cultural or political sophistication and were essentially raiders, swooping down from their hills to plunder the rich cities of the plains. They may have been the very first Indo-European entrants into the West Asian arena, though it's difficult to say, since they arrive on the scene nearly 1,500 years earlier than Indo-Europeans elsewhere in the region. They have also sometimes been called the ancestors of the Kurdish people and are described in clay tablets from the time as being light-skinned.

But to come back to where we started, it's very possible that this shift in power from the plains to the hills prompted the building of Dar Untash, along with a re-arranging of the Elamite pantheon to reflect a changing regional reality. Elamite highland or Anshan deities began taking precedence over lowland Susha ones and even though Susha's patron god Insusinak remained the most celebrated god in the Elamite pantheon for most of Elamite history, from the Middle Elamite Period onwards, he had to share his throne with Kirmasir and Napirisha, strictly Elamite gods from Anshan and beyond. Elamite kings began referring to themselves as 'servants of Kirmasir' and King Untash-Napirisha's name is, of course, a testament to his loyalty to Napirisha the god. At Chogha Zanbil, half of the 26 gods mentioned are Suso-Mesopotamian while the other half are Elamite, and the ziggurat is dedicated jointly to Napirisha and Insusinak, to represent, equally, the cities of Ashan and Susa. This new, fused pantheon, not unlike the Hindu pantheon, is officially unveiled here at Dur Untash.

My guide leads me through the outer wall of the ziggurat towards the southwestern corner of the structure, which is oriented to the cardinal points of the globe. Large circular objects like the bases of pillars are situated all around it and I'm told these are altars to lesser gods. The entire structure is surprisingly modern—it's square and step-pyramidal, with hard edges and terraces that look like they were designed according to the principles of Cubism. It's also remarkably well built, and displays none of the signs of decay you would expect in a building that has stood for more than 3,000 years. The bricks look nearly new, and the laying of them almost industrially accurate. There is a set of stairs on the side running all the way to the top, but it's closed off with a steel grill that must've been installed to prevent tourists from indulging in the desire to climb them, like I'm experiencing at the moment. Quintessential Iranian arches form doorways and gates to all the terraces and it's clear that some of the design features that have become standard Persian had their origins in Elamite architecture. Glazed and painted tiles, for instance, were used here and their slight remnants can still be seen on a brick or two. The ziggurat has largely collapsed, but it once had four terraces in descending size, topped by an altar to Napirisha and Insusinak together.

All along the building, running all the way through the main and peripheral structures is a ring of inscribed bricks. Every eleventh row of bricks is inscribed in cuneiform script and the Elamite language with a dedication to the 'Lord of Susa' Insusinak. It's an attractive and subtle feature, and a forebearer of the inscribed dedications to Allah on the walls of mosques across the Muslim world. There are drainage channels all around and through all the terraces of the structure that look like they are designed to catch rainwater, but a more sinister outlook might lead one to believe that they were designed to channel blood from the top of the temple, where presumably a human or animal sacrifice or two would take place. No such evidence exists, of course, but Elamite values differ from ours enough to make such an abomination possible. For example, according to the Encyclopedia Iranica, Elamite royal succession followed a pattern that many of us would find particular revolting today:

> *The succession to the throne was based on male primogeniture, with, however, an important additional element: the different degrees of legitimacy exemplified by the primacy of endogamy over exogamy. The child born to a union of the king with an Elamite princess, that is, a foreigner, was legitimate. The child born to a union of the king with his own sister had a higher degree of legitimacy. An elder son born to the marriage of a sovereign with a princess outside the family (exogamy) thus had to cede the throne to a younger brother born to a later union of the king and his sister (endogamy). The supreme degree of legitimacy was accorded to the son born to a union of the king with his own daughter. That was the case some centuries later with Hutelutuš-Inšušinak, who seems to have been the son of Šutruk-Nahhunte by his daughter Nahhunte-utu.*

Today only about two and a half terraces are intact, standing 25 metres high instead of the 60 metres it occupied when it was built; the rest of the ziggurat has collapsed into itself and looks like it was smashed with a very large mallet before being covered over with mud. None of the decorative and commemorative items that were discovered here are kept on site; they have been preserved in various museums around the world. Votive figurines and fragments of an inscribed faience bull, seals, inscribed bricks, doorknobs, pottery, amulets and the remains of two panels in ivory mosaic found at the site give us a sense of what life was like during the relatively brief period, only about 200 years, that Dur Untash was in use. But it was not expected to have such a short life. Untash-Napirisha went to great lengths to ensure its survival by commissioning one of the earliest known attempts at redirecting a river. A 50-kilometre channel connected a tributary of the river Karun to a massive reservoir, from where nine aquaducts took water to a central basin in Dur Untash (the remains of which are still visible). It's a staggering feat of engineering, and along with the ziggurat, which is the largest in the world, testimony to the wealth and the industriousness of the kingdom of Elam.

I walk around the structure, guide in tow, who tells me about the smaller temples on the northern side and the solitary footprint in clay, that is said to be of an Elamite child from the 11th century BC. I check out the storehouses and their enormous bolts, where perhaps grain, gold or tributes were stored, and soak in the feeling of walking around in a place that was among the crowning achievements of an extremely powerful civilisation that is now completely extinct. It's a peculiar sensation, as though you can never be powerful enough to prevent yourself from disappearing into obscurity, and as I walk back towards the taxi I wonder what will become of our own civilisations, four, maybe five thousand years from now.

Shush

I get back to Shush bus stop where I take a taxi into town and ask to be dropped off near the tomb of Daniyal. It's the centre of town where, my guidebook tells me, budget accommodation will be available and the ruins of the Achaemenid city of Susa will be within walking distance. The taxi pulls up next to what looks like an 18th-century European castle on my left and a strange, bare, conical structure on my right. It has a decorated gate and I see people entering it with a reverence normally shown to a shrine or a temple. I ask after it, and sure enough it *is* the tomb of Nabi Daniyal, the Hebrew prophet Daniel. Ever since I arrived in Western Iran, I've been in places that feature in Jewish holy literature, and a Semitic, particularly Hebrew, frame of reference is becoming increasingly evident. I am, of course, very close to the Biblical heartlands and the events and characters captured in scripture are beginning to coincide with archeological historicity.

Shush and Elam are both mentioned in Hebrew religious literature; in fact, Elam is the name of Noah's grandson, one of Shem's five son's—Elam, Asshur, Arfachshad, Lud, and Aram. Shem, or Sem, is the reason his descendants are called Semites, and his sons are supposedly the ancestors of the Elamites, the Assyrians and the Arameans, corresponding to Elam, Asshur and Aram. I can hear my Arab-Iranian taxi driver at Chogha Zanbil agree. But none of this is anthropologically verified, of course. The Jews and Arabs supposedly descend from Arfachshad, who was an ancestor of the prophet Abraham and a founder of the city of Ur, the centre of a kingdom called Uruk, from which Iraq takes its name. True or not, all of it makes for an interesting origin story for the people of the Fertile Crescent, whose collective offspring influenced and are probably still influencing the way we broadly understand the word 'civilisation'.

As I mentioned a while back, the Jewish book of Ezra confirms that Cyrus was instrumental in restoring the Jews to their homeland, but it also talks about Darius and Athaxerxes. It tells us Cyrus helped to build the Second Temple, which was completed by his successor, Darius the Great (or a subsequent Darius), who also ordered his subjects to help the Jews financially in this task. It then says Arthaxerxes, descendent of Darius and a follower of Zoroaster, set the Prophet Ezra on his mission by making him responsible for 'religious affairs' in the Persian province of Judah, and gave him wealth and state patronage to help him spread the word of his God, the same God that became Allah in Arabic. He told him:

Appoint magistrates and judges to administer justice to all the people of the region—all who know the laws of your God.

The Achaemenids were friends and patrons of the Jews, a fact that stands in stark contrast to the relationship between Israel and Iran today. In the Jewish book of Ester, set in Shush in the 5th century BC, we discover that a Persian king, either Xerxes or Athaxerxes, marries Ester, a Jewish woman from among the exiled Jews now living in the Achaemenid realm. We also learn of the plot by a Persian noble, Haman, to exterminate the Jews after becoming resentful of the rise of Mordecai, Ester's Jewish guardian and now someone close to the royal couple. Through various machinations, a plot is hatched but foiled after it is discovered by the Persian king and queen, who support Mordecai and put the scheming Persian nobleman to death. It leads to an interracial bloodbath, in which the Persians come off the worst, yet in the interest of justice, the Achaemenids allow it and do nothing in retaliation against the Jews. This event is celebrated by Jews today as Purim. Ester and Mordecai lived out their lives peacefully in the Persian realm and are said to be buried together in Hamedan where Iranian Jews, who claim descent from Ester, still go to pay their respects.

The Book of Daniel is also set in Shush, which brings us back to the point of this elaborate Jewish tangent, but at an earlier age. According to scripture, Daniel, or Daniyal, a victim of the Babylonian Captivity, was installed in a Babylonian court in Shush as a soothsayer, before the Persians overran Babylon and established their own empire. Daniyal predicted this event, and he tells the last Babylonian king that he will be defeated and killed by an Aryan warlord. This comes to pass, and the Aryan king, referred to in the book as Darius even though this is chronologically incongruent, retains Daniyal's services in his own court. Daniyal, being non-Persian, becomes an object of hatred for other officials, who plot his demise by playing on the Persian king's vanity. They make him decree that no one other than himself is worthy of any sort of worship for 30 days, knowing that Daniyal prays to Allah three times a day and will certainly violate this order. He does and is punished by being thrown into a den of lions, but emerges the next day miraculously unharmed. This impresses the king greatly, who decides that Daniyal's God is a real one, and reinstates him with full honours.

Daniyal's eventual death is a mystery, as is the location of his remains. At least three tombs around the world are dedicated to him. According to some traditions he died in Shush while according to others, in Israel. A peculiar account by Benjamin of Tudela, the 12th-century Jewish traveller, written in 1167 in Shush, gives us some indication of where Daniyal might be buried.

In front of one of the synagogues is the sepulchre of Daniel of blessed memory. The river Tigris divides the city, and the bridge connects the two parts. On the one side where the Jews dwell is the sepulchre of Daniel. Here the market places used to be, containing great stores of merchandise, by which the Jews became enriched. On the other side of the bridge they were poor, because they had neither market places nor merchants there, only gardens and plantations. And they became jealous, and said: 'All this prosperity enjoyed by those on the other side is due to the merits of Daniel the prophet who lies buried there.' Then the poor people asked those who dwelt on the other side to place the sepulchre of Daniel in their midst, but the others would not comply. So war prevailed between them for many days, and no one went forth or came in on account of the great strife between them. At length both parties growing tired of this state of things took a wise view of the matter, and made a compact, namely the coffin of Daniel be taken for one year to the one side and for another year to the other side. This they did, and both sides became rich.

Benjamin then tells us that the Seljuq sultan at the time put Daniel's wooden coffin inside a crystal coffin and suspended it from the middle of the bridge. How it got from there to the tomb I'm standing in front of, after what sounds like centuries of unrest, is anyone's guess.

The tomb looks like any Persian mosque or mazaar, with *kashi* tiles and mirrors for decoration, a central courtyard with an ablution fountain, and a vaulted gate, but with one major and conspicuous exception—it has no dome but is finished off with a huge inverted cone that has a step-like, serrated surface. It's not decorated but plain, and resembles the top of certain Hindu temples in Bengal. A man dressed like an Ayatollah and another like an Arab Sheikh, with their wives covered in full black chador, enter through the gate. Though Nabi Daniyal is not mentioned in the Quran, Muslims consider him a prophet, and I follow them towards the courtyard.

It's very hot and I've been lugging my backpack around all day, so I head straight for the ablution fountain in the middle of the courtyard to wash up and cool down. I sit by the tank of water for a bit, just taking in my surroundings when I notice a young man looking at me with a gaze that signals both affection and concern. I greet him, he greets me and discovers that I'm not a local, which he must've already gathered by my quite obvious appearance as a traveller. He tells me his name is Jasim, and that he isn't a local either but also a traveller, from Basra, Iraq. We try to converse a little in whatever combination of Farsi, English and Arabic we can manage and he tells me to follow him, in that uniquely Arab sort of urgency that spawned the expression '*yalla, yalla*'. We go inside the shrine, and he helps me with my backpack as I remove my shoes. There is something genuine and thoughtful about this person.

The metal cage-like structure that encases most Shia mazaars, like the one at Imam Reza's tomb, surrounds Daniyal's grave as well. It's ornately decorated, as is the niche in which it sits, which is covered in mirrors. Inside, the sarcophagus is draped in velvet cloth. There is nothing Jewish about it at all; in fact, it's overwhelmingly Islamic in its appearance. Visitors hang on to it, rocking back and forth on their heels. Some weep softly, others pray with cupped hands. A contingent of military men in uniform is praying in congregation in front of the grave. I ask Jasim about it and he tells me soldiers like to visit Nabi Daniyal before being sent on missions as it reminds them of his courage in the lion's den. Jews come too, but there are none here today. I pray with Jasim—he does it the Shia way and I do it the way I'm used to, but we do it together. I feel a bond with this man whom I have only just met.

After we pray, we sit for a while as Jasim tells me he's on ziyarat to Imam Reza's tomb. I'm reminded again of my travelling companion in Balochistan and the poor, unfortunate Hazara pilgrims who were slaughtered on the way to their own ziyarat, from the other end of Iran. Jasim tells me he's staying with some family friends who are Arab-Iranian and live around the corner. He asks me to join him for tea, I try to decline, he insists, I'm too tired for *tawrouf* so I accept and we head towards the house, passing the bridge where Nabi Daniyal's remains were sacrilegiously suspended for a period of time.

The neighbourhood consists of rows of houses and shops, some painted but most unfinished, and their concrete exoskeletons remind me of small towns in rural Bangladesh or India. These are new developments that were just barely finished before becoming old and lived in—almost overnight. Past a nice park, we turn into a street and stop in front of a large corrugated iron gate, which Jasim pounds on while shouting something in Arabic. The gate opens, Jasim is greeted with on his cheeks, I'm greeted with a handshake, and we're led into the compound. At the far end is a long room next to a small house and to the right are some trees and vegetation. Beside the gate there's an outhouse, some rubble and the general articles of an untended plot.

The long room is laid out like a divan, with a mattress along one wall and Persian rugs covering the whole floor. I meet Jamil, who greets me cordially but with surprise, and I hear the words 'Muslim?' and 'Shia?' being uttered as parts of questions being placed to Jasim in hushed Arabic after I sit down. *'Na'am'* and *'La'* are offered as replies, at which Jamil, the person in charge of the room and possibly the house, pauses for the briefest of seconds before declaring with an exaggerated gesture, 'Muslim is Muslim. Welcome, *akhi'*. I'm immediately made to feel like part of the group and if there was a conversation in progress before I arrived, it gets thrown out in favour of their curiosity about the stray Jasim had brought in, who speaks neither Arabic nor Farsi, but knows enough words in both to understand a little of what is being said to him. I'm reminded of the boys in Neyshabur and experience a similar sensation of disjointed yet barely intelligible conversation.

They offer me tea and ask me numerous questions about myself, some of which I understand and try to answer in a way that might also be understood, while at others I just nod along or shrug my shoulders. The room is spartan, with grey cement walls made colourful in places by pictures, posters or articles of faith. A verse from the Quran in calligraphy hangs alongside a picture of Ayatollahs Khamenei and Khomeini, beside a poster of a man in a green turban and an angelic expression. I'm told it's a representation of Imam Ali and the parallels between how he is depicted and how Christ is often shown are unmistakable. In fact, at first glance it's very easy to think it's a picture of Jesus himself. Other items include family pictures, a bright orange clock and a string of yellow plastic flowers hung over everything like a *matra*. There is a set of shelves and a television in the corner. The room is otherwise completely empty, allowing its occupants to sprawl out across it—reclining, sitting or lying down flat.

A few more people arrive after us, including a very friendly and flamboyant young man called Shuaib. He greets everyone, including me, with kisses, and I notice that Arab-Iranians have a different way of doing it—instead of three kisses, beginning and ending on the left cheek, they kiss either cheek and end by kissing the left shoulder, an unusual gesture and one I've only ever seen done in Shush. They all do it here, and at first it's quite confusing. After greetings, people settle in and break off into smaller, individual conversations, catching up on the day's events, most likely. It's clear that these people spend a lot of time together and this is probably their standard winding down ritual. The only thing different today, of course, is me, yet in no time, they are as comfortable with me as they are with each other, language barriers notwithstanding. It's very homey and I feel ensconced in familiarity, though well aware of how impossible that actually should be. Tea arrives, and the communal ceremony that tea drinking is everywhere, commences. Afterwards, someone turns on the TV; a Premier League football match is on and we all get drawn into it. Language barriers melt away, football being a planet of its own, and universally recognisable sounds rings out across the room.

'*Uff, Passpasspasspasspass! Goaaaa … nononoooo … ohhhh! Uffffff.*'

It's getting late, so I indicate that I want to head off and find a hotel for the night, but my hosts insist I stay for dinner. I recognise it as courteousness but feel conscious about imposing and am also keen to find a room before it's too late. They continue to insist and so I relent—I'm not quite sure why, but I find it difficult to say no, maybe because I fear it might offend them, but also, and perhaps more importantly, because I feel very genuinely looked after. Dinner is a full spread—Arabian bread, olives, cheese, salad, chicken and lamb. It's a feast, and in *dastarkhana* style we sit across each other along a long plastic mat spread out in the middle of the room. More people arrive and are waved in welcomingly as they take their place in front of paper plates. The atmosphere turns festive and food is passed around along with various muttered expressions of satisfaction and gratitude. Everyone, it seems, is welcome, even strange foreigners like me.

I discover over dinner that the people who live here, and many of the visitors, are refugees, Shias from neighbouring Iraq. They live on the fringes of Shush's society and are poor by Iranian standards, but you wouldn't know it by the way they are making their home and kitchen abundantly available to everyone. It's only men in this room and the food comes from the main house, where the women are. I chat with the people on either side of me. One of them is wearing a blue *dishdasha*; he's middle-aged and very good looking but his eyes house a sadness that confirms the horrors he's fled in Basra, where he grew up. I imagine he's witnessed the Iran–Iraq War, the first and second Gulf wars and the crippling sectarian violence that is currently tearing his country apart, but when I ask him about these he just smiles as if to say 'What do you think?' His name is Hanif, and he's a thoroughly dignified gentleman.

After dinner, Hanif, Shuaib and some others, including Jasim, head out, leaving me in the care of our hosts, Jamil and his younger brother Mohammed. Their youngest brother Malik, an adorable nine-year-old, is with us too, and they ask me to join them as they go out to get some dessert. I agree, seeing it as a chance to also find a place to stay for the night, and we walk out to the end of the street where a friend of theirs offers us a lift in his car. We pass the city centre and a few guesthouses along the way. I make a mental note of them, hoping to be able to walk down from wherever we stop and book myself into a room. But we don't stop nearby; instead we are taken to a large amusement park further from the city centre, where the car drops us off and leaves. It's about 9 pm already and I'm starting to worry. The park is open, surprisingly, and full of visitors. Jamil explains that it's the one day of the week that the park is open at night and buys us all tickets to go in. I'm not allowed to pay for mine and even though I'm concerned about the time, I can't refuse to join them after all the hospitality I've already been shown.

We go on a number of rides—the Ferris wheel, the revolving tea cups, bumper cars, even a terrifying pendulum ride which almost relieves me of my dinner. We go on a few of them twice, three times even, and are transformed into a bunch of very small boys with every successive turn. The delight is completely basic and needs no interpretation—we look at each other with wide eyes and wide smiles, screaming together like we grew up playing in the same yard. After rides, we walk around the park feeling giddy and excited; it's a wonderful experience, honest and innocent, and I can feel years of cynicism miraculously falling off me as I soak up the company of these charming boys, who seem to have nothing jagged about them at all.

Afterwards, we walk towards a large field where families have come for an evening out. A sign tells me it's called Wendi Park. True to Iranian form, some of them are picnicking on the grass with their teapots and *calyans*, while others are playing badminton or football. There are floodlights, and the grounds look tended and clean. We buy ice-cream and sit together on a steel rail fence, enjoying it as Jasim and Shuaib return from where they had gone after dinner and join us. A group of middle-aged men are playing football. They aren't dressed for it—one of them is even wearing a thobe and they are all barefoot, but they play with all their heart and it fills their souls, and mine, with joy.

I finally work up the courage to say I have to leave and that I would like to book a room nearby, but I'm met with the stiffest resistance. There's no way around it either, since I have no idea where the hotels are and it's almost 11 pm. I plead a little but they implore better, and we look for a taxi to take us back to the house. I'm slightly frustrated; I was looking forward to a room and a bath, having not slept on a bed the previous night, but can't really be upset about it considering the spirit in which it is being denied to me. We find a taxi; the driver is in the nearby shop and comes out as we approach. He fusses about the number of passengers but something is said in Farsi at which he laughs and nods. His bearing suggests he's not Arab-Iranian but Persian—the gestures are more superfluous and he carries himself with a sense of entitlement that makes my companions feel slightly submissive. He *is* Persian, as it turns out, and chatty, and the cab fills up with conversation before it fills up with people. There are subtle differences in the way Iranian Arabs and Persians carry themselves—the Persian penchant for dramatic overstatement is not shared by their Arab compatriots, who seem more conservative generally.

At the house, blankets and pillows have already been provided, which Jamil and his brothers spread out like mattresses. I'm invited to occupy one set while Jasim and the three brothers occupy the other four. Shuaib leaves soon after, Malik and Muhammed watch a bit of TV and Jasim chats with Jamil in low, private tones. The lights are turned off and a bit later the TV as well. I'm already dozing off when I hear Jamil saying, 'Good night, Mr. Zeeshan', with the familiarity of an old friend or a relative, humbling me profoundly and forcing me to wonder whether I, or anyone I know, would ever have extended this sort of unreserved, unquestioning hospitality to a total and foreign stranger. I'm almost certain that most of us wouldn't, but it seems like nothing out of the ordinary for my hosts.

Hammurabi

We wake up early the next morning, some of us earlier than others, and when I open my eyes I find Jasim and Jamil already up and walking around outside. It's about 7 am, and after the rest of us get up and put our bedding away, tea is brought to the room. I go to wash up outside as a steady stream of the same people from dinner pour back into the room for breakfast—once again a full spread— with cheese, olives, bread and honey.

Jasim, Jamil and Muhammed head towards the vegetable market and ask me to join them, so I do. Shuaib meets us along the way and as we walk into town he looks for opportunities to make a bit of early morning money. A man struggling with a large piece of metal piping comes into view and Shuaib offers to take it off his shoulders for a small fee. The man agrees but Shuaib nearly buckles under the weight, causing everyone present to have a good laugh at his expense. He shakes his head and apologises, and then offers to help the man carry it for free, so the two of them carry the pipe for about half a kilometre up the road where they part ways.

At the market I discover that Jamil has another brother, an older one, who works at one of the vegetable stalls. While Jasim does some grocery shopping, Jamil and Muhammed help their brother unload and display produce. I go with Jasim to try and contribute to the grocery bill but predictably, he won't have it, so I go back to the stall and help with the vegetable stacking. On the way back to the house, I learn that Jamil and Muhammed have yet another brother, who lives and works in Iraq, and that their father was an Iraqi soldier who was killed during the Iran-Iraq War. It's a complete and utter travesty that Shia Iraqis had to fight Shia Iranians in a war that started, partly at least, as an attempt to contain Shi'ite Iran's influence in the Arab world. Even more ironic is the fact that Jamil's family, and many others like his, have sought and received refuge in the very Iran that was once their father's adversary.

At home, Jasim lets me know that I can have a bath if I want to. In fact, he doesn't even imply I have a choice, which is wonderfully thoughtful and mildly insulting all at the same time. I'm sure I do smell terrible, but I'm also sure that's not why he offered it. I'm grateful for the opportunity and get some fresh clothes and toiletries out of my bag as Jamil shows me to the bathroom inside the main house. The hushed voices of women can be faintly heard along the dark, narrow corridor. In beautiful feminine Arabic, Jamil is instructed to take the towels and soap provided by shy hands from behind barely opened doors, and asked to tell me I should let the water run for a bit before using it. He leaves me at the bathroom as the voices slowly taper off and I disrobe inside, doubly shielded by the purdahs of their minds that add an extra layer of privacy to the atmosphere. When I finish, I shout '*Shukran*' at the closed doors to a volley of muffled giggles, and then an '*Afwan akhi*' is cheerfully returned.

We eat lunch soon after and it's all very fresh; there is fish too, deliciously baked, along with a range of other treats like raw kibbeh and hummus—a complete feast, and the *dastar* is spread out once more so the community can gather around to eat together. Over lunch, Jasim tells me that he will not be going to Mashhad after all and will have to return to Iraq shortly since his father has called him back. He is sad about this, and I feel sorry for him. He also mentions something about not having anyone to go with, and I consider going with him but it's not an option, unfortunately, as my visa will run out before I can make it back across virtually all of Iran again. I'm surprised I even thought about it, but I'm desperate to do something for these wonderful people who have virtually adopted me without any questions and without a single stitch of suspicion. After lunch, I announce that I will leave in the evening and say an emotional goodbye to people I won't see before I go, like Shuaib and Hanif. Even though we've known each other for less than 24 hours, for some inexplicable reason this is a reasonably sad moment for all of us. I then set off to visit the ruins at Shush, and Muhammed, Malik and Jamil decide to join me.

The ruins of ancient Susa lie sprawled out across a considerable expanse, but hardly any of it is extant, except for a few base stones and the outlines of structures. Its original layer is thought to be even older than the region's Elamite heritage, and was the capital of a state called Sushan, which struggled to survive as an independent entity between Elam, Sumer and Akkad—three much more powerful countries. It was conquered by the Akkadians around 2300 BC but managed to shrug off Sargon the Great's expansionism and reassert its independence only to be conquered again, first by the Sumerians and finally by Elam, which turned it into an entirely Elamite country by 2000 BC. After that it was an integral part of Elam and one of its capital cities. The Assyrians laid total waste to it in the 6th century BC, taking great joy in doing so, and

Ashurbanipal, the Assyrian conquerer-king, boasted of his exploits in a tablet that contains the following:

Susa, the great holy city, abode of their gods, seat of their mysteries, I conquered. I entered its palaces, I opened their treasuries where silver and gold, goods and wealth were amassed.... I destroyed the ziggurat of Susa. I smashed its shining copper horns. I reduced the temples of Elam to naught; their gods and goddesses I scattered to the winds.

Neither Shush not Elam ever recovered from the Assyrian onslaught, and it wasn't until Parsa emerged a century or so later that Shush was on the map again, this time as the winter capital and the second most important city in the Achaemenid realm. Darius the Great is said to have rebuilt it entirely and restored it to its former glory, and in December 330 BC Alexander the Great plundered the city, making off with 40,000 talents of gold and silver from its treasury.

The excavation of Shush began over 150 years ago. The Frenchman Jacques de Morgan was the most enthusiastic archaeologist on the site and excavated extensively during the late 1800s, but he also committed the unpardonable sin of destroying historical artefacts while attempting to uncover them. It wasn't just accidental, either—the area is dominated by a huge castle built by de Morgan using bricks from Chogha Zanbil and Darius's palace. The very French-styled castle, which was built to serve as a base and a museum, also sits on a mound that may contain an important historical structure. It's hard to understand why de Morgan would do such things though it smacks of imperial pomposity, the sort that stems from an envious admiration of greatness.

But in 1901, this French archaeological mission at Shush succeeded in making perhaps one of the most important discoveries of all time—a stele containing the entire code of Hammurabi, one of the oldest surviving sets of laws in the world. It exists in the form of a 7-feet-tall finger, easily mistakable for a giant flick off, but is actually an index finger and has a carved relief of Hammurabi being given the laws by Samash, the Akkadian god of justice, on the fingernail. All over it, the laws are written in cuneiform text. It probably stood in a temple at Babylon before it was taken to Shush by the Elamite King Shutruk-Nahhunte in the 12th century BC, when he plundered Babylonia. It now lives at the Louvre Museum in France and when you consider the irreparable damage Islamists and Imperialists alike are doing to the archaeology of the Middle East lately, it's very good that it does too.

Hammurabi was the sixth king of the city state of Babylon, and rose to power around 1790 BC. He was a contemporary of Prophet Abraham, who lived not far from Babylon, in Harran. It was Hammurabi who began annexing his neighbours in a state-building project that would, some centuries later, become the Babylonian Empire and make the word 'Babylon' synonymous with the word 'authority'. He called his country Mat Akkadi, in deference to the Akkadians, the first empire-builders in the region, but history has mostly recorded it as Babylonia. The Hammurabi Code was, for all intents and purposes, the constitution of this country, one of the very first constitutions in recorded history. Though Hammurabi was a consummate conqueror, attacking enemies and allies alike, many of the laws he laid down are so universally recognisable that he features on the walls of the US Supreme Court building as one of 18 prominent lawgivers who have influenced the American political and legal systems. Interestingly enough, Muhammad and Moses are also included in this list, but Jesus and Abraham are not. He also features on the walls of the US House of Representatives, for his contribution to the foundations of statecraft.

The Hammurabi Code has detailed rules for a range of issues including commerce, contracts, filial conduct, crimes and punishment, fines, sexual behaviour, judicial processes, agricultural practices, false testimonies, duties of care, prices, payments, medical malpractice—a whopping 282 rules in total, and is prefaced with this noble sentiment:

When Marduk sent me to rule over men, to give the protection of right to the land, I did right and righteousness ... and brought about the well-being of the oppressed.

Some of the rules are incredibly sophisticated for their time, and lay down principles that are still honoured by societies today, like the presumption of innocence and proportionate retribution, while others are quite harsh and even unfair by modern standards. But there is a clear inclination towards justice, governance, fair trade, social and familial harmony and a host of other values that drive societies even now. There are also rules that are remarkable for their fairness to women, such as these,

142. If a woman quarrel with her husband, and say: 'You are not congenial to me,' the reasons for her prejudice must be presented. If she is guiltless, and there is no fault on her part, but he leaves and neglects her, then no guilt attaches to this woman, she shall take her dowry and go back to her father's house.

156. If a man betroth a girl to his son, but his son has not known her, and if then he defile her, he shall pay her half a gold mina, and compensate her for all that she brought out of her father's house. She may marry the man of her heart.

Other rules attempt to deal justly between citizens by establishing standards of conduct, such as the following,

5. If a judge try a case, reach a decision, and present his judgement in writing; if later error shall appear in his decision, and it be through his own fault, then he shall pay twelve times the fine set by him in the case, and he shall be publicly removed from the judge's bench, and never again shall he sit there to render judgement.

48. If any one owe a debt for a loan, and a storm prostrates the grain, or the harvest fail, or the grain does not grow for lack of water; in that year he need not give his creditor any grain, he washes his debt-tablet in water and pays no rent for this year.

191. If a man, who had adopted a son and reared him, founded a household, and had children, wish to put this adopted son out, then this son shall not simply go his way. His adoptive father shall give him of his wealth one-third of a child's portion, and then he may go.

The rules, but more importantly the values they codify, reflect Hammurabi's attempts at establishing a just country (albeit with different rules for free people and for slaves) and seek to validate his claim that his reign was divinely ordained. Over a thousand years later, Kurosh will attempt to do the same through his edicts and will make the same claim of being divinely appointed using the same God, Marduk.

But Hammurabi's code isn't the oldest set of laws discovered. In fact it's not even that unique for its times. It belongs to a body of work called Cuneiform Law, as they were written in cuneiform, and exist as a precursor to later Middle Eastern lawmaking efforts, including the Indo-European Hittite Laws, Achaemenid Law and, most significantly, Mosaic Law. The oldest set of these laws discovered goes back to about 2400 BC and is Sumerian, but it's possible that older laws exist too; we just haven't found them yet. Even though they span a vast period of time, many of the legal codes have common rules and have almost certainly borrowed from and influenced each other. They were, after all, developed in the same small geographic area by people who had languages and cultures that were not drastically different from one another. Most of them were, in fact, Semitic, with the exception of the Sumerians, the Hittites and the Persians. One very noteworthy difference, however, between Cuneiform Law and Mosaic Law is that the latter also contains punishments for offences against God rather than just against society—an adaptation that has wreaked havoc on the moral compasses of Muslims, Jews and Christians everywhere and for all time.

So the legal codes espoused by the Abrahamic faiths may have as much to do with Mesopotamian lawmakers like Hammurabi, Ur-Nammu, Eshnunna and Lipit-Ishtar, as they do with Abraham, as he lived in an environment that was steeped in these pre-existing systems. To be more controversial, I'd even go as far as to say there is nothing unique about his or any subsequent prophet's claims that God spoke to them and inspired their words; Hammurabi, at least, was as convinced as Moses was that his instructions came from above and said so on his stele,

... then Anu and Bel called by name me, Hammurabi, the exalted prince, who feared God, to bring about the rule of righteousness in the land, to destroy the wicked and the evil-doers; so that the strong should not harm the weak....

Bel is none other than the Arabic Ba'al in Akkadian, a name used both as a generic term for 'gods' and for the specific god that is mentioned in the Quran as a discarded deity. Since we're on the topic, even the root word for 'Ilah', which becomes Elah in Aramaic and Eloh in Hebrew, is 'El', and was used in a similar fashion, that is, both generically and as the name of a deity, for whom images exist. Well before the time of Hammurabi, and eons before Islam inherited the name, Ilah was worshipped as a Middle Eastern deity, evidenced in the name 'Babylon' which began life as 'Bab Illahni' or the 'Gate of of the Gods' in Akkadian, a Semitic tongue.

The ruins at Shush remind me of the ruins at Pataliputra, that is to say there is hardly anything to see. A few outlines of structures, piles of stones and marble, a single reasonably intact Achaemenid bull capital and a piece of a pillar are all that remain of Darius's buildings. There's nothing left of the palaces and halls that Daniyal, Mordecai, Ester and Xerxes once graced. Beyond the palace grounds, a large area identified as the ancient city remains covered in soil, waiting to be discovered. I want to walk around in it, but my companions are growing impatient as they have to get to work and I have to find a seat on a bus going north so decide to head back to the house to collect my gear. On the way I meet yet another Afghan refugee, a shopkeeper, who looks just like my neighbourhood shop-keeper in Dhaka.

The Iraqis and I take pictures together and exchange email addresses when it's time to leave, and I become emotionally over-whelmed. After nearly a month on my own through an unknown country, the spontaneous hospitality I have received from these amazing people has been nothing short of a godsend. They've treated me like a brother or a son and I became very comfortable among them, as though I could live here forever. It's a matter-of-fact sort of hospitality too, the type that you can take for granted once it's been offered, which seems to me to be a very Arabic thing. Nearly all of my encounters with Arabs, from good friends to total strangers, have revealed an understated, unexaggerated quietness, especially in regards to magnanimity. It's markedly different from South Asian or Persian varieties of the same quality, which are often accompanied by much fanfare and considerable embarrassment for the guest. By contrast, Arabs seem almost uninvolved, almost as though they consciously don't want to take any credit for it—as though it's not their hospitality that is being enjoyed, but hospitality in general, of which they too are recipients. I will miss this, and this family, immensely.

I go back to Ahvaz in a shared taxi and head to the main bus terminal where the usual hyperactivity of Iranian bus stations prevails. I want to go to Esfahan again, to do some gift shopping, but the buses are full so I buy a ticket to Tehran instead. I hadn't really intended to visit the Iranian capital, but I'm curious to see what it's like and it also gets me back on my route to Turkey. Settling in for the long night journey, I reflect on the experience I've just had and how completely unusual such a high level of hospitality really is. In a more cynical world we forget that people can be this open with their lives, and the only way to close these circles is to pay it forward so that more people can experience the soul-quenching qualities of compassion—kindness begets kindness, or so it certainly should.

Tehran
Day 50

The bus pulls into Tehran's southern bus terminal just after dawn and the place is already bustling with commuter activity. It's immediately apparent that this is a proper metropolis—the urban landscape is dominated by tall buildings in mostly grey and white, and the bleating sounds of car horns accompany gridlocked expressways several lanes wide. Iran's infrastructure is modern throughout the country but Tehran's is very much like cities in more developed parts of the world. It's not particularly ugly, just a bit stark, but the Alborz mountains to its north frame it very beautifully indeed. Standing above its skyline is the Milad Tower, the fourth-tallest tower in the world.

Compared to many other Iranian cities, Tehran has no historical depth to speak of, but is located very close to a place called Rey, which is mentioned in Zoroastrian epics as well as in the *Shahnameh*. In fact, some consider Rey the very birthplace of Zoroaster. Until the 1700s Tehran was just a small village when, in 1776, the Qajar Dynasty made it Iran's capital—the thirty-second city chosen for the job in Iran's long and complex history. Much of Qajar Tehran was then demolished by the Pahlavis in the 1920s and 1930s to make way for the rebuilding of the city in contemporary style, but with certain pre-Islamic architectural features. It has continued to grow along the path it was set upon by the Shah, and even though it was bombed repeatedly during the Iran-Iraq War, it managed to expand into a spawning city of about 14 million people.

I get a taxi to take me to a hotel which is centrally located and mid-ranged in price. I don't intend to stay long in Tehran, and I'm not keen on doing much sightseeing either. I also have very little time left on my visa and want to go to Tabriz via Esfahan before I leave Iran. The hotel is small but clean and the receptionist speaks good English, which is always a plus. It's also on a narrow street with small shops and teahouses on both sides, giving it a very bohemian feel. I get something to eat and then head towards an internet cafe where I see a number of other foreigners but few who look like tourists. Most look like young professionals or people who have come to Tehran on work. At the internet cafe, I get information about how to get around and where to go, and am told to use the metro system which covers much of the city. I also learn that I'm close to the Treasury of National Jewels, or the Jewellery Museum, which contains one of two diamonds in the world that might be the Darya-i-Noor, cousin of the famous Koh-i-Noor, so I decide I owe it to India to pay her a visit.

The museum is housed in a large vaulted area beneath the Iranian Central Bank, which is only accessible after passing through several checks. I'm not allowed to take my camera, bag or mobile phone in, and the staircase that leads me into the vault is behind a set of heavy doors guarded by burly men in dark suits. It's all appropriately intimidating and very weighty, heightened by the maximum security in and around the country's national vault, alongside, curiously, this very public tourist attraction. The vault is climate-controlled and low-lit, with spotlighting on the reinforced glass display cases that are protected by a series of sensitive alarms. I am told not to touch anything because they are ear-piercing, and setting them off will lead to my imminent arrest.

Iran's crown jewels are among the largest, if not the largest, set of state-owned jewels on display in any one place in the world. They are so valuable, in fact, that Iran's currency is backed up by them and government representatives are required to be present when they go on display three days a week, for only two hours a day. Luckily, it's one of those days and I'm just in time. An all-girl school trip is also taking place and teachers are telling their students about the history, the aesthetics and the worth of the items they stop in front of. I eavesdrop now and then, my broken Farsi allowing me partial access to the wealth of knowledge being imparted, but thankfully there are English labels as well.

Iranians take their love affair with their national jewels very seriously, which is not surprising considering how easily they seem to fall under the spell of all things glamorous. But these are not only astronomically expensive objects of adornment; they are also symbols of Iran's imperial might and cultural sophistication. The fawning labels speak glowingly about the various rulers who 'acquired' some of these items from neighbouring kingdoms throughout the ages, notably from Mughal India and Central Asia, and often through enormous bloodshed. But most are originally Iranian, like the globe made from 35 kilograms of pure gold and the 51,366 jewels commissioned by Naser al-Din Shah of the Qajar Dynasty. The water is emerald and the earth is ruby but Iran, Britain, France, and parts of South Asia are made entirely of diamonds. Equally impressive are the Pahlavi Crown and the Imperial Sword, each encrusted with thousands of diamonds (3,380 in the crown alone) and hundreds of pearls, emeralds, sapphires and rubies. The sword, also called the Shahi Sword, is 103 centimetres long and has over 3,000 stones on it. There are tiaras, necklaces, rings, watches, bejewelled robes, turbans, brooches, armbands, plates, weapons and various other pieces of treasure that glitter under their spotlights, but I'm not one for so much ostentation and feel distinctly underwhelmed even as the schoolgirls in the room ooh and aah at every case.

I am, however, drawn to two items here, but for very different reasons. There is a throne in a display case, and believing it to be the famous Peacock Throne of Delhi, I go towards it with feelings of entitlement. One of the teachers, surmising that I am South Asian and noticing the scowl on my face, tells me it's not the Peacock Throne but another one, called the Naderi Throne. She tells me the original Peacock Throne was indeed brought to Iran after it was plundered from India in 1739, but was stolen again after Nader Shah's assassination and was most likely smashed into pieces to be sold off, bit by bit. Each piece alone must've fetched a large fortune as the Peacock Throne cost twice as much as the Taj Mahal to make, and was perhaps one of the most opulent objects ever to have been created anywhere in the world. Though this information is meant to assuage me, it makes me feel annoyed—I'd much rather have believed that the throne was still intact and on display in an Iranian vault.

Nader Shah's plunder of Delhi is a watershed event, marking the beginning of the end of Muslim rule in India. It's the last high note of an age that went right before the age of European imperialism, when South and West Asian Muslim empires were the global superpowers of their day. Just 18 years after Nader Shah sacked Delhi, Robert Clive took Murshidabad in Bengal, and made the single largest haul in the entire history of European colonisation, anywhere in the world. Nothing of the details about the treasures he stole is known, but among the treasures looted by Nader Shah were two large diamonds, the Koh-i-Noor and the Darya-i-Noor.

The story of the Koh-i-Noor is well known. After it was taken to Iran, it was grabbed by the Durrani ruler of Afghanistan who gifted it to Maharaja Ranjit Singh as a gesture of peace when the two were determining where to draw the borders between them. It was then looted by the British when they captured Punjab and made it a part of their crown jewels, residing now as it did then, in the Tower of London. The story of the Darya-i-Noor, however, is much murkier. According to the Iranian version, it never left Iran but was cut into two, becoming the Darya-i-Noor and the Noor-ol-Ein, both of which are part of the Iranian crown jewels. But this could be a case of mistaken identity as a third diamond, the Great Table, may have also been among the plundered Mughal treasure, and it may have been that one and not the Darya that was cut into two pieces. Certainly the description of the Great Table by the French jeweller Tavernier in 1642 when he saw it on Mughal Emperor Shah Jahan's crown, is consistent with the pink diamond I am looking at today, in the vault.

The South Asian version of the story has the Darya-i-Noor travelling back to India with the Koh-i-Noor and also falling into the clutches of the British, whereupon it was taken to London, exhibited, and then auctioned off in Kolkata during the 1800s. The winning bid was made by the Nawab of Dhaka at the time, Khwaja Alimullah; the Darya was kept in Kolkata until 1947 when it was transferred to Dhaka, and is now said to be in a vault in the Bangladesh government's state-run Sonali Bank! Its authenticity was supposedly verified by a team of experts in 1985 and that's the last anyone in Bangladesh, and possibly even the entire region, has ever heard of it. It sits unsung and undisplayed in a loveless vault somewhere in an uninterested bank, but it's thrilling to think that the actual Darya-i-Noor might be in my very own Dhaka, while the one in Tehran is just an impostor! When I suggest this to a teacher there she rebuffs me and says it's just a British rumour, but I certainly prefer this version, so that's the story I'll be going with. I leave the bank while it's still light outside and stroll around a Tehran that's rumbling with the rush of commuters returning home from work.

I spend the next two days exploring the city at an easy pace. Having spent almost a month appreciating Iran's historical and archaeological legacy, I am more interested in enjoying Iran in the present tense here in its modern capital, and make no attempt at all to visit anything particularly old. I consciously skip the Qajar's Golestan Palace because the pictures I've seen tell me it's slightly gaudy and over-the-top, and may not live up to the elegance of the palaces I've seen in other Iranian cities—although gaudy and over-the-top is quite often the measure of Iranian taste. They seem to like a bit of what we might call '*khayt*' in Bangladesh and elevate it to a level of high culture, employing kitsch in a way that Muslim Indian culture tends to do as well. But I'm also not a big fan of the Qajars and don't want to waste my time fawning over their finery.

Instead, I walk around modern Tehran and find myself at a paved square which resembles the paved squares of various European cities. The whole area looks very much like Europe, in fact—the buildings, street signs (which are also in English) and the layout are typical of parts of Paris or London. There's a sculpture of a set of firemen on one end of the square, which is actually more of a triangle, putting out an imaginary fire made of sheets of steel. It's very nicely made and a fine tribute. Iran has sculptures all over the place and public art is certainly a very big thing here, but few are as modern or pop-art-like as this one. On the other corner of the triangle is a tall transparent structure, which, on closer inspection, turns out to be a bicycle parking tower where bikes are stacked flat on top of each other and lifted up mechanically. I've only ever seen anything like it before in Holland, and it wasn't as sophisticated. There's also a metro station nearby so I duck into it to experience Tehran's underground.

The Tehran Metro, like the Delhi Metro, is a work in progress. It was begun in 1985 and has many lines, with more being added in phases. The trains are clean, punctual and like Delhi, have a women-only car as well. I buy a prepaid travel card, as these can also be used on buses, and ride the trains with no particular destination in mind. The stations sport impressive artwork on their walls and in small showcases, some modern and some traditional. There are replica Achaemenid reliefs, tile work, calligraphy, and even carpet prints, all with good, informative labelling. Metro Art has become a genre in its own right, and many places in the world now use their commuter transit systems to highlight their histories and cultures as well as their national icons. It's a most interesting way to learn about a place, and subtly brings the present into close contact with the timeless, stitching together, appropriately, the journey of a nation.

I alight at a randomly selected station and find myself in what looks like an area where textbooks are sold or copied. The place is bustling with students and features the sort of thing you find at most places like these: fliers stuck to lamp posts and walls, advertising rooms for rent, books for sale, furniture to buy and tuition to be offered. I walk around and then out of the area towards a roundabout, which is adorned with a large statue of a mythical hero slaying a ferocious crocodile with a spear. The road becomes uninteresting beyond that, so I turn around and go back into the trenches to come out at another part of the city.

Missing, a little bit, the internationalised world to which I belong, I decide to check out the Tehrani version of this sub-culture, which lives in North or New Tehran, and head to Gandhi Shopping Centre, on Gandhi Street, where my guidebook tells me a good cup of coffee and a decent Thai meal can be had. I decide to miss the meal but step into a charismatic cafe, where the first person my eyes fall upon has a formidable moustache, thick and curled at the edges, and the din of vociferous conversation makes the atmosphere inviting and lively. Many English words are used the way we use them in anglicised Bengali or Hindi, and the people and place resemble similar people and places back home. I also recognise the pretentiousness—a sort of pride in their acquired poshness that suggests they are thrilled to be able to feel like a better class of Iranian, what with their English words and their deftly displayed trappings of globalisation.

After a good pot of Iranian tea, I decide to call it a day and while leaving the shopping centre, I overhear bits of what sounds like an interesting conversation between a group of anglicised Iranian boys and some of their foreign friends, standing in a huddle, the way most boys their age do.

... yeah, they think it's like 300 or something. One of them can take out thousands of us. Why don't they come and we'll see?

Tehran has lots of parks and open spaces where one can sit and take in the view, but its most attractive features, for me anyway, are its murals. I've seen beautiful wall art all over the world, from graffiti along train tracks to professional pieces commissioned by cities, but Tehran's massive, three-dimensional murals are really something special to behold. Painted along the sides of multi-storeyed buildings, these beautiful works of art create optical illusions that make a dead end look like a road to a meadow or a flat wall appear like a street corner. They are mostly the work of an artist called Mehdi Ghadyanloo, who answered the municipality's call for muralists in 2006 and won the right to be a part of the city's beautification project. He was given a free hand and proceeded to create a series that would, in his own words, 'gladden the spirit'.

One of them shows a pair of men walking in a meadow with children on their shoulders, which is so realistic you could easily walk right into the wall if you didn't know any better, while another features stairs coming up from the pavement with life-sized people standing on landings, painting a rainbow. They're extraordinary and there are loads of them all over the city, making it look like something out of a psychedelic film set. Other types of murals, not as surreal, exist as well; most of them are contemporary but some employ traditional Persian styles, splashed across the side of 20- or 30-storeyed buildings. Some are religious, some political but most are just plain fun, and very modern renditions of that old Iranian habit of covering the exterior of their structures with art.

The least attractive feature of Iranian society is the abundance of nose jobs. Throughout the country, but more so in Tehran, women can be seen with white bandages on their noses—telling signs of their plastic ambitions. Even worse, getting a nose job has become a prestige event and many women wear bandages just to look like they have had one, because it means they are well-off enough to be able to afford it. It's quite a sickness and even men are afflicted by this terrible disease. I've seen at least four men with bandages over their noses, three in Tehran alone.

On my last day in the city I check out the National Museum, which houses a large collection of Iranian artefacts from as long ago as the Palaeolithic Era. Many of the items are from places I have already travelled through and I have seen similar ones in local museums or on site. Still, to have it all displayed as a chronological story is enjoyable, and I spend a few hours looking at Elamite, Achaemenid, Parthian and Sassanian relics in sequence. There's even a very macabre display of a man's head and parts of his limbs, which are said to have been found preserved in salt mines near Zanjan province. A separate museum houses Iran's Islamic heritage and is right next door, but I decide to skip it. Instead I look at the pieces of contemporary art by a Tabrizi sculptor called Ahad Hosseini, being displayed at this museum, which includes many impressive sculptures in bronze, one of which shows mankind devolving from club-wielding cave dwellers to ferocious creatures armed with powerful missiles. Iran's art and public messaging often include a rejection of violence, and a poster near the entrance of the museum makes an appeal for multicultural harmony, stating that the only way people will stop destroying one another is if they can be made to fall in love with each other's cultures. The poster features beautiful Persian calligraphy set against an image of an ornately decorated dagger hilt, with the blade broken off.

Tabriz

My last few days in Iran are a blur as I rush through to Esfahan and Tabriz with virtually no time left on my visa. It's foolhardy to do it this way, but I'm stubborn and trust my calculations, which should get me out of Iran with literally just hours to spare. I check out of my hotel in Tehran at noon, walk around all day and take a 9:30 pm bus to Esfahan, which arrives at dawn. I shower at the bus station, buy a ticket to Tabriz for the same evening, and spend the day at Imam Square buying gifts for my family and flirting with

Mahsa from the restaurant. With nowhere to really rest for virtually the entire day, I head for the *chaikhaneh* to put my feet up, while the wonderful people at a carpet shop agree to let me leave my backpack at their store. In the evening I catch the bus to Tabriz and arrive in Irani Azerbaijan just as the sun is coming up over the mountains. I can only spend one day here and will have to be on my way to Van, in Turkey, by the evening, if I'm to stay within the limits of my visa. Speed travelling at its most hectic.

My first impression of Tabriz is that it's quite definitely not Persian in its orientation. The taxi drivers who accost me as I alight from the bus are much rougher and don't bother with the usual pleasantries that go with most interactions in Persia proper. They are Azeris, related to the Turks, and I suspect they are a sterner lot than the people I've been living among for the last month. The place is colder as well, and more rugged. First things first, I buy a ticket on an overnight bus to Van, 11 hours, which seems like a lot for a distance of only 340 kilometres, and check into a hotel to try and get some rest during the day. It's a modern and mid-ranged place called the Park Hotel. The hotelier is friendly and speaks English so while I check in we talk about languages to satisfy my curiosity about Azeri and its relationship with both Iran and the Republic of Azerbaijan. He tells me that it's not quite Turkic but a hybrid, although more closely related to Turkish than Farsi. We talk about linguistic nationalism and I tell him about how perhaps this side of Azerbaijan is a bit like Indian Bengal, while Azerbaijan the country is Bangladesh. He doesn't agree completely. I ask him if they face pressure to assimilate and he tells me they can all speak Farsi so that's not an issue, but there's no question whatsoever of abandoning Azeri.

'Languages are not just for communication; they are points of view, interpretations of the world. I will always have an Azeri point of view which sustains the language and is also sustained by it.'

Eloquently put and I couldn't agree more. I want to learn much more about Azeri identity and nationalism but after two nights without a room, all I can think about is a hot shower and a soft bed. I turn the TV on for company, and after a bit of channel-surfing, find Amitabh Bachchan's *Kala Patthar* playing—in Farsi! It's a complete surprise but the Bachchan looks perfectly natural speaking it and certain words like '*barabar*', '*rubaru*' and '*tanha*' didn't even need dubbing at all. Sleep finds me amidst images of colourfully dressed Indian women with large bangles and my last thought is how much I miss the vibrancy of South Asian cultures.

I wake up around 2 pm and decide that I should at least attempt to explore Tabriz in the few hours that I have here, and step outside to look for things of interest. I'm happy enough just being here, frankly, seeing that Shams, the eccentric and indomitable dervish who awakened Rumi's dormant mysticism, was born and grew up in this town. Where he died, though, is a complete mystery. I've already come across one potential grave in Multan, while a second one is said to be in Khoy, on the outskirts of Tabriz. I won't have time to visit it, but seeing that Shams was a Qalandar, I'm sure he has as little need for a grave in death as he did for a home during his life. Or perhaps, true to his wanderings, he has several.

Shams-i-Tabrizi is one of Sufism's more controversial characters. His story is full of conflict, and he cuts a figure quite unlike the serene and sedate soul-men we have come to expect all Sufis to be. He is abrasive and aggressive, and is associated with the colour black, which he is said to have worn most of the time. He spoke cuttingly, and would go straight to the sordid heart of matters, making kings, teachers, imams and pimps alike, extremely uncomfortable. His demeanour was deliberately affronting and he challenged established hierarchies that were not biased towards the less fortunate. He was also most unconventional in his religiosity and would make it a point to attack every flimsy, untested belief, questioning the legitimacy of anything that blurred the line between superstition and real faith. In short, he was a relentless, raging force for Truth, stopping at nothing to make it known, and in his brief time on earth, he managed to make many enemies. But he was also deeply revered, most prominently by Jalaluddin Rumi, who is said to have fallen completely under his sway.

Shams's association with Rumi has been subject to much controversy—Rumi's own family questioned the nature of their relationship, implying that it was lewd and homoerotic, but the truth is probably far more complex. They were lovers, that is true, but lovers in spirit—two souls in love with the Divine, who were, through their affections, submission and intense spiritual conversations or *sohbets*, attempting to expand themselves to be able to grasp more and more of God's essence. The trouble was, just as everything creates an equal and opposite reaction, their expansion created a constriction in the hearts of Rumi's wife, son and disciples, all of whom felt jealous about the exclusive nature of this relationship and Rumi's total, almost obsessive, devotion to Shams's eccentricities.

The result of this unwarranted negative energy has never been conclusively ascertained. Some say Shams was murdered by Rumi's disciples, others that he left in the dead of the night without saying goodbye, leaving Rumi with an intense feeling of loss—the inspiration for his phenomenally profound poetry. The truth of this matter determines his gravesite—if he was killed in Konya it's likely that the one that's said to be near Rumi's tomb is the real one. If not, it's anyone's guess. But the ending of that story isn't what became of Shams; it's what became of Rumi, who, by both having and losing 'The Sun of Tabriz', was transformed from a clerical scholar into an ocean of mystic love, one which seekers from all faiths and walks of life have been baptised in, for centuries.

I walk around Tabriz looking for traces of this man Shams, but there's none of it here, except perhaps in the almost rude straightforwardness of the Azeri people. They are quite curt in their manner and unlike the Persians, generally a bit severe. There are a lot of stiff older men in suits and moustaches, serious in their grave and grey attire, and I don't see too many colourful young Iranians carrying on in that supple, flirtatious manner of theirs. It's the Turkic element, I think, present in Pakistanis too, that makes them a bit cold, and seeing as I'm going deeper into Turko-sphere, I start to feel a bit nostalgic for playful Persia. I walk past a music store and hear Azeri music coming out of it, which is nice, so I decide to buy some, along with some Persian santoor music. Afterwards, I step into a restaurant, an elegant old converted house and hamaam, for my last Persian meal in Iran. Here I meet a Polish and Indian couple who are going the in opposite direction, towards India. They've just arrived in Tabriz from Van so I ask them about the route. They tell me it's very picturesque and that Van is also worth exploring for its history as a major city in the Assyrian and Urartu Empires. After my meal I go down to the bus terminal and head out to Turkey.

There are only three other passengers on the bus, a couple and their small daughter. The large, spacious Volvo bus is completely empty otherwise, so I presume it will stop to pick up passengers along the way, accounting for the long duration of the journey perhaps. I'm not fussed; it's a night bus so I will sleep all the way anyway. But it turns out to be something completely different. It's not a passenger service at all but a petrol-smuggling run, and we're just the cover! Instead of stopping for passengers, the bus stops at various petrol stations, where large barrel drums are stealthily filled and stowed away in the cargo space. This is repeated at various pumps, accompanied by cash payments for complicit pump operators. Petrol in oil-rich Iran is much cheaper than in Turkey, but embargoes and sanctions make it difficult, if not impossible, for it to be exported legally. It's entertaining, but also a bit worrying as an interception by the police on either side of the border will make it difficult to get to Van at this time of night. The bus also stops for long periods of time, for no apparent reason at all, and it's become perfectly clear now, why a journey that should only take five or six hours will take 11.

We reach the border around midnight and join a queue of vehicles—buses and trucks mostly—all waiting to enter Anatolia. It's quite a dramatic frontier, amidst hills and crags, with flags of the respective countries flying triumphantly over them. The walls and gates of the border are also painted in their national colours. An enormous picture of Mustafa Kemal Ataturk, modern Turkey's founder, features. Land borders are great places to observe the arbitrary and absurd nature of national standard times. Turkey is one and a half hours behind Iran, so I set my watch accordingly and wait to be transported back in time, to yesterday even, the moment the bus crosses over the border line. In fact, if I really want to have fun with it I can run from the front of the bus to the back of it at that exact moment, and go straight into the future. The immigration building on the Iranian side of the border is reminiscent of a hospital waiting room; everyone disembarks and sits on rows of fixed plastic chairs, takes a number and waits to be called to an immigration booth. When it's my turn, I enthusiastically approach the window, eager for a chance to tell the authorities in Iran how much I loved my stay in their country. The officer, a young, unofficiously dressed man, just like the man at the entrance gates in Zahedan, smiles and tells me to come again then, as soon as I can. Our luggage is then taken out of the bus and checked under the open air by a customs officer who insists I take everything out of my backpack. It's starting to drizzle so I look at him as if to say, 'seriously, brother?' at which he just rifles through some of my things instead, and says, 'okay, go'.

I board the oil carrier masquerading as a bus and we set off towards Turkey. Just before we cross, I look back at Iran as though I am leaving home and can almost conjure up a large family standing at the gates waving me goodbye. It feels as though I'm coming away from a precious reunion with loved ones, after decades apart, and I experience a sort of separation anxiety that makes me feel slightly forlorn. I will never be able to leave Iran; the memory of its exceptionally warm and hospitable atmosphere will keep my spirit sated, hundreds of miles away. I will certainly return, and if there was ever a perfect occasion to use the Bangla expression for 'goodbye', which is not really a goodbye at all but more like an 'I'll be back', it would be this one.

Ashi.

Suggested Readings

Facts and references in this book have been collected from a number of sources, including, but not exhaustively, the following (in no specific order):

Aspects of Indian History and Civilisation (1965), Buddha Prakash; *Birth of the Persian Empire, Volume 1: Idea of Iran, (2005),* Vesta Sarkhosh Curtis, Sarah Stewart; *Our Oriental Heritage (1935)* Will Durant; *Cyropaedia of Xenophon; The Life of Cyrus The Great,* Xenophon; *Great Tang Records on the Western Regions,* Hieun Tsiang; *The Rise of Islam and the Bengal Frontier, 1204–1760,* *(1996)* Richard Eaton; *Mughal Empire in India: A Systematic Study Including Source Material, Volume 1 (1999),* S.R. Sharma; *Indica,* Megathenes; *Arthashastra,* Kautilya; *Tabaqat-i-Nasiri,* Minhaj-i-Siraj; *The Code of laws promulgated by Hammurabi, King of Babylon, B.C. 2285-2242 (1903)* Claude Hermann Walter Johns; *An Islamic Utopian: A Political Biography of Ali Shari'ati (1998),* Ali Rahnema; *The Itinerary of Benjamin of Tudela (1907)* Marcus Nathan Adler; *The Mahabharata,* Ved Vyasa; *The Argumentative Indian (2005)* Amartya Sen; *Baburnama,* Zahiruddin Muhammed Babur; *Humayun Nama,* Gulbadan Begum; *Orientalism (1978)* Edward W. Said; *Zoroastrians: Their Religious Beliefs and Practices (1979)* Mary Boyce; *The Sword of Persia: Nader Shah, from Tribal Warrior to Conquering Tyrant (2006)* Michael Axworthy; *Aśoka and the Decline of the Mauryas, (1998)* Romila Thapar; *Early India: From Origins to AD 1300 (2002)* Romila Thapar; *The Great Indian*

Novel (1989) Shashi Tharoor; *Universities in ancient India, (2010 reprint)* D.G. Apte; *The Alchemy of Happiness,* Abu Hamid Al Ghazali; *The Incoherence of the Philosophers,* Abu Hamid Al Ghazali; *The Incoherence of the Incoherence,* Ahmed Ibn Rushd; *The Muslim Mystic Movement in Bengal: 1301–1550 (1993)* Sk. Abdul Latif; *Siyastnama,* Nizam al-Mulk; *Kitab al- Tawasin,* Mansur Al-Hallaj; *The Arctic Home in the Vedas (1903)* Bal Gangadhar Tilak; *On the City Wall (1898)* Rudyard Kipling; *Asterisk in Bhāropīyasthān: Minor Writings on the Aryan Invasion Debate (2007)* Koenraad Elst; *The Quran; The Tanakh; The Rig Veda; The Avesta; Late Victorian Holocausts: El Niño Famines and the Making of the Third World (2000)* Mike Davis; *Minute on Education (1835)* Tomas Babington Macaulay; *Shunya Purana,* Ramai Pandit; *Buddhist Monks and Monasteries in India (1988)* Sukumar Dutt.

About the Author

Zeeshan Khan is a journalist, currently working in communications with the International Organisation for Migration. He was born in the UK and raised in Bangladesh, but spent a part of his childhood in Mauritius. He studied in Canada and Australia and worked in Europe before returning to Bangladesh, where he currently resides. He is passionate about history, religions, cultures and languages, and has an active interest in mysticism, particularly in Sufism. He is also interested in international and current affairs and writes about these for a living as a journalist. Zeeshan is obsessed with overland travel. His other pursuits include sports, photography, reading and appreciating music.